BASIC STATISTICS FOR SOCIAL RESEARCH

BASIC STATISTICS FOR SOCIAL RESEARCH

ROBERT A. HANNEMAN
AUGUSTINE J. KPOSOWA
MARK RIDDLE

Cover image: ©track5/istockphoto
Cover design: Mike Rutkowski

Published by Jossey-Bass
A Wiley Imprint
One Montgomery Street, Suite 1200, San Francisco, CA 94104-4594—www.josseybass.com

Library of Congress Cataloging-in-Publication Data
Hanneman, Robert.
Basic statistics for social research / Robert A. Hanneman, Augustine J. Kposowa, and Mark Riddle.
p. cm.
Includes index.
ISBN 978-0-470-58798-0 (pbk.); ISBN 978-1-118-22055-9 (ebk.);
ISBN 978-1-118-23415-0 (ebk.); ISBN 978-1-118-24930-7 (ebk.)
1. Social sciences—Statistical methods. I. Kposowa, Augustine J. II. Riddle, Mark, 1957-
III. Title.
HA29.H2494 2013
519.5—dc23

2012011790

Printed in the United States of America

FIRST EDITION
PB Printing 10 9 8 7 6 5 4 3 2 1

CONTENTS

Tables and Figures ix
Preface xv
About the Authors xix

PART I UNIVARIATE DESCRIPTION 1

Chapter 1 Using Statistics 3
Why Study Statistics? 4
Tasks for Statistics: Describing, Inferring, Testing, Predicting 4
Statistics in the Research Process 9
Basic Elements of Research: Units of Analysis and Variables 14

Chapter 2 Displaying One Distribution 25
Summarizing Variation in One Variable 26
Frequency Distributions for Nominal Variables 26
Frequency Distributions for Ordinal Variables 32
Frequency Distributions for Interval/Ratio Variables 38
Summarizing Data Using Excel 43

Chapter 3 Central Tendency 81
The Basic Idea of Central Tendency 82
The Mode 83
The Median 88
The Mean 95

Chapter 4 Dispersion 113
The Basic Idea of Dispersion 114
Dispersion of Categorical Data 115
Dispersion of Interval/Ratio Data 121

Chapter 5 Describing the Shape of a Distribution **149**
The Basic Ideas of Distributional Shape 150
The Shape of Nominal and Ordinal Distributions 152
Unimodality 158
Skewness 163
Kurtosis 169
Some Common Distributional Shapes 175

Chapter 6 The Normal Distribution **187**
Introduction to the Normal Distribution 188
Properties of Normal Distributions 189
The Standard Normal, or Z, Distribution 192
Working with Standard Normal (Z) Scores 194
Finding Areas "Under the Curve" 197

PART II INFERENCE AND HYPOTHESIS TESTING **209**

Chapter 7 Basic Ideas of Statistical Inference **211**
Introduction to Statistical Inference 212
Sampling Concepts 214
Central Tendency Estimates 219
Assessing Confidence in Point Estimates 229

Chapter 8 Hypothesis Testing for One Sample **247**
Hypothesis Testing 248
The Testing Process 250
Tests about One Mean 258
Tests about One Proportion 267

Chapter 9 Hypothesis Testing for Two Samples **279**
Comparing Two Groups 280
Comparing Two Groups' Means 280
Comparing Two Groups' Proportions 289
Nonindependent Samples 296
Using Excel for Two-Sample Tests 301
Interpreting Group Differences 302

Chapter 10 Multiple Sample Tests of Proportions: Chi-Squared **313**
Comparing Proportions across Several Groups 314
Testing for Multiple Group Differences 315
Describing Group Differences 327

Chapter 11 Multiple Sample Tests for Means: One-Way ANOVA **337**
Comparing Several Group Means with Analysis of Variance 338
Analyzing Variance and the F-Test 339
Analyzing Variance 342
The F-Test 350
Comparing Means 356

PART III ASSOCIATION AND PREDICTION **369**

Chapter 12 Association with Categorical Variables **371**
The Concept of Statistical Association 372
Association with Nominal Variables 375
Association with Ordinal Variables 391

Chapter 13 Association of Interval/Ratio Variables **425**
Visualizing Interval/Ratio Association 426
Significance Testing for Interval/Ratio Association 434

Chapter 14 Regression Analysis **453**
Predicting Outcomes with Regression 454
Simple Linear Regression 454
Applying Simple Regression Analysis 465
Multiple Regression 469
Applying Multiple Regression 474

Chapter 15 Logistic Regression Analysis **489**
Predicting with Nonlinear Relationships 490
Logistic Regression 492
The Logistic Regression Model 492
Interpreting Effects in Logistic Regression 493
Estimating Logistic Regression Models with Maximum Likelihood 495
Applying Logistic Regression 496
Assessing Partial Effects 498
Extending Logistic Regression 499

APPENDIX

Chi-Squared Distribution: Critical Values for Commonly Used Alpha = 0.05 and Alpha = 0.01 **505**

F-Distribution: Critical Values for Commonly Used Alpha = 0.05 and Alpha = 0.01 **507**

Standard Normal Scores (Z-Scores), and Cumulative Probabilities (Proportion of Cases Having Scores below Z) **511**

Student's t-Distribution: Critical Values for Commonly Used Alpha Levels **517**

Index 519

TABLES AND FIGURES

TABLES

Table 1.1 Levels of Measurement and Their Characteristics 18
Table 2.1 Frequency Chart for a Nominal Variable 28
Table 2.2 Nominal Frequency Chart with Relative Frequencies: Marital Status in the 1978–1998 General Social Survey 30
Table 2.3 Respondent's Highest Degree, U.S. 1978–1998 (General Social Survey) 34
Table 2.4 GNP in Five Categories 41
Table 2.5 GNP in Nine Categories 41
Table 3.1 Region of Interview 85
Table 3.2 Frequency Chart of Educational Attainment, 2008 General Social Survey 90
Table 3.3 Why Rounding Cumulative Percentages Is Problematic 91
Table 3.4 Attitudes about Court Sentencing 93
Table 3.5 Monthly Earnings of Students 93
Table 3.6 Birthrates 94
Table 3.7 Age Distribution of Students in Basic Statistics 101
Table 4.1 Guessing Strategies Compared 117
Table 4.2 How Maximum Dispersion Depends on the Number of Categories 118
Table 4.3 Frequencies of Marital Status Categories 119
Table 4.4 Hypothetical Distribution of Gender by Occupation 120
Table 4.5 Adjusting Frequencies to Obtain Equal Proportions 121
Table 4.6 Difference in Proportions as a Measure of Dispersion 121
Table 6.1 Calculation of Z-Scores for Some Values of Median Income 196

Table 6.2 Proportions of Cases Having Values Lower and Higher Than Selected Values of Median Income 196
Table 8.1 SPSS One-Sample t-Test Results 261
Table 8.2 SPSS Results for Testing a Proportion Using a Dummy Variable t-Test of Means 270
Table 9.1 Descriptive Statistics for Two Groups 284
Table 9.2 SPSS Output for Two-Group Mean Hypothesis Test 285
Table 9.3 Descriptive Statistics for Two-Group Comparison Using Dummy Variables 292
Table 9.4 Two-Sample Test for Proportions Using Dummy Variables 292
Table 9.5 Descriptive Statistics for Nonindependent Samples 299
Table 9.6 Test for Difference of Group Differences 300
Table 10.1 Multiple Group Proportions of Marital Status by Race 315
Table 10.2 Frequencies Observed and Expected Assuming Independence 319
Table 10.3 Pearson (and Other) Chi-Squared Test Results: Marital Status by Race 320
Table 10.4 Educational Degree by Race, General Social Survey 1993, Observed Frequencies 325
Table 10.5 Educational Degree by Race, General Social Survey 1993, Expected Frequencies 326
Table 10.6 Educational Degree by Race, General Social Survey 1993, Residuals 326
Table 10.7 Educational Degree by Race, General Social Survey 1993, Chi-Squared Test 327
Table 10.8 Differences in Proportions: Marital Status by Race 328
Table 10.9 Differences in Proportions between "White" and "Black" 329
Table 10.10 Analyzing Residuals to Describe Group Differences 330
Table 12.1 Cross-Tabulation of Region of Residence by Race 373
Table 12.2 Association between Marital Status and Race 380
Table 12.3 Chi-Squared Tests for the Association of Marital Status and Race 380
Table 12.4 Chi-Squared-Based Measures of Association for Marital Status by Race 383
Table 12.5 PRE Measures of Association between Marital Status and Race 384
Table 12.6 Marital Statuses by Class Identification, General Social Survey 1996 390
Table 12.7 Religious Service Attendance by Highest Educational Degree 392

Table 12.8 Perfect Positive Rank-Order Correlation: All Pairs Concordant 395
Table 12.9 Perfect Negative Rank-Order Correlation: All Pairs Discordant 396
Table 12.10 Less Than Perfect Positive Rank-Order Correlation 396
Table 12.11 Rank-Order Correlation with Ties on Y 397
Table 12.12 Relationship between Conservativism and Sentencing Attitudes 401
Table 12.13 Counts of Pairs for the Relationship between Conservativism and Sentencing Attitudes 402
Table 12.14 Partial Listing of Raw Infant Mortality and Fertility Data 403
Table 12.15 Calculation of Differences in Ranks 404
Table 13.1 Ordinal Association of Infant Mortality and Life Expectancy 426
Table 13.2 Spreadsheet Calculations for the Relationship of Property Crime and Unemployment Rates (Partial Listing) 443
Table 14.1 Number of Class Factions and Anti-Instructor Comments (Hypothetical Data) 456
Table 14.2 Income and Education: Goodness of Fit Model Summary 466
Table 14.3 Income and Education: Effects Analysis 467
Table 14.4 Residuals for 10 Cases after Predicting Income with Education and Age: The 2008 General Social Survey 473
Table 14.5 Income, Education, and Age: Goodness of Fit 475
Table 14.6 Income, Education, and Age: Partial Effects 476
Table 14.7 Income, Education, Age, and Occupational Status: Goodness of Fit 477
Table 14.8 Income, Age, Education, and Occupational Status: Partial Effects 478
Table 15.1 How Odds and Probabilities Are Related 494
Table 15.2 Goodness of Fit in Predicting Support for Decriminalization 497
Table 15.3 Partial Effects on the Odds of Favoring Decriminalization of Marijuana 498

FIGURES

Figure 2.1 Marital Status in the 1978–1998 General Social Survey 30
Figure 2.2 Modified Bar Charts 31
Figure 2.3 Marital Status in the 1978–1998 General Social Survey 32
Figure 2.4 Respondent's Highest Degree, General Social Survey 1978–1998 36
Figure 2.5 Respondent's Highest Degree, General Social Survey 1998 37

Figure 2.6 Numbers of Siblings, General Social Survey 1998 42
Figure 2.7 Cumulative Numbers of Siblings, General Social Survey 1998 42
Figure 3.1 Marital Status in the 2008 General Social Survey 84
Figure 3.2 Opinions about a Mediocre Class 86
Figure 3.3 Strong, Opposite Opinions about a Handout 86
Figure 3.4 Ranked Data and Median Height 88
Figure 3.5 Median When the Two Middle Scores Have the Same Value 89
Figure 3.6 Median When the Two Middle Scores Have Different Values 89
Figure 3.7 Educational Attainment 90
Figure 3.8 Educational Attainment in Years 96
Figure 3.9 The Sum of Deviations from the Mean 97
Figure 3.10 Squared Deviations from the Mean versus Other Squared Deviations 98
Figure 4.1 Religious Affiliations in Two Different Communities, A and B 115
Figure 4.2 Religious Affiliations in Two Different Communities, C and D 116
Figure 4.3 Age of Respondent 126
Figure 4.4 Means and Variability in Numbers of Siblings 135
Figure 5.1 Income Distribution for Nonblack Families 150
Figure 5.2 Income Distribution for Black Families 151
Figure 5.3 Box-and-Whiskers Plots of Educational Attainment by Race 153
Figure 5.4 The Effect of Having More or Fewer Categories on the Mode 162
Figure 5.5 Skewness Displaces the Mean toward the Longer Tail 164
Figure 5.6 Respondents' Ages in the General Social Survey 165
Figure 5.7 Effect of Skewness on the Location of Central Tendency Statistics 166
Figure 5.8 Distribution of Literacy Levels versus Normal Distribution 167
Figure 5.9 A Standard Normal Curve, and Positive and Negative Kurtosis 170
Figure 5.10 Respondents' Ages in the General Social Survey 171
Figure 6.1 Theoretical Standard Normal Curve and Random Normal Data 189
Figure 6.2 Median Household Income, 1995 195
Figure 6.3 Area of the Standard Normal Curve above +1 Standard Deviation 198
Figure 6.4 The Normal Distribution Function in Excel 199
Figure 6.5 Area Between the Mean and +1 Standard Deviation 200
Figure 6.6 Finding the Area between Two Scores 201
Figure 8.1 Sampling Distribution of a Normally Distributed Statistic 252

Figure 8.2 Areas under the Normal Curve of the Sampling Distribution of a Statistic 253
Figure 8.3 Visualizing the Meaning of the t-Test Results 261
Figure 8.4 Visualizing the Z-Test Results 269
Figure 12.1 Comparative Bar Chart of the Association between Race and Region of Residence 376
Figure 12.2 Comparative Pie Charts of the Association between Region of Residence and Race 377
Figure 13.1 Interval/Ratio Association of Infant Mortality and Life Expectancy 427
Figure 13.2 Relationship of Infant Mortality to Education with Linear Regression Line 430
Figure 13.3 Relationship of Infant Mortality to Education with Nonlinear Regression Line 431
Figure 13.4 Property Crime Rates by Unemployment Rates in the United States 442
Figure 14.1 The Best-Fitting Equation and the Regression Line for Predicting Anti-Instructor Comments 459
Figure 15.1 Logistic Curve Showing the Relationship between Age and Percent of Homeowners 491

PREFACE

There are numerous textbooks in statistics that have "basic" or "introductory" in their titles, but these words are often misleading. A quick glance at the first few chapters reveals that there is hardly anything basic about them. They're often full of concepts that a first-year undergraduate student with a limited mathematics background may find difficult to comprehend. As a result, many students, already frightened by numbers and mathematics, throw in the towel even before trying. For them, a required statistics course is a major obstacle that appears to have been placed in the path of doing other courses in their major, with the goal of causing much pain and suffering. This book grew out of two decades of teaching undergraduate and graduate statistics where the authors have seen the frustration in the eyes of students. We decided to write a book that assumes only that students are able to add, subtract, multiply, and divide.

A unique feature of this book, designed to be used mainly by undergraduate students, is that we have taken an applied perspective, wherein examples aim at solving real-world (everyday) problems. In addition, we have been very mindful of advances in information technology, including the omnipresence of computing software. Thus, elaborate and tedious hand calculations are held to a minimum. This does not mean that the book is an exercise in using statistical software. Rather, concepts and theories behind techniques are explained in detail, along with the potential pitfalls and abuses of those techniques. Worked-out examples are provided, and statistical software is used. We believe that de-emphasizing tedious hand calculations saves time, and given that use of software will increasingly become widespread in statistics, we have tried to maintain a balance. We also worry about the increasing cost of software licensing. Given that many—if not most—undergraduate students lack financial resources to purchase personal licenses, and some colleges and universities are also under severe budgetary constraints, we have avoided sole reliance on SPSS. Instead, many chapters take students through calculations using Microsoft Excel, which is more widely accessible to students worldwide.

In the book we provide coverage of the most commonly used approaches in the social sciences to univariate and bivariate descriptive and inferential statistics.

Chapter 1: Importance and use of statistics in research is presented, using everyday examples of how consumption of statistical information has become prevalent in the twenty-first century. Concepts typically met in descriptive and multivariate statistics are presented and defined, and examples are provided. The chapter closes with a step-by-step overview of the research process and the role of statistical analysis in it.

Chapter 2: The idea of distributions is defined and their functions are also offered. In addition, for each type of measurement, the appropriate distribution is presented in numerical and graphical forms. This chapter introduces students to the use of Excel and SPSS software in displaying data.

Chapter 3: Summarizing data is crucial in statistical analysis. In this chapter, students are introduced to the concept of central tendency. In a step-by-step presentation, each measure is given, along with the type of variables for which a given measure is appropriate. Excel and SPSS examples are also given.

Chapter 4: The concept of spread of data points is presented by measurement levels of variables using examples that students can relate to. Clear distinctions are made between central tendency and dispersion measures. Students are taken through step-by-step calculations, and at the end of the chapter, a section illustrates how Excel can be used for calculating measures of dispersion.

Chapter 5: Distributions and their shapes are presented to students using pictorial diagrams as appropriate for each level of measurement. Extensive illustration is accomplished using data from the U.S. Census.

Chapter 6: The normal distribution is covered here, with regard to its definition, properties, relevance in hypothesis testing, and finding areas under the curve. Extensive use is made of Excel.

Chapter 7: Students are introduced to the concept of statistical inference by way of examples from research results presented in the media. Distinctions are made between sample values and characteristics (statistics) and population values and characteristics (parameters). The notion of sampling error is presented in a simple fashion using examples. Illustrations of statistical inference are made via Excel.

Chapter 8: This chapter tackles hypothesis testing using t-distributions and Z-distributions when there is only one sample. Ideas covered in Chapter 7 are put into practice in Chapter 8. Selection of alpha levels is discussed, along with the meaning, assumptions, and interpretation of null and research hypotheses.

Chapter 9: Hypothesis testing for two samples is discussed, and calculations are done for the independent sample t-test using Excel.

Chapter 10: The chapter discusses multiple sample tests of proportions, including the use of the chi-squared test of independence. Students are taken through hypothesis setup, analysis, and presentation of results using data from the U.S. General Social Surveys.

Chapter 11: Multiple sample tests of means are presented and discussed in this chapter, including a detailed presentation of the theory, assumptions, and application of analysis of variance (ANOVA).

Chapter 12: The notion of statistical association is introduced in this chapter. The idea of association is fundamental to all advanced statistical techniques. Association between nominal-level variables is presented using visualization before moving to numerical measures. Association between ordinal-level variables is also discussed by way of visual displays and numerical measures.

Chapter 13: Statistical association of interval/ratio variables is discussed using illustrative visual examples. Students are taken on a tour of detecting association through scatter plots. Correlation is presented, along with related hypotheses, computation, and interpretation of results.

Chapter 14: This chapter is a didactic discussion of linear regression as both an explanatory and a predictive technique, beginning with a definition of the simple linear model, uses of linear regression, assumptions, and consequences of their violation. The chapter goes through a detailed step-by-step computation of the simple linear model. Multivariate regression is presented, and analysis of the U.S. General Social Survey is discussed in a detailed manner.

Chapter 15: This final chapter in the book is an extension of Chapter 14, and deals with prediction when the outcome or dependent variable is nonlinear. Emphasis is on logistic regression, including its meaning, application, and presentation of results. Maximum likelihood is discussed, and a detailed application of the technique is illustrated using the 2008 U.S. General Social Survey.

Appendix Tables: We have included some basic tables of cumulative probabilities and/or critical values of the Z, t-, chi-squared, and F-distributions. Excellent and (usually, but not always) accurate tables for test statistics are also easy to find on the web. The tables here, though, should be sufficient for all the problems and illustrations in the book.

INSTRUCTIONAL TOOLS

Each chapter contains pedagogical features to aid students in understanding and mastering the various statistical approaches presented in the book:

- Learning objectives
- Check quizzes after many sections and an answer key at the end of the chapter
- Summary
- Key terms
- End-of-chapter exercises
- SPSS exercises (select chapters)

There are also ancillary materials for both the student and the instructor to accompany this book. For instructors, there is a test bank.

ACKNOWLEDGMENTS

We thank Quincy A. Edwards, Helen Kwan, and Steven Stack, who read the first drafts and made invaluable comments and suggestions that greatly improved the manuscript. We also thank students at the University of California, Riverside, who have been used as unwitting samples on which the CD version of the book was tested for six years. Through annual usage of the draft on CD, we were able to get valuable comments and feedback that were used to revise the draft and make it suitable for publication.

ABOUT THE AUTHORS

Robert A. Hanneman is a professor of sociology at the University of California, Riverside. Most of his work is in the areas of mathematical and simulation modeling as a way of building and experimenting with theories of processes of social change. He has done a number of empirical studies of organizational change in educational, medical, military, and economic organizations. He also works extensively in the area of applied social network analysis.

Augustine J. Kposowa is a professor of sociology at the University of California, Riverside. Dr. Kposowa's line of research adopts a multidisciplinary approach that encompasses demography, epidemiology, political economy, and racial/ethnic inequality. In addition to doing basic research, Dr. Kposowa is convinced that sociological findings must and should influence public policy in order to uplift the human condition and for sociology to remain relevant in the twenty-first century and beyond. Thus, his findings have received extensive media coverage nationally and internationally. Dr. Kposowa is currently involved in research that investigates long-term consequences of the Sierra Leone civil war on population health. Recent publications have appeared in *Social Science & Medicine*, *Journal for the Scientific Study of Religion*, *Journal of Community Psychology*, *Social Psychiatry & Psychiatric Epidemiology*, and *Social Science Quarterly*.

Mark Riddle is the Director of Institutional Research at Antioch University Los Angeles, where he puts the techniques you'll find in this book to use on a daily basis. Prior to his return to Southern California, he was a member of the sociology faculty at the University of Northern Colorado in Greeley, Colorado, where he taught research methods and courses on institutions for six years. Dr. Riddle received his MA and PhD degrees from the University of California, Riverside. He lives in Long Beach, California, and spends time away from computers on bicycles or making sawdust.

BASIC STATISTICS FOR SOCIAL RESEARCH

PART I

Univariate Description

Chapter 1

USING STATISTICS

LEARNING OBJECTIVES

When you have finished this chapter, you will be able to:

- Distinguish the uses of statistics for description, inference, hypothesis testing, and prediction.
- Distinguish between the exploratory and confirmatory uses of statistics.
- Understand the distinction between sample statistics and population parameters.
- Understand how statistics are related to the process of constructing and verifying theory.
- Know how to write a report using statistical information.
- Identify units of analysis and cases in research problems.
- Understand variables and apply the notion of levels of measurement.

WHY STUDY STATISTICS?

Whether you wish it or not, you are a consumer of statistics. The news media present a constant flow of information, with government officials and pundits often throwing out number after number, ranging from current unemployment figures to opinion poll results about how some administration is doing in office. During football season, colleges are ranked based on polling coaches and feeding statistical data into computers. In newspapers, leading economic indicators, corporate performance and profits, results of studies both social and medical, car sales, and weather forecasts are all presented to the public in statistical language.

How does one process information and cope with the relentless barrage of statistical data without becoming overwhelmed? And, perhaps even more importantly, how does one become an intelligent and critical user of statistical information? Statistics are used not only to inform us, but to influence us. As a common aphorism puts it: "Statistics don't lie, but liars use statistics."

For a student of statistics, the answer lies in becoming an informed and discerning user of numerical information. The job of a student of statistics is to derive useful and usable information from a flood of data too large and complicated to be understood without being summarized. Learning to discern what is essential and what is not in quantitative data is an art and craft that requires practice and experience. But it is cultivated through careful learning. Some people devote their entire careers to accomplishing this and becoming experts—for example, university professors. Unless he or she is a statistics major, an undergraduate student does not have the time to devote a career to learning statistics in the four years of study for the BA or BS degree. Nevertheless, the crucial tools of becoming an informed user of statistical data can be learned in an introductory-level course in statistics in the time span of a quarter or a semester.

This book has been written to guide you through your first course in statistics at the undergraduate level. The only assumption that the authors have made is that everyone is capable of learning statistics. Accordingly, the book is not a textbook in mathematics. Formulas have been kept to a minimum. Where their use is unavoidable, the authors have gone to great lengths to explain every component and guide you through their application. Mathematical proofs are deliberately avoided throughout the book. Students who wish to learn proofs and acquire higher levels of statistics knowledge will find many courses on their campus that will satisfy their intellectual curiosity. The goal of the book is to help you learn and become an informed user of statistics whether your eventual plan is to obtain a degree and get employed or to undertake graduate work.

TASKS FOR STATISTICS: DESCRIBING, INFERRING, TESTING, PREDICTING

A first step in learning statistics is to appreciate the human capacity to summarize information through visual inspection and numerical indicators. Graphs and other charts can be used to summarize lots of information that would require many pages if each piece of information were written down without graphs. Through visual inspection, the statistician can begin to lock for patterns or trends in data to explore the possibility of uncovering relationships. In addition to visual inspection, the statistician uses simple arithmetic to compute single numbers (indexes or numerical indicators) that summarize data and buttress results derived from visual gleaning.

Having described the data in summary form, the next major goal of the statistician is to draw inferences or arrive at conclusions using simple mathematical calculations. In an increasingly complex world, rarely do researchers use the entire population or universe of cases to conduct a study. Instead, they use a subset of the population. This subset is called a sample. For instance, a researcher wishing to study risk factors for divorce in the United States will most likely not have time, money, and resources to study the entire population of couples who married at some point and divorced at a later time. In research, what frequently happens is that a researcher obtains a representative sample of couples that he or she studies.

While every research project is unique, we can summarize the four main ways that statistics are used in social research.

Describing Variation and Covariation

Descriptive statistics are tools that are used to summarize and index various things about the variation in the distribution of the scores of cases on one (or more) variable(s). This is one of our main tasks: to summarize large amounts of information in such a way that we can quickly, accurately, and honestly communicate about the main patterns that are present in the data.

There are a huge number of descriptive statistical indexes and visualizations. In this book, we provide only an introduction. Underlying all statistical description are a few—and only a few—very important ideas. If you grasp these ideas, you may always consult a textbook on the technical details of their application. In the first portion of the book we focus on these core ideas: the frequency distribution, central tendency, dispersion, and distributional shape. Later on, we will introduce the other core concept of descriptive statistics: association or covariation.

Inferring to the Population

In most social science applications of statistics, we observe only a ***sample*** of cases from a larger ***population***. We talk *to* some students, but would like to talk *about* all students. We talk *to* some citizens in a survey, but we want to make a generalization *about* all citizens. The second major task of statistics is to make inferences about variation and covariation in a population, based on the information available from a sample drawn from that population.

A number that summarizes variation or covariation in a sample is referred to as a ***statistic.*** If a number is calculated using the population, it is described as a ***parameter.*** For example, suppose researchers take a sample from the 2010 United States Census of Population, calculate the percentage of married individuals, and arrive at a figure of 50 percent; this would be a statistic, since they did not use the entire census. However, if they do the same computations on the full census and report a figure of 47 percent, in this case the 47 percent constitutes a parameter, since it was based on the entire population.

There are two aspects to this task: making an estimate of the value of some statistic and assessing how confident we are about the estimate. Estimating the value of a population parameter (e.g., the proportion of all Americans who are currently married) based on sample information (e.g., the proportion of the respondents to the General Social Survey [GSS] of the National Opinion Research Center [NORC] at the University of Chicago who say that they are married) is often quite straightforward for basic statistics. Determining how confident we are in making that inference is a bit more complicated, and is the main subject of ***inferential statistics.***

Almost all the statistical procedures we discuss in this text assume that, when we have selected a sample of cases from a defined population, we have used *probability sampling methods.* That is, we can state precisely what the likelihood is that a given case was selected from the population to be in the sample. If we select one student at random from a class of 10, the probability of any one student being selected is exactly 0.10.

CHECK QUIZ 1.1

1. Statistics are to parameters as
   a. samples are to populations.
   b. populations are to samples.
   c. medians are to standard deviations.
   d. standard deviations are to medians.
2. The goal of all techniques for selecting probability samples is to select samples that are
   a. very large.
   b. nonrandom.
   c. easily located.
   d. representative.
3. We use inferential statistics
   a. to make generalizations to a sample from a population.
   b. when we are working with data from a census.
   c. when we are using nonprobability sampling methods.
   d. to make generalizations to a population from a sample.

Probability sampling methods are often used in social science research to try to ensure that a sample is representative of the population from which it was drawn. Not all social science research, however, uses probability sampling (and there are often very good reasons for not doing so). While we may use descriptive statistics to describe variation and covariation in nonprobability samples, we mostly cannot use inferential statistics with them.

Testing Hypotheses

The third major task of statistics is to test hypotheses. As we will see shortly, statistical analysis in the social sciences is usually part of a larger intellectual project to develop and verify theories—explanations of how the social world works that go beyond a particular sample or even a particular population.

Descriptive statistics are often used to explore a set of observations and make effective summaries or empirical generalizations. That is, one way to do statistics is to start with the data and move toward more abstract and general statements. ***Hypothesis testing***, however, uses a different logic. It begins with a speculation about how the social world works (based on prior research, observation, and previous empirical work). Using this prior theory, we logically deduce what we should observe in a particular sample if the theory is correct, and what we might observe if it is not correct. That is, we make a hypothesis about the values of sample statistics in advance, and then we evaluate whether the evidence from the sample is consistent with our expectations.

Hypothesis testing uses both descriptive and inferential statistics to assess whether a set of observations is consistent with a theory. Rather than an *exploratory* application of statistics, it is a *confirmatory* application; that is, we seek to (dis)confirm theories using sample observations. Note that a characteristic of a sample is typically called a statistic, and a characteristic of a population from which that sample was derived is called a parameter. In hypothesis testing, we use sample statistics (characteristics) to arrive at best guesses or estimates of population parameters.

Predicting

In addition to describing, inferring, and hypothesis testing, statistical techniques are used for making predictions. In the use of statistics for ***prediction***, we create a *model* that describes our knowledge of how one or more causes (or predictors or independent variables) produce an outcome (or dependent variable). We then use the model to describe the patterns that we see in our sample. We evaluate whether our model does a good job or a poor job of describing the sample data. If the *goodness of fit* is adequate, we can then use the model to make predictions—either about the individual cases in the sample or with regard to new cases.

Models for statistical prediction, like the regression models that we examine near the end of this text, apply description, inference, and hypothesis-testing tools. The goal of the analysis, however, is to create a formal and mathematical description of social processes (the model), and see what this model can (and can't) help us explain about our current observations and predict about new observations that we might make.

Each of the four main tasks of statistics builds on the previous one. First we describe and explore observations in a sample. Then we infer how confident we are that the sample may generalize to a population. Then we may use statistics to test whether theories are consistent with our observations. Finally, we may use statistics to build predictive models of the social processes that produce variation and covariation.

CHECK QUIZ 1.2

1. The statement that "49 percent of the state's likely voters support Melvin, with a 3 percent margin of error" corresponds to which of the tasks of statistics?
   a. describing variation and covariation
   b. inference to the population
   c. testing a hypothesis
   d. prediction
2. The statement that "grades in statistics courses are directly proportional to the amount of time spent studying statistics" corresponds to which of the four tasks of statistics?
   a. describing variation and covariation
   b. inference to the population
   c. testing a hypothesis
   d. prediction
3. The statement that "contrary to our prediction, we found no association between the volume of chocolate consumed and one's grade on the midterm" corresponds to which of the four tasks of statistics?
   a. describing variation and covariation
   b. inference to the population
   c. testing a hypothesis
   d. prediction
4. The statement that "scores on the midterm ranged from a low of 12 to a high of 14" corresponds to which of the four tasks of statistics?
   a. describing variation and covariation
   b. inference to the population
   c. testing a hypothesis
   d. prediction

STATISTICS IN THE RESEARCH PROCESS

Statistics are used for describing, inferring, hypothesis testing, and prediction in almost every area of modern society. Businesses, government agencies, and nongovernmental organizations all collect and analyze data to understand patterns and trends. Scientific researchers do many of the same things using statistical techniques. But, in addition, research scientists use statistics as part of the process of developing and testing theories.

If you are reading this book, you are probably taking a basic course in statistics as part of your introduction to one of the social sciences. The fundamental goal of the social sciences is to create theories that help us to understand and explain the social world. Statistics play a key role in this enterprise. In this section, we briefly examine the ways that statistics fit in the research process. Then, we show what this looks like in practice—how research scientists apply statistics to problems and report their results.

Theories and Social Research

In social research, the use of statistics is never an end in itself, but rather a means to achieving an end. That end is the construction and validation of theory.

A theory is simply a proposed explanation or story about why something is the way it is, or works the way it does. Everyone develops theories all the time, in this very general sense of the word. So what makes a social-scientific theory different from any commonsense explanation? One important distinction is that a scientific theory is a *proposed* explanation. Scientific theories are never *proven* to be true. Theories can be useful or not; they can be shown by evidence to be consistent with particular observations or not. But theories are always tentative explanations that might apply to help us understand something. Another important distinction between a scientific theory and some other kinds of explanations is that scientific theories can be evaluated as useful or not by observation following intersubjective methods. That is, any two people following the same rules of observation and analysis can arrive at the same conclusion about whether a theory is a useful explanation of some phenomenon. This is part of why you are studying statistics. Statistics are part of the tool kit of shared methodologies that scientists use to connect theory and observation.

Scientific theories are general or abstract statements that provide proposed explanations for whole classes of specific phenomena. Our observations of the social world are much more specific and narrow, so there is always a gap between an abstract general explanation of a whole population or class of phenomena and our particular observations. While there are many issues in making valid connections between abstract theories and concrete observations, statistical tools address some of the issues of inference from samples to more general populations.

Social science research can begin with abstract theory, but most often it begins with an observation of a particular phenomenon in a particular place and time. That is, most social science research begins with *observing a datum.* To try to make sense of our observation, we always make comparisons—we may observe the same phenomenon over time, we may compare it to other phenomena that are similar to it, or we may compare the phenomenon to others that differ from it. We *form empirical generalizations* by making comparisons. That is, we see patterns, similarities, and differences.

The next step, having made some empirical generalization, is to develop a tentative explanation of it—a theory. We may draw on previous theories of the same phenomenon or theories about other phenomena that seem similar, or we may imagine wholly new concepts and ways of thinking about our observations. There are only three rules that the scientist needs to follow at this step: the theory we develop must apply to a general class of phenomena, we must be able to devise ways in which we can share an intersubjective understanding of the phenomenon, and it must be possible for us to prove that our theory fails or is not useful in explaining the phenomenon.

Once we have a proposed theory, we develop a *research hypothesis.* A hypothesis in research is a statement of an expected relationship between variables. If a researcher has a hunch that people with more education tend to have more income, the hypothesis implied here is that the higher the educational attainment, the higher the income. The researcher must first place this hypothesis within a broader scheme as to why and how those with higher educational attainment might earn more income. In other words, the researcher has to come up with some plausible explanations that elucidate the expected relationship between education and income. The researcher might argue, for example, that education is a form of investment that people make in themselves. Formal education through schooling takes a long time, but during that process, individuals learn skills and knowledge that can later be used on a job. Accordingly, those who have acquired more skills through attending school for longer periods are rewarded by society for their perseverance and higher skill levels through higher income.

The research hypothesis tells us what we should do empirically if a theory is useful, and if it is not. The human capital theory of education suggests that people who have more schooling should also earn higher incomes. We can look at real-world data and determine that this is wrong—and hence the theory is not helpful. Or we can look at real-world data and see that (in one sample) the human capital theory provides an explanation. Based on the results of our investigation, we may revise the theory or suggest an alternative theory.

Where do statistics fit in?

In the *exploratory* phase of research we collect data and seek to find patterns and make empirical generalizations. While there are many methods for doing this, descriptive statistics are often a very helpful tool. Often our exploratory data are not collected using probability samples or even highly standardized measurement tools—so inferential statistics are not very relevant, and we cannot apply hypothesis testing and prediction.

Once we have developed a theory and deduced a research hypothesis, we enter the *confirmatory* phase of research. Using research methodology tools, we make our theoretical concepts operational and develop measurable variables. Using research design and sampling, we collect systematic data, usually using probability or random assignment methods. With our data in hand, we can formally test hypotheses leading to verification of the theory and use statistical models to make predictions.

CHECK QUIZ 1.3

1. Social scientists use statistics to
   a. prove that research theories are true.
   b. manage and analyze data.
   c. maintain the status quo in the research community.
   d. assure that no errors were made in research design.
2. In the research process, theory
   a. is unnecessary.
   b. is always fully developed before any data are gathered.
   c. is developed only after the data have been completely analyzed.
   d. attempts to explain the relationship between phenomena.
3. A hypothesis differs from a theory in that
   a. it is testable.
   b. it is true.
   c. it is more speculative.
   d. it is more abstract.

The Research Report

Most of your professors have at one time or another written scientific research papers that have been published in professional or peer-reviewed journals. Conducting research and disseminating findings is a fundamental job requirement of the professoriate in most research universities in the United States and around the world. As undergraduate students, you have probably heard the expression that professors must either "publish or perish." Outside of the university, anyone who works with data must also, in a sense, publish or perish. Your boss will want you to examine some data for patterns and make a report; you may collect data on customer preferences to be used for marketing; you may evaluate whether one program of medical treatment produces better results than another. Applied statisticians must also report their results.

While the details will vary with your problem and your context, reporting the results of research that uses statistics almost always follows a common format. In preparing answers to many of the chapter exercises in this book, you can also use the following template.

The Research Problem

Research reports generally begin with a clear statement of the aim, objective, or purpose of the study. Hypotheses or expected patterns are clearly stated in a testable format. Since precision is crucial in the scientific enterprise, concepts should also be defined. The research problem answers the question: what does the researcher wish to explain, predict, or investigate? A typical research problem could be stated as: "The aim of this research is to investigate whether divorced men are more likely to commit suicide than divorced women."

Methods

Next the researcher indicates the nature and source of data to be used in bringing evidence to bear on the research problem and related hypotheses. Analysts can either use primary data that they collect, for instance through surveys, or rely on secondary data (collected by others) that exist in many data archives. For example, the National Center for Health Statistics (NCHS; part of the U.S. Department of Health and Human Services) collects and disseminates several data sets that are freely available at the organization's website (www.cdc.gov/nchs). Students interested in studying issues of health, fertility, family growth, morbidity, and mortality will find rich data sets at the NCHS site. An especially useful data set is the National Health Interview Survey. Other data archives include the Integrated Public Use Microdata Series (IPUMS) project at the University of Minnesota (www.ipums.org). Here one finds census data for the United States from earliest times to the latest decennial census of population. Many social scientists rely on data from the Inter-University Consortium for Political and Social Research (ICPSR) at University of Michigan. Data from ICPSR are available to researchers (including students and faculty) at universities that are members of the consortium and pay their regular dues. The United States Bureau of the Census (under the U.S. Department of Commerce) is a great source of information on the U.S. population. To determine what is available, visit the Internet site at www.census.gov. Two notable sets of data collected by the census bureau are the Current Population Surveys and the American Community Surveys.

In the methods section of the research report, it is not enough merely to indicate the type and source of one's data. The researcher must clearly state which variables were used and how they were measured. Where applicable, distinctions should also be made between dependent and independent variables. It is advisable to specify the dependent variable first, followed by your primary independent variable(s). It is also in the methods section of the research paper that the analyst indicates which statistical technique was used in order to test hypotheses and answer the research problem. Material that you are learning in this class will find their greatest application in the methods section of a research paper. It is required that the researcher state not only the statistical technique(s) used to address the research problem, but the appropriateness of the technique(s). As you study and apply statistics using this book, we will make it clear under what circumstances certain techniques are appropriate or not appropriate. Data analysis and statistical computations done on the data will be mentioned in this section of the paper as well, along with any known shortcomings of selected statistical technique(s).

Results

After analyzing the data, findings are presented in this section of the research paper. Depending on the research problem and the statistical technique(s) used, the researcher presents his or her results with the aid of statistical tables and charts. In this section, one must indicate which hypotheses were supported by the data analysis and which ones were not. It is not enough to merely present results; they must be interpreted in an objective manner for the intended audience. It is a good idea to keep tables to a minimum and to write out the findings as clearly as possible.

Discussion

In this section of the report, the researcher summarizes the findings and then goes on to place them within the context of the research problem and any relevant theories. The analyst also indicates the implications of the findings for past and future research. It is good discipline for a researcher to point out unique contributions made by his or her study. In this regard, an important question that should be addressed in the discussion is the following: What do we know as a result of this research that we did not know beforehand? The analyst must also indicate whether and how the findings are consistent with past studies. In addition, he or she should note existing studies that contradict the findings, and try as much as possible within the context of the data analysis to suggest possible reasons for inconsistencies.

Depending on the nature of the research question, it is a good idea for a researcher to suggest policy implications of the findings. Questions such as the following could be addressed: How could findings be used to improve the human condition? How might findings be used to solve specific problems in society? What is currently going on that needs to be reexamined and perhaps stopped as a result of findings from this study? Finally, the researcher should close by acknowledging any limitations of his or her study and offer caution (if appropriate) about the extent to which results might be generalized.

At the end of the research process, the author must communicate the findings to a wider audience. This can be done in several ways. The author could submit the article to a scientific journal for peer review and publication. Some researchers may decide to give a lecture within the university, in the community, or at another university, organization, or agency. Still others might decide to issue a press release, although it is advisable to issue a press release only upon the article's acceptance by a journal. Greater credence is given to the results if an article has gone through the peer-review process, is about to be published, or has already been published.

BASIC ELEMENTS OF RESEARCH: UNITS OF ANALYSIS AND VARIABLES

Researchers using statistical method use empirical observations—or data—to describe, infer, test hypotheses, and predict. But what are data?

Data are information, but they are more than that. Data are the result of using systematic methods of research design, sampling, and measurement guided by research hypotheses derived from theories. Because the information is collected with a method and plan, it has a structure. Data are scores on variables, observed across units of analysis.

Units of Analysis

Units of analysis in research are the carriers of information. They are the entities that the researcher studies, and upon which he or she collects data and makes generalizations. In a study that seeks to explain why higher educational attainment leads to higher income, if a researcher collects data on persons, then individuals comprise units of investigation. Similarly, in a study to determine whether poverty rates in cities contribute to higher crime rates, cities would be units of observation or study.

An important principle in statistics is that conclusions based on one unit of observation may not be generalized to other units. For example, if a researcher uses cities to study crime rates and finds that cities with high levels of poverty tend to have higher crime rates, it would be a mistake to conclude on the basis of the same study that poor people are committing the crimes. This is an example of a logical error, called the *ecological fallacy*.

Social scientists may study different units of analysis. Individual persons are the most obvious unit of analysis, but research might focus on families, groups, church congregations, neighborhoods, cities, political units like states or nations, or whole societies. What is important is that the unit of analysis be consistent with the theory, and that we use systematic methods to identify the elements of the population of units (i.e., be able, in principle, to list each member of the population).

Generally, social scientists, as we discussed earlier, don't collect information from every member of a population of units of analysis. Instead of doing a census, they usually draw a sample. The *cases* or *observations* or *units of analysis* in data, then, are usually elements selected from some homogeneous and bounded population to which the researcher wants to generalize.

CHECK QUIZ 1.4

1. A "case" in statistics refers to
   a. something to keep your calculator and pencil in.
   b. one in a set of variables (e.g., gender).
   c. an entity for which we have some data.
   d. one in a set of values (e.g., male).
2. A case is also known as
   a. an observation.
   b. a variable.
   c. an association.
   d. a difficult situation.

Variables

Statisticians collect information or data on characteristics or attributes of units of analysis. These characteristics are referred to as ***variables.*** A variable is a characteristic or attribute that can take on different values (or vary) across cases. It changes from person to person, from county to county, from city to city, or from country to country. A variable can be distinguished from a ***constant,*** which does not vary across observations. In the General Social Survey, for example, all cases share the same score on the attribute "resident in the United States," since the study is conducted only in the United States. Research aims at explaining change or variation. Since constants by definition do not change, they cannot be objects of study.

Every variable is made up of *levels* or *values.* The levels or values of a variable are the scores that cases might have on an attribute. The variable "sex" might have two levels, male and female. The variable "income" might have many values: $3,426.27 and $105,232.16 are two examples.

Kinds of variables are often distinguished by the role they play in research questions (dependent or independent), whether their scales of measurement are discrete or continuous, and their levels of measurement.

Dependent and Independent Variables

A ***dependent variable*** is the entity that a researcher wishes to explain or predict. For example, if an analyst wishes to explain why workers have different earnings, then earnings comprise the dependent variable. Other names that are used in statistics to describe dependent variables are outcome or response variables. An ***independent variable*** is a variable that is believed to explain or predict the variation in the dependent variable. Other names that are used to describe independent variables are explanatory variables, predictors or predictor variables, covariates, and prognostic factors.

To differentiate between independent and dependent variables, think again about factors that explain earnings differences among workers. Suppose a sociologist was to propose a hypothesis that educational attainment influences one's earnings. Educational attainment would be the independent variable and earnings would be the dependent variable.

It is important to realize that no variable is inherently dependent or independent. Whether a given variable is independent or dependent is dictated by the research objectives. In one research a variable might be independent, but in another the same variable could be dependent.

Discrete and Continuous Variables

Variables can be described as *discrete* or *continuous* depending on their unit of measurement. A variable is considered a ***discrete variable*** if its unit of measurement cannot be broken down or subdivided into finer or smaller units. For example, the variable "children ever born per woman" is discrete. Its unit of measurement is human beings or persons, and these exist only as whole numbers (integers). Children ever born could take on values ranging from 0 (no children), 1 child, 2 children, or 3 children to the highest possible number of children born, but this variable will never take on values such as 0.1 children or 2.5 children. Other examples of discrete variables are household size, number of living children, number of married couples, number of cars per garage, and so on.

Continuous variables are those whose numerical values can be broken down or subdivided into finer units almost indefinitely. Age qualifies as an example of a continuous variable in that it could be broken down into years, months, days, and beyond. Other examples are weight, height, time, income, educational attainment, and so on. Many other continuous variables are formed by taking ratios or rates. The homicide rate (homicides per 100,000 residents) is a continuous variable because it divides homicides by population, and the calculation could be carried out to any number of decimal points. One hallmark of continuous variables is that in addition to a researcher's ability to break them down into finer gradations, they can assume decimals. In practice, many researchers end up rounding their values to one or two decimal places.

Levels of Measurement

The way in which we attach scores to attributes when we measure phenomena is very important. The ***level of measurement*** of a variable describes the kind and amount of information it contains; it also affects what kinds of operations we can perform on the variable, and the types of statistics that are appropriate.

There are four main levels or types of measurement: nominal, ordinal, interval, and ratio. The level or type of measurement to use on a variable is determined by noting the

CHECK QUIZ 1.5

1. A variable contains
   a. cases.
   b. values.
   c. statistics.
   d. observations.
2. Which of the following could *not* be a value?
   a. twelve (12)
   b. tall
   c. hairy
   d. often
   e. All of these could be values.
3. A researcher asks: "Are men or women more likely to become depressed?" The dependent variable is ________, and the independent variable is ________.
   a. women; men
   b. depressed; not depressed
   c. sex; depression
   d. depression; sex
4. The number of points that Kobe Bryant scores in a particular game is a(n) ________ variable; Kobe's scoring average for the whole season is a ________ variable.
   a. independent; dependent
   b. discrete; continuous
   c. outcome; predictor
   d. continuous; discrete
5. Suppose I am studying why some men drop out of high school and others don't. Dropping out of high school is a(n) ________, and sex is a(n) ________.
   a. constant; variable
   b. variable; constant
   c. independent variable; dependent variable
   d. dependent variable; independent variable

presence or absence of four characteristics: distinctiveness, ordering in magnitude, equal intervals, and an absolute or natural zero. Table 1.1 summarizes how levels of measurement distinguish types of variables.

Sometimes the levels of measurement are referred to in somewhat different ways. A variable that distinguishes kind but not amount is often referred to as "qualitative" or "categorical." Nominal and ordinal variables are qualitative—we can tell whether two cases

TABLE 1.1 Levels of Measurement and Their Characteristics

Characteristic	Nominal	Ordinal	Interval	Ratio
Distinctiveness	Present	Present	Present	Present
Ordering in magnitude	Absent	Present	Present	Present
Equal intervals	Absent	Absent	Present	Present
Absolute zero	Absent	Absent	Absent	Present

are of the same type but not the amount of the difference between them. A variable that distinguishes the amount of difference between cases is sometimes called "quantitative." Interval and ratio variables are quantitative.

Nominal variables have only the characteristic of distinctiveness. A nominal variable measures identity or category. In this level of measurement, numbers serve merely as labels or names to identify items, classes, or categories of the concept being measured. For example, if we are studying religion, we may sort our sample of people into categories and assign a number to each category, with 1 = Protestant, 2 = Catholic, 3 = Muslim, 4 = other, and 5 = none. These numbers serve to identify people by their religion. Apart from this, they mean nothing. For example, although the Catholic score is given as 2 and the Protestant score is 1, it does not make sense to assume that Catholics have more religion than Protestants, that there are twice as many of them, or any other conclusion based on the numbers 1 and 2.

A nominal variable that has only two categories (e.g., true/false, present/absent, yes/no, agree/disagree) is a *binary* (i.e., two-value) variable or ***nominal dichotomy variable type.*** Usually one category is given the numerical value of 1, and the other category is given the value of 0. When scores are assigned this way, the variable is often called a *dummy variable.* A nominal variable that has more than two categories may be called a ***nominal polyotomy variable type*** (i.e., many types). Religion, for example, is a nominal polyotomy.

Ordinal variables indicate not only distinctiveness, but also ordering in magnitude. In such a case, larger numbers represent more of the concept or phenomenon being measured than smaller numbers. Numbers reflect the rank order of the concept. For example, suppose we want to measure the concept social class; we might divide our sample into 1 = lower, 2 = middle, and 3 = upper. It is clear that there is an ordering in magnitude, with those given 3 being of a higher class than those with 2. At the same time, the distance (or amounts) between classes are not necessarily equal. In this example, not only have we divided a concept (social class) into categories, but we have also shown that there are degrees of class.

Most ordinal variables used in social research are ***grouped ordinal variable type.*** There are a limited number of ranks, and many cases may have the same rank on a grouped ordinal variable. In survey research, for example, respondents are asked whether they "strongly disagree," "disagree," "feel neutral," "agree," or "strongly agree" with a statement. We can order the respondents from low to high agreement, so the variable is ordinal. But many

CHECK QUIZ 1.6

1. The values "left-handed," "right-handed," and "ambidextrous" form
   a. a nominal dichotomy.
   b. a nominal polyotomy.
   c. a grouped ordinal variable.
   d. a full rank-order scale.
2. The values "Green Party," "Democratic Party," "Republican Party," and "Chaos Party" form
   a. a nominal dichotomy.
   b. a nominal polyotomy.
   c. a grouped ordinal variable.
   d. a full rank-order scale.
3. The values "tallest in class," "second-tallest in class," and "shortest in class" suggest the use of
   a. a nominal dichotomy.
   b. a nominal polyotomy.
   c. a grouped ordinal variable.
   d. a full rank-order scale.
4. If a variable contains the values "failing course," "just barely passing course," and "doing really well in course," it is probably
   a. a nominal dichotomy.
   b. a nominal polyotomy.
   c. a grouped ordinal variable.
   d. a full rank-order scale.
5. The original data had a variable called "Party" that contained the values "Green Party," "Democratic Party," "Republican Party," and "Chaos Party." We created three new variables out of the original variable. Now we have a "Green" variable (1 = Green Party, 0 = other), a "Democrat" variable (1 = Democrat, 0 = other), and so on. Forming variables in this way is known as
   a. stupid coding.
   b. ridiculous coding.
   c. dummy coding.
   d. Morse coding.
6. If you ask "How many years of school have you completed?" on a survey, this variable will be
   a. an interval/ratio variable.
   b. a full rank-order ordinal variable.
   c. a nominal dichotomy.
   d. a nominal polyotomy.

respondents can give the same answer, forming a group. *Full rank-order ordinal variables* are less common in social research. On a ***full rank-order ordinal variable***, each case has a distinct rank. The order of finish in a race (first, second, third, . . .) is a full rank-order ordinal variable because only one case can be at each level of the variable.

Interval variables have the characteristic of distinctiveness, ordering in magnitude, and, in addition, equal intervals. The variable age is an example of an interval variable. Imagine three people, one 16 years old, another 17 years old, and the third 18 years old. The three ages are different (and hence the distinctiveness quality exists). In addition, 17 is greater than 16, and 18 is greater than both 16 and 17. Thus there is ordering in magnitude with higher numbers denoting more age. What distinguishes this level of measurement from the rest is that in addition to the two aforementioned characteristics, there are equal intervals or equal distances between numbers. For instance, the distance (interval) between 16 and 17 is the same as that between 17 and 18.

Ratio variables have all the qualities previously stated (distinctiveness, ordering in magnitude, and equal intervals). Additionally, they have what is called an absolute or natural zero. This simply means that a zero represents a complete absence of the phenomenon or property in question. For example, in talking about income, zero income implies complete absence of money and hence income would qualify as a ratio level variable.

Take a minute, before moving on, to be sure you understand the distinctions among the levels of measurement that are used in statistical measures.

SUMMARY

The purposes of this chapter have been to clarify the role that statistics play in the process of scientific inquiry, and to review some basic concepts and terminology that you need to know before beginning to study statistics.

Knowledge of the logic and some of the technique of statistical analysis is simple cultural literacy in contemporary society. Statistics are used for a number of purposes: describing the variation and covariation of variables across cases, making inferences from observations in a sample to larger populations from which the sample was taken, testing hypotheses derived from theories of how the social world works, and making predictions based on models of the relationships among variables.

In this book we discuss statistics as a set of tools that support scientific inquiry. Scientific inquiry is primarily concerned with developing theory and validating theory by empirical observation. Statistics play roles both in creating theory and in validating theory by observation. The former (exploratory) role uses statistics as a tool to summarize data and find patterns so empirical generalizations can be made, which then beg theoretical explanation. The latter (confirmatory) role involves using theory to make predictions—hypotheses—about what we should observe in new samples if a theory is valid (or not), and then using statistics to determine the confidence we have in asserting that observations are (or are not) consistent with theoretical expectations.

In this chapter, we've also provided an outline of how statistical information is used in writing a research report. Statistics are not an end in themselves, and the research report is a good example of how they are actually used in practice in social-scientific research.

Statistics are operations performed on data. Data are information describing scores on variables that are attributes of units of observation. *Cases*, *units*, and *elements* are terms used to identify the units of observation in data. Social scientists may study many different kinds of units.

Each unit of observation is measured, and then assigned scores to describe its attributes. Measured attributes that may differ from one unit of observation to another are called variables. Variables have levels or scores that indicate the possible states of each attribute. It is often useful to distinguish between independent and dependent variables, discrete and continuous variables, and qualitative and quantitative variables.

Each variable has a level of measurement or scale. The scale used to assign numbers to the levels of a variable is important because different scales contain different kinds of information and allow different kinds of statistical procedures. We discussed nominal, ordinal, interval, and ratio scales for the levels of variables.

We've finished with the preliminaries, so let's start doing some statistics!

KEY TERMS

dependent and independent variables

descriptive statistics

discrete versus continuous variables

full rank-order ordinal variable type

grouped ordinal variable type

hypothesis testing

inferential statistics

interval variable type

levels of measurement or scale

nominal dichotomy variable type

nominal polyotomy variable type

prediction

ratio variable type

sample and population

statistic and parameter

variable versus constant

CHECK QUIZ ANSWERS

Quiz 1.1 Answers: 1. (a); 2. (d); 3. (a)
Quiz 1.2 Answers: 1. (b); 2. (d); 3. (c); 4. (a)

Quiz 1.3 Answers: 1. (b); 2. (d); 3. (a)
Quiz 1.4 Answers: 1. (c); 2. (a)
Quiz 1.5 Answers: 1. (b); 2. (e); 3. (d); 4. (b); 5. (b)
Quiz 1.6 Answers: 1. (b); 2. (b); 3. (d); 4. (c); 5. (c); 6. (a)

EXERCISES

1. What are descriptive statistics used for? What are inferential statistics used for? Provide an example of each.
2. For each of the following scenarios, determine whether the use of statistics being described is descriptive or inferential.
   a. The average age of students in a class is found to be 19.4 years.
   b. A poll of public opinion reports that 38 percent of the population supports ballot proposition B, with a margin of error of 3 percent.
   c. The annual family incomes of persons applying for disability income in San Rafael during 2003 ranged from $15,437 to $234,550.
   d. Based on a sampling of students enrolling in 15 classes taught in a large lecture hall, the registrar estimates that 38 percent of all students enrolled in classes in the lecture hall are "extremely dissatisfied" with the acoustics.
3. Here are a number of variables that are used in the General Social Survey. For each variable, indicate the level of measurement (nominal, ordinal, or interval/ratio) and whether the variable is continuous or discrete.

Variable	Level of Measurement	Continuous or Discrete
What is your sex? (Male or female)		
How many siblings (i.e., brothers and sisters) do you have?		
What social class would you say your family is? (Upper, middle, working, or lower)		
Do you believe in life after death? (Yes, not sure, no)		
What is your current grade point average (GPA)?		
What is your mother's occupation?		
How many years of schooling did your father complete?		
The death penalty for murder should be used in all states. (Strongly agree, agree, neutral, disagree, strongly disagree)		
How many times per year do you attend religious services?		

4. For each of the variables listed, state the level of measurement and whether the variable is continuous or discrete.

Variable	Level of Measurement	Continuous or Discrete
Student's age, measured in years		
Proportion of the students in classes at the university who are women		
Student's class (e.g., first-year, senior)		
Self-identified national origin (e.g., United States, Cambodia, Senegal)		
Father's education (less than high school, high school, some college, completed college, or graduate work)		
Support for the war in Iraq (strongly support, support, neutral, oppose, strongly oppose)		
Grade point average, measured to two decimal places (e.g., 3.45)		
Member of fraternity or sorority (yes, no)		
Number of times per week that you eat at an on-campus dining facility		
Number of persons in your immediate family		

5. The following are some short descriptions of research studies. For each, identify the variables that are being used, describe the level of measurement of each, and determine whether the variable is being used as an independent or a dependent variable:
   a. A student was recently arrested for hacking into the database used to conduct elections for officers of the senior class. The campus newspaper has asked you to do a study to determine how other students feel about this—that is, how many students feel that this is a very serious crime, not a serious crime, or not really a crime at all. The editor thinks that computer science students and business students are less likely than other students to view the hacking as a serious crime.
   b. The campus computing service personnel are interested in how aware students are of the services they offer. They ask a sample of 500 students whether they are aware (yes, maybe, no) of each of 10 different services, and count up how many are chosen. To try to target future advertising, they also ask respondents to report their sex, age, and year in school, and whether they own a computer.
   c. A political economist has derived the hypothesis that "the greater the level of income inequality, the greater the political instability." To test this hypothesis, she collects data on the percentage of all income that is controlled by the richest 5 percent of families in each of 100 nations in the year 2000. The researcher measures

the concept of "political instability" as a count of the number of changes in government between 2001 and 2004.

d. A researcher thinks that police-community relations are affected by city size and racial heterogeneity. The researcher measures the quality of police-community relations by doing a survey in each of 30 cities, asking the question: "How would you rate your local police? (Excellent, good, fair, poor)." City size is measured by the number of people in the city as reported by the census. Racial heterogeneity is measured by the ratio of nonwhite persons to white persons.

6. The following are some short descriptions of research studies. For each, identify the variables that are being used, describe the level of measurement of each variable, and determine whether each variable is being used as an independent or a dependent variable:
   a. A researcher is interested in understanding why some students earn higher grades than others. One possible explanation is that performance in college is a continuation of earlier academic performance. The researcher collects information on a sample of students, measuring their current GPAs and their high school GPAs.
   b. Some communities have higher rates of crime than others. Our researcher thinks that high average income and high average education of the families in communities may decrease the rates of some crimes (e.g., family violence), but increase rates of other crimes (simple theft).
   c. As organizations become larger, they need to become more vertically differentiated (i.e., have more levels of management). A researcher collects information on the total employment of universities and the number of levels of administration in order to test this hypothesis.
   d. Does ethnic identity become less the longer a family has been in the United States? A researcher asks a series of questions designed to measure ethnic consciousness in people of Japanese origin whose families have been resident in the United States for one, two, three, four, or more generations.

Chapter 2

DISPLAYING ONE DISTRIBUTION

LEARNING OBJECTIVES

When you have finished this chapter, you will be able to:

- Lay out a frequency chart properly for nominal, ordinal, and interval/ratio variables.
- Display value labels, frequencies, and relative frequencies for nominal variables.
- Use a bar chart and a pie chart to graph nominal variables.
- Add cumulative relative frequencies for the frequency charts of ordinal and interval/ratio variables.
- Use histograms and stacked bar charts to graph ordinal and interval/ratio variables.
- Determine midpoints and class boundaries for interval/ratio variables.
- Use histograms, frequency polygons, and cumulative frequency polygons to graph interval/ratio variables.

SUMMARIZING VARIATION IN ONE VARIABLE

Researchers use statistics to describe phenomena in ways that can be readily understood by others; statistics are a tool for telling the story about one's discoveries. We begin by considering some of the basic tools used to tell the simplest stories, those that involve a single distribution of scores.

When we are trying to describe the scores of a sample of ***cases or observations*** on a variable, we could simply list them. For example, if we were describing the distribution of the variable "age" for a sample of students in a class, we could present something like: 18, 19, 17, 22, 33, 19, 22, 23, 18, 24.

A simple list like this provides full information about the variable, but it is hardly a summary. If we had many cases (and sociological studies often have thousands), a list would be almost completely useless (although the length of the list would suggest sample size, but even that wouldn't give us a precise measure).

If we sorted the cases in the list, we would be somewhat better off. The ages of students in the class could be arranged from low to high: 17, 18, 18, 19, 19, 22, 22, 23, 24, 33. This is more informative because it gives us some idea of sample size (the length of the list); the sample's minimum score (17) and maximum score (33); and which scores are most common (18 occurs twice, 19 occurs twice, and 22 occurs twice).

But we can do much better than a sorted list to summarize the distribution of the scores on a variable in our sample. One very useful thing to do is to prepare a frequency chart. The ***frequency chart*** is a numerical summary of the number of cases and their relative frequencies. Another useful approach is to present the same information in the form of graphical displays such as pie charts and bar charts.

Variables measured at the nominal, ordinal, and interval/ratio levels contain different kinds and amounts of information. Because of this, the approaches to constructing and interpreting frequency charts and graphics differ somewhat, depending on the level of measurement. We discuss how to approach the frequency chart and graphics for nominal, ordinal, and interval/ratio variables in the sections in this chapter.

FREQUENCY DISTRIBUTIONS FOR NOMINAL VARIABLES

Nominal variables allow us to classify cases into categories, but not to rank the cases or describe a degree of difference between the cases in different categories.

We can summarize the information about the scores of the cases in our sample by presenting a simple tabulation of how many cases there are that have each possible score. The frequency chart is the normal way of presenting this information.

It is also helpful to understand the relative frequencies of the scores on a nominal variable. For example, are there more men or more women in the sample? To make comparisons across several samples (e.g., a class in the College of Liberal Arts versus a class in the College of Engineering), expressing relative frequencies as ***percentages*** or proportions is helpful.

Frequency Chart Rules

There are better (and worse) ways of making a chart to display the frequencies of the scores on a nominal variable. Here are some best practices.

- A frequency chart should have a title that describes the variable and sample.
- A frequency chart should describe the source of the data. This is often done in the footer of the chart.
- If there are cases in the sample that have not been included in the chart (for example, "refused to answer" might not be reported), or if the scores in the chart have been modified in some way (for example, combining certain categories), these need to be reported—either in the text or in a note to the table.
- The categories of the variable being described (sometimes called the *levels* or *values* of the variable) must be mutually exclusive and jointly exhaustive. That is, no case in the sample belongs in more than one category, and there is a category for every case.
- The frequency chart must have at least two columns. Each column must have a title describing the contents of the column.
- The leftmost column uses the name of the variable being described as its title. Each value of the variable is listed in the leftmost column as a row of the chart. For a nominal variable, the order in which we list the values does not matter.
- The next column of the frequency chart uses "Frequency," "*N*," "Count," or "*f*" as its title. In each row, the count of the number of cases having each value is presented.
- The last row of the table, which is called the "column marginals," is labeled as "Total" and gives the total number of cases.

That's a lot of rules. Let's look at a simple frequency table created by IBM SPSS (Table 2.1) (Analyze → Descriptive statistics → Frequencies) to illustrate.

We'll talk about the "Percent" "Valid Percent" and "Cumulative Percent" columns later—for now just ignore them.

The table provided by SPSS is pretty good, but it doesn't follow all of our rules.

The table has a title ("Marital Status"). Actually, we should probably say more than this to tell readers where (United States) and when (1978–1998) the sample was drawn. We should probably also add a footnote citing the data source (General Social Survey), and describing how many cases were left out and why.

Helpful hint: While it is possible to edit tables in SPSS (double-clicking on them in the output window brings up some editing tools), it's usually easier to copy them to the

TABLE 2.1 Frequency Chart for a Nominal Variable

		Marital Status			
		Frequency	Percent	Valid Percent	Cumulative Percent
Valid	Married	816	54.4	54.4	54.4
	Widowed	150	10.0	10.0	64.4
	Divorced	199	13.3	13.3	77.7
	Separated	45	3.0	3.0	80.7
	Never married	290	19.3	19.3	100.0
	Total	1,500	100.0	100.0	

clipboard in SPSS and paste them into a spreadsheet program like Microsoft Excel, where it's easy to make modifications. It is also possible to paste directly into MS Word, but if you need to clean up the table by deleting cells, dealing with merged cells can be frustrating.

Notice the categories. Every person in the sample can be classified in one, and only one, category (the categories are mutually exclusive). Notice that the table reports the ***marginal*** total at the bottom. Also notice that it really would not matter what order we use to report the categories—these are simply different groups of respondents, and they are not ranked.

Finally, notice that the columns have labels to describe what information is being reported (actually, we should probably put "marital status" in the column header for the value labels). And note that we report the number or frequency.

The table reports there were 1,500 respondents overall, and that 816 said they were married, 150 said they were widowed, and so on. This is obvious but important information.

Relative Frequencies (Percentages and Proportions)

The frequency chart presents useful information about the total number of cases and the number of cases in each category of a nominal variable. It is also useful to describe the sizes of the groups relative to one another: Which is the biggest group? The smallest? How much bigger is the biggest group?

In one sample, we can easily answer these questions simply by looking at the frequencies. There are 199 divorced persons and 45 separated persons, for example, so there are roughly four times as many divorced persons as separated persons. Using relative frequencies is preferred to looking at raw frequencies in order to make comparisons across groups and to make comparisons to other samples (that probably have different total numbers of cases).

Relative frequencies are the frequencies in each category divided by the total frequency. The formal way of saying this is shown in Formula 2.1.

$$p_K = \frac{f_K}{N} \tag{2.1}$$

Helpful hint: If, when seeing that formula, you thought to yourself, "Sure, the proportion of things in one category is equal to the number of things in that category divided by the total number of things," then you can skip the rest of this paragraph. If, however, you felt a little tightening in your chest at seeing this, the first of many formulas in this text, you're not alone: not everyone grasps this stuff at the beginning. Don't panic; just take a deep breath and work your way through it.

p (in this case) stands for a given proportion, like the proportion of people in the sample who are married.

Subscripts (the little letters or numbers like the 2 in H_2O) are used to differentiate between different things or sets of things. In this case, *K* is a placeholder that means something like "The name of the thing we care about goes here when you actually use this equation." If we are talking about the proportion of men in a sample, we might use the notation p_{men}.

f stands for a frequency (a count), and it has the same subscript as the *p* because it refers to the same set of things.

N stands for the total number of things. Capital *N* usually stands for the total number of items in a sample; lowercase *n* is sometimes used that way, but can also refer to the number of items in a subsample.

So, if we were talking about the married people in our sample, the formula would be as shown in Formula 2.2.

$$p_{married} = \frac{f_{married}}{N} \tag{2.2}$$

If we simply divide the number of cases (frequency, or *f*) in one category (*K*) by the total (*N*) (e.g., 816 married divided by 1,500 total = 0.544), we are expressing the relative frequency as a proportion. Often we multiply the proportions by 100 to express them as a percentage (e.g., 54.4 percent), as in Formula 2.3.

$$\%_K = \left(\frac{f_K}{N}\right) \times 100 \tag{2.3}$$

The relative frequencies for nominal variables are almost always reported in a third column of a frequency chart (the first column is the value label, while the second is the raw frequency), as shown in Table 2.2.

Graphical Displays

For a nominal variable, we've seen that it is important to report the total number of cases and to report what the categories are and their relative frequencies. A frequency chart with percentages or proportions is a simple and elegant way to do this.

TABLE 2.2 Nominal Frequency Chart with Relative Frequencies: Marital Status in the 1978–1998 General Social Survey*

Marital Status	*f*	%
Married	816	54.4
Widowed	150	10.0
Divorced	199	13.3
Separated	45	3.0
Never married	290	19.3
Total	1,500	100.0

*U.S. sample only.

FIGURE 2.1 Marital Status in the 1978–1998 General Social Survey

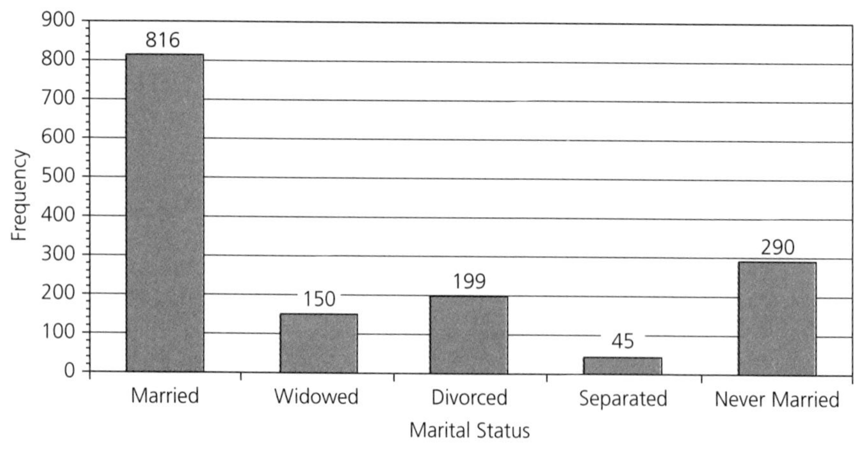

$N = 1{,}500$; U.S. sample only.

Pictures (visualizations) of our data, though, are often even more effective ways of conveying the same information. Two kinds of statistical graphics (***graphs***) are commonly used to report on nominal variables: the bar chart and the pie chart. These are not easy to draw by hand, but spreadsheet and statistical software packages make them very easy to prepare.

Bar charts are widely used. You've seen them in newspapers and magazines, as well as in scientific reports. Bar charts are very easy to interpret, and provide information on both the frequencies and the relative frequencies of a nominal variable.

While bar charts are pretty simple, there are some better and some worse ways of preparing them. Figure 2.1 shows a bar chart drawn by SPSS of the same data we examined earlier in the frequency table.

FIGURE 2.2 Modified Bar Charts

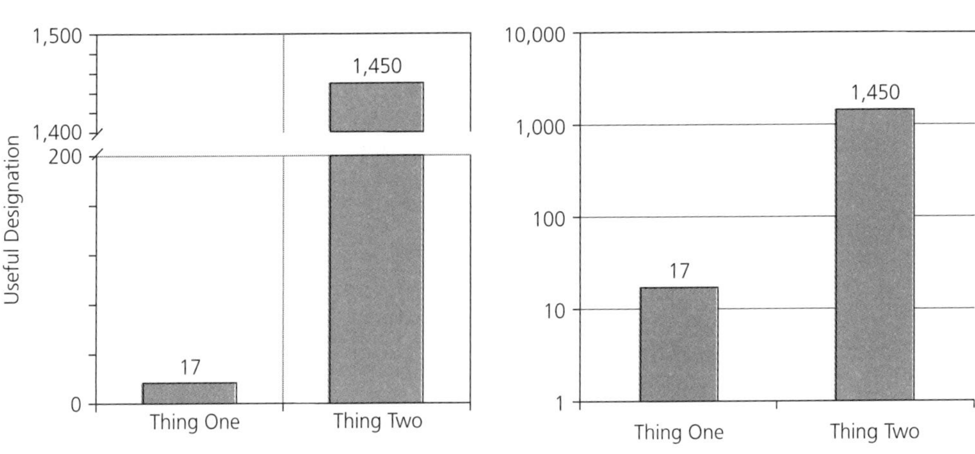

Like a frequency table, a bar chart should have a title and should identify the source of data and anything special that was done to the data (e.g., combining categories or leaving out missing data).

The *x*-axis (the horizontal dimension) of the bar chart contains one bar for each category of the nominal variable. Each bar is labeled with the name of the category it represents. Notice that the bars do not touch one another; this is because we don't want to suggest that the categories are really adjacent to one another. This differs from the graphics that we use for ordinal and interval variables. Again, since the variable is nominal, the order in which the bars are arranged doesn't affect interpretation.

The *y*-axis (the vertical dimension) is labeled to tell us what is being graphed (frequency). Notice that the intervals between the points on the scale are equal in size, and that they begin at zero and extend slightly beyond the highest value (married = 816). If values differ a great deal (some very large, others relatively small), it may be necessary to use a broken vertical axis. In the first graph in Figure 2.2, if the axis weren't broken, the "Thing One" bar wouldn't show up at all. However, when a broken axis is used, it may give the impression that smaller categories are larger than they actually are.

In some bar charts, we might want to use some other kind of scale (e.g., sometimes the logarithm of the frequency is graphed). Using a nonlinear scale is not wrong if there is a reason to do so and the axis is clearly labeled. Generally, though, equal intervals on a linear scale are best. The first panel of Figure 2.2 shows an example of breaking the axis so it is clear that the relative sizes of the bars need to be studied closely; the second panel shows the use of a logarithmic scale. These are two ways that bar charts can be modified to be useful when the relative frequencies of the categories are very different from one another.

FIGURE 2.3 Marital Status in the 1978–1998 General Social Survey

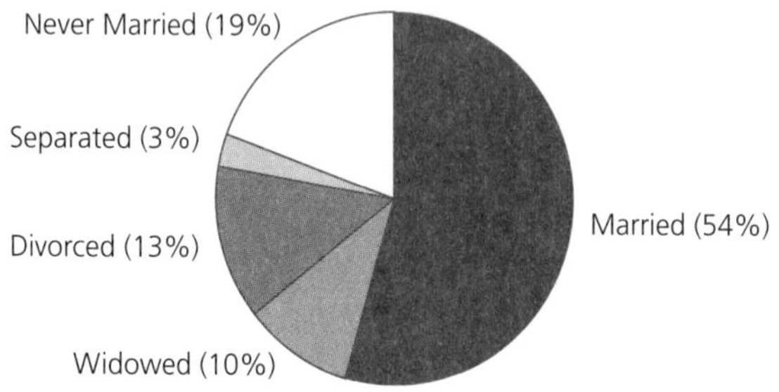

U.S. sample only.

Bar charts can also be presented horizontally rather than vertically (horizontal bar chart), and can even be presented with the bars hanging down from the *x*-axis (icicle chart), rather than rising above it. But, unless there is a good reason not to do it the conventional way, keep it simple!

The bar chart shows us the relative sizes of the groups, but emphasizes the frequency in each category, which we can see by looking at the scale on the vertical axis. Another commonly used graphic for nominal data—the pie chart—provides exactly the same kind of information but emphasizes the relative frequencies. Figure 2.3 is a pie chart of exactly the same data (again, drawn by SPSS).

The pie chart is better than the bar chart for showing the sizes of the groups as parts of the whole sample. It is *not* as good at showing the actual frequencies (though they can be reported in the labels).

Like all other statistical charts and tables, a pie chart should have a title and explanatory notes, if needed. The slices of the pie can be arranged in any order, without affecting our impression of which are the biggest and smallest groups.

In this section we've covered quite a bit of information about how to use charts and graphics to describe the distribution of a nominal variable. Take the short quiz and see if you've mastered all of this. Then we will take a look at how frequency charts and graphics for ordinal variables are the same—and different.

FREQUENCY DISTRIBUTIONS FOR ORDINAL VARIABLES

Ordinal variables have more information than nominal variables. In addition to telling us which category each case falls into, the value of an ordinal variable on a particular case tells us if it is ranked more highly, the same, or less highly than another case.

CHECK QUIZ 2.1

1. When we say that the categories of a nominal variable should be mutually exclusive, we mean that
   a. we have no leftover cases that don't fit in any of our categories.
   b. one case shouldn't fit in more than one category.
   c. we should not use rank-order data when interval/ratio data are available.
   d. all variables should fit (mutually) in our coding scheme.
2. When we say that the categories of a nominal variable should be jointly exhaustive, we mean that
   a. we have no leftover cases that don't fit in any of our categories.
   b. one case shouldn't fit in more than one category.
   c. we should not use rank-order data when interval/ratio data are available.
   d. all variables should fit (mutually) in our coding scheme.
3. A frequency chart
   a. should clearly identify the variable it is describing.
   b. should list all values in the first column.
   c. should show the column marginals in the bottom row.
   d. should indicate the source of the data.
   e. all of the above.
4. To find the relative frequency of a value
   a. divide the total number of cases by the number of cases with that value.
   b. divide the number of cases with that value by the percentage of cases with other values.
   c. divide the number of cases with that value by the total number of cases.
   d. subtract the number of cases with the value from the total number of cases, and divide by 6.
5. You can convert a proportion into a percentage by
   a. taking the square root.
   b. moving the decimal two places to the right.
   c. dividing by 100.
   d. multiplying by 100.
   e. b and d.
6. Bar charts are (usually) better than pie charts at
   a. emphasizing the actual number of cases with each value.
   b. emphasizing the relative proportion of cases with each value.
   c. holding the reader's attention.
   d. emphasizing the level of measurement.
7. Pie charts are (usually) better than bar charts at
   a. emphasizing the actual number of cases with each value.
   b. emphasizing the relative proportion of cases with each value.
   c. holding the reader's attention.
   d. emphasizing the level of measurement.

To summarize the distribution of an ordinal variable, we use the same tools—the frequency chart and graphical displays—but we make a few changes to take into account that the scores represent ranks.

There are two kinds of ordinal variables: grouped and full rank-order. In this section, we apply the ideas of a frequency chart and associated graphics only to the grouped ordinal scale. A variable that is measured on a full rank-order scale (like the order by which people enter a room with a narrow doorway: one person enters first, another second, yet another third, with no ties) does not lend itself to being summarized in a frequency chart, since there are as many categories as cases, and all (untied) categories have the same frequency (i.e., one case).

Frequency Chart Rules

A proper frequency chart for a grouped ordinal variable follows all the same rules as one for a nominal variable, with just one change. Because the categories of the variable are ranks, the order in which we present them makes a difference. As a general rule, the category representing the "highest" or "most" amount of the variable we are measuring should be the first (top) row of the frequency chart of a grouped ordinal variable. The next highest level is the second row, and so on until the lowest possible rank is given. Consider the example of the edited output from SPSS in Table 2.3.

The highest level of education a respondent has attained is a grouped ordinal variable. The categories or levels (i.e., "graduate," "bachelor," etc.) can be ranked to place respondents higher or lower on the dimension of the amount of education obtained. The intervals between levels, though, do not necessarily represent equal amounts of difference in education, so the variable is ordinal, not interval/ratio.

We have arranged the rows of the chart to represent the ranking of the levels of the variable, with the highest at the top of the chart. For some charts, starting with the lowest category at the top makes more sense; we don't recommend that practice, but it is not wrong.

TABLE 2.3 Respondent's Highest Degree, U.S. 1978–1998 (General Social Survey)

	Frequency	Percent	Valid Percent	Cumulative Percent
Graduate	103	6.9	6.9	6.9
Bachelor	204	13.6	13.6	20.5
Junior college	70	4.7	4.7	25.2
High school	790	52.7	52.7	77.9
LT high school	331	22.1	22.1	100
Total	1,498	99.9	100	
NA	2	0.1		
	1,500	100		

LT—less than; NA—not applicable.

Notice that the categories, as always, are mutually exclusive and jointly exhaustive. There is a category for each possible case, and each case falls into only one category.

As with a nominal variable, the frequency chart tells us the total number of cases, and the number of cases in each level of the variable. As with a nominal variable, it is useful to report the relative frequencies, either as a proportion or as a percentage of the total number of cases. We may also want to report some other frequencies.

Valid Frequencies (or in SPSS, *Valid Percent*)

In Table 2.3, notice that, out of the 1,500 subjects, two respondents (one-tenth of 1 percent of the total) gave an answer other than a level of education in response to this question. The "Percent" column reports these two cases in the context of the whole sample: 0.1 percent. There are times, however, when an investigator might want to focus solely on subjects whose answers are directly related to the question at hand (in this case, highest level of education achieved), so subjects who answered "not applicable" or "unknown" or for whom data are missing are removed from the analysis. The N is reduced by this number, and the percentages of subjects in categories that matter (valid responses) sum to 100.

Sometimes variables may have large amounts of missing or invalid responses. Honest reporting of your results may require that you report and discuss why the data are missing, and whether this could be a problem for interpretation. In cases like this, reporting the total and valid relative frequencies can be important.

Cumulative Relative Frequencies

It is often helpful to add a new column to the chart when describing a grouped ordinal variable. Because the categories are ranked, we may wish to describe the percentage or proportion of cases that have scores higher or lower than some level. For example, we might want to point out that about a quarter (25.2 percent) of General Social Survey respondents have some kind of college degree (i.e., junior college, bachelor, or graduate degree).

The ***cumulative percentage*** associated with each level of the variable is the percentage of all cases that have the level in question or more. Looking at Table 2.3, you can see how cumulative percentages are calculated. Starting at the highest category (graduate degree), we know that 6.9 percent have this level or more (obviously, since this is the highest level, the "or more" doesn't mean anything here). The percentage having a bachelor's degree or more is the percentage with a graduate degree plus the percentage with a bachelor's degree (6.9 percent plus 13.6 percent equals 20.5 percent). We proceed until we reach the lowest level of the variable, where it must be true that 100 percent of the cases have this level or more.

Cumulative relative frequencies are a special case of the idea of the percentiles of a distribution. We look at percentiles in more detail in the next chapter.

Graphical Displays

Pictures of the distribution may provide a quicker and more compelling summary than the frequency chart. With ordinal variables, we modify the bar chart and pie chart somewhat so we can visually represent the ranking in the data.

Rather than a bar chart, with ordinal (and interval/ratio) data we use a very similar graphic called the frequency histogram (or simply histogram). Figure 2.4 shows a histogram, drawn by SPSS, of the data we examined in the frequency chart.

At first glance, the histogram looks exactly like a bar chart. In fact, a ***histogram*** is very much like a bar chart, with just two small changes.

The first difference is that the order in which we array the categories along the *x*-axis matters. With an ordinal variable, the category with the lowest rank (which was given the numerical score of zero in the General Social Survey coding, to mean "less than high school") is at the origin of the *x*-axis and *y*-axis. As we move from left to right across the graphic, the levels of the variable increase. We do it this way simply because we are used to the Cartesian coordinate way of representing and reading quantitative information—where scores increase as we move from bottom to top or from left to right. We should note in passing that this is a cultural artifact; this is the "right" way to organize data only because it is easier and more convenient for most of this book's readers to understand.

The second difference between a bar chart and a histogram for grouped ordinal data is that in a histogram the bars are shown as touching one another; in a bar chart there are empty spaces between the bars. The reason for this difference is that with a nominal variable the bars represent groups that are simply different from one another, so each is separated from the others. With grouped ordinal scores, the categories represent amounts of the same

FIGURE 2.4 Respondent's Highest Degree, General Social Survey 1978–1998

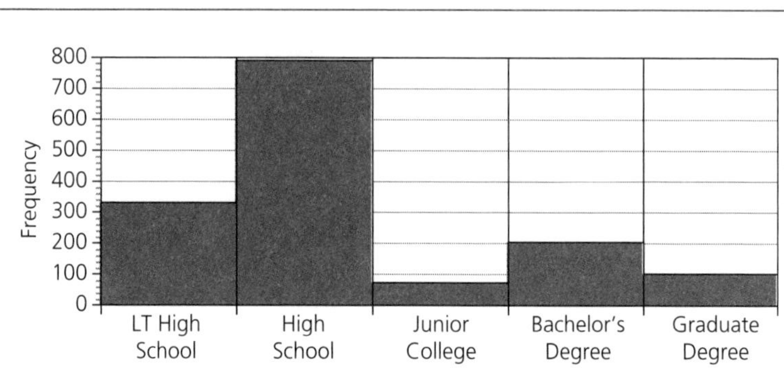

U.S. respondents; $N = 1{,}498$; LT—less than.

FIGURE 2.5 Respondent's Highest Degree, General Social Survey 1998

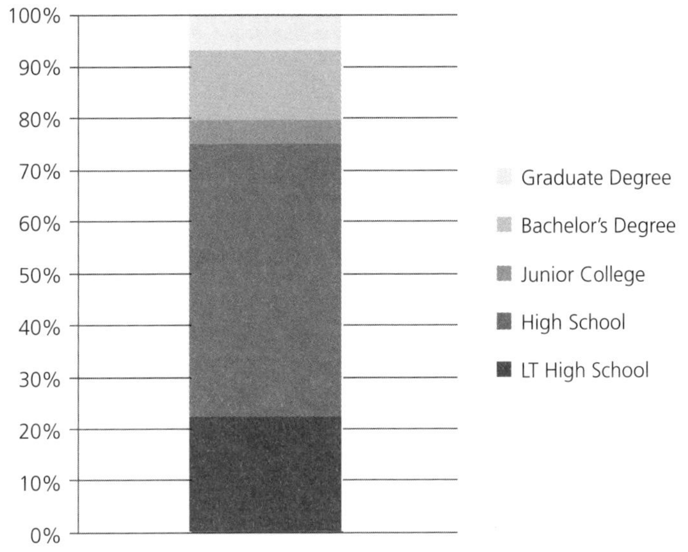

N = 1,498; LT—less than.

thing (in our example, amounts of education). Having the bars adjacent to one another suggests that there is an underlying continuity to the scale.

With a nominal variable, we suggested that the pie chart was probably a better graphic than the bar chart to emphasize the relative frequencies. With a grouped ordinal variable, we use the *stacked bar* chart to emphasize relative frequencies, clearly showing the ranking of the categories. SPSS does not draw very good stacked bar charts, so we've used Excel to prepare the example (Figure 2.5).

The stacked bar chart, like the bar chart, shows the sizes of groups by the sizes of bars. But the bars have been stacked on top of one another, beginning with the lowest score at the bottom of the stack. A legend or labels tell us which group each slice in the stack represents. By looking at the labels on the y-axis, we can easily read the cumulative relative frequencies of the variable.

The tools that are used to display the distribution of the scores on a grouped ordinal variable are very much like those for describing a nominal variable. But there are a few subtle variations in technique that are very helpful to make the rank ordering of the categories more obvious. Techniques for interval/ratio variables again follow all the same rules, but with some small changes—which we will see in the next section. But, before you go there, take the quick check quiz to make sure you've mastered the ideas of how to represent grouped ordinal variables.

CHECK QUIZ 2.2

1. One way to tell the difference between the frequency charts for nominal and grouped ordinal data is
   a. charts for grouped ordinal data have labels under the *x*-axis.
   b. charts for grouped ordinal data show the percentages in that category and above.
   c. SPSS can't produce frequency charts for nominal data.
   d. the bars in the chart for nominal data don't touch each other.
2. It doesn't make much sense to create a frequency chart or a bar chart of full rank-order ordinal data because
   a. each ranking would typically have only one case assigned to it.
   b. researchers don't care about full rank-order data.
   c. one shouldn't use full rank-order data when interval/ratio data is available.
   d. it doesn't make sense to make a bar chart of any ordinal data.
3. In order to show the distribution of value graphically for nominal data, one constructs a bar chart; for grouped ordinal data, one constructs
   a. a histogram.
   b. a stacked bar chart.
   c. an inverted pie chart.
   d. a or b.

FREQUENCY DISTRIBUTIONS FOR INTERVAL/RATIO VARIABLES

Interval/ratio scales let us measure cases as falling in one or another category (like nominal variables), and these categories are ranked from high to low (like ordinal variables). But, in addition, we know that the scores of an interval/ratio variable are measures of actual quantity that can be added and subtracted, and they can be multiplied and divided in meaningful ways. For example, we can say that someone who weighs 220 pounds is twice as heavy as someone who weighs 110 pounds, or that someone with $1.50 in her pocket has six times what someone with $0.25 has.

The additional information that we get about cases' scores when we measure a variable on an interval/ratio scale present some special challenges when we are trying to summarize the information with a frequency chart or graphical display. On an interval/ratio scale, it is often the case that there are many values. For example, the interval/ratio variable "number of children in the family" might be 0, 1, 2, and so on, up to quite a large number. Some interval/ratio variables, for example the sex ratio (number of females per 100 males) in a number of cities, can have as many distinct values as there are cases.

In order to summarize the distribution of an interval/ratio variable using the frequency chart and graphics, we often must first collapse the values into summary categories (e.g., 0–2 children, 3–5 children, 6 or more children).

So, we first need to examine how to collapse interval/ratio data into categories. Once we've done that, we will see that the frequency charts and graphics we use to present interval/ratio variables are very similar to those that we use with grouped ordinal variables.

Forming Categories

There is no absolute right way to collapse the range of values of an interval/ratio variable into a set of categories that we can use for frequency charts and graphics, but there are some very good rules of thumb that you should apply.

*Categories should be **jointly exhaustive**.* As with nominal and ordinal variables, we should include categories that allow us to classify all observations in the sample. Sometimes, the score zero needs special consideration. For example, if we are talking about the numbers of children in families, we might want to leave zero out (and present charts labeled "numbers of children in families with children"). Sometimes, the highest scores on a variable might be very far away from the others, so we might want to have a top category that is, for example, "100 or more." There are no absolute rules here, except that we must be able to put each case in a category.

*Categories should be **mutually exclusive**.* As with nominal and ordinal variables, we don't want to double-count observations by having them appear in more than one category. With interval/ratio data, this requires careful attention. Suppose that Fred has an income of $10,000. Now, suppose that we are designing categories and we propose "up to $10,000" and "$10,000 or more" as our two groups. We wouldn't know where to put Fred—he could fall into both categories, because the endpoints overlap.

Therefore, when we design the categories or classes for our frequency charts and graphics, we must set ***real class boundaries*** that enable us to avoid this problem. These boundaries must be precise enough to unambiguously classify each case. If we say "up to $10,000" and "more than $10,000," we would solve the problem of where to put Fred. Technically, the upper bound of the first category is $10,000.00; the lower bound of the second category is $10,000.01. The class boundaries must always be set with a level of precision that allows an unambiguous assignment of each case to exactly one category.

Categories (sometimes called bins) should be equal in size. Each category should include the same amount of the number line of the scale of a variable. For the number of children in families, we might choose 0, 1, 2, 3, 4, . . . , or we might choose 0–2, 3–4, 5–6, . . . ; but we shouldn't choose 0, 1–2, 3–8, . . . children.

Not using equal-sized intervals can result in very serious misperception of the shape and relative frequencies of a distribution. In fact, not using equal category intervals is one of the most common ways that some people (but not you!) "lie with statistics." We can make a distribution look much more or less equal than it really is by manipulating intervals.

With many interval/ratio variables, we can't completely follow this rule of thumb. With the variable income, for example, we might know only that family income is more than some amount. Or it may be that the distribution is extremely skewed—and we don't want to have lots of categories with no observations. We will discuss these issues a bit more in Chapter 5 on the shape of distributions.

How many categories should be used to summarize an interval/ratio variable so that we can create charts and graphs? There is no one right answer, but there is some good advice.

If an interval/ratio variable is discrete and has a limited number (not more than 20) values, we may wish to use each value as a category. In representing the distribution of the number of children in families, this might be a good choice—no information is lost. In representing the ages of persons in a population (measured to the nearest year of age), we could make a reasonable graphic using all category values, but we would probably want a smaller number of categories for a frequency chart.

In general, we want to use enough categories to tell the truth about the shape of the distribution of a variable. Dividing incomes into "high" and "low" is too crude to tell the whole story about the shape of the distribution. Dividing incomes into categories of $100 increments would result in hundreds of categories, and we wouldn't be able to see the patterns. So, judgment and trial and error are needed. For many variables, no fewer than five and no more than 20 categories are a good choice. Remember that the goal is to summarize but not misrepresent the relative frequencies across the full range of scores.

Frequency Chart Rules

Once we have decided on the categories that we will use to collapse the scores on an interval/ratio variable into ordered categories of equal size, we construct the frequency chart exactly as we would for a grouped ordinal variable.

The category labels need to be carefully designed so that they describe unambiguous lower and upper category boundaries. The categories should be arrayed in order from highest to lowest. And we should present frequencies, relative frequencies, and cumulative relative frequencies.

Tables 2.4 and 2.5 show frequency charts of the gross national product (GNP) per capita in nations of the world in the mid-1990s. GNP per capita is an interval variable, and every one of the 142 nations on which we have data has a different value. So, we need to group the observations into categories. The first chart groups the nations into five categories, and the second chart groups the nations into nine categories.

Both charts are correct, but they do give slightly different impressions. Where the data are presented in fewer (cruder) categories, there is the appearance of somewhat greater equality (the relative frequencies in the categories are somewhat more equal). Both charts make it quite clear that most nations are quite poor. But, among the more fortunate nations, the different numbers of categories might suggest greater or less inequality. So, how many categories one chooses can have an effect on the way results are interpreted.

TABLE 2.4 GNP in Five Categories

		Frequency	Percent	Valid Percent	Cumulative Percent
Valid	$40k+	3	1.7	2.1	2.1
	$30–39.9k	3	1.7	2.1	4.2
	$20–29.9k	10	5.7	7.0	11.3
	$10–19.9k	10	5.7	7.0	18.3
	$0–9.9k	116	66.7	81.7	100.0
	Total	142	81.6	100.0	
Missing	System	32	18.4		
Total		174	100.0		

TABLE 2.5 GNP in Nine Categories

		Frequency	Percent	Valid Percent	Cumulative Percent
Valid	$40k+	1	0.6	0.7	0.7
	$35–39.9k	2	1.1	1.4	2.1
	$30–34.9k	3	1.7	2.1	4.2
	$25–29.9k	8	4.6	5.6	9.9
	$20–24.9k	2	1.1	1.4	11.3
	$15–19.9k	6	3.4	4.2	15.5
	$10–14.9k	4	2.3	2.8	18.3
	$5–9.9k	4	2.3	2.8	21.1
	$0–4.9k	112	64.4	78.9	100.0
	Total	142	81.6	100.0	
Missing	System	32	18.4		
Total		174	100.0		

To be sure that you noticed: the degree of inequality in the market value of economic activity per capita is remarkably high—regardless of how one might categorize the data.

Graphical Displays

The histogram and stacked bar charts that we learned about for grouped ordinal variables are also good devices for presenting visualizations of interval/ratio variables. It is also possible to modify these graphics somewhat to emphasize the continuous nature of interval/ratio variables. Examine the graph in Figure 2.6, drawn with SPSS (Graphs → Linechart) of the frequency distribution of the numbers of siblings reported by respondents.

We could have used a histogram to present these data (and that would be perfectly all right). But, by drawing a line between the midpoints of each class interval and connecting them into a ***frequency polygon***, we create a line graph that suggests the more continuous nature, rather than ranked categories nature, of the variable. We can use the same approach

FIGURE 2.6 Numbers of Siblings, General Social Survey 1998

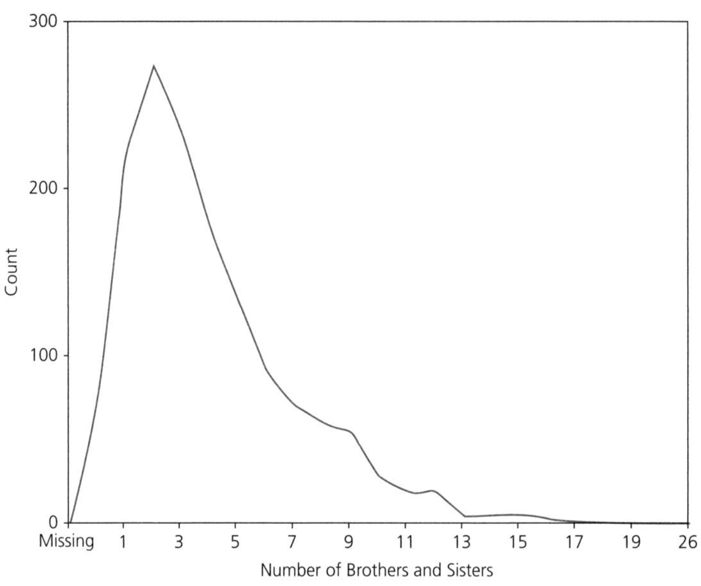

FIGURE 2.7 Cumulative Numbers of Siblings, General Social Survey 1998

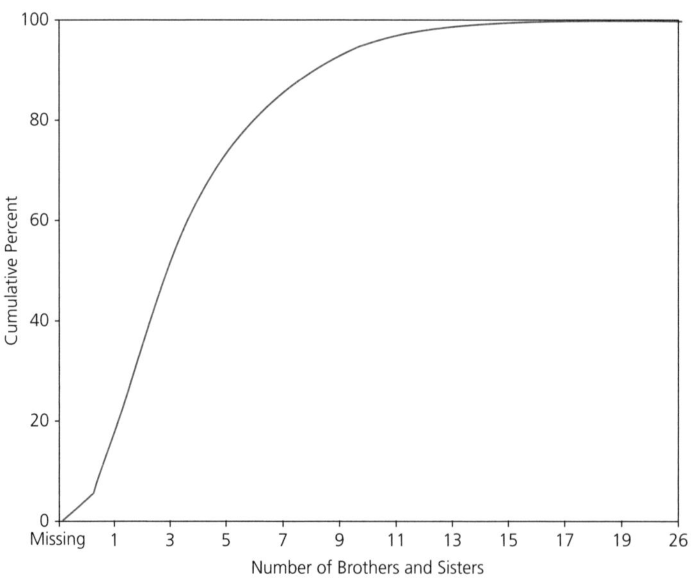

CHECK QUIZ 2.3

1. Investigators studying arguments in marriage rated them as minor, intermediate, or major. What kind of data are we dealing with?
   a. nominal
   b. ordinal
   c. rank-order
   d. interval/ratio
2. An investigator wants to describe the distribution of GPAs at your school. She proposes to create the following categories: 0–1.49, 1.5–2.99, 3.0–4.0+. You protest, based on which of these issues?
   a. jointly exhaustive
   b. mutually exclusive
   c. equal-sized categories
   d. meaningful/appropriate number of categories
3. The investigator, heeding your advice, creates categories for every tenth of a grade point (0.0, 0.1, 0.2, 0.3, . . . , 3.8, 3.9, 4.0). Assuming that 4.0 is the highest GPA available, you might raise the issue of
   a. jointly exhaustive.
   b. mutually exclusive.
   c. equal-sized categories.
   d. meaningful/appropriate number of categories.
4. Frequently, researchers will show a line graph instead of a histogram to emphasize
   a. the shape of the distribution.
   b. the continuous nature of the distribution.
   c. the width of the distribution.
   d. the categories with missing data.

to graph the cumulative frequencies; this is also a simple option in SPSS (Graphs → Linechart), as in Figure 2.7.

With this line chart, we can easily see that, for example, about half of the population have four or fewer brothers and sisters. We could have used a stacked bar chart to make the same point, and that would be perfectly all right. But using a cumulative frequency polygon is probably better because it suggests the continuous interval/ratio nature of the variable we are describing.

SUMMARIZING DATA USING EXCEL

Excel has some good tools for constructing and working with frequency distributions. Many of the things we need to do can be done using simple built-in functions. There are also some useful tools in the Excel add-in toolpack for statistics.

Working with Excel Functions to Summarize Data

The data should be arranged so that the variable of interest is in one column:

C
shoes
2
3
3
3
4
4
4
5
6
6
6
7

(Of course, if we had such a small amount of data, we wouldn't need Excel to do the figuring for us, so imagine that the data are more extensive than this.)

In a nearby column, make a list of the values you're interested in tabulating. You could sort the data in the data column (as in the example) to see what the highest and lowest values are, and use those two values and all the values between them. Excel will refer to this list as the "bins_array" into which the numbers are sorted.

C	D
shoes	bins
2	2
3	3
3	4
3	5
4	6
4	7
4	
5	
6	
6	
6	
7	

Next, we'll insert a formula in the column to the right of the bins to count each occurrence of each value. It is easiest to let Excel enter the formula using the Wizard, because it will take care of the cell references.

Set the insertion point in the cell immediately to the right of the first cell containing a bin label, and (Mac) select Insert → "Function . . .", or (PC) with the Formulas tab showing, click on Insert Function.

The Formula Builder should appear. We're going to use the Frequency key word. You can either scroll down the list until you see it, or (Mac) start typing "frequency" in the search box at the top of the window and the Frequency function will appear on the list, or (PC) type "frequency" in the search box and click Go.

Double-click the Frequency item in the list. Two pieces of information need to be filled in. First, Excel needs to know where the data are.

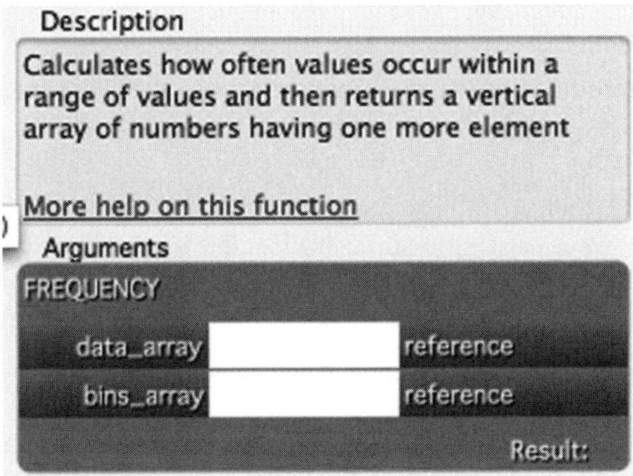

The insertion point should be flashing in the box labeled "data_array." Drag through the data part of your variable column (don't include the heading);

C
shoes
2
3
3
3
4
4
4
5
6
6
6
7

doing so will put the cell references into the data_array box:

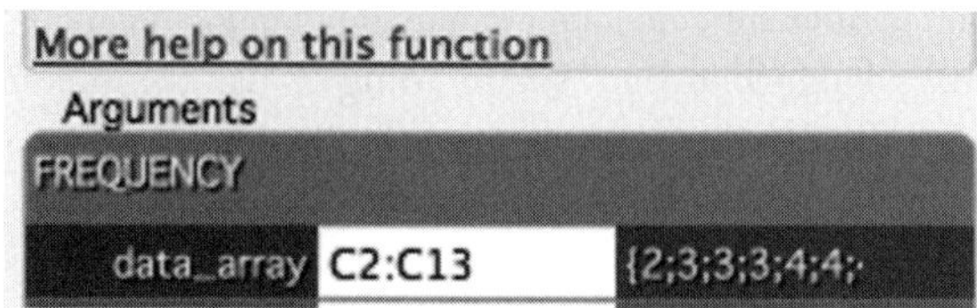

If you have a lot of data, scrolling through the data may be something of a nuisance; in this case, you can type the cell references into the data_array box; it's in the form "top cell of data: bottom cell of data."

Next, set the insertion point in the bins_array part of the Formula Builder, and drag through the bins section; again, only drag through the numbers:

D
bins
2
3
4
5
6
7

The bins_array part of the Formula Builder will get filled in:

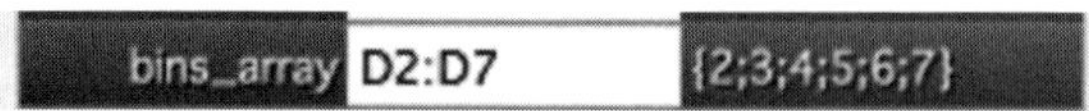

Hitting Enter/Return will set the formula in the cell. If you have the formula bar showing and click on the cell, it should look something like this:

Next, some voodoo. Ordinarily, we might just select the cell with the formula in it and drag its handle to fill the cells below, but we need to maintain the array structure of the bins, so this approach won't work.

Click on the cell with the formula and continue holding down the mouse button while you drag down to select all of the cells next to the bins:

D	E
bins	counts
2	1
3	
4	
5	
6	
7	

Click Control-u (hold down the Control key and type "u" (lowercase, without quotation marks). (The data and bin arrays will be highlighted, and the formula will appear in its cell.)

Click Command-Return/Enter; the counts should appear next to the bins:

C	D	E
shoes	bins	counts
2	2	1
3	3	3
3	4	3
3	5	1
4	6	3
4	7	1
4		
5		
6		
6		
6		
7		

Adding a cumulative frequency column to the table is straightforward.

We need to know how many elements there are, so we'll begin by summing the counts. First, add the label "Total" at the bottom of the bins column. Click in the cell to the right of the label (immediately under the counts) to set the insertion point, then type an equal sign, type the keyword "sum," and then click and drag through the counts:

C	D	E
shoes	bins	counts
2	2	1
3	3	3
3	4	3
3	5	1
4	6	3
4	7	1
4	Total	=sum(E2:E7)
5		
6		
6		
6		
7		

In the screen shot, you can see that Excel indicates which cells are selected (E2:E7), and Excel is also showing the contextual help for the "sum" keyword.

Press Return/Enter. With just a little luck, the number that appears is the number of items in your data set (we'll call it *N*) for the remainder of this exercise.

Next, we'll create a column for the percentages.

Label the next column to the right "Percentage."

- Click in the cell to the right of the first count, and type an equal sign.
- Click in the cell to the left of this cell (the first actual count) to add this cell reference to the formula.
- Type "/" (a division sign).
- Type the total *N* that appears next to the Total label.
- Type "*100" and hit Return/Enter. A number should appear in the cell. If you click on the cell, the formula bar should show something like:

E	F
counts	frequency
1	=E2/12*100
3	
3	
1	
3	
1	
12	

If you click on the cell, a small handle will appear at the lower right of the cell; clicking and dragging will paste the formula into the cells below:

D	E	F
bins	counts	frequency
2	1	8.33333333
3	3	25
4	3	25
5	1	8.33333333
6	3	25
7	1	8.33333333
Total	12	100

Next, label the next column to the right "Cumulative %."

The first cell in this column is really just a repeat of the cell next to it:

- Click in the cell to the right of the first percentage, and type an equal sign.
- Click in the cell to the left of this cell (the first percentage) to add this cell reference to the formula.
- Type Enter/Return.

The two adjacent cells (top of the Percentage column and top of the Cumulative % column) should now have the same value. Don't worry about all the extra decimal places; we'll fix them later.

Next we add a formula that adds the next row's percent to the cumulating percent.

- Click in the next cell down.
- Type an equal sign.
- Click in the cell to the left of the current cell to add its reference to the formula.
- Type a plus sign (+).
- Click in the cell above to add its cell reference to the formula, and hit Return/Enter.

If you click in the cell into which you just entered a formula, a small handle will appear at the lower right-hand corner of the cell; clicking and dragging down will paste the formula into the cells below:

D	E	F	G
bins	counts	Percentage	Cumulative %
2	1	8.3	8.33333333
3	3	25.0	33.3333333
4	3	25.0	58.3333333
5	1	8.3	66.6666667
6	3	25.0	91.6666667
7	1	8.3	100
Total	12		

We can clean up the extra decimals in the percentage and cumulative percentage column by selecting those cells, choosing Format → "Cells . . ."; select Number from the Category list, and set the number of decimals to something reasonable (like 1).

Note: If you didn't multiply the count/*N* amount by 100, you could use the Format → "Cells . . ." percent category to get the numbers to display properly.

From here, a little tidying up will give you a table that's easy to read (one that conforms to the rules laid out in Chapter 2):

Student's Responses to the Question: "How Many Shoes Are in Your Closet?"

No. of Shoes	Frequency	Percentage	Cumulative %
2	1	8.3	8.3
3	3	25.0	33.3
4	3	25.0	58.3
5	1	8.3	66.7
6	3	25.0	91.7
7	1	8.3	100.0
Total	12	100.0	

Summarizing Data Using Excel's Analysis ToolPak

The Analysis ToolPak may not be available in your computer lab's installation of Excel, and it is not currently available on the Macintosh platform.

Click on the Data Tab in Excel. If you don't see the Data Analysis block and icons shown here, follow the set of instructions for installing the Analysis ToolPak.

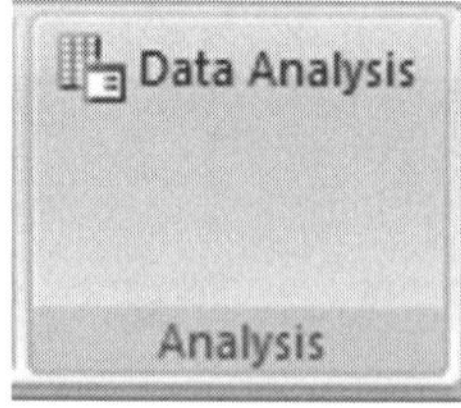

To install the Analysis ToolPak:

- Click on the Office button (upper left-hand corner of window).
- Select Excel Options at bottom of dialogue.
- Choose Add-Ins from menu on left. It looks as if you should be able to double-click on Analysis ToolPak, but don't bother: that doesn't do anything. Instead:
- At the bottom of the dialogue box, there is a drop-down menu titled "Manage:" that defaults to Excel Add-Ins; click the button "Go" next to it.
- In the dialogue box that appears, click the check box by Analysis ToolPak (not Analysis ToolPak – VBA), and click OK.

Once the Analysis ToolPak is installed, here is how to create a summary table using the Analysis ToolPak.

Before you begin, you'll need to have your data in one column, and your bins (the categories you're going to have Excel summarize by) in another:

E	F
data	bins
3	3
4	4
5	5
5	6
6	7
6	8
6	
7	
7	
7	
8	

Interesting/helpful note: Excel's bins are upper cutoffs. If you are using decimal values, this means that the value 3.1 would be assigned to the "4" category rather than the "3" category, because it is greater than 3 (which is an upper cutoff for that category) and less than 4.

If you need to group the data into larger bins (e.g., age ranges or dollar amounts that include more than a single value), just adjust the bins accordingly (e.g., instead of 1, 2, 3, 4, . . . your bins might be 4, 8, 12, 16, . . .).

Once your data and the bins have been created, click on the Data Analysis icon:

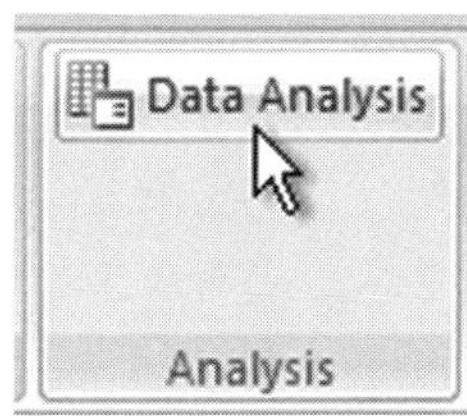

Select "Histogram" from the list in the dialogue box that appears, and click OK.

- Set the insertion point in the box labeled "Input Range"; click and drag through your data, from the top cell (containing a number, not the label) through the bottom-most cell.
- Set the insertion point in the box labeled "Bin Range," and click and drag through the bins (again, not including the bin label).
- Click the check boxes beside Cumulative Percentage and Chart Output.
- Excel will put the output in a new worksheet ply (page) by default; if you want it somewhere else, use the controls in the middle of the dialogue.

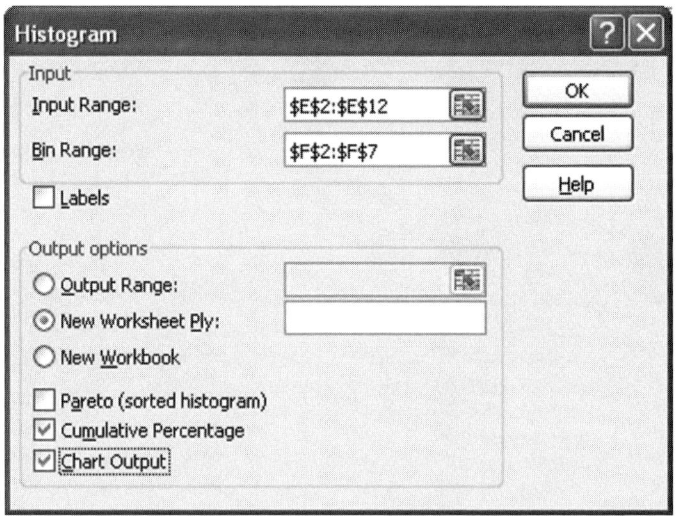

- Click OK.

You'll be rewarded for your labor with a chart and a graph:

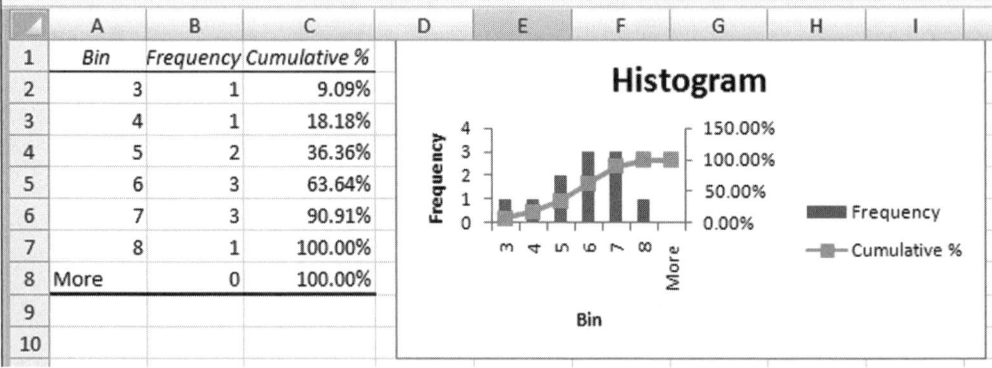

	A	B	C
1	*Bin*	*Frequency*	*Cumulative %*
2	3	1	9.09%
3	4	1	18.18%
4	5	2	36.36%
5	6	3	63.64%
6	7	3	90.91%
7	8	1	100.00%
8	More	0	100.00%
9			
10			

If you've planned your bins properly (so the highest-valued bin contains the highest value in your data), you don't need the row labeled "More." Click on the row heading for the row (the cursor should change to a right-facing arrow) and delete it (click on Delete in the Cells section of the Home tab).

In order to create a frequency table like those described in Chapter 2, you will want to add a Percentage column to the table Excel provides:

Switch to the Home tab, if you're not already there.

Before we can add a column with percentages, we need to know the total *N*:

Add a row label ("Total") for the row beneath the largest bin label.

Next, we'll use a formula to sum the frequencies:

- Set the insertion point at the intersection of the new Total label and the Frequency column.
- Type an equal sign.
- Add the keyword "sum" (without the quotation signs).
- Click and drag through the frequencies column from top to bottom (not including the heading; stop before you get to the cell we're working in). This will fill in the cell references for our formula; the formula bar should show something like:

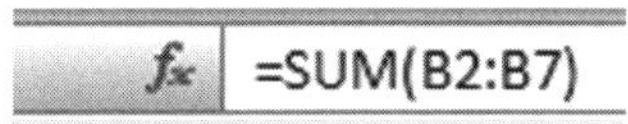

- Click Enter/Return.

At this point, your chart should look something like this:

	A	B	C
1	*Bin*	*Frequency*	*Cumulative %*
2	3	1	9.09%
3	4	1	18.18%
4	5	2	36.36%
5	6	3	63.64%
6	7	3	90.91%
7	8	1	100.00%
8	Total	11	

To insert a column for the percentages, click on the column heading for the Cumulative % column (in this example, click on the C right above "Cumulative %." In the Cells section of the toolbar, select Insert (with a column selected, it knows that you want to insert a column, and Excel inserts to the left of selected columns).

Add a label for the new column: "Percentage."

Set the insertion point in the cell below the label. We'll insert another formula to compute the percentages.

- Type an equal sign.
- Click on the cell to the left to put its cell reference in our formula.
- Type a division sign (/).
- Type the total number of items (*N*, from the last formula entered), in this case the number 11.

The formula bar ought to look something like this:

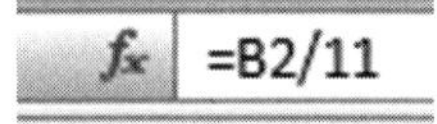

- Hit Enter/Return.

Now, to fill all the cells below with the same formula:

- Select the cell to which you just added the formula.
- Click and hold down the mouse on the little handle at the lower right-hand corner of the cell.
- Drag the handle down until the selection includes the "Total" row.

To format the cells to have percentages instead of decimals:

- Select the cells to format by clicking and dragging through them. (Since one digit to the right of the decimal is plenty for most cases, select the cells in the Cumulative % column, too.)
- Choose the Format drop-down menu from the Cells part of the toolbar, and select Format Cells.
- Choose Percentage from the Category list, and choose one decimal place.
- Click OK.

At this point, your table should look something like this:

	A	B	C	D
1	*Bin*	*Frequency*	*Percentage*	*Cumulative %*
2	3	1	9.1%	9.1%
3	4	1	9.1%	18.2%
4	5	2	18.2%	36.4%
5	6	3	27.3%	63.6%
6	7	3	27.3%	90.9%
7	8	1	9.1%	100.0%
8	Total	11	100.0%	

You can copy the table to MS Word, and make the final modifications:

Student's Responses to the Question: "How Many Shoes Are in Your Closet?"

No. of Shoes	Frequency	Percentage	Cumulative %
3	1	9.1	9.1
4	1	9.1	18.2
5	2	18.2	36.4
6	3	27.3	63.6
7	3	27.3	90.9
8	1	9.1	100.0
Total	11	100.0	

SUMMARY

In this chapter we have shown how to do the first step in univariate descriptive statistics—summarize the distribution of the scores of the cases in our sample. This basic information is usually examined using both numerical displays (frequency charts) and visualizations (graphics).

All of the specific techniques we've examined are intended to help us summarize some key information: How many cases are there in the sample? How many cases are there with each score (or range of scores)? Which categories have more or fewer cases than others? And, for variables that we can rank or arrange on an interval scale: what proportions of cases have scores above or below a certain value or rank?

Clear labeling (titles, explanatory notes, references to the sources of data, value labels, column headers, etc.) is essential to a good frequency chart or clear graphic.

For nominal variables, the frequency chart contains frequencies, and may contain relative frequencies in the form of percentages or proportions. Bar charts and pie charts are good tools for visualizing the frequencies and relative frequencies of nominal variables.

For grouped ordinal variables, we can add cumulative relative frequencies to our frequency chart. The order in which we display categories matters for ordinal variables. High ranks should be displayed at the top of the frequency chart and at the right for graphical displays. The ranked categories of an ordinal variable are adjacent, so histograms are better than bar charts. Stacked bar charts are a good choice for displaying cumulative relative frequencies of grouped ordinal variables.

For interval/ratio variables, we often must collapse the actual scores into a smaller number of categories. There are better and worse ways of doing this task. Once the data are arranged this way, the frequency charts of interval/ratio variables are the same as those for grouped ordinals—but we must be sure to label the categories to indicate the upper and lower boundaries of the class intervals. Histograms can be used to visualize relative frequencies. Often, though, frequency polygons (a type of line graph) are a more effective display for interval/ratio data. Stacked bar charts could be used to display cumulative relative frequencies, but a line chart of cumulative relative frequencies is often a better choice for interval/ratio variables.

Before you go on to the next chapter, you may want to take some time to read further about SPSS at the end of this chapter. If you have access to the SPSS statistical package (or any other, as all the packages are pretty similar), we provide an introduction about how to use software to do frequency charts and graphics. Frequency charts and graphics are very easy to prepare using software, and you can even exercise some artistic skills that will make your reports far more effective!

KEY TERMS

case or observation

cumulative percentage

frequency chart

frequency polygon

graph

histogram

jointly exhaustive and mutually exclusive

marginal

percentage

real class boundary

valid percent

CHECK QUIZ ANSWERS

Quiz 2.1 Answers: 1. (b); 2. (a); 3. (e); 4. (c); 5. (e); 6. (a); 7. (b)
Quiz 2.2 Answers: 1. (d); 2. (a); 3. (d)
Quiz 2.3 Answers: 1. (b); 2. (c); 3. (d); 4. (b)

EXERCISES

1. Consider the following data, and answer the questions that follow:

Property Crimes by Type, United States, 1990 and 1998

Type of Crime	Offenses 1990 (×1,000)	Offenses 1998 (×1,000)
Robbery	639	447
Burglary	3,074	2,330
Larceny	7,946	7,374
Motor vehicle theft	1,636	1,241
Total	13,295	11,392

Source: Statistical Abstract of the United States, 2000, Table 337.

a. What was the percentage of all property crimes that were burglaries in each year?
b. What was the ratio of larceny to motor vehicle theft in each year?
c. What proportion of the property crimes in each year were robberies?
d. What percentage of all motor vehicle thefts shown in the table occurred in 1998?
e. What was the ratio of robbery and burglary to larceny and motor vehicle theft in each of the two years?
f. What was the percentage rate of change in robbery between 1990 and 1998? That is, how much and in what direction did the number of robberies change as a percentage of the number in 1990?
g. For which type of crime what there the greatest percentage rate of change between 1990 and 1998? (Show your evidence.)
h. Was the distribution of various types of property crimes different in 1998 than it was in 1990? (Show your evidence.)

2. Here is some information on school enrollments and the cost of education in the United States since 1990. Use this table to answer the questions that follow.

Fall Enrollments in Millions of Persons

	1990	1995	2000	2001	2002
Grades K–8	34.0	38.8	38.4	38.5	38.4
Grades 9–12	12.5	13.7	14.8	15.0	15.1
Higher education	13.8	14.3	15.3	15.4	15.6
Education Expenditure in Billions of Constant (2001–2002) Dollars					
Primary and secondary	331	367	437	454	NA
Higher education	218	244	289	291	NA

Source: Statistical Abstract of the United States (website).

a. What was the percentage of all school enrollments that were enrollments in higher education in each year?
b. What was the ratio of primary school to secondary school enrollment for each year?
c. What proportion of all enrollments were enrollments in grades 9 to 12 each year?
d. What were the levels of expenditure, per capita, for primary and secondary and for higher education for each year?
e. What was the percentage rate of change between 1990 and 2001 for enrollments in higher education?
f. What was the percentage rate of change in expenditure for higher education between 1990 and 2001?

3. Consider the following table, and answer the questions that follow:

United States: School Enrollments by Type and Level, 1980 and 2000

	1980	2000
K–8 public	27,647,000	33,875,000
K–8 private	3,992,000	4,646,000
Grades 9–12 public	13,231,000	13,658,000
Grades 9–12 private	1,339,000	1,360,000
College public	9,457,000	11,750,000
College private	2,640,000	3,322,000
Population ages 5–24	77,429,000	78,005,000

Source: Statistical Abstract of the United States, 2000, Table 239 and population tables.

a. Calculate the rates (per 100,000 persons ages 5 to 24) of enrollments for each school type and level for 1980 and 2000.
b. Have the rates of enrollment at the primary (K–8), secondary (grades 9–12), and higher education levels changed? What is your evidence?

c. How have the rates of enrollment in public versus private schools at each of the three levels changed? What is your evidence?

4. Here is listing (created with the SPSS "case summaries" procedure) of 25 cases taken from the General Social Surveys of 1978–1998.

This codebook describes the variables (short names) and the values:

- Age of respondent (age): age in years.
- Highest year of school completed (educ): last year completed, in years.
- Respondent's sex (sex): female or male.
- Political party affiliation (partyid): strong Democrat, not strong Democrat, independent near Democrat, independent, independent near Republican, not strong Republican, strong Republican, other.

Case Summaries

Respondent ID Number	Age of Respondent	Highest Year of School Completed	Respondent's Sex	Political Party Affiliation
1,067	26	10	Female	Independent near Dem.
1,404	68	12	Male	Independent near Dem.
1,085	54	12	Female	Independent near Rep.
786	36	15	Male	Not strong Republican
1,342	61	12	Female	Independent near Dem.
127	42	12	Male	Independent near Dem.
579	59	4	Male	Strong Democrat
1,054	40	12	Male	Independent near Dem.
472	33	12	Male	Independent near Dem.
585	25	12	Female	Independent near Rep.
482	29	16	Male	Independent near Dem.
1,041	32	12	Male	Independent
1,280	69	12	Female	Not strong Democrat
567	89	8	Male	Not strong Democrat
889	26	16	Male	Strong Democrat
132	26	11	Female	Independent
1,405	80	16	Female	Independent
750	32	12	Male	Independent near Rep.
339	31	18	Male	Not strong Democrat
963	45	9	Male	Not strong Democrat
475	43	12	Male	Strong Democrat
664	25	12	Female	Strong Democrat
642	27	13	Female	Independent near Rep.
687	81	8	Male	Strong Republican
448	25	14	Female	Not strong Democrat

a. For each variable, create a frequency chart that includes relative frequencies and cumulative relative frequencies. These may be prepared by hand, but you could also use a program like SPSS.
b. For each variable, prepare either a pie chart or a bar chart to display the distribution. These may be drawn by hand, but it is better to use a spreadsheet program like Excel.

5. Here are some data from the General Social Survey conducted by the National Opinion Research Center (NORC), a social science research center at the University of Chicago, for the year 1998. The variables displayed are described in the codebook as:
   - Race of respondent: white, black, or other.
   - Respondent's highest educational degree.
   - Number of children in respondent's family.

Data from 1998 General Social Survey

Respondent ID Number	Race of Respondent	R's Highest Degree	Number of Children
1,433	Black	Junior college	2
2,344	White	Bachelor	0
878	Other	High school	1
337	White	LT high school	2
431	White	High school	1
181	White	High school	1
2,408	White	High school	4
2,302	White	High school	0
2,799	Other	High school	0
601	Black	High school	0
657	White	High school	1
1,605	White	High school	0
671	White	LT high school	4
1,655	White	High school	3
2,795	White	Graduate	2
391	Other	High school	0
2,045	White	LT high school	5
146	White	LT high school	2
2,727	White	High school	2
1,920	White	High school	0

LT—less than.

a. For each variable, create a frequency chart that includes relative frequencies and cumulative relative frequencies. These may be prepared by hand, but you could also use a program like SPSS.
b. For each variable, prepare either a pie chart or a bar chart to display the distribution. These may be drawn by hand, but it is better to use a spreadsheet program like Excel.

AN INTRODUCTION TO SPSS

SPSS is what's known as a statistical package, software designed both to manage data and to analyze it. We like it for applied statistics courses because of its interface: the raw data are easily accessible, and analysis is performed by means of menus and dialogue boxes, rather than by typing what can seem like obscure commands.

We have developed some exercises to familiarize you with the SPSS interface and with techniques required to create tables and graphs.

For these exercises, we will be using the 2008 General Social Survey data from the NORC website; your instructor may have another data set for you to use. We will assume that you're using SPSS in a campus lab, on a computer running some version of the Windows operating system.

Your instructor will need to tell you where to find the data for this exercise; save it to a location where you can easily find it, like the desktop or your documents folder.

Double-clicking on the data file should launch SPSS, assuming that SPSS is installed on the computer.

If SPSS is installed but doesn't launch, it may be because the security settings in your campus computer lab don't allow it, in which case you should start SPSS from the Windows Start menu.

If you must launch SPSS from the Start menu, one of two things will happen, depending on the installation:

1. You may see a large dialogue box with several options, one of which is to open a data set; choose this option, navigate to your data file, and open it.
2. You may see a large, empty spreadsheet. In this case, use the File menu to choose File → Open → Data.

You'll see arrow notation throughout this book. The first element ("File") is the menu item, and additional items represent choices you will make in hierarchical menus.

Chances are that the process of opening the data file brought up two windows. The Output window may have appeared to tell you that SPSS successfully opened the requested data file, along with the Main window (which is labeled with the name of the file you just opened).

If you see an asterisk (*) before the title of either of those windows, it means that the current contents have not been saved. If you find yourself wondering, "Have I saved this file recently?" just look to the window title to find out.

The Main window is designed for looking at and managing your data. It has two views, which are always available by means of the tabs at the lower left-hand corner of

(continued)

the window; they are labeled Data View and Variable View. If it is not already selected, choose Data View.

Data View is basically a spreadsheet containing your data. It shows cases in the rows, and variables in the columns. If you were going to enter data by hand, this is where you would do it. If there are value labels associated with variables in your data set, you can show these by clicking on the little icon (that looks like a price tag) on the tool bar:

The button is a toggle; clicking it again will return the display to the former view.

ANCESTRS	ANHEAT	ANSCITST
4	1	1
0	0	1
4	8	4
4	0	0
0	3	4
4	9	4
4	0	0
8	8	4

ANCESTRS	ANHEAT	ANSCITST
No, definitely ...	Long ears ...	Strongly agree
IAP	IAP	Strongly agree
No, definitely ...	DONT KN...	Strongly disag...
No, definitely ...	IAP	IAP
IAP	A long nos...	Strongly disag...
No, definitely ...	NA	Strongly disag...
No, definitely ...	IAP	IAP
DONT KNOW	DONT KN...	Strongly disag...

Variable View is where information about the variables is maintained. Click on the Variable View tab at the lower left-hand corner of the Main window.

Each row contains information about a single variable.

- The Name column contains the variable's name. This name must conform to some simple rules, the most important of which are that variable names can't start with a number or nonletter character, and they can't contain spaces. These are usually mnemonic: good variable names remind us of what is stored in the variable, so "sex" is a better variable name than "v26." If the variable Label field (see next paragraphs) is left blank, the variable name will appear on the output. SPSS also uses the variable names in dialogue boxes that perform analyses.
- The Type column tells SPSS what kind of information is contained in the data cells. If you click on a cell in this column, shading will show that it is selected, and a box with an ellipsis (three dots) will appear:

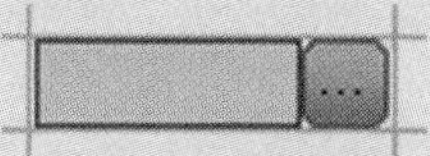

Clicking on the box with the ellipsis will bring up a dialogue box with additional options. For an introductory statistics course, you will probably use only two of these: numeric and string. Numeric data means just numbers (and decimal points, if needed): no dollar signs, no commas, no letters, and so on. String data means "Treat the entry as if it is text and not a number." You will use this only if you are storing information that is text and it doesn't make sense to code it numerically. So, if you are using your subjects' names as identifiers (Bob, Ted, Carol, Alice, etc.), you might set the type to string and use the names themselves in the data, rather than using numerical codes (1 = Bob, 2 = Ted, etc.).

- The Width column is a holdover from earlier computing days; you can ignore it.
- The Decimal column is where you set how many decimal places to display in Data View. If you don't need any showing, set this to 0 (zero).
- The Label column is used to specify variable labels in output. Since a variable label can contain spaces (unlike the variable name), you can use it to make your output more understandable than it would be if only the variable name were used (see earlier discussion of the Name column).

So, imagine that you have asked an attitude question about penguins. You might create a variable named "att_peng"; that is, "att_peng" appears in the Name column.

(*continued*)

If you leave the Label column blank, your output will say "att_peng" whenever this variable is used, which may make sense to you, but perhaps not to others (or not even to you if you don't look at this project for a while). If you use the Labels column to say something like "Attitudes toward Penguins," your output will be labeled in a way that makes sense to you and to others.

- The Values column is where you tell SPSS how to translate variables that are stored as numbers into the categories and values that the numbers represent. So, if your variable records a subject's response to a yes/no question, you might have coded "yes" as 1 and "no" as 0 (zero). Click in the cell to select it, then on the ellipsis box, and a dialogue box appears. Numbers go in the Value box, words go in the Label box, and then click on Add to move the pairing into the working box:

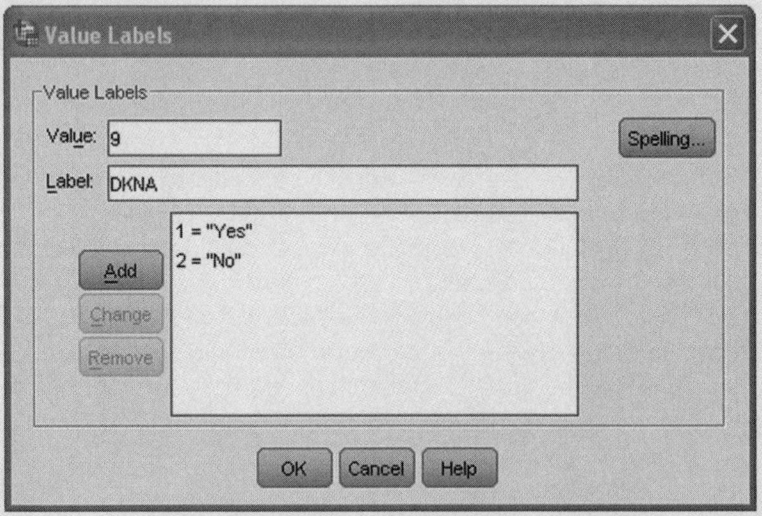

- The Missing values column is where you tell SPSS if there are values that should be ignored during analysis. For example, if you have a variable that holds subjects' ages and you used the value "−1" or maybe "999" for subjects who refused to reveal their ages, you wouldn't want those values included if you were going to have SPSS compute the average age.
- The Columns column is another holdover from bygone days.
- The Alignment column controls the horizontal alignment of data in the Data View.
- The Measure column tells SPSS whether the data should be treated as scale (what we call interval/ratio), ordinal, or nominal.

Exercises with SPSS

Now that you've got the basics of running SPSS and documenting your data, you'll want to prepare frequency charts and graphics to display your variable's distributions.

Exercise 1: Frequency Tables

In this exercise, we will be creating output with SPSS, and then using MS Excel and MS Word to dress up the output. While it is possible to annotate output in SPSS and to delete tables that someone else (e.g., your instructor) may not want to see (like Case Processing Summaries), it is easier to achieve professional-looking results in other programs.

Choose a variable measured at the nominal level from the data set.

If you don't have the codebook for your data set in front of you, go to the Main window and click on the Variable View tab in the lower left-hand corner, if it's not already showing. You may make the Label column wider by grabbing the divider and dragging to the right (roll the cursor over the divider to the right of the word "Label" until the cursor turns into a double-headed arrow, and then click and drag):

Label
AMOUNT OF F...
FEE GIVEN TO...
INTERVIEW D...
HOW OFTEN ...
PARTICIPATIO...
SIZE OF PLAC...
EXPANDED N....

Label
AMOUNT OF FEES PAID(GROUPED)
FEE GIVEN TO GET CASE
INTERVIEW DONE IN-PERSON OR OVER THE PHONE
HOW OFTEN DOES R TAKE PART IN RELIG ACTIVITIES
PARTICIPATION/RECORDING CONSENT
SIZE OF PLACE IN 1000S
EXPANDED N.O.R.C. SIZE CODE

(continued)

Once you've found a likely-looking variable for analysis, check the Values column entry to be sure that it is measured at the nominal level.

We want to make a frequency table, so choose: Analyze → Descriptive Statistics → Frequencies. This brings up a dialogue box.

In case you missed it earlier, we use arrow notation throughout this book. The first element ("Analyze") is the menu item, and additional items represent subsequent elements in hierarchical menus.

If you appreciate shortcuts or want to reduce mouse usage some, you can use the Alt key on your keyboard to select menu items. Notice the underlined "A" in the Analyze menu? Hit Alt-a to bring down that menu; then notice that Descriptive Statistics has an underlined "e," so you can hit Alt-e to reach the next menu, and so on. On the left-hand side of the dialogue box is a list of variables in the data set. By default, variables are listed in the order they appear in the data set, so if the variable you care about is near the top of the list in Variable View, it will be near the top of this list, too. It's also possible (Edit → Options → General) to display them in alphabetical order, or by measurement level ("Measure"; see earlier discussion).

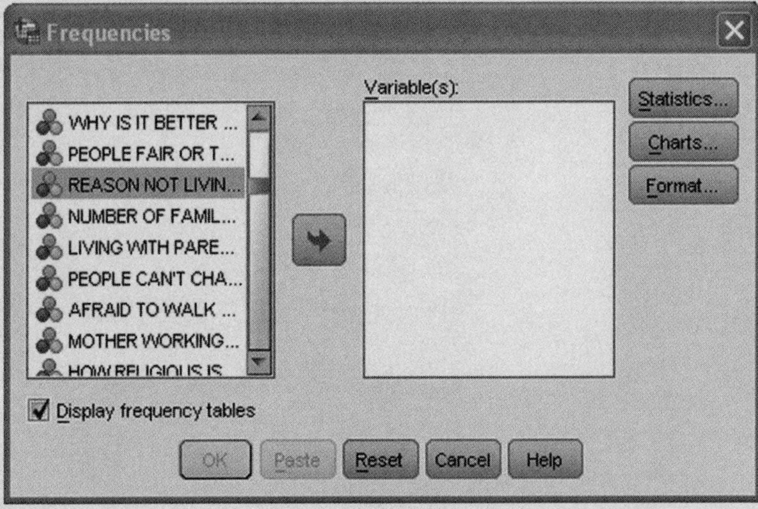

It's possible to make the whole dialogue box wider so you can see more of the variable information, but rolling your cursor over an item in the list will result in a brief glimpse of the whole description:

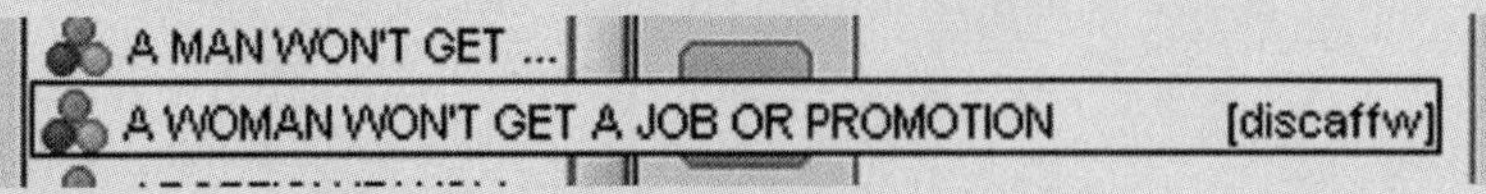

On the right-hand side of the dialogue box is the working box (in this dialogue, it's labeled "Variable(s)"), which is the to-do list of variables you want to analyze. You can move variables into this list either by double-clicking on them in the left-hand list or by single-clicking to select the variable and then using the little "transport" arrow to move the selected variable into the working box:

You may select multiple items simultaneously from the left-hand list in the same way as you might in other programs. To select a set of contiguous items, select one, then shift-click on another, and all variables between the two will also be selected. To select noncontiguous items, select the first with a mouse click, then hold down CTRL and click on additional variables.

Here is another potentially helpful navigational aid: If you know the first few letters of the variable label, you can type these while the list on the left is selected, and the list will scroll to the first occurrence of these letters. If the list is showing variable names rather than variable labels, type the first few letters of the name.

With the desired variable in the working box (we've chosen "Feelings about the Bible"), click OK:

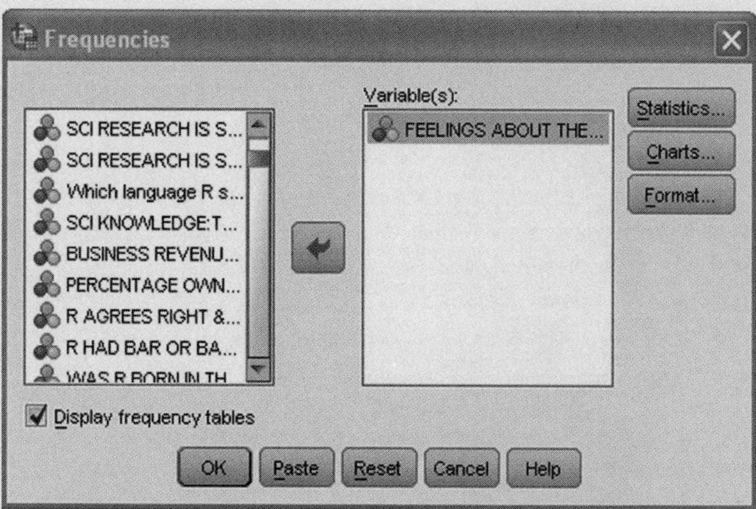

(*continued*)

The Output window will likely come to the front, and will display the output from this procedure:

Frequencies

[DataSet1] C:\Documents and Settings\mark\Desktop\2008gss.sav

Statistics

N	Valid	1987
	Missing	36

Feelings about the Bible

		Frequency	Percent	Valid Percent	Cumulative Percent
Valid	WORD OF GOD	639	31.6	32.2	32.2
	INSPIRED WORD	924	45.7	46.5	78.7
	BOOK OF FABLES	392	19.4	19.7	98.4
	OTHER	32	1.6	1.6	100.0
	Total	1987	98.2	100.0	
Missing	DK	23	1.1		
	NA	13	.6		
	Total	36	1.8		
Total		2023	100.0		

A word about the output before moving on: "Frequencies" is the name of the procedure. A note about what data file is associated with the procedure follows, as does a report about how many cases were processed (both those with data for the variable and those that were missing data), followed by the table we care about.

We'll begin by moving this table into MS Excel in order to make some modifications. Right-click in the middle of the last table of output, and select Copy.

Alternately, with the Output window in front, choose File → Export; choose Word/RTF in the Document type drop-down menu; use the "Browse . . ." button to name the exported file and choose a destination. You can open this file in MS Word, but you'll still want to copy this table to the clipboard and paste it into Excel.

Launch MS Excel. Right-click on any cell (probably near the upper left of the spreadsheet) and choose Paste.

The table ought to look like it did in SPSS (or Word). Rather than making changes to the original table, we will work on a copy; that way, if things go awry, we still have access to the original without having to return to SPSS.

Start by copying part of the table to the clipboard. We're going to click and drag through a selection of cells. Click and hold down the mouse button in the cell above the first value label (in this example, it's the blank cell above the phrase "Word of God." Don't let up on the mouse button as you drag over to the column labeled "Valid Percent," and down to the bottom-most cell (which should contain the number 100.0). Let up on the mouse button; you should have this much selected:

	Frequency	Percent	Valid Percent
WORD OF GOD	639	31.6	32.2
INSPIRED WORD	924	45.7	46.5
BOOK OF FABLES	392	19.4	19.7
OTHER	32	1.6	1.6
Total	1987	98.2	100

Right-click somewhere in the middle of the selected portion, and select Copy. Select a cell in a free area (below the original table), right-click again, and choose Paste.

We won't include the various percentages of missing data—the "don't know" (DK) and "not applicable" (NA) categories—in our table, so we will delete the Percent column and use only the Valid Percent column. Click and hold down the mouse on the column label "Percent" (not "Valid Percent"; we need that), and continue to hold down the mouse as you drag down to the bottom of that column. Let up on the mouse button. Right-click in the middle of the selected cells, and choose "Delete . . ."; a dialogue box will appear, asking what you wish to do with cells adjacent to those deleted:

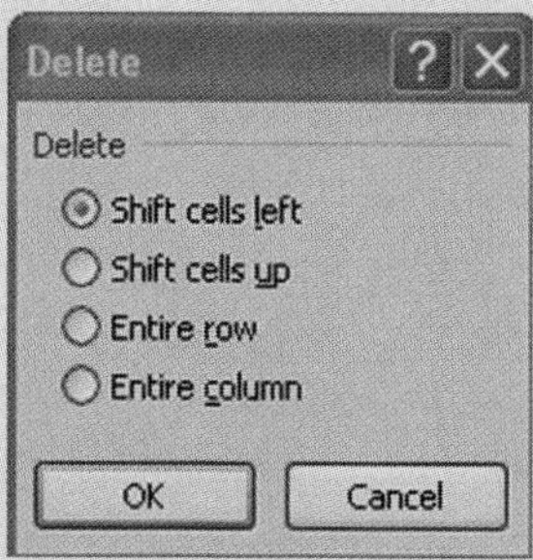

"Shift cells left" will be selected by default; click OK.

(continued)

Our table is down to three columns now:

	Frequency	Valid Percent
WORD OF GOD	639	32.2
INSPIRED WORD	924	46.5
BOOK OF FABLES	392	19.7
OTHER	32	1.6
Total	1987	100

Save your Excel file; Exercise 2 uses this spreadsheet.

Select these cells (by using the drag-through technique you've been using), and launch MS Word.

When a new page opens in MS Word, hit Enter a couple of times. If you don't, adding text above the table you're about to paste will be troublesome. Right-click (or use the Edit menu) and Paste.

	Frequency	Valid Percent
WORD OF GOD	639	32.2
INSPIRED WORD	924	46.5
BOOK OF FABLES	392	19.7
OTHER	32	1.6
Total	1987	100

Next, we'll make modifications to give the table more visual appeal, and for clarity:

- Use the "Change Case . . ." command to change the case of the values to title case (first letter capitalized, subsequent letters lower case).
- Click and drag on the cell borders to customize cell widths.
- Use the alignment tools to center the last two columns horizontally.
- Use the table formatting tools to make cell spacing consistent.
- Add a title that includes information about the table's content.
- Add a footnote with the data source and any other pertinent information.
- Use the Table AutoFormat to reduce the number of lines.

Exercise 2: Pie Chart

If you saved the spreadsheet from Exercise 1, open it. Otherwise, create a new spreadsheet with the values you wish to graph, arranged like the following table (labels in one column, values in the next column to the right). Select the cells that contain the value labels and the frequencies. (If you're using the spreadsheet from Exercise 1, be sure *not* to select the cell with the total frequency.)

WORD OF GOD	639
INSPIRED WORD	924
BOOK OF FABLES	392
OTHER	32

There are several ways to tell MS Excel to make a graph; unfortunately, the particulars keep changing with each new version. In the current version, once the proper cells are selected (see previous paragraph), click on the Insert tab, and then click on the Pie Chart icon; we selected 2-D Pie from the drop-down menu. Clicking on the chart will activate contextual tools with which you may modify your chart.

Once your graph is complete, you can copy it to the clipboard and paste it into Word, where you can add titles and footers.

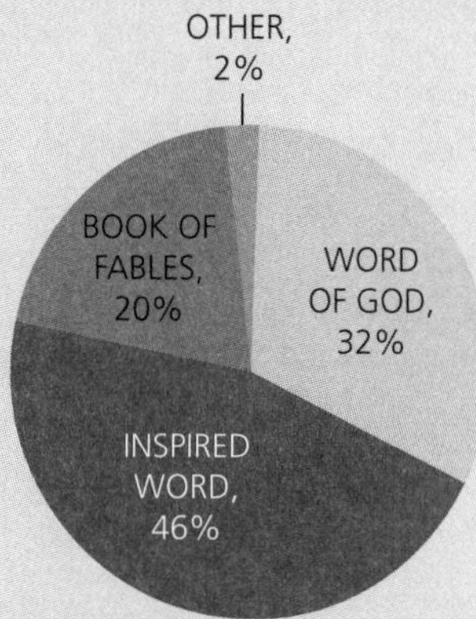

Source: 2008 General Social Survey. Data were missing for 36 cases.

Exercise 3: Bar Chart

Make a bar chart of a nominal variable from the data set; the process is exactly the same as that for making a pie chart, except that you will choose Bar Chart from the gallery of chart types.

(*continued*)

- Experiment with the options for showing values.
- Figure out how to give the vertical and horizontal axes labels. This may require a trip to the Help file.
- Add a title and any required footer text.

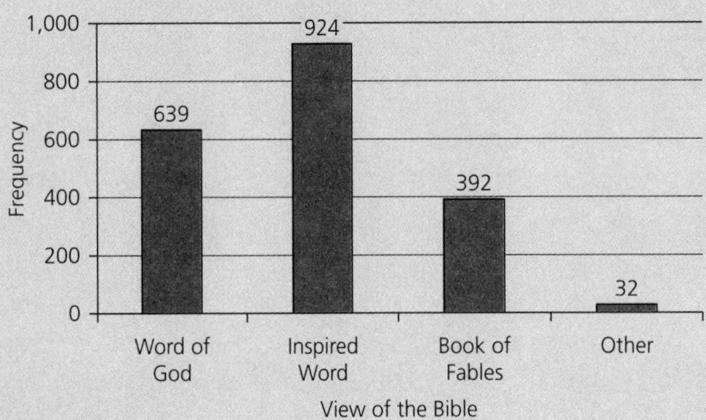

Source: 2008 General Social Survey. Data were missing for 36 cases.

Exercise 4: Recoding into Fewer Categories (Preliminary Work toward Displaying Interval/Ratio Data Summaries)

As the book suggests, a frequency table that shows all values of an interval/ratio variable is not much more useful than the list of values itself. Consider the socioeconomic index (SEI) from the 2008 General Social Survey (GSS); it has 1,911 cases distributed across ~230 values; to show the complete frequency distribution would take several pages, and it would not be a useful summary of the data.

Let's say that, rather than 230 categories, we want to summarize this distribution in five categories. Since the index runs from 0 to 100, with one decimal point of precision to create real class intervals, we will divide the values up into the following categories:

0–20
20.1–40
40.1–60
60.1–80
80.1–100

Now, we could just have SPSS create a frequency chart and we could then tabulate the frequencies of our new categories by hand, but this is tedious. The preferred method is to tell SPSS to recode the original values into a new variable that keeps track of the new categories.

So, where the original ("SEI") variable had any value between 0 and 20, the new variable will contain the value "1"; where the original variable had any value between 20.1 and 40, the new variable will have the value "2"; and so on.

Original Values Between	Examples of Original Values	New Variable's Value	New Variable's Value Label
0 and 20	17.1, 19.6	1	"0–20"
20.1 and 40	22, 23	2	"20.1–40"
40.1 and 60	42, 44.5	3	"40.1–60"
60.1 and 80	63.4, 78	4	"60.1–80"
80.1 and 100	80.1, 99	5	"80.1–100"

Once the transformation is complete, instead of a frequency chart that goes on for pages and pages,

Respondent Socioeconomic Index

		Frequency	Percent	Valid Percent	Cumulative Percent
Valid	17.1	8	.4	.4	.4
	17.6	1	.0	.1	.5
	18.5	1	.0	.1	.5
	19.4	1	.0	.1	.6
	20.1	5	.2	.3	.8
	21.1	2	.1	.1	.9
	21.2	14	.7	.7	1.7
	21.3	1	.0	.1	1.7
	21.6	1	.0	.1	1.8
	22.5	14	.7	.7	2.5
	22.6	3	.1	.2	2.7
	22.7	5	.2	.3	2.9
	22.9	4	.2	.2	3.1

we will have a tidy summary of the data.

In SPSS, choose Transform → Recode into Different Variables.

As you can see from the menu, it's possible to "Recode into Same Variables," which replaces the original values of the variable with the new values. If something

(continued)

goes awry in the process, however, the original values are lost, and there's no way to recover them, so it's usually best to "Recode into Different Variables."

This brings up a dialogue box:

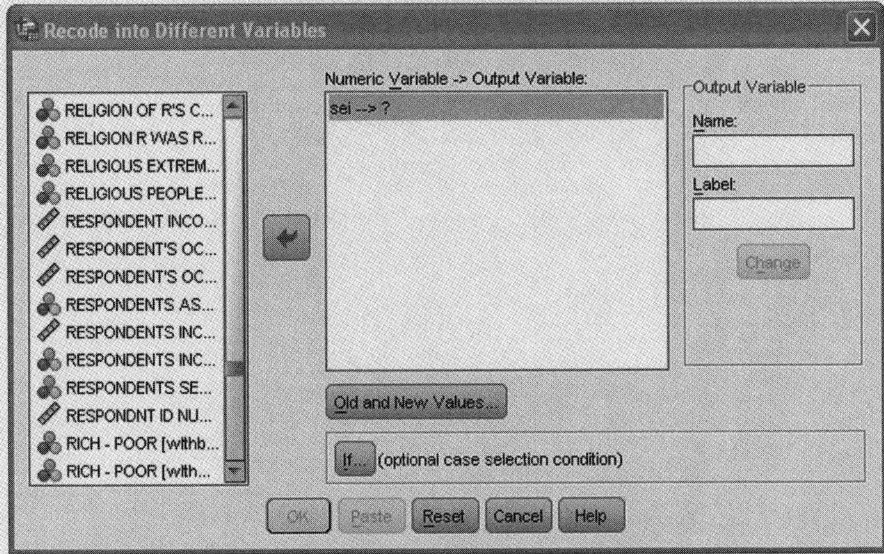

Choose the source variable (the original one, with too many values) from the list, and move it into the working box (here labeled "Numeric Variable → Output Variable") by double-clicking on it or by selecting it and using the transport arrow to the right of the variable list.

Next, give the new variable (the variable that will keep track of the five categories of SEI) a name (since this is SEI in five categories, we'll call it "SEI_5cats"), and type it into the Name box. You have the option of creating a label for the variable at this time, and you can type that in the Label box:

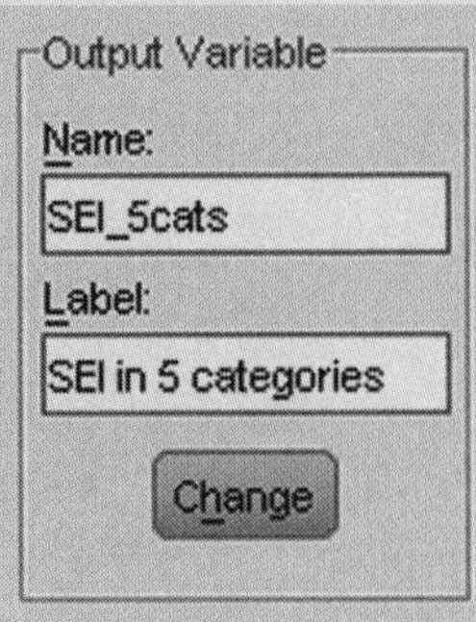

Just typing into these boxes doesn't actually do anything; you must click the Change button below the Label box to move this part of the instruction into the working box. Notice that when you do, the working box changes from this:

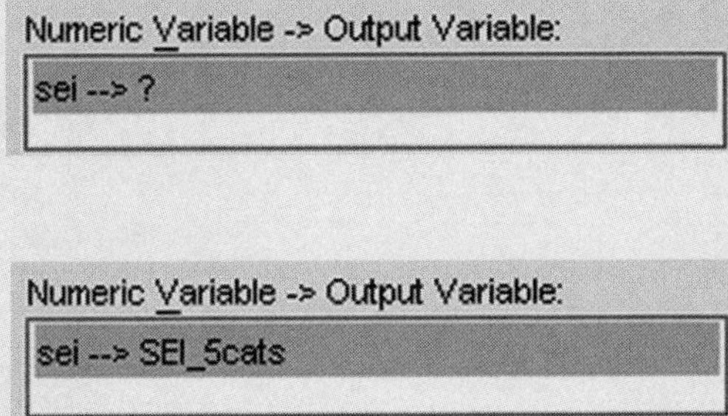

to this:

This shows that SPSS is getting reading to use values from SEI to create values for SEI_5cats.

Next, we need to tell SPSS how to make the transformation. Click on the button labeled "Old and New Values." This brings up a dialogue box:

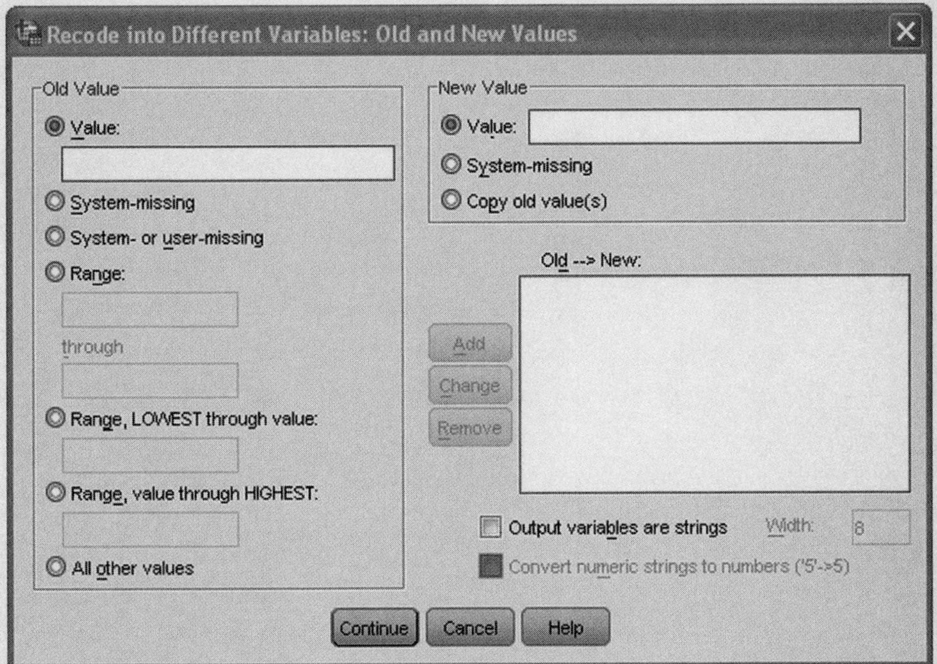

(continued)

This dialogue is a little busier than the ones we've seen so far. The entire left side is devoted to telling SPSS about the value or values of the original variable ("Old Value"). The top of the right side is for telling SPSS about the associated value of the new variable, and at the bottom of the right side is the working box, showing what SPSS will do once we're done defining the transformation.

It's helpful to make yourself a table with the transformation values on it to keep track of the transformations:

SEI	**SEI_5cats**
0–20	1
20.1–40	2
40.1–60	3
60.1–80	4
80.1–100	5

Start at the top of your list. We need to tell SPSS that for any value of the original variable that falls between 0 and 20 (inclusive), it should put the value "1" into the new variable.

A look at the frequency distribution tells us that the lowest value of SEI is 17.1. There are two ways this information could be used to enter the range of SEI values that will become "1" in the new variable.

We could use the Range function. Select the radio button next to the word "Range," and enter the actual values at either end of the range (17.1 through 20):

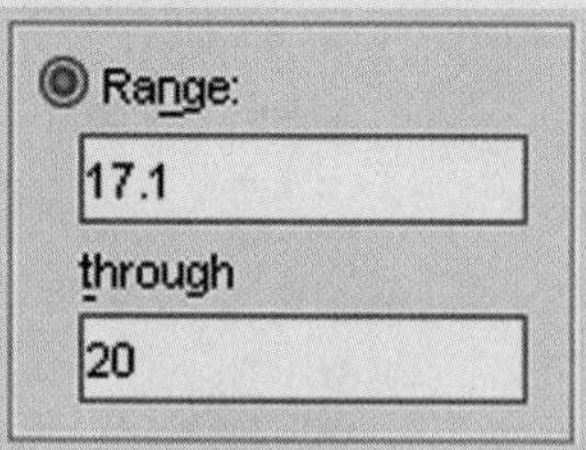

Since these are the bottom values of SEI, we could tell SPSS to select any values it finds that are less than or equal to 20. To do this, select the radio button next to "Range, LOWEST through value":

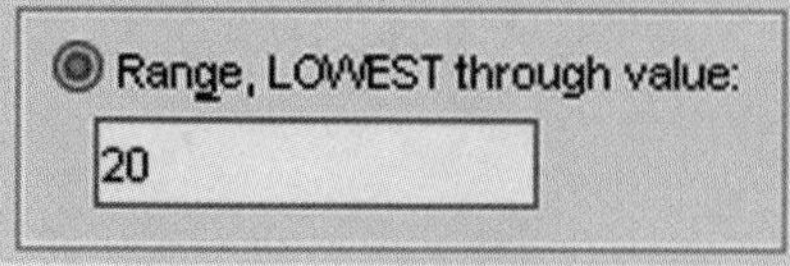

Either method accomplishes the same thing, but if you only knew that 20 was the upper cutoff for this category, it might be safer to use the second method.

Next, we tell SPSS what value to assign to the new variable by typing in the New Value box. By default, the radio button next to "Value" is selected; type "1" into this box:

Once again, just typing into the boxes doesn't actually accomplish anything. In order to put this work into the working box, you must click the Add button:

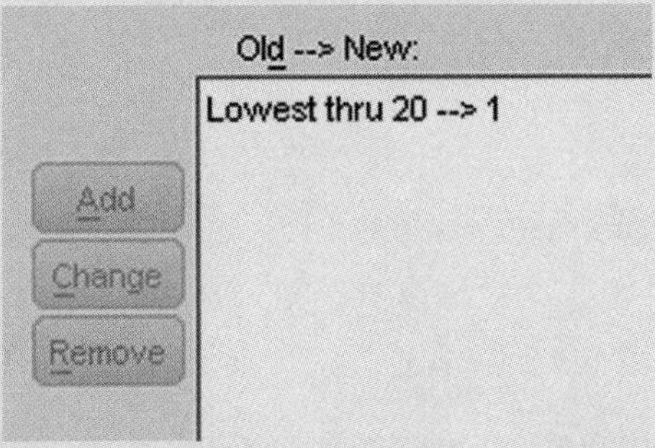

If you find that you've made a mistake, you can select entries in the working box, and either delete the whole entry by clicking Remove or modify the parts by reentering numbers and clicking Change.

For the middle categories, we must use the Range technique:

On the Old Values side:	On the New Values side:	Working box, after clicking Add:
Range: 20.1 through 40	New Value Value: 2	Old --> New: Lowest thru 20 --> 1 20.1 thru 40 --> 2 Add
Range: 40.1 through 60	New Value Value: 3	Old --> New: Lowest thru 20 --> 1 20.1 thru 40 --> 2 40.1 thru 60 --> 3 Add

(continued)

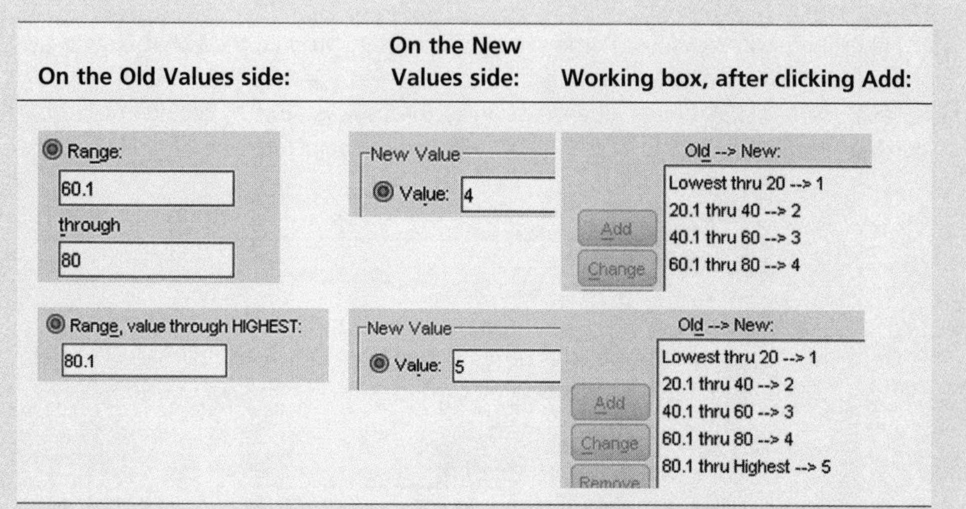

It's good practice to tell SPSS to take any missing values it finds in the original variable and create missing values in the new value:

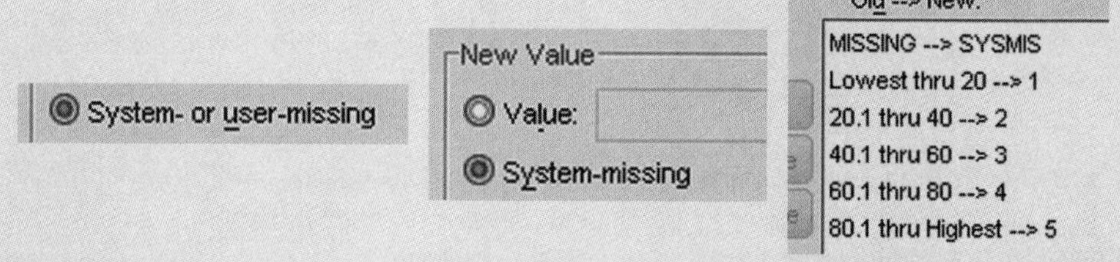

After you've taken care of everything on your list and the missing values, click Continue. This brings you back to the earlier dialogue box, where you can click OK.

We've told SPSS to recode into a new variable, but it doesn't know what the values of the new variable mean, so output we create at this point will be a little dodgy:

SEI in 5 categories

		Frequency	Percent	Valid Percent	Cumulative Percent
Valid	1	11	.5	.6	.6
	2	970	47.9	50.8	51.3
	3	243	12.0	12.7	64.1
	4	532	26.3	27.8	91.9
	5	155	7.7	8.1	100.0
	Total	1911	94.5	100.0	
Missing	System	112	5.5		
Total		2023	100.0		

We need to tell SPSS what the values 1 to 5 mean, so the output will be more useful.

Go to Variable View on the Main window, and scroll to the bottom of the list of variables; SPSS always creates new entries at the bottom.

Go over to the Values column, click on the cell to activate it, and then click on the box with the ellipsis. Here's where you will define the values (see Exercise 1 for more detailed instructions):

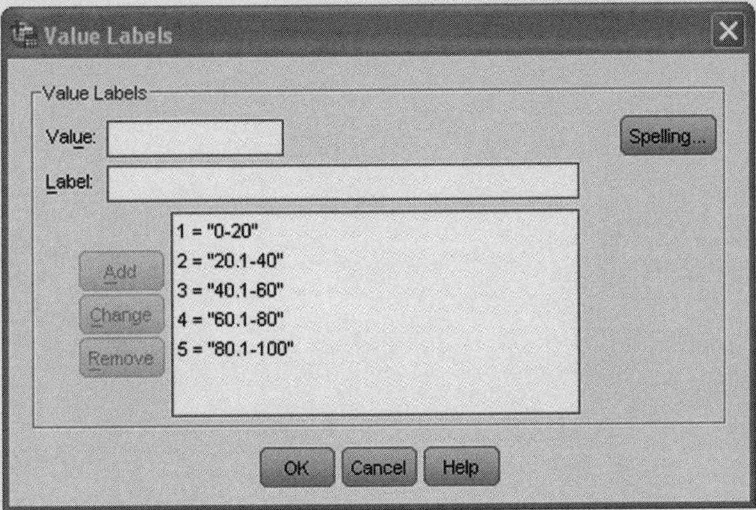

With the values defined, it's time to create the frequency chart:

SEI in 5 categories

		Frequency	Percent	Valid Percent	Cumulative Percent
Valid	0–20	11	.5	.6	.6
	20.1–40	970	47.9	50.8	51.3
	40.1–60	243	12.0	12.7	64.1
	60.1–80	532	26.3	27.8	91.9
	80.1–100	155	7.7	8.1	100.0
	Total	1911	94.5	100.0	
Missing	System	112	5.5		
Total		2023	100.0		

Once you have created a well-labeled table, you can use the techniques outlined earlier to dress up the table, or you can create a graph.

Chapter 3

CENTRAL TENDENCY

LEARNING OBJECTIVES

When you have finished this chapter, you will be able to:

- Explain the general idea of the central tendency of a distribution for nominal, ordinal, and interval/ratio data.
- Identify the mode of a distribution, and explain its meaning.
- Identify the median of a distribution from raw data and from grouped data, and explain its meaning.
- Calculate the mean of a distribution from raw data and from grouped data, and explain its meaning.
- Use a spreadsheet program or statistical software package to calculate the mode, median, and mean.

THE BASIC IDEA OF CENTRAL TENDENCY

In Chapter 2, we learned to describe the entire distribution of a variable with the frequency table and some graphical tools. Chapters 3, 4, and 5 discuss statistics that describe particular aspects of the distribution in more detail—central tendency, dispersion, and shape.

Measures of central tendency are particularly important because they are used to summarize and convey what people want to know most about the distribution of scores on a variable—what is the typical score? Measures of central tendency are also important because many of the tools of bivariate and multiple variable analyses focus on central tendency.

One of the main purposes of statistical tools is to summarize information about many cases in hopes of identifying patterns in our data; measures of central tendency focus on what is "typical," "normal," "most commonly occurring," or "most likely" in our sample.

When considering the distribution of the variable "sex" in a sample (or describing a party to someone who missed it), the first thing people want to know is whether there were more women or more men. One notion of ***central tendency*** is the most common, most typical, or most likely score; this is the *mode.*

When you hear about fluctuations in housing prices, it's rare to hear about the most common price; in fact, there may not be any single price that occurs more than once. News accounts of new home sales typically report the ***median*** house price, the one in the middle of the distribution.

Part of a job I held years ago was holding retreats for high school kids. Before I could publicize a retreat, I'd have to come up with a budget. Some costs (like the retreat center) were fixed, but I'd have to guess how much meals would cost. Without knowing who was coming, it was hard to predict how much food would be required. Eventually, I settled on a system: I could put together a breakfast that would average $3 per kid, a lunch for $4 per kid, and a dinner for $5 per kid. The system worked because most kids did eat close to the ***mean or average*** amount, and the (fewer) kids who ate more balanced out the (fewer) kids who ate less.

The basic idea of central tendency is what is typical of the distribution of scores on a variable. But, as we've seen, there are three main ways of defining what this might mean: the most common score, the middle-ranking score, or the average score.

In this chapter, we will learn about specific statistics that are helpful for operationalizing each of these concepts. Deciding what specific statistic (or statistics) to use for a particular problem depends on two things—what we mean by "typical," and how we have measured the variable we want to describe.

If a variable is measured at the nominal level, the only definition of central tendency that makes any sense is the most common score. I can describe which religion—Protestant, Catholic, or Jewish—is most common in my sample (i.e., the most typical score on the variable "religious identification"). But can I tell you which religion is the middle-ranking religion? Can I tell you which religion is the average religion? I can't, because nominal variables simply don't tell me about whether scores are higher or lower, or by how much.

If a variable is measured at the ordinal level, we can still apply the definition that central tendency means the most common score. Any variable that is ordinal can also be treated as nominal. But, if we know that the cases are in ranked categories (not just categories), then we can apply the idea of central tendency as the middle-ranking score. That is, if I rank the cases from low to high and find the middle-ranking case, what is its score? In looking at the distribution of letter grades in my class, I can tell you both the most common grade and the grade of the person at the middle rank in the class. They might be the same thing, or they might not.

If a variable is measured at the interval/ratio level, we can apply all three definitions of central tendency. Any variable that is interval/ratio is also ordinal; any variable that is interval/ratio is also nominal. With a variable measured at the interval/ratio level, in addition to telling you what is the most common score and what is the middle-ranking score, I can also tell you the average or balance point. In looking at the grades on the midterm exam, I can tell you what the most common score was and what the score of the person at the middle rank in the class was. But I can go further and also tell you the balance point at which 50 percent of the differences in people's scores were above and 50 percent of the differences in people's scores were below that point. This may sound like an abstract idea (it is, actually), but the idea of an "average" score is one that we use all the time.

So, the level of measurement of a variable affects how we approach creating statistics to assign a value to the idea of central tendency. In the remainder of this chapter, we examine each of the levels in more detail.

THE MODE

The ***mode*** is the most frequent value (or category) of a distribution. The fact that one value appears more often than others means that it is the most likely outcome of a random observation.

The mode is an appropriate measure of central tendency for nominal data. Sometimes, the mode may also be useful with ordinal or interval/ratio variables as well.

The Mode and Nominal Data

Consider the bar graph of the distribution of the nominal variable "marital status," shown in Figure 3.1.

If I had to make just one simple statement to try to describe the most important thing about this graph, I would probably say, "In this sample, there are more married people than any other kind." That is, the most typical score on the variable is "married." The category "married," then, is the central tendency of the distribution of marital status.

FIGURE 3.1 Marital Status in the 2008 General Social Survey

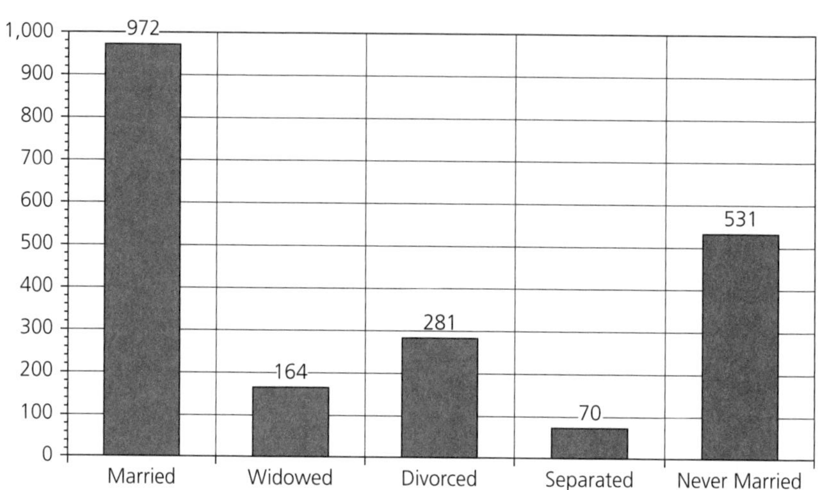

Another way of thinking about this is to ask: If I closed my eyes and picked just one case at random, what is the most likely (most probable) score of that case? Of course, I might actually choose someone from any of these categories, but the most likely outcome of a random draw would be a person who is married. This is another way of defining the central tendency of a nominal variable—the maximum likelihood outcome or expected value.

So, by looking at Figure 3.1, we see immediately that the category with the largest number of cases (and largest percentage of the cases) is "married." So, the mode of the distribution of the variable "marital status" is the value "married."

Note that the value of the mode is (ordinarily) not a number; it is the name of a category. You might be tempted to say something like "The mode is 972," but it's not: the mode is "married"; 972 is the frequency of the modal category.

A properly constructed bar chart makes it easy to identify the mode. It is also easy to identify the mode from a frequency table. Consider Table 3.1.

Since the mode is the category with the largest relative frequency, and the South Atlantic had the largest valid percent of cases, the mode of the variable "region of interview" is "South Atlantic."

While the mode is the name of the single largest category, it is sometimes helpful to go one step further in reporting the central tendency of a nominal variable. If instead of saying that the modal category in Table 3.1 is "South Atlantic," suppose that I said: "The modal category in Table 3.1 is 'South Atlantic' and it contains 21 percent of the cases." Reporting the relative frequency in the modal category can often be much more informative when there are many categories.

TABLE 3.1 Region of Interview

		Frequency	Percent (%)
Valid	New England	16	5.4
	Middle Atlantic	40	13.6
	E. North Central	45	15.3
	W. North Central	21	7.1
	South Atlantic	62	21.0
	E. South Central	19	6.4
	W. South Central	36	12.2
	Mountain	23	7.8
	Pacific	33	11.2
	Total	295	100.0

Source: General Social Survey, 1998.

The Mode and Ordinal Data

The mode is the only useful measurement of central tendency for nominal data, whether dichotomous (two categories) or polyotomous (three or more categories), but it can be a useful statistic for ordinal or interval/ratio data, too.

Remember, though, that there are two kinds of ordinal data: full-rank and grouped. In full-rank data, every case has an individual ranking. Imagine the order of people coming through a door into a classroom. If the door is not wide enough to allow two people through at the same time, there will only be one first person through the door, one second person through, one third person, and so on. If there's only one of every category, it would be appropriate to say that the mode is undefined. Even if ties are allowed (two people manage to cram themselves through the door at once), the mode is not very useful (although it might be entertaining to describe the day four people attempted to get through the doorway at the same time).

In contrast to full-rank data, it is very useful to examine the mode for a grouped ordinal variable. For example, when evaluating the usefulness of a handout, we might tally responses to the question: "How helpful were the instructions? Would you say that they were: very unhelpful, unhelpful, neutral, helpful, or very helpful?"

If the handout were neither excellent nor horrible, we might see a distribution like the one in Figure 3.2.

If this is the case, knowing that more people responded "neutral" than any other category is probably helpful information (although we might be better off reporting the median; more about this later).

Knowing which answer occurred most frequently may be useful, but it is not necessarily the case that this most common answer is also close to or typical of most people. Imagine that, instead of being mediocre, the instructions had struck some as brilliant and some as terrible (see Figure 3.3).

FIGURE 3.2 Opinions about a Mediocre Class

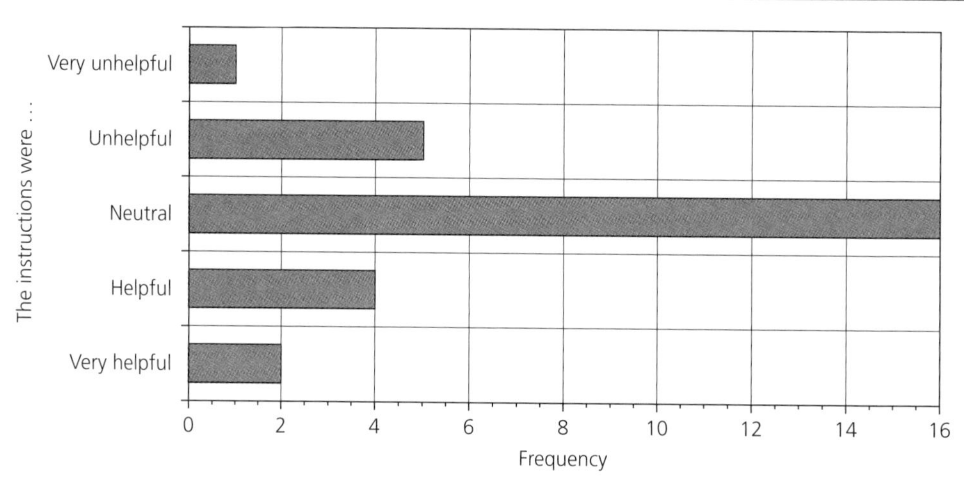

FIGURE 3.3 Strong, Opposite Opinions about a Handout

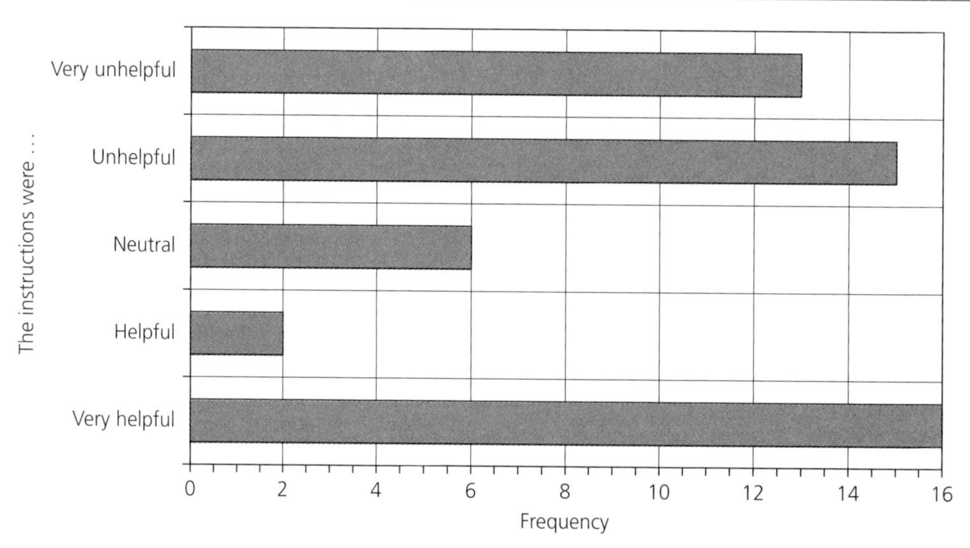

Notice that while "very helpful" is the modal category; most of those asked thought that the instructions were "unhelpful" or "very unhelpful." In this case, whereas it is accurate to state that the mode is "very helpful," it is probably more accurate to describe the distribution as bimodal, having two modes.

The Mode and Interval/Ratio Data

The central tendency of the distribution of an interval/ratio variable can also be described with the mode. As is the case with ordinal data, sometimes this is helpful, and sometimes it is not.

If there are many values but little duplication of values in an interval/ratio distribution, the mode probably won't be very helpful. Imagine the sales prices of homes, for example. In a sample of thousands of home prices, there might be only two homes that sold for the

CHECK QUIZ 3.1

1. The mode is
   a. midway between the highest and lowest scores.
   b. the only measure of central tendency appropriate for use with nominal data.
   c. useless when talking about interval/ratio variables.
   d. the arithmetic average of a variable's values.
2. Look at Figure 3.1 again. If the "married" category were eliminated, which category would be the mode?
   a. widowed
   b. separated
   c. divorced
   d. never married
3. Figure 3.1 shows that the "married" category is the mode for this distribution, so if you closed your eyes you would probably pick a married person. If this is the case, then if you were to walk around campus with your eyes closed, why would you be more likely to run into a never-married person?
   a. because the distribution of the variable "marital status" is different on campus than it is in the GSS sample
   b. because married people on campus are all indoors
   c. because there are more single people who go to school
   d. all of the above
4. Which of the following is *not* a nominal-level variable?
   a. zip code
   b. occupation
   c. level of education
   d. make of automobile
5. Choose the nominal-level variable:
   a. number of students in class
   b. hair color of students in statistics class
   c. time it takes to commute to school
   d. your weight

same exact price, while all the other prices were unique. The price those two houses sold for is the mode, but it doesn't help much in describing the distribution of housing prices.

On the other hand, it may make sense to report the mode of an interval/ratio variable with relatively few values. Take the number of children in families: it might be useful to know that families with two children are more frequent than families with zero, one, three, and more children.

It is always a good idea to look at a bar graph or frequency table for a variable before deciding whether the mode is a useful summary of central tendency. If there are multiple categories with about the same relative frequency, reporting a single one may be misleading.

THE MEDIAN

We've already said that there is no way to talk about the middle value of a nominal variable, since any arrangement of the categories is arbitrary. If a variable has been measured at the ordinal level, however, its scores tell us more than whether one case is the same or different from another; the scores indicate a rank ordering from less to more of the thing we are measuring. When the cases may be ranked from low to high or less to more, central tendency can be defined as the middle-ranking score. Since interval/ratio variables also rank things from low to high or less to more, it is also possible to talk about the median of interval/ratio variables.

Consider height (a variable measured at the ratio level). If you want to know what the median height is in a classroom, you could line everyone up from shortest to tallest. If the number of students is odd, the middle-most student's height is the median, as in Figure 3.4.

Note: Michelle might be the middle-most student, but it's her height (5′5″) that's the median, not her.

If there's an even number of students, then (by convention) the median is the value that lies midway between the two middle-most values. If those two values are the same, that's the median, as in Figure 3.5.

If those values are different, we take the average, as in Figure 3.6.

FIGURE 3.4 Ranked Data and Median Height

FIGURE 3.5 Median When the Two Middle Scores Have the Same Value

Michelle and Gladys are both 5′5″.

FIGURE 3.6 Median When the Two Middle Scores Have Different Values

(5′5″ + 5′6″)/2 = 5′5½″

The Median and Ordinal Data

Consider the distribution of formal education among adults in the United States (from the General Social Survey, 2008), ranked according to the highest level of educational credentials that are held, as shown in Figure 3.7.

The cases here are classified in ranked groups, from fewer educational credentials (at the bottom of the graph) to more. As we saw in Chapter 2, stacked bar charts, like Figure 3.2, are a good way to display the frequency distribution of ordinal variables. If we start with the person with the lowest education and go up the distribution until we find the midpoint, we see that the score of the middle-ranking person is "high school." Of course, we could start at the top and work down, too, to find the middle-ranking person.

Another way of thinking about the median is to say that it's the 50th percentile. The 50th percentile of a distribution is the value at which 50 percent of the distribution lies at or below that value. Other percentiles work the same way: the 10th percentile is the value at which 10 percent of a distribution lies at or below that value. When you took achievement tests in high school and your mother beamed, "She's in the 94th percentile," it meant that 94 percent had a lower score than you did or the same score.

This suggests that the 50th percentile of the distribution can also be located using a frequency chart instead of a graphic display. While it's possible to figure out where the median falls using the actual frequencies, it's easier to use cumulative percentages reported in stat package output.

FIGURE 3.7 Educational Attainment

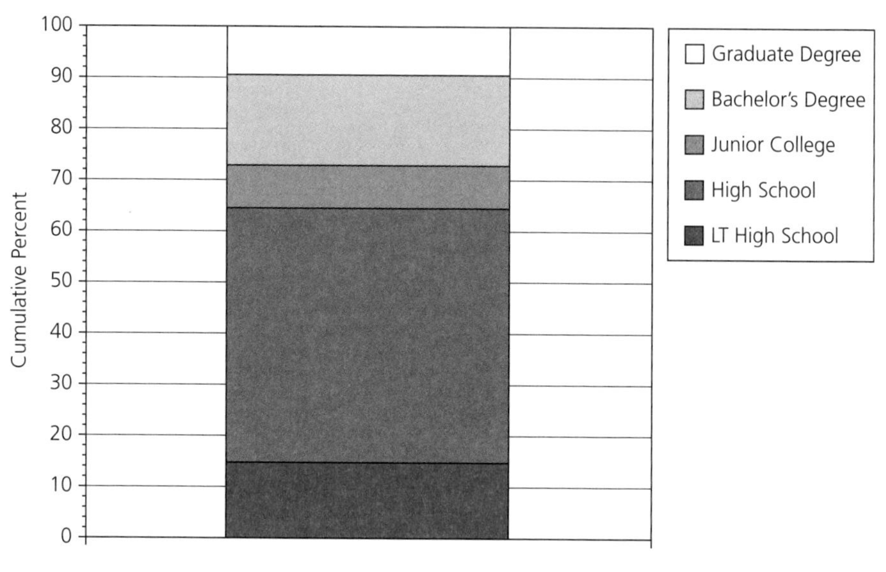

TABLE 3.2 Frequency Chart of Educational Attainment, 2008 General Social Survey

		Frequency	Percent	Valid Percent	Cumulative Percent
Valid	LT high school	297	14.7	14.7	14.7
	High school	1,003	49.6	49.6	64.3
	Junior college	173	8.6	8.6	72.8
	Bachelor's degree	355	17.5	17.6	90.4
	Graduate degree	194	9.6	9.6	100.0
	Total	2,022	100.0	100.0	
Missing	DK	1	0.0		
	Total	2,023	100.0		

LT—less than; DK—don't know.

First, a word about cumulative frequencies. The idea here is that the percentages cumulate (gather together and combine) with each category added. Start at the top of Table 3.2: respondents with less than high school account for 14.7 percent of valid cases. When we add high school grads to the less than high school respondents, we've accounted for 64.3 percent of the valid cases.

TABLE 3.3 Why Rounding Cumulative Percentages Is Problematic

		Cumulative Percent
Valid	Strongly disagree	14.7
	Disagree	49.2
	Neutral	72.8
	Agree	90.4
	Strongly agree	100.0

So, using the cumulative percentages, we can see that the 50th percentile falls in the category "high school." The key to finding the median is to look for the first entry in the cumulative percent column that is 50 percent or larger.

Helpful hint: There are some places where rounding can get you into trouble. If you were looking for the median in Table 3.3, you might be tempted to say to yourself, "Since 49.2 is nearly 50, I'll just round up and call 'disagree' the median." Don't; 49.2 isn't large enough to accommodate the 50 percent required for the 50th percentile, so "neutral" is the median value of this distribution (even though it's quite a bit larger than 50 percent).

The Median and Interval/Ratio Data

We can identify the median of an interval-level variable. Cases can be ranked as higher or lower according to their exact scores on an interval variable, so we can find the 50th percentile (the median). It can very useful to calculate the median of an interval variable—as we will discuss in the next section on the central tendency of interval variables.

The median is the score of the case at the 50th percentile of ranked data. If there is an uneven number of cases, there will always be exactly one case that falls in the middle (e.g., if there are seven people, ranked from low to high or high to low, the median is the score of the fourth person, counting either up from the bottom or down from the top). If there is an even number of cases, though, the 50th percentile will fall between two cases (e.g., if there are eight ranked cases, the 50th percentile falls between the fourth and fifth cases). If the two cases adjacent to the 50th percentile have the same score (e.g., both are "high school"), there is no problem—the median is the score that they both have.

But what if the two cases adjacent to the 50th percentile have different scores? If we happen to be using the median with interval-level data, then we would define the median as the average of the two scores adjacent to the 50th percentile. If the 50th percentile falls on the boundary line between two ranked categories (e.g., the 50th percentile falls above "high school" but below "junior college"), we just have to say: "The median falls between high school and junior college."

CHECK QUIZ 3.2

1. For which of the following variables would one *not* use the median as a measure of central tendency?
   a. income
   b. miles from home to school
   c. race
   d. satisfaction with a course (not, some, very, . . .)
2. In addition to saying that one case is different from another, the ordinal level of measurement allows us to
   a. order categories from high to low.
   b. measure the distance between high and low.
   c. say that one case is more or less than another.
   d. do both a and c.
3. Variables measured at the ordinal level are limited to which of the following mathematical operations?
   a. addition and subtraction
   b. multiplication
   c. ranking cases higher or lower, more or less
   d. counting the number of cases per category
4. The variable "socioeconomic status" ranges from upper class to lower class and is an example of
   a. nominal level of measurement.
   b. ordinal level of measurement.
   c. interval/ratio level of measurement.
   d. ratio level of measurement.

Example

FINDING THE MEDIAN IN GROUPED ORDINAL DATA

The median is the score of the case that lies in the middle of the distribution—that is, at the 50th percentile. If we have a list of all the individual cases' scores on a variable, we can create a sorted list and then find the middle case's score (or average the two middle cases' scores if there is an even number of cases).

But often we are confronted with either (1) data that have already been grouped into ranked categories in a frequency table or (2) grouped ordinal data. How can we find the median in such cases? In both of these cases, the median is defined as the name of the class or category that contains the 50th percentile. A couple of examples can clarify.

Example

Suppose that we asked the following question on a survey (the data are fictitious): "How do you feel about how our courts deal with criminals? Would you say the courts are much too harsh, too harsh, about right, too lenient, or much too lenient?" We have compiled the results in a proper frequency chart for an ordinal variable and have calculated relative frequencies and cumulative relative frequencies (see Table 3.4).

TABLE 3.4 Attitudes about Court Sentencing

Courts Too Harsh?	Frequency	Percentages	Cumulative Percentages
Much too harsh	348	13.5	13.5
Too harsh	432	16.8	30.3
About right	668	26.0	56.3
Too lenient	278	10.8	67.1
Much too lenient	843	32.8	100.0
Total	2,569	100.0	

Source: Data are not real.

What was the answer given by the person who fell in the middle of the distribution of attitudes? Using the cumulative percentages, we can see that the person at the 50th percentile fell in the category "about right." So, "about right" is the median.

What if we want to find the median of an interval-level variable that has been grouped into categories? Suppose we collected information from some students on their monthly earnings last month, and compiled the data into a frequency chart (Table 3.5; again, we add both percentages and cumulative percentages).

TABLE 3.5 Monthly Earnings of Students

Earnings in Dollars	Frequency	Percentages	Cumulative Percentages
$2,000 or more	3	3.1	3.1
$1,500 to $1,999	13	13.5	16.6
$1,000 to $1,499	28	29.2	45.8
$500 to $999	37	38.5	84.3
$0 to $499	15	15.6	100.0
Total	96	100.0	

Source: Data are fictitious.

Using the cumulative percentages, we can see that the 50th percentile falls somewhere in the category "$500 to $999." It seems likely that the real median falls near the upper limit of this interval (i.e., closer to "$1,000 to $1,499" than to "$0 to $499), but we really can't say this for sure. So the most honest way to identify the median is to say that it falls in the range "$500 to $999."

Example

FINDING THE MEDIAN IN A LIST OF VALUES

Finding the value of the median from a list of values can be tedious, but is logically pretty simple.

Remember that the median is the score of the case that is in the middle of the distribution when the cases are ranked from low to high. It's the score at which 50 percent of the cases have scores the same or lower, and 50 percent of the cases have scores higher.

Table 3.6 presents some data on the crude birthrates of some countries during the mid-1990s. We've added a column that assigns the ranks to the cases from lowest to highest (sorting the list first would make this easier!).

TABLE 3.6 Birthrates

Country	Birthrate per 1,000 People	Rank
Afghanistan	53	25
Argentina	20	9
Armenia	23	13
Australia	15	7
Austria	12	1.5
Azerbaijan	23	13
Bahrain	29	16
Bangladesh	35	19
Barbados	16	8
Belarus	13	3.5
Belgium	12	1.5
Bolivia	34	18
Bosnia	14	5.5
Botswana	32	17
Brazil	21	10.5
Bulgaria	13	3.5
Burkina Faso	47	24
Burundi	44	21.5
Cambodia	45	23
Cameroon	41	20
Canada	14	5.5
Cent. Afri. R.	44	21.5
Chile	23	13
China	21	10.5
Colombia	24	15

Example

Notice that some cases are tied; that is, they have the same rank. For example, both Belgium and Austria have birthrates of 12.0, making them the lowest two cases on the list. These cases would get the ranks "1" and "2," but we don't know in what order. So, we assign "1.5" to both cases. The next highest case then is rank "3." There are a number of examples of tied scores in the list—take a moment to see how we assigned rank scores.

There are 25 cases on the list. So the middle case would be the 13th case because it has 12 cases with lower scores and 12 cases with higher scores. The 13th case, as it turns out, is Chile, with a crude birth rate of 23 per 1,000 people. So, that's the median—23 births per 1,000 people.

Sometimes a list of cases will have an even number of cases. In this case, the middle actually will fall between two scores. Where a list has an even number of cases, the numerical average of the two adjacent scores is reported as the median.

THE MEAN

If a variable has been measured at the interval/ratio level, its scores tell us more than whether one case is the same as or different from another, or which case ranks higher. Interval/ratio variables measure the amount or quantity of something on a scale with equal intervals. When the scores of cases can be compared using ratios (e.g., "Susan's income is twice as much as Bill's") then the variable has been measured at the interval/ratio level, and central tendency can be defined as the average score.

Consider the distribution of formal education among U.S. adults (pooled General Social Surveys from 1978 to 1998) recorded as the number of years completed, as shown in Figure 3.8.

The cases here are classified according to the exact number of years of schooling completed. Since "years of schooling" is a continuous variable, a histogram is the most useful graphic to display the full distribution of scores. As there are only 20 scores, we have not had to group the cases.

We could characterize the central tendency of this distribution with the mode (in this case, 12 to 13 years of education). We could also find the case that falls at the 50th percentile, or the median. In this case, the median happens to be 12. However, because the data are interval/ratio, we can define the central tendency more precisely.

Using Figure 3.8, try to imagine that the bars are sitting on a teeter-totter (the *x*-axis). Now, think about where one would put the balance point of this teeter-totter in order to make the beam balance. The answer is not entirely obvious. There are more cases at higher levels of education (say 12 to 20 years) than at lower education (say 0 to 8 years). To make the beam balance, the balance point is going to have to be moved toward these upper values. But, if we do that, the cases with very low scores will now be further away from the balance point. When cases are further from the balance point, they have greater influence. This suggests that the balance point might need to be lower.

FIGURE 3.8 Educational Attainment in Years

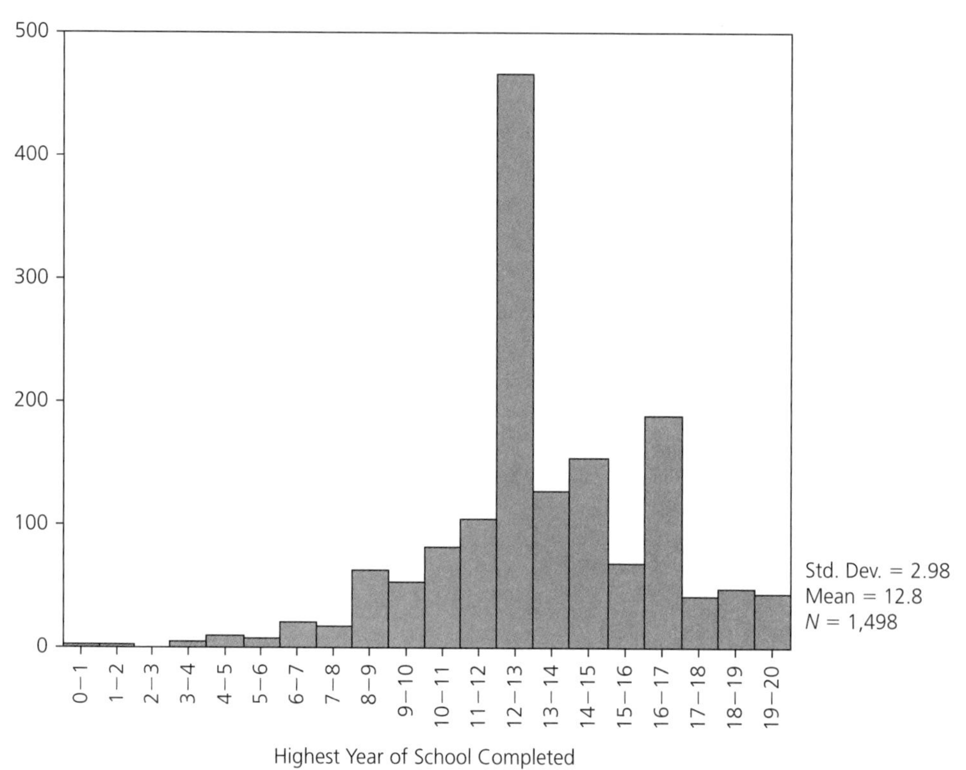

The basic idea of central tendency measures for interval/ratio data is to find the point where the influences or distances of cases above the balance point and below the balance point are equal—that is, to try, in a sense, to find the point where the distances above and below the central tendency are in balance.

The arithmetic mean (or usually just "mean" or "average") is the most common statistic used to index the balance point. By the way, the mean for the "years of schooling" variable turns out to be 12.8 in this case.

The Mean and Interval/Ratio Data

The arithmetic mean is a statistic that you have used for years; you know it by the name "the average." Mathematically, the mean is defined as shown in Formula 3.1:

$$\bar{X} = \frac{\sum_{i=1}^{N}(X_i)}{N} \tag{3.1}$$

The mean of the values in a sample is usually indicated by the letter X with a bar (the symbol is called X bar).

The formula's numerator has a big Greek letter sigma, which means to take the sum of whatever follows it, in this case X_i (x sub i). The subscript i is an index, or counter; X_1 is the first X in a list, X_2 is the second, and so on.

The notation $i = 1$ below the sigma and the N above the sigma are there to specify what to sum. Taken together, they mean, "Take a sum: start with the first X (X_1) and keep adding x's until you've added X_N (x sub N); that is, $X_1 + X_2 + X_3 \cdots + X_N$." (In cases like this, in which it's pretty obvious what you should be summing, the start/stop notation is sometimes left off, as is the index on the X.)

After the sum has been computed, the quantity is then divided by the sample size (the same N that's above the sigma).

There is nothing new in this. You've calculated averages before, and that's what the mean is. The notation (X bar, the summation sign, and the use of the subscript i to refer to individual cases) may be new. Try to get comfortable with it—this kind of notation is used throughout basic statistics.

The arithmetic mean has two interesting mathematical properties that help to explain why it is useful to think of the mean as the balance point of a distribution.

1. The sum of all of the distances of cases from the mean is zero.
2. The sum of the squared distances of cases from the mean is smaller than the sum of the squared distances from any other value.

If we took each case's value and subtracted the mean from it (that is, calculated the deviation from the mean), cases with scores above average would be positive, while cases with below average scores would be negative. The sum of these positive and negative deviations will always be zero (see Figure 3.9).

This means that the mean has as much deviation above it as below it—so it is reasonable to think of it as a central point in the distribution. The mean, then, is the score at which the sum of positive and negative deviations from it is zero.

FIGURE 3.9 The Sum of Deviations from the Mean

2	2 − 5 = −3	−3
6	6 − 5 = 1	1
+7	7 − 5 = 2	+2
15 ÷ 3 = 5		0

FIGURE 3.10 Squared Deviations from the Mean versus Other Squared Deviations

Squared deviations from $\bar{x}$			Squared deviations from 6		
$2 - 5 = -3$	$-3^2 = 9$	9	$2 - 6 = -4$	$-4^2 = 16$	16
$6 - 5 = 1$	$1^2 = 1$	1	$6 - 6 = 0$	$0^2 = 0$	0
$7 - 5 = 2$	$2^2 = 4$	+4	$7 - 6 = 1$	$1^2 = 1$	+1
		14			17

Instead of calculating the deviation of each case from the mean, we could square these deviations. Since any number squared is positive, the sum of the squared deviations of the cases from any score will always be a positive number (or, trivially, zero if all cases have the same score). The mean is the score at which this sum of squared deviations is smaller than it would be if we selected any other value to calculate deviations.

Consider these three numbers 2, 6, and 7 again. The mean is 5. The sum of squared deviations from the mean is 14 (see Figure 3.10).

Now, both 6 and 7 are higher than the mean, so you might imagine that we could minimize squared deviations by choosing one of them. Let's try 6 (right panel, Figure 3.10).

The squared deviation from 6 is reduced to zero, and the squared deviation from 7 is only 1; but the squared deviation from 2 is 16. When we take the sum of these squared deviations (17), it's larger than the squared deviations from X bar. It turns out that no other value will give us smaller squared deviations than does the mean.

The mean, in a sense, comes closer on average to all the individual values than any other possible score—it has the "least squared deviations." This will become an important fact when we discuss analysis of variance (ANOVA) and regression analysis in later chapters.

The mean, then, is a summary of the central tendency in terms of a balance point, or a point that comes closer to all the cases than any other possible score. When we use the word *average*, we are really describing these more complicated mathematical ideas.

Working with the Mean

The mean, median, and mode will not always give us the same answer about the central tendency of the distribution of an interval/ratio variable. The mode is sometimes useful. But, if there are many different scores on X (and sometimes each case has a unique score), the mode may not fall anywhere near the balance point.

Often, the median and the mean will give us very similar values for the central tendency. But it is not necessarily true that the middle-ranked case is at the balance point of the distribution. Because the mean is the point where the sums of positive and negative deviations are equal, the mean is affected by how far cases are from it. The median is not, because the median treats all distances between adjacent cases as equal. As a result, the mean of a distribution is pulled toward the end of the distribution that has a longer tail (see Chapter 5 on distributional shape) in a skewed distribution. Indeed, we can tell if a distribution is skewed, and in which direction, by comparing the mean and median. If the mean is higher than the median, the distribution is positively skewed; if the mean is lower than the median, the distribution is negatively skewed.

When the mean and the median are not the same, you should usually report both. Many variables that we encounter in social science analysis are skewed (e.g., the distribution of income and wealth, the distribution of life expectancies, counts of the number of crimes across cities, etc.).

When a variable is skewed, the median may be the more helpful measure of central tendency. Consider the variable "life expectancy." We could describe the central tendency of life expectancy by calculating the average age at which people die (the mean). Or we could describe the central tendency as the age at which 50 percent of the population has died (the median). The median is usually used because then we don't have to wait for everyone in a group to die before we can calculate it, and because the distribution of age at death is severely positively skewed (that is, there is a long tail toward upper ages) in most populations.

Sometimes, we do not have the score of each individual available. Instead the data have been grouped (as in a frequency table). To calculate the mean from grouped data, we treat each case as though it is at the midpoint of the class interval in which it falls. The midpoints of the intervals are multiplied by the number of cases in the interval for all intervals, and then summed. This sum is then divided by the total number of cases. The result is only an estimate of the mean, but will be a reasonable one if there are a quite a few categories. A special problem happens when a category is unbounded (e.g., "more than $1,000,000 in income").

It should be obvious from the example that this approach to estimating the mean only gives *an estimate*, not the true value of the mean. In the example, the students in the category "age 10–19" are probably older than 15 on average—so by using the midpoint of the interval, we may be underestimating the overall mean. Still, since we don't know any better, this is a reasonable approach.

If you have estimated the mean from grouped data, be sure to say so—don't say that your value is "the mean."

Another problem often comes up in estimating the mean from grouped interval data. What to do if the data contain classes that are open-ended (i.e., "less than ... " or "more than ... "? We don't know what the midpoints of these open-ended categories are, so we can't apply the simple method just described.

CHECK QUIZ 3.3

1. Prejudice, when measured on a scale ranging from "most prejudiced" to "least prejudiced," is an example of what level of measurement?
   a. nominal
   b. ordinal
   c. interval/ratio
   d. ratio
2. When using interval/ratio data, the distance between the scores is
   a. always two units.
   b. always one standard deviation.
   c. exactly defined.
   d. not always clear.
3. Which of the following can be treated as interval/ratio data?
   a. student identification numbers
   b. zip codes
   c. ages
   d. eye colors
4. The number of hours that a student spends in the library is an example of
   a. nominal-level data.
   b. ordinal-level data.
   c. interval/ratio-level data.
   d. ordinary-level data.

Example

CALCULATING THE MEAN FROM A LIST OF VALUES

The arithmetic mean of a list of values is equal to the sum of the values, divided by the number of values.

Suppose we had the values 10, 12, and 20. The sum of the three values is $10 + 12 + 20 = 42$. There are three values. So, the arithmetic mean is 42/3 or 14.

If you have more than a few cases, it's best to use a spreadsheet or statistical package to calculate the mean. Excel, for example, has a built-in function to calculate the mean. But we can do means by hand (or with a calculator).

Here are the test scores of 20 students on the first midterm examination in a basic statistics class:

70	62	73	92
87	68	67	83
50	50	65	73
79	83	81	73
65	52	75	71

Example

If we sum across X from $i = 1$ to $i = N$ (i.e., add up the scores for all 20 individuals), the result is 1,419.

The number of observations is 20.

So, dividing 1,419 by 20, we get: 1,419/20 = 70.95. The arithmetic average, or mean, of the scores on the midterm was about 71.

There are some other summary statistics that are also means. The harmonic mean and geometric mean are calculated somewhat differently, so be a bit careful. Usually, unless we say differently, it's assumed that the mean is the arithmetic mean.

To calculate an estimate of the mean in this kind of circumstance, we do need to make an assumption about the midpoint of the open-ended category. There is no one best way to do this. You need to use your judgment and your knowledge of the particular data to make a reasonable choice for the estimated midpoint of an open-ended interval. Once you've done this, you can proceed as described earlier.

Be sure to report what you have done—both that the mean has been estimated from grouped data, and what values you assumed for the midpoints of open-ended intervals.

Example

CALCULATING THE MEAN FROM GROUPED DATA

It's not unusual to have interval data presented to us in the form of an already compiled frequency chart or table. We cannot exactly calculate the mean of data that have already been grouped, but we can get an estimate.

We can estimate the mean for grouped interval data by assuming that all cases in an interval fall at the midpoint of that interval. We find the midpoint of each interval and multiply it times the frequency in the interval. Sum these values (there will be as many values as there are intervals). Then, divide the sum by the total number of cases (not the number of intervals). We are calculating a weighted average.

Suppose we had the frequency chart shown in Table 3.7 (we've added the last two columns to show the calculations; they are not part of a regular frequency chart).

TABLE 3.7 Age Distribution of Students in Basic Statistics

Interval	Frequency	Midpoint	Midpoint Frequency
Age 40–49	3	45	135
Age 30–39	7	35	245
Age 20–29	12	25	300
Age 10–19	54	15	810
Total	76		1,490

Source: Fictitious data.

Since there are $N = 76$ students in the sample, we divide 1,490 by 76, which yields an estimated mean age of 19.6 years in the class.

SUMMARY

The general idea of central tendency measures is to assign an index number to summarize the most typical values in a distribution. When applied to nominal data, central tendency can be defined as identifying the most frequent or common types of cases that occur; when applied to ordinal data, central tendency describes the values of cases that have midlevel ranking; when applied to interval/ratio data, central tendency refers to the balance point where the weight of the cases with higher scores equals the weight of the cases with lower scores.

With nominal data, the central tendency of the distribution is most often measured with the mode. The mode is the value of the category with the greatest relative frequency. The mode may also be used with grouped ordinal and interval/ratio data, but caution is necessary when applying it to other data types.

With ordinal data, central tendency is most often measured with the median. The median is the value of the case that falls at the midpoint (50th percentile) when the cases are ranked from lowest to highest. For grouped ordinal data, the median is defined as the score of the category containing the 50th percentile. The median should not be used with nominal data. The median may sometimes be useful with interval/ratio data; in fact, reporting the median for an interval/ratio variable is recommended if the distribution of that variable is not symmetric.

With interval/ratio data, central tendency is most often measured with the average, or arithmetic mean. The mean is the balance point or score at which the sum of the distances from it to all cases below it is equal the sum of the distances between it and all cases above it. The mean is also the point where the sum of the squared distances of all other data points from it is at a minimum. The mean is intuitively understood as the average.

The central tendency of a distribution of scores is one of the most important concepts in descriptive statistics. Usually the first thing we want to describe about a set of scores is what's typical. Central tendency measures are also important because most advanced statistics are concerned with the central tendencies of distributions.

What's a typical score, though, is not the only aspect of the frequency distribution that deserves special attention. In the next chapter, we examine another important concept—dispersion—and how it is measured.

Before you go to the next chapter, though, you might want to read the two sections (following the exercises) that show how you can use spreadsheets (like MS Excel) and statistical software packages (like SPSS) to calculate measures of central tendency.

KEY TERMS

central tendency

mean or average

median

mode

CHECK QUIZ ANSWERS

Quiz 3.1 Answers: 1. (b); 2. (d); 3. (a); 4. (c); 5. (b)
Quiz 3.2 Answers: 1. (c); 2. (d); 3. (c); 4. (b)
Quiz 3.3 Answers: 1. (b); 2. (c); 3. (c); 4. (c)

EXERCISES

1. Here is an extract of the General Social Survey codebook. For each variable, indicate which measure of central tendency is optimal.

Variable	Codes	Measure of Central Tendency
Marital status	1 = married	
	2 = widowed	
	3 = divorced	
	4 = separated	
	5 = never married	
Number of brothers and sisters	1 = one	
	2 = two etc.	
Highest educational degree	0 = less than high school	
	1 = high school	
	2 = junior college	
	3 = bachelor's	
	4 = postgraduate	
Total family income	1 = less than $1,000	
	2 = $1,000 to $2,999	
	3 = $3,000 to $3,999	
	4 = $4,000 to $4,999	
	5 = $5,000 to $5,999	
	6 = $6,000 to $6,999	
	7 = $7,000 to $7,999	
	8 = $8,000 to $9,999	
	9 = $10,000 to $14,999	
	10 = $15,000 to $19,999	
	11 = $20,000 to $24,999	
	12 = $25,000 or more	
Race of respondent (R)	1 = white	
	2 = black	
	3 = other	
Size of place where R lives	1,000s of persons	

(continued)

Variable	Codes	Measure of Central Tendency
How would you say our courts are dealing with criminals?	1 = too harsh 2 = about right 3 = not harsh enough	
Hours per day watching TV	number of hours	
Marijuana should be made legal	1 = strongly disagree 2 = disagree 3 = neutral 4 = agree 5 = strongly agree	
Religious preference	1 = Protestant 2 = Catholic 3 = Jewish 4 = none 5 = other 6 = Buddhism 7 = Hinduism 8 = other Eastern 9 = Muslim/Islam 10 = Orthodox Christian 11 = Christian 12 = Native American 13 = interdenominational	

2. The following are some data extracted from the pooled General Social Surveys of 1978 to 1998. For each variable, calculate the appropriate measure of central tendency.

Case Summaries

	Marital Status	R's Highest Degree	Number of Brothers and Sisters
1	Divorced	LT high school	5
2	Married	High school	4
3	Married	High school	3
4	Married	High school	0
5	Married	High school	12
6	Married	High school	8
7	Married	LT high school	4
8	Married	High school	5
9	Separated	High school	10
10	Married	High school	10
11	Never married	Bachelor's	2
12	Married	High school	2
13	Married	High school	4

	Marital Status	R's Highest Degree	Number of Brothers and Sisters
14	Married	LT high school	4
15	Married	Bachelor's	2
16	Married	LT high school	9
17	Never married	Bachelor's	2
18	Married	High school	5
19	Divorced	Graduate	0
20	Married	LT high school	8
21	Married	High school	9
22	Never married	High school	1
23	Married	High school	4
24	Married	LT high school	6
25	Married	High school	2

3. Below are some data from the General Social Survey of 1998. The political party affiliation scale ranks people from "strong Republican" through "independent" to "strong Democrat." For each variable, calculate the appropriate measure of central tendency.

Race of Respondent	Political Party Affiliation	Age of Respondent
White	Independent, near Dem.	26
White	Independent, near Dem.	68
White	Independent, near Rep.	54
White	Not strong Republican	36
White	Independent, near Dem.	61
White	Independent, near Dem.	42
Black	Strong Democrat	59
White	Independent, near Dem.	40
White	Independent, near Dem.	33
White	Independent, near Rep.	25
White	Independent, near Dem.	29
Black	Independent	32
White	Not strong Democrat	69
White	Not strong Democrat	89
White	Strong Democrat	26
White	Independent	26
White	Independent	80
White	Independent, near Rep.	32
White	Not strong Democrat	31
White	Not strong Democrat	45

Source: General Social Survey, 1998.

4. Has the average value of agricultural exports from selected U.S. states changed between 1995 and 1999? Using the following table, calculate the mean and the median value, and comment.

Value of Agricultural Exports (in $ millions) in Selected U.S. States

State	1995	1999
Alabama	467	366
Alaska	0.1	0.2
Arizona	420	333
Arkansas	1,631	1,220
California	6,968	6,932
Colorado	945	828
Connecticut	47	93
Delaware	108	107
Florida	1,201	1,118
Georgia	1,126	867
Hawaii	109	108
Idaho	930	789

Source: Statistical Abstract of the United States, 2000, Table 1327.

5. Here are some data on the rates of crime in several U.S. states in 1996, 1997, and 1998 (crimes known to the police per 100,000 population).

State	1996	1997	1998
Massachusetts	3,837	3,675	3,436
Michigan	5,118	4,917	4,683
Minnesota	4,463	4,414	4,047
Mississippi	4,523	4,630	4,384
Missouri	5,084	4,815	4,826
Montana	4,494	4,409	4,071
Nebraska	4,437	4,284	4,405
Nevada	5,992	6,065	5,281
New Hampshire	2,824	2,640	2,420
New Jersey	4,333	4,057	3,654
New Mexico	6,602	6,907	6,719
New York	4,132	3,911	3,589
North Carolina	5,526	5,492	5,322

Source: Statistical Abstract of the United States, 2000, Table 331.

a. Calculate the mean and median crime rate for each year.
b. Comment on your result. What happened to average crime rates in this sample of states during this three-year period? Do the mean and the median give the same impression?

6. Does the typical age of persons with work disability differ by race? Calculate the mean, median, and mode for each race from the table, and use the result to answer the research question.

U.S. Number of Persons with Work Disabilities by Age and Race, 1999

Age	White	Black	Hispanic
16 to 24	903	329	176
25 to 34	1,521	537	237
35 to 44	2,905	867	396
45–54	3,517	806	438
55–64	4,034	878	475
Total (in thousands)	12,879	3,418	1,723

Source: Statistical Abstract of the United States, 2000, Table 619.

7. The amount of air pollution generated by automobiles depends on the ages of the vehicles. Here are some data on the number of motor vehicles, classified by their ages in the United States in 1980 and 1995. Calculate the mean, median, and modal age of motor vehicles for the two years. Comment on your result.

Cars (millions) in Use in the United States, by Age of Vehicle

Age of Car	1980	1995
Zero to five years old	52.3	46.2
Six to eight years old	25.2	26.9
Nine to 11 years old	14.6	23.3
Twelve to 15 years old	12.5	26.8
Total	104.6	123.2

Source: Statistical Abstract of the United States, 2000, Table 1031.

USING MS EXCEL TO FIND MEASURES OF CENTRAL TENDENCY

While it's easy to have SPSS or other statistical packages compute measures of central tendency (see the next section), sometimes we don't have such software at our disposal. In this case, it's only a little more time-consuming to find these using a spreadsheet program.

Finding the Mode of Nominal Data

If your data are measured at the nominal level, the only measure of central tendency that applies is the mode. If this is the case, Excel may be of relatively little help, since its strengths in dealing with nonnumeric data lie elsewhere. There are at least three possibilities, however, for using Excel in this context.

The first is to create a variable that maps numbers onto the categories of your original variable (1 = apple, 2 = pear, etc.), and then use the techniques described here for summarizing ordinal and interval/ratio data. This could be done by sorting the original variables alphabetically (to force categories into adjacent cells), and then typing numbers into an adjacent column (you'll want to explore Excel's ability to fill adjacent cells by clicking and dragging). This could also be accomplished using the find-and-replace capability (copy your data into another column, so if something goes awry, you still have the original data intact).

The second possibility is to sort the data, and then count the number of cells associated with each category. This is probably a good idea only if you have some serious procrastinating to do. (There are some functions that can help, but the process is tedious at best, and prone to errors.)

The third possibility is to use Excel's database functions to create a lookup table, but unless you use this method frequently, the trial-and-error process will use even more time than the second possibility described, so it's not recommended.

Finding the Mode and Median of Ordinal and Interval/Ratio Data

Finding the mode of ordinal or interval/ratio data requires finding the most common value(s). The exercises in the previous chapter show how to make graphs from summarized data, and graphs make it easy to find the mode(s).

The simplest means of finding the median of an ordinal or interval/ratio variable is to look at the cumulative frequencies on a frequency chart. This can be done by hand, or refer to the exercises in the previous chapter for an Excel solution.

Finding the Mean of an Interval/Ratio Variable

Set the insertion point in an empty cell where you wish the mean to appear.

- Type an equal sign (to tell Excel that this is the beginning of a function).
- Type the keyword "average" (without the quotes).
- Drag through your data to add their cell references to the formula.
- Type Enter/Return.

Use the cell's formatting menu items (or icons) to set the number of decimals.

USING SPSS TO FIND MEASURES OF CENTRAL TENDENCY

A cautionary note: As a researcher, it's up to you to remember which measures are appropriate for each level of measurement. SPSS will gladly report the mean for a nominal variable; we just got it to tell us that the mean of a variable that identifies which part of the country respondents are from (1 = East, 2 = Midwest, 3 = South, and 4 = West) was 2.57, but we're pretty sure that doesn't mean that the average respondent is from Tucson.

Finding the Mode of Variables

Finding a mode for nominal, ordinal, and interval/ratio variables requires creating a frequency chart.

Select: Analyze → Descriptive Statistics → Frequencies

In the dialogue box that appears, move the variable(s) of interest from the complete list of variables (in the left-hand pane) to the working list by double-clicking on the variable, or by single-clicking to select the variable and then clicking the "move-it" arrow between the panes.

Helpful hint: Multiple selections work in SPSS as they do in other programs. You may select contiguous items by clicking on the first item, and then shift-clicking on the last item; this will select both clicked-on variables and everything in between. You may select noncontiguous items by control-clicking on each item. Use the "move-it" arrow after making your selection.

It's possible to have SPSS report the mode (see next paragraph), but, as the text suggests, there may be multiple modes, and SPSS will report only the most frequent value. One handy feature of SPSS is its ability to order frequency chart output by the frequency of values. To access this feature, click on the Format button (in the Frequencies dialogue box). This brings up a new dialogue box:

(continued)

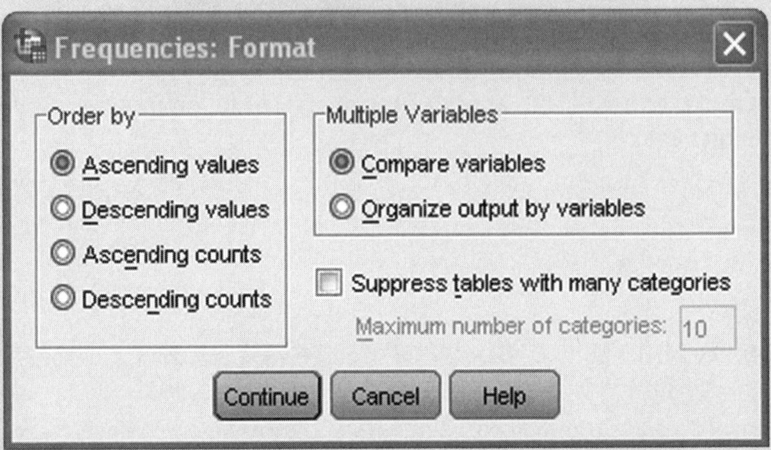

By default, SPSS formats frequency tables by ascending values (so if you coded 1 = East, 2 = Midwest, etc., the table will list East first, Midwest second), but you can get it to list categories/values by descending counts by clicking the appropriate radio button. This will force the true mode to the top of the table and values with smaller counts just beneath it, down to the least frequent values.

You can have SPSS create graphs at the same time by clicking the "Charts..." button:

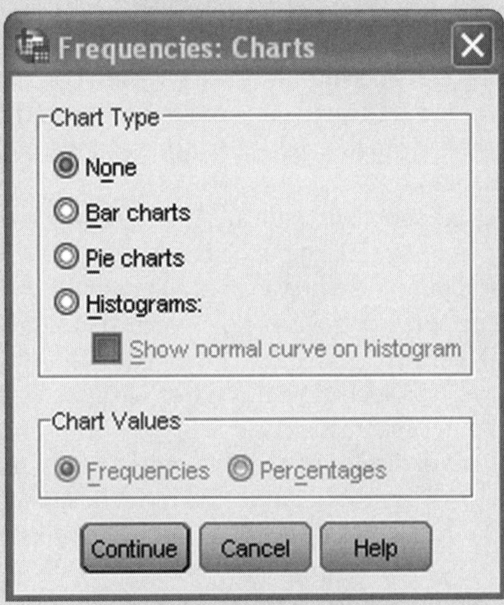

By default, SPSS doesn't make graphs, but you can tell it to make bar charts, pie charts, and histograms using this dialogue box.

Finding the Median of a Distribution

When exploring a variable, it's often a good idea to have SPSS generate a frequency table (and perhaps a simple graph; see preceding) so you can get a feel for the range of values and how cases are distributed among them. Having done so, you can use the cumulative frequencies column to locate the median of a distribution (remember that it's the first category that's big enough to contain 50 percent of cases). Be sure that the table is ordered by ascending or descending values, not by ascending or descending frequencies (SPSS defaults to listing by ascending values, and this is fine).

It's also possible to have SPSS report the median of a distribution directly. While creating a frequency table (Analyze → Descriptive Statistics → Frequencies), click on "Statistics . . .", and the following dialogue box will appear:

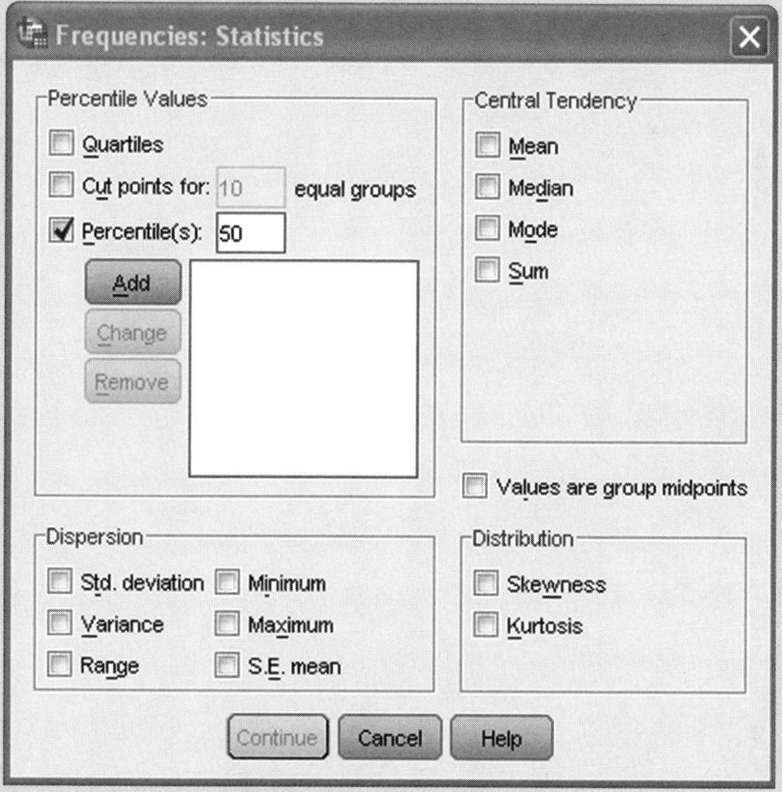

(continued)

Choose the median from the list of central tendency measures. Sometimes the median and its check box are grayed out (not available). In this case, it's still possible to obtain the median. Remember, the median is the 50th percentile, so you can check the Percentile(s): box, type a "50" into the adjacent text box, and click the Add button to add it to the list of percentiles to identify.

Finding the Mean of a Distribution

Several routines in SPSS report the mean of a distribution. If you are already creating a frequency chart, click on the "Statistics..." button in the Frequencies dialogue box, and check the Mean button.

If you want SPSS to report the mean but don't want a frequency chart, select Analyze → Descriptive Statistics → Descriptives. Choose the variable(s) of interest from the list, and click on the "Options..." button; in the dialogue box that appears, select Mean.

Chapter 4

DISPERSION

LEARNING OBJECTIVES

When you have finished this chapter, you will be able to:

- Understand and explain the idea of the dispersion of a distribution.
- Calculate and interpret measures of dispersion used with categorical (nominal and grouped ordinal) variables.
- Calculate and interpret measures of dispersion used with interval/ratio variables.

THE BASIC IDEA OF DISPERSION

One main purpose of descriptive statistics is to help us quickly and accurately summarize many observations. In the previous chapter, we learned some tools to describe central tendency—that is, what is a typical or most common score.

If everyone in a sample had exactly the same score, we could describe central tendency and there would be nothing more to say. But, of course, samples of social actors don't all have the same scores—they display diversity. Indeed, it is this diversity among social actors that social sciences are trying to understand and explain.

The diversity of scores of the observations in a sample, then, is a very important aspect of the distribution of scores. The statistical term that is most commonly used to get at the idea of diversity is *dispersion.*

The statistical concept of ***dispersion*** corresponds very closely to the everyday language of variation, variability, diversity, and difference. That is, it refers to the idea that all the cases do not have the same score—their scores vary from one another.

Sociology and the other social sciences are fundamentally concerned with trying to understand and explain diversity, difference, and variation among social actors. Why is it that more people die at early ages in one place than another? Why do people have different attitudes and beliefs? Why are some organizations big and others small? Why do students score differently on class examinations?

Sociology and the other social sciences often focus specifically on describing and explaining inequalities. If you think about it for a moment, you can see that *inequality* is another word for dispersion. If one person or group controls most of the wealth in a society and other groups have very little, then wealth is concentrated or not dispersed among the groups. If all groups have equal wealth, then wealth is dispersed.

Nominal variables describe whether two cases are the same or different, but do not describe ranking or amounts of difference between cases. For nominal variables, the idea of dispersion can be translated as the extent to which cases are equally distributed across all possible scores. This may not be an obvious idea at first glance. We'll look a bit more closely at this in the next section, "Dispersion of Categorical Data."

If cases are measured on a full rank-order scale (i.e., first, second, third, etc.), the distribution of their scores has the maximum possible dispersion. That is, all possible scores have the same relative frequency (i.e., one). Because of this mathematical property of a full rank-order variable, it is not useful to try to define measures of dispersion for variables measured on this kind of scale.

If the cases are measured on a grouped ordinal scale, dispersion is a useful idea. If we asked people about their attitudes toward something and recorded their answers as 5 = very favorable, 4 = favorable, 3 = neutral, 2 = opposed, and 1 = very opposed, we would have a grouped ordinal scale. If 95 percent of all people answered "neutral," there would be very little diversity or dispersion in people's answers. For purposes of examining and describing the degree of dispersion, grouped ordinal variables are treated in the same way as nominal variables. There are no widely used measures of dispersion that take the rank order of cases into account. This is just one of those peculiarities about the way that social scientists have come to use statistical tools.

If a variable is measured at the interval/ratio level, there are a number of tools available to measure dispersion. One way to understand (and remember) the differences among the measures of dispersion for interval/ratio variables is to think of them as being of two different kinds.

One type of measure focuses on how far the scores at (or near) the top of the distribution are from the scores of those cases at (or near) the bottom of the distribution. The idea is simple, but useful: if the high and low scores are very far apart, then there must be more dispersion than if the high and low scores are close together.

The other type of measure of dispersion for interval/ratio variables focuses on how far cases are from the central tendency. This idea, once you get it, is also pretty simple. If cases are, on average, pretty far away from the average score, then there is high dispersion. If cases are, on average, not very far away from the central tendency, then there is low dispersion. We will examine a number of measures of dispersion for interval/ratio variables of both kinds later in the chapter.

DISPERSION OF CATEGORICAL DATA

Imagine two communities; parts of each are shown in Figure 4.1. In community A, there are 100 people, and all are Catholics. Community B is larger, and has 1,000 residents. In community B, 500 people are Catholics and 500 are Protestants. Which community displays the greater diversity with respect to religion?

Since everyone in community A is Catholic, there is no diversity or variability in religion. In community B, there are members of two religions present—so there is greater diversity. Community B is more diverse because it displays variability in scores on the

FIGURE 4.1 Religious Affiliations in Two Different Communities, A and B

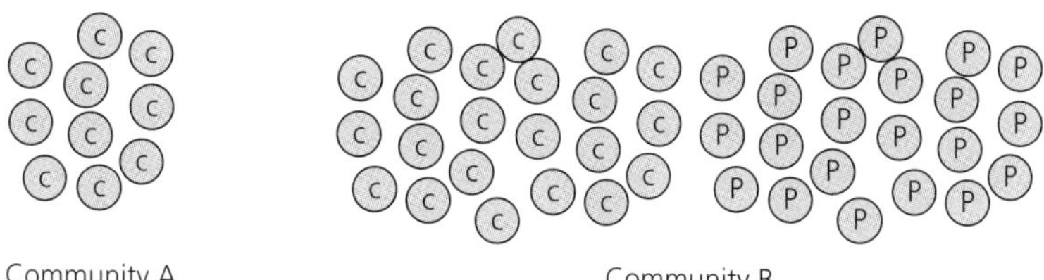

FIGURE 4.2 Religious Affiliations in Two Different Communities, C and D

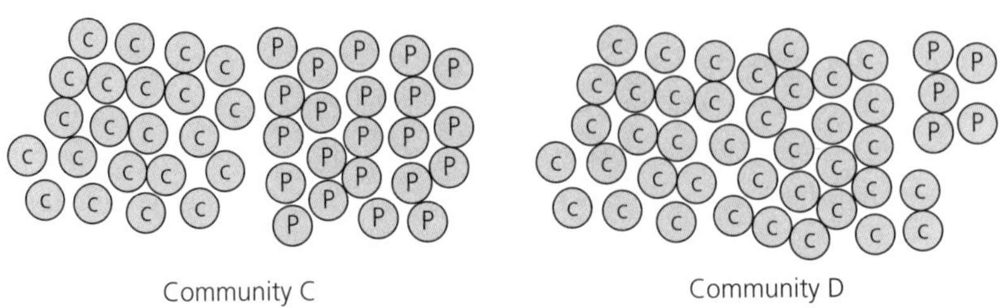

variable "religion," while community A does not. This is a reasonable conclusion about the two communities, even though there are more Catholics in community B than in community A.

So, one measure of diversity (or dispersion) for a categorical variable like religion might be the number of kinds or types or levels of the variable that actually occur in our sample.

This approach, though, is pretty crude. Think about two more communities, as shown in Figure 4.2. In community C there are 500 Protestants and 500 Catholics. In community D there are 100 Protestants and 900 Catholics. Which community has the greater diversity?

The comparison of the amount of dispersion or variation in religion between communities C and D is a little less obvious. But think of it this way: if I had to guess each person's religion in community C (knowing nothing about the people, but knowing that there were 500 Protestants and 500 Catholics in the town), what should I guess?

One strategy would be to guess the same religion for everyone.

If I guessed "Protestant" for everyone, I would be wrong 50 percent of the time (see Strategy A in Table 4.1); that is, there's a 50 percent chance that I'm wrong. (Of course, I'd also be wrong half of the time if I guessed "Catholic" every time). I would get the same results if I guessed "Protestant" half the time and "Catholic" half the time (see Strategy B).

Now, if I played the same guessing game in community D, where there are 100 Protestants and 900 Catholics, it would be reasonable to guess "Catholic" 90 percent of the time, and "Protestant" 10 percent of the time.

If I did this, I would guess Catholic 900 times, but 10 percent of these guesses (90 guesses) would likely be wrong. I would guess Protestant 100 times, but 90 percent of these guesses would likely be wrong. In total, I'd probably be wrong $90 + 10 = 100$ times out of 1,000 guesses, an error rate of 10 percent.

This example does have a point. It is this: The greater the equality in the distribution of cases across categories, the greater the uncertainty in predicting any one case's score, and the greater the diversity or dispersion of scores.

There are a number of statistics that can be used to describe of the degree of dispersion in the distribution of scores on a categorical variable. All of them, however, are based on this

TABLE 4.1 Guessing Strategies Compared

	Strategy A: Guess Modal Category		Strategy B: Guess Known Percentages	
Actual Religion	**My Guess**	**Outcome**	**My Guess**	**Outcome**
P	P	Right!	P	Right!
P	P	Right!	C	Wrong.
P	P	Right!	P	Right!
P	P	Right!	C	Wrong.
C	P	Wrong.	P	Wrong.
C	P	Wrong.	C	Right!
P	P	Right!	P	Right!
C	P	Wrong.	C	Right!
C	P	Wrong.	P	Wrong.
P	P	Right!	C	Wrong.
C	P	Wrong.	P	Wrong.
P	P	Right!	C	Wrong.
P	P	Right!	P	Right!
P	P	Right!	C	Wrong.
P	P	Right!	P	Right!
C	P	Wrong.	C	Right!
C	P	Wrong.	P	Wrong.
C	P	Wrong.	C	Right!
C	P	Wrong.	P	Wrong.
C	P	Wrong.	C	Right!
		50% right		50% right

same idea of how equally cases are distributed across categories. For describing dispersion, the same approaches are used with both nominal and grouped ordinal variables.

The Proportion in Nonmodal Categories

The amount of dispersion in a categorical variable is at its maximum when the frequencies are equal across categories. One very simple index of dispersion would be to subtract the proportion in the modal category from 1. If all the cases were in one category, then the index would be $1 - 1$, or zero, reflecting no variation or dispersion.

The problem with this very simple approach is that the maximum possible value of the index of the amount of dispersion would depend on the number of categories. If there were two categories, the maximum possible dispersion would be 0.50; if there were three categories, the maximum would be 0.66, and so on, as in Table 4.2.

So, using the proportion of cases that are not in the modal category as a measure of dispersion makes sense—but the value of the statistic depends on the number of categories.

TABLE 4.2 How Maximum Dispersion Depends on the Number of Categories

Number of Categories	Proportion in Each Category at Maximum Dispersion	Crude Dispersion Measure: $1 - P_{mode}$
2	0.50, 0.50	0.50
3	0.33, 0.33, 0.33	0.66
4	0.25, 0.25, 0.25, 0.25	0.75

In one case 0.50 might mean maximum possible dispersion, whereas in another case 0.50 might not. We can do better than this.

Index of Qualitative Variation

The ***index of qualitative variation*** (IQV) is a useful measure of dispersion for any categorical variable (nominal dichotomy or polyotomy, or grouped ordinal variable). It ranges from a value of zero (no dispersion) when all the cases fall in a single category to 1 (maximum dispersion) when the cases are equally distributed across all available categories.

Formula 4.1 is the formula for the IQV:

$$\text{IQV} = \frac{k(N^2 - \sum f^2)}{N^2(k-1)} \tag{4.1}$$

where k is the number of categories in the variable (include all the categories, even if some have zero frequency!), N is the total number of cases, and f is the number of cases in a particular category. The first step of the formula tells us to take is to take the number of cases in each category and square it, and then sum across the k categories.

Suppose we had the frequency chart shown in Table 4.3 (calculated by SPSS from a General Social Survey sample).

The number of categories, k, is five ("married," "widowed," . . . "never married").

The sample size, N, is 1,498; N squared is 1,498 times 1,498 or 2,244,004.

To calculate the sum of the frequencies, squared:

$$f_{\text{married}^2} = 886 \times 886 = 784{,}996$$
$$f_{\text{widowed}^2} = 132 \times 132 = 17{,}424$$
$$f_{\text{divorced}^2} = 164 \times 164 = 26{,}896$$
$$f_{\text{separated}^2} = 49 \times 49 = 2{,}401$$
$$f_{\text{never\_married}^2} = 267 \times 267 = 71{,}289$$

So, $784{,}996 + 17{,}424 + 26{,}896 + 2{,}401 + 71{,}289 = 903{,}006$.

TABLE 4.3 Frequencies of Marital Status Categories

	Frequency	Percent	Valid Percent	Cumulative Percent
Valid Married	886	59.1	59.1	59.1
Widowed	132	8.8	8.8	68.0
Divorced	164	10.9	10.9	78.9
Separated	49	3.3	3.3	82.2
Never married	267	17.8	17.8	100.0
Total	1,498	99.9	100.0	

Using these values, we can calculate the IQV:

$$\begin{aligned} \text{IQV} &= [5(2{,}244{,}004 - 903{,}006)]/[(2{,}244{,}004(4)] \\ &= 0.747 \end{aligned}$$

The math is a bit tedious and involves big numbers, but is really pretty simple. The final result (0.747) tells us that this distribution has quite a lot of dispersion. You can verify this by looking at the percentages. The modal category (married) contains about 60 percent of the cases. The other categories have many fewer cases—so there is quite a lot of inequality, diversity, or dispersion in marital status.

Segregation Index (or Index of Dissimilarity)

The ***segregation index*** (also known as the index of dissimilarity) is an extension of the same basic idea of the IQV. The segregation index is used to describe how different the distribution of cases in one population is from the distribution in another population. In one famous application in sociology, the researchers used this measure to describe how much the distribution of black persons differed from the distribution of white persons across the spatial areas (census tracts) of cities, but it can be used to gauge differences in all kinds of groups.

Consider the segregation of men and women in different jobs (see Table 4.4).

It looks as if the distribution of men and women is not the same across all job categories. Let's use the segregation index to explore these numbers.

The segregation index looks like Formula 4.2:

$$I = \frac{1}{2}\sum_{i=1}^{n} \left| M_i - F_i \right| \tag{4.2}$$

Notice that, at the heart of the equation, we'll be subtracting the proportion of women in a job category from the proportion of men in the same category. We will sum the absolute value of those differences, and then take half of that sum as the value of the index.

TABLE 4.4 Hypothetical Distribution of Gender by Occupation

	Welder	Barista	Mime	Total
Females	2	40	60	**102**
Males	30	4	10	**44**
Total	**32**	**44**	**70**	**146**

The proportions of men and women are given by Formula 4.3:

$$M_i \equiv \frac{m_i}{m} \text{ and } F_i \equiv \frac{f_i}{f} \tag{4.3}$$

This means that we will divide the number of men in a category by the total number of men in our sample, and do the same with women.

$$\begin{aligned}
s &= 0.5\left\{\sum_{i=1}^{3}\left|\frac{m_i}{m}-\frac{f_i}{f}\right|\right\} \\
&= 0.5\left\{\left|\frac{m_1}{m}-\frac{f_1}{f}\right|+\left|\frac{m_2}{m}-\frac{f_2}{f}\right|+\left|\frac{m_3}{m}-\frac{f_3}{f}\right|\right\} \\
&= 0.5\left\{\left|\frac{30}{44}-\frac{2}{102}\right|+\left|\frac{4}{44}-\frac{40}{102}\right|+\left|\frac{10}{44}-\frac{60}{102}\right|\right\} \\
&= 0.5\{|0.6818-0.0196|+|0.0909-0.3922|+|0.2273-0.5882|\} \\
&= 0.5(0.6622+0.3013+0.3609) \\
&= 0.5(1.3244) \\
&= 0.6622 \text{ or } 66.22\%
\end{aligned}$$

This means that, in order for the proportions of men and women to be the same, we would have to move 66 percent of the people in one sex into other job categories. So, for example, let's move the women around. In order to have the same proportion of women in each job, we'd need to move 67.5 women to other categories (66.2 percent of the 102 women). Let's add 67 women welders and get rid of 31 women baristas and 36 women mimes, as in Table 4.5.

The 66.22 percent of 102 total women is approximately 67, which is the number of women who would have to change jobs for men and women to have these jobs in the same proportions.

TABLE 4.5 Adjusting Frequencies to Obtain Equal Proportions

	Welder	Barista	Mime	Total
Females	2 + 67 = 69	40 − 31 = 9	60 − 36 = 24	**102**
Males	30	4	10	**44**
Total	**99**	**13**	**34**	**146**

TABLE 4.6 Difference in Proportions as a Measure of Dispersion

Scores on X	Low	Medium	High	Total
Actual	0.25	0.50	0.25	1.00
Theoretical	0.33	0.33	0.33	1.00
Absolute difference	0.08	0.17	0.08	0.33

If we add the differences in the women's cells (69 + 24 = 134), we'll need to divide by 2 (134/2 = 67), since otherwise, we would be counting each woman twice (once when she left one job, and again when she joined another.)

So, if $S = 0$, that would mean that no one in either group (sex, race, etc.) would have to change occupations (or regions, etc.) to have the same proportion. If $S = 1$, then a number equivalent to the total number of persons in one group would have to move in order for all occupations to have the same proportions.

One drawback of this method is that, while similar proportions could be achieved by moving the proportion indicated by the index, the whole job market would also have to change in order to reach those proportions. Note that under the proposed reallocation of women we would end up with more welders (and fewer baristas) than we need (we will let you decide how many mimes society needs).

A variation on the segregation index is to compare the proportional distribution of one group across categories of X to a theoretical distribution of equal distribution, as in Table 4.6.

The sum of the absolute difference of the proportions (0.08 + 0.17 + 0.08) is 0.33. One-half of this difference is 0.165. So, 16.5 percent of all the actual cases would have to be moved to different categories to make the distribution the same as a perfect dispersion or equality.

DISPERSION OF INTERVAL/RATIO DATA

When we apply the basic idea of dispersion or variability to interval/ratio variables, our approach is somewhat different than with categorical variables.

CHECK QUIZ 4.1

1. True or False: A nominal variable achieves maximum variation if all of its categories are equally represented (e.g., there are exactly the same numbers of Democrats, Republicans, Green Party members, etc.).
2. True or False: Guesses about the value of a case drawn at random are more likely to be correct when the variable in question displays less variability.
3. True or False: Values of the index of qualitative variation and the segregation index may range from −1 to 1.
4. True or False: In the absence of any other information, the best strategy for guessing the value of a randomly drawn case measured at the nominal level is to guess the modal category.

With categorical variables, we ask (in a variety of ways): "How close is the observed distribution of cases across categories to one of complete equality?" The closer to equality, the greater the dispersion.

With interval/ratio variables, there are two somewhat different approaches to measuring dispersion that take advantage of the fact that we can measure *how* different the scores of cases are, rather than just *whether* the cases are different.

The first approach asks: "If I compare the scores of cases at the top of the distribution to those of cases at the bottom of the distribution, how different are the scores?" If the scores at the top and bottom of the distribution are very not far apart, then there isn't much variation; if the scores at the top and bottom of the distribution are further apart, there is more dispersion. The range and interquartile range are measures of dispersion that use this approach.

The second approach to indexing dispersion with interval/ratio variables asks, "How much do scores of cases vary, on average, from the central tendency?" With an interval/ratio variable, if every case had the same score (i.e., no dispersion or variation), then every case would have the same score as the mean. This is because the mean is defined as the balance point or average of the scores. If the scores of cases differ from the mean only a little, then there is little variation or dispersion; if the scores of cases differ from the mean a great deal, then there is more dispersion. The mean absolute deviation, variance, standard deviation, and coefficient of variation are measures of dispersion that use this approach.

The Range

It is very easy to calculate the statistic called the ***range***. Simply take the lowest score and subtract it from the highest score in the sample. For example, if the lowest income in a community was $5,000 and the highest was $100,000, then the range would be $95,000.

The distance between the highest and lowest scores in a sample is a useful rough-and-ready measure of dispersion. If the extreme values in sample A are further apart than they are in sample B, it is reasonable to say that there is more variation or dispersion in sample A.

The Interquartile Range

There are a couple of problems with the range as a measure of variability or dispersion. While we usually do report the range, it can sometimes be misleading.

One problem is that the range looks only at the highest and the lowest scores in the sample. What if the highest score is an extreme outlier that is not really typical of most of the high scores? If we were measuring income, for example, we might have one very rich person (say, for example, Bill Gates, the founder of Microsoft) who is far richer than most of the other rich people. Of course, the same kind of problem could happen at the bottom of the distribution. The lowest score might not really be typical of low scores in general.

To correct the potential problem that the highest and/or lowest scores are extreme and not typical of high and low scores generally, we might decide to trim the distribution of cases by ignoring a certain percentage of the highest- and lowest-scoring cases. For example, we might trim the distribution by ignoring the top 5 percent and bottom 5 percent, and then calculate the range. In most samples, doing this will get rid of extreme outliers. The resulting measure tells us how far apart the scores of cases at the 5th and the 95th percentiles are.

While you might have a good reason for trimming some arbitrary proportion of values from the top and bottom of a distribution, one widely used approach is to calculate the ***interquartile range***, which trims 25 percent off both the top and the bottom. Finding the interquartile range involves finding the values of the 75th and 25th percentiles, and subtracting the latter from the former.

The interquartile range is useful as a measure of dispersion because it almost always solves the problem of extreme outliers. It is also helpful because the value of the interquartile range is a meaningful number; it describes how different the scores are at the top and bottom of the middle half of all scores. So, in a certain sense, the interquartile range describes how much diversity there is in the scores of the "middle class" of the distribution.

It is useful to examine both the range and the interquartile range. The range tells us something about the distance between the scores at the very top and very bottom. If we were discussing the distribution of wealth, the range would tell us how far apart the really rich and the really poor are. The interquartile range would focus our attention on how much variation there is among the people in the middle class. Both measures can be useful.

Even so, both the range and the interquartile range have an important limitation. Measures based on the range really only use information about two cases (e.g., the highest and lowest or the case at the 25th and 75th percentiles). Why not use all the data? Measures based on deviations from the mean like the absolute deviation, variance, standard deviation, and coefficient of variation do this. But first, let's see some examples of working with ranges.

Example

FINDING QUARTILES AND CALCULATING THE INTERQUARTILE RANGE

Calculating the range for an interval variable is easy. You find the maximum value and subtract the minimum value (these can be found by sorting the list of scores, using a statistics package, or just plain inspection by eye). The range is simply the maximum score minus the minimum score.

Finding the interquartile range can be a bit more complicated. The interquartile range is the difference between the 75th percentile and the 25th percentile. It is easy enough, if we know these values.

With a large amount of data, use a computer. But for small data sets, we can find these percentiles by hand.

Here's a data set on infant mortality rates in 47 randomly selected countries. We used a statistics program data editor to sort the values from high to low.

Afghanistan	168.0
Somalia	126.0
Rwanda	117.0
Uganda	112.0
Tanzania	110.0
Burundi	105.0
India	79.0
Cameroon	77.0
Egypt	76.4
Senegal	76.0
Bolivia	75.0
Nigeria	75.0
Iraq	67.0
Peru	54.0
Nicaragua	52.5
China	52.0
Dominican Republic	51.5
El Salvador	41.0
Botswana	39.3
Ecuador	39.0
Russia	27.0
Malaysia	25.6
Bahrain	25.0
Georgia	23.0
Latvia	21.5

Example

Barbados	20.3
Belarus	19.0
Lithuania	17.0
Chile	14.6
Poland	13.8
Kuwait	12.5
Cuba	10.2
Czech Republic	9.3
Croatia	8.7
Greece	8.2
United States	8.1
Italy	7.6
Australia	7.3
Belgium	7.2
United Kingdom	7.2
Canada	6.8
Austria	6.7
Netherlands	6.3
Norway	6.3
Hong Kong	5.8
Sweden	5.7
Japan	4.4

The 25th percentile is the case that has 25 percent of all cases below it. With 47 cases, 25 percent of the cases is 11.75. So, we would start at the bottom of the list and find the 12th case from the bottom. This happens to be the United States with a value of 8.1. So, 8.1 is the 25th percentile.

The 75th percentile will be the same distance from the top of the distribution. If we start at the top of the list, and find the 11.75 (or 12th) case down, we locate Nigeria with a score of 75.0. The 75th percentile then is 75.0.

The interquartile range, then, is 75.0 − 8.1 or 66.9 infant deaths per 1,000 live births.

You can follow the same strategy with a list of any length. Determine how many cases need to fall below the 25th percentile by multiplying the list size by 0.25. Count up the list, and locate the score at the 25th percentile. Then, start at the top of the list and go down the same amount to find the 75th percentile. The difference between the two values is the interquartile range.

Example

FINDING THE INTERQUARTILE RANGE USING A FREQUENCY CHART

Quartiles are named starting at the small end of values, so the first quartile is the 25th percentile, the second quartile (aka the median) is the 50th percentile, and the third quartile is the 75th percentile.

Finding quartiles using a frequency chart involves the same logic as finding the median (see Chapter 3), as they all involve percentiles. Arrange the values from low to high. To find the first quartile (the 25th percentile), look down the cumulative percentages for the first category that is large enough (without rounding) to accommodate 25 percent of the sample; the value that's associated with this category is the first quartile. In the example in Figure 4.3, the first cumulative percentage large enough to fit 25 percent is 26.4 percent; the value associated with that percentage is 34 years, so 34 is the first quartile.

The third quartile (the 75th percentile) is the value associated with the first cumulative percentage large enough to accommodate 75 percent of the sample; in the example, 75.7 percent satisfies that condition, and the associated value is 60 years.

To find the interquartile range, we subtract the first quartile from the third: 60 – 34 = 26.

FIGURE 4.3 Age of Respondent

Age of Respondent

		Frequency	Percent	Valid Percent	Cumulative Percent
Valid	18	6	.3	.3	.3
	19	31	1.5	1.5	1.8
	20	28	1.4	1.4	3.2
	21	21	1.0	1.0	4.3
	30	27	1.3	1.3	19.2
	31	47	2.3	2.3	21.5
	32	22	1.1	1.1	22.6
	33	36	1.8	1.8	24.4
	34	40	2.0	2.0	26.4
	35	41	2.0	2.0	28.4
	36	45	2.2	2.2	30.7
	37	44	2.2	2.2	32.8
	57	41	2.0	2.0	71.5
	58	24	1.2	1.2	72.7
	59	20	1.0	1.0	73.7
	60	40	2.0	2.0	75.7
	61	36	1.8	1.8	77.5
	62	34	1.7	1.7	79.2
	63	19	.9	.9	80.1

Mean Absolute Deviation

A limitation of the range and interquartile range is that they pay attention to the scores of only two cases and ignore all the others. The range looks only at the scores of the very top case and the very bottom case; the interquartile range looks only at the score of the case at the 75th percentile and the score of the case at the 25th percentile. Wouldn't it be better if our measure of dispersion used information from all of the cases? There are a number of approaches based on deviations from the sample mean that take this approach. The one that is easiest to understand (but not the most widely used) is the mean absolute deviation (MAD).

The ***mean absolute deviation*** is defined as in Formula 4.4:

$$\text{MAD} = \frac{\sum |X_i - \overline{X}|}{N} \tag{4.4}$$

To calculate the mean absolute deviation, we first find the mean. Then, we subtract the mean from each score, ignoring whether the difference is positive or negative (i.e., we take the absolute value, which is symbolized with the vertical bars in the formula). Then, take the average, or mean, of these absolute deviations by summing them and dividing by the number of cases.

The resulting index, the mean absolute deviation, has an easy and appealing interpretation. It tells us how far, on average, cases are away from the mean. If cases are far away from the mean, on average, there is more dispersion. If all cases have the same score, the MAD would have a value of zero; as the MAD becomes a larger and larger positive number (prove to yourself that it can never be a negative number), it is indexing increasing variation.

CALCULATING THE MEAN ABSOLUTE DEVIATION

Example

Again, the mean absolute deviation has the formula:

$$\text{MAD} = \frac{\sum |X_i - \overline{X}|}{N} \tag{4.4}$$

Formula 4.4 instructs us to subtract the first case's score (X_i) from the mean and treat the result as a positive number (i.e., take the absolute deviation), and then to

(continued)

Example

repeat this process across all the cases and sum the result. The mean absolute deviation is then calculated by taking the average of the absolute deviations. This is done by dividing the sum of the absolute deviations by the number of cases.

Here's an example using the Excel spreadsheet. We've collected information about the average number of children ever born to women in a sample of 49 nations.

Country	**Fertility**	**Deviation** $x - \bar{x}$	**Absolute Deviation** $\lvert x - \bar{x} \rvert$
Afghanistan	6.9	3.573	3.573
Argentina	2.8	−0.527	0.527
Armenia	3.2	−0.137	0.137
Australia	1.9	−1.427	1.427
Austria	1.5	−1.827	1.827
Azerbaijan	2.8	−0.527	0.527
Bahrain	4.0	0.633	0.633
Bangladesh	4.7	1.373	1.373
Barbados	1.8	−1.547	1.547
Belarus	1.9	−1.447	1.447
Belgium	1.7	−1.627	1.627
Bolivia	4.2	0.883	0.883
Botswana	5.1	1.773	1.773
Brazil	2.7	−0.627	0.627
Bulgaria	1.8	−1.527	1.527
Burkina Faso	6.9	3.613	3.613
Burundi	6.8	3.473	3.473
Cambodia	5.8	2.483	2.483
Cameroon	5.7	2.373	2.373
Canada	1.8	−1.527	1.527
Cent. Afri. R.	5.4	2.093	2.093
Chile	2.5	−0.827	0.827
China	1.8	−1.487	1.487
Colombia	2.5	−0.857	0.857
Costa Rica	3.1	−0.227	0.227
Croatia	1.7	−1.677	1.677
Cuba	1.9	−1.427	1.427
Czech Rep.	1.8	−1.487	1.487
Denmark	1.7	−1.627	1.627
Dominican R.	2.8	−0.527	0.527
Ecuador	3.1	−0.247	0.247
Egypt	3.8	0.443	0.443
El Salvador	3.8	0.453	0.453

Example

Country	Fertility	Deviation $x - \bar{x}$	Absolute Deviation $\lvert x - \bar{x} \rvert$
Estonia	2.0	−1.327	1.327
Ethiopia	6.8	3.483	3.483
Finland	1.8	−1.527	1.527
France	1.8	−1.527	1.527
Gabon	4.0	0.643	0.643
Gambia	6.3	2.963	2.963
Georgia	2.2	−1.147	1.147
Germany	1.5	−1.857	1.857
Greece	1.5	−1.827	1.827
Guatemala	4.8	1.433	1.433
Haiti	5.9	2.613	2.613
Honduras	4.9	1.573	1.573
Hong Kong	1.4	−1.927	1.927
Hungary	1.8	−1.527	1.527
Iceland	2.1	−1.217	1.217
India	4.5	1.153	1.153
Count	49.0	Sum	74.047
Mean	3.3	Average	1.511163

Here are the eight steps we went through:

1. We used a function =count( ) to count the number of cases, which turned out to be 49.
2. We used a function =average( ) to calculate the mean of the values, which turned out to be 3.327.
3. Then we calculated the deviation of the first case from the mean (6.9 − 3.327) = 3.573.
4. Copying the formula, we calculated the deviations for all of the remaining cases.
5. Using a function =ABS( ), we calculated the absolute value of the first deviation: ABS(3.573) = 3.573.
6. Copying the formula, we calculated the absolute value of the deviation for all the other cases.
7. Using the sum( ) function, we summed the column of absolute deviations (74.047).
8. Using the avg( ) function, we calculated the average of the absolute deviations.

The result is that average absolute deviation in the average number of children born to women is about one and one-half children.

Variance

In calculating the mean absolute deviation, we measure how far cases are from the mean (mean deviations, or just deviations). If we added up these deviations without taking the absolute value, the sum would be zero—regardless of how much variation there was in the scores. This is because the mean is the balance point of the distribution, and the deviations below it equal the deviations above it. We solved this problem by taking absolute values.

There is a second way of solving the problem that the sums of the deviations above and below the mean are equal. This is to take the square of each deviation. Positive deviations, squared, are positive; negative deviations, squared, are also positive. So, by squaring deviations from the mean before summing, we also get an index of variation that ranges from zero (no variation) to increasing positive values as variability increases. This particular statistic is called the variance (see Formula 4.5).

$$s^2 = \frac{\sum (X_i - \overline{X})^2}{N} \tag{4.5}$$

The variance is a very important statistic because it is used extensively in inferential statistics and in statistical analysis of many problems with several variables (e.g., correlation, regression, and analysis of variance that we will discuss in later chapters). The ***sample variance*** is usually referred to by the notation s^2.

If the variance is zero, there is no variation—all cases have the mean score. The variance cannot be a negative number (it wouldn't really make sense to talk about "negative diversity"). As the variance gets bigger, it means that diversity or variation is increasing.

As important as the variance is, it is not very easy to talk about and to interpret its value. Let's suppose we find that the variance of some variable in some sample is 81. We could say that the average *squared* distance of cases from the mean is 81 units. This does make some sense, but people just don't easily grasp the idea of a *squared* distance.

Standard Deviation

The variance is an important measure of dispersion, but it is difficult to interpret because it talks about squared deviations. This is a problem that we can easily overcome by simply taking the square root of the variance. The resulting statistic is called the ***standard deviation***, shown in Formula 4.6:

$$s = \sqrt{VAR} \tag{4.6}$$

or Formula 4.7:

$$s = \sqrt{\frac{\sum (X_i - \overline{X})^2}{N}} \tag{4.7}$$

The standard deviation is the most widely used statistic for summarizing the degree of dispersion in interval/ratio variables. Like the variance, it has the value zero when there is no dispersion (all cases have the mean score); its value becomes increasingly positive as dispersion increases.

But we can go further in interpreting the numerical value of the standard deviation, and this is what makes it more useful as a summary statistic than the variance. Earlier we gave the example of a variable that had a variance of 81. We said that this could be interpreted as "the average *squared* distance of cases from the mean is 81 units."

Now, suppose that we turn this variance into a standard deviation by taking sqrt (81) = 9. Now we could say that "the average distance of a case from the mean is 9 units." Since most people understand the idea of an average distance, this is a much better way of describing dispersion.

You'll see two versions of the formula for the standard deviation in later sections of this book. The first is the one we've already seen, and this is sometimes referred to as the "population" standard deviation. When we're dealing with samples, we make a slight adjustment to the formula, as shown in Formula 4.8:

$$s = \sqrt{\frac{(x_i - \bar{x})^2}{n - 1}} \tag{4.8}$$

Notice that the denominator has been changed in two ways. First, instead of a capital N (which frequently designates the total number of cases), there's a lowercase n, which designates a sample.

Second, $n - 1$ has taken the place of N. What's going on here? This is an adjustment we make in recognition that there's less certainty in samples than there is in whole populations. If we were reporting the standard deviation of an entire census (all inhabitants of Sri Lanka, or all the trees in a given forest), we could say with certainty, "The standard deviation of (this variable) is (some number)." When we're taking a sample, the value we obtain from the sample is our best estimate of the parameter, but it's only an estimate, and it could be wrong. When we're estimating the variance using samples, then, we take a conservative approach, and suppose that there may be more variation in the population than we find in the sample. This formula does that for us: by making the denominator a little smaller, it makes the whole term a little larger.

Example

CALCULATING THE VARIANCE AND STANDARD DEVIATION

Again, Formula 4.5 is the formula for the variance:

$$s^2 = \frac{\sum (X_i - \overline{X})^2}{N} \tag{4.5}$$

The standard deviation (*s*) is just the square root of the variance.

Calculating the variance is tedious, and is best done with a spreadsheet if you have more than just a few cases. The five steps are very simple, as shown by the formula:

1. Calculate the mean of the cases ($\overline{X}$).
2. Calculate the deviation of each case ($X_i - \overline{X}$) from the mean by subtracting the mean from the case's score.
3. Square the deviation of each case.
4. Add up the squared deviations.
5. Divide by the number of cases.

The most common error in calculating the variance is to sum the deviations and then square the quantity—rather than squaring each deviation and then summing. Doing this wrong will give you a wrong answer!

Here is an example of calculating the variance and standard deviation using a spreadsheet to do the calculations. The data refer to the mean fertility of women in nations of the world during the mid-1990s, and are measured as the average numbers of children ever born to women. We've added our calculations to the original data.

Country	Fertility	Deviation	Squared Deviation
Afghanistan	6.9	3.6	12.96
Argentina	2.8	−0.5	0.25
Armenia	3.2	−0.1	0.01
Australia	1.9	−1.4	1.96
Austria	1.5	−1.8	3.24
Azerbaijan	2.8	−0.5	0.25
Bahrain	4.0	0.7	0.44
Bangladesh	4.7	1.4	1.96
Barbados	1.8	−1.5	2.31
Belarus	1.9	−1.4	2.02
Belgium	1.7	−1.6	2.56
Bolivia	4.2	0.9	0.83

Example

Country	Fertility	Deviation	Squared Deviation
Botswana	5.1	1.8	3.24
Brazil	2.7	−0.6	0.36
Bulgaria	1.8	−1.5	2.25
Burkina Faso	6.9	3.6	13.25
Burundi	6.8	3.5	12.25
Cambodia	5.8	2.5	6.30
Cameroon	5.7	2.4	5.76
Canada	1.8	−1.5	2.25
Cent. Afri. R.	5.4	2.1	4.49
Chile	2.5	−0.8	0.64
China	1.8	−1.5	2.13
Colombia	2.5	−0.8	0.69
Costa Rica	3.1	−0.2	0.04
Croatia	1.7	−1.7	2.72
Cuba	1.9	−1.4	1.96
Czech Rep.	1.8	−1.5	2.13
Denmark	1.7	−1.6	2.56
Dominican R.	2.8	−0.5	0.25
Ecuador	3.1	−0.2	0.05
Egypt	3.8	0.5	0.22
El Salvador	3.8	0.5	0.23
Estonia	2.0	−1.3	1.69
Ethiopia	6.8	3.5	12.32
Finland	1.8	−1.5	2.25
France	1.8	−1.5	2.25
Gabon	4.0	0.7	0.45
Gambia	6.3	3.0	8.94
Georgia	2.2	−1.1	1.25
Germany	1.5	−1.8	3.35
Greece	1.5	−1.8	3.24
Guatemala	4.8	1.5	2.13
Haiti	5.9	2.6	6.97
Honduras	4.9	1.6	2.56
Hong Kong	1.4	−1.9	3.61
Hungary	1.8	−1.5	2.25
Iceland	2.1	−1.2	1.42
India	4.5	1.2	1.39
Count	49.0	Sum	148.63
Mean	3.3	Variance	3.03
	St. dev.	1.74	

(*continued*)

Example

Using functions and formulas, and copying these over the range of values, can save a lot of time and effort in doing the tedious calculations.

We see that the variance turns out to be 3.03 children, and the standard deviation to be 1.74 children (this value is a little larger than the mean absolute deviation for these data).

We would say, then, that the average country differs from the mean fertility (3.3 children) by about 1.74 children. This suggests quite a bit of heterogeneity, inequality, or variance in fertility rates across nations in the world.

Coefficient of Variation

Suppose that we were interested in studying differences in family structure among American ethnic groups. As part of the study, we are looking at the numbers of siblings in families. To see whether there is more or less variation across groups, we've calculated the standard deviation in the number of brothers and sisters reported by respondents to the General Social Survey. We discover:

$$s \text{ for whites} = 2.998$$
$$s \text{ for blacks} = 3.815$$

The numbers of brothers and sisters in white families differ from the mean by about three siblings. There is more variation in the numbers of siblings in black families, where the families differ from the mean by 3.8 siblings. Clearly there is more variability in the numbers of siblings in black families than in white families. But is that the whole story?

We also happened to notice that the mean number of siblings differs between white and black families:

$$X \text{ for whites} = 3.78$$
$$X \text{ for blacks} = 5.50$$

That is, the average number of siblings is considerably larger in black families than in white families. This fact might lead me to think about the issue of variability a bit differently. While the average variation in the number of siblings for white families (2.998) is smaller than for black families (3.815), the variability (5.50) is quite high relative to the smaller average size of white families (3.78). (See Figure 4.4.)

In fact, for white families, the standard deviation (2.998) is 79.3 percent of the size of the mean; while for black families, the standard deviation is only 69.4 percent of the size of

FIGURE 4.4 Means and Variability in Numbers of Siblings

s_{whites}	2.998
$\bar{X}_{whites}$	3.78
s_{blacks}	3.815
$\bar{X}_{blacks}$	5.50

the mean. Relative to the size of the mean, the variation in white family size is actually greater than in black families!

The operation of dividing the standard deviation by the mean and expressing the result as a percentage creates a statistic called the ***coefficient of variation*** (CV). The CV is defined as shown in Formula 4.9:

$$CV = \frac{s}{\bar{X}} \times 100 \tag{4.9}$$

The coefficient of variation tells us the amount of variation in what we are measuring as a percentage of the average score of what we are measuring. For example, a coefficient of variation of 10 tells us that the average case differs from the mean by 10 percent of the value of the mean. This can be quite helpful for two different purposes.

First, as we saw in the preceding example, the coefficient of variation allows us to compare the amount of variability in the scores of several samples that have different average scores. If groups of cases have quite different average scores, it is sometimes useful to think about variation within each group relative to what is typical *for that group*.

Second, if we are trying to compare the amount of variability in two or more variables (rather than two or more samples of cases with the same variable), the coefficient of variation can be quite helpful. In the General Social Survey, the coefficients of variation for two variables are:

$$\text{CV number of siblings in family} = 78.7(s = 3.162, \bar{X} = 4.02)$$
$$\text{CV years of education of head of household} = 23.4(s = 2.981, \bar{X} = 12.76)$$

If we were interested in what factors might best describe how American families differ, it is clear that there is more relative variation in the numbers of siblings in families than there is in the education of the head of the household.

Example

CALCULATING THE COEFFICIENT OF VARIATION

The coefficient of variation describes the amount of variation in an interval/ratio variable relative to the mean of that variable. That is, it expresses the variation in variable relative to the typical score on the variable.

To calculate the coefficient of variation, you need to first find the mean and find the standard deviation of the variable. The coefficient of variation is then, very simply:

$$\text{CV} = (s/\overline{X}) \times 100$$

That is, first divide the standard deviation of the variable by the mean of the variable. Then, multiply the result by 100, to express the standard deviation as a percentage (rather than as a proportion) of the mean.

Here are some data on the percentage of the people in U.S. states (in 1996) who were age 65 or older.

	State	Percent of Population Older than 65, 1996
1	Florida	18.50
2	Pennsylvania	15.90
3	Rhode Island	15.60
4	Iowa	15.20
5	West Virginia	15.20
6	North Dakota	14.50
7	South Dakota	14.40
8	Arkansas	14.40
9	Connecticut	14.30
10	Massachusetts	14.10
11	Maine	13.90
12	New Jersey	13.80
13	Missouri	13.80
14	Nebraska	13.80
15	Kansas	13.70
16	Oklahoma	13.50
17	New York	13.40
18	Ohio	13.40
19	Oregon	13.40
20	Wisconsin	13.30
21	Montana	13.20
22	Arizona	13.20
23	Alabama	13.00

Example

	State	Percent of Population Older than 65, 1996
24	Hawaii	12.90
25	Delaware	12.80
26	Indiana	12.60
27	Kentucky	12.60
28	Illinois	12.50
29	North Carolina	12.50
30	Tennessee	12.50
31	Michigan	12.40
32	Minnesota	12.40
33	Mississippi	12.30
34	Vermont	12.10
35	South Carolina	12.10
36	New Hampshire	12.00
37	Washington	11.60
38	Maryland	11.40
39	Louisiana	11.40
40	Idaho	11.40
41	Nevada	11.40
42	Virginia	11.20
43	Wyoming	11.20
44	New Mexico	11.00
45	California	11.00
46	Texas	10.20
47	Colorado	10.10
48	Georgia	9.90
49	Utah	8.80
50	Alaska	5.20
Total *N*	50	
Mean	12.7000	
Std. deviation	2.01909	

On average, 12.7 percent of the population of states were age 65 or older (mean). The average difference between the mean and the score for individual states was 2.0 percent.

The coefficient of variation, then, is:

$$\begin{aligned} \text{CV} &= (2.0/12.7) \times 100 \\ &= (0.15748) \times 100 \\ &= 15.748 \end{aligned}$$

States, on the average, differed from the mean by about 16 percent of the value of the mean.

CHECK QUIZ 4.2

1. Reporting the range of a distribution may be problematic because
   a. we don't always know what it is.
   b. the extreme values may be far from the majority of values.
   c. it is difficult to compute for large populations.
   d. it is often confused with other statistics with similar names.
2. The interquartile range is the difference between the 75th percentile and the 25th percentile. What statistic is the same as the 50th percentile?
   a. mean
   b. mode
   c. median
   d. medium
3. What is the advantage to reporting the interquartile range over the simple range?
   a. It is less sensitive to outliers (extreme values).
   b. It is easier to compute.
   c. It makes it look as though the researcher knows what he or she is doing.
   d. It conveys more information.
4. Why must one take the absolute value of difference scores when computing the MAD?
   a. The sum will always be positive.
   b. The sum will always be negative.
   c. The sum will always be indeterminate.
   d. The difference scores always sum to 0.
5. What is the relationship between the MAD and the variance?
   a. To get the variance, one sums the squared difference scores.
   b. To get the variance, one sums the square root of the difference scores.
   c. To get the variance, one adds the difference scores.
   d. To get the variance, one consults a medium.
6. The standard deviation is equal to
   a. the average absolute deviation from the mean.
   b. the average squared deviation from the mean.
   c. the average deviation from the mean.
   d. the mean deviation from the average.
7. What is true about the variance and the standard deviation?
   a. They must both be negative numbers.
   b. The variance cannot be smaller than the standard deviation.
   c. The standard deviation cannot be smaller than the variance.
   d. The variance is the square root of the standard deviation.
8. The coefficient of variation expresses the average deviation of cases from the mean as a percentage of
   a. the standard deviation.
   b. the variance.
   c. the mean.
   d. the interquartile range.

A couple of comments:

The coefficient of variation is sometimes used to assess whether there is enough variation in a variable to analyze. While this is a questionable practice, the rule of thumb often used is that the amount of variation in a variable should be at least 20 percent of the value of the mean.

It is quite possible for a coefficient of variation to exceed the value of the mean—that is, for the CV to be greater than 100. This is relatively uncommon, though, and should cause you to look closely for outliers or errors in the data.

There are two kinds of measures of dispersion for interval/ratio variables. One type is based on the range, the other on average deviations. We've discussed several variations on each of these.

SUMMARY

Dispersion is the name that statisticians use to refer to diversity, variation, or inequality—the fact that cases have different scores on a variable. Some variables show very little variation (almost everyone has the same score); some variables show a great deal of variation. With categorical data, dispersion refers to the extent to which cases are concentrated in a single category or equally spread among many categories. Ordinal data is usually treated like nominal data in measuring dispersion. With interval/ratio data, dispersion refers to the average distance of cases from the central tendency.

For categorical variables, there are a number of possible indexes to describe dispersion. The proportion of cases not in the modal category is the simplest measure. Two measures that take into account the whole distribution across categories are the index of qualitative variation and the segregation index or index of dissimilarity.

With interval/ratio variables, there are also a number of indexes of dispersion that are widely used. The simplest is the range—the distance between the lowest and highest scores in the sample. The range may be affected by extreme scores, so sometimes the distance between the 25th and 75th percentiles—called the interquartile range—is used. Several measures of variation from the mean are also important, because they use all sample information; they are widely used in more advanced statistics. The mean absolute deviation, variance, standard deviation, and coefficient of variation all measure the amount of distance of cases from the mean.

Central tendency and dispersion are the two most important specific aspects of the shape of frequency distributions. Most advanced statistics focus their attention on these aspects of distributional shape. There are some other things about the shape of distributions, though, that are worth noting and indexing. We'll look at some of these other aspects of the shape of distributions in the next chapter.

Before moving on, though, you may want to study how you can set up a spreadsheet program to calculate measures of dispersion more easily (and with fewer errors!).

KEY TERMS

coefficient of variation

dispersion

index of qualitative variation (IQV)

interquartile range

mean absolute deviation

range

sample variance (s2)

segregation index

standard deviation

CHECK QUIZ ANSWERS

Quiz 4.1 Answers: 1. (T); 2. (T); 3. (F); 4. (T)
Quiz 4.2 Answers: 1. (b); 2. (c); 3. (a); 4. (d); 5. (a); 6. (c); 7. (b); 8. (c)

EXERCISES

1. Here is an extract from the General Social Survey codebook. For each variable, select an appropriate measure of dispersion.

Variable	Codes	Measure of Dispersion
Marital status	1 = married	
	2 = widowed	
	3 = divorced	
	4 = separated	
	5 = never married	
Number of brothers and sisters	1 = one	
	2 = two etc.	
Highest educational degree	0 = less than high school	
	1 = high school	
	2 = junior college	
	3 = bachelor's	
	4 = postgraduate	
Total family income	1 = less than $1,000	
	2 = $1,000 to $2,999	
	3 = $3,000 to $3,999	
	4 = $4,000 to $4,999	
	5 = $5,000 to $5,999	
	6 = $6,000 to $6,999	
	7 = $7,000 to $7,999	
	8 = $8,000 to $9,999	

Variable	Codes	Measure of Dispersion
	9 = $10,000 to $14,999	
	10 = $15,000 to $19,999	
	11 = $20,000 to $24,999	
	12 = $25,000 or more	
Race of respondent	1 = white	
	2 = black	
	3 = other	
Size of place where respondent lives	1,000s of persons	
How would you say our courts are dealing with criminals?	1 = too harsh	
	2 = about right	
	3 = not harsh enough	
Hours per day watching TV	number of hours	
Marijuana should be made legal	1 = strongly disagree	
	2 = disagree	
	3 = neutral	
	4 = agree	
	5 = strongly agree	
Religious preference	1 = Protestant	
	2 = Catholic	
	3 = Jewish	
	4 = none	
	5 = other	
	6 = Buddhism	
	7 = Hinduism	
	8 = other Eastern	
	9 = Muslim/Islam	
	10 = Orthodox Christian	
	11 = Christian	
	12 = Native American	
	13 = interdenominational	

2. Here are some data extracted from the pooled General Social Surveys of 1978 to 1998. For each variable, calculate an appropriate measure of dispersion.

Case Summaries

	Marital Status	R's Highest Degree	Number of Brothers and Sisters
1	Divorced	LT high school	5
2	Married	High school	4
3	Married	High school	3

(continued)

	Marital Status	R's Highest Degree	Number of Brothers and Sisters
4	Married	High school	0
5	Married	High school	12
6	Married	High school	8
7	Married	LT high school	4
8	Married	High school	5
9	Separated	High school	10
10	Married	High school	10
11	Never married	Bachelor	2
12	Married	High school	2
13	Married	High school	4
14	Married	LT high school	4
15	Married	Bachelor	2
16	Married	LT high school	9
17	Never married	Bachelor	2
18	Married	High school	5
19	Divorced	Graduate	0
20	Married	LT high school	8
21	Married	High school	9
22	Never married	High school	1
23	Married	High school	4
24	Married	LT high school	6
25	Married	High school	2

3. Here are some data extracted from the pooled General Social Surveys of 1978 to 1998. The political party affiliation scale ranks people from "strong Republican" through "independent" to "strong Democrat." For each variable, calculate an appropriate measure of dispersion.

Race of Respondent	Political Party Affiliation	Age of Respondent
White	Independent, near Dem.	26
White	Independent, near Dem.	68
White	Independent, near Rep.	54
White	Not strong Republican	36
White	Independent, near Dem.	61
White	Independent, near Dem.	42
Black	Strong Democrat	59
White	Independent, near Dem.	40
White	Independent, near Dem.	33
White	Independent, near Rep.	25

Race of Respondent	Political Party Affiliation	Age of Respondent
White	Independent, near Dem.	29
Black	Independent	32
White	Not strong Democrat	69
White	Not strong Democrat	89
White	Strong Democrat	26
White	Independent	26
White	Independent	80
White	Independent, near Rep.	32
White	Not strong Democrat	31
White	Not strong Democrat	45

4. Has the dispersion of agricultural exports from selected United States changed between 1995 and 1999? Using the following table, calculate the standard deviation and coefficient of variation for each year. Comment on your results.

Value of Agricultural Exports (in $ millions) in Selected United States

State	1995	1999
Alabama	467	366
Alaska	0.1	0.2
Arizona	420	333
Arkansas	1,631	1,220
California	6,968	6,932
Colorado	945	828
Connecticut	47	93
Delaware	108	107
Florida	1,201	1,118
Georgia	1,126	867
Hawaii	109	108
Idaho	930	789

Source: Statistical Abstract of the United States, 2000, Table 1327.

5. Here are some data on the rates of crime in several U.S. states in 1996, 1997, and 1998 (crimes known to the police per 100,000 population).

State	1996	1997	1998
Massachusetts	3,837	3,675	3,436
Michigan	5,118	4,917	4,683

(continued)

State	1996	1997	1998
Minnesota	4,463	4,414	4,047
Mississippi	4,523	4,630	4384
Missouri	5,084	4,815	4,826
Montana	4,494	4,409	4,071
Nebraska	4,437	4,284	4405
Nevada	5,992	6,065	5,281
New Hampshire	2,824	2,640	2,420
New Jersey	4,333	4,057	3,654
New Mexico	6,602	6,907	6,719
New York	4,132	3,911	3,589
North Carolina	5,526	5,492	5,322

Source: Statistical Abstract of the United States, 2000, Table 331.

a. Calculate the range, interquartile range, and standard deviation for each year.
b. Comment on your results. What happened to dispersion of crime rates in this sample of states during this three-year period?

USING EXCEL TO COMPUTE MEASURES OF VARIATION

The most commonly used measures of variation (e.g., the variance and standard deviation) are usually available as built-in functions in statistical software and spreadsheets. Some of the other measures discussed in this chapter may have to be computed by hand. It is fairly easy, however, to use a spreadsheet like MS Excel to do the tedious calculations.

The Index of Qualitative Variation

How much variation is there on the variable "race and ethnicity" for undergraduate students on your campus? There's a good chance that the "Common Dataset" is available on your campus website. You might find it on a page for prospective students, or it might be hidden among the pages devoted to institutional research. Find the table for Race/Ethnicity, and compute the IQV for this variable on your campus. How racially and ethnically diverse is your campus, compared to some other campus?

It's possible to compute the IQV by hand using a frequency table and the formula from the chapter, but this is the sort of thing at which MS Excel excels. The following data are from the University of California–Riverside, 2009 undergraduate enrollment (for which the IQV was computed to be 0.84).

◇	A	B	C
1	**Race/Ethnicity**	**freq**	**freq^2**
2	African American / Black	1336	=B2^2
3	American Indian / Alaskan Native	63	=B3^2
4	Asian / Pacific Islander	6785	=B4^2
5	Hispanic	4907	=B5^2
6	White	2881	=B6^2
7	International	261	=B7^2
8	Race/Ethnicity Unknown	763	=B8^2
9	Total/Sum	=SUM(B2:B8)	=SUM(C2:C8)
10			
11	N^2	=B9^2	
12	k	=COUNT(B2:B8)	
13	k-1	=B12-1	
14			
15			
16	Numerator	=B12*(B11-C9)	
17	Denominator	=B11*B13	$IQV = \frac{k(N^2 - \sum f^2)}{N^2(k-1)}$
18			
19	IQV	=B16/B17	
20			

Start by arranging the categories and frequencies in adjacent columns, and then build the formulas using this screen shot as a guide. Note that if you have a different number of categories (or start elsewhere on the spreadsheet), your cell references (e.g., "B2:B8") may be somewhat different.

Note: If you experience trouble with functions, you can use the Excel options to turn on "show formulas" while proofreading (like we did for the screen shots).

The formulas/functions and keywords for this example include:

sum( )	adds together the cells in the cell reference. You may type the cell reference directly into the function, or you may click and drag through the range of cells.
count( )	counts the number of cells containing numbers (so use zeros when needed)
*	sign for multiplication
/	sign for division
^2	sign for squared (raise to second power)
–	sign for subtraction

The Segregation Index/Index of Dissimilarity

Compute and interpret the segregation index for some classification system. We compared three categories of the 1988 U.S. Census job codes from the 2008 General

(continued)

Social Survey (variable named "isco88") across sexes ($S = 0.28$), but you could compare the sexes on handedness in your class (e.g., left-handed, right-handed, or ambidextrous), hair color, or some other variable.

Again, using Excel is a good strategy, both because the measure is not available directly in SPSS or SAS, and because it's easy to be sure that you've summed everything that ought to be summed.

	A	B	C	D	E	F	G	H
1		Males	Females	Pmale	Pfemale	'male - Pfemal	abs(Pm-Pf)	*S*
2	Social work professionals	7	12	=B2/$B$5	=C2/$C$5	=D2-E2	=ABS(F2)	
3	H.S. teachers	5	17	=B3/$B$5	=C3/$C$5	=D3-E3	=ABS(F3)	
4	Technical & commercial sales reps	10	6	=B4/$B$5	=C4/$C$5	=D4-E4	=ABS(F4)	
5	Total	=SUM(B2:B4)	=SUM(C2:C4)				=SUM(G2:G4)	=0.5*G5
6								

Start by arranging the data in columns, and then form the functions around the data. The only new Excel keyword here is ABS( ), which returns the absolute value of the expression inside the parentheses.

Absolute cell references (see columns D and E in the screen shot): Excel defaults to using "relative" cell references. This means that if you entered the expression "=B2/B5" into cell D2 and wanted to drag that formula to fill the cells below, you would end up with:

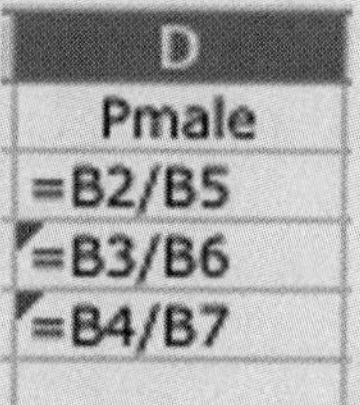

D
Pmale
=B2/B5
=B3/B6
=B4/B7

We want to divide each frequency by the contents of B5 (the total number of men), but because Excel defaults to relative cell references, it wants to divide by the next cell down in each case (e.g., B6 and B7). Since those cells are empty, this generates "divide by 0" errors. In order to fix this, we tell Excel to divide by the contents of a particular cell by using "absolute" cell notation, inserting a dollar sign before the row designation and the column designation: $B$5.

Of course, with so few categories, you could just type the cell reference in or click on the cell in question to insert a reference in each formula, but this increases the chances of error along the way.

The Mean Absolute Deviation and Standard Deviation

Construct the following table in Excel:

◇	A	B	C	D	E
1		value	deviation	abs dev	squared deviation
2		6.4	=B2-$B$13	=ABS(C2)	=C2*C2
3		6.5	=B3-$B$13	=ABS(C3)	=C3*C3
4		6.5	=B4-$B$13	=ABS(C4)	=C4*C4
5		2	=B5-$B$13	=ABS(C5)	=C5*C5
6		6.5	=B6-$B$13	=ABS(C6)	=C6*C6
7		6	=B7-$B$13	=ABS(C7)	=C7*C7
8		8	=B8-$B$13	=ABS(C8)	=C8*C8
9		6.5	=B9-$B$13	=ABS(C9)	=C9*C9
10		6.5	=B10-$B$13	=ABS(C10)	=C10*C10
11		6.6	=B11-$B$13	=ABS(C11)	=C11*C11
12					
13	mean:	=AVERAGE(B2:B11)	=AVERAGE(C2:C11)	=AVERAGE(D2:D11)	=AVERAGE(E2:E11)
14	sum:				=SUM(E2:E11)
15	pop s.d.				=SQRT(E13)
16	sample s.d.				=SQRT(E14/(COUNT(E2:E11)-1))
17	MAD				=D13
18					

Experiment: Change the values, and notice how more or less variation in the values affects the MAD, the sample standard deviation, and the population standard deviation.

The Coefficient of Variation

Construct the following table in Excel:

◇	A	B	C
1		Group 1	Group 2
2		2	4
3		3	6
4		3	6
5		3	9
6		4	9
7		4	9
8		5	8
9		5	6
10		5	6
11			
12			
13	s.d.	=STDEV(B2:B10)	=STDEV(C2:C10)
14	mean	=AVERAGE(B2:B10)	=AVERAGE(C2:C10)
15	C.V.	=(B13/B14)*100	=(C13/C14)*100
16			

(*continued*)

Note that the keyword "stdev" is used to compute the sample standard deviation; if you wish to use the population standard deviation, use the keyword "stdevp."

Experiment with the values of each group: change the values so that:

- Both the standard deviation and the mean of Group 1 are larger than the values for Group 2.
- The mean of Group 1 is larger, but the standard deviation of Group 2 is larger.

Watch what happens to the relative coefficient of variation of both groups.

Chapter 5

DESCRIBING THE SHAPE OF A DISTRIBUTION

LEARNING OBJECTIVES

When you have finished this chapter, you will be able to:

- Know how to construct and interpret the box-and-whiskers diagram.
- Describe the shape of a distribution as unimodal or multimodal.
- Describe the distributions of ordinal or interval/ratio variables in terms of kurtosis and skewness.
- Interpret the coefficients of kurtosis and skewness for interval/ratio variables.
- Recognize the shapes of several basic distributions used in many statistical procedures.

THE BASIC IDEAS OF DISTRIBUTIONAL SHAPE

In the preceding two chapters we studied tools for examining two aspects of distributions—central tendency and dispersion. When we are describing the distributions of social phenomena, these two aspects of the shape of the distribution of scores in a sample are usually our main focus. When we are using statistics to test hypotheses derived from theories, we are usually interested in central tendency and dispersion; most hypotheses make predictions about these aspects of distributions.

There are some other aspects of the shape of distributions that are sometimes of interest, as well. In this chapter, we examine three more concepts about the shape of distributions: modality, skewness, and kurtosis. Familiarity with these concepts may help you to see important patterns when you look at the distribution of a single variable, or when you compare multiple distributions. We also briefly look at the shapes of some commonly used "ideal type" distributions, and learn a new graphical tool, the box-and-whiskers plot, for displaying distributional shape.

Look at the two histograms presented in Figures 5.1 and 5.2. These show the distributions of family incomes for nonblack and black American families (classified by race of head of household) from the 2000 U.S. Census (calculated from the public use samples of the census).

FIGURE 5.1 Income Distribution for Nonblack Families

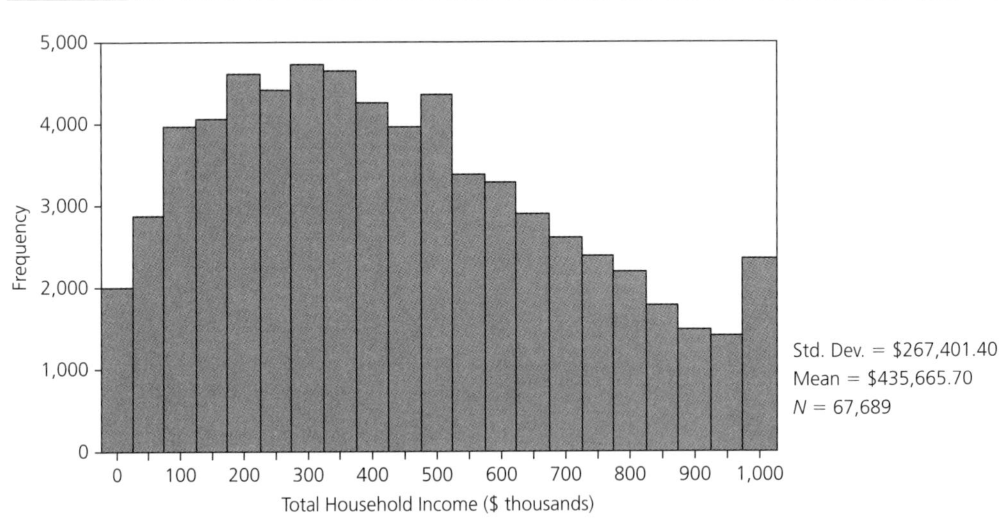

Source: PUMS data, U.S. 2000.

FIGURE 5.2 Income Distribution for Black Families

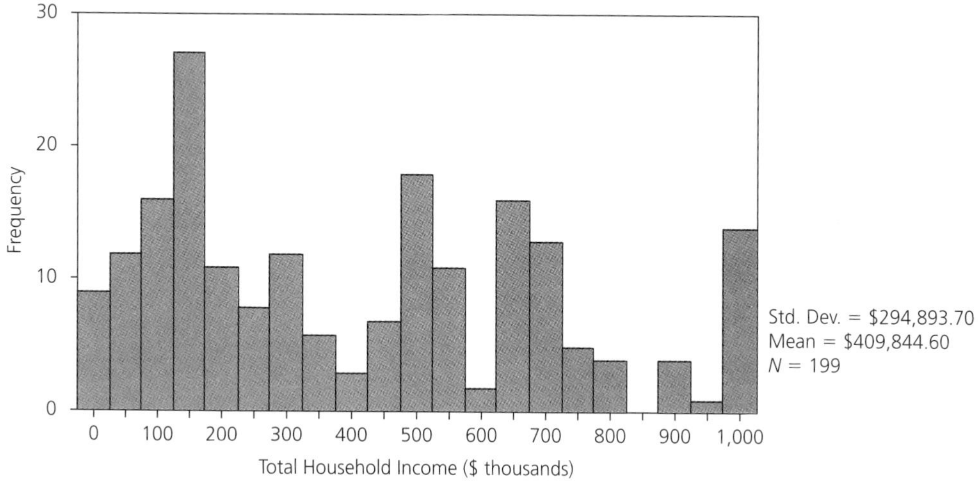

Source: PUMS data, U.S. 2000.

The distribution of income is clearly quite different for these two samples. One obvious difference is that the samples have different sizes. In the graphics we've hidden that fact by showing the groups in separate charts. The chart for black Americans is less smooth because the sample size (199) is much smaller than for nonblack Americans (67,689).

What do you see when you compare the two distributions?

You might notice that the two distributions are different in the number of high points or lumps in the shape of the curve. The nonblack distribution is *unimodal.* That is, it has a single range of values with higher relative frequencies (ignoring the 1,000,000 or more category). The distribution for blacks has two relatively high points, which shows rather clearly the gap between the black lower and middle classes in the United States. In statistical jargon, the black distribution is *bimodal*, whereas the nonblack distribution is *unimodal.* The difference in the shape of these two distributions is, in fact, very important in understanding the issues of race relations in the United States.

A difference between the normal (bell curve) distribution and the distributions of income (Figures 5.1 and 5.2) is that the peak or mode of the ***normal distribution*** is right in the middle. But the mode of the income distribution is more to the left, over lower scores. Whether the mode of a distribution is in the middle (like in a normal distribution) or more off-center can be an important fact in describing social variables. The peak of the income distribution is to the left; this means that there are more people with lower incomes than there would be if income had a normal distribution. This "off-center" idea is referred to statistically as ***skewness.***

The normal distribution as a theoretical baseline has a particular shape. If one starts at the midpoint and moves in either direction, the way that the relative frequencies change is the same. That is, the distribution is symmetric; one side of it is just a mirror image of the other. In the normal distribution, as one moves away from the center point to the right, the shape of the curve resembles an S shape; the curve goes down slowly at first, then accelerates, and then flattens out again. If a distribution changes much more rapidly around its center point than is the case for a normal distribution, the distribution is said to have high ***kurtosis.*** In a distribution with high kurtosis, the tails of the distribution are thinner or have fewer cases than in a normal distribution. Social scientists don't use kurtosis very frequently in their work, but it can be an important social fact.

As a first step toward summarizing the shape of a distribution, we'll look at a graphical tool, the box-and-whiskers plot. This tool is a very useful one for seeing the main features of the shape of the distribution of interval/ratio variables. Though it isn't used with categorical variables, it helps to give an intuitive grasp of some of the basic ideas.

While graphics are great for getting a feel for our data, we often want to calculate numerical indexes to be more precise in our descriptions. Assessing unimodality is a judgment call, but there are good statistical indexes of skewness and kurtosis that we will examine.

In the last part of this chapter, we briefly consider a few distributions that are commonly used in statistical work, and that we will encounter again as we discuss hypothesis testing.

THE SHAPE OF NOMINAL AND ORDINAL DISTRIBUTIONS

The distribution of a nominal variable can be described as unimodal or multimodal. Nominal variables can also be described in terms of central tendency and dispersion. Since order in which we display the levels of a nominal variable is arbitrary (they aren't ranked or scaled), comparing the distribution of a nominal variable to that of a normal variable doesn't make much sense. So we don't use the ideas of kurtosis and skewness with nominal variables.

When the levels or categories of a variable can be ranked from low to high (i.e., the variable is ordinal or interval/ratio), the ideas of unimodality, central tendency, and dispersion all make sense. With an ordinal variable, we can describe the distribution by its ***skew*** and kurtosis—but only in an informal way, because the normal distribution that we are using for comparison is an interval/ratio distribution.

For nominal and grouped ordinal variables, the best description of the shape of the distribution is often a graphic display like a bar chart or pie chart. Such pictures, along with measures of central tendency and dispersion, can give us a quite complete understanding of distributional shape.

With interval/ratio variables, we can do quite a lot more. A good place to start with interval/ratio variables is visualizing the distribution.

Visualizing Shape with the Box-and-Whiskers Plot

A good graphic can quickly show us many of the most important things about the shape of the distribution of interval/ratio variables. Histograms are very useful, but there is another graphical tool that you ought to know about. This is called the ***box-and-whiskers plot***. Figure 5.3 shows three box-and-whiskers plots to compare the

FIGURE 5.3 Box-and-Whiskers Plots of Educational Attainment by Race

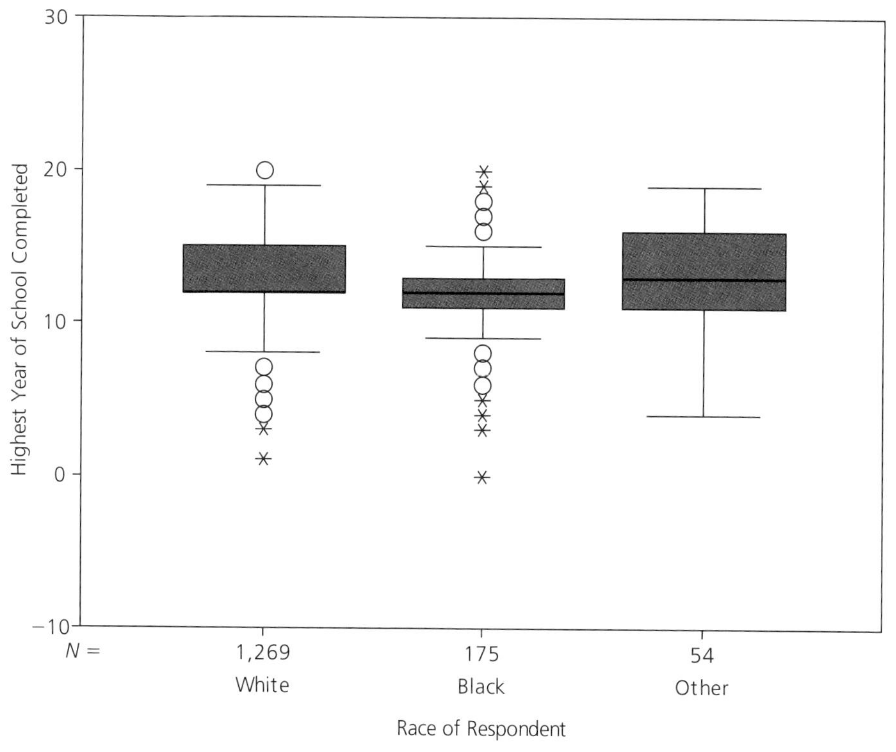

Source: General Social Survey, 1998.

distributions of formal schooling attained by three racial groups. These plots were produced by SPSS.

The box-and-whiskers plot is used for interval/ratio variables, and shouldn't be used for nominal or grouped ordinal data. Rather than drawing a picture of the actual relative frequencies (i.e., a histogram), the box-and-whiskers plot is a picture of summary statistics about central tendency, dispersion, and shape.

In Figure 5.3, we are comparing the distribution of the highest level of education completed by respondents in three samples: people who identify themselves as "white," those who identify themselves as "black," and those who identify themselves as anything else (an extremely diverse group, but probably including mostly Latino and Asian-Americans).

The "box" of the box-and-whiskers plot encloses the scores between the 25th and 75th percentiles (also called the "hinges"). The "box then shows the interquartile range. The line crossing the box shows the value of the 50th percentile, or median. In our example, you can immediately tell that the central tendency value for "other" is higher than for "white" or "black," and that the central tendency for the latter two groups does not differ very much. You can also immediately see that the amount of dispersion is greatest among those in the "other" group. That is, the vertical size of the box is equal to the interquartile range—one useful measure of dispersion. Dispersion is least among black persons.

Extending out from the top and bottom of the box are the "whiskers." In SPSS's version of the box-and-whiskers plot, the whiskers show us where the highest and lowest data values are—excluding extreme values or outliers. An "outlier" or "extreme value" is usually defined as a case that has a score more than 1.5 times the interquartile range above or below the median. Some versions of the box-and-whiskers plot draw the whiskers all the way out to the highest and lowest values, whether these are outliers or not. In our example, we can see that the upper and lower tails (i.e., the values from the 75th percentile to the top value, and the values from the 25th percentile to the bottom value) are longest for the "other" group, next longest for whites and shortest for blacks. This suggests different amounts of kurtosis in the three distributions (with the black group having the shortest and thickest tails in its distribution).

The box-and-whiskers plot does not give us the precise numerical values that statistical measures like the mean, standard deviation, and coefficient of skewness do. It does not give us a complete picture of the whole distribution, like a histogram of a stem-and-leaf diagram. But, the box-and-whiskers plot does quickly and easily convey a lot of information about central tendency, dispersion, skew, and kurtosis, and it allows us to make qualitative group comparisons that can be very important in sociological research.

MAKING BOX-AND-WHISKERS PLOTS BY HAND

John Tukey invented the box plot, or box-and-whiskers plot, in the 1970s. The box part is always bounded by the 25th and 75th percentiles. If the median falls between (rather than at one of) these two values, it is represented by a horizontal line drawn at a point between the other two. Sometimes the mean of the distribution is represented by an X, but often it is not.

The whiskers—the lines extending away from the box—can represent a variety of values. One school of thought (the five-number summary approach) uses the whiskers to represent the highest and lowest values of the distribution, with the 25th, 50th, and 75th percentiles serving as the other three key values.

We use the approach taken by Tukey for the whiskers, which places the ends of the whiskers at values in the data that lie a step (1.5 times the interquartile range) above and below the box.

To draw the plot by hand, start by finding (by looking on the frequency chart) or computing the following values:

25th percentile	Find
50th percentile	Find
75th percentile	Find
Interquartile range (75th percentile minus 25th percentile)	Compute
One step (1.5 times the interquartile range)	Compute
Two steps (3 times the interquartile range)	Compute
Upper fence (add one step to 75th percentile)	Compute
Lower fence (subtract one step from 25th percentile)	Compute
Upper adjacent (see the following)	Find
Lower adjacent (see the following)	Find
Upper outlier boundary: 75th percentile + two steps	Compute
Lower outlier boundary: 25th percentile − two steps	Compute
Up to five extreme values at either end (see the following)	Find

Statistical packages don't draw the fences and boundaries on the plot, but they're helpful when constructing these plots by hand.

(continued)

Example

The fences (see the drawing) help in locating the adjacents (the lines at the end of the whiskers); the whiskers can (potentially) extend all the way to the fences from the box, but not beyond.

- For the upper adjacent, if there's a value in your frequency chart that is equal to the value of the upper fence, that's the upper adjacent. If there is not, then the next actual *smaller* value in your data is the upper adjacent.
- For the lower adjacent, if there's a value in your frequency chart that is equal to the value of the lower fence, that's the lower adjacent. If there is not, then the next actual *larger* value in your data is the lower adjacent.

After you've assembled those values, the plot is easily drawn:

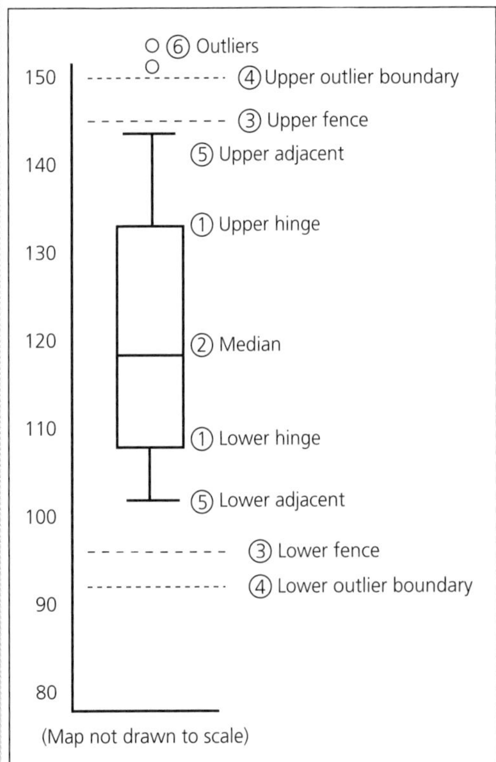

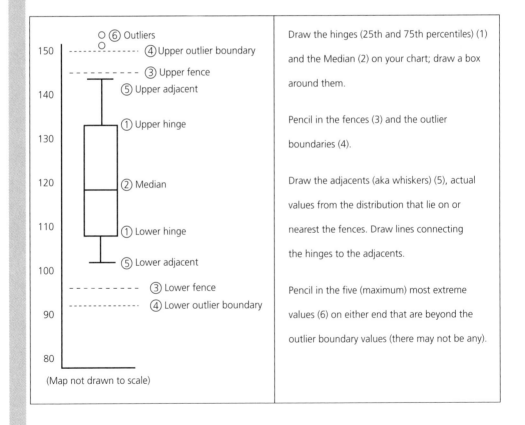

Draw the hinges (25th and 75th percentiles) (1) and the Median (2) on your chart; draw a box around them.

Pencil in the fences (3) and the outlier boundaries (4).

Draw the adjacents (aka whiskers) (5), actual values from the distribution that lie on or nearest the fences. Draw lines connecting the hinges to the adjacents.

Pencil in the five (maximum) most extreme values (6) on either end that are beyond the outlier boundary values (there may not be any).

Example

Let's try it with some actual data:

Hours Worked in the Last Week (from Cumulative GSS)

Value	Frequency	Valid Percent	Cumulative Percent
0	7	.0	.0
1	11	.0	.1
2	25	.1	.2
3	35	.1	.3
4	72	.3	.6

(Data omitted)

20	815	3.0	9.8
21	73	.3	10.0
22	72	.3	10.3

(Data omitted)

36	292	1.1	24.5
37	321	1.2	25.7
38	499	1.9	27.5
39	94	.4	27.9
40	9,470	35.4	63.3

(Data omitted)

47	133	.5	73.5
48	782	2.9	76.4

(Data omitted)

64	45	.2	94.4
65	299	1.1	95.5

(Data omitted)

25th percentile:	37
50th percentile:	40
75th percentile:	48
Interquartile range (75th percentile minus 25th percentile):	11
One step (1.5 times the interquartile range):	16.5
Two steps (3 times the interquartile range)	33
Upper fence (add one step to 75th percentile):	64.5
Lower fence (subtract one step from 25th percentile):	20.5
Upper adjacent	64
Lower adjacent	21
Upper outlier boundary: 75th percentile + two steps	81
Lower outlier boundary: 25th percentile–two steps	4

(*continued*)

Example

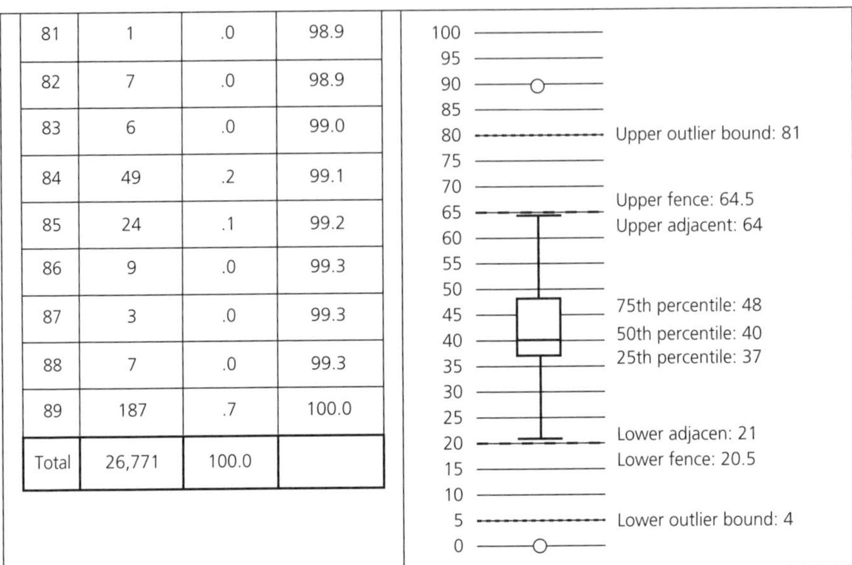

81	1	.0	98.9
82	7	.0	98.9
83	6	.0	99.0
84	49	.2	99.1
85	24	.1	99.2
86	9	.0	99.3
87	3	.0	99.3
88	7	.0	99.3
89	187	.7	100.0
Total	26,771	100.0	

Many people find locating the adjacents problematic. The upper fence is computed to lie at 64.5. A quick look at the frequency distribution confirms that the value 64.5 does not appear in the data (if it did, we would use it for the upper adjacent). We then look in the frequency chart for the next smaller value that actually appears in our data; a larger value would lie on the wrong side of the fence. The next smaller value in the data is 64, so that's the upper adjacent.

The same logic is used to find the lower adjacent. The fence is computed to lie at 20.5, but 20.5 does not occur in the frequency chart. We're looking for the next value that is in our data, which also lies inside (on the box side) of the fence, and 21 fills the bill.

Fairly often in social science (and other) data, the lower fence will lie at a negative number, and the first value that actually appears in the data will be zero (0).

Graphical displays are always an excellent starting point for examining the shape of distributions. Often, though, we may wish to characterize the various aspects of distributional shape with numerical indexes so that we can make comparisons among distributions. The next sections show how we can describe modality, skewness, and kurtosis with convenient index numbers.

UNIMODALITY

The question that we ask most frequently of our data is: "What is a typical score?" In Chapter 3, we studied statistical measures of central tendency that can give precise answers to

CHECK QUIZ 5.1

FIGURE 5.3 Box-and-Whiskers Plots of Educational Attainment by Race

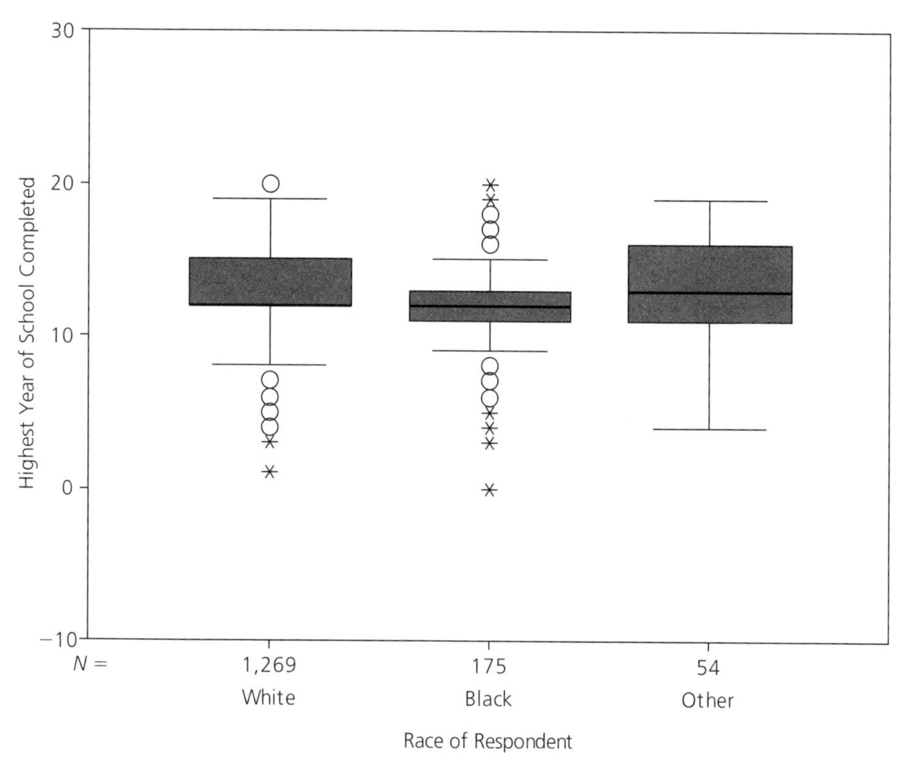

Source: General Social Survey, 1998.

1. Look again at Figure 5.3, the box-and-whiskers plot of years of education completed by race = white. Why is the thick line that represents the median touching the lower edge of the box?
   a. because there are missing values
   b. because there are so many outliers
   c. because so many people go to college
   d. because both the median and the 25th percentile contain the same value
2. Look at the box-and-whiskers plot again: What is the substantive meaning of the finding from the last question?
   a. At least 25 percent of whites in the sample ended their education at grade 12.
   b. About 75 percent of whites in the sample completed some college.
   c. Most whites in the sample completed more than grade 6.
   d. There is no substantive meaning.

3. If you consider only the interquartile range, which of the three categories shows the least skewness?
   a. white
   b. black
   c. other
   d. a and b

this question. In Chapter 4, we saw that the idea of dispersion speaks to the question: "How typical is this typical score?" In thinking about answering this most important question of what is typical, we also need to ask a third question: "Does the distribution have a single typical score, or is there more than one score that is typical?"

The Basic Idea

Looking at a bar chart (for a nominal variable) or a histogram (for a grouped ordinal or interval/ratio variable), we will immediately notice whether there is one category that is much bigger than the others, or whether there are two or more categories that have large relative frequencies.

The formal name for what we are noticing about how many lumps or high points there are is whether the distribution is ***unimodal*** (one high point), ***bimodal*** (two high points), or ***multimodal*** (more than two high points).

How many modes there are (and where they are located, and how big they are) can be quite important in describing how social structures differ from one another, and in understanding and making predictions about the behavior of the actors in those social structures. A community with two equal modal categories of religious affiliations may behave very differently from a community with one modal category of religious affiliation, for example.

Applying the Idea

While the idea of whether a distribution is unimodal or multimodal is very simple in the abstract, it is not always so simple to apply in real cases.

For a nominal variable, the relative frequency in one category may be larger than any other. If the relative frequency in the largest category is much, much larger than the relative frequency in any other, it is reasonable to describe the distribution as unimodal. If we had three categories and the cases were distributed 90 percent, 5 percent, and 5 percent, it would be reasonable to describe the distribution as unimodal. If the relative frequencies were 45 percent, 45 percent, and 10 percent, it would be reasonable to describe the distribution as bimodal. But what if the distribution were 47 percent, 43 percent, and 10 percent?

CHECK QUIZ 5.2

1. True or False: A distribution of scores will always have only one mode.
2. The mode may be a useful tool in describing variables measured at which of the following levels?
   a. nominal
   b. ordinal
   c. interval/ratio
   d. all of these
3. True or False: The mode is a useful tool in describing full rank-order ordinal data.
4. True or False: When we say that a distribution is bimodal, we don't necessarily mean that the same exact number of cases fall into each of the two high-frequency categories.

The distributions of nominal variables in the real world are rarely exactly unimodal, exactly bimodal, or exactly multimodal. And there are no firm rules that one can apply.

Clearly, if one category is much bigger than any of the others, unimodal is a reasonable description. We might go even further and describe just how much unimodal the distribution is by telling what percentage of cases are in this largest category. When there is more than one category with higher relative frequencies, you need to exercise your judgment. You might want to report the percentages of cases that fall in the categories that are larger than the others as a way of telling the story.

For grouped ordinal variables, the same issues arise. But the ordering of the cases can help in making a decision about how to describe the relative frequencies. When we look at the histogram of a grouped ordinal variable, there may be several categories that have higher than average frequencies. But if all of these categories are adjacent, it is reasonable to describe the distribution as unimodal.

For interval/ratio variables, describing the distribution as having one or more modes can be a little tricky. The impression that we have can depend on how we have decided to create class intervals (see the discussion in Chapter 2). The more categories there are, the more likely it is that the distribution will have more modes. If we have classified all the cases into only a few categories, the data are more likely to appear to be unimodal. The two histograms in Figure 5.4 illustrate this problem.

In the second panel of Figure 5.4, we have created larger classes (e.g., grouping together ages 1, 2, 3, and 4). When we do this, we hide the fact that there actually two modes in these data (age 2 and age 4).

If the high points in the distribution are adjacent to one another, we might describe them as forming a single mode (note that we are using the word *mode* in a less formal and

FIGURE 5.4 The Effect of Having More or Fewer Categories on the Mode

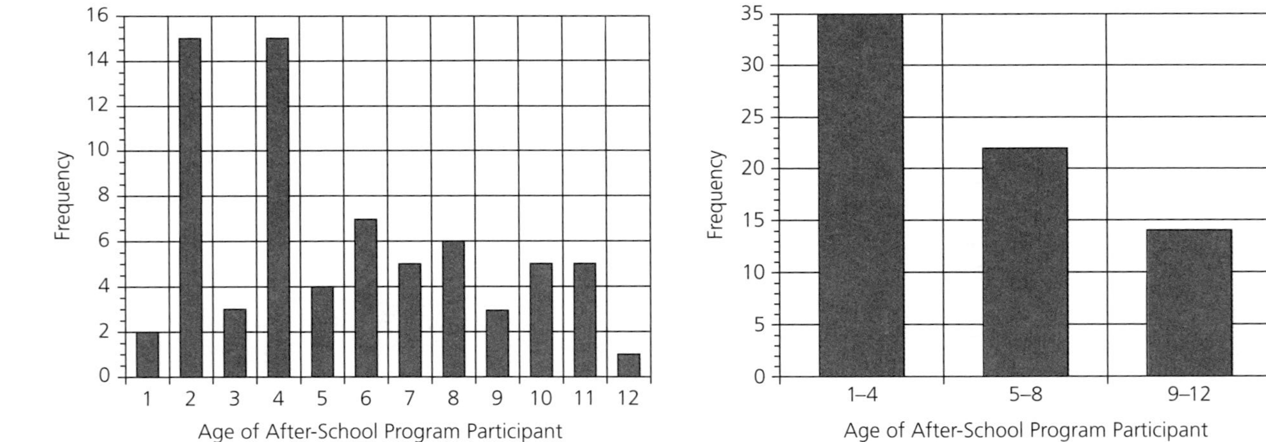

precise way here than we did in the chapter on central tendency, though the ideas are similar). Again, there is no single right answer to this dilemma. You will have to use your judgment in light of the particular problem.

Here are just a few quick questions to be sure that you have the idea of how to describe a distribution in terms of modes. When you've mastered this, you should go on to looking in a little more detail at the idea of "skew" in the next section.

SKEWNESS

Many of the variables of interest to social scientists have distributions that resemble the bell curve—they are unimodal and symmetric. Scores on most tests and responses to attitude surveys often have such distributional shapes. But many of the variables that are of interest do not have symmetric distributions. It is generally true that the distribution of anything that is socially valued—money, fame, power—is not only unequal (displays dispersion) but also nonsymmetric.

Consider the distribution of income that we saw in Figure 5.1 for nonblack Americans. It is "off center." More families are located near the lower end of the distribution than near the upper end. This is not just a statistical peculiarity; it is a very important social fact. If the distribution were symmetric, we would have a society with a large middle class and equally sized lower and upper classes. In the United States (and everywhere else, too), the families that earn middle-ranking incomes are very different from the rich, and not very different from the poor. The extent to which the central tendency is off center can tell us quite a lot about inequality in groups, and many other important social phenomena.

The Basic Idea

To determine whether the distribution of an interval/ratio variable is skewed, we compare the distribution of a variable that we are studying to a theoretical "pure type" of distribution—the normal curve. The normal or bell-shaped curve is perfectly symmetric, so its central tendency is at the high point in the middle of the distribution.

If a distribution is skewed, it isn't symmetric, and the high point has been pushed off the center in one direction or the other. Skewness of a distribution describes how far off center the midpoint of the distribution is (i.e., the amount of skewness), and whether the high point of the distribution has been deflected toward lower or higher values (***positive skew*** or ***negative skew***).

Since the normal curve describes a theoretical distribution of an interval/ratio variable, the idea of skewness really doesn't apply to nominal variables. While formal statistical measures of skewness don't apply to grouped ordinal variables, we can note that the peak of the distribution of a grouped ordinal variable is centered (or not).

FIGURE 5.5 Skewness Displaces the Mean toward the Longer Tail

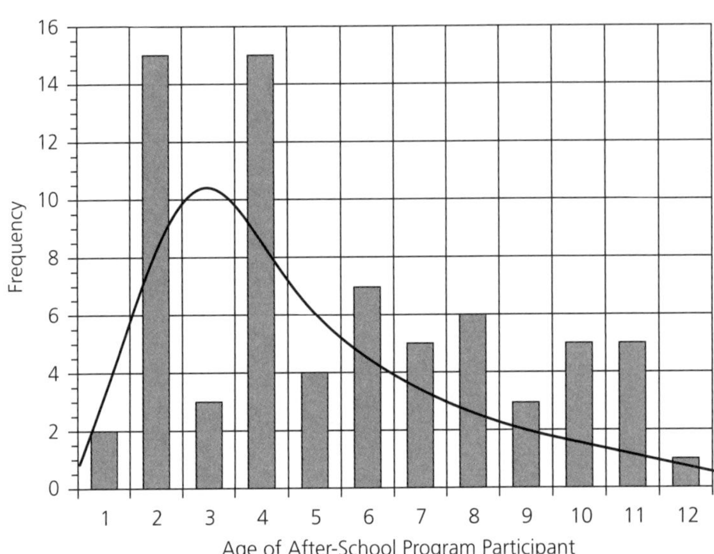

For interval/ratio variables, there are formal measures that describe both the extent and the direction of skewness in the shape of the distribution.

Statistical Measures of Skewness

Statisticians have developed a number of different ways of measuring the degree and direction of skewness. One approach is to subtract the median from the mean. The mean will always be pulled away from the median in the direction of the longer tail, so the difference between the mean and the median tells us the direction of the skew, and how much the central tendency has been displaced by skewness.

In Figure 5.5, the mean is 5.5; the median is 5; 5.5 minus 5 = 0.5. The sign (positive) tells us which way the mean has been shifted due to the distribution's skew (to the right). The difference (0.5) is 9 percent of the mean.

Technically, skewness is the "third moment" of the distribution, and it can be indexed by summing the cubed differences between each score and the mean, and dividing the result by the standard deviation cubed. Frankly, this is not as intuitive or useful as comparing the median and mean (see Formula 5.1).

$$\text{Skewness} = \frac{\sum (x - \bar{x})^3}{(n-1)s^3} \tag{5.1}$$

Take a look at the age distribution from the General Social Survey in Figure 5.6.

FIGURE 5.6 Respondents' Ages in the General Social Survey

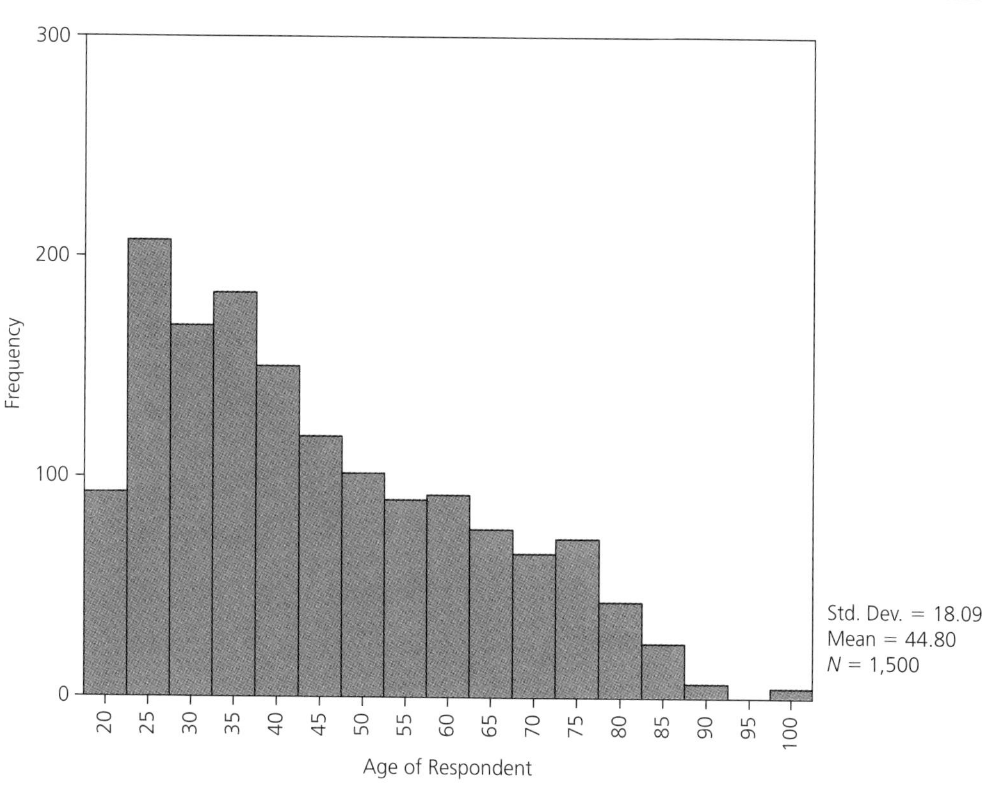

Your eye should tell you that this distribution has a skewed shape. Since the long tail is toward the right, or higher, values, the distribution is *positively* skewed.

Helpful hint: The long tail always points in the direction of skew. If it points to the right (the positive direction on a number line), the skew is positive; if it points to the left, the skew is negative.

The coefficient of skewness for this variable is reported by SPSS to be 0.592. The coefficient of skewness is zero when there is no skew, increasingly negative when the long tail is to the left (lower values), and increasingly positive when the long tail is to the right (positive values).

Right now, you are probably asking yourself: "Why in the world should I care about whether a distribution is skewed, how much, and in what direction?"

There are two reasons why it is important to examine the skewness of the distribution of variables, and interval/ratio variables in particular.

First, the direction and degree of skew may describe something that is quite important to understanding a social phenomenon. The distribution of income and wealth in most societies has a very substantial positive skewness. That is, there is a long, thin upper tail of

FIGURE 5.7 Effect of Skewness on the Location of Central Tendency Statistics

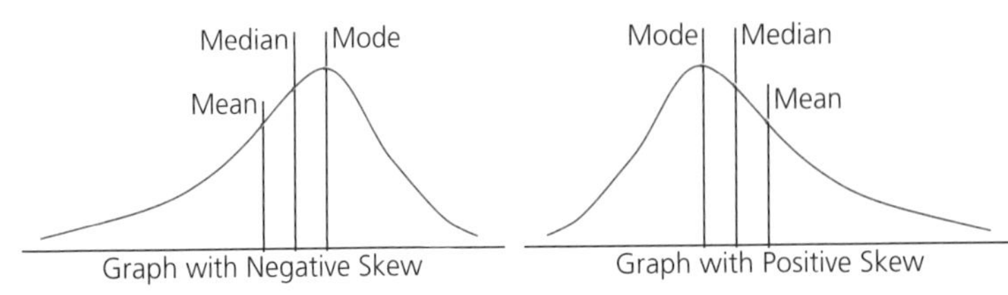

very wealthy people, while large portions of the population are concentrated at relatively low incomes. If we were to compare two nations or two communities, however, we would probably find that they differ in the skewness of their distributions. This statistical fact is describing an important difference between the class structures of the two nations or communities.

Second, skewness is important for a narrower, technical reason. In the perfect normal distribution, the mean, median, and mode all fall at the same score. But if a distribution is skewed, the three measures of central tendency will have different values. In particular, the mean will always be higher than the median when a distribution is positively skewed; the mean will be lower than the median when a distribution is negatively skewed. This effect is illustrated in Figure 5.7.

If a variable has a quite skewed distribution, the mean can actually be quite far away from the median and mode. When this is the case, the mean is still telling us the truth about central tendency, but it's not telling us the whole truth. When a variable is quite skewed, it is a good idea to report both the median and the mean.

Take a moment now to check your knowledge about skewness with a quick quiz. When you're done, you should go on to the next section.

CHECK QUIZ 5.3

1. If the long tail of a distribution points to the left, we say that it is
   a. negatively skewed.
   b. symmetric.
   c. positively skewed.
   d. positively marvelous.
2. The age at which students graduate from college is a variable; what is the likely shape of its distribution?
   a. positively skewed
   b. normal/symmetrical
   c. negatively skewed
   d. long torso, short legs

Example

THE COEFFICIENT OF SKEWNESS

The coefficient of skewness measures the extent (and direction) of asymmetry distribution of an interval/ratio variable. A value of zero indicates that the distribution is symmetric, like that of the standard normal distribution. A negative value (negative skewness) indicates that the long tail of the distribution is located toward lower values; a positive value indicated that the long tail of the distribution is located toward higher values.

Consider the distribution of levels of literacy in nations of the world during the mid-1990s. Figure 5.8 shows a histogram (drawn by SPSS frequencies) with an overlay of a normal distribution with the same mean and standard deviation (the black continuous curve).

FIGURE 5.8 Distribution of Literacy Levels versus Normal Distribution

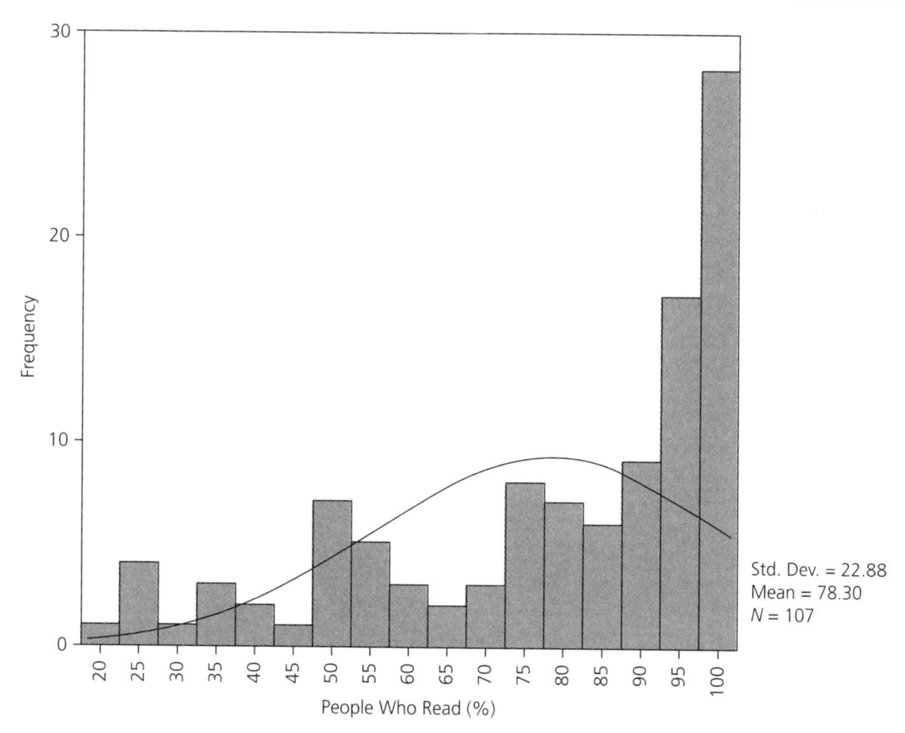

Compared to a normal distribution with the same mean and standard deviation, the distribution of literacy shows a mode at very high values that exceeds what a normal curve would predict. It also shows a longer tail of low values; that is, there are more cases at low values than the normal curve would predict.

(continued)

Example

The modal area of the curve has been pushed to the right, leaving a long tail to the left, or toward lower values. So, this distribution has a *negative* skewness. There are a couple of different ways to describe the amount and direction of skewness.

We could compare the mean and the median. Because the mean finds the balance point in the distribution where the sums of the deviations above and below it are equal, its value is affected by the shape of the distribution. Specifically, the mean will be pulled in the direction of the long tail. The median, which does not pay attention to distances (only rank), is less affected by skewness.

One way to index skewness is to take the mean and subtract the median. If the mean is higher than the median (which means the long tail is to the right, or positive), the difference between the mean and the median will be a positive number—indicating a positive skew.

In our example, the mean is 78.3; the median is 88.0. Subtracting the median from the mean gives us a negative value (78.3 − 88.0 = −9.7), indicating a negative skeweness. Whether the skewness is big or small can be roughly indexed by examining the size of the difference between the mean and median, as a percentage of the mean. Here, −9.7/78.3 = −12 (or the difference between the mean and the median) is negative, and 12 percent of the value of the mean.

A more formal method for indexing skewness is to calculate the "third moment" of the distribution. This descriptive statistic is called the coefficient of skewness, and has the advantage of having known estimates of its sampling variability—so we can use inferential logic to decide whether the amount of skewness in the distribution is significant (in the statistical inference sense of the term).

Again, Formula 5.1 is the formula for the coefficient of skewness:

$$\text{Skewness} = \frac{\sum (x_i - \bar{x})^3}{(n-1)s^3} \tag{5.1}$$

The numerator is similar to the mean and the variance, except that the deviation of each case from the mean is raised to the third power. The denominator is the sample size, less 1, multiplied by the standard deviation (s) raised to the third power.

For our example, the sample (N) is 107, so $N - 1$ is 106. The standard deviation is 22.883, so $s^3 = 11{,}982.3$. We calculated the deviations $(x_i - \bar{x})$ using a spreadsheet, and found the sum of cubed deviations to be −1,239,288.7.

$$\begin{aligned}\text{Skewness} &= -1{,}239{,}288.7/(106 \times 11{,}982.3)\\ &= -1{,}239{,}288.7/1{,}270{,}123.8\\ &= -0.976\end{aligned}$$

The numerical magnitude of the coefficient of skewness does not have any easy interpretation. However, it does indicate, in this case, a negative skewness. Values 2 or above are generally considered skewed.

KURTOSIS

Modality speaks to the question: "How many central tendencies are there?" Skewness asks whether the central tendency (assuming that there is one!) is in the middle of the distribution.

In addition to knowing these things about central tendency, it can be important to know whether most of our observations are close to the central tendency or large proportions of cases are not well described by the central tendency.

The notion of dispersion that we studied in Chapter 4 describes, in a general way, the amount of variation around the mean of interval/ratio distributions. So, measures of dispersion like the standard deviation give answers to the question of how typical the central tendency is.

The statistical measure of kurtosis is intended to answer the same question of dispersion around the central tendency. It does this in a different way than the variance or standard deviation: by comparing an observed distribution to the standard normal curve.

The Basic Idea

The basic idea of kurtosis is to compare the distribution of a variable that we are studying to a theoretical "pure type" of distribution—the normal curve. In a normal bell-shaped curve, the relative frequencies of cases decline as we move away from the mean. The normal curve is defined, in part, by the mathematical rule (or function) that describes how rapidly the frequencies decline. Kurtosis measures whether the frequencies of an actual distribution decline more or less rapidly than a standard normal curve. A distribution displays *negative kurtosis* when frequencies decline less rapidly than in the bell curve; a distribution displays *positive kurtosis* when frequencies decline more rapidly than in a bell curve. Normal, positive, and negative kurtosis are illustrated in Figure 5.9.

A distribution that is flatter than expected compared to the normal curve (has negative kurtosis) is called ***platykurtic***. A distribution that has a higher peak than expected compared to a normal curve is called ***leptokurtic***. (These are just some fancy Greek-derived words to impress your nonstatistician friends with!)

Since the normal curve describes a theoretical distribution of an interval/ratio variable, the idea of kurtosis doesn't actually apply to nominal variables. It doesn't really apply to grouped ordinal variables, either. But, we can note that the peak of the distribution of a grouped ordinal variable is very high (or not).

Statistical Measures of Kurtosis

If our distribution has a higher peak than a theoretical normal distribution of the same central tendency and dispersion (don't worry about the details of that assumption), then we

FIGURE 5.9 A Standard Normal Curve, and Positive and Negative Kurtosis

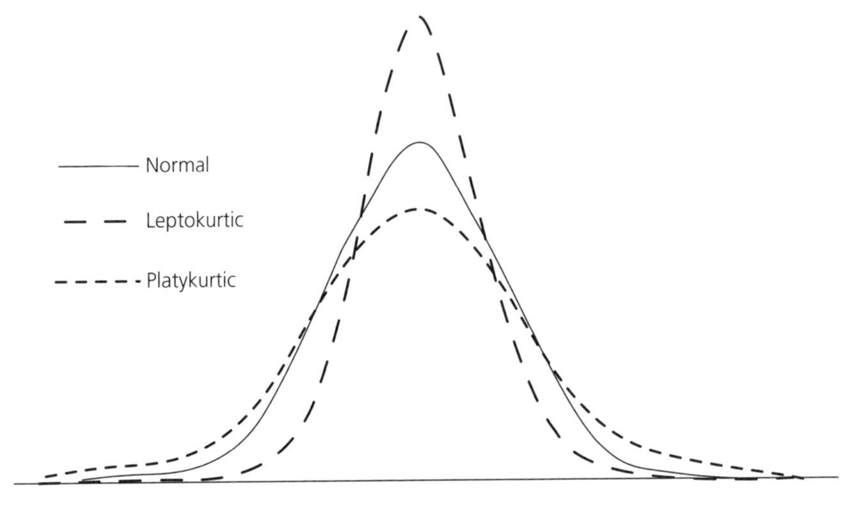

describe the distribution as leptokurtic. That is, the tails of the distribution are thinner and relative frequencies decline more rapidly than normal as we move away from the mean. If the peak is lower than that of a theoretical normal distribution, we describe our distribution as platykurtic.

For interval/ratio data, a statistic called the *coefficient of kurtosis* has been developed, and is calculated by most computer packages. The mathematical definition of kurtosis is the "fourth moment" of a distribution. The coefficient of kurtosis is mathematically equal to the sum of the deviations of each case from the mean, raised to the fourth power, with the resulting quantity divided by the standard deviation raised to the fourth power. For scaling reasons, 3.0 is subtracted from the result (see Formula 5.2).

$$Kurtosis = \frac{\sum_{i=1}^{n} (x_i - \bar{x})^4}{(n-1)s^4} \qquad (5.2)$$

The coefficient of kurtosis has a value of zero when the tails of the distribution have the same thickness as those for a standard normal distribution. Positive values of the coefficient of kurtosis indicate that the distribution has thinner tails than a standard normal distribution—that is, the distribution is more peaked than expected (leptokurtic). Negative values of the coefficient of kurtosis indicate the distribution has thicker tails than the standard normal distribution. That is, it is flatter than expected, or platykurtic. Let's look again at our distribution of respondent's ages from the General Social Survey (see Figure 5.10).

FIGURE 5.10 Respondents' Ages in the General Social Survey

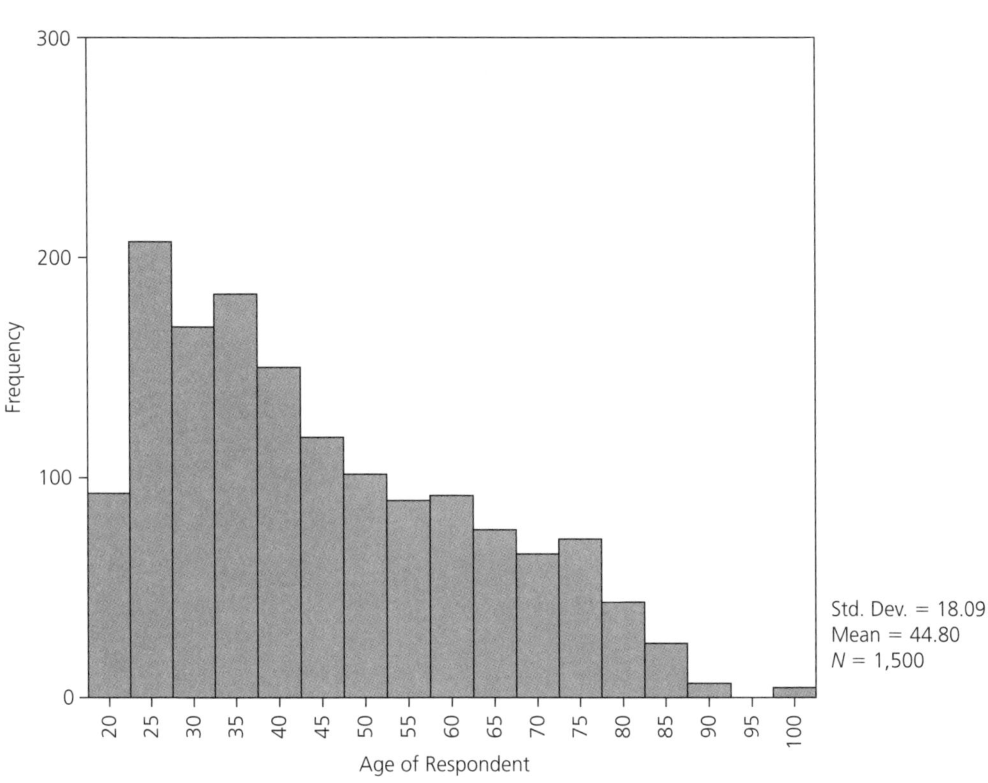

The distribution of respondents' ages from the General Social Survey is clearly not a normal distribution, because it is quite skewed, as we saw in the previous section. The coefficient of kurtosis for this distribution is −0.620, indicating that the tails are thicker and the distribution less peaked than one would expect if respondent age were a normal bell curve.

This is not a surprising result if you think about it a bit. In the General Social Survey, no people under age 18 were interviewed—cutting off the lower tail. Also, while the normal distribution goes on forever in both directions, humans' ages don't—they cannot be below zero and rarely exceed 100. So, the coefficient of kurtosis is telling us something about the distribution of ages that is useful, even if it might have been fairly obvious.

Helpful hint: Even if a distribution has only one thick tail, statistical packages will report that the distribution is platykurtic. If the distribution is also skewed, it's a safe bet that the thick tail will be on the side of the distribution opposite the long tail.

Here are just a few quick quiz questions so you can be sure that you've mastered the idea of kurtosis.

CHECK QUIZ 5.4

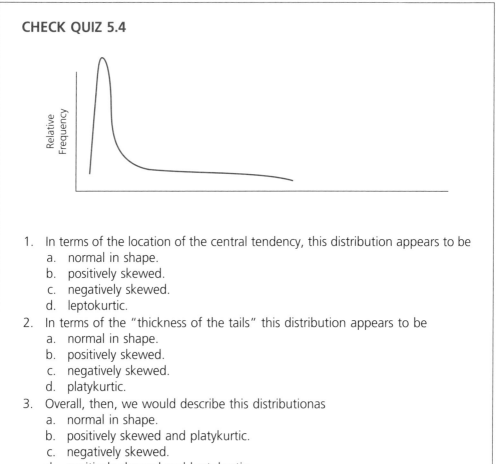

1. In terms of the location of the central tendency, this distribution appears to be
   a. normal in shape.
   b. positively skewed.
   c. negatively skewed.
   d. leptokurtic.
2. In terms of the "thickness of the tails" this distribution appears to be
   a. normal in shape.
   b. positively skewed.
   c. negatively skewed.
   d. platykurtic.
3. Overall, then, we would describe this distributionas
   a. normal in shape.
   b. positively skewed and platykurtic.
   c. negatively skewed.
   d. positively skewed and leptokurtic.

Example

THE COEFFICIENT OF KURTOSIS

Kurtosis refers to how peaked a distribution is, when compared to the shape of the standard normal distribution.

The following histogram shows the distribution of the percentage of the population who can read, across a sample of 107 nations during the mid-1990s. A normal curve with the same mean and standard deviation as the sample data has been superimposed on the histogram (black continuous curve).

Example

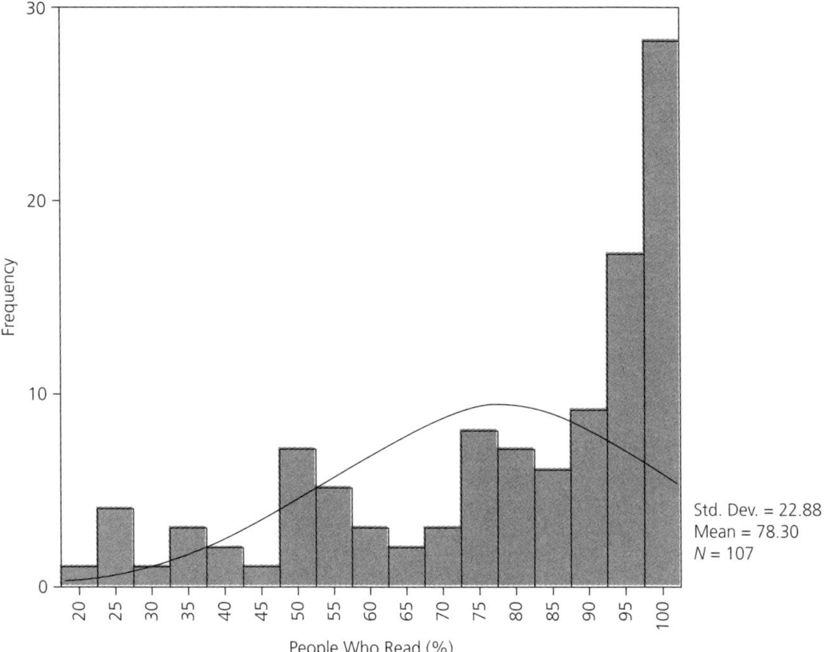

Kurtosis may be summarized as the "fourth moment" of the distribution. That is, the formula for the calculation of the coefficient of kurtosis (Formula 5.2) uses the fourth power of deviations from the mean:

$$Kurtosis = \frac{\sum_{i=1}^{n} (x_i - \bar{x})^4}{(n-1)s^4} \tag{5.2}$$

The coefficient of kurtosis that is usually reported (by SPSS, for example) adjusts the formula by subtracting 3.0, which is the kurtosis of a normal distribution. This adjustment to make the measure one of excess kurtosis yields a measure that takes on negative values for a distribution that is flatter than the standard normal distribution, and positive values for a distribution that is more peaked than a standard normal distribution.

In our example data, the mean is 78.3 (i.e., on average across nations, 78.3 percent of the population can read). The number of cases is 107 in our sample. The standard deviation, calculated elsewhere, is 22.88. Raising the standard deviation to the fourth power, we get 274,190.15. Using a spreadsheet (not shown here), we computed the deviation of each case from the mean, raised the result to the fourth power, and then summed the values. The sum of the deviations raised to the fourth power for these data is 80,398,877.61.

(continued)

Example

Substituting these values into the formula, we obtain:

$$\begin{aligned}\text{Kurtosis} &= 80{,}398{,}877.61/(106 \times 274{,}190.15)\\ &= 80{,}398{,}877.61/29{,}064{,}156\\ &= 2.766\end{aligned}$$

Adjusting this to the standard normal distribution by subtracting 3.0, we obtain:

$$\begin{aligned}\text{Kurtosis} &= 2.766 - 3.0\\ &= -0.234\end{aligned}$$

As with skewness, the numerical value of the coefficient does not lend itself to a simple and intuitive interpretation beyond the obvious fact that it is negative—indicating that the distribution is somewhat flatter than a standard normal curve of the same mean and standard deviation.

Example

SKEWNESS AND KURTOSIS TOGETHER

Frequently, data collected in social science projects exhibit both skew and kurtosis: there will be a long (often thin) tail on one side of the distribution, and a thick tail on the other side. Consider the distribution of ages in the General Social Survey from earlier in this chapter:

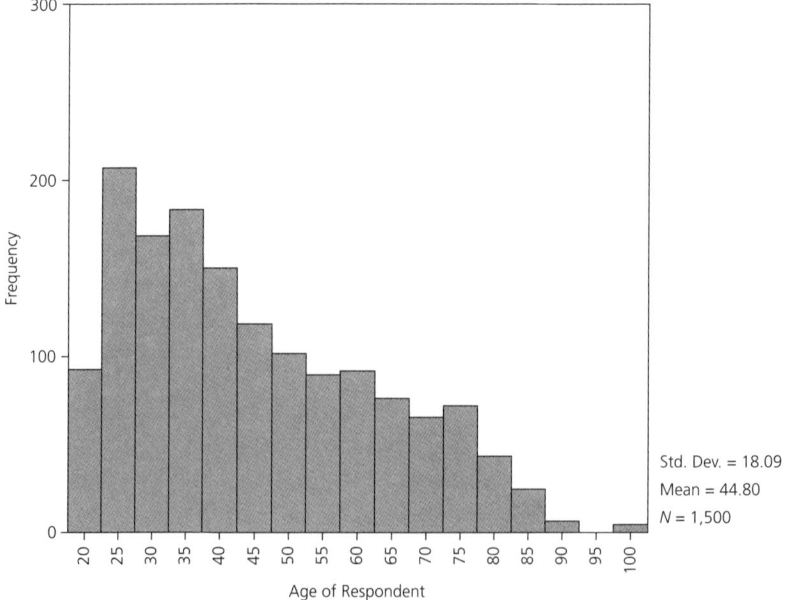

Example

The researchers at the National Opinion Research Center (NORC) who sponsor the General Social Survey limit survey participants on the basis of age: only people 18 and above are allowed to respond to the survey, but they (obviously) get a fair number of respondents at that lower end of the age continuum. In contrast, there are relatively few people at the other extreme. It is reasonable, then, that the graph shows positive skew (the long tail, which is not all that thin in this case, points off to the right), and shows many cases piling up on the left side. In this case, you should expect SPSS to report a negative score for kurtosis, suggesting a platykurtic distribution. Even if the distribution is skewed such that the opposite tail is thin, a distribution with one thick tail will result in a negative kurtosis score.

Using Excel to Calculate Skewness and Kurtosis

The coefficients of skewness and kurtosis are easily calculated using functions in the Excel spreadsheet.

The keywords for skew and kurtosis in MS Excel are:

Skew = skew( )
Kurtosis = kurt( )

Just type an equal sign, the keyword, and an opening parenthesis into a cell (type "=" and select the function from the functions menu).

Type the range of the data between the parentheses, or (better) click and drag through the data, and then type a closing parenthesis.

SOME COMMON DISTRIBUTIONAL SHAPES

So far in this chapter, we've talked about some features of distributions that we often want to describe statistically—in addition to the central tendency and dispersion. The general ideas of how many modes a distribution has, skewness, and kurtosis have been explained.

In describing the shape of a distribution, statisticians tend to use the normal or bell-shaped distribution curve as a point of comparison. This is because the normal distribution is a particularly important distribution in statistics (particularly in inferential statistics). Because the normal distribution is so important, we will spend a whole chapter on it (Chapter 6).

But there are a number of other distributional shapes that you will want to have some familiarity with, both because they actually occur in many social science variables and because they play important roles in inferential statistics.

The purpose of this brief section is just to introduce you, in a quite informal and nonmathematical way, with some of the distributions that you will encounter when you describe real variables, or when you do statistical inference.

Equal Probabilities

If I flipped a coin 100,000 times and recorded how many times it came up heads and came up tails, the result would be pretty close to a 50,000-to-50,000 split; if I made a bar chart of this result, the two bars would be very close to being equal in height. If I tossed a die, I would end up with a bar chart with six bars of about equal height. Both of these are examples of distributions where all the possible outcomes are equally likely.

Most social phenomena that we study in the real world do not turn out to have distributions with equal probabilities. Even the distribution of the variable "sex" usually has unequal probabilities (in most places and times, women live longer than men, so there are usually more women than men in most populations). Indeed, much of what social science attempts to do is to provide testable explanations of why outcomes are *not* equally likely in the real world.

A distribution in which every outcome is equally likely is rarely observed with real nominal or grouped ordinal variables. But it is often useful to compare observed distributions to this ideal type, just as we often compare observed distributions of interval/ratio variables to the ideal type of the normal distribution. Distributions where all outcomes are equally likely occur frequently in statistics as a baseline against which we can compare observed distributions.

Exponential Distributions

The bell curve has its greatest relative frequency at its midpoint, and the relative frequencies become smaller the further we move from the midpoint. In the equal probabilities distribution, the relative frequencies are the same across the entire distribution. Both of these are symmetric. That is, the shape of the distribution above and below the midpoint are mirror images of one another.

Many social science variables do not have symmetric distributions. Many variables cannot be symmetric because the thing they are measuring cannot be. Consider the variable "number of children in your family." Many variables in social sciences have limits on the range of possible scores, and often have their highest relative frequency at the minimum or maximum score.

There are a number of different "ideal type" distributions that are sometimes used to describe variables like these. Probably the most common are exponential, power, and reciprocal ($1/x$). We won't make much further use of these in statistical analysis in this book. But it is important for you to remember that many social science variables can be described with simple mathematical tools—and that not all social science variables are normally distributed.

Some Statistical Distributions: Z, t, F, and Chi-Squared

In inferential statistics we often compute a test statistic from our sample data. This test statistic is then compared against an ideal type of distribution called a sampling distribution. We'll have much more to say about all of this, beginning in Chapter 7.

There are a number of "ideal type" distributions (in addition to the normal distribution and the equal probabilities distribution) that are used in inferential statistics. The most common ones are:

The t- or Student's t−distribution is really a family of distributions. Individual t-distributions are selected for comparison with sample data on the basis of sample size. Every member of the family is much like the standard normal distribution, in that all are unimodal, continuous, and symmetrical, and all have a mean of 0. When used for comparison with large samples, the t-distribution is shaped just like the Z distribution; as sample sizes decrease, the shape of the t-distribution used for comparison becomes more and more platykurtic. This distribution is often used instead of the Z distribution when we are working with small samples.

The F-distribution is another family of distributions, all of which contain only positive values, and all have varying degrees of skewness and kurtosis, depending on the problem under consideration. The F-distribution is used when we are studying differences between several groups on an interval/ratio variable.

The chi-squared distribution is yet another family of distributions. It is like the F family in that it is limited to positive values and has a varying degree of skewness and kurtosis depending on the number of groups that we are comparing. We will be using it when we study differences among several groups on nominal variables.

SUMMARY

The central tendency and dispersion of a distribution are usually the two most important aspects of the shape of the distribution. Usually these are the main things that we want to describe, and they are usually what our theoretically derived hypotheses make predictions about. But other aspects of distributions can be important as well.

The box-and-whiskers plot is a very useful graphical device for visualizing most aspects of the shape of an interval/ratio variable. It can be particularly useful for describing similarities and differences in the shape of the distributions of a variable between several samples or groups of observations.

Distributions can be described in terms of how many high points they have. Many distributions, like the normal distribution, have a single area where relative frequencies are highest—unimodal. Some distributions may have more than one relatively large group of cases—bimodal or multimodal.

Distributions of variables that can be ranked or measured on an interval scale may differ in skewness—the extent to which the central tendency is not in the center of the distribution of scores.

Distributions of variables that can be ranked or measured on an interval scale may differ in kurtosis—the extent to which the numbers of cases in the tails of the distribution are greater or less than in a standard bell curve.

There are a number of "ideal type" distributions that play important roles in descriptive and inferential statistics, because they serve as standards against which we compare the distributions of observed variables, or statistics computed from observed variables. The standard normal distribution, equal probabilities distribution, exponential distributions, and certain specialized statistical distributions (t, F, chi-squared) are among the most important of these theoretical baseline distributions.

Of all the distributions that we've examined, the normal or bell curve distribution plays the most important role in statistical analysis. In the next chapter, we will learn more about this distribution.

KEY TERMS

bimodal

box-and-whiskers plot

kurtosis

leptokurtic

multimodal

normal distribution

platykurtic

positive and negative skewness

skew/skewness

unimodal

CHECK QUIZ ANSWERS

Quiz 5.1 Answers: 1. (d); 2. (a); 3. (b)
Quiz 5.2 Answers: 1. (F); 2. (d); 3. (F); 4. (T)
Quiz 5.3 Answers: 1. (a); 2. (a)
Quiz 5.4 Answers: 1. (b); 2. (d); 3. (b)

EXERCISES

Using data from the 2000 U.S. Census Bureau's Public-Use Microdata Samples (PUMS) data, a researcher has used SPSS to prepare a histogram of total family incomes of respondents (excluding respondents with incomes of $1,000,000 or more). A baseline normal curve has been added to the graphic.

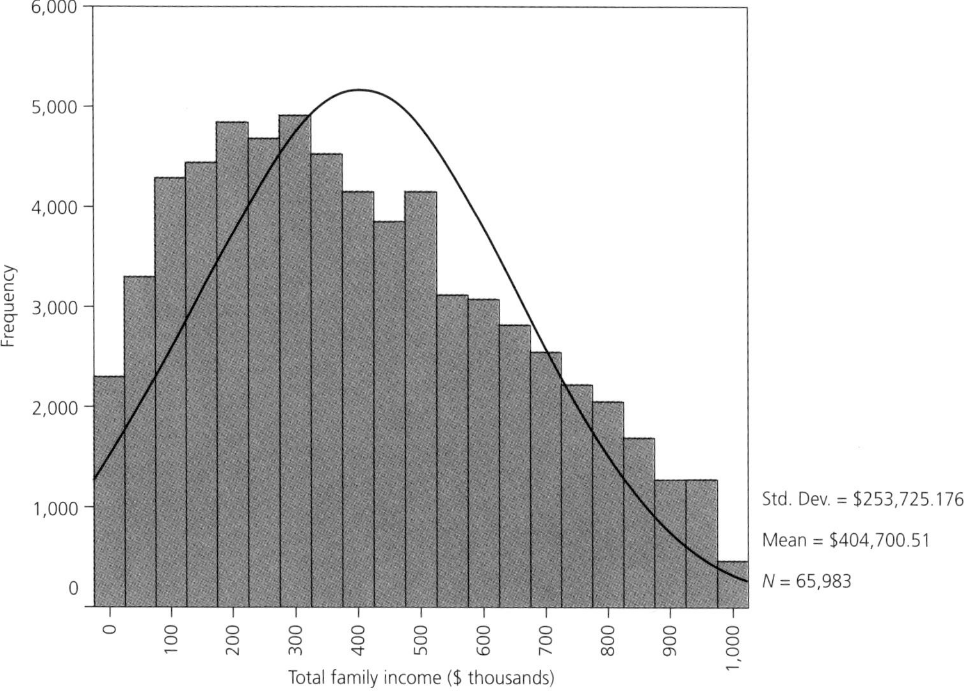

1. Describe the distribution in terms of its mode(s).
2. Describe the distribution in terms of its skewness.
3. Describe the distribution in terms of its kurtosis.

Here are the descriptive statistics, calculated with SPSS, that go with the graphic:

Statistics: Total Family Income

N	65,983
Mean	404,700.51
Median	371,000.00
Standard deviation	253,725.176
Skewness	0.390
Std. error of skewness	0.010
Kurtosis	−0.774
Std. error of kurtosis	0.019

4. Compare the mean and median to describe the skewness of the distribution.
5. Provide a short interpretation of the value of the coefficient of skewness.
6. Provide a short interpretation of the coefficient of kurtosis.

A researcher has examined the distribution of the variable "average years of school completed" measured across 162 nations in the world during the mid-1990s. Using SPSS, the following histogram was produced. Use this histogram to answer the questions.

World Data Set ca. 1995

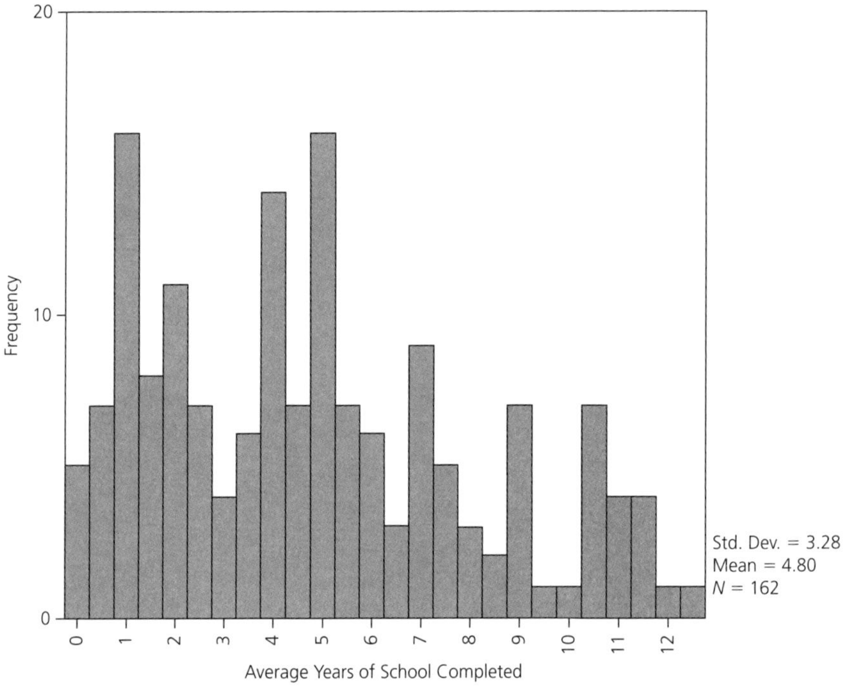

7. Describe the shape of the distribution in terms of its modes.
8. Describe the shape of the distribution in terms of its skewness.
9. Describe the shape of the distribution in terms of its kurtosis.

SPSS was also used to calculate descriptive statistics for the distribution of average years of schooling across world nations. Here is an edited table of the results. Use this table to answer the questions that follow it.

Average Years of School Completed

	Statistic	Std. Error
Mean	4.8000	0.25742
Median	4.4500	
Std. deviation	3.27644	
Skewness	0.517	0.191
Kurtosis	−0.651	0.379

10. Compare the mean and median to describe the skewness of the distribution.
11. Provide a short interpretation of the value of the coefficient of skewness.
12. Provide a short interpretation of the coefficient of kurtosis.

The following is a box-and-whiskers plot that compares the family incomes (from the 2000 U.S. Census PUMS, excluding incomes over $1,000,000) of households where heads of households identified themselves as "black or African American" or not black.

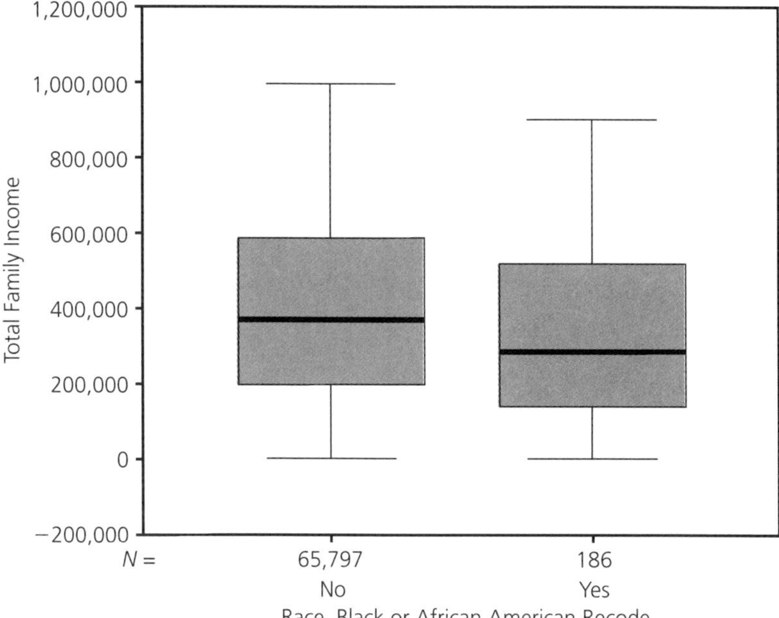

13. How do the central tendencies of the distributions of income differ between the two groups? What is your evidence?
14. How does the degree of dispersion of incomes differ between the two groups? What is your evidence?
15. How do the distributions of income of the two groups differ in terms of their skewness? What is your evidence?

Our researcher has grouped the nations of the world into four very large regions (Asia, Africa, Europe, and the Americas). The researcher then created a box-and-whiskers plot to compare the average years of school completed across the regions. Here is the result. Use this to answer the questions that follow the graphic.

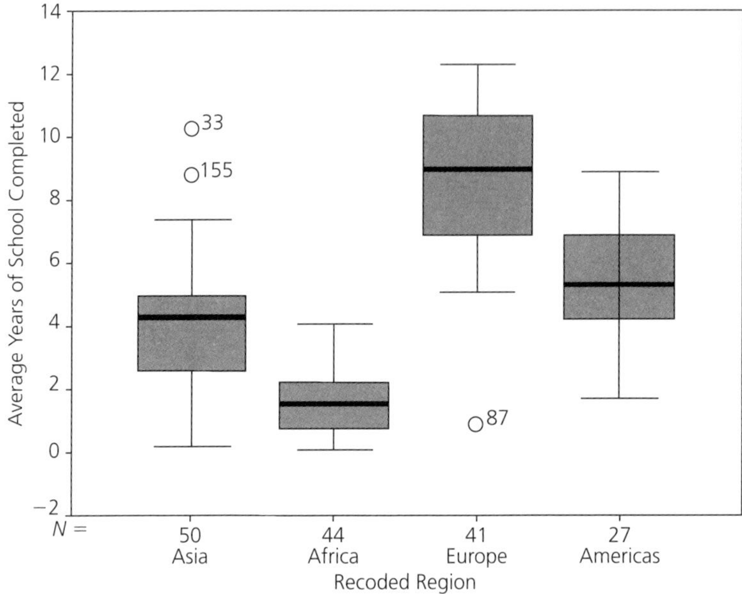

16. How do the central tendencies of the distributions of average years of schooling differ among the regions? What is your evidence?
17. How does the degree of dispersion in the distributions of average years of schooling differ among the regions? What is your evidence?
18. How do the shapes of the distributions of average years of schooling differ among the regions in terms of their skewness? What is your evidence?

USING SPSS FOR COMPARING NUMERICAL INDEXES AND GRAPHICS OF DISTRIBUTIONAL SHAPE

For this discussion, we will generate statistics about a distribution and compare them to a graph of the distribution.

To follow along, you could open one of the data sets available to you in SPSS and choose an interval/ratio variable for analysis.

Potentially helpful hint: At the far right-hand side of the window in Variable View is a column devoted to "Measure." It can be set to nominal, ordinal, or scale (what we refer to as "interval/ratio"). The folks at NORC, who provide the General Social Survey, are reasonably careful about setting the measure descriptor for each variable, but other sources generally aren't. This means that it's a good idea to look at a frequency chart of a variable that's listed as scale before you decide that it actually is one.

In SPSS, choose Analyze → Descriptive Statistics → "Explore..."

- Move the variable of interest into the dependent list.
- Click the "Statistics..." button.
  - Make sure that "Descriptives" is selected; click Continue.
- Click the Plots button.
  - Select stem-and-leaf and histogram; click Continue.
- Click OK.

The output should look something like the following:

Descriptives

			Statistic	Std. Error
AGE OF 1ST PERSON	Mean		49.38	.383
	95% Confidence interval for Mean	Lower Bound	48.63	
		Upper Bound	50.13	
	5% Trimmed Mean		48.98	
	Median		48.00	
	Variance		281.028	
	Std. Deviation		16.764	
	Minimum		18	
	Maximum		97	
	Range		79	
	Interquartile Range		25	
	Skewness		.291	.056
	Kurtosis		−.628	.112

(continued)

Where is the mean in relation to the median? Remember, if the distribution is skewed, the mean will usually pull in the direction of the skew. In this case, the mean is a little larger than the median, suggesting that there is some positive skew. Note at the bottom of the table that the skewness measure confirms this.

Note that when extreme values have been trimmed from the top and bottom, the resulting mean ("5% Trimmed Mean") is a little smaller, another sign that in the untrimmed distribution the mean is getting tugged to the right.

The kurtosis value is negative, suggesting that there is at least one fat tail, which we will expect to find opposite the long tail (that is, we'll probably see it on the left side of the distribution).

Having checked the statistics, it's time to look at the graph:

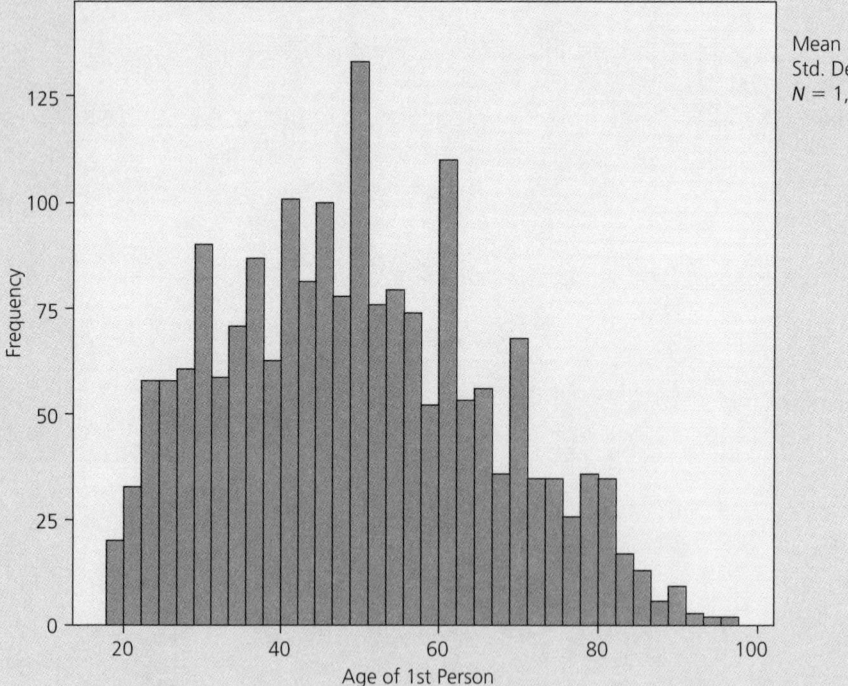

The histogram shows a distribution that is skewed to the right, and, while both tails are fairly thick, the left tail is decidedly fatter than the right tail.

A similar picture is given by the stem-and-leaf plot:

```
AGE OF 1ST PERSON Stem-and-Leaf Plot

Frequency      Stem  &  Leaf

    11.00         1 .  8999
   100.00         2 .  0001111122222233333333334444444
   149.00         2 .  5555555556666666666777777777788888888899999999
   155.00         3 .  00000000000011111122222222233333333333444444444444
   185.00         3 .  5555555555556666666666666777777777777777888888888899999999999
   182.00         4 .  000000000000111111111122222222222223333333333333333444444444444
   230.00         4 .  5555555555555555666666666666666666677777777777777888888888888888999999999999999999
   197.00         5 .  0000000000000001111111111122222222222222333333333333333444444444444
   165.00         5 .  555555555555566666666666667777777777788888889999999999
   163.00         6 .  0000000000011111111111111111122222222233333333334444444444
   113.00         6 .  55555555555556666666777777888889999999
   101.00         7 .  0000000001111112222222333344444444
    78.00         7 .  55555666777778888889999999
    52.00         8 .  00001111122233334 4
    21.00         8 .  55666789
    11.00         9 .  0013&
     4.00         9 .  5&

Stem width :    10
Each leaf :     3 case (s)
```

This plot, or graph, is another invention of John Tukey.

The first thing to notice is that the overall shape of the stem-and-leaf plot is the same as that of the histogram, although it has been turned 90°.

The main feature of this kind of graph is that it shows the actual values in the data, although it takes a little getting used to in order to see them.

This particular plot is of ages. The ages in question all take two digits to represent (e.g., 18, 50, 65). The first of these two digits is displayed under the Stem heading. The second of these two digits is displayed under the Leaf heading.

Before we go any further, note that at the bottom of the plot, SPSS reports that each leaf represents three cases; in actuality, each leaf may represent fewer cases.

At the top of the chart, the "1" under the Stem heading is the 1 of 18 and 19. Since there's one 8 in the Leaf section, we know that there are (approximately) three cases of age 18; the three 9s mean that there are (up to) nine (three symbols × three cases per symbol) cases of age 19.

After this, each decade of age is broken up into two parts, the first part with digits 0 to 4, and the second part with digits 5 to 9, with each part occupying one line in the plot. So, the three zeros (0s) in the first 2 stem mean that there are about nine 20s in the data.

This graph makes it easy to see that there are many cases with age 55, but only three (or so) of age 87.

As with the histogram, it's easy to see that people pile up on the younger end of things, while there are fewer people with extreme ages on the older side of things in the sample distribution.

Chapter 6

The Normal Distribution

LEARNING OBJECTIVES

When you have finished this chapter, you will be able to:

- Describe the general characteristics of the histogram of a normal distribution.
- Define the unique properties of the standard normal (Z) distribution.
- Convert the scores of any interval/ratio variable into standard normal (Z) scores.
- Find the percentile of any case, and the percentage of cases that fall above any chosen value or between any two chosen values of a normally distributed variable.

INTRODUCTION TO THE NORMAL DISTRIBUTION

In the preceding chapter we learned some tools for describing the shape of the frequency distribution of scores on a variable. Some distributions of scores are unimodal, and some are not; some are skewed positively, some negatively, and so on.

In this chapter we are going to take a closer look at one particular distributional shape that is widely used in both descriptive and inferential statistics: the normal or Gaussian or Laplacian distribution. The normal distribution is used with variables measured at the interval/ratio level.

In this chapter, we will focus on how the normal distribution can be useful in describing the distributions of scores of cases in a sample. The normal distribution is also used as a tool in inferential statistics in a somewhat different way. We will study the use of the normal curve in inferential statistics in the next several chapters.

You are probably already familiar with the normal distribution, because it is a widely used ideal type in both scientific and not-so-scientific discussions. The normal curve is also commonly called the "bell-shaped curve" or "bell curve," because the histogram of a normal distribution looks something like the silhouette of a bell (at least some bells). We will describe the features of this curve in a general way, using the somewhat more precise language that we learned in the previous chapter for describing the shape of distributions.

It's actually a misstatement to talk about the normal curve. The normal distribution is a family of distributions with the same bell shape, but different central tendencies and dispersion. One particular normal curve—the normal curve that describes a distribution with a mean of zero and a standard deviation of 1—is so widely used that it has been given the name of the ***standard normal distribution***. In statistics, the standard normal distribution is also referred to as the Z distribution.

The Z distribution is useful because we know what percentages of all the cases fall above, below, or between any two values of this distribution. In a Z distribution, for example, we know that only about 5 percent of all cases have scores that are smaller than -2.0 or bigger than $+2.0$.

The Z distribution turns out to be more generally useful, because other nonstandard normal distributions can be converted into standard or ***Z-score*** form. We look at the relationship between any normal distribution and the standard normal distribution a little more closely. We then discuss how the distribution of any interval/ratio variable can be converted to Z-scores. We will see how this is useful to describe the location of a case as a percentile, and to find the percentages of cases that have any values we might choose to describe.

These tools are useful for describing the location of a case in a normally distributed variable, and they will also be used (many times!) in the chapters that follow on statistical inference and hypothesis testing.

PROPERTIES OF NORMAL DISTRIBUTIONS

The bell-shaped or normal curve is an ideal type of frequency distribution that serves as a reference point. It also happens to be a reasonably good description of the actual distributions of scores on many interval/ratio variables used by social scientists. Scores on many educational tests, and people's responses to questions in attitude surveys, for example, are often normally distributed (at least approximately). In Figure 6.1, we've used SPSS to draw an "ideal type" normal curve (the solid curved line) based on data that we generated randomly using the mathematical equation that describes the probability density function for a standard normal distribution. Note that the actual distribution (the histogram) looks like a bell-shaped curve generally, but isn't perfect. Even though a variable may really be normal if we observed every possible outcome, the distribution may not be exactly normal in any one real-world sample.

The ***normal distribution*** is actually a family of distributions that have the same bell shape, but differ in their central tendency (mean) and dispersion (standard deviation). The particular normal distribution that we have graphed happens to have a mean of −0.01 and a standard deviation of 0.96.

All normal distributions share a number of common features that make them quite useful.

FIGURE 6.1 Theoretical Standard Normal Curve and Random Normal Data

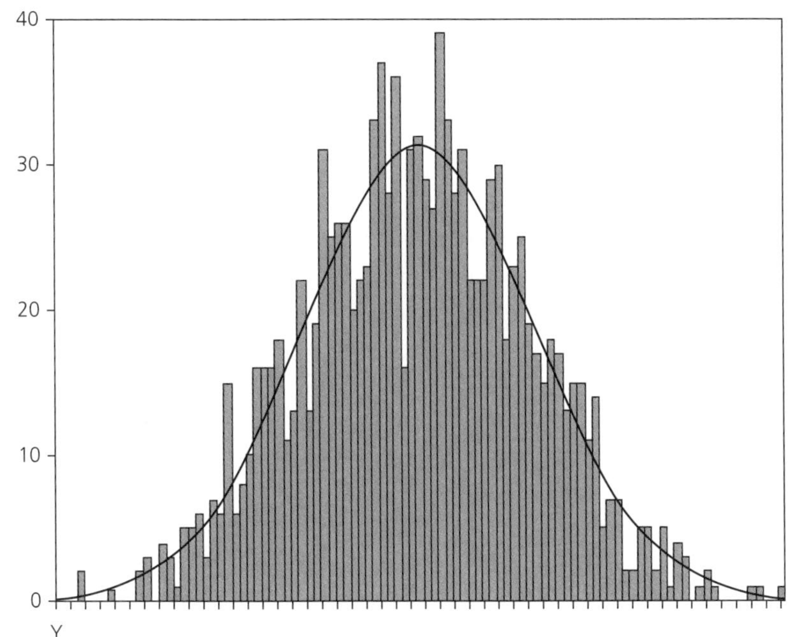

Range

The normal distribution covers the full range of possible positive and negative values. While most of the cases cluster around the central tendency of the normal distribution, the expected frequency of any score is nonzero.

This feature of the normal distribution makes it very useful for representing "ideal type" or theoretical distributions where any score is possible. The real distributions of measured attributes in samples, however, are often bounded—scores below or above certain values are just not possible. So the distributions of real data are often only approximately normal.

Symmetry

A very important feature of the normal distribution is that it has the same shape on both sides. If we started at the middle of the distribution (i.e., at the mean), the shape of the curve above the mean (i.e., as we move to the right) is a mirror image of the shape of the curve below the mean.

The symmetry of the normal distribution turns out to be a useful property. Cases that are above and below the mean by the same amount are also mirror images of each other in terms of the proportions of all cases that fall above or below them. So, when we are working with the normal distribution, we only need to describe one-half of the distribution; the other half is simply its mirror image. This makes doing calculations with the normal distribution easier.

Unimodality

The normal distribution is unimodal. That is, there is a concentration of cases at just one point along the range of possible values.

The mode of the normal distribution falls at the mean and median. Since the distribution is symmetric and has a mode right at its central tendency, the mode, median, and mean of a normal distribution all have the same value.

Not all empirical distributions, of course, are unimodal, let alone normal. Among empirical distributions that are unimodal, the mode does not necessarily fall at the middle of the range. But many social science variables have distributions that are approximately normal, and the normal distribution can be a useful tool for describing and studying them.

Shape

The shape of the curve of the histogram of the normal distribution is what makes it unique. Most cases are near the middle of the distribution. As we move away from the mean, the number of cases becomes fewer. At first, the change is slow; there are almost as many cases near the mean as at the mean. As we go a bit further, the frequencies begin to drop very rapidly. As we go further still, the rate of decline in frequencies slows—as the expected frequencies get closer and closer to zero.

Imagine that you were shooting at a target, but that you were not a perfect marksman. Most of your shots would be on or quite close to the bull's-eye. As you got further away from the center of the target, the density of shots would become less and less. It turns out that many processes that are aimed at a target (the central tendency or true score—the bull's-eye), but are subject to random error, will be well described by normal distributions.

The shape of this curve, or function, can be described mathematically with a rather complicated equation. The key things about the equation are that the shape of any particular normal distribution can be calculated directly if we know the mean and the standard deviation. That is, any possible normal distribution's curve is completely determined if we know these two parameters (if a curve is describing a population) or statistics (if the curve describes a sample).

CHECK QUIZ 6.1

1. All normal distributions cover the range of values
   a. from zero to positive infinity.
   b. from negative infinity to positive infinity.
   c. from −1.96 to +1.96.
   d. from zero to 2.56.
2. The normal distribution is symmetric; the values below ________ are distributed in the same way as those above it.
   a. the mean
   b. the median
   c. the mode
   d. all of these
3. The mean of a normally distributed variable is equal to
   a. zero.
   b. one.
   c. the median and mode.
   d. the standard deviation.
4. In a normal distribution, most of the scores are
   a. near the central tendency.
   b. located at the extreme values.
   c. equally distributed across all possible values.
   d. positive.

THE STANDARD NORMAL, OR Z, DISTRIBUTION

One particular version of the normal distribution, called the "standard normal" or "Z" distribution, is widely used in statistics as a tool for working with any normal (or approximately normal) variable.

Properties of the Z Distribution

The standard normal, or Z, distribution is a normal distribution with a mean of zero and a standard deviation of 1.

In a standard normal distribution, then, a case that is at the mean of a variable has a score (called a standard normal score or ***Z-score***) of zero. If a case has a score that is above the mean, its standard normal score will be a positive number. If a case has a score below the mean, its Z-score will be a negative number.

Suppose that the average grade point average (GPA) in a class is 2.87. Sandra happens to have a GPA equal to the class mean. Sandra's standard normal score or Z-score is zero. Fred's GPA of 2.54, sadly, is below the class average. Fred's standard normal score will be a negative number.

Z-scores, or standard normal scores, tell us how far from the mean a case falls—measured in standard deviation units. If a case has a score that happens to fall exactly one standard deviation above the mean, its Z-score is +1.0.

Suppose I have an IQ score of 115; if the mean score of IQ is 100 and the standard deviation of IQ scores is 15, then my Z-score is +1.0. If my IQ score happens to be 85, it is one standard deviation (i.e., 15 points) below the mean (i.e., 100), so my Z-score would be −1.0.

The standard normal distribution is helpful in describing where a case falls relative to the mean of the distribution. Positive scores fall above the mean, and negative scores fall below the mean. How far above or below the mean is expressed in terms of units of variation of the distribution—the standard deviation. So, Z-scores tell me how many standard deviations above or below the mean a case falls.

If we are comparing the scores of cases on different variables that are measured with different scales, Z-scores can be a very useful tool. I might say, "Sally has an IQ of 115, and achieved 16 years of formal education." This makes sense, and does describe Sally's scores on two important variables. But, suppose I said that "Sally has a Z-score of +1.0 on IQ, and also has a Z-score of +1.0 on education." This would tell me that Sally's scores were above average on both variables. In fact, they would say that her scores were one standard deviation above average on both variables. This is a useful way of talking about Sally—because it tells us whether she is above or below the average, and by how much.

In fact, we can go further than saying that a case falls above or below the mean by a given amount of standard deviation units. This is because we know what proportions of cases fall above and below any given score in the Z distribution. So, in addition to saying that "Sally is one standard deviation above the mean," I can go further and say that "84 percent of people have scores lower than Sally; only 16 percent of people have scores that are higher"—or Sally is at the 84th percentile.

We can make this statement because we know, for any standard normal distribution:

- Approximately 68 percent of cases have scores that fall within one standard deviation of the mean (i.e., between Z-scores of -1.0 and $+1.0$).
- Approximately 95 percent of cases have scores that fall within two standard deviations of the mean (i.e., between Z-scores of -2.0 and $+2.0$).
- Approximately 99 percent of cases have scores that fall within three standard deviations of the mean (i.e., between Z-scores of -3.0 and $+3.0$).

So, if we know the Z-score of a case on any variable (assuming that the variable is approximately normally distributed), we can say what proportion of all cases have higher or lower scores.

Z-Scores Defined

Because it is possible to find the proportion of cases in a standard normal distribution that fall below or above any given Z-score, it is useful to be able to express the real score of any case as a Z-score. This can be done very easily by applying a simple formula (Formula 6.1):

$$Z_i = \frac{X_i - \overline{X}}{s} \tag{6.1}$$

What the formula says is: the Z-score of any individual on the variable X (Z_i) can be found by subtracting the mean of X ($\overline{X}$) from the person's score (X_i), and dividing the result by the standard deviation of X (s).

What this formula does is convert the scores of any distribution to scores on a standard distribution.

In the numerator, we subtract a case's real score from the mean. The result is a positive number if the case is above the mean, or a negative score if the case is below the mean.

After we have deviated scores from the mean—that is, expressed how far they are from the mean in the positive or negative direction—the formula says that we should divide the mean deviation by the standard deviation. This expresses the deviation of a case from the mean in terms of multiples of the standard deviation. For example, if the standard deviation of a given distribution is 20 and a case falls 20 points above the mean (i.e., the mean deviation is +20), then the Z-score will be +1.0 (i.e., 20/20).

CHECK QUIZ 6.2

1. The standard normal distribution has a mean of ________ and a standard deviation of _________.
   a. one, zero
   b. zero, zero
   c. one, one
   d. zero, one
2. What is the (approximate) percentage of cases that have values between the Z-scores of -2 and $+2$ of a normal distribution?
   a. 100 percent
   b. 66.7 percent
   c. 95 percent
   d. 99 percent
3. Fred got a Z-score of -1.0 on his first midterm. This means that
   a. his score was at the class average.
   b. his score was above the class average.
   c. his score was below the class average.
   d. his score is mathematically impossible!

Now you can find the Z-score for any case's real score—if you know the mean and the standard deviation. If you know a case's Z-score, you can find out the proportion of cases above or below it. We'll show how in the next section.

WORKING WITH STANDARD NORMAL (Z) SCORES

If the distribution of an interval/ratio variable is approximately like that of the normal (bell-shaped) curve, we can use Z-scores to determine the proportion of cases that have scores below any score we happen to choose, or that have scores higher than any score we happen to choose. We can also find the proportion of all cases that fall between any two scores or outside of the interval between any two scores.

Calculating Standard Normal (Z) Scores

Z-scores (aka standard normal scores) describe the location of a score in terms of how many standard deviations it lies above or below the mean of the variable. This can be seen from the formula for calculating a Z-score (Formula 6.1):

$$Z_i = \frac{X_i - \overline{X}}{s} \tag{6.1}$$

The first step in calculating a Z-score for a particular case (call it case "*i*") is to take the score of the case we are interested in (X_i) and subtract the mean ($\bar{X}$). This is the *deviation of the case from the mean*, and will be negative if the case falls below the mean, and positive if the case falls above the mean.

The second step is to take the deviation, and divide it by the standard deviation of the variable (s). This converts the deviation into multiples of the standard deviation.

If we do this transformation (i.e., subtract the mean and divide by the standard deviation) for all cases in a sample, the resulting normal variable will have a mean of zero (because we deviated all cases from the mean), and a standard deviation of 1.

The distribution of the median household incomes across the 50 U.S. states is approximately normal, as shown in the Figure 6.2. The average across the states was \$33,875.40, and the standard deviation was \$5,183.52.

Let's calculate the Z-scores for a number of different points on the distribution in Table 6.1.

If the median income in a state happened to be \$20,000, we would first subtract the mean (\$33,875.40). This yields a deviation of −\$13,875.40. We then divide this deviation

FIGURE 6.2 Median Household Income, 1995

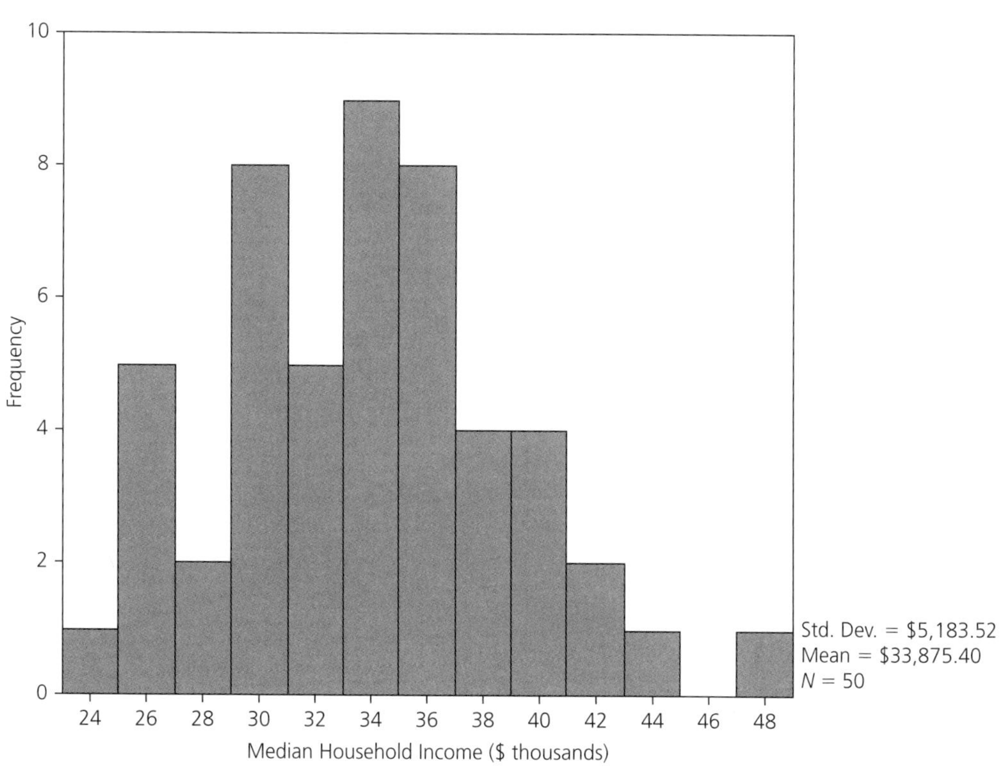

TABLE 6.1 Calculation of Z-Scores for Some Values of Median Income

Median Income ($)	Mean ($)	Deviation ($)	Std. Dev. ($)	Z-Score
20,000	33,875.4	−13,875.4	5,183.52	−2.677
25,000	33,875.4	−8,875.4	5,183.52	−1.712
30,000	33,875.4	−3,875.4	5,183.52	−0.748
35,000	33,875.4	1,124.6	5,183.52	0.217
40,000	33,875.4	6,124.6	5,183.52	1.182
45,000	33,875.4	11,124.6	5,183.52	2.146

TABLE 6.2 Proportions of Cases Having Values Lower and Higher Than Selected Values of Median Income

Median Income ($)	Mean ($)	Deviation ($)	Std. Dev. ($)	Z-Score	Lower	Higher
20,000	33,875.4	−13,875.4	5,183.52	−2.677	0.004	0.996
25,000	33,875.4	−8,875.4	5,183.52	−1.712	0.044	0.956
30,000	33,875.4	−3,875.4	5,183.52	−0.748	0.227	0.773
35,000	33,875.4	1,124.6	5,183.52	0.217	0.587	0.413
40,000	33,875.4	6,124.6	5,183.52	1.182	0.881	0.119
45,000	33,875.4	11,124.6	5,183.52	2.146	0.984	0.016

by the standard deviation ($5,183.52) and the result is −2.677. An income of $20,000 falls 2.677 standard deviations below the mean. We've shown the Z-scores for a few other values. Obviously, you could calculate the Z-score for any particular income you were interested in, using the same algorithm.

Finding the Percentile of a Score Using Z-Scores

Once the score of a case has been transformed into a Z-score, we can use a table of areas under the standard normal (Z) distribution to find the proportion of cases that have scores lower or higher than it has.

Using the table of Z-scores and probabilities in the Appendix, we've looked up each of the Z-scores we calculated in Table 6.1, and added the proportion of cases with lower scores to our table. If we know the proportion of cases that have lower scores, we can easily calculate the proportion of cases that have higher scores—because the proportions below and above any score must sum to 1.00. Table 6.2 presents the results.

If a state had an average income of, for example $30,000, it has a Z-score of −0.748, about three-fourths of one standard deviation below the mean. The table helps us determine that 0.227 (22.7 percent) of all states would have median incomes less than this; so 0.773 (or 77.3 percent) of states would have higher incomes.

CHECK QUIZ 6.3

1. To find the Z-score of a case, we follow the algorithm:
   a. Subtract the mean from the score, and divide by the standard deviation.
   b. Subtract the score from the mean, and divide by the standard deviation.
   c. Subtract the standard deviation from the score, and divide by the mean.
   d. Subtract the score from the standard deviation, and divide by the mean.
2. Hector scored 55 on the statistics exam. The class average was 50, with a standard deviation of 5. Hector's Z-score on the exam was:
   a. 0
   b. −1
   c. +1
   d. One cannot tell from the information given.

Once we've found the proportion of cases that fall below any particular scores, we can find the area that falls between them. Suppose that we wanted to know what percentage of states had incomes between $35,000 and $45,000. Starting with the $45,000 state, we know that 98.4 percent of all cases will have scores lower than it. 58.7 percent of all cases will have scores below $35,000. So, it must follow that the percentage of cases with scores between $35,000 and $45,000 is 98.4 − 58.7 or 39.7 percent. Since all cases must fall somewhere, 100 − 39.7 or 60.3 percent of the cases have incomes either below $35,000 or above $45,000.

FINDING AREAS "UNDER THE CURVE"

The main purpose of calculating Z-scores is to be able to describe the location of cases in terms of percentiles.

Rather than saying that a person has a score of 115 on a variable where the mean is 100 and the standard deviation is 15, we could say that the person's Z-score is +1.0. That won't speak to most people, though. If, instead, we said, "This person has a score of 115, which means that this person's score is higher than about 85 percent of the other people in the sample" (or this person is at the 85th percentile), this is usually a more effective way of communicating about the location of a case.

If we know that a variable has an approximately normal distribution, we can use Z-scores to find the percentage of cases that have lower scores or the percentage of cases that have higher scores. We can also find out what percentages of cases have scores between any two values, or outside of the range between two values. We do this by finding the percentage of cases that fall in ***areas "under the curve"*** for the normal distribution.

Finding any given area in a normal distribution is a pretty easy process:

First, calculate the Z-score value of the score or scores that you are interested in. You can do this by hand, make a formula in a spreadsheet of a mathematical program, or have a statistical program calculate and save the Z-scores of the cases' values.

Second, draw a little sketch of a bell curve, and make a mark that shows where the value or values that you are interested in lie; shade the area of interest (that is, the area above or below a point, the interval between two points, or the area outside an interval). Making a little sketch will keep you from getting confused as you go through the process.

Third, use mathematical, statistical, or spreadsheet software to look up the probability density below (or above, or between the value and the mean of) the Z-score of interest. There is a table for doing this in the Appendix. Almost all printed statistics textbooks have tables of Z-scores and probabilities, or you can easily locate one on the web (try a Google search for "Z-scores" or "standard normal probabilities").

Last, once you've found probabilities associated with the value or values of interest, do whatever simple math is necessary to come to your final answer. Let's look at some examples of how to do problems of this type.

Areas Beyond (More Extreme Than) a Score

Suppose that we were interested in a variable that happened to have a mean of 100 and a standard deviation of 20.

Now, suppose that we wanted to know: "What percentage of people have scores more than 120?"

We first calculate the Z-score of 120 by subtracting the mean ($120 - 100 = 20$) and then dividing by the standard deviation ($20/20 = +1.0$).

Second, we make a little sketch (see Figure 6.3). A Z-score of +1.0 is one standard deviation above the mean. We are interested in the area above that.

FIGURE 6.3 Area of the Standard Normal Curve above +1 Standard Deviation

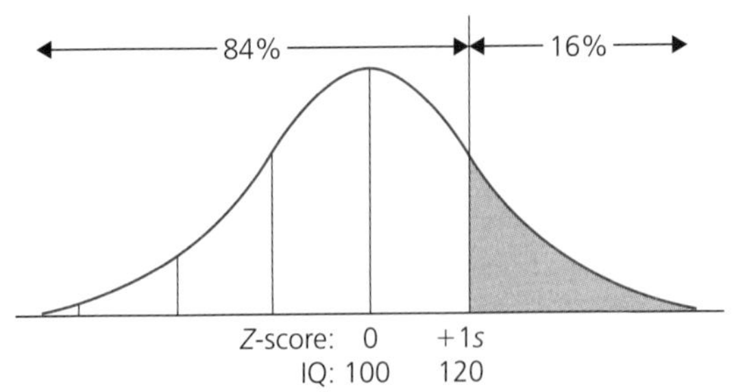

FIGURE 6.4 The Normal Distribution Function in Excel

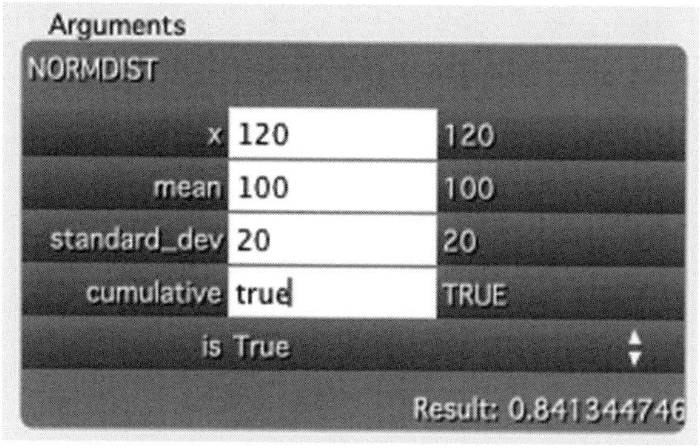

Arguments
NORMDIST
x 120 120
mean 100 100
standard_dev 20 20
cumulative true TRUE
is True
Result: 0.841344746

Look up the probability associated with the Z-score. There are lots of ways to do this; one good way is to use Excel's statistical functions (NORMDIST), as shown in Figure 6.4.

We entered the value we were interested in, the mean, the standard deviation, and the word "TRUE" (to tell Excel to calculate the probability). When we clicked on OK, Excel returned the value 0.84134474. Note that this is the area up to a Z-score of +1.0. So, about 84 percent of the cases fall below the Z-score of +1.0.

We're interested in the percentage above this score. Since the probabilities must add up to 1.00, if 0.84 of cases fall below a Z-score of +1.0, then 0.16 must fall above this value.

Remember that the normal distribution is symmetric! If we know that the proportion of cases with scores bigger than 1.0 is 0.16, then we know that the proportion of cases with scores less than −1.0 is also 0.16.

Areas between the Mean and a Score

We know that the mean of a normal distribution falls at the 50th percentile (because the normal distribution is symmetric), and has a Z-score of zero.

Suppose, for example, we are interested in the value 120 in a distribution where the mean is 100 and the standard deviation is 20. We want to know what percentage of all cases fall between the mean (100) and 120.

First, draw a little sketch (as in Figure 6.5). Make one mark at the value we're interested in. Make a second mark at the mean. Shade the area between these two points—so we know what we are trying to find.

Second, calculate the Z-scores. This time, we need two Z-scores: the Z-score of 120 and the Z-score of the mean. Earlier, we already calculated the Z-score and probability for the value of 120. For the mean, we don't have to do any calculations. We know that the mean's Z-score is zero (by definition). And we know that 50 percent of the cases fall below this

FIGURE 6.5 Area Between the Mean and +1 Standard Deviation

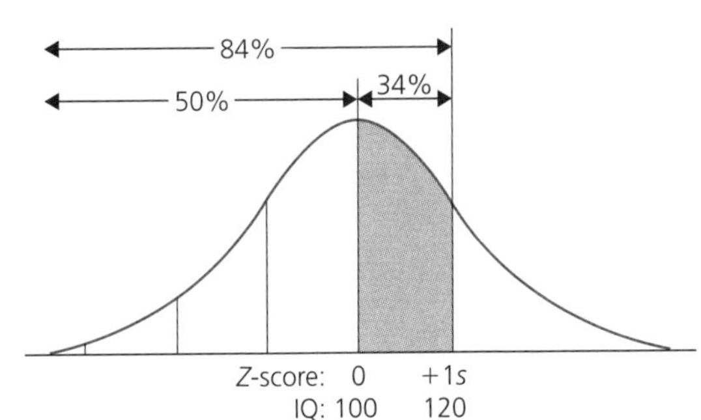

value—because the mean and median of a normal distribution have the same value (by definition).

Third, get the probabilities. We know from doing the earlier calculation that 84 percent of the cases have values less than +1.0. We also know, by definition, that 50 percent of the cases have values below 0.

Fourth, find the proportion of cases falling between the mean and a score of 120. Since 84 percent of all cases fall below 120 and 50 percent of cases fall below 100 (the mean), the area has to be equal to 84 percent minus 50 percent or 34 percent. That is, 34 percent of the cases fall between the mean and the Z-score value of +1.0.

What percentage of the cases would fall between the mean and plus or minus one standard deviation? Sixteen percent of the cases fall above +1.0 (because 84 percent of the cases fall below it). But the distribution is symmetric; so 16 percent of the cases must fall below a Z-score of −1.0. Therefore, about 32 percent of cases have scores that are more than one standard deviation away from the mean.

Areas between Two Scores

Using the same approach, we can calculate the percentage of cases that fall within or without any interval we might choose. Here's an example using some different numbers.

Suppose we have a variable, X, with a mean of 3.0 and a standard deviation of 0.50 (the variable X might be, for example, GPA values of students in this class).

Let's suppose, for some reason, that we wanted to know the percentage of cases that had scores greater than 2.0 but less than 3.5.

First, draw a little sketch (see Figure 6.6). On the normal curve, mark the mean as being 3.0 (the mean), and draw lines at +1.0 and −1.0 standard deviations (that is, 3.0 + 0.5 or 3.5; 3.0 − 0.5 or 2.5). On the little sketch, shade the area we're interested in: the area between 2.0 and 3.5.

FIGURE 6.6 Finding the Area between Two Scores

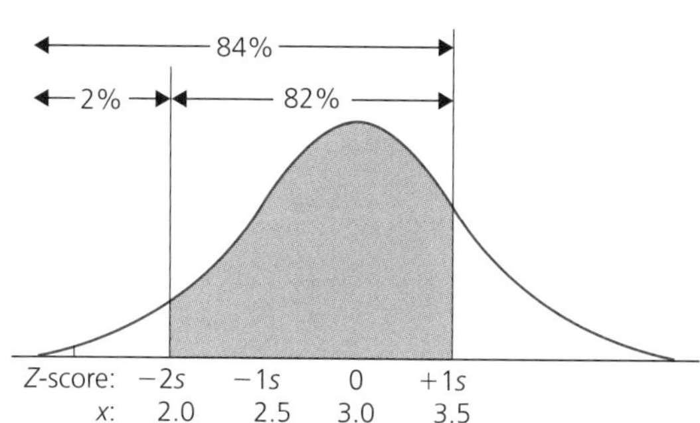

Second, calculate the Z-scores of each of the points of interest. The Z-score for 2.0 is:

$$(2.0 - 3.0)/0.5 = -1.0/0.5 = -2.0$$

(Note that the Z-score is a negative number, because 2.0 is below the mean.)

The Z-score for 3.5 is:

$$(3.5 - 3.0)/0.5 = 0.5/0.5 = +1.0$$

So, we are trying to locate the proportion of cases that fall between Z-scores of −2.0 and +1.0.

Using either tables or software, we find that the proportion of cases falling below −2.0 is 0.02275 and the proportion of cases falling below +1.0 is 0.841345. That is, only about 2 percent of cases fall below the lower boundary of the interval of interest; 84 percent fall below the upper boundary of the interval of interest.

So, the area in the interval is the difference, or about $0.84 - 0.02 = 0.82$. Thus, about 82 percent of the cases fall between 2.0 and 3.5.

You'll need to practice in order to master the skill of finding areas under the normal curve. Do the problems, and study the examples! It's important to master these ideas by doing some problems by hand. In the real world, we usually use spreadsheets or statistical software to find areas under the curve.

SUMMARY

In this chapter we've examined one "ideal type" distribution quite closely. The normal distribution in general, and the standard normal or Z distribution in particular, are so widely used in statistics that you need to be pretty comfortable with them.

We began by examining the normal distribution's general properties. We noted that it is a distribution that includes all possible positive and negative values. It is symmetric (that is, the shape above and below the central point are mirror images of each other). It is unimodal, and the mode equals the median and the mean. It has a distinctive shape that has most cases fairly close to the mean. In fact, we saw that any normal distribution has about two-thirds of its cases within one standard deviation of the mean, about 95 percent of its cases within two standard deviations, and over 99 percent of the cases within three standard deviations of the mean.

The normal distribution is an ideal type. All normal distributions have the same shape, but they may differ according to the value of the mean and the value of the standard deviation.

One particular normal distribution, with a mean of zero and a standard deviation of 1, has been chosen as the standard normal distribution. This particular normal distribution is also called the Z distribution.

Any distribution can be expressed as a function of the standard normal distribution by adjusting its mean and its standard deviation. This means that any score in any distribution can be expressed as a normal or Z-score. We saw that the Z-score is calculated by subtracting the mean from a particular score and dividing the result by the standard deviation. The Z-score expresses how many standard deviations above (positive scores) or below (negative scores) the mean a given case falls.

Calculating Z-scores is worth doing because they enable us to find the proportions of cases that fall above or below any particular score we may choose. When working with Z-scores, it is a good idea to draw a little sketch of a normal distribution, locate the mean and standard deviations, and mark the value or values of interest. Once one has calculated Z-scores, the percentage of cases falling above or below the score, or between the score and the mean, can be calculated by hand, with a spreadsheet, with statistical or mathematical software, or with printed tables.

By working with the percentages of cases that fall above or below given Z-scores, you can calculate the proportion of cases that fall in any area of a normal distribution that you might choose. This is often a very useful way of describing the location of a case or range of cases relative to others.

Z-scores are a useful tool for describing the locations of cases. We will shortly see that Z-scores are also used extensively in inferential statistics and hypothesis testing.

KEY TERMS

areas "under the curve"

normal distribution

standard normal distribution

Z-score

CHECK QUIZ ANSWERS

Quiz 6.1 Answers: 1. (b); 2. (d); 3. (c); 4. (a)
Quiz 6.2 Answers: 1. (d); 2. (c); 3. (c)
Quiz 6.3 Answers: 1. (a); 2. (c)

EXERCISES

1. Here are some data on the sex ratio (number of females per 100 males) in a sample of world nations in the mid-1990s. You will note that the distribution is not exactly normal due to outlier cases, but most of the cases are pretty much normally distributed. The mean and standard deviations of the distribution are given in the output that follows.

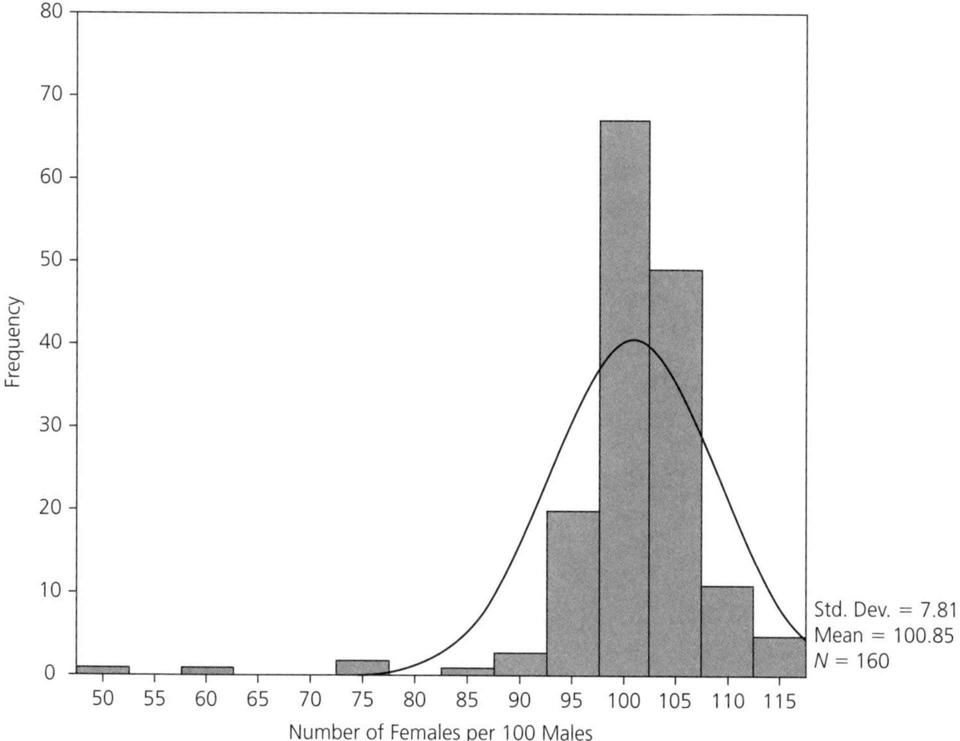

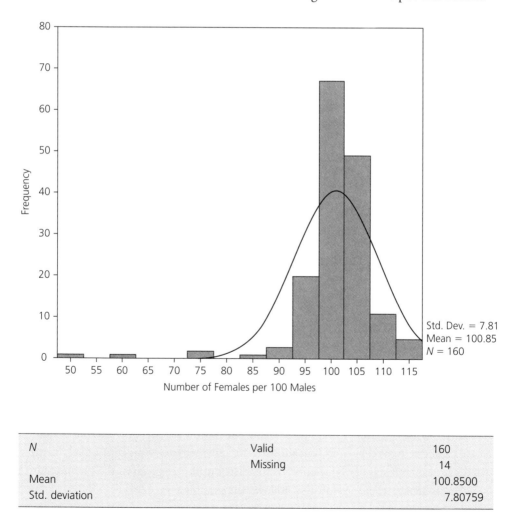

N	Valid	160
	Missing	14
Mean		100.8500
Std. deviation		7.80759

If the distribution of the variable "#females per 100 males" was normal, complete the following table:

Observed Sex Ratio	Z-Score	Proportion of Countries with Lower Sex Ratios	Proportion of Countries with Higher Sex Ratios
80			
85			
90			
95			
100			
105			
110			
115			
120			

2. On a midterm examination, the distribution of scores is approximately normal, with a mean of 80 and a standard deviation of 10. Calculate the percentage of students who scored:
   a. Below 60.
   b. Below 70.
   c. Below 80.
   d. Below 90.
   e. Above 65.
   f. Above 75.
   g. Above 85.
   h. Above 95.
   i. Between 63 and 82.
   j. Between 70 and 90.
   k. Between 60 and 100.
   l. Between 76 and 86.

Here are some data on the number of abortions per 1,000 live births in the 50 states of the United States during 1992. You will note that the distribution is not exactly normal due to outlier cases, but most of the cases are pretty much normally distributed. The mean and standard deviation of the distribution are given in the graphic. Use these data to answer the question that follows the graphic.

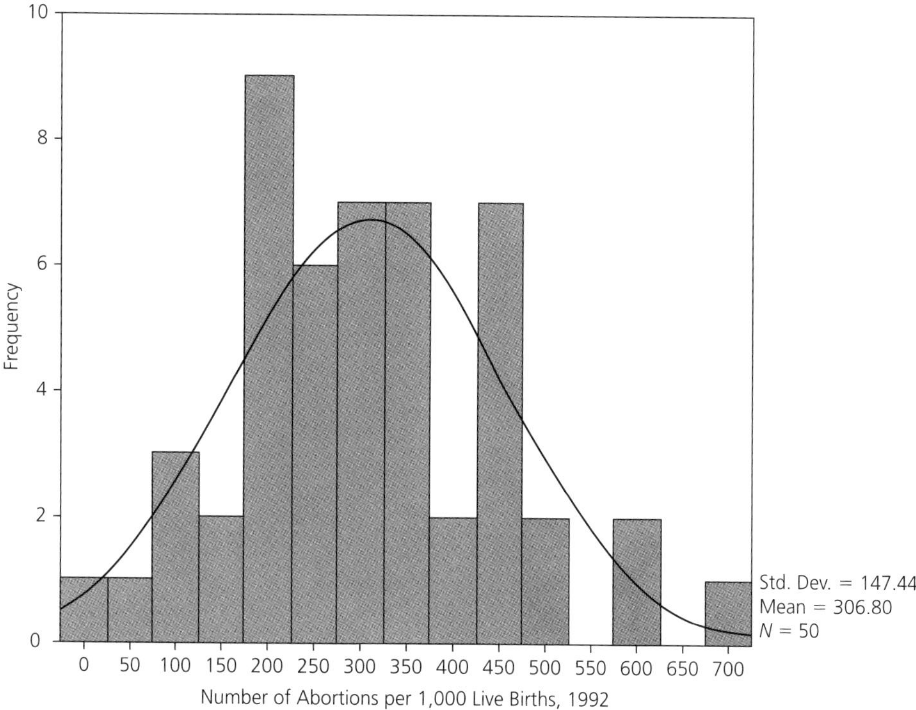

3. Let's accept the idea that the distribution of the variable "abortion rates" is approximately normal. Using the information in the graphic and the table of probabilities for the standard normal distribution, complete the following table.

Abortion Rate	Z-Score	Percentage of States with Lower Abortion Rates	Percentage of States with Higher Abortion Rates
100			
150			
200			
250			
300			
350			
400			
450			
500			

4. In the United States during 1995, there was a good bit of variation among the states in the rates of poverty. Across all 50 states, the average percentage of families who had incomes below the poverty level was 12.9 percent. The standard deviation was 4.1 percent. If this variable was normally distributed, what percentage of all states would be estimated to have poverty rates that were:
   a. Below 12.9 percent.
   b. Below 10 percent.
   c. Below 5 percent.
   d. Above 12.9 percent.
   e. Above 15 percent.
   f. Above 20 percent.
   g. Between 5 and 10 percent.
   h. Between 10 and 15 percent.
   i. Between 15 and 20 percent.

USING EXCEL TO WORK WITH THE NORMAL DISTRIBUTION

MS Excel has some easy functions to find areas under the curve of any distribution or the Z distribution, and to create Z-scores.

In MS Excel, the =normdist( ) formula returns the "normal cumulative distribution" when given an arbitrary value, the mean, and the standard deviation of a distribution. This is the same value shown in the Standard Normal Scores (Z-Scores) table in the Appendix, which is the area under the curve to the left of an arbitrary value.

The "standardize" formula returns a Z-score after you've given it an arbitrary value, and the mean and standard deviation of the distribution from which that value might have been selected.

The "normsdist(z)" formula (notice the keyword is normsdist) will return the area under the curve for any Z-score that you place between the parentheses.

The keywords for Z-score functions are:

Standard normal cumulative distribution	=normdist(x,mean,sd,True)
Z-score	=standardize(x,mean,sd)
To find the standard normal cumulative distribution if you know Z	=normsdist(z)

You can set up a spreadsheet to show areas under the curve. The value that appears in the cell labeled "to left" is the proportion of the distribution to the left of the arbitrary value. Here is an example of a worksheet:

	A	B	C	D
1	Case no.	Calories		
2	1	186		
3	2	181		
4	3	176		
5	4	149	Mean	=AVERAGE(B2:B25)
6	5	184	sd	=STDEV(B2:B25)
7	6	190		
8	7	158	value?	150
9	8	139	Z:	=(D8-D5)/D6
10	9	175	to left:	=NORMDIST(D8,D5,D6,TRUE)
11	10	148	to right:	=1-D10
12	11	152		
13	12	111		
14	13	141	lower value?	140
15	14	153	upper value?	150
16	15	190	outside:	=(NORMDIST(D14,D5,D6,TRUE)+(1-NORMDIST(D15,D5,D6,TRUE)))
17	16	157	between:	=(NORMDIST(D15,D5,D6,TRUE))-(NORMDIST(D14,D5,D6,TRUE))
18	17	131		
19	18	149		
20	19	135		
21	20	132		
22	21	173		
23	22	191		
24	23	182		
25	24	190		
26				

For questions about what proportion of the distribution lies above or below an arbitrary number, put the arbitrary value in the cell next to the "value?" label.

For questions about what proportion of the distribution lies between two values or beyond both values, use the lower two cells in column D. The cell labeled "outside:" shows the proportion of the distribution that is less than the lower value *or* greater than the upper value. The cell labeled "between:" shows the proportion of the distribution that lies between the two values.

Note: Be sure to put the smaller of the values in the "lower value?" cell, or you'll get strange results.

PART II

Inference and Hypothesis Testing

Chapter 7

Basic Ideas of Statistical Inference

LEARNING OBJECTIVES

When you have finished this chapter, you will be able to:

- Explain and apply the key ideas of sampling variability, sampling distributions, and standard errors.
- Understand the idea of a point estimator of a population parameter, and the properties of unbiasedness and efficiency.
- Apply these ideas to calculate the standard errors of population means and proportions.
- Determine confidence intervals around population means and population proportions.

INTRODUCTION TO STATISTICAL INFERENCE

It's pretty common to hear something like this:

"A new survey, out today, indicates that 63 percent of the American public feels the President is doing a good job. The margin of error in the poll is plus or minus 2 percent."

How do the people who did this survey know that "the American public" feels this way? Did they actually get the opinions of every member of the public? Of course not. That would be impractical. Instead, they talked to a small random sample of people. And, on the basis of that sample, the survey takers made an *inference* about the feelings of the people in the whole population.

Since the pollsters didn't talk to everyone, they don't know that the real percentage is exactly 63 percent. This is their best guess. But, the pollsters are also able to say that they are pretty sure that the real percentage in the whole population is probably pretty close (plus or minus 2 percent) to this value.

The pollsters are using the tools of ***statistical inference*** to make a best guess about the value of a ***population parameter*** (the true proportion of the whole population who feel the President is doing a good job) on the basis of a ***sample statistic*** (the proportion who feel this way among those polled). The statistical term for this is the ***point estimate*** of the population parameter.

The pollsters are also using the tools of statistical inference to tell us how accurate the results are likely to be. They are giving us a margin of error, so that we know the chances that they might be wrong, and by how much. The statistical term for this the ***confidence interval.***

In this chapter, you'll master all of these ideas, and apply them to assessing the confidence we have in estimating population means and proportions from the information in simple random samples.

The Basic Problem of Inferential Statistics

When we execute a particular study, there is usually a gap between the cases that we observe directly and those that we would like to generalize to. When I perform an experiment in the social psychology laboratory with 100 first-year students, how do I know that the result would be similar to what I would have observed if I had chosen a different set of 100? If I do a ***sample survey***, how do I know that the 1,000 respondents are typical of all the people whom I might have interviewed?

If I make an empirical generalization as the result of studying some people, how can I be sure that the result is really typical of all people? For example, I may note that the social networks of middle-class persons that I asked contained a smaller proportion of kinship ties than the social networks of working-class persons I interviewed. This is an interesting result. But, since I didn't actually talk to *all* middle-class people and all working-class people, how do I know that my result generalizes?

When I use empirical observations to test a hypothesis, how do I know that I would get the same result if I chose new observations? If my theory predicts that men will score higher on a test of "propensity to take risks" than women, and the results are consistent with this idea in one sample of persons, can I be confident that it will also be true in the next group I sample?

When we make observations in the social sciences, we are almost always using samples. Our interest, though, is usually broader; we would like to make generalizations about the populations that we took the samples from.

The bad news is that we can never be certain that the results we observe in a sample are really true for the whole population from which we took the sample. The only way to be sure is to do a census—study every member of the population of interest. This is almost always impractical or impossible in social science work.

The good news is that under some circumstances we can use the tools of statistical inference to have a better knowledge of how much confidence we should place in our results. We can never be sure that the results from a sample are right. Sometimes, though, we can be rather precise about the chances that they are.

In this chapter we introduce the basic ideas of inferential statistics. The "inference" that we are talking about is inferring the values of parameters in the whole population on the basis of the statistics from a single sample. When we report the results of a study using statistics that describe the sample we studied, we can sometimes go further—and also report how confident we can be that we would get similar results if we did the study again on a different sample. This helps us, and our readers, to know just how much faith to put in the results. If we can never be sure, at least we can know how unsure we are!

Uses of Inferential Statistics

Inferential statistics are used in two main ways: setting confidence intervals and performing hypothesis tests. Both are applications of the same basic ideas. We study the idea of confidence intervals in this chapter; we will turn to hypothesis testing in Chapter 8 (and beyond).

Confidence intervals (like the statement about "margin of error" in the previous example) are important because they allow us report how confident we (and our readers) should be about the results from a sample. If I told you, in one case, that the mean income of students in a sample was $15,000 and I was 95 percent sure that the population mean fell between $5,000 and $25,000, you shouldn't be very impressed. There is a wide margin of error. If, instead, I was able to say that the mean income of students in the sample was $15,000 and I was 95 percent sure that the population mean fell between $14,500 and $15,500, this is much more useful because the result is pretty reliable and precise.

Confidence intervals are an important tool for honest scientific reporting about results. When we share our results, we should also report how confident we are about them.

Hypothesis testing uses the same ideas, but turns them upside down. We begin with a guess about what the population value should be, derived from a theory (not from the sample data). We then look at the sample data and ask, "How likely is it that my hypothesis about the true population value is wrong—given what I see in the sample?" Obviously, if the sample looks very different from our prediction about the population, the theory that led to the prediction is probably (but not for sure) not a helpful one. If the values in the sample are a likely outcome if the theory about the population is true, then the theory is supported (but not proven). Inferential statistics are also used for this type of hypothesis testing.

Before we can learn to use confidence intervals or hypothesis tests, we need a bit of basic theory and terminology about inference.

SAMPLING CONCEPTS

In this section we introduce the most important concepts and terminology that you need to know to understand how we can make an inference from a sample statistic to a population parameter, and assess our confidence in that estimate.

There are many ways to draw samples. Indeed, entire courses are devoted to exploring different approaches to sampling. In your introductory methodology course, you probably discussed simple random sampling, systematic random sampling, stratified sampling, and cluster sampling. The appropriate methods of statistical inference do depend on how a sample is performed. In this book, we assume that simple random sampling has been used. This is a common approach in laboratory and small-scale empirical research. Simple random sampling is also assumed by most computer statistics packages.

Kinds of Probability Sampling

Social science research always involves observing empirical data. But we rarely actually observe every case (or every possible case) of the phenomena we are studying. Almost all social science research uses samples in one way or another.

The formal tools of statistical inference apply only to ***probability samples***. They should not be used when samples have been drawn by ***nonprobability*** means (e.g., purposely selecting typical cases, selecting high and low extreme score cases, etc.). This does not mean that nonprobability samples are a bad thing. Nonprobability samples have many very valuable uses in social sciences. But one should not apply inferential statistical tools to data arising from these kinds of samples.

The simplest kinds of probability samples are ones in which every sample element (i.e., case) of a bounded population has a known and equal probability of selection. For example, if there are 100 students in my class and I select 10 at random (with replacement) for a study, each of the 100 students has a 10/100 or 10 percent chance of being selected. The probability that any given student will be selected is known, and it is the same for all students. For another example, suppose that 50 students volunteer for my social psychology experiment, and I randomly assign 25 to the control group and 25 to the treatment group. The students who volunteered for the experiment are not a probability sample of all students; but the members of the treatment and control groups are random samples of the population of students participating in my study.

Simple random samples and systematic random samples are the most common kinds of "equal and known probability" samples. These are the kinds of samples we discuss in this chapter.

There are other kinds of samples that are probability samples and are widely used in the social sciences. While we won't talk much more about these here, a couple of words about stratified and cluster samples are in order. Though we cannot apply the techniques discussed here directly to stratified and cluster samples, we do know how such samples tend to differ from simple random sampling. So, it is often helpful to calculate inferential statistics for stratified and cluster samples as if they were random samples. But, let me emphasize, such results are only for the researcher's insight—they are not correct in any strict sense.

A ***stratified sample*** is one in which the population is first divided into groups (strata) on the basis of some known criteria (e.g., gender, age, community of residence, etc.). Samples are then drawn from each stratum with known probability. Usually, the probabilities are not the same across the strata. Stratified samples are most often used to assure that we have enough cases of each type (i.e., drawn from each stratum) to make comparisons between the groups. Stratified samples are particularly common when one stratum is a small percentage of the population and a simple random sample would not yield enough cases to represent the group.

Stratified samples are usually (but not necessarily) as good as or better than simple random samples in terms of assessing how confident we can be in making an inference from a sample to a population. The standard inferential statistics printed by computer packages are usually conservative estimates of how confident we can be when the data are drawn from a stratified sample (there are, however, cases in which this is not true—you should consult an expert).

A ***cluster sample*** is one where the population is already naturally divided into subpopulations; we first select subpopulations with known probability, and then select cases from each selected subpopulation with a known probability. If, for example, I wanted to draw a sample of students in a school district, I might select 10 of the 50 schools, and select 20 students from each of the schools I chose. Cluster samples are usually used when no list of the whole population is available, and/or where it is too expensive to use a full equal-probability sample.

Cluster samples are usually (but not necessarily) not as good as simple random samples in terms of assessing how confident we can be in making an inference from a sample to a population. The standard inferential statistics printed by computer packages are usually too liberal estimates of how confident we can be when the data are drawn from a sample involving clustering (there are, however, cases in which this is not true—you should consult an expert).

For the remainder of this book, we are going to assume that we are working with data from a sample that has been drawn with equal probabilities of selection.

Sampling Error

Let's suppose that my class has 100 students, and that exactly 50 are male and 50 are female. The population parameter of the variable "proportion of females," then, is 0.50.

Since it is too costly for me to study all 100 students, I decide to randomly select 10 to interview. I assign a random number to each of the 100 students, and use statistical software or a table (you can easily find tables of random numbers on the Internet) to select 10 people at random.

From the data that I collect from my sample of 10 students, I can calculate the sample statistic of the variable "proportion of females." If my sample is, in fact, exactly representative of the population, I will have randomly selected five males and five females, and my sample statistic of the proportion of females will be 0.50. That is, the sample statistic is (in this example) exactly equal to the population parameter.

But, am I certain that I will actually get a proportion of 0.50 in the sample that I drew? The answer is no. Since there are more than 10 women in the population, there is some chance that my sample proportion of women will be 1.00. There is also a chance that my sample includes no women at all—that the sample estimate of the proportion of women could be 0.00. And every outcome in between could have happened; I could have observed 0.00, 0.10, 0.20, . . . , 0.80, 0.90, or 1.00 in my sample. So, the sample statistic (in this case, a proportion) will not necessarily be equal to the population parameter.

The difference between the value of a sample statistic and the population parameter it is trying to estimate is called "sampling error." That is, the sample statistic may be wrong because I happened to draw a sample that wasn't exactly representative of the population. This is not a methodological flaw. Sampling error is normal, even if I have done everything exactly right in drawing my sample.

So, we have a dilemma. When I draw a sample and calculate a statistic, it is likely that the value of that statistic isn't the same as the real value of the population parameter. That is, the value of any sample statistic is an estimate of the population parameter, but is likely to differ from the true population value by some amount due to sampling error.

So, we can never be sure that the value of a sample statistic (it could be a count, a proportion, a mean, a partial correlation coefficient, or whatever) is really close in value to the true population value—the value that I would have found if I had actually done a census instead of using a sample.

Inferential statistics are really all about figuring out how far off my sample value might be, and the probability that it is wrong by various amounts. Once we know these things, we know how much confidence we should have in the results from our sample.

Sampling Distributions

To figure out how much confidence we should have in sample statistics as estimates of population parameters, we need to know more about the sampling errors that might have occurred. How can we figure out the likely size of our sampling error, so that we know how confident to be about how far our sample result might be from the population parameter?

This takes a little explanation, so be patient. Let's go back to the example of drawing a sample of 10 students from the 100 in my class and recording the sample statistic "proportion of females." Let's suppose that I draw one sample, and the proportion of females happens to be 0.40.

Now, let's draw another sample (using the full 100 cases again). The value of the sample statistic "proportion of females" in sample number two turns out to be 0.60. I draw a third sample, and the proportion of females turns out to be 0.40 again.

Imagine doing this many, many times; and each time, we record the value of the sample statistic "proportion of females." Sometimes this value will be 0.50, sometimes 0.60, sometimes 0.20, and so on. In fact, let's imagine that we drew every possible different sample of 10 people from my population of 100, and recorded the statistic "proportion of females" every time (this is a lot of samples!).

I can summarize the outcomes of the values of a statistic on repeated sampling with a frequency distribution. This distribution is called the sampling distribution of the statistic.

The ***sampling distribution*** of a statistic is simply the frequency distribution of the values of a statistic across all possible samples from a population. It is important because it shows us the distribution of the outcomes of the value of a statistic that would occur just by chance from one sample to another. That is, it gives us a picture of the ***sampling variability*** (or sampling error) of a statistic.

The sampling distribution of a statistic is like a regular frequency distribution of a variable in that it describes the distribution of scores across a sample. But it is quite different in that, in a sampling distribution, we are describing variation in a statistic across samples; in a regular frequency distribution, we are describing the variation of scores on a variable across individual cases.

Standard Errors

Because the sampling distribution of a statistic is itself a frequency distribution, we can use the same tools we would normally use to summarize it. That is, the sampling distribution of a statistic has central tendency, dispersion, and shape, just like the frequency distribution of cases' scores on a variable.

In order to avoid the confusion that can arise in working with "sample distributions of values of cases" versus "sampling distributions of the values of a statistic," some special terminology is used to describe sampling distributions.

The mean of the sampling distribution of a statistic is called the ***expected value of the statistic***. That is, if we were to take just a single sample (which is what we, in fact, do most of the time), the value of the statistic that we expect to find—the value that is most likely—is the average or mean of the sampling distribution. The mean of the sampling distribution of a statistic is the most likely outcome when we collect one sample and calculate the statistic in that one sample.

The standard deviation of the sampling distribution of a statistic is called the standard error of the statistic. The ***standard error*** of a statistic (just like the standard deviation of a

CHECK QUIZ 7.1

1. In terms of our confidence in making inferences from sample to population, stratified samples are usually __________ simple random samples; cluster samples are usually __________ simple random samples.
   a. not as good as; not as good as
   b. as good as; not as good as
   c. not as good as; as good as
   d. as good as; as good as
2. In a sampling distribution of sample means, most of the sample means will
   a. cluster around the true population value.
   b. be below the population mean in value.
   c. be above the population mean in value.
   d. not follow any particular pattern.
3. The mean age of all mall employees is 25. If the population distribution is normal, the mean of any sampling distribution of sample mean ages of mall employees will be
   a. within ± 1 standard deviation of 25.
   b. close to 25.
   c. 25.
   d. determined by the size of the distribution.
4. The standard error of the mean is the same thing as
   a. the standard deviation of the sample.
   b. the standard deviation of the population.
   c. the standard deviation of the sampling distribution.
   d. the variance of the sample.

variable) describes the average difference between any one sample statistic and the central tendency of the sampling distribution. This is important because the standard error of a statistic is measuring how different the value of a statistic in any one sample is likely to be from the average value of the statistic across all possible samples.

The standard error is a measure of expected sampling variability. It tells us how far the value of a statistic in any one sample is likely to be from the true value of the population parameter (assuming the statistic is unbiased—which we will discuss in the next section). This is really important! So let's illustrate this idea.

For example, suppose I told you that the mean income of students in a sample drawn from my class was $15,000, and that the standard error of this estimate was $5,000. What this means is that, if I drew another sample from the class and calculated the mean income in that sample, I might expect it to vary from the first sample by $5,000. That is rather a lot, so I shouldn't be too confident that the estimate of $15,000 is very accurate. If I told you that the mean income was $15,000 and that the standard error of this statistic was $500, you would be more confident in my estimate. That is, if I took another sample, the average income would probably be within $500 of what I got in the first sample. So, my confidence about the value of the statistic is greater.

We'll be more precise about the idea of confidence in our predictions a bit later in this chapter. For the moment, stop and take the check quiz to make sure you've mastered the ideas in this section.

CENTRAL TENDENCY ESTIMATES

So far we've been talking abstractly about the sampling distribution, expected value, and standard error of *any* statistic. You've got the general theory. But now we need to get specific and talk about *particular* statistics. We are going to focus on the statistics that describe the central tendency of variables in samples—means and proportions.

Studying the sampling distributions, expected values, and standard errors of means and proportions will teach you the ideas of statistical inference and how they are used. Different statistics (e.g., the standard deviation, the correlation coefficient) have different-looking sampling distributions and different formulas for calculating standard errors that we won't study closely. Statistical software will usually calculate and report standard errors of statistics. You need to know what they mean, and how to use them.

In this section, we focus on two ideas about how sample statistics relate to population parameters—bias and efficiency—that we can now describe rather precisely using the concepts of sampling distributions.

We will also see how standard errors of central tendency statistics (means and proportions) can be estimated from a sample.

Point Estimates

If you've been following the arguments we've been making about sampling variation and how the value of a statistic may differ from one sample to the next, you may be a bit puzzled about why any of this is useful.

The sampling distribution, expected values, and standard errors all refer to what we observe if we draw lots and lots of samples and examine the distribution of the values of a statistic (say a mean or a proportion) across all of these samples.

The problem is: when we do research, we don't take all possible samples—we usually take just a single sample. So, how is the idea of a sampling distribution useful if we have only one sample?

The answer is: statisticians have very carefully studied the relationship between the values of certain statistics in a single sample, and the overall sampling distributions of those statistics. When we use statistical inference tools, we are relying on the findings of past researchers about how the data in one sample can tell us about the sampling distribution.

One key question is about the relationship between the value of a statistic (say a mean or a proportion) in one sample and the population parameter that corresponds to the sample statistic.

For means and proportions, the value of the statistic that we calculate in a sample is our ***unbiased point estimate*** of the corresponding population parameter. That is, the mean from a single sample is our best guess about the population mean; a proportion calculated in a single sample is our best guess about the population proportion.

The reason that we can make the assertion that the value of a mean or a proportion in one sample is our best estimate of the population mean or proportion is that statisticians have proven these point estimators to be unbiased and efficient.

Bias and Efficiency

A sample statistic is an unbiased estimator of the population parameter if the expected value of the sampling distribution of the statistic is equal to the population parameter. This is a fancy way of saying that if, across many samples, the average value of a sample statistic converges toward the true population parameter, then the statistic is unbiased.

The normal formulas for calculating sample means and sample proportions give rise to unbiased estimators of population means and proportions. The formulas for some other statistics (like standard deviations, for example) need to have certain adjustments to be unbiased.

The fact that sample means and proportions are unbiased estimators of population means and proportions is important because it tells us that the value of a mean or a proportion that we calculate from a single sample is the best guess we can make about the value of the corresponding population parameter.

So, even though the value of a mean or a proportion will vary from one sample to another drawn from the same population, any one sample's result is a fair guess about the true population parameter.

Of course, since there is sampling variability, even though the result from one sample is a reasonable guess about the population parameter, it is not necessarily really equal to the population parameter.

When there is more than one way to estimate a population parameter with a sample statistic, the different approaches may have different standard errors. Smaller standard errors are more desirable, because that means that our sample statistics will usually be closer to the true population value than statistics with larger standard errors. Statistics that have smaller standard errors than others are said to be more ***efficient estimates***. In basic statistics, there is usually one accepted way of doing most tasks, and this way is usually the most efficient (in terms of having the smallest average errors).

For means and proportions, the sample estimators (i.e., the way we've learned to calculate these statistics) have been proven by statisticians to be unbiased and efficient. In very advanced statistical techniques, careful attention needs to be paid to bias and efficiency. For all of the statistics that we'll study in this book, we need not worry about this any further.

Standard Error of the Mean

So, we know that the sample mean is our best guess about the population mean. We know that the sample proportion is our best guess about the population proportion. They are unbiased and efficient.

But, how efficient are these statistics? That is, since we know that any one sample mean or proportion will differ from the true population parameter, the key question is: "How much?" Statisticians have developed a formula that estimates the size of the sampling variability—the standard error—of a mean based on the information that we have available in a single sample.

This is an extremely useful result, because it means that we can estimate the accuracy or efficiency of a sample mean as an estimator of a population mean from information we have available. Formula 7.1 is the critical formula:

$$\hat{\sigma}_{\overline{Y}} = \frac{S_Y}{\sqrt{N}} \tag{7.1}$$

The formula says: The estimated standard error of the mean ($\hat{\sigma}_{\overline{Y}}$) is equal to the standard deviation of the variable Y in the sample (S_Y), divided by the square root of the sample size.

Notice the notation in the formula. "Sigma hat" tells us this is a population value (because we are using Greek letters) and that it is an estimate (because we are using the "hat" or "carat" notation). Sigma, as we've seen before, refers to the population standard deviation.

It is the population standard deviation of the sample means (the subscript $\overline{Y}$). Terms on the right-hand side (the standard deviation of *Y*, and *N*) are things that we can observe from the one sample we have taken.

The formula is saying two important things about the standard error:

First, as the size of the sample we use increases, the size of the standard error decreases (at a decreasing rate). Very simply: the larger the sample, the more confident we are that the value of the mean in the sample is close to the true population mean. This should make sense. The more cases we observe, the more likely it is that the average of those cases presents a typical picture of the central tendency. It turns out that increasing sample size from very small to slightly larger makes a big difference in our confidence. If we already have a big sample, however, making it bigger still doesn't reduce our uncertainty much more.

Also note that the estimated standard error does not depend of what percentage of the cases in the population we observe—only on the number of cases observed. This is not intuitive, but it is very important. It means that we can get (close to) the same confidence about the population mean of a population of 100,000 people as we can about the mean of a population of 300,000,000 people using samples of the same sizes! Only in the case where the sample actually includes a substantial portion of a population does the proportion sampled matter.

The second important thing about the formula is: as the variability of the variable we are studying gets bigger (S_Y), the standard error gets bigger. This is a bit less obvious, but think about it for a moment. If we are studying a phenomenon that varies only a little from person to person (say, for example, the age of college freshmen), a small sample will probably give a pretty accurate answer about the mean age. If I were studying the ages of persons in a sample where there was more variation (for example, the entire population of the city I live in), there is more chance for sampling error in calculating the mean from a small sample.

Almost all of the statistics we will study have formulas that can be used to estimate standard errors from the information in a single sample. Statistical software packages routinely present the values of these estimates. Almost all of these formulas teach the same lessons: if the thing you are studying has more variation, you need to study more cases; and, regardless, big samples are always better than small samples.

Example

CALCULATING THE ESTIMATED STANDARD ERROR FOR A MEAN

The standard error (i.e., standard deviation of the sampling distribution) of a mean can be estimated from the information in a single sample. For large, simple random samples, the estimation formula is Formula 7.1:

$$\hat{\sigma}_{\overline{Y}} = \frac{S_Y}{\sqrt{N}} \tag{7.1}$$

Using the formula is quite simple:

1. Find the standard deviation of the case's scores on Y in the sample, in the usual way.
2. Find the square root of the sample size.
3. Divide the standard deviation by the square root of the sample size.

Suppose we were interested in the mean of the variable "blacks as a percentage of the population." We selected a sample of 20 U.S. states and collected information on the percentage of the population who were black. Here are the data. We've used SPSS, but you could also do this with just paper and pencil.

Case Summaries

	Name	Blacks as % of Population, 1994
1	Maine	0.40
2	New Hampshire	0.60
3	Vermont	0.30
4	Massachusetts	6.00
5	Rhode Island	4.70
6	Connecticut	9.00
7	New York	17.40
8	New Jersey	14.30
9	Pennsylvania	9.60
10	Ohio	11.10
11	Indiana	8.10
12	Illinois	15.30
13	Michigan	14.40
14	Wisconsin	5.40
15	Minnesota	2.70
16	Iowa	1.90
17	Missouri	11.00
18	North Dakota	.60
19	South Dakota	.60
20	Nebraska	3.80
Total *N*	20	
Mean	6.8600	
Std. deviation	5.64012	

The first step in calculating the estimated standard error of the mean is to calculate the standard deviation. This can be done by hand, but doing so is tedious. So, we've used the computer to estimate $s = 5.64012$.

(*continued*)

Example

The next step is to find the value of the square root of the sample size. The sample size is 20. Using a calculator, we find this value to be 4.47.

Last, we divide *s* by the square root of the sample size: 5.64012/4.47 = 1.26.

The estimated standard error of the mean, then, is 1.26 percent (since the variable was measured was "blacks as a percentage of the population"). That is, on average, we might expect that the mean percentage of blacks will vary from sample to sample (independent simple random samples of size 20) by 1.26 percent.

Example

USING EXCEL TO CALCULATE THE STANDARD ERROR OF A MEAN

MS Excel has no built-in formulas for computing the standard error of the mean, but you can cobble formulas together to accomplish this task. Here we want to calculate the standard error of the mean of the number of pizza boxes used on 25 days. The first panel shows how to calculate the count of the number of cases and the standard deviation. Then we use the square root function and a division to calculate the standard error.

◇	A	B	C
1	Pizza boxes		
2	76		
3	43		
4	6		
5	54		
6	8		
7	67	n:	=COUNT(A2:A25)
8	79	sd:	=STDEV(A2:A25)
9	36	sq rt of n:	=SQRT(C7)
10	9	SE:	=C8/C9
11	40		
12	3		
13	88		
14	64		
15	91		
16	40		
17	3		
18	91		
19	4		
20	74		
21	68		
22	41		
23	75		
24	14		
25	14		
26			

And here is the result:

◇	A	B	C
1	Pizza boxes		
2	76		
3	43		
4	6		
5	54		
6	8		
7	67	n:	24
8	79	sd:	31.5
9	36	of n:	4.9
10	9	SE:	6.4
11	40		
12	3		
13	88		
14	64		
15	91		
16	40		
17	3		
18	91		
19	4		
20	74		
21	68		
22	41		
23	75		
24	14		
25	14		
26			

Standard Error of a Proportion

There is also a simple formula for estimating the standard error of a population proportion (Formula 7.2):

$$\hat{\sigma}_{P_I} = \sqrt{\frac{P_u(1 - P_u)}{N}} \qquad (7.2)$$

Formula 7.2 looks rather different from the formula for the standard error of a mean, but it is actually the same—logically. In the denominator we have the sample size. So, again, the larger the sample, the more efficient the estimate.

The numerator says to take the proportion of cases in the sample that fall into the category of interest (P_u) and multiply it times the proportion not in that category ($1-P_u$). This is a measure of the variability in the scores in the sample. If 99 percent of the cases were in the category of interest and 1 percent were not, the result of the numerator would be $0.99 * 0.01 = 0.0099$. If 50 percent were in the category of interest and 50 percent were not, the result of the numerator would be $0.5 * 0.5 = 0.25$. The more equal the distribution of cases between categories, the greater the variability.

Researchers often use 0.50 instead of the actual sample value of P_u, to be conservative. The numerator is an estimate of the expected variability in the proportion we are trying to estimate. The greater this variability, the bigger the standard error, and the less confidence we have.

Example

CALCULATING THE ESTIMATED STANDARD ERROR OF A PROPORTION

When we are talking about the central tendency of a categorical variable (nominal dichotomy, nominal polyotomy, or grouped ordinal variable), we usually report the proportion of cases in the largest category as our measure of central tendency.

If we are working with data from a sample, the proportion that we observe in the sample is only an estimate of the population proportion. It is useful to index how reliable this estimate is by calculating the standard error (i.e., standard deviation of the sampling distribution) of the proportion. We can do this using the information that is available in our sample. Here's a formula to do this:

$$\hat{\sigma}_{P_l} = \sqrt{\frac{P_u(1 - P_u)}{N}} \tag{7.2}$$

The left-hand side of Formula 7.2 indicates that we are making an estimate ("hat") of the population value of the standard deviation (sigma) of sample proportions (subscript P_l).

Most of the formula for the estimator is simple; the square root and sample size (N) are obvious. The top part $P_u(1-P_u)$ isn't. It is an estimator of the variance of the population proportion. There are three possible approaches to this part:

1. If, somehow, we happen to know what the true population proportion of cases is that fall in the category we're interested in, we can use this for P_u in the formula. If we knew this, though, we wouldn't need to be doing inference—so this approach rarely applies.

Example

2. We can use the proportion of cases in the category of interest in our sample as an estimator of the population proportion. For example, if we were calculating the standard error of the proportion of persons who are black, and 10 percent of the people in our sample happened to be black, we could use $P_u = 0.10$.
3. If we want to be conservative, we can assume that $P_u = 0.50$. This is sometimes done with dichotomous variables, particularly. This assumption is using the maximum possible value of the numerator of the formula $P_u(1 - P_u)$.

Let's illustrate the latter two approaches.

In a data set drawn from the General Social Survey, 11.7 percent of the respondents report themselves to be "black." The number of respondents to the survey is 1,500.

If we take 11.7 percent (expressed as a proportion = 0.117) as our estimate of P_u (the population proportion) we would get:

$$\begin{aligned}
\text{Standard error} &= \text{Square root of } [0.117(1 - 0.117)]/1{,}500 \\
&= \text{sqrt } (0.117 * 0.883)/1{,}500 \\
&= \text{sqrt } (0.1033)/1{,}500 \\
&= \text{sqrt } 0.00006887 \\
&= 0.0083
\end{aligned}$$

That is, on the average, we would expect the proportion of persons reporting themselves to be "black" to vary by about eight-tenths of 1 percent from one survey to another (with simple random sampling, and sample sizes of 1,500).

If we chose the more conservative approach of estimating P_u as 0.50 (not a very sensible approach in this particular case, since we know that P_u is really much smaller), we would get:

$$\begin{aligned}
\text{SE} &= \text{sqrt } [0.50(1 - 0.50)]/1{,}500 \\
&= 0.0129
\end{aligned}$$

That is, the much more conservative estimate suggests that the proportion "black" might vary by as much as 1.3 percent from sample to sample (with simple random samples of 1,500 people).

CHECK QUIZ 7.2

1. When we say that a sample statistic is a "point estimate," we mean that it is
   a. a sample taken at a given point in time.
   b. our best guess about the value of a given case.
   c. our best guess of a population parameter.
   d. a statistical measure of error.
2. Simply put, "bias" means that our sample statistic is not a good estimate of the corresponding population parameter. Which of the following situations might lead to bias?
   a. taking a nonrepresentative sample
   b. adding 3 to each measurement
   c. cluster sampling
   d. all of the above
3. If "bias" refers to whether or not our estimate is a good predictor of a population parameter, "efficiency" refers to
   a. how easily a statistic is computed.
   b. whether the estimate is too large or too small.
   c. a downstairs apartment.
   d. how far our estimate is likely to deviate from the population parameter.
4. Having the square root of *N* in the denominator of the formula for the standard error of a mean means that
   a. as *N* gets larger, the standard error will get smaller.
   b. as *N* gets larger, the standard error will get larger, too.
   c. when *N* is negative, the standard error will also be negative.
   d. the smaller the population, the larger the deviance.
5. From a sample of 200 private college students, you found that the average number of hours of study time each week is 25 with a standard deviation of 6. A point estimate of the average study time for all private college students would be
   a. 6.
   b. 25.
   c. 200.
   d. 12.5 $\pm$ 1 standard deviation.
6. Two sample statistics are unbiased estimators. They are
   a. means and proportions.
   b. means and standard deviations.
   c. medians and modes.
   d. proportions and percentages.

7. An estimator is unbiased if the mean of its sampling distribution is equal to
   a. the midpoint of the distribution.
   b. the sample mean.
   c. the population value.
   d. the population median.
8. The more efficient the estimate, the more the sampling distribution
   a. is evenly spread from the mean to ±2 standard deviations.
   b. becomes flatter.
   c. clusters to the right of the mean.
   d. is clustered around the mean.

ASSESSING CONFIDENCE IN POINT ESTIMATES

The idea of a sampling distribution points out that we can expect the value of a sample statistic to vary around the true value of the population parameter about which we are trying to make an inference.

The idea of a standard error is very helpful, because it lets us measure the expected amount of that variability. Big standard errors mean that we can't be very confident about our estimates of population parameters; small standard errors mean that our sample results are probably pretty close to the true population values.

The formulas for estimating the standard errors of means and proportions from a single sample mean allow us to be quite precise about the accuracy and confidence that we have in our sample estimates of population means and proportions. The procedure for making statements about our confidence is called "setting confidence intervals."

There are two parts to the process of setting confidence intervals. First, we need to decide just how confident we want to be. Second, we use the estimated standard errors to construct statements like: "I'm 95 percent sure that the true population mean falls between $14,500 and $15,000."

Selecting an Alpha Level

When we report on a mean or proportion, we can say that the value we observe in the sample is our best unbiased estimate of the population mean or proportion.

But, because of sampling variability, we know that the mean or proportion that we observe in a particular sample is probably not exactly equal to the true population mean or proportion.

The way that we deal with this uncertainty about the true population parameter is to state that, with a certain degree of confidence, we predict that the population parameter falls within a confidence interval of values between a ***lower bound*** and an ***upper bound***. For example, we might state: "With 90 percent confidence, the population proportion of persons who are women falls between 0.49 and 0.56."

The degree of confidence (90 percent in this example) is called the confidence level.

Sometimes, instead of talking about how confident we are, we talk instead about the chance that our predictions about the population parameter are in error. If I am 90 percent confident that the proportion of women in the population falls between 0.49 and 0.56, then there is also a 10 percent chance that this prediction is wrong—that the proportion of women falls outside this range, either less than 0.49 or more than 0.56.

The probability that the population parameter falls outside of the confidence interval is called the ***alpha level*** or type I error level (there is also a type II error level that we won't discuss here). Very frequently, you will see reports that "We are confident about our result at the 0.05 alpha level." What this is saying is that we are 95 percent sure and there is a 5 percent chance that we are wrong when we make our inference about the population parameter.

We can figure out the range of values—the confidence interval's lower and upper bounds—for any confidence or error level we might desire (we'll show how in the next section). But what level should we select? There is no one right answer to this question, but there are some guidelines.

The most commonly used alpha level is 0.05. That is, we want to be 95 percent sure that the confidence interval contains the real population value. This is simply a tradition that reflects the fact that we want to be pretty sure about assertions that we make about populations on the basis of samples from them.

Sometimes, we are willing to live with higher probabilities of error (but rarely more than alpha = 0.10). If we know little about a phenomenon and are looking for leads, we might be willing to follow up on false leads. If the costs of an error are not high, we may be willing to take a bigger chance of being wrong. That is, we would accept a larger alpha level. But, if people's lives are directly affected by the results of our study and its recommendations, then a much higher level of confidence (e.g., alpha = 0.01 or even alpha = 0.001) might be a better choice.

Confidence Intervals

There is a direct relationship between how confident we need to be and the size of the confidence interval. If we need to be very sure that the range of values in the interval includes the mean or proportion, then we will have to include a wider range of values. If we are willing to take a bigger chance of being wrong, then the range of predicted values will be smaller.

But how can we determine the boundaries of the confidence interval, once we have decided on how confident we need to be? This turns out to be pretty simple, using the estimated standard errors we've already discussed, and one new—and pretty important—fact:

The sampling distributions of means and proportions are approximately normal in shape. The larger the sample, the more closely the sampling distributions of means and proportions approximate "normal." That is, the way in which the values of means and proportions in samples vary from the true population parameter can be described as a bell-shaped curve. Most samples' means and proportions will be quite close to the true population parameters; smaller and smaller percentages of sample means and proportions will be further and further away from the true population parameters.

This is a comforting result, because it tells us that most means or proportions in samples are likely to be fairly close to the true population parameter values, and that really big sampling errors are relatively unlikely (not impossible, but not likely).

But we can go further than this by combining the idea of a standard error with what we learned earlier about normal distributions.

Any standard normal distribution has known proportions of cases that fall at various distances from the mean. Recall that we determined that about two-thirds of all cases in a normal distribution fell within one standard deviation (plus or minus) of the mean; about 95 percent of all cases fell within plus or minus two standard deviations, and so on.

The standard error is the standard deviation of the sampling distribution of a statistic. So, if the sampling distribution is normal, about two-thirds of all samples will have statistics that fall within one standard error of the true population parameter; about 95 percent of the statistics from samples will fall within two standard errors of the population parameter.

In fact, if we know that the sampling distribution of a statistic is normal in shape (and this is true for means and proportions—but not for all statistics), and, if we know the standard error (and we have formulas to estimate this for means and proportions), then we can calculate the percentage of sample outcomes that can be expected to fall at any given distance from the mean or proportion.

Confidence Intervals for Means

Here is a formula that can be used to calculate the confidence interval of a mean.

$$\mathrm{CI} = \overline{Y} \pm Z_{\alpha}\left(\frac{s}{\sqrt{N}}\right) \tag{7.3}$$

Formula 7.3 says that the confidence interval (for some value of alpha) around the estimate of the population mean is equal to the sample mean ($\overline{Y}$) plus or minus a quantity. We know that the sample mean is an unbiased estimator of the population mean, so the sample mean will fall at the middle of our confidence interval, and is our "maximum likelihood" point estimator of the population mean.

Since the sampling distribution of means is normal, we know that it is symmetric. So the confidence interval will extend equally far from the sample mean in both directions—hence the "plus or minus" part of the formula. The mean plus some quantity gives us the upper bound of the confidence interval. The mean minus the same quantity gives us the lower bound.

How far the confidence interval extends in each direction from the sample mean is determined by Z and by the quantity inside the parentheses.

You might recognize the quantity in the parentheses. It is the estimated standard error of the mean that we discussed earlier in this chapter. So, the formula is saying that the confidence interval starts at the sample mean, and extends some number (Z) of standard error units in either direction. Since the standard error is a measure of sampling variability, this part of the formula is telling us that the confidence interval starts at the observed mean, and includes units of sampling variability in either direction. Actually, that should make sense—the confidence interval is talking about how far a sample might fall from the true population value as a result of sampling variation.

The last quantity in the formula is "Z." Z is a standard normal score that we use to set the alpha or confidence level.

Suppose, for example, we wanted to be 95 percent sure that the confidence interval around the mean included the true population value. What Z-score would I have to choose to find the middle 95 percent of a standard normal distribution? Using a statistical table or software, we can determine that the area of the standard normal distribution between a Z-score of (approximately) -1.96 and $+1.96$ includes the middle 95 percent of scores.

So, to find the range of values that includes 95 percent of possible outcomes for the sample mean, we would substitute 1.96 for Z and the estimated standard error (s divided by the square root of N).

If we wanted to be more confident than 95 percent, alpha would have to be smaller. Using a table of Z-scores or software, we would find the value that cuts off the desired percentage of error in the two tails of the distribution, and substitute that Z value.

Note that the level or degree of confidence that we select determines the width of the confidence interval and the precision of the estimate (e.g., the mean). If the degree of confidence is only 90 percent, the resulting confidence interval will be wide and the calculated estimate will not be as precise. As the level of confidence increases, (e.g., from 90 percent to 99 percent), the calculated confidence interval (boundaries around the estimate) becomes narrower, and the estimate derived improves in precision. Selecting a 90 percent confidence level implies that we could be wrong in estimating the true value in the population by 10 percent. Selecting a 95 percent confidence level narrows the confidence interval and also decreases our error (of being wrong) to 5 percent, and finally, selecting a 99 percent confidence level substantially reduces our confidence interval, since we are accepting an error rate or chance of the true value falling outside the confidence interval by only 1 percent. There is thus an inverse relationship between the width of a confidence interval and the degree of confidence selected.

That's the basic idea. To become comfortable in figuring out and understanding confidence intervals for means, you really do need to study the examples closely, and work some problems.

CALCULATING THE CONFIDENCE INTERVAL FOR A MEAN

Example

To calculate the confidence interval for a mean, you need to assemble some information. You will need to know:

- What is the sample mean?
- What is the sample standard deviation?
- What is the sample size?
- What level of confidence do you want? Conversely, what is the alpha or error level that you are willing to risk in setting the interval?

Once you have this information available, you can use Formula 7.3 to set the confidence interval:

$$\mathrm{CI} = \overline{Y} \pm Z_{\alpha}\left(\frac{s}{\sqrt{N}}\right) \tag{7.3}$$

The confidence interval for a mean is reported as the values of the lower bound and upper bound of the interval. To find these, we start with the sample mean ($\overline{Y}$ in the formula) and subtract (to find the lower bound) and add (to find the upper bound) a value that we calculate according to the formula.

Part of the formula should be familiar as the estimate of the standard error of the mean (i.e., s divided by the square root of N).

The "Z" part of the formula is where we take the confidence level into account. Suppose that we want to be 95 percent confident that the interval of values we estimate includes the true population mean. This means that alpha is 0.05, or we are willing to take a 5 percent chance that the true population value falls outside of the interval.

Since the true population mean could be outside either the lower bound or the upper bound, half of the error (i.e., 2.5 percent or 0.025) falls on either side of the mean. Using the table of Z values, we look up the Z value that corresponds to 0.025. We find that the Z value is -1.96 for the lower tail; so, it must be $+1.96$ for the upper tail. This value of Z then gets plugged into the formula. Of course, if we wanted to be more confident, a higher Z value would be used.

(continued)

Example

Here's an example. We have collected information on 109 nations in the world during the mid-1990s. We find that that average life expectancy for females is 70.16 years, with a standard deviation of 10.572 years. We want to set a 95 percent confidence interval around the mean.

Substituting into the formula, we get:

$$\begin{aligned}
95\%\ \text{CI} &= 70.16 \pm 1.96[10.572/\text{sqrt}\,(109)] \\
&= 70.16 \pm 1.96(10.572/10.440) \\
&= 70.16 \pm 1.96(1.013) \\
&= 70.16 \pm 1.98 \\
\text{Lower bound} &= 70.16 - 1.98 \text{ or } 68.18 \\
\text{Upper bound} &= 70.16 + 1.98 \text{ or } 72.14
\end{aligned}$$

So, we are confident at the 95 percent level that the true population mean life expectancy for women falls between 68.18 and 72.14 years.

If we wanted to be more confident than this, we might choose the 99 percent level. Everything would remain the same except the Z-score. Using the *Z* table, we need to find the value that cuts off one-half of 1 percent (0.005) of the distribution (that is, one-half, or the lower tail of the alpha level of 0.01). This turns out to be −2.575, so we use $Z = 2.575$ in our calculations of the 99 percent confidence interval.

Example

USING EXCEL TO CALCULATE THE CONFIDENCE INTERVAL FOR A MEAN

MS Excel has a formula to find the part of the confidence interval formula that is to the right of the ±.

The keywords for confidence intervals are:

Confidence interval for mean (part added and subtracted from the mean)	=confidence(alpha,s.d.,n)

Use the confidence formula to solve problems on confidence intervals around means, as in this example. The first panel shows the Excel formula, and the second shows the results.

Example

	A	B	C
1	Cheesy movies		
2	456		
3	574		
4	359		
5	304		
6	383		
7	313		
8	522		
9	401		
10	439		
11	445		
12	534		
13	518		
14	617		
15	650		
16	407		
17	661	alpha:	0.05
18	695	s.d.	=STDEV(A2:A25)
19	383	n:	=COUNT(A2:A25)
20	493	x-bar	=AVERAGE(A2:A25)
21	301	confidence'	=CONFIDENCE(C17,C18,C19
22	499		
23	309	lower bound:	=C20-C21
24	419	upper bound:	=C20+C21
25	368		

	A	B	C
1	Cheesy movies		
2	456		
3	574		
4	359		
5	304		
6	383		
7	313		
8	522		
9	401		
10	439		
11	445		
12	534		
13	518		
14	617		
15	650		
16	407		
17	661	alpha:	0.05
18	695	s.d.	117.56
19	383	n:	24.00
20	493	x-bar	460.42
21	301	confidence'	47.03
22	499		
23	309	lower bound:	413.38
24	419	upper bound:	507.45
25	368		

Confidence Intervals for Proportions

Setting the confidence interval around our estimate of a population proportion follows exactly the same logic as with a mean. The only thing that differs is our estimate of the standard error—because we use a different formula to estimate the standard error of a mean and a proportion. Formula 7.4 is one formula for calculating the upper and lower bounds of the confidence interval of a proportion:

$$\mathrm{CI} = P_s \pm Z_\propto \sqrt{\frac{P_u(1 - P_u)}{N}} \tag{7.4}$$

The midpoint of the confidence interval is the value of the proportion that we observe in the sample. This is because the sample proportion is our best guess about what the true population proportion is. Since we know that sampling errors will be normally distributed around this value, we select a Z-score (plus or minus) of whatever size we need to include the desired percentage of outcomes within the confidence interval. This Z-score is then multiplied times our estimate of the standard error of the proportion. P_u is the proportion that we observe in the sample, or 0.50 (if we want to be most conservative).

Some analysts prefer to always use the most conservative method for setting confidence intervals around estimates of population proportions. They argue that we really don't know what the population proportion (P_u) is, so we ought to use an estimate of it that is as conservative as possible. Since a 50–50 split in the population is the upper-bound estimate of variability in proportions, these more conservative analysts will use Formula 7.5 instead:

$$c.i. = P_S \pm Z_\propto \sqrt{\frac{.50(1 - .50)}{N}} \tag{7.5}$$

In most real cases, unless we are studying events that are pretty rare (say if more than 90 percent fall in one category and less than 10 percent are not in that category) you will usually get pretty much the same answer using either the more conservative approach or the less conservative approach. There isn't a right or wrong way.

Example

CALCULATING THE CONFIDENCE INTERVAL FOR A PROPORTION

When we want to present information about the distribution of a categorical variable (nominal dichotomy, nominal polyotomy, grouped ordinal) we most often will report the proportion of cases that fall in some category. For example, to characterize the gender distribution in a basic statistics class, saying that "74 percent of the students are women" provides a good general summary.

Proportions observed in simple random samples are unbiased and efficient estimators of population proportions. But it is useful to know how reliable or precise the sample proportions are as population parameter estimators. A good way of reporting this information is by providing the confidence interval.

Here is Formula 7.4 once more to calculate the confidence interval for a proportion:

$$\mathrm{CI} = P_s \pm Z_\alpha \sqrt{\frac{P_u(1 - P_u)}{N}} \tag{7.4}$$

The formula is easy to use. We require only two pieces of information from the sample in order to make the calculations. N is the sample size. P_s is the sample estimator of the population proportion in question. With the standard approach, P_s is also used for the P_u in Formula 7.4. With the more conservative approach, P_u is 0.50. We also require a decision. What level of confidence do we want to have, and what is the associated Z-score?

Let's suppose that we were working with the General Social Survey, and we observed that 11.7 percent of 1,500 respondents characterized themselves as "black." We have decided that we want to calculate the 99 percent confidence interval.

P_s is 0.117, the proportion actually observed in our sample.

N is 1,500.

To find the Z-score that we need, we reason this way: We want 99 percent confidence; therefore, alpha is equal to 1 percent or 0.01; since the error could be in either the low tail or the high tail, we need to find a Z-score that cuts off one-half of alpha, or 0.005. Using the table of Z values and probabilities, we find that a Z-score of −2.575 has 0.005 of the distribution below it (and, of course, a Z-score of +2.575 has 0.005 of the distribution above it). So, for the 99 percent confidence level, we should use the Z-scores of plus and minus 2.575.

$$\begin{aligned}
\mathrm{CI} &= 0.117 \pm 2.575 * \text{sqrt}\ \{[0.117(1 - 0.117)]/1{,}500\} \\
&= 0.117 \pm 2.575 * \text{sqrt}\ [(0.117 \times 0.883)/1{,}500] \\
&= 0.117 \pm 2.575 * \text{sqrt}\ [(0.1033)/1{,}500] \\
&= 0.117 \pm 2.575 * \text{sqrt}\ (0.00006887) \\
&= 0.117 \pm 2.575 * 0.008299 \\
&= 0.117 \pm 0.0214
\end{aligned}$$

So, the lower bound of the 99 percent confidence interval is 0.117 − 0.0214 or 0.0956; the upper bound of the 99 percent confidence interval is 0.117 + 0.0214 or 0.1384.

We may be 99 percent confident that the true population proportion of black persons falls between 9.56 percent and 13.8 percent.

Example

USING EXCEL TO CALCULATE THE CONFIDENCE INTERVAL FOR A PROPORTION

To find confidence intervals for proportions, you might put together a spreadsheet like this:

◇	A	B	C
1	left-handed		
2	1		
3	1		
4	1		
5	0		
6	0		
7	0	n:	=COUNT(A2:A17)
8	0	obs. Proportion:	=AVERAGE(A2:A17)
9	0	Z:	=1.96
10	0	Pop. Prop.	0.5
11	0		
12	1		
13	0	confidence'	=C9*(SQRT(C10*(1-C10)/C7))
14	0	lower bound:	=C8-C13
15	1	upper bound:	=C8+C13
16	1		
17	1		
18			

Notice that the data are dummy-coded: a "1" means that the subject is left-handed, and a "0" means that the subject is not. This allows us to obtain the proportion easily.

In the cell labeled "*Z*:," use the appropriate *Z* value for the desired level of confidence. If the population proportion is known (or you'd like to make a guess of some sort), put that in the cell labeled "Pop. Prop."

◇	A	B	C
1	left-handed		
2	1		
3	1		
4	1		
5	0		
6	0		
7	0	n:	16.00
8	0	obs. Proportion:	0.44
9	0	Z:	1.96
10	0	Pop. Prop.	0.50
11	0		
12	1		
13	0	confidence'	0.25
14	0	lower bound:	0.19
15	1	upper bound:	0.68
16	1		
17	1		
18			

If we were trying to find the proportion of a variable with some categorical value (the word "left" for left-handed, say), it would also be possible to use the countif( )

Example

function to count particular values, and then divide by *n* (probably using the count( ) function). The countif formula looks like this:

$$=\text{countif}(\text{range of cells, criteria})$$

If we wanted to count the number of 1's in the preceding example, we could have used:

$$=\text{countif}(\text{a2} : \text{a17,1})$$

Of course, you will get nearly the same confidence interval if you dummy-code your variable of interest and use the spreadsheet for finding the confidence interval for means.

CHECK QUIZ 7.3

1. The probability that an interval estimate does *not* include the population value is called
   a. the margin.
   b. alpha.
   c. an error.
   d. the odds.
2. In the social sciences, researchers frequently set alpha at 0.05; in drug tests, we might expect researchers to set their alpha at
   a. 0.1.
   b. 0.5.
   c. 0.05.
   d. 0.01.
3. If we are confident about an estimate at an alpha level of 0.1, this means
   a. that we will probably be wrong about 10 percent of the time.
   b. that we will probably be wrong about 0.1 percent of the time.
   c. that our estimate may be off by as much as 10 percent.
   d. that we will probably be right about 10 percent of the time.
4. The confidence interval for the point estimate of mean of a population centers on the sample
   a. standard deviation.
   b. mean.
   c. median.
   d. cumulative frequency.
5. The confidence interval for the mean of a population takes into account the sample mean, the Z-score for the level of confidence, and
   a. the size of the population.
   b. the estimated standard error of the mean.
   c. the cycle of the moon.
   d. the standard deviation of the population.

6. There is always a chance that a sample will not be representative; because of this, alpha cannot be
   a. known.
   b. 1.0.
   c. 0.0.
   d. less than 0.1.

SUMMARY

This chapter has provided an introduction to the basic ideas and concepts of inferential statistics. Then these ideas were applied to seeing how we can make precise statements about our confidence in making inferences about the values of population means and proportions on the basis of sample statistics.

Most social science research uses samples, rather than studying whole populations. Samples can be drawn in many ways, depending on the purpose of the research. The tools of statistical inference discussed in this chapter are useful only for probability samples. The specific techniques in this book are appropriate for data collected from simple random samples. We briefly discussed stratified and cluster sampling, and pointed out that our inferential confidence is sometimes stronger with stratified than with simple random samples; our inferential confidence is usually less with cluster samples than with simple random samples.

The value of a statistic calculated from sample data is likely to differ from the true population parameter that it estimates because of random variability in drawing cases into the sample. This sampling error or sampling variability is the fundamental inferential problem: how can I make a statement about a population parameter when the sample estimate is most likely in error to some degree?

The sampling distribution of a statistic is the frequency or probability distribution of the values of that statistic calculated across all possible samples drawn from a population. The sampling distribution describes the distribution of sampling errors. The central tendency of the sampling distribution of a statistic is called the "expected value." When the expected value of a statistic is equal to the true population parameter, the statistic is said to be "unbiased."

The standard deviation of the sampling distribution of a statistic is called the "standard error." The standard error indexes the amount of variation in the value of a statistic that can be expected from one sample to another simply as a result of random sampling variation. Statistics that have smaller standard errors are said to be more efficient than statistics with larger standard errors.

The sample mean and sample proportion statistics are unbiased and efficient point estimators of the corresponding population parameters.

The standard error of the sampling distributions of means and proportions can be estimated from the values measured in a single sample. The formulas for estimating the standard errors suggest that the greater the variability of the variable, the greater the standard error, and the greater the sample size, the smaller the standard error.

The sampling distributions of means and proportions are normal in shape. Using this fact and the estimate of the standard deviation of the sampling distribution (i.e., the standard error), one can calculate the percentage of the statistics from all possible samples that would be expected to fall at any chosen distance from the true population parameter.

Using this idea, a confidence interval described by a lower and an upper boundary value can be calculated for estimates of population means and proportions at any given level of confidence (or the opposite of confidence, which is the alpha error level).

Reporting the confidence interval (for a given alpha level) for estimates of population means and proportions is an important thing to do, so that we can be more honest about how much faith we should place in estimates of population means and proportions.

There is a second major way in which the core ideas of inferential statistics (i.e., sampling variability, sampling distributions, expected values, and standard errors) are used in applied statistics in the social sciences. In addition to using these ideas to set confidence intervals, inferential statistics are used to test hypotheses. That is, inferential statistics play a role in helping us to decide whether our empirical data are or are not consistent with theories. In the next several chapters, we will examine the use of inferential statistics for hypothesis testing.

KEY TERMS

alpha level

bounds (lower and upper) of a confidence interval

cluster sample

confidence interval

efficient estimates

expected value of a statistic

point estimate

population parameter

probability (and nonprobability) samples

sample statistic

sample survey versus population census

sampling distribution

sampling variability

standard error

statistical inference

stratified sample

unbiased point estimate

CHECK QUIZ ANSWERS

Quiz 7.1 Answers: 1. (b); 2. (a); 3. (c); 4. (c)
Quiz 7.2 Answers: 1. (c); 2. (d); 3. (d); 4. (a); 5. (b); 6. (a); 7. (c); 8. (d)
Quiz 7.3 Answers: 1. (b); 2. (d); 3. (a); 4. (b); 5. (b); 6. (c)

EXERCISES

A statistician at UNESCO is examining the levels of schooling attained in nations of the world in the mid-1990s. Data are available on 162 nations, and are displayed in this histogram.

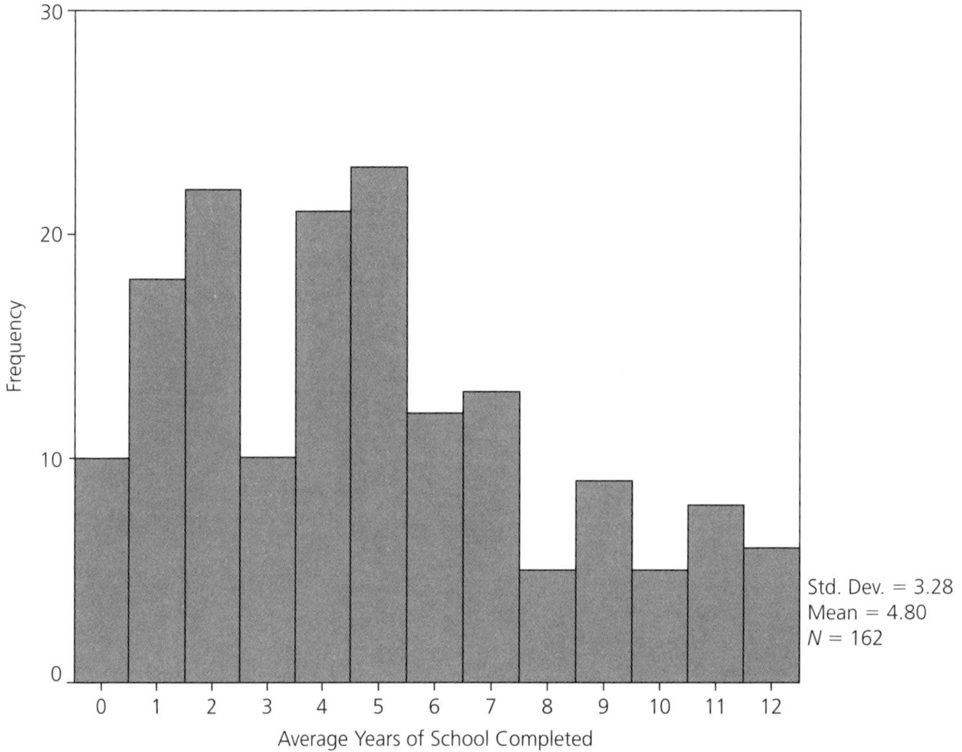

The statistician asks: "How accurate a picture would I get about the real population average value (4.8 years of schooling) if I took a simple random sample of about 10 percent of the cases ($n = 16$), rather than examining them all?"

To find out, the statistician draws 30 samples of 16 cases each, and calculates the mean years of schooling across the nations in each sample. The results of the 30 trials are shown here:

4.79	5.69	3.63
6.51	4.87	4.22
4.46	2.70	5.00

5.62	6.02	5.76
4.58	3.43	4.22
4.96	4.93	4.85
5.05	3.56	5.32
4.97	3.57	6.35
4.02	4.18	5.52
5.38	3.62	6.55

1. Is the population distribution of the years of schooling approximately normal, or is it skewed? How much variability is there in education levels in the population distribution?
2. Construct a histogram or frequency chart that shows the distribution of the values of the mean, calculated from the 30 samples. This is the sampling distribution of the mean years of schooling. You may wish to use SPSS or Excel, or you can also do this by hand.
3. Calculate the mean of the values in the sampling distribution. If we take this average or expected value of the sampling distribution as an estimator of the true population mean, how close is it?
4. Calculate the mean of the first 10 samples, the second 10 samples, and the last 10 samples. Are these means of the sampling distributions closer or less close to the population parameter than the result using all 30 samples?
5. Calculate the standard deviation of the sampling distribution. This value is also called the "estimated standard error" of the mean.
6. Which is larger: the standard deviation of the population distribution or the standard deviation (standard error) of the sampling distribution of the mean?
7. Provide a brief interpretation of the meaning of the value of the standard error.
8. A random sample of 100 college students were asked: "How many times in the past week did you eat fast food?" The average number of times turned out to be 2.37, with a standard deviation of 0.30. Estimate the confidence interval for the value of the population mean at the 95 percent and 99 percent confidence levels.
9. We have taken a simple random sample of 500 residents of a city, and asked them whether they will vote for the incumbent mayor in the upcoming election. Of the 500 residents, 287 indicate that they will vote for the mayor.

   On the basis of this poll, how confident can the mayor be that she will be reelected (that is, get at least 51 percent of the vote, since there are only two candidates in the election)? Can she be 99 percent sure? 95 percent sure? 90 percent sure? Construct the confidence intervals around the proportion for these alpha levels, and see if they include any outcomes in which the mayor would get less than 51 percent.

10. The means of two demographic variables (age, in years; whether a respondent is female or not) have been calculated from an extract of the pooled General Social Surveys from 1978 to 1998; here are the results.

Descriptive Statistics

	N	Minimum	Maximum	Mean	Std. Deviation
Age of respondent	1,500	18	99	44.76	18.090
Respondent is female	1,500	0.00	1.00	0.5633	0.49614
Valid N (listwise)	1,500				

a. What is the value of the unbiased point estimator of the population mean for age? For the proportion who are female?
b. Calculate the 95 percent confidence interval for the variables "age" and "female."

The following histogram shows the distribution of the percentage of the population of the 50 U.S. states that are of Hispanic origin during the 1990s.

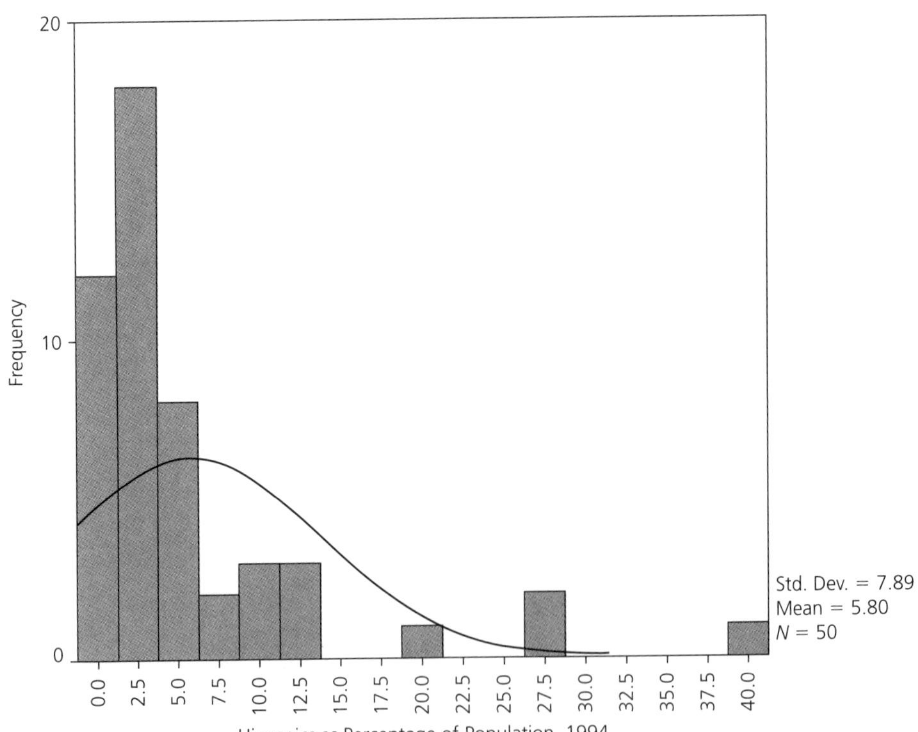

The statistician asks: "How accurate a picture would I get about the real population average value (5.8 percent Hispanic) if I took a simple random sample of 30 cases, rather than examining all 50?"

To find out, the statistician draws 20 samples of 30 cases each, and calculates the mean percentage Hispanic across the cases in each of the samples. The result is:

Sample Number	Mean Percent Hispanic	Sample Number	Mean Percent Hispanic
1	5.59	11	5.20
2	6.01	12	6.56
3	5.09	13	5.61
4	4.41	14	4.20
5	5.98	15	6.28
6	5.56	16	5.83
7	5.38	17	5.70
8	7.14	18	5.80
9	4.43	19	4.93
10	7.91	20	4.91

11. Is the population distribution of the percentage Hispanic approximately normal, or is it skewed?
12. Construct a histogram or frequency chart that shows the distribution of the values of the mean, calculated from the 20 samples. This is the sampling distribution of the percentage Hispanic. You may wish to use SPSS or Excel, or you can also do this by hand.
13. Calculate the mean of the values in the sampling distribution. If we take this average or expected value of the sampling distribution as an estimator of the true population mean, how close is it to the population parameter?
14. Calculate the standard deviation of the sampling distribution. This value is also called the "estimated standard error" of the mean.
15. Provide a brief interpretation of the meaning of the value of the standard error.
16. A simple random sample of 200 registered Republican voters in California were asked: "What was your family income, from all sources, last year?" The mean income reported was $175,000, with a standard deviation of $25,000. Calculate the 90 percent and the 95 percent confidence intervals around the estimate of the population mean.
17. We have taken a simple random sample of 1,000 residents of a county, and asked them whether they will vote for incumbent sheriff in the next election. Of the 1,000 residents, 475 indicate that they will vote for the sheriff.

    On the basis of this poll, how confident can the sheriff's campaign be that he will carry the county (that is, get at least 51 percent of the vote, since there are only two candidates in the election)? Can the campaign be 99 percent sure? 95 percent sure?

90 percent sure? Construct the confidence intervals around the proportion for these alpha levels, and see if they include any outcomes where the sheriff would get less than 51 percent.

18. Using the General Social Survey (pooled 1978–1998), the chronological age of the respondent is measured, and analyzed using SPSS. Here is the resulting table.

Descriptive Statistics

	N Statistic	Mean Statistic	Std. Error
Age of respondent	1,500	44.76	0.47

What is the unbiased point estimator of the population age? Provide a short (one- or two-sentence) interpretation of the meaning of the "Std. Error" (i.e., the standard error of the estimated population mean).

Chapter 8

Hypothesis Testing for One Sample

LEARNING OBJECTIVES

When you have finished this chapter, you will be able to:

- Understand how hypothesis testing connects theory and observation.
- Properly state a null hypothesis and its corresponding one-sided and two-sided alternative hypotheses.
- Set alpha (type I) error levels and understand the relationship between type I and type II errors.
- Test a hypothesis about the value of one population mean using the Student's t-distribution.
- Test a hypothesis about the value of one population proportion using the standard normal distribution.

HYPOTHESIS TESTING

In the first chapter we made the assertion that the goal of the social sciences is empirically supported general explanations, or theories, of social behavior. We argued that statistics play a role in connecting empirical observations to theory in two ways. First, statistics are used to summarize patterns in data, which aids in forming empirical generalizations. Empirical generalizations, in turn, lead to efforts at explanations or proposed theories. Second, statistics play a role in the verification or validation of theories, through aiding us in assessing whether empirical observations are consistent with theoretical explanations.

So far, we've been mostly concerned with statistical techniques that enable us to summarize and describe trends and patterns in our data. In the last couple of chapters, we've learned the basic ideas of inferential statistics. Now we are ready to turn more serious attention to how statistics are used in confirming and disconfirming theories.

When statistics are used as tools for testing the utility or validity of theories, the process is called ***hypothesis testing***.

In this chapter we first discuss the process of hypothesis testing in general. We then see how this process is used for two very common kinds of hypotheses: hypotheses about the value of a single mean and hypotheses about a single proportion. Before we get to these specific applications, though, a few words about the whole idea of hypothesis testing are in order.

In the preceding chapter we looked at how inferential statistical tools could be used to set confidence intervals. The basic issue in this use of inferential statistics was that we couldn't be sure about the value of population parameters, given that we had only observed a sample. In a sense, we were inferring from the sample to the population. In hypothesis testing, we use inferential tools to go in the other direction—from population to sample.

Hypothesis testing begins with theory. The researcher proposes that a general explanation can account for some class of phenomena. For example, one might argue that as rational organizations get larger they become more vertically differentiated, because more levels of management are necessary to coordinate the activities of larger numbers of persons.

This explanation is quite general, it is intended to cover or explain the behavior of all rational organizations. We might think of this theory as being a statement or expectation about a population of phenomena (in this case, a population of rational organizations).

Without a demonstration that the theory is consistent with empirical data, though, the theory is just speculation. So, we really need to test our theory by applying it to a sample of observations (in this case, we need to observe some rational organizations). When we attempt to validate our theory by looking at new evidence, we are (almost always) looking at a sample of cases. So, theories are about populations, but our observations are usually about samples.

When we set about the task of observing a sample of cases to validate a theory, the theory guides what we need to observe, and gives us some very specific prior expectations about what we should see when we look. These prior expectations about what we should see in a sample, if the theory is true for a population, are called the "research hypothesis." In statistics, the "research hypothesis" is actually what is called the "alternative hypothesis" in hypothesis testing. To continue our example, we might very well propose the research hypothesis that, in a sample of organizations, those that are larger will also be more vertically differentiated.

Armed with a research hypothesis about what we should see in a sample if the general population theory is true, we are almost ready to look at the data. But, there is one more step: creating the null hypothesis.

A ***null hypothesis*** is a statement of what we would expect to see when we look at the data and the theory is *wrong*. For example, if our theory leads us to the research hypothesis that "larger organizations will have more levels of vertical differentiation than small organizations," then the null hypothesis would be that "larger organizations will not have more levels of vertical differentiation than small organizations." Often, the null hypothesis takes the form of stating that there is "no difference" (e.g., big and small organizations have the same number of levels of hierarchy).

When we do hypothesis testing with statistics, we seek to invalidate the null hypothesis. We require that the evidence tells us that the null hypothesis is probably wrong. We seek to reject the null hypothesis, rather than directly testing the idea that the research hypothesis is right. This sounds odd, and can create a lot of confusion. The reason that we use evidence to evaluate the null hypothesis rather than the research hypothesis is that we can never be sure that a theory is true; future observations (new samples) could always result in overthrowing our current knowledge. So we cannot confirm the research hypothesis. But, if the evidence tells us that the null hypothesis is consistent with the data, we can reject the theory or research hypothesis—because we have found a case where the evidence does not support it.

So, somewhat oddly, hypothesis testing seeks to reject the null hypothesis. If we do reject the null hypothesis, then the research hypothesis is supported—but not proven.

Suppose that the evidence from the sample seems to be consistent with the theory. Can we conclude with certainty that the theory is correct? Not necessarily. There is some probability that the outcome we see in the sample is not true in the population. That is, there is a chance of a "false positive" result. In the language of hypothesis testing, this kind of an error is called a *type I (or alpha) error*. The data in one sample lead us to believe that the alternative (research) hypothesis is correct, and we "reject the null." But, had we looked at all possible samples from the population, we would not have reached this conclusion.

A type I (or alpha) error is the worst kind for a scientist to make, because it leads us to believe that a theory is valid and useful when, in fact, it is not. In science, we need to remain skeptical—we should be slow to believe that we have a valid theory.

When we look at the data, there is also a ***type II (or beta) error***—a "false negative" result. That is, the sample data are inconsistent with the theory, but this is an accidental result for one sample, and the theory really is valid for the whole population in general.

A type II error is less serious from the point of view of scientific method. We are left believing that we still have a puzzle to solve, rather than believing that we have solved a puzzle when we haven't.

There is a trade-off between type I and type II errors in doing hypothesis testing. Lessening the chance of making one kind of error tends to increase the chance of making the other.

In this chapter we are going to first discuss the process of hypothesis testing in a bit more detail. Then we will apply the general logic to two very commonly used tests for hypotheses about the value of population mean, and about the value of a population proportion.

THE TESTING PROCESS

Hypothesis testing is fundamental to how statistics are used to connect empirical observations to theories. Virtually all of the more advanced statistical techniques in this book and more advanced texts are really about testing hypotheses of various sorts. There are a wide variety of specific hypothesis tests, depending on the sort of data we are working with and our research question. Hypotheses must be declared in advance—that is, prior to engaging in statistical analysis.

Underneath the complexity, there is a fairly simple and straightforward logic to setting up hypothesis testing problems and solving them. In this section, we discuss this general process in the abstract. Later in the chapter, we will apply the general process to two particularly important kinds of hypotheses.

Step 1: Null Hypothesis

Hypothesis testing always begins with a theory. A theory is an explanation, stated in abstract, general concepts. No observation can prove a theory to be right (because theories apply to whole populations, and we can only observe samples). But a single observation can cast doubt on the utility, if the theory fails to be consistent with the observed data.

Hypothesis testing, then, is really about disconfirming theories, rather than proving them. Because of this, the first step in the process is to make a statement about what we could observe that would disconfirm the theory.

A null hypothesis is a statement of the values of the sample statistics that, if we did observe them, would lead us to conclude that the theory was incorrect. A null hypothesis is deduced from theory, but is stated in terms of expectations about the value of a particular sample statistic.

It's easier to see this with an example.

Suppose I believe that, as organizations get larger, they become more vertically differentiated. This is a theory about the relationship between two concepts (organizational size and vertical differentiation) in the population of all organizations.

Now, what might I observe that would tend to disconfirm the utility of my theory? If large organizations are no different from small ones, then the theory would appear to be wrong. I can state this as a null hypothesis:

> H_0: Population mean vertical differentiation of large organizations = population mean vertical differentiation of small organizations.

or:

> H_0: The difference between the mean vertical differentiation of the population of large organizations and the mean vertical differentiation of the population of small organizations is zero.

Notice that null hypotheses are indicated with an *H* sub zero, colon, notation.

The null hypothesis makes a statement about population parameters, not sample statistics. What we want to be able to do is to conclude, on the basis of a sample of observations, that there is little chance that the null hypothesis is true in the population. Also note that the null hypothesis makes a statement about specific values of some statistic (here, we say that one mean is equal to another mean). Actually, the null hypothesis is really about population values—but the population values are being used to make predictions about the most likely sample outcome if the null hypothesis is true.

Null hypotheses are the starting point. They are derived by reasoning from a theory, and lead to a prediction about what specific values of sample statistics are most likely if the theory is, in fact, false.

Step 2: Alternative Hypotheses

Suppose that the values of statistics that we observe in a sample are very much different from what we would expect if the null hypothesis were true in the population. For example, let's suppose that the mean number of vertical levels in large organizations in my sample turns out to be 12, and the mean number of vertical levels in small organizations turns out to be 3.

If the null hypothesis about the population were correct, observing the sample statistics of 12 and 3 is quite unexpected. So, we would tend to disbelieve (or reject) the null hypothesis. If we reject the null hypothesis, what's left? What's left is the ***alternative hypothesis***. The second step in the hypothesis testing process is to specifically state the alternative hypothesis—this is what is left if we reject the null hypothesis. For our example:

> H_a: Population mean vertical differentiation of large organizations > population mean vertical differentiation of small organizations.

or:

> H_a: Population mean vertical differentiation of large organizations is not equal to the population mean vertical differentiation of small organizations.

(Note the notation of H_a.)

The alternative to the null hypothesis states the conclusion that we will reach if we become convinced that the null hypothesis is very unlikely. For many null hypotheses, there may be a need to select between two different alternative hypotheses. These are the ***one-tailed*** and the ***two-tailed*** versions of the alternative hypothesis.

Suppose that the number of vertical levels in small organizations was 12, and the number of vertical levels in large organizations was 3. Would this lead us to reject the theory that as organizations get larger, they become more vertically differentiated? Yes. While the null hypothesis appears to be wrong (because the means for small and large organizations are not the same), our research (alternative) hypothesis is clearly not correct—because the difference we are observing is in the opposite direction of what our theory would predict! So, only differences between the means in one direction lead to rejection of the null hypothesis in favor of the first alternative hypothesis. The first alternative hypothesis is a one-tailed alternative.

If all we needed to know was that large and small organizations were different (but we didn't care which had more vertical levels) in order to reject the null hypothesis, then the second alternative hypothesis would be sufficient. Here, a difference in either direction (two-tailed) would reject the null.

We can state the ideas of null and alternative hypotheses somewhat more clearly with a graphic display (see Figure 8.1). And this display also helps make clear the difference between a one-tailed and a two-tailed alternative hypothesis.

FIGURE 8.1 Sampling Distribution of a Normally Distributed Statistic

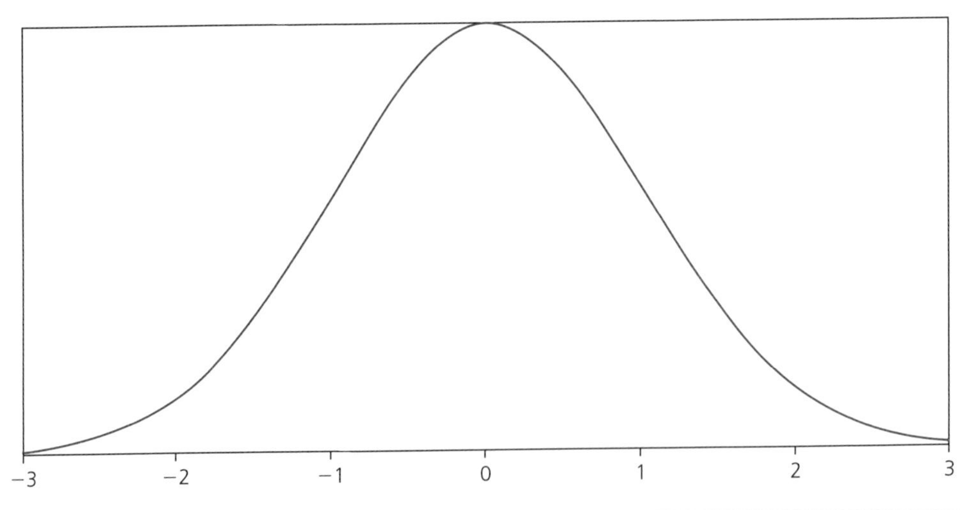

Imagine that the null hypothesis was, in fact, true in the population. This would lead to the null hypothesis that we would expect that the difference between the mean number of levels in small organizations and the mean number of levels in large organizations is zero.

We can't observe the whole population. We can only observe a sample. But there are many samples that one might randomly choose. We can draw a picture of the sampling distribution of the difference in the mean number of vertical levels between large and small organizations. It turns out that the sampling distribution for the difference between two means is approximately normal with large samples (more on this in the next chapter). And, of course, the sampling distribution has a standard error that measures the amount of difference between the two sample means that we could expect to occur just as a result of sampling variability.

By imagining that the null hypothesis is true, we are saying that the center of the sampling distribution of the statistic falls at zero. That is, if the null hypothesis was true, the mean of the population would fall at zero, and most observations of differences between samples of large and small organizations would vary only a little bit from that value.

When we observe a sample statistic that is quite far away from the null hypothesis value, it is unlikely that such an event could have happened by chance if the null hypothesis is correct; therefore, the null hypothesis may be wrong.

Let's suppose that we observed a difference of two units between the mean vertical differentiation of large and small organizations. Let's also suppose that the standard error of the sampling distribution was one unit. This would mean that our result was located at the heavy vertical line in the sampling distribution (see Figure 8.2).

How often would an outcome of two or more occur in a sample if the null hypothesis was actually true? The probability of such an event is the area to the left of the heavy vertical

FIGURE 8.2 Areas under the Normal Curve of the Sampling Distribution of a Statistic

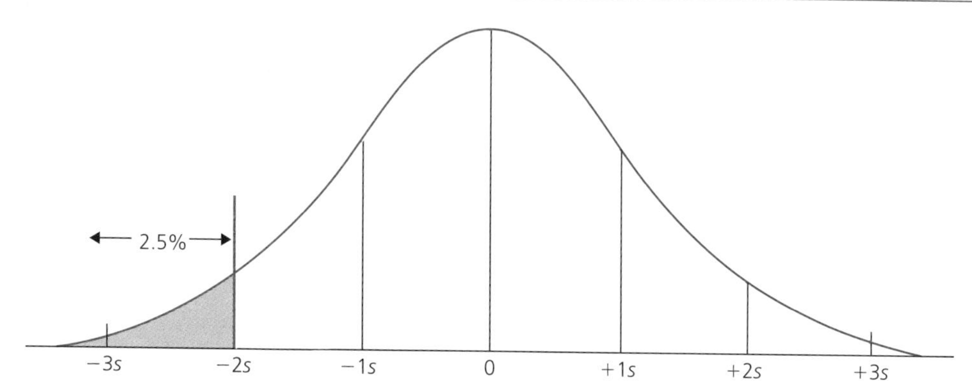

mark in the drawing—which is about 2.5 percent of the area. Since an outcome of a difference of two or more vertical levels of hierarchy would occur only a small percentage of the time if the null hypothesis were true, it is unlikely that the null hypothesis is true, and we would reject it in favor of the alternative that the vertical differentiation of large organizations is greater than the vertical differentiation of small organizations.

In doing hypothesis testing, we decide in advance how different a sample result must be from the prediction of the null hypothesis in order for us to reject the null hypothesis. This decision is based on how large a shaded area we are willing to tolerate (our alpha or "p" value). The dividing line between the region where we accept the null and where we reject it (the boundary between the white and shaded regions under the curve) is called the ***critical value***. The shaded area under the curve, where we are led to reject the null hypothesis, is called the ***rejection region***.

The logic of hypothesis testing asks: "What is the probability that we could observe what we did in the sample if the null hypothesis is true in the population?" If what we observe would be very unlikely if the null hypothesis were true, then the null hypothesis is probably not true, and we reject it.

To compare the null and alternative hypotheses in a formal way, we need to satisfy certain assumptions and make some prior decisions.

Step 3: Assumptions

Before we can do formal hypothesis testing to compare the null and alternative hypotheses, we do need to be sure that we have satisfied certain assumptions. While the assumptions for various tests differ, they almost always include:

- The sample was selected with simple random sampling.
- The variable or variables are measured at the appropriate level for the test in question.
- The shape of the sampling distribution of the statistic is known.

Without simple random sampling, the results of hypothesis tests that are calculated by the standard formulas, by spreadsheets, and by statistical packages are incorrect. In many cases, the error might lead us to accept a theory as useful when it is not—a type I error.

If we are doing a test about means, of course we must have measured our variables at the interval/ratio level; if our hypothesis is about proportions, then categorical variables are okay. This sounds obvious—but the use of the wrong statistic for a task will result in an incorrect hypothesis test.

We must also know the shape of the sampling distribution of the statistic about which we are hypothesizing. The reason that we spent a good bit of time studying the normal distribution earlier is that many statistics have been proven to have normal-shaped sampling distributions. In this chapter we will look at a test about a single proportion. That test has a normal sampling distribution. We will also look at a hypothesis test about one mean. The sampling distribution for that test is not normal—but it is known to be a Student's t-distribution. The correct distribution must be used, or the hypothesis test will be wrong.

Step 4: Selecting an Error Level

After we have clearly stated our null and alternative hypotheses, and have checked to make sure that we have satisfied the assumptions for the kind of hypothesis test we want to do, there is one more thing we need to do before looking at the data. We need to decide, in advance, how we are going to read the evidence. Specifically, we need to set our type I or alpha error level for the test. This is also, confusingly, called selecting the ***"p-level"*** for a test. In most statistical software results, you will see "*p*" rather than "alpha."

Let's suppose that we look at the evidence, and it suggests that the value of the sample statistic we are observing could occur 3 percent of the time if the null hypothesis were true (that is, the size of the shaded or rejection region in Figure 8.1 includes 3 percent of the area under the curve). Is this evidence good enough to reject the null hypothesis and tentatively accept our alternative?

There isn't any simple way to answer this question. Most of the time, by convention, we insist that the type I error level (or alpha level, or *p*-level) be 0.05 or less. That is, we want to be 95 percent confident that the null hypothesis is wrong before we reject it; we want to take no more than a 5 percent chance of being wrong if we do reject it.

In cases of exploratory analysis, and/or where there are no significant negative consequences if we are wrong, a higher alpha level (say 10 percent or 0.10) may be acceptable. In testing theories under controlled conditions and/or where the costs of making a wrong decision are high, a smaller alpha level (say 1 percent or even 0.1 percent) may be selected.

In any case, the error level (or alpha level, type I error level, *p*-level, or significance level) needs to be decided before we look at the evidence. Peeking first is not acceptable.

Step 5: Calculating Test Statistics

After all these preliminaries, we are finally ready to calculate the hypothesis test. We will calculate a ***test statistic*** and use the value of the test statistic to make a decision about whether we must accept the null hypothesis or can reject it.

Each particular hypothesis test has a particular test statistic. In the chapters that follow, we will see test statistics for hypotheses about the values of one, two, and many means; we will see test statistics for hypotheses about one, two, and many proportions; we will also see hypothesis test results for measures of association. Each of these hypothesis tests has a different formula. Fortunately, statistical software can usually be used to calculate the right test once you've thought carefully about the steps of the process.

Almost all hypothesis test statistics, though, do have the same form in the abstract. In the abstract, most test statistics are calculated by formulas that look like Formula 8.1:

$$\text{Statistic} = \frac{(\text{Observed} - \text{Null})}{\text{Standard error}} \tag{8.1}$$

That is, most of the formulas for specific hypothesis tests compare the observed value of a sample statistic to the value we would expect if the null hypothesis were true, and divide the result by the estimated standard error of the statistic.

From this general formula, we can see that the values of hypothesis test statistics get bigger as there is a bigger difference between what we observe in our sample and what the null hypothesis predicts. So, the bigger the test statistic, the less likely it is that the null hypothesis is true, and the smaller the probability of error (alpha or p) if we reject the null hypothesis.

How big is big? That's what dividing by the standard error of the statistic is for. The standard error measures how much variation there will be in the value of a statistic from one sample to the next, due only to sampling variation, if the null hypothesis were actually true. So, when we divide the size of the difference between the observed value and the null hypothesis value by the standard error, we are saying: "How big is the observed difference relative to what would happen just as a result of sampling variation, and if the null hypothesis was really true?"

If the difference between the sample statistic and the null hypothesis value is, for example, 2.0 standard errors, we would be saying that the difference is twice as large as we would expect (on average) as a result of sampling variation.

Since we know the shape of the sampling distribution (assumptions), we can then find the probability associated with a difference as big as the one we're observing. For example, if our test statistic is 2.0 and we know its distribution is normal, then only about 5 percent of the time would we observe test statistics this big if the null were true. Here, we are using our knowledge of how to find areas under the curve.

Different test statistics have different specific formulas. Some have sampling distributions that are normal (Z), whereas others are distributed as t, F, or chi-squared. But the logic is always the same: the bigger the test statistic, the less likely it is that the null hypothesis is correct.

Step 6: Making a Decision

The last step in the hypothesis testing process is to make a decision about whether we accept the null hypothesis or reject it in favor of the alternative hypothesis. If we've done everything carefully up to this point, the final decision is easy.

If the probability of our test statistic is greater than the alpha level we set, we do not reject the null hypothesis. A probability bigger than our alpha level means that there is more than an "alpha" percent chance that the null hypothesis is true. If the probability of our test statistic is greater than the alpha level we set, we do reject the null hypothesis in favor of the alternative. A probability level smaller than alpha means that there is a small chance that the null hypothesis is true.

Another way is often used to describe this process. We identify the value of the test statistic that is big enough to reject the null hypothesis—the critical value (the boundary between the shaded and unshaded regions under the curve in Figure 8.2). If our test statistic falls into the shaded area (the rejection region or critical region), we reject the null hypothesis. If it doesn't, we fail to reject the null hypothesis. Never say that we "accept the null hypothesis." We should either reject it or fail to reject it.

If we reject the null hypothesis, this means that we have found that the evidence supports, or is consistent with, our theory. We've not proved the theory right, but it has withstood a test, and we are now more convinced that it is a useful explanation.

If we fail to reject the null hypothesis, this means that the evidence does not support our theory. There is always a chance that the theory is right and that the statistical test is wrong. But we have found at least one sample where the theory is not helpful—and this suggests that we need to rethink either the theory or its scope conditions.

In deciding whether to reject or fail to reject the null hypothesis in favor of the alternative, we need to keep in mind whether the alternative hypothesis is one-tailed or two-tailed. Consider this example:

Let's suppose that our null hypothesis is: "Families have, on average, 2.1 children—about the number needed to replace the population at current mortality rates."

Let's first suppose that we observe in our sample that families have, on average, three children. This is an outcome that is pretty unlikely if the null hypothesis is true, so we are likely to reject the null hypothesis. But what is the probability that the null hypothesis is wrong? It depends on the alternative hypothesis.

If the alternative hypothesis were two-tailed: "Families do not have an average of 2.1 children," then a sample outcome that is either much higher than this (say 3) or much lower (say 1.2) would lead to rejection of the null hypothesis. So, we need to ask: "What percentage of outcomes are more than 0.9 children away from the null hypothesis value?" That is, we need to consider the probabilities in both tails of the distribution. Here, there are two critical values and two rejection regions. If our alternative hypothesis was one-tailed: "Families have more than 2.1 children," then we would need to consider only the probability of an outcome of 3 or larger—one tail, one critical value, and one rejection region.

This section has looked at the general logic and steps involved in doing hypothesis testing. In the next couple of sections we will study two particular hypothesis tests. As we do, some of the abstract ideas about hypothesis testing in general will become clearer.

But, before you do move on to study tests about one mean and one proportion, pause and take the check quiz to see how well you've mastered the general ideas of the hypothesis testing process.

CHECK QUIZ 8.1

1. In hypothesis testing, the __________ is the critical assumption, the assumption that is actually tested.
   a. research hypothesis
   b. null hypothesis
   c. assumption of a normal sampling distribution
   d. assumption that the sample was randomly selected
2. Which assumption must be true in order to justify the use of hypothesis testing?
   a. random sampling
   b. interval/ratio level of measurement
   c. very large samples
   d. samples have been stratified
3. If we reject the null hypothesis of "no difference" at the 0.05 level,
   a. the odds are 20 to 1 in our favor that we have made a correct decision.
   b. the null hypothesis is true.
   c. the odds are 5 to 1 in our favor that we have made a correct decision.
   d. the research hypothesis is true.
4. Given the same alpha level or *p*-level, the one-tailed test
   a. makes it harder to reject the H_0.
   b. does not affect the probability of rejecting the H_0.
   c. makes it more likely that the H_0 will be rejected.
   d. is less dependable than the two-tailed test.
5. A one-tailed test of significance could be used whenever
   a. the researcher can predict a direction for the difference.
   b. the researcher feels like it.
   c. the null hypothesis is thought to be true.
   d. the alpha level exceeds 1.0.

TESTS ABOUT ONE MEAN

Sometimes researchers may be interested in the question of whether the central tendency of a sample that they are observing differs from some known value. If the variable they are interested in is measured at the interval/ratio level, this research question becomes a hypothesis test about one mean.

For example, we might want to know whether the average number of siblings in families in one community differs from the national average—which we know with certainty from the national census. Or we might be interested in whether the average number of siblings for all families differs from some specific value that we have deduced from a theory.

Single-sample tests involve comparing a statistic observed in one sample to a test value or criterion.

Step 1: Null Hypothesis

The American stereotype is a family with two children. Of course there are many families with more and many with fewer. But we can use this hypothetical value as a baseline. That is, we can test whether the empirical evidence about real American families shows a mean of two children. Our researcher, the skeptical sociologist, believes that the two-child family is a myth and a cultural stereotype, not reality. So, the researcher believes that the real average number of children is not 2.0. The first step then is to state what evidence would convince us that our research hypothesis was wrong.

Let's test whether the mean number of children in American families is, in fact, equal to 2.0, using data from the 1998 General Social Survey (GSS).

Our null hypothesis will be:

H_0: Population mean = 2.0.

Note that the null hypothesis is a single value predicted for the population mean, derived from some prior theory or criterion.

Step 2: Alternative Hypotheses

Our theory is stated very generally, and says only that the average number of children in American families is not at this level. This statement suggests that if we find that the mean number of children is either much higher or much lower than 2.0, we will reject the null hypothesis.

H_a: Population mean is not equal to 2.0.

This is a two-tailed alternative, because a difference in either direction from the null hypothesis value would lead to rejection of the null in favor of the alternative.

Perhaps, though, our theory could be more specific. We might suppose that, because the American population has been aging and its wealth and education have been increasing, family sizes are now less than the *Ozzie and Harriet* stereotype.

H_a: Population mean is less than 2.0.

This is a one-tailed alternative. The mean number of children in the sample must differ from 2.0 in the negative direction for us to reject the null. If it turns out that the number is greater than 2.0, we will not reject the null in favor of this alternative hypothesis.

Step 3: Assumptions

We will be using data from the General Social Survey, 1998, which is an (approximately) equal-probability sample of the American population. So, it is reasonable to assume random sampling.

The variable that we are interested in, the number of children, is an interval/ratio variable, so it is appropriate to do a test about means.

What do we know about the shape of the sampling distribution of means? With large samples (say greater than 100 cases) we know that the sampling distribution of means is very close to normal in shape. In small samples, though, the ***Student's t-distribution*** is a better approximation to the shape of the sampling distribution. With large samples, the t-distribution is almost identical to the normal distribution, so we will use the t-distribution for any sample size.

The shape of the Student's t-distribution depends on the number of cases; it has degrees of freedom equal to the sample size less 1. When you consult a statistical table (like the Student's t-Distribution table in the Appendix) for a t-distribution, you need to be sure to use the correct critical values that depend on the degrees of freedom.

Step 4: Selecting an Error Level

Since we don't have any strong reason to choose otherwise, we will set our alpha (or type I error level or *p*-level) at 0.05. That is, we will insist that there be less than a 5 percent chance that the null hypothesis is true before we reject it.

Step 5: The t-Test

The formula for testing a hypothesis about a single population mean is Formula 8.2:

$$t_{N-1} = \frac{\overline{Y} - \mu_0}{s/\sqrt{N-1}} \tag{8.2}$$

where t is our test statistic. It has the subscript of $N - 1$ to remind us that this is the degrees of freedom that we will use in evaluating the probability of the values of t.

The numerator is the difference between our observed sample mean ($\overline{Y}$) and the hypothesized population mean (in this case, 2.0). The more different the sample mean is from the value proposed by the null hypothesis, the greater the magnitude of the test statistic; if the sample mean is bigger than the null hypothesis, t becomes a bigger positive number; if the sample mean is smaller than the null hypothesis, t becomes a bigger negative number.

The denominator is the standard deviation in the sample divided by the square root of the sample size less 1. This denominator is our sample estimator of the standard error of a mean. That is, it is a measure of how much we would expect sample means to vary from sample to sample as a result of random variation. The less efficient our statistic is (i.e., the bigger the standard error), the smaller the value of our test statistic, and the less likely we are to reject the null hypothesis. In this hypothesis test, we use $N - 1$ instead of N in our estimate of the standard error of the mean because we are using up a piece of information by estimating the sample mean. Remember that when we are simply describing the standard error of a mean, we use N.

TABLE 8.1 SPSS One-Sample t-Test Results

One-Sample Statistics

	N	Mean	Std. Deviation	Std. Error of Mean
Number of children	294	1.77	1.669	0.097

One-Sample Test

Test value = 2.0

	t	*df*	Sig. (2-tailed)	Mean Difference	95% Confidence Interval of the Difference: Lower	95% Confidence Interval of the Difference: Upper
Number of children	−2.342	293	0.020	−0.23	−0.42	−0.04

Using SPSS, we perform the one-sample t-test, and get the results shown in Table 8.1.

The results tell us that we have a sample of size of 294 (note that the degrees of freedom reported in the second part of the display is 293, one less than the sample size).

We observe that the mean in the sample is 1.77, which is −0.23 children below the prediction of the null hypothesis (called the "test value" by SPSS).

The mean number of children might be expected to vary from sample to sample, on average, by about 0.097 children (standard error of the mean).

The difference between the observed sample mean and the null hypothesis (−0.23), divided by the standard error (0.097), gives us a t statistic of −2.342. What does this mean? Sometimes a little visualization is helpful, as in Figure 8.3.

FIGURE 8.3 Visualizing the Meaning of the t-Test Results

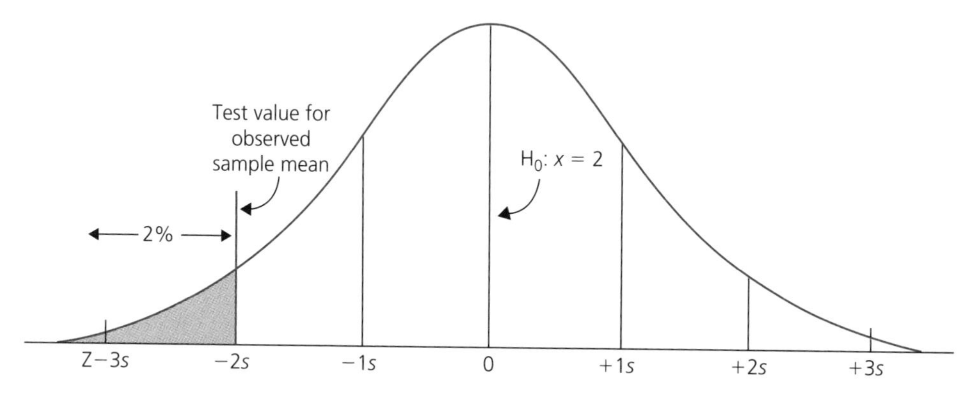

The t statistic is telling us that the observed sample mean falls 2.342 standard errors below the mean proposed by the null hypothesis.

The output also gives us the alpha (or type I error, or *p*-level) as the significance (two-tailed). The value is 0.020. This is telling us that 2 percent of all sample means would be expected to fall 2.342 standard errors from the hypothesized value just by chance. With this information, we can make a decision about whether we should accept or reject the null hypothesis in favor of the alternative.

Step 6: Making a Decision

The significance level for a two-tailed test is given as 0.02. This means that 2 percent of samples might have means that are as far or farther away from the null hypothesis about the mean just by chance.

If we reach the conclusion that the null hypothesis is false (that is, that the population mean is *not* 2.0), there is a 2 percent chance that we will be making an error. Or another way of thinking about it is to say that the significance or *p*-level is the probability that the null hypothesis is really true.

We had decided, in advance, that we were willing to take up to a 5 percent chance of being wrong in rejecting the null hypothesis in favor of the alternative. Since the result is telling us that we would be wrong only 2 percent of the time, we would reach the conclusion that we can reject the null hypothesis with an acceptable margin of error.

If we reject the null hypothesis (remember that the null hypothesis was that the mean number of children was 2.0), then we are accepting the alternative hypothesis.

Earlier we suggested that there were two possible alternative hypotheses—one-tailed and two-tailed. Our statistical software has reported the significance level for a two-tailed test. It is saying that there is a 2 percent chance of observing a mean that is 2.34 standard errors away from the null hypothesis *in either direction.* So, the p-level (or significance level, or alpha error level) for the two-tailed alternative is 2 percent (actually, statisticians almost always say $p < 0.02$, rather than 2 percent).

If we were only interested in the probability that the sample mean was *less than* 2.0 (i.e., a one-tailed alternative), the *p*-level would be only 1 percent—because only about 1 percent of all sample results will be greater than 2.34 standard errors in the negative direction. So, the significance level for the one-tailed alternative is $p = 0.01$. We can be even more confident that the population mean is below 2.0 than we are with the more general alternative that it is not equal to 2.0.

Most statistical software reports *p* for two-tailed tests. If your alternative hypothesis is one-tailed, you can simply divide the reported *p*-level by 2 in order to get the significance level for a one-tailed test (if the difference is in the direction specified by the one-tailed alternative hypothesis!).

Hypothesis tests about the central tendency of a single mean can be quite useful when we want to know whether the value in a sample is truly different from some comparison value. To be really sure that you understand the lessons of this section, you will need to take the time to study the examples and to work some problems. But why not take a second now to see how well you do on the check quiz—and see if you should reread this section?

CHECK QUIZ 8.2

1. A sample of people attending a professional football game averages 13.7 years of formal education while the surrounding community averages 12.1 years. The difference is significant at the 0.05 level. What could we conclude?
   a. The null hypothesis should be accepted.
   b. The research hypothesis should be rejected.
   c. The sample is significantly more educated than the community as a whole.
   d. The alpha level is too low.
2. A researcher is interested in the effect that neighborhood crime-watch efforts have on the crime rate in the inner city, but he is unwilling to predict the direction of the difference. The appropriate test of a hypothesis would be
   a. one-tailed.
   b. two-tailed.
   c. descriptive.
   d. symmetrical.
3. Do sex education classes and free clinics that offer counseling for teenagers reduce the number of pregnancies among teenagers? The appropriate test of a hypothesis would be
   a. a one-tailed test.
   b. a two-tailed test.
   c. cross-sectional.
   d. participant observation.
4. When reading output from SPSS, in order to find the significance of a one-tailed test for a difference in means, one needs to
   a. multiply the significance of the two-tailed test by 2.
   b. multiply the significance of the two-tailed test by 0.5.
   c. take the square root of the one-tailed test.
   d. take the last train to Clarksville.
5. When H_a is that the mean is "greater than" some value, you have a __________; when H_a is that the mean is "not equal to" some value, you have a __________.
   a. one-tailed test; two-tailed test
   b. two-tailed test; two-tailed test
   c. normal distribution; standard error
   d. problem; solution

Example

COMPUTING A SINGLE-SAMPLE TEST ABOUT A MEAN

In the mid-1990s, the life expectancy of women born in the United States was about 75 years. That is, 50 percent of the women born in 1995 could expect to live at least this long. Given the remarkable material wealth of the United States compared to many other nations, we might expect that life expectancy in the United States is notably higher than the average of other nations. But, since we do not have information on all nations and some of the data that we do have may be somewhat unreliable, we want to use a hypothesis test to determine how much confidence we should have if we want to assert that female life expectancy in the United States is higher than the average of other nations.

First, we set up the problem:

Female life expectancy is measured in years at the interval level, so a test of means is a reasonable approach. We will assume that we have observed a random sample of nations (though this is probably not strictly true).

Let's set up the null hypothesis that the mean female life expectancy in world nations is three years lower than it is in the United States. Note that the most common null hypothesis would be that the mean female life expectancy in world nations was no different than in the United States—but we want to make our example a little more interesting.

Next, we need to set up the alternative hypothesis. Our theory about material wealth leads us to believe that, if anything, life expectancy is greater in the United States than the world average. This would lead us to the alternative hypothesis that the mean for the world nations is more than three years lower than the mean for the United States, or less than 72 years. This is a one-tailed alternative hypothesis, since only differences in one direction lead to the rejection of the null in favor of the alternative. A two-tailed alternative would suggest, more simply, that the mean of world nations was different (higher or lower) than that of the United States.

Last, we need to decide, in advance, how confident we want to be in accepting the alternative hypothesis instead of the null. Or what chance are we willing to take of being wrong if we choose to reject the null? Let's choose a stringent alpha (or *p*) level of 0.01.

Here's Formula 8.2, the formula for a single sample test about a mean, again:

$$t_{N-1} = \frac{\overline{Y} - \mu_0}{s/\sqrt{N-1}} \tag{8.2}$$

Example

We need to know several things in order to do the test. We've calculated this elsewhere: The sample size (N) is 109. The standard deviation (s) of female life expectancy in the sample is 10.572 years. The sample mean life expectancy is 70.16 years. Our null hypothesis value about the mean is the value for the United States, less the three-year difference we had proposed ($75 - 3 = 72$ years).

The calculation is very easy:

$$\begin{aligned}\text{Test statistic} &= (70.16 - 72)/[10.572/(\text{sqrt}108)] \\ &= -1.84/(10.572/10.392) \\ &= -1.84/1.02 \\ &= -1.80\end{aligned}$$

Next, we need to evaluate the probability of observing a test statistic this large, if the null hypothesis is true. We need to use the t distribution with 108 degrees of freedom ($N - 1$).

We use the table of critical values of t provided in the Appendix. We are doing a one-tailed test. Our desired alpha level is 0.01. Our degrees of freedom are 108. Using the table, we see the critical value for $df = 60$ is 2.39; the critical value for $df = 120$ is 2.36.

Since our test statistic is not as large as the critical value, we must accept the null hypothesis. That is, we cannot be 99 percent confident that the average life expectancy of women in other world nations is more than three years lower than it is in the United States.

So, even though the world nations sample mean (70.16 years) does appear to be lower than the criterion of 72 years (that is, the United States' value of 75 years, less three years), we cannot be confident that this difference was not due to sampling variability.

Just a few comments about this example are in order. The sample of nations is not really random—poor nations are underrepresented in the sample. The sample of 109 nations includes a substantial proportion of the population of nations, and we might want to apply a "finite population correction" to the result. Our choice of a three-year difference was pretty arbitrary—we don't have any particular theory about this. Last, our demand for 99 percent confidence is quite stringent. These comments suggest an important thing about real-world hypothesis testing. Test results depend on assumptions, data quality, and our decisions. When someone tells you a result is "significant" you need to ask a lot of questions!

Example

USING EXCEL FOR ONE-SAMPLE T-TESTS OF MEANS

Here's one way of setting up a spreadsheet to perform a one-sample test for a mean:

	A	B	C
1	Delinquent frogs		
2	376		
3	491		
4	236		
5	633		
6	540		
7	514		
8	471	y-bar:	=AVERAGE(A2:A25)
9	352	hypothesized mean:	475
10	328	n-1	=COUNT(A2:A25)-1
11	229	sd	=STDEV(A2:A25)
12	505	t	=(C8-C9)/(C11/SQRT(C10))
13	486	P (2-tailed):	=TDIST(ABS(C12),C10,2)
14	393		
15	205		
16	587		
17	421		
18	664		
19	413		
20	348		
21	492		
22	641		
23	463		
24	336		
25	521		

Enter mu (the hypothesized value for the population mean) in C9, and you'll get the Student's t and a *p*-value from the sheet. Here's the result:

	A	B	C
1	Delinquent frogs		
2	376		
3	491		
4	236		
5	633		
6	540		
7	514		
8	471	y-bar:	443.54
9	352	hypothesized mean:	475.00
10	328	n-1	23.00
11	229	sd	127.28
12	505	t	-1.19
13	486	P (2-tailed):	0.25
14	393		
15	205		
16	587		
17	421		
18	664		
19	413		
20	348		
21	492		
22	641		
23	463		
24	336		
25	521		

Note: You can use the same spreadsheet to do tests about one proportion. All you need to do is to code the variable of interest as a dummy (i.e., 0 or 1) variable!

TESTS ABOUT ONE PROPORTION

If we interested in the central tendency of a categorical variable (nominal or grouped ordinal), we usually use proportions as our descriptive statistic. We frequently want to compare the value of a proportion in a sample to some standard or baseline value. For example, we might be interested in whether the proportion of people who are "black" in a sample that we have taken in our community differs from the national percentage—which we know with some certainty from the U.S. Census. Or, we might be interested in whether the proportion of students in a sociology class who are women is greater than the proportion in the undergraduate population—which we know with certainty from the school registrar's records.

Tests about a single proportion can be done in two ways. One approach is to directly calculate a Z-test based on observed sample proportions. A second approach is to transform the variable we are interested in into a "dummy" variable, and use the t-test for means that we described in the previous section. We'll show you both approaches.

Step 1: Null Hypothesis

The null hypothesis for a test about a single proportion proposes that the proportion in question is equal to some specific value in the population.

As an example, let's look at some data from the 1998 General Social Survey. A problem that sometimes arises in survey research is that women tend to be overrepresented in survey research samples. This is probably because women may be slightly more likely to be at home when survey takers call or may be slightly more willing to answer questions than men. We might hypothesize, on the basis of these arguments, that women are likely to be overrepresented among respondents to the 1998 General Social Survey.

What does *overrepresented* mean? Women constitute somewhat more than half of the U.S. population. For the purposes of this exercise, let's assume that we know with some certainty that the proportion of women in the population is 0.52 (actually, it is a bit higher than this). Our null hypothesis, then, would be that there is no difference between the population proportion and the sample proportion, or:

$$H_0 : P_s = 0.52$$

Step 2: Alternative Hypotheses

Our theory about response rates to surveys leads us to predict that the proportion of women among survey respondents may be *higher* than the proportion in the population:

H_a: $P_s > 0.52$, or the difference between the criterion (0.52) and the sample value is greater than zero.

This is a one-tailed alternative. We will need to keep this in mind when interpreting the results of the test.

Step 3: Assumptions

The observations must be from a random sample. While the General Social Survey is not really a simple random sample, it has been carefully designed to approximate one. So, we will live with the assumption of random sampling.

The variable in question, gender, is nominal with two categories, so tests for proportions as measures of central tendency are appropriate. With nominal variables with multiple categories, one would combine the categories into two for the purpose of hypothesis testing: a focal group or groups versus all other categories combined. For a grouped ordinal variable, combining the proportions in all of the categories up to a certain level (e.g., "disagree" = strongly disagree + moderately disagree) and contrasting this proportion with the proportion in the remaining categories (e.g., neutral + moderately agree + strongly agree).

The sampling distribution of a proportion is known to be approximately normal in large samples (at least 100 cases). The classic test for proportions uses the normal sampling distribution. An alternative approach, using dummy variables, is really a test for means, and a t-distribution is more appropriate. When the size of the sample is small (less than 100) it is wise to use an exact test that can be calculated in most statistical software.

Step 4: Selecting an Error Level

Let's suppose that we've decided, in advance, that we are willing to take a 10 percent chance of being wrong if we decide to reject the null hypothesis that the General Social Survey proportion's of female respondents is equal to 0.52. So, we are setting our confidence level for the test at 90 percent, or our alpha level, *p*-level, or significance level at 0.10.

Step 5: The Test Statistic

Here's Formula 8.3, the formula for a large-sample hypothesis test about a single sample proportion:

$$Z = \frac{P_S - \rho_0}{\sqrt{P_S(1 - P_S)/N}} \tag{8.3}$$

In the numerator we have the difference between the observed proportion in the category of interest in the sample (P_S) and the null hypothesis value about the population proportion (ρ_0). Like most hypothesis tests, the numerator gets larger as the difference between the null and alternative hypotheses gets bigger.

In our example, it turns out that the proportion of female respondents in the 1998 General Social Survey was 0.539. This contrasts with the null hypothesis value of 0.52. So, the numerator of the Z-test in our example has the value of 0.019.

In the denominator of the formula, we are calculating an estimate of the standard error of the proportion. This can be estimated by multiplying the proportion in the category of interest (P_S) times the proportion not in that category, dividing the result by the sample size, and then taking the square root. This is our regular formula for the standard error of a proportion.

In our example, P_s is 0.539, so the result of doing the math is 0.029. That is, we would expect the proportion of females among General Social Survey respondents to vary, on average, by 0.029 from sample to sample.

The Z-test statistic is the size of the difference between the observed proportion and the null hypothesis proportion, divided by the expected sampling variability of the proportion.

In our example, this is $0.019/0.029 = 0.655$.

It is always useful to visualize our results in terms of the sampling distribution of the null hypothesis proportion, as in Figure 8.4.

Your intuition should be telling you that the difference we've observed (0.019) relative to the expected sampling variability (0.029) is not big enough for us to be confident that the sample differs from the null hypothesis. But we'll return to this decision in a minute.

First, let's look at a slightly different way of solving this problem using a test of means, rather than a test of proportions.

Suppose that we turned the variable "gender" into a numerical variable called "female" by giving a score of one point to persons who were females and a score of no points to a person who was not a female. This particular approach is called creating a dummy variable.

FIGURE 8.4 Visualizing the Z-Test Results

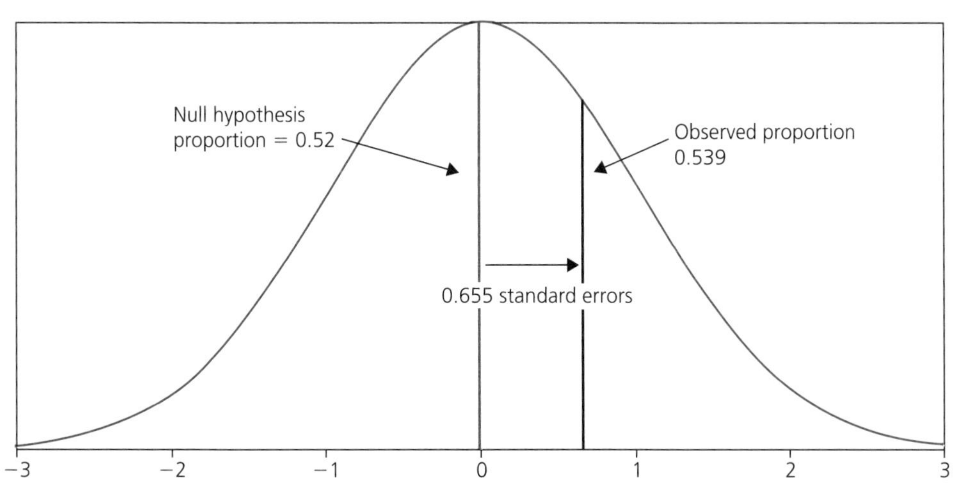

A dummy variable is simply a variable that gives a score of 1 to cases that satisfy some criterion and a score of 0 to all others.

Now that we have created the dummy variable "female" (remember, 0 = nonfemale, 1 = female), let's calculate the mean. This is legitimate because the variable is now an interval/ratio variable—it just happens to only have one interval, the interval from zero to one. The mean of a dummy variable is equal to the proportion of cases that are scored 1 on that variable. When I calculate the mean, I add up the scores of all the cases. These are either 0 (for males) or 1 (for females), so the sum of the variable is actually a count of the number of females. Then, in calculating the mean, I divide by the total number of cases. Thus, I'm dividing the number of females by the total number of persons, which equals the proportion of persons who are females.

Once I've done this dummy coding, I can apply the t-test for hypotheses about one mean. Table 8.2 presents the results, calculated by SPSS.

The mean in the sample is 0.539, which is the proportion female. The estimated standard error of this mean (0.02907) is very close to the estimated standard error using the Z formula approach. The t-statistic (0.653) is very close to—a little more conservative than—the Z-statistic (0.655).

Step 6: Making a Decision

Now that we have performed the test, using either Z for a proportion or t for a mean, we need to reach a conclusion about rejecting or accepting our null hypothesis.

SPSS reports the two-tailed significance as 0.514. Since our alternative hypothesis is that the proportion of females may be higher than 0.52 (not just different from 0.52), we are doing a one-tailed test. So, our significance level, alpha level, or *p*-level is actually 0.257.

TABLE 8.2 SPSS Results for Testing a Proportion Using a Dummy Variable t-Test of Means

One-Sample Test

	N	**Mean**	**Std. Deviation**	**Std. Error of Mean**
Dummy variable for female	295	0.5390	0.49933	0.02907

One-Sample Test

Test value = 2.0

	t	***df***	**Sig. (2-tailed)**	**Mean Difference**	**95% Confidence Interval of the Difference** Lowers	Upper
Dummy variable for female	0.653	294	0.514	0.0190	−0.0382	0.0762

CHECK QUIZ 8.3

1. All other things being equal, with which of the following alpha levels would we be most likely to reject the null hypothesis?
   a. 0.01
   b. 0.001
   c. 0.05
   d. 0.10
2. Rejecting the null hypothesis means
   a. accepting defeat.
   b. accepting the alternative hypothesis.
   c. finding insignificance.
   d. that we haven't done the test properly.
3. Under what conditions might we use proportions rather than means as the test statistic?
   a. when sample size is very small
   b. when sample size is very large
   c. when the variable of interest is only interval/ratio in level of measurement
   d. when the variable of interest is only nominal in level of measurement
4. From a random sample of size 200 drawn from a local community, 120 respondents identify themselves as Democrats. For the community as a whole, 75 percent of the residents classify themselves as Democrats. If the null hypothesis is that $P_s = P_u$, the alternative hypothesis might be
   a. $P_u - P_s = 0.15$.
   b. $P_u - P_s > 0.14$.
   c. $P_s < 0.60$.
   d. any of the above.
5. When solving the equations for the test statistic, one should perform ___________ first.
   a. operations in parentheses
   b. multiplication
   c. division
   d. addition
6. In the Z-test example for difference in proportions given in the text, in order for us to have rejected the null hypothesis, the Z-score should have been
   a. closer to the mean for the distribution.
   b. farther to the left of the distribution.
   c. farther to the right of the distribution.
   d. a t-score.

Example

COMPUTING A SINGLE-SAMPLE TEST ABOUT A PROPORTION

In the United States at about 1980, roughly 62 percent of the adult population was married. We have all heard that "the institution of marriage is declining." What does the evidence say?

Using a sample from the General Social Survey in 1998 ($N = 295$), we observe that 47.8 percent of the respondents report that they are currently married. This suggests that the proportion of the population who are married has, indeed, declined. But the 1998 figures are based on a sample. Can we be confident that the difference is real, and not due to sampling variability?

The variable "married or not" is categorical, so a test about a proportion is a reasonable approach. We will assume that the General Social Survey sample is similar to a simple random sample, and we note that there is a large sample size.

Our null hypothesis is that the proportion of the adult population who are married in 1998 does not differ from the 1980 value of 0.62 (62 percent).

Our alternative hypothesis, based on the theory that marriage is declining as a social institution, is that the proportion of the adult American population who were married in 1998 will be less than 0.62. Note that this is a one-tailed test (a two-tailed alternative would propose simply that the proportion in 1998 was different from that in 1980).

Let's suppose that we want to be 95 percent confident should the evidence suggest that we ought to reject the null hypothesis, or, alternatively, that we are willing to take no more than a 5 percent chance of being wrong if we reject the null in favor of the alternative.

Our test statistic is calculated by Formula 8.3.

$$Z = \frac{P_S - \rho_0}{\sqrt{P_S(1 - P_S)/N}} \tag{8.3}$$

P_S is the proportion that we observed in our sample (0.478 or 47.8 percent married in 1998). N is the sample size (295). The null hypothesis about the population value (in the numerator of the formula) is that the proportion is 0.62 (what we know it was in 1980). Thus, we can calculate:

$$\begin{aligned}\text{Test statistic} &= (0.478 - 0.62)/\text{sqrt}\{[0.478(1 - 0.478)]/295\}\\ &= (0.142)/\text{sqrt}[(0.478 \times 0.522)/295]\\ &= -0.142/\text{sqrt}(0.0008458)\\ &= -0.142/0.029\\ &= 4.897\end{aligned}$$

Example

Since the test statistic is a standard normal variable (that is, a Z-score), we could use the Appendix table of areas under the standard normal curve to find the probability. The table goes only as high as 3.00, which shows a probability of 0.0013. Since this *p*-level is less than the alpha level we had set (95 percent confidence, so alpha = 0.05), we have passed the critical value and can reject the null hypothesis.

That is, we can be confident (at the 95 percent level) that the proportion of adult Americans who were married in 1998 was less than 0.62.

One comment is in order. Does this result prove that the institution of marriage is in trouble? No. The result does say, however, that a prediction from a theory of institutional decline appears to be consistent with the data. Until a better theory comes along, we tentatively conclude that the theory may be a useful explanation of the data. There may be other theories that are also consistent with the data.

There are several correct ways of thinking about this:

- About 25.7 percent of the time we would observe proportions of females in samples that are higher than the baseline of 0.52 as much as the current sample is—just by chance.
- There is a 25.7 percent chance that the null hypothesis is actually correct.
- We would be taking a 25.7 percent chance of being wrong if we decided to reject the null hypothesis.

We had decided, before we did the test, that we were willing to take as much as a 10 percent chance of being wrong. All of our results suggest that we would be taking a bigger chance than 10 percent if we rejected the null hypothesis. So, we have no choice but to fail to reject the null hypothesis.

We must conclude, then, that we cannot be 90 percent confident that the proportion of females responding to the General Social Survey differs from 0.52. Substantively, we do not have very good grounds for questioning the gender representativeness of the GSS sample.

So, hypothesis tests about a single proportion are very much like hypothesis tests about a single mean. In fact, one approach to dealing with a single proportion is to turn it into a dummy variable and use the t test for means.

We've covered a lot of material in this chapter. You will need to work through the examples and do some problems to make sure you've mastered the key ideas of hypothesis testing, and their application to hypotheses about a single-sample central tendency. For now, take the quick check quiz to see if you grasped the main points about hypothesis tests for a single proportion.

SUMMARY

In this chapter we've introduced the logic of hypothesis testing, and applied the basic ideas to two particular tests: tests of hypotheses about a single sample mean and tests of hypotheses about a single sample proportion.

Hypothesis testing uses the same inferential statistics ideas as confidence intervals, but in a different way. In setting confidence intervals, we examine data in a sample and make an inference about the most likely values of population parameters. In hypothesis testing, we begin by making an assumption about the true value of a population parameter, and then evaluate how likely a given sample result is if that assumption is correct.

Hypothesis testing is designed to see if data are consistent with the expectations of theory. Working with theory, we develop a null hypothesis—which, if true in the population, would suggest that our theory was wrong. After developing the null hypothesis, we consider the alternatives—what we are led to conclude if we are able to reject the null hypothesis with a desired level of confidence.

By making assumptions about random sampling, correct levels of measurement, and the shape of the sampling distributions of statistics, we can then apply inferential tools to determine the probability that the results in a sample could be the result of drawing that sample from a population where the null hypothesis is, in fact, true.

If the results are very unlikely under the assumption that the null hypothesis is true, we are led to reject the null hypothesis in favor of the alternative. However, we are never certain, so we must set a type I error level, alpha error level, *p*-level, or significance level (or their opposite—a confidence level) to make the decision to accept or reject the null.

The next-to-last step in the hypothesis testing process is to compute a test statistic. There are different test statistics for different kinds of hypotheses. Most test statistics measure how different a sample statistic is from the null hypothesis value for the population parameter. The size of this difference is then expressed in units of standard errors of the statistic in question.

Since we know the shape of the sampling distribution of the statistic, we can determine the probability that a sample statistic could have occurred by chance, given the null hypothesis. If that probability is less than our alpha level, we reject the null hypothesis and conclude that the alternative hypothesis is supported.

These basic ideas were applied to hypotheses about a single mean and a single proportion. The test for a single proportion can also be converted into tests for means by using dummy variables.

Tests about a mean or a proportion have a baseline or test value that is determined by theory. The null hypothesis is that the value of the mean or proportion in a sample does not differ from the baseline value, which is the null hypothesis value. Test statistics are calculated that measure the difference between the sample statistic and the hypothesized population parameters. Using estimates of the standard error and assumptions about the shape of the sampling distribution (t with $N - 1$ degrees of freedom, or Z), the probability of the sample statistic can be determined. The probability of the sample statistic depends, as well, on whether the alternative hypothesis is one-tailed or two-tailed.

The basic ideas of hypothesis testing are quite important for all advanced statistics. Almost all advanced statistics may be thought of as performing hypothesis tests of various levels of complexity. In the next chapters we will look at just a few more examples of hypothesis testing, all having to do with central tendency.

KEY TERMS

alternative hypothesis: one-tailed and two-tailed

critical value

hypothesis testing

null hypothesis

rejection region

Student's t-distribution

test statistic

type I (alpha) error or "p-level"

type II (beta) error

CHECK QUIZ ANSWERS

Quiz 8.1 Answers: 1. (b); 2. (a); 3. (a); 4. (c); 5. (a)
Quiz 8.2 Answers: 1. (c); 2. (b); 3. (a); 4. (b); 5. (a)
Quiz 8.3 Answers: 1. (d); 2. (b); 3. (d); 4. (d); 5. (a); 6. (c)

EXERCISES

1. Let's suppose that we know, from a survey, that 10 percent of the residents of San Bernardino have suffered a property loss due to crime in the past five years. In a new study, we discover that 14 percent of 527 residents who are over the age of 65 have suffered property losses. Can we be 95 percent confident that the rate of crime victimization of older residents is higher than the population percentage?
2. A political poll taker finds that 54 percent of the respondents in a sample of 300 people report that they will vote for the incumbent in an upcoming election. Can the poll taker be 95 percent confident that more than 50 percent of the population will vote for the incumbent? Can we be 99 percent confident?
3. A random sample of 425 residents of a city have finished an average of 12.7 years of schooling, with a standard deviation of 1.7 years. In the state as a whole, we know that the average years of schooling completed is 12.2 years. Can we be confident (at the alpha = 0.05 level) that the average education in the city is higher than the average for the state as a whole?
4. A sample of 100 sociology majors is asked to report their grade point averages (GPAs). They report an average of 2.87, with a standard deviation of 0.30. The registrar of the university tells me that the average GPA of all students on campus is 2.75. Can I be confident at alpha = 0.05 that sociology majors have a higher grade point average than the campus average?

5. A random sample of 26 psychology majors at the local college scored an average of 458 on the Graduate Record Examination verbal skills test, with a standard deviation of 20. The national average score on this test for all psychology majors is 440. Can we be confident, at $p = 0.05$, that the average score at the local college is higher than the national average?
6. Assume that the 15 students in a criminal justice class are a random sample of all criminal justice students. These students report that they work on average 18 hours per week, with a standard deviation of 4 hours. Can I be confident, at $p < 0.05$, that criminal justice students work less than 25 hours a week?
7. We are concerned that the General Social Survey sample may not be exactly representative of the whole adult U.S. population in terms of gender. In the entire population, we know that 53 percent are female (from the U.S. Census). We create the variable "female" that has the value of 1 if a person is female, and 0 otherwise. Then we use SPSS to do a single-sample test. Here are the results.

One-Sample Test

	N	Mean	Std. Deviation	Std. Error Mean
Female	1,500	0.5633	0.49614	0.01281

One-Sample Test

Test value = 0.53						
					95% Confidence Interval of the Difference	
	t	*df*	Sig. (2-tailed)	Mean Difference	Lower	Upper
Female	2.602	1,499	0.009	0.0333	0.0082	0.0585

   a. What is the null hypothesis being tested here?
   b. Can we be 95 percent confident in rejecting this null hypothesis? What is your evidence?
   c. What conclusion do you reach regarding the representativeness of the General Social Survey?
8. We are concerned that some data we are using from the General Social Survey may not be representative of the true proportion of persons in the United States who are classified by the U.S. Census as "black." We know from the Census that the population proportion who are "black" in the U.S. adult population is 13 percent.

We code black persons as 1 and nonblack persons as 0. Then we run SPSS one-sample tests, and obtain the following output:

One-Sample Statistics

	N	Mean	Std. Deviation	Std. Error Mean
Person is black	1,500	0.1167	0.32113	0.00829

One-Sample Test

Test value = 0.13					95% Confidence Interval of the Difference	
	t	*df*	Sig. (2-tailed)	Mean Difference	Lower	Upper
Person is black	1.608	1,499	0.108	−0.0133	−0.0296	0.0029

a. If our null hypothesis is that the proportion of GSS respondents is 0.13, do we accept or reject this hypothesis at $p = 0.05$? What is your evidence?
b. Would you conclude that the GSS sample is probably representative?

9. Do the respondents to the General Social Survey, on average, have a greater than high school education (i.e., completed 12 years of schooling)? Here is the necessary analysis from SPSS.

One-Sample Statistics

	N	Mean	Std. Deviation	Std. Error Mean
Highest year of school completed	1,498	12.76	2.981	0.077

One-Sample Test

Test value = 12					95% Confidence Interval of the Difference	
	t	*df*	Sig. (2-tailed)	Mean Difference	Lower	Upper
Highest year of school completed	9.924	1,497	0.000	0.76	0.61	0.92

a. Can we be confident at the 95 percent level that the sample value differs from 12 years? What is your evidence?
b. Can we be confident at the 95 percent level that the sample value is greater than 12 years? What is your evidence?

10. We know that, on average across all 50 U.S. states, the percentage of the population who were younger than 19 years of age in 1996 was 26.09 percent.

    We've drawn a sample of 29 states, and calculated the mean percentage who are age 19 or less. To determine whether our sample is representative, we've tested whether the mean in the sample is equal to 26.09 percent, the true population value in 1996. Here are the results:

One-Sample Statistics

	N	Mean	Std. Deviation	Std. Error Mean
Percent of population younger than 18, 1996	29	25.5586	1.22693	0.22784

One-Sample Test

Test value = 26.09						
	t	*df*	Sig. (2-tailed)	Mean Difference	95% Confidence Interval of the Difference	
					Lower	Upper
Percent of population younger than 18, 1996	−2.332	28	0.027	−0.5314	−0.9981	−0.0647

What is your conclusion? Is our sample representative of the population? What is your evidence?

Chapter 9

Hypothesis Testing for Two Samples

LEARNING OBJECTIVES

When you have finished this chapter, you will be able to:

- Understand the null and alternative hypotheses for two-sample tests for differences in means.
- Select the appropriate two-sample means test based on the Levene homogeneity test for the equality of population variances.
- Perform a two-group mean difference test and interpret the results.
- Understand and perform the test for the difference between two group proportions, and the alternative approach of dummy variables.
- Know when to use the nonindependent (repeated measures, within subjects) test for the difference between two means, and interpret the results.
- Understand the difference between statistical significance and substantive significance, and use differences in means and differences in proportions to discuss effect size.

COMPARING TWO GROUPS

In this chapter we apply the ideas of hypothesis testing to the case in which we want to compare the central tendencies (either means or proportions) of two groups to each other. The basic logic of hypothesis testing with two groups is very much like comparing one group to a baseline, like we did in the preceding chapter. But there are some differences, because we are concerned with two samples, not just one.

Two-sample tests are very common in the social sciences. In experiments, we very often want to compare the mean outcome of a treatment group to that of a control group. In quasi-experimental work, we may wish to compare some outcome for two communities or two treatment programs. Many nonexperimental questions involve comparing means or proportions between two naturally occurring populations: men versus women, persons of color versus persons of European ethnicity, nations in the core of the world system versus those on the periphery.

So far in this book we have been doing univariate statistics—first descriptive, then inferential. That is, we were looking at one variable at a time, or just one sample.

For the remainder of this book, we will be doing bivariate statistics. That is, we will be examining how the scores of cases on two variables go together or "covary." In this chapter and the next, we will look at a very common kind of bivariate statistics: group comparisons. In later chapters, we will extend this to the more general idea of studying the association between variables.

If we compare the scores of men and women on some outcome variable, we are, in fact, considering two variables. One variable, obviously, is the outcome (or dependent) variable. The other variable, not so obviously, is the variable group. The actual variable here is "gender," and people's scores on this variable vary—a person may be either a male or a female. So, when we compare two groups, we are actually doing a bivariate analysis in which we see how scores on one variable (what group you are in) tend to go with scores on another (means or proportions on the outcome).

COMPARING TWO GROUPS' MEANS

Tests to compare two-group means follow the same process of hypothesis testing as one-group tests. First we establish our null and alternative hypotheses, examine the assumptions, and select an error level. Then we look at the data by computing a test statistic. Using the appropriate sampling distribution, we find the probability that the null hypothesis is true in the population, and reach a decision to accept or reject the null hypothesis.

Step 1: Null Hypothesis

Usually theories offer explanations of why two groups differ from each other. Sometimes the theories may go further, and suggest that one group's mean is higher or lower than the other's. Less commonly, a theory may suggest that the means of two groups differ by a particular amount.

The simplest and most common null hypothesis for comparing the means of two groups would be:

$$H_0 : \mu_A = \mu_B$$

We can also express this (perhaps a bit more simply) as:

$$H_0 : \mu_A - \mu_B = 0$$

This null hypothesis would let us test whether the means of the two groups were simply different from one another (a two-tailed alternative), or whether one mean was greater than the other (a one-tailed alternative).

By stating hypotheses about two means in terms of the size of the difference between them, we can also test null hypotheses about the difference being more than some amount. Suppose, for example, we wanted to reject the idea that group A was three points higher than group B, in favor of the alternative that group A was more than three points higher than group B. We could use the null hypothesis:

$$H_0 : \mu_A - \mu_B = 3.0$$

By using a one-tailed alternative (that the difference was greater than +3.0), we could then test the hypothesis that group A was significantly more than three points higher than group B.

Notice that all the null hypotheses are stated in terms of population means, not sample means. Remember that what we are doing is assuming that the null hypothesis is true for the populations, and then asking: "How likely is it that populations for which the null is true could have produced the samples we see?" If it is very unlikely that the sample data could have been produced by populations in which the null hypothesis is true, we will reject the null hypothesis. When we reject (or accept) the null hypothesis, we are making an inference about the populations.

Step 2: Alternative Hypotheses

For any null hypothesis about the size of the difference between two population means, we could suggest either a one-tailed or a two-tailed alternative. A two-tailed alternative hypothesis is simply that the difference between sample means is significantly different from (greater or less than) the value specified in the null hypothesis. A one-tailed alternative hypothesis is simply that the difference between the means is significantly different from the value specified in the null hypothesis—in one direction (i.e., either a positive amount or a negative amount, but not both).

As with hypotheses about one mean, it is generally easiest to set the null hypothesis, perform the test and recover the two-tailed significance level (which is what most software will print), and then decide—depending on the kind of alternative hypothesis you chose—whether to divide the error level in half (if a one-tailed hypothesis) or to leave it as it is (if a two-tailed hypothesis).

Step 3: Assumptions

The hypothesis tests for differences between means assume that random sampling has been used to select cases from each of the two populations.

The tests that we examine in this section assume that the sampling of cases from one population is independent of the sampling of cases from the other. Most surveys and archival data use independent samples; for example, the fact that a particular male person happens to have been selected for inclusion in the study has no effect on the probability of a particular female being included. But if females were selected randomly and then each was asked to nominate a male to be in the study, the samples would not be independent. Studies with matched subjects or with before-and-after experiments do not have independent samples. A different approach is used with nonindependent samples (discussed later in the chapter).

Since we are examining a difference between means, it is important that the outcome variable has been measured at the interval/ratio level, and that the mean is a reasonable summary of central tendency. If the distributions are multimodal or highly skewed, one might not want to use the two-sample tests described here (and it might be advisable to consult an expert).

We must also make an assumption about the shape of the sampling distribution of the difference between two means. For large samples ($N_1 + N_2 > 100$), it is reasonable to assume that the sampling distribution of the difference between two means is normal. For smaller samples, it is generally recommended that we use the t-distribution with $(N_1 + N_2 - 2)$ degrees of freedom. Actually, since the t-distribution becomes very similar to the normal distribution as sample sizes increase, many analysts just use the t-distribution for all tests of differences between means, regardless of sample size.

There is one additional complexity in examining the difference between two means. Generally it is assumed that the variances of the outcome variable are the same in the two populations being compared. The hypothesis tests for small samples discussed later assume equal variances. It is a good idea to examine the sample standard deviations and see if they are approximately equal. There is also a test, called the ***Levene test*** for the equality of variances, that can be done before the actual hypothesis test. If it is not reasonable to assume that the variances are the same across the two groups, then the pooled estimator that is usually used for large samples should probably be used regardless of sample size—because it is a more conservative approach.

Step 4: Selecting an Error Level

There is nothing new about selecting an alpha level (aka *p*-level, type I error level, or significance level) for a test of the difference between two means. The same considerations about the costs and benefits of selecting a strict and demanding criterion for rejecting the null hypothesis (i.e., 0.01 or 0.001) apply to all hypothesis testing.

Step 5: Computing Test Statistics: Z and t

If both of the samples being compared are fairly large (i.e., if the combined sample size is greater than 100, and there are at least 30 cases in each group), we know that the sampling distribution of the difference between population means is approximately normal, and a Z-test statistic can be used, as in Formula 9.1:

$$Z = \frac{(\overline{Y}_1 - \overline{Y}_2) - (\mu_{0_1} - \mu_{0_2})}{\sigma_{\overline{Y}_1 - \overline{Y}_2}} \tag{9.1}$$

The numerator here says: Compare the difference that we observe between the two sample means ($\overline{Y}_1$ and $\overline{Y}_2$) to the size of the difference stated by the null hypothesis (mu sub zero, population 1 minus mu sub zero, population 2). If we are simply testing for a difference between two population means, the null hypothesis difference is zero, and this term drops out.

The numerator then is: How different is the sample result from our hypothesis about the population parameter? The bigger the numerator, the less likely it is that the null hypothesis can be true. So, as the test statistic gets bigger, we are more and more likely to conclude that the null hypothesis must be wrong.

The denominator in Formula 9.1 is the standard error of the difference between the two population means. We don't know this value (we would have to actually measure the populations), but we can estimate it, as in Formula 9.2:

$$\sigma_{\overline{Y}_1 - \overline{Y}_2} = \sqrt{\frac{S_1^2}{N_1 - 1} + \frac{S_2^2}{N_2 - 1}} \tag{9.2}$$

This formula—called the "pooled estimator," does not assume equal population variances, and gives generally smaller estimates of standard errors than a formula that does assume equal variances. Generally, in large samples, it is reasonable to assume equal variances. If the sample standard deviations are very different (say one is twice as large as the other or more), you should use the t-test (Formula 9.3) that has been designed for small samples.

For small samples, the test statistic is:

$$t = \frac{(\overline{Y}_1 - \overline{Y}_2) - (\mu_{0_1} - \mu_{0_2})}{\sigma_{\overline{Y}_1 - \overline{Y}_2}} \tag{9.3}$$

The estimate of the standard error for the small sample t-test is as shown in Formula 9.4:

$$\sigma_{\overline{Y}_1 - \overline{Y}_2} = \sqrt{\frac{N_1 S_1^2 + N_2 S_2^2}{N_1 + N_2 - 2}}\sqrt{\frac{N_1 + N_2}{N_1 N_2}} \tag{9.4}$$

This formula assumes equal population variances, and generally gives larger estimates of standard errors. This t-test has degrees of freedom equal to the sum of the two sample sizes, less 2.

To make the discussion here a little easier, let's look at an example. Table 9.1 presents some results generated by SPSS using random subsamples of self-identified "white" and "black" persons in 1998. The subjects were asked to report the highest year of schooling they had completed. Theory would suggest that, for a number of reasons, we would expect the mean educational attainment of black persons to be less than that of white persons. Therefore, we might set up the null hypothesis of "no difference" between the two groups, and contrast this against the one-tailed alternative hypothesis that the mean for whites is higher than the mean for blacks.

The sample data would seem to be consistent with our theory's predictions: the sample mean for whites (13.98 years) is higher than the sample mean for blacks (12.72 years). The difference, though, is not large. What is the probability that a sample difference of this size could have happened just as a result of sampling variation, when in fact there was no difference between the population means?

Another thing to notice is that the sample variation of scores for whites (standard deviation = 8.5 years) is much larger than the sample variation for blacks

TABLE 9.1 Descriptive Statistics for Two Groups

Group Statistics: Highest Year of School Completed				
Race of Respondent	***N***	**Mean**	**Std. Deviation**	**Std. Error Mean**
White	226	13.98	8.527	0.567
Black	54	12.72	2.602	0.354

TABLE 9.2 SPSS Output for Two-Group Mean Hypothesis Test

Independent Samples Test: Highest Year of School Completed									
	Levene's Test for Equality of Variances		t-Test for Equality of Means					95% Confidence Interval of the Difference	
	F	Sig.	t	*df*	Sig 2-tailed	Mean Difference	Std. Error Difference	Lower	Upper
Equal variances assumed	1.491	0.223	1.073	278	0.284	1.26	1.175	−1.052	3.572
Equal variances not assumed			1.885	264.193	0.061	1.26	0.669	−0.056	2.577

(standard deviation = 2.6 years). This may raise a question about the assumption of equality of population variances.

Table 9.2 presents the test results from SPSS.

SPSS first reports the Levene test, which asks: What is the chance we are wrong if we reject the idea that the two population variances are equal? This particular test happens to have an F-distribution, but the important result is that $p = 0.223$. This says we would be taking a large chance of being wrong if we rejected the idea of equal variances in favor of unequal variances. So, even though the sample standard deviations do appear quite different, we cannot be confident that the population variances are unequal.

So, it is proper to use the "equal variances assumed" or "small sample" test. In this example, it is important to examine this assumption—because we arrive at different conclusions to our hypothesis test with the two approaches.

Step 6: Making a Decision

The difference between the two sample means is 1.26 years of schooling (with whites having more). If we take the "large sample" approach, the estimated standard error of the difference between the means is 0.669 years of schooling and our t-test statistic is 1.885. If we take the "small sample" approach that assumes equal variances, the estimated standard error of the difference between the means is much larger (1.175) so the t-statistic is considerably smaller (1.073).

Since we had decided beforehand that we wanted to examine the one-tailed alternative that the mean of whites was higher than the mean of blacks, we may divide the significance

CHECK QUIZ 9.1

1. The central problem in the case of two-sample hypothesis tests is to determine
   a. if the samples are random.
   b. if sample statistics are the same as those of the sampling distribution.
   c. if the parameters are representative of the populations.
   d. if two populations differ significantly on the trait in question.
2. When testing for the significance of the difference between two means, which is the proper assumption?
   a. random sampling
   b. ordinal level of measurement
   c. that degrees of freedom are zero
   d. that samples are independent as well as random
3. When random samples are drawn so that the selection of a case for one sample has no effect on the selection of cases for another sample, the samples are
   a. dependent.
   b. independent.
   c. simple.
   d. systematic.
4. If the Levene test in SPSS output reports an outcome with significance less than our alpha (say, 0.05), we should probably
   a. ignore the results.
   b. not assume that the two samples' variances are equal.
   c. assume that the two samples' variances are equal.
   d. rerun the test.
5. SPSS reports significance levels for two-tailed tests by default; to find the significance of one-tailed tests,
   a. divide the two-tailed significance by 2.
   b. divide the two-tailed significance by 5.
   c. look in the next column over.
   d. multiply the two-tailed significance by 2.

levels printed for the two tests in half. So, for the large sample approach, $p = 0.03$; for the small sample approach, $p = 0.14$.

Using the large sample approach, where $p = 0.03$, we would arrive at the conclusion that we can reject the notion that the means of blacks and whites are the same, in favor of the alternative that the mean for whites is larger (with 95 percent confidence). Using the small sample approach, we cannot be so sure; we would be taking a 14 percent chance of being wrong if we rejected the null hypothesis of equal means.

What should one do? There isn't really a single correct answer. Generally, when we get different answers with slightly different statistical assumptions we should err in the direction of being conservative and requiring more proof before we believe our theory is supported.

The tests for differences between two population means are a little more complicated than tests about one population mean. But, once you have mastered this section, you will have no trouble with the next section on differences in proportions.

To make sure that you are ready to move on, take a few minutes to do the check quiz, and review if you need to.

Example

TESTING A HYPOTHESIS ABOUT THE DIFFERENCE BETWEEN TWO GROUP MEANS

Differences among societies in population growth rates are a result of many factors. One influence may be differences among the predominant religious institutions of the societies. We will compare a sample of nations where the predominant religion is Roman Catholic to a sample where the predominant religion is Islam.

The average annual population growth rate in a sample of 41 Catholic countries during the 1990s was 1.403 percent, with a standard deviation of 0.984 percent. The average annual population growth rate in a sample of 27 Islamic nations was 2.844 percent, with a standard deviation of 0.988 percent. Can we be confident at the 99 percent level that these growth rates differ? Can we be confident at the 99 percent level that the population growth rate of the Catholic nations was lower?

The dependent variable (annual population rate of change) is an interval-level variable, so it is appropriate to compare means. The total sample size is 68 (41 Catholic and 27 Muslim). It is suggested that a small sample test be used. But, to illustrate, we will calculate both a large sample test and a small sample test.

Our null hypothesis is that the means of the populations of Catholic and Muslim nations are the same, that is, that $\mu_{Catholic} = \mu_{Muslim}$. A simpler way to say this is that the difference between the means, under the null hypothesis, is zero.

We will examine two different alternative hypotheses. The first is a two-tailed alternative: the mean population growth rates are not the same. The second is a one-tailed alternative: the mean population growth rate of Catholic nations is lower than that of Muslim nations.

As always, we must decide our alpha level for the rejection of the null hypothesis in advance. For this example, let's use the conventional $p < 0.05$ level.

(continued)

Example

Large Sample Test

Again, Formula 9.1 is the formula for the test statistic:

$$Z = \frac{(\overline{Y}_1 - \overline{Y}_2) - (\mu_{0_1} - \mu_{0_2})}{\sigma_{\overline{Y}_1 - \overline{Y}_2}} \tag{9.1}$$

Here, the difference between the means for Catholic and Muslim nations is 1.403 – 2.844 or –1.441. Our null hypothesis is that the population means are the same, or the difference between the population means is zero. So, the second part of the numerator ($\mu_{Catholic} - \mu_{Muslim}$) is zero. Thus, the numerator is –1.441.

The denominator is an estimator of the standard error of the difference between the two means.

$$\sigma_{\overline{Y}_1 - \overline{Y}_2} = \sqrt{\frac{S_1^2}{N_1 - 1} + \frac{S_2^2}{N_2 - 1}} \tag{9.2}$$

Formula 9.2 uses the variance (s^2) for each sample, and the sample size for each sample. We know that $s_{Catholic} = 0.984$, so s^2 is 0.968. We know that $s_{Muslim} = 0.988$, so s^2 is 0.976. There are 41 Catholic nations and 27 Muslim nations. Doing the math:

$$\begin{aligned} \text{Estimated standard error} &= \text{sqrt}[(0.968/40) + (0.976/26)] \\ &= \text{sqrt}(0.0242 + 0.0375) \\ &= 0.248 \end{aligned}$$

So, the test statistic is –1.441/0.248 = −5.810

Since this test statistic is distributed as a standard normal (Z) variable, 5.8 is very much larger than the critical value for a two-tailed test ($Z = -1.96$) or for a one-tailed test ($Z = -1.645$). We may therefore reject the null hypothesis of no difference between Catholic and Muslim nations with 95 percent confidence. We may accept either the alternative that there is a difference or the stronger alternative that the mean for Catholic nations is lower than the mean for Muslim nations.

Small Sample Test

Given the sample sizes in this case, we should probably use the small sample test. The difference between the two tests is in how the estimate of the standard error is

(continued)

Example

constructed. In addition, we use the t-distribution to evaluate the significance of the test result. The basic test statistic formula is the same (Formula 9.3).

$$t = \frac{(\overline{Y}_1 - \overline{Y}_2) - (\mu_{0_1} - \mu_{0_2})}{\sigma_{\overline{Y}_1 - \overline{Y}_2}} \tag{9.3}$$

So, the numerator remains –1.441.

The standard error of the difference between the means is estimated with Formula 9.4:

$$\sigma_{\overline{Y}_1 - \overline{Y}_2} = \sqrt{\frac{N_1 S_1^2 + N_2 S_2^2}{N_1 + N_2 - 2}} \sqrt{\frac{N_1 + N_2}{N_1 N_2}} \tag{9.4}$$

$$\begin{aligned}
\text{Estimated standard error} &= \text{sqrt}\{[(41)(0.968) + (27)(0.976)]/(41 + 27 - 2)\} \\
&\quad \times \text{sqrt}[(41 + 27)/(41 \times 27)] \\
&= \text{sqrt}[(39.688 + 26.352)/66] \times \text{sqrt}(68/1{,}107) \\
&= \text{sqrt}(66.04/66) \times \text{sqrt}(0.061) \\
&= 1.000 \times 0.247 \\
&= 0.247 (\text{note how similar this is to the large sample result!})
\end{aligned}$$

So the test statistic is:

$$t = -1.441/0.247$$
$$t = -5.834$$

Using our table of critical values of *t*, we note that for a one-tailed test, with alpha = 0.05, and $N_1 + N_2 - 2$ (that is, 66) degrees of freedom, the critical value is about 1.671. For a two-tailed test, the critical value is about 2.000.

Since our test statistic is larger than the critical value for either the one-tailed test or the two-tailed test, we reject the null hypothesis in favor of the alternative.

COMPARING TWO GROUPS' PROPORTIONS

When we are comparing two groups and the outcome variable is categorical (nominal or grouped ordinal), we should measure the central tendency of the two groups using proportions. In addition, we need a slightly different form of our two-sample test to make the comparison.

An alternative approach is to dummy code the outcome variable. This means that the difference between proportions becomes the same thing as the difference between means, and we can apply the tests discussed in the previous section.

Step 1: Null Hypothesis

The null hypothesis for the two proportions test is that the difference between the two proportions in the populations is equal to some amount. Most commonly, the null hypothesis is that there is no difference in the proportions between groups.

Step 2: Alternative Hypotheses

As with the other tests we've looked at, we may reject the null hypothesis of a specific difference between population proportions in favor of either a two-tailed or a one-tailed alternative hypothesis. The two-tailed alternative asserts that the difference between the two population proportions is greater in magnitude (either positive or negative) than the null hypothesis proposes. The one-tailed alternative asserts that the difference in population proportions is larger than the null proposes, but in either a positive or a negative direction (but not both).

Step 3: Assumptions

We assume independent random sampling. That is, the method for selecting cases into one group was not connected to the method for selecting cases into the other (e.g., no matching of subjects).

The outcome variable, since we are using proportions, should be a nominal dichotomy.

There is only one commonly used test for the equality of two population proportions. It assumes relatively large samples, so the sampling distribution of the difference between the two proportions can be assumed to be normal in shape. If this does not seem reasonable, one can convert the outcome variable into a dummy variable and apply the small-sample t-test for means to get a more conservative test.

Step 4: Selecting an Error Level

No new tricks. One needs to be sure to set the acceptable significance level for the test before doing the statistics. Unless we have a good reason to do otherwise, it is usually reasonable to insist on 95 percent confidence in rejecting the null hypothesis, or significance at the 0.05 level.

Step 5: Computing Test Statistics: Z and t

To calculate the test statistic, one first needs to estimate the proportion falling in the category of interest on the outcome variable for the whole population. You may calculate this separately. Or, if you have the information of the proportion in each group and each group's size, you can calculate the population proportion as a weighted average using Formula 9.5:

$$P_o = \frac{N_1 P_{S_1} + N_2 P_{S_2}}{N_1 + N_2} \tag{9.5}$$

Once the overall proportion of cases in the category of interest (P_u) has been calculated, we estimate the standard error of the difference of proportions using this Formula 9.6:

$$\sigma_{P_1 P_2} = \sqrt{P_u(1 - P_u)}\sqrt{(N_1 + N_2)/N_1 N_2} \tag{9.6}$$

The formula for the standard error of the difference between two population proportions involves the sample sizes and the proportions in, and not in, the focal category of the outcome variable. Suppose we were testing a hypothesis about the proportion of the populations of men and women who supported a Republican for Congress. The weighted average of the proportions (P_u) turns out to be .60. The first term of the estimator of the standard error of the difference in proportions would be the square root of (.60 times .40). A more conservative estimator of the standard error is to assumes that the proportions are 0.50, which gives the largest possible estimated standard error for given sample sizes (so that the first term in Equation 9.6 would be the square root of .50 times .50).

With these preliminaries out of the way, we can calculate the test statistic using Formula 9.7:

$$Z = \frac{(P_{S_1} - P_{S_2}) - (P_{0_1} - P_{0_2})}{\sigma_{P_1 - P_2}} \tag{9.7}$$

This test statistic is, logically, like all the others we've considered. The numerator compares the size of the sample difference in proportions to the null hypothesis about the difference. So, the more different the sample results are from what the null hypothesis proposes, the bigger the test statistic and the higher the probability of rejecting the null hypothesis.

To convert the size of the difference into units of standard errors, the denominator divides the difference in proportions by the estimated standard error.

The one-tailed or two-tailed probabilities of type I error can then be directly found with a table, spreadsheet, of statistical package.

As an alternative, we could convert the outcome variable into a dummy variable and apply the t-test for the difference between means.

The General Social Survey has asked respondents whether they believe in life after death. We might hypothesize that there is a gender difference in this belief, with females being more likely to hold this belief. Using SPSS, we converted "belief in life after death" into a dummy variable (1 if you do believe, 0 if you don't). Table 9.3 presents the proportions (means of the dummy variables) for men and women.

The proportion believing in life after death (79.83 percent) in the sample of women is very slightly higher than the proportion (79.81 percent) in the sample of men. But is this difference one that could have happened just as a result of sampling variation—when, in fact, the proportions in the populations of women and men are exactly the same? Let's perform the test for the difference between the two means (which are proportions because of the dummy coding). (See Table 9.4.)

Step 6: Making a Decision

Levene's test very strongly suggests we would be wrong if we rejected the null hypothesis of equal group variances (F is essentially zero, and p is .990). This makes a lot of sense, as the sample standard deviations (0.40179 and 0.40159) are nearly identical. So, we should use the equal variances test.

TABLE 9.3 Descriptive Statistics for Two-Group Comparison Using Dummy Variables

Group Statistics: Dummy Variable for Belief in Life after Death				
Respondent's Sex	***N***	**Mean**	**Std. Deviation**	**Std. Error Mean**
Male	530	.7981	0.40179	0.01745
Female	689	.7983	0.40159	0.01530

TABLE 9.4 Two-Sample Test for Proportions Using Dummy Variables

Independent Samples Test: Dummy Variable for Belief in Life after Death									
	Levene's Test for Equality of Variances		**t-Test for Equality of Means**					**95% Confidence Interval of the Difference**	
	F	**Sig.**	**t**	***df***	**Sig. (2-tailed)**	**Mean Difference**	**Std. Error Difference**	**Lower**	**Upper**
Equal variances assumed	0.000	0.990	−0.006	1,217	0.995	−0.0001	0.02321	−0.04568	0.04539
Equal variances not assumed			−0.006	1,137.805	0.995	−0.0001	0.02321	−0.04568	0.04539

CHECK QUIZ 9.2

1. When looking at a difference in proportions between two populations, to be wrong in rejecting the null hypothesis means that
   a. there is a significant difference between the groups.
   b. we accept the null hypothesis.
   c. there is not a significant difference between the groups.
   d. b and c.
2. Samples from two high schools are being tested for the difference in their levels of prejudice. One sample contains 39 respondents, and the other contains 47 respondents. The appropriate sampling distribution is
   a. the t-distribution.
   b. the Z distribution.
   c. the F-distribution.
   d. any of the above.
3. When solving the formula for finding *Z* with sample proportions in the two-sample case, we must first estimate
   a. the standard deviation of the population.
   b. the population proportion.
   c. the ratio of the sample proportions.
   d. the critical region.
4. When testing the significance of the difference between two sample proportions, the null hypothesis is
   a. $P_{s1} = P_{s2}$.
   b. $P_{s2} = P_{s1}$.
   c. $P_u = (1 - P_u)$.
   d. $P_{u1} = P_u$.
5. From a university population, random samples of 145 men and 237 women have been asked if they have ever cheated in a college class. Eight percent of the men and 6 percent of the women say that they have. What is the appropriate test to assess the significance of this difference (assuming that no dummy coding has been done)?
   a. Test for the significance of the difference between two sample proportions, large samples.
   b. Test for the significance of the difference between two sample proportions, small samples.
   c. Test for the significance of the difference between two sample proportions, matched samples.
   d. Test for the significance of the difference between two sample means.
6. For all tests of hypotheses, the probability of rejecting the null hypothesis is a function of
   a. the size of the observed difference.
   b. the alpha level and the use of one- or two-tailed tests.
   c. sample size.
   d. all of the above.

Since we hypothesized that the proportion of women believing in life after death would be higher than for men (not just different from men), we can use a one-tailed test. So, we can divide the observed *p*-level (0.995) in half. This gives us a *p*-value of 0.4975.

This says that there is an almost 50/50 chance that the null hypothesis is actually true: that the proportions of males and females who believe in life after death are the same. We would be taking a 50 percent chance of being wrong if we rejected this null hypothesis. Therefore, we cannot reject the null hypothesis of equal group proportions with the required 95 percent confidence.

The process of reaching a decision and interpreting the results, then, is identical for tests of the difference between two population means or for tests of the difference between two population proportions.

Take a minute now to do the check quiz. Next, we're going to take a look at two issues that sometimes come up in group comparisons: nonindependent sampling and the question of what it means to say that there is a "significant" difference between two groups.

Example

TESTING THE DIFFERENCE BETWEEN TWO GROUPS' PROPORTIONS

Each year that the General Social Survey is collected, it asks respondents about their marital status. A number of theories based in the feminist perspective and in modernization/secularization theory suggest that being married will become less common over time.

In 1988, 51.6 percent of 322 respondents to the survey reported that they were married. A decade later, in 1998, only 47.8 percent of 295 respondents indicated that they were married.

Can we be 99 percent confident that the population (not sample) proportions married were different between 1988 and 1998? Can we be 99 percent confident that the prevalence of marriage was lower in 1998 than in 1988?

We will set our null hypothesis to be: "The proportion of the population that was married was the same in 1988 and 1998. Or, the difference between the population proportions, predicted by the null hypothesis, is zero."

We will examine both the one-tailed alternative hypothesis that marriage prevalence was lower in 1998 and the weaker two-tailed alternative hypothesis that marriage prevalence was simply different in 1998 than it was in 1988.

Formula 9.7 is used for computing a test statistic for hypotheses about differences between two proportions:

$$Z = \frac{(P_{S_1} - P_{S_2}) - (P_{0_1} - P_{0_2})}{\sigma_{P_1 - P_2}} \tag{9.7}$$

Example

The numerator is the difference between the observed proportions (0.478 – 0.516 = –0.038) less the difference expected by the null hypothesis. Here, the null hypothesis is "no difference," so the second part of the numerator is zero, and the numerator is simply –0.038.

The denominator asks for an estimate of the standard error of the difference in proportions. To compute this, we first need to use sample information to estimate the overall population proportion under the null hypothesis. That is, if the null hypothesis of no difference were true, then the proportion married is the same in both samples and is equal to the weighted average of the observed values.

$$P_o = \frac{N_1 P_{S_1} + N_2 P_{S_2}}{N_1 + N_2} \tag{9.5}$$

Using Formula 9.5, this works out to:

$$P_u = (322 \times 0.516) + (295 \times 0.478)/322 + 295$$
$$P_u = 0.498$$

Once we've got an estimate of the population proportion, we can calculate the estimated standard error of the difference using Formula 9.6:

$$\sigma_{P_1 P_2} = \sqrt{P_u(1 - P_u)}\sqrt{(N_1 + N_2)/N_1 N_2} \tag{9.6}$$

Here, this works out to:

$$\begin{aligned}\text{Estimated standard error} &= \text{sqrt}[0.498 \times (1 - 0.498)] \\ &\quad \times \text{sqrt}[(322 + 295)/(322 \times 295)] \\ &= \text{sqrt}(0.25) \times \text{sqrt}(0.0065) \\ &= 0.50 \times 0.0806 \\ &= 0.0403\end{aligned}$$

The test statistic, then is:

$$Z = -0.038/0.0403$$
$$Z = -0.943$$

The probability of a Z-score this small or smaller if the null hypothesis is true is 0.1736. So we would be taking a 17 percent chance of being wrong if we rejected the

(continued)

Example

null hypothesis in favor of the alternative that there had been a decline in marriage. This risk of error is more than the 1 percent we had decided beforehand would be acceptable. Since the one-tailed test is more conservative than the two-tailed test, we also fail to reject the null in favor of the two-tailed alternative.

In sum, we cannot say with 99 percent confidence that the proportion married in the population differed between 1988 and 1998. Nor can we say with 99 percent confidence that the proportion married declined from 1988 to 1998.

NONINDEPENDENT SAMPLES

There are many research designs followed by social science researchers that lead to nonindependent samples. When the members of the two groups being compared are not sampled independently, the approaches we've discussed in the previous sections should not be used. But there is another approach based on comparing the "mean differences" instead of the differences in means.

Research Designs with Nonindependent Samples

Nonindependent samples are very common in experimental research. For example, we might give a "pretest" to a group of subjects, then give them a treatment, and then observe their scores on a "posttest." The analysis of these data would test a null hypothesis of "no change" in the sample means from pretest to posttest. But, since the group of subjects who took the pretest (sample 1) are the same subjects as those who took the posttest (sample 2), obviously the samples are not independent.

Many experimental designs reuse the same sample of subjects to collect scores on different variables. Sometimes the same subjects are measured with the same instrument two (or more) times under different conditions; designs like this are called "repeated measures" designs. More generally, whenever we compare the score of an individual subject on one variable to the same subject's score on another variable, we are examining a "within subjects" factor of an experiment. Since we are reusing the same subject, the samples are not independent.

Nonindependent sampling is also widely used in nonexperimental research, when "paired subjects" or "paired comparisons" are used. For example, if I wanted to see whether husbands and wives had different perceptions of the fairness of the division of household labor, it would be a better research design to compare the scores of husbands and wives who were married to each other, rather than independent samples of persons who were husbands and others who were wives.

In quasi-experimental research, paired designs are often used to select subjects. It is not unusual to randomly select one sample (say from school A), but then to select students from school B by identifying students there who are the same as each individual in the sample from school A on traits such as age, sex, ethnicity, social class, and so on. Paired designs like this lead to samples that have different people in the two groups being compared, but each individual in one group is linked to or matched with a particular person in the other group. Thus, the observations in the two samples are not independent.

Nonindependent Samples Test for Difference in Mean Differences

When we were comparing the means or proportions in two independent samples, we made a null hypothesis and an alternative hypothesis about the difference between the sample means or proportions. In working with nonindependent samples, we proceed somewhat differently and make hypotheses regarding the mean of the differences between the observations in the two samples.

For example, suppose that I had a sample of couples, and I was interested in comparing the mean score of husbands to the mean score of wives. I would begin by calculating the difference between the score of each husband and the score of the wife that he was paired with—let's call this D_i (the difference in scores for pair i).

I could also calculate the mean of the pairwise differences. Let's call this quantity $\bar{D}$. And I could calculate the variance or standard deviation of the pairwise differences. Let's call this quantity S_D.

Having done these calculations on the pair-by-pair differences in scores, I can prepare a test statistic that looks like Formula 9.8:

$$t_{N-1} = \frac{\bar{D} - \bar{D}_0}{S_D/\sqrt{N-1}} \qquad (9.8)$$

In the numerator, we have the average of the differences between the scores of the members of each pair ($\bar{D}$). If there is no systematic difference between the members of the pairs, this quantity will be zero. For example, if husbands have, on average, the same scores as their wives, the $\bar{D}$—the average of the differences across the couples—will be zero. But, if husbands more often score higher than their wives, the mean difference would not be zero.

Our null hypothesis about paired means or proportions is usually that there is no difference between the scores of the samples. This is the same as saying that the mean of the pairwise differences in scores is hypothesized to be zero. The second term in the numerator of the formula ($\bar{D}_0$) states our null hypothesis about the average pairwise difference. If we wanted to test for differences that were greater than some amount, the null hypothesis quantity would be that amount.

So, the numerator of this test statistic is like all the others. It compares that actual sample statistic ($\bar{D}$) value of the average pairwise difference to a null hypothesis about that difference ($\bar{D}_0$). The bigger the difference between the sample value and the

CHECK QUIZ 9.3

1. In twins studies, in which one twin is assigned to one group and one to another, the selection of subjects is
   a. not independent.
   b. twisted.
   c. independent.
   d. stratified and random.
2. Why do the degrees of freedom matter when performing t-tests?
   a. If you don't know how many degrees of freedom there are, you might be doing a Z-test.
   b. The shape of the t-distribution differs for different degrees of freedom.
   c. Calculating the denominator of the test statistic requires knowing the degrees of freedom.
   d. Freedom is everything, baby.
3. Our null hypothesis about paired means or proportions is usually that there is no difference between
   a. the scores in the population.
   b. the scores in the sampling distribution.
   c. the scores of the samples.
   d. the two populations.
4. In the section example, we tested for difference in means between two non-independent groups. What could we have done if the variable of interest were categorical instead of interval/ratio?
   a. We could have converted the outcome into a dichotomy and assigned dummy coding scores.
   b. We could have converted the outcome to a proportion and tested for a mean difference.
   c. We could have multiplied the outcome by a constant and treated it as a interval/ratio measurement-level variable.
   d. a and c

null hypothesis, the bigger the test statistic and the greater the likelihood of rejecting the null hypothesis in favor of the alternative.

The denominator, as always, is an estimator of the standard error. In this case, it is an estimator of the standard error of the mean pairwise difference. The estimate is derived by taking the average variability in the pairwise differences (S_D) and dividing it by the square root of the number of pairs less 1.

It is important to remember that the number of cases, or N, in paired or repeated measures analysis is the number of pairs—not the number of individual observations in the two samples.

The test statistic that results from this is distributed like "t" with degrees of freedom equal to the number of pairs, less 1. A "significant" result means that the sample data are so different from what the null hypothesis proposed that we can reject the null hypothesis with whatever level of confidence we have selected.

Example

TESTING TWO NONINDEPENDENT MEANS

In one offering of a statistics class, there was a midterm and a final exam. Both exams had the same number of total possible points, and the instructor is interested in determining whether students did better, on average, on the final than they did on the midterm.

The instructor might be tempted to simply calculate a two-sample t-test for the difference between the mean score on the midterm (which happened to be about 35 points) and the final (which happened to be about 51 points). But, since it was the same students who took both tests, it would be better to test the null hypothesis that the average difference between individuals' midterm and final exam scores was zero against the alternative that the average difference of individuals' scores was not zero.

Using SPSS compare means, paired samples procedure, we obtained the results presented in Table 9.5.

We see that the average score on the midterm was about 35, and the average score on the final was about 51. Note that the 96 people who took the tests, though, are not independent samples—they are the same 96 people.

The "paired samples correlation" reported is a measure of how similar the scores were on the two tests (more on this in Chapter 15). It shows that, on average, people who got high scores on the midterm were more likely to get high scores on the final.

TABLE 9.5 Descriptive Statistics for Nonindependent Samples

Paired Samples Statistics

		Mean	***N***	**Std. Deviation**	**Std. Error Mean**
Pair 1	Midterm	35.02	96	8.837	0.902
	Final	51.08	96	13.980	1.427

Paired Samples Correlation

		N	**Correlation**	**Sig.**
Pair 1	Midterm and final	96	0.683	0.000

(continued)

Example

TABLE 9.6 Test for Difference of Group Differences

Paired Samples Test									
		Paired Differences Mean	Std. Deviation	Std. Error Mean	95% Confidence Interval of the Difference Lower	Upper	t	*df*	Sig. (2-tailed)
Pair 1	Midterm and final	–16.07	10.235	1.045	–18.14	–13.99	–15.381	95	0.000

The statistical test is performed by first calculating the average difference between the midterm and final exam scores (the mean of the paired differences). (See Table 9.6.) On average, students scored 16.07 points lower on the midterm than on the final. The standard deviation of the pairwise differences is 10.235 points, which (along with the sample size of 96), lets us calculate the estimated standard error of the mean difference as 1.045 points.

The mean difference was –16.07 points, and the amount that we could expect this to vary just by sampling variability is 1.045 points, so the t-test statistic is –15.381. The *p*, or alpha, or significance level of the test is smaller than 0.000.

What should we conclude? The average difference between individuals' midterm and final exam scores (–16 points) was much greater than the amount we would expect due to sampling variability (1.045 points). It is very unlikely ($p = 0.000$) that a difference this large could be observed just by chance when there really was no average difference between individuals' midterm and final exam scores. So, we can reject the null hypothesis of no difference with a great deal of confidence. The alternative is that there is a difference on average across individuals in their midterm and final exam scores.

In our example, we have used a t-test for differences in means. If the outcome of interest is categorical, we can still apply this test by first converting the outcome into a dichotomy and assigning dummy coding scores.

Nonindependent samples, "repeated measures," and "within subjects" research designs are very common and very useful in social science research. Because the sampling is not independent, we need to show some care to properly analyze the results. If we assume independent sampling when the sampling is, in fact, not independent, we will make inferential errors. Often these errors will lead to the conclusion that there are effects when in fact there are none—a very serious kind of error.

USING EXCEL FOR TWO-SAMPLE TESTS

Two-sample t-tests are the sort of thing at which Excel excels. Set up a spreadsheet like this:

◇	A	B	C	D	E
1	first set	second set			
2	24	18			
3	26	16			
4	24	16			
5	24	15			
6	25	17			
7	26	18		s.d.(1)	=STDEV(A2:A15)
8	25	18		s.d.(2)	=STDEV(B2:B12)
9	28	20		equal variances?	=IF(MAX(E7:E8)>2*MIN(E7:E8),"no","yes")
10	30	23			
11	18	23			
12	20	24		independent, eq variance:	=TTEST(A2:A15,B2:B15,2,2)
13	20			independent, non-eq variance:	=TTEST(A2:A15,B2:B12,2,3)
14	21			dependent/paired:	=TTEST(A2:A15,B2:B15,2,1)
15	21				
16					

◇	A	B	C	D	E
1	first set	second set			
2	24	18			
3	26	16			
4	24	16			
5	24	15			
6	25	17			
7	26	18		s.d.(1)	3.36
8	25	18		s.d.(2)	3.14
9	28	20		equal variances?	yes
10	30	23			
11	18	23			
12	20	24		independent, eq variance:	0.00
13	20			independent, non-eq variance:	0.00
14	21			dependent/paired:	0.00
15	21				
16					

Note: The formulas on the right of this spreadsheet are set up to do independent and dependent t-tests; just be sure to select all of the data cells for whichever test you're doing.

Unpaired or Independent t-Tests

We suggest some rules of thumb for choosing whether to use the pooled estimator denominator or the unpooled estimator. One has to do with size; if the samples are of size 30 or more, it's probably okay to assume equal variances. With smaller samples, if one sample's standard deviation is less than twice the other's standard deviation, it's probably okay to assume equal variances. The cell labeled "equal variances?" checks for this second rule. In this example, since it says that the variances are equal ("yes"), it's probably safe to use the *p*-value from the "independent, eq variance:" row (which, you see, is identical to the "independent, non-eq variance:" row, so this doesn't seem like much of a stretch).

Paired Sample t-Tests

Read the *p*-value for the test from the cell labeled "dependent/paired." The screen shot shows "#N/A" for this number because the cell selections in each set need to contain the same numbers of cells; just select an equal number of cells for this test.

Tests of Proportions

The same spreadsheet can be used for tests of proportions, but the variables need to be dummy coded (category of interest = 1, otherwise 0) for the category of interest.

Excel Wizardry

MS Excel's if( ) formula takes the basic form:

$$= \text{if}(\text{condition, value-if-true, value-if-false})$$

In this case, we define *equal variances* as one variance being less than two times the other variance. (You might not want to use this definition if you're sharing a plate of food "equally" with a friend.)

In MS Excel, we use the max( ) function to choose the larger of two values, and the min( ) function to choose the smaller, and use the greater-than comparison to see if the larger value was greater than two times the smaller value. If it is, then we want to answer the question "equal variances?" with "no"; if it's not, then we want Excel to show "yes."

$$= \text{if}(\text{max(range-of-cells)} > 2 \times \text{min(range-of-cells)}, \text{"no"}, \text{"yes"})$$

INTERPRETING GROUP DIFFERENCES

Comparing the central tendency of the scores in one sample to those in another sample is fundamental to all hypothesis testing. Hypothesis testing is fundamental to doing empirical science, where theories about populations must be subjected to testing (and possible rejection) by observing samples.

Inferential statistics are a powerful tool for letting us assess how much confidence we have in reaching conclusions that sample results are, or are not, consistent with the predictions of theories.

But, it is also possible to get a little carried away by inferential statistics, and to lose sight of the bigger issues of why we are doing them in the first place. In this section, we want to take just a few minutes to examine this issue.

The Power of Tests

Hypothesis testing, or significance testing (as it is often called), has the useful task of guarding against the possibility of believing that a theory helps explain an observation when the observation could have been a chance occurrence due to sampling variation. This is an important safeguard, because social science research is very often based on samples, and sampling variation can be a problem in reaching valid conclusions about theories.

We shouldn't forget, though, that there are other problems that can arise in the research process in the social sciences that are often even more troubling than sampling variation. Bad research design, poor measurement, biased observations or sampling, and poorly formed hypotheses can all lead to incorrect conclusions from observations—and have nothing to do with sampling variability.

Assume, however, that none of these other issues are a problem. Let's suppose we've conducted a Z-test for the difference between two sample means, and we've concluded that the result is significant at the 95 percent confidence level.

It's important to examine the factors that go into making a significant hypothesis testing result. It might be helpful to look at Formula 9.9 for the two-sample means:

$$Z = \frac{(\overline{Y}_1 - \overline{Y}_2) - (\mu_{0_1} - \mu_{0_2})}{\sqrt{\frac{S_1^2}{N_1 - 1} + \frac{S_2^2}{N_1 - 1}}} \tag{9.9}$$

There are a number of factors, according to the formula, that can lead to a larger test statistic (Z), and a more significant result.

First, there is the size of the difference between the sample means. The larger the difference, the less likely it is that the null hypothesis is true. This makes a great deal of sense—the more inconsistent the observed data are with the predictions of the null hypothesis, the less likely it must be that the null is true.

Second, there is the size of the difference hypothesized under the null hypothesis. We can get a more significant result by using a less demanding null hypothesis. I can easily reject the null hypothesis that the income of the population of students in my class is zero. It is not as easy to reject the null hypothesis that the mean income is $10,000. So, a statistically significant result may not mean much if the null hypothesis is not a very demanding one.

Now, turn to the denominator, which is an estimator of the standard error of the difference between the means.

Third, sample size matters. The bigger the samples, the more significant is the result, holding everything else constant. Indeed, it is possible to make almost any difference significant at almost any *p*-level if we have a sufficiently large sample. And the bigger the sample, the smaller the actual difference that is necessary to give a significant test result.

Fourth, the sample variability of the thing being studied matters. The larger the sample standard deviations in Formula 9.9, the less significant is the result (holding everything else constant). If we are studying a phenomenon that displays a great deal of variability, we can observe a seemingly large difference between the means of two samples that fails to be significant.

Now that we have the test statistic, there are two more factors that enter into determining how significant our result really is.

Fifth, what alpha level have we used to decide that a result is significant? The same test result may be significant at $p = 0.05$, but not significant at $p = 0.01$.

Sixth, what is the alternative hypothesis? Is it one-tailed or two-tailed? One-tailed alternative hypotheses are more likely to result in significant findings than two-tailed alternatives are.

So, there are a number of factors that go into generating a significant result of a hypothesis test. When we determine that a result is statistically significant. we need to remember that this outcome is a result of all of these factors.

Significance and "Significance"

The preceding discussion suggests that a "statistically significant" difference may not really be a very substantively meaningful difference. Just because a difference was probably not the result of sampling variability, this does not mean that the difference makes a difference.

This also suggests that a difference that is not "statistically significant" may still be of some interest and importance. If small samples were used, for example, quite large differences may not be statistically significant. But one must be very cautious about taking seriously any difference that could be due to sampling variation. Even a large difference could easily be a sampling accident.

So, if "significance" is not the same thing as "importance," how should we think about importance? After all, we are not doing research in order to reach statistical conclusions; we are doing research to try to reach conclusions about the social world.

If a result is not statistically significant, one probably should not regard it as being important. It can be interesting, though—and we may want to replicate the study with better samples. But if observations can't pass a test of statistical significance, they can't be taken too seriously.

Even if results do pass a test of statistical significance, they are not necessarily important.

A result that has important consequences in terms of people's well-being is an important result. A result that leads to improvement in theory is an important result. But how do we tell whether a result is important in this sense? There isn't a perfect answer to the question, but here are a couple of suggestions.

Effect Sizes

In later chapters, we will look at the idea of "statistical association" between two variables. For the moment, we can think of association as the extent to which the scores on one variable tend to systematically correspond to scores on the other variable. Variables that are strongly associated enable us to be quite certain about the score on the second if we know the first. For example, "sex" (male or female) and "body height" are rather strongly associated. That is, if I told you that a person is 7 feet tall, there is a very good chance that this person is male (but it isn't certain!).

One way of assessing the importance of a significant result is to ask if knowing the score on one variable makes the other highly predictable. If knowing what group a person is in enables me to make a strong and accurate prediction about their score on outcome, this is an important result. Statistical results can be significant without being strong associations in this sense.

Another approach to evaluating the importance of group differences that are statistically significant is to examine the actual size of the difference between the groups. If the mean income of group A is $10,000 and the mean income of group B is $20,000, this would seem to be a more important difference than if the mean of group A was $18,000 and the mean of group B was $20,000. We may be confident that the means of the groups are different in both cases—that is what the tests of statistical significance tell us.

So, in addition to reporting that the difference between two means or two proportions is significant, it is important to report the means or the proportions themselves. The difference between the means or proportions is often called the "effect" of being in one group or the other. In our first example, the effect of group is $10,000; in the second case, the effect of group is $2,000.

It may also be useful to express this effect relative to the size of the mean or proportion in one of the groups. For example, if the effect of group was $10,000 but the means of the two groups were $200,000 and $210,000, this would mean something different than an effect of $10,000 when the group means were $10,000 and $20,000. In the first case, the difference of $10,000 is only 5 percent of the mean in the lower group ($200,000). In the second case, the difference of $10,000 is equal to 100 percent of the mean of the lower group.

Reporting the effects and/or the size of the effects relative to the means of proportions does not answer the question of what is an important difference. That ultimately is a matter of judgment. But examining effect sizes (and association) can be helpful in deciding whether a "statistically significant" result is also an "important" result.

Please take minute now to quiz yourself on this section. If you've grasped it, then go on to the chapter summary for a final review.

CHECK QUIZ 9.4

1. The higher the alpha level,
   a. the lower the probability of rejecting the null hypothesis.
   b. the smaller the sample size has to be to reject the null hypothesis.
   c. the greater the probability of rejecting the null hypothesis.
   d. the more desirable the two-tailed test.
2. Four tests of significance were conducted on the same set of results: for test 1: alpha = 0.05, two-tailed test; for test 2: alpha = 0.10, one-tailed test; for test 3: alpha = 0.01, two-tailed test; for test 4: alpha = 0.01, one-tailed test. Which test is most likely to result in a rejection of the null hypothesis?
   a. test 1
   b. test 2
   c. test 3
   d. test 4
3. The value of all test statistics is directly proportional to
   a. the sampling distribution used.
   b. the alpha level chosen.
   c. the size of the rejection region.
   d. sample size.
4. The larger the sample size,
   a. the more important the observed difference.
   b. the more likely we are to reject the null hypothesis.
   c. the less likely we are to reject the null hypothesis.
   d. the lower the Z-score.
5. A difference between samples that is shown to be statistically significant may also be
   a. practically insignificant.
   b. theoretically insignificant.
   c. sociologically insignificant.
   d. all of the above.
6. If a difference between samples is not statistically significant, it is almost certainly ___________. On the other hand, a statistically significant difference is not necessarily ___________.
   a. important; due to random chance
   b. unimportant; large
   c. important; unimportant
   d. unimportant; important

SUMMARY

Often our research question involves asking whether the central tendency of a variable for one group differs meaningfully from that of another. Does the treatment group differ from the control group? Are the pretest scores lower than the posttest scores? Are the incomes of minority persons lower than the incomes of majority persons?

Tests for differences between two population means or two population proportions follow the same logic as other hypothesis tests. We first set a null hypothesis about the value of the difference in the populations and then we look at the difference between the samples. Usually, the null hypothesis suggests that the difference between the means or proportions of the two groups is zero or some specific amount. If the differences that we observe between the sample means or proportions are so large that they are very unlikely assuming that the null hypothesis is true, we can reject the null in favor of the alternative.

In examining the difference between two independent sample means, either Z-tests or t-tests are used (Z-tests for large samples, t-tests for small samples). There are different estimators of the standard error of the difference between the means, depending on whether it is reasonable to assume that the variances in the two groups are equal (which is the default approach) or unequal. The Levene test can be helpful in deciding which estimator of the standard error of the mean difference is most appropriate.

Tests for the difference between proportions in two independent samples can be done as tests of means if the variable defining the groups is properly coded as a dummy variable. Alternatively, a Z-test for the difference of independent proportions is used.

Sometimes research designs create nonindependent samples. "Matched subjects" designs or "repeated measures" designs lead to samples from two groups such that the cases in one sample are paired with cases in the other sample. In these cases, the sample size is the number of pairs, not the number of total observations. And we do not test the difference between means of the samples. Rather, we test the mean of the differences between the members of the pairs.

Statistical significance of hypothesis tests is important, because we should not believe that we have found important differences between groups if the differences we observe could have been produced by sampling variability. But just because a result is statistically significant, that does not mean that it is important. We reviewed a number of factors that affect statistical significance, and found that many of these factors are design and sampling issues that don't necessarily inform us about the theory that led us to predict that the groups would be different.

Even if a result is statistically significant and the research design is sound, the difference between the groups is not necessarily very important. There is no definite procedure for determining that a statistically significant result is also an important result. Examining the strength of association (which we will discuss in Chapters 12 to 15) and examining the effect sizes are good approaches to help to make a judgment about importance.

In Chapter 8, we examined one-sample tests for central tendency. In this chapter, we have examined two-sample tests. The next logical step is to examine tests that we can use for comparing any number of groups. This is the subject of the next two chapters, which deal with multiple sample tests for means and multiple sample tests for proportions.

KEY TERMS

Levene test

nonindependent samples

CHECK QUIZ ANSWERS

Quiz 9.1 Answers: 1. (d); 2. (d); 3. (b); 4. (b); 5. (a)
Quiz 9.2 Answers: 1. (c); 2. (a); 3. (b); 4. (d); 5. (a); 6. (a)
Quiz 9.3 Answers: 1. (a); 2. (b); 3. (a); 4. (a)
Quiz 9.4 Answers: 1. (c); 2. (b); 3. (d); 4. (b); 5. (d); 6. (d)

EXERCISES

1. Do members of college fraternities and sororities party more than nonmembers? A recent (fictitious) survey shows the average numbers of parties that students attended during the last school term to be:

	Members	**Nonmembers**
Mean	12.3	10.3
Standard deviation	4.2	2.7
N	55	40

   Can we be confident, at the 95 percent level, that the means of the two groups are different in the whole populations of members and nonmembers? Show your calculations and evidence.

2. Is support for college athletics equal between men and women, as required by legislation? In 1997–1998, a sample of 100 men's NCAA basketball teams had an average of 16.1 players, with a standard deviation of 0.5; an independent sample of 100 women's NCAA basketball teams had an average 14.4 players, with a standard deviation of 0.7.

   Can we be confident, at $p < 0.05$, that the mean sizes of men's and women's teams differ? Can we be confident, at $p < 0.05$, that women's teams are smaller than men's?

3. Was there a gender gap in support for Bill Clinton in the 1992 election? The General Social Survey shows that 46 percent of 372 men supported Clinton, while 59 percent of 458 women supported Clinton.

   Can we be confident at the 95 percent level that the support for Clinton was at least 10 percent higher among women than it was among men in the whole population?
4. A researcher hypothesizes that women are more likely than men to seek help from physicians. In the 1991 General Social Survey, adult men and women were asked whether, within the past year, they had been "ill enough to see a doctor." Of the sample of 417 men, 44.4 percent said "yes"; 62.8 percent of the sample of 596 women said "yes."

   Can the researcher be confident, at the 99 percent level, that the population of women are more likely to say "yes" than the population of men? Show your calculations and briefly describe your findings.
5. Are men or women more politically conservative? The General Social Survey uses a scale that rates people from low (1 point) to high (7 points) on political conservativism. Here is a set of computer output testing the difference in mean conservativism by sex.

Group Statistics: Think of Self as Liberal or Conservative

Respondent's Sex	N	Mean	Std. Deviation	Std. Error Mean
Male	593	4.19	1.318	0.054
Female	683	4.06	1.324	0.051

Independent Samples Test: Think of Self as Liberal or Conservative

	Levene's Test for Equality of Variances		t-Test for Equality of Means					95% Confidence Interval of the Difference	
	F	Sig.	t	*df*	Sig. (2-tailed)	Mean Difference	Std. Error Difference	Lower	Upper
Equal variances assumed	1.410	0.235	1.656	1,274	0.098	0.12	0.074	−0.023	0.268
Equal variances not assumed			1.656	1,250.504	0.098	0.12	0.074	−0.023	0.268

a. Should we use the "equal variances assumed" test or the "equal variances not assumed" test?
b. Can we conclude, with 95 percent confidence, that men and women differ in their political conservatism?
c. Can we conclude, with 95 percent confidence, that men are more conservative than women?

6. Do female and male parents have different values for child rearing? A study (using the 1991 General Social Survey) asked male and female adults whether teaching children that "helping others" was the most important value in child rearing, or whether any one of a list of other values was most important. The researcher suspects that there may be a gender difference, but doesn't have a prediction about whether male or female parents are more likely to endorse "helping others" as the most important value in child rearing. Respondent's answers were coded 1 if "helping others" was the most important goal; the responses were coded 0 is any other goal was selected as most important. Here are the results of this two-sample test of proportions:

Group Statistics: Helping Others Is Most Important

Respondent's Sex	*N*	Mean	Std. Deviation	Std. Error Mean
Male	636	0.0849	0.27896	0.01106
Female	881	0.0817	0.27410	0.00923

Independent Samples Test: Helping Others Is Most Important

	Levene's Test for Equality of Variances		t-Test for Equality of Means					95% Confidence Interval of the Difference	
	F	Sig.	t	*df*	Sig. (2-tailed)	Mean Difference	Std. Error Difference	Lower	Upper
Equal variances assumed	0.196	0.658	0.221	1,515	0.825	0.0032	0.01437	−0.02500	0.03137
Equal variances not assumed			0.221	1,354.006	0.825	0.0032	0.01441	−0.02509	0.03145

a. State the null and research hypotheses.
b. Is this research (alternative) hypothesis one-tailed or two-tailed?

c. According to the results of the Levene test, should the researcher use the "equal variances assumed" or the "equal variances not assumed" version of the hypothesis test? (Show evidence.)
d. Should the researcher accept or reject the null hypothesis at the 95 percent confidence level? (Show evidence.)
e. What conclusion should the researcher reach about the research question?

7. Obtaining some amount of formal education beyond high school is very important to one's economic success in the United States. Here are some data from the General Social Survey on the proportions of white and black sample respondents who had completed more than a high school education.

Group Statistics: Completed More Than High School

Race of Respondent	*N*	Mean	Std. Deviation	Std. Error Mean
White	1,271	0.2691	0.44366	0.01244
Black	175	0.1257	0.33248	0.02513

It appears that the proportion who have completed high school may be much higher for "whites" than for "blacks." But can we be confident at the 95 percent level that this is really true in the entire populations? Here are some test results.

Independent Samples Test: Completed More Than High School

	Levene's Test for Equality of Variances		t-Test for Equality of Means					95% Confidence Interval of the Difference	
	F	Sig.	t	*df*	Sig. (2-tailed)	Mean Difference	Std. Error Difference	Lower	Upper
Equal variances assumed	104.352	0.000	4.118	1,444	0.000	0.1434	0.03481	0.07507	0.21166
Equal variances not assumed			5.112	267.572	0.000	0.1434	0.02805	0.08815	0.19858

a. Do the standard deviations of the two groups appear to be similar? What does the Levene test say about this?
b. What is the null hypothesis being tested?

c. Can we reject the null hypothesis at alpha = 0.05?
d. What conclusion do you reach about the educational attainments of "white" and "black" Americans?

8. In the 1991 General Social Survey, researchers asked independent samples of male and female respondents whether they would describe their lives as "exciting," "routine," or "dull." This ordinal variable was coded 1, 2, 3, with high scores meaning "dull." Assuming that it is appropriate to treat this variable as interval, the researchers tested the hypothesis that women perceived their lives to be less exciting than men's. Here are the results:

Group Statistics: Is Life Exciting or Dull?

Respondent's Sex	*N*	Mean	Std. Deviation	Std. Error Mean
Male	425	1.53	.554	.027
Female	555	1.65	.576	.024

Independent Samples Test: Is Life Exciting or Dull?

	Levene's Test for Equality of Variances		t-Test for Equality of Means					95% Confidence Interval of the Difference	
	F	Sig.	t	*df*	Sig. (2-tailed)	Mean Difference	Std. Error Difference	Lower	Upper
Equal variances assumed	0.292	0.589	−3.480	978	0.001	−0.13	0.036	−0.199	−0.055
Equal variances not assumed			−3.498	929.251	0.000	−0.13	0.036	−0.198	−0.056

a. State the null and research hypotheses.
b. Is the research (alternative) hypothesis one-tailed or two-tailed?
c. According to the results of the Levene test, should the researcher use the "equal variances assumed" or the "equal variances not assumed" version of the hypothesis test? (Show evidence.)
d. Should the researcher accept or reject the null hypothesis at the 95 percent confidence level? (Show evidence.)
e. What conclusion should the researcher reach about the research question?

Chapter 10

Multiple Sample Tests of Proportions: Chi-Squared

LEARNING OBJECTIVES

When you have finished this chapter, you will be able to:

- Understand the null and alternative hypotheses of the Pearson independence chi-squared test.
- Explain the logic and perform the calculation of the Pearson chi-squared test.
- Determine the significance level of the test using the proper degrees of freedom, and interpret the test results.
- Summarize the strength and form of the significant differences between multiple groups' proportions.

COMPARING PROPORTIONS ACROSS SEVERAL GROUPS

In the previous two chapters we have seen how the main ideas of statistical inference (sampling variability, standard errors, and confidence levels) can be used to test hypotheses about one or two groups' measures of central tendency (means or proportions) on a variable.

In this chapter and the next, we will extend these basic ideas to situations in which there are more than two groups (or populations) to be compared. In this chapter, we focus on the ***Pearson chi-squared test of independence***. This test is used when we are comparing two or more groups on an outcome (i.e., dependent variable) that is categorical (nominal or grouped ordinal). In the next chapter, we'll examine the one-way analysis of variance (ANOVA). That is used when we are comparing two or more groups, and the outcome (i.e., dependent variable) is interval/ratio.

Suppose that I had the hypothesis that organizations' sizes at the time of founding affected their survival rates (organizations that are large at the time of founding are hypothesized to have higher chances of survival). Using data on the founding and survival of organizations in an industry, I divide the cases into three groups: those that were small at the time of founding, those that were average size, and those that were larger than average. We examine what proportion of the organizations in each size class survives for five years.

To test my hypothesis in this example, I would need to compare the proportion of cases that survive to the age of five years across three groups—those that were small, average, or large at the time of founding. How can I do this?

Knowing what we know so far, I could try to solve the problem by doing three two-group tests of proportions, like those we studied in the preceding chapter. First I could compare the proportion surviving of small to average-sized organizations; then I would compare small to large organizations; finally, I would compare average-sized to large organizations.

It would seem that we could compare any number of groups we wanted by doing them two at a time. So, why should we go to the trouble to learn a new approach for comparing multiple groups all at once? There are two answers.

One answer is that it is a lot less work to do a single comparison rather than multiple comparisons. Suppose that I had five groups instead of three. I would have to do 10 comparisons $[K^* (K-1)]/2$, where K is the number of groups.

The other answer is that we need a new approach because the statistical answer we get from doing multiple comparisons pairwise will be wrong! In fact, the results will be biased in favor of finding at least one significant pairwise difference. This is because the formulas for the standard errors of the differences between two proportions assume that the two samples are independent. But, when we do multiple comparisons with the same samples (e.g., compare A to B, A to C, and B to C), the samples are not independent—we are reusing the same data for multiple tests. We don't really have as much data as the standard formulas for two-sample tests assume—so our results are too optimistic.

To guard against this kind of inferential error and to do all the comparisons at once, we need some new techniques for comparing multiple groups. In this chapter, we examine the Pearson chi-squared test of independence that is used to compare multiple groups when the outcome or dependent variable is categorical (nominal or grouped ordinal).

TESTING FOR MULTIPLE GROUP DIFFERENCES

In Table 10.1, we compare the marital statuses of respondents to the General Social Survey (1978–1998) by self-reported race. There are number of reasons to expect that the proportions of people with various marital statuses will differ by race. Different racial groups have quite different demographic compositions; they differ in their economic circumstances; and they differ in cultural and historical ways.

By comparing the percentages of people with different marital statuses across the racial groups, we can see that there are some notable differences. For example, almost 60 percent of white respondents report they are married, while less than 40 percent of black respondents do.

Comparisons across multiple groups are very common in experimental, quasi-experimental, and nonexperimental social science research. While our example has three levels of the "group" variable (i.e., white, black, other), other research questions may call for comparisons across many groups.

The outcomes on which we want to compare the groups are often categorical. Marital status is a nominal variable with (in this case) five levels (i.e., married, widowed, divorced, separated, never married). In many cases, the categorical outcome may have only two categories (yes or no, is or isn't, did or didn't happen, etc.), but many variables of interest have multiple possible outcomes.

If we think about the example problem a bit more abstractly, we can see that we are interested in comparing more than two groups (three, in this case), and that we are interested

TABLE 10.1 Multiple Group Proportions of Marital Status by Race

Marital Status by Race of Respondent (General Social Survey, 1978–1998)				
	White	**Black**	**Other**	**Total**
Married	727 (57.2%)	67 (38.3%)	22 (40.7%)	816 (54.4%)
Widowed	122 (9.6%)	22 (12.6%)	6 (11.1%)	150 (10.0%)
Divorced	173 (13.6%)	18 (10.3%)	8 (14.8%)	199 (13.3%)
Separated	24 (1.9%)	17 (9.7%)	4 (7.4%)	45 (3.0%)
Never married	225 (17.7%)	51 (29.1%)	14 (25.9%)	290 (19.3%)
Total	1,271 (100.0%)	175 (100.0%)	54 (100.0%)	1,500 (100.0%)

in whether these groups have different proportional distributions on some outcome (i.e., marital status in this case).

Let's see how the now-familiar steps of hypothesis testing can be applied to problems like this.

Step 1: Null Hypothesis

Usually our theory would lead us to predict that the groups we are comparing will differ in their distributions across the available outcomes. Theory would usually lead us to hypothesize that the treatment groups will differ from the control group, that the new program intervention group will differ from the old program recipients, or that the members of one social group will differ from another. Sometimes we may have more specific ideas about which groups will differ from which other groups and in which ways.

But, before we worry about which groups differ from which others in which ways, we need to be confident that there are, indeed, group differences. We can't be sure just by looking at the data, because the data are (usually) from a sample; our hypothesis is a prediction about the population from which the sample is drawn.

Usually, then, our null hypothesis for comparing multiple groups on categorical outcomes will be:

> H_0: The proportions of cases having each of various outcomes are the same across the populations being compared.

In the case of our example, the null hypothesis might be stated:

> H_0: The proportions of persons who are married, widowed, separated, divorced, and never married are the same across the populations of white, black, and other races.

As we will see, the Pearson chi-squared statistic (χ^2—the Greek letter "chi" squared) is used for hypothesis testing. This statistic has the value of zero when there are no differences in group proportions. So, the null hypothesis could also be stated as:

$$H_0\colon \chi^2 = 0$$

Step 2: Alternative Hypothesis

Of course, if our theory is correct, then we ought to be able to reject the null hypothesis based on our observation of the sample data. If we do reject the null hypothesis, what are we accepting instead?

In general, the alternative or research hypothesis would be:

> H_a: One or more proportions differ between two or more groups.

Or, in this case:

H_a: Not all proportions of persons in various marital statuses are the same across all groups.

The alternative hypothesis is a very general one. It really just states that there is some difference between some groups. We need to be sure this is the case, though, before we can worry about specific differences.

The chi-squared statistic never has negative values. As the differences in proportions between groups become larger, the chi-squared statistic becomes larger. So, an alternative way of stating the alternative hypothesis is:

$$H_a : \chi^2 > 0$$

Step 3: Assumptions

There are several important assumptions that need to be satisfied to produce valid results with the Pearson chi-squared statistic.

Both variables must be measured at the nominal or grouped ordinal level. As usual, the levels of each variable must be mutually exclusive and jointly exhaustive.

The observations should be from simple random samples from the populations of each of the groups being compared. The chi-squared test should not be used with "paired" or "matched" observations (e.g., spouses, twins, cases where one subject is selected because that subject is similar to another).

The samples are large enough to yield expected frequencies (we will explain this shortly!) in most cells of the cross-tabulation that are at least five cases. In cases where we are comparing two groups on two outcomes (a 2×2 cross-tabulation), this assumption is very important. If you do not have expected frequencies of at least five cases in each cell, you should use *Fisher's exact test* instead of chi-squared. In cases where we are comparing more groups and/or more outcomes, it is usually satisfactory if the assumption is approximately met. It is often recommended that at least 80 percent of the cells have expected frequencies of five or more.

Step 4: Selecting an Error Level

The null and alternative hypotheses for the Pearson independence chi-squared test are very simple. Either the proportions on the outcomes are the same for all groups (i.e., the null hypothesis) or they are not (i.e., the alternative). So the chi-squared test is necessarily a one-tailed test.

Our usual rules of thumb apply in selecting error levels. The most common practice is to insist that we be 95 percent sure the null hypothesis is wrong before we reject it (alpha or p is less than or equal to 0.05). If we are doing exploratory work, a larger error rate might be acceptable. If mistakes are costly, a smaller p is usually selected.

Step 5: Calculating the Pearson Chi-Squared Test of Independence

The Pearson chi-squared test of independence (you should use the full name, even though it is long, because there are other kinds of chi-squares—not Pearson—and other kinds of tests—not independence—that are done with them) provides a direct test of the null hypothesis of no group differences.

The formula for the test is as shown in Formula 10.1:

$$\chi^2_{(r-1)(c-1)} = \sum_{i=1}^{rc} \frac{(f_o - f_e)^2}{f_e} \tag{10.1}$$

Again, the symbol at the left is the Greek letter "chi" squared. The complicated subscript of the test statistic is simply the degrees of freedom for the particular problem. If we were working with at 2×2 table, the subscript would simply be 1. If we were working with a 3×5 table, the subscript would be 8 (remember why?).

The right-hand side of the equation shows how this test statistic is computed.

The key part of the formula is the numerator. It says: "Take the number of cases actually observed in a cell of the table (f sub o), subtract from it the expected number of cases for that cell (f sub e), and square the result. So, the chi-squared test statistic will get bigger as the difference between the "observed" and "expected" cell frequencies gets big. But what are these observed and expected cell frequencies?

The ***observed cell counts or frequencies*** are exactly that—the number of cases that actually occur in a given cell (e.g., the number of married white persons is 727).

The ***expected cell counts or frequencies*** are hypothetical numbers. They are the number of cases that should have occurred in a given cell if the null hypothesis of no group difference were, in fact, true. The expected frequencies can be computed by applying the proportions for the whole sample to compute the expected numbers for each cell.

For example, overall, 54.4 percent of all persons were married (see Table 10.1). If there were no group differences, 54.4 percent of white persons, black persons, and all other persons would be married. Since there were 1,271 white persons overall, there should have been $1{,}271 \times 0.544 = 691.4$ married white persons if there were no group differences. There should have been $175 * 0.544 = 95.2$ married black persons, and so on for all the cells. The expected counts for our example, along with the actual counts, are shown in Table 10.2 (computed with SPSS).

We want the chi-squared test statistic to get larger as the difference gets larger between the actual frequencies and the frequencies expected if there were no group differences. To make all the differences between observed and expected positive numbers, the differences are squared.

TABLE 10.2 Frequencies Observed and Expected Assuming Independence

Marital Status * Race of Respondent Cross-Tabulation

			Race			
			White	**Black**	**Other**	**Total**
Marital Status	**Married**	Count	727	67	22	816
		Expected count	691.4	95.2	29.4	816.0
	Widowed	Count	122	22	6	150
		Expected count	127.1	17.5	5.4	150.0
	Divorced	Count	173	18	8	199
		Expected count	168.6	23.2	7.2	199.0
	Separated	Count	24	17	4	45
		Expected count	38.1	5.3	1.6	45.0
	Never Married	Count	225	51	14	290
		Expected count	245.7	33.8	10.4	290.0
	Total	Count	1,271	175	54	1,500
		Expected count	1,271.0	175.0	54.0	1,500.0

The other parts of the formula for the chi-squared statistic tell us to divide each difference between observed and expected frequency by the expected frequency. This takes into account the fact that the cells in the table are not equal because some are expected to have more cases than others. Last, the formula tells us to do the calculation of observed minus expected, squared, divided by expected for each cell in the table, and add them up. In our example, there are 15 cells in the table, so we would do the calculation shown 15 times, and then add up the results to give the final test statistic that we use to make our decision.

Step 6: Making a Decision

The important thing to remember about the chi-squared test statistic is that it is a measure of how different the actual data are from what we should have observed if the null hypothesis of no group difference were true.

So, the bigger the chi-squared test statistic, the less likely it is that the null hypothesis of no group differences is true. As chi-squared gets bigger, the probability that the null is true (our *p*-level) gets smaller. If the probability falls below the critical level we set before doing the test (usually 0.05), we reject the null hypothesis (no group difference) in favor of the alternative (at least one group difference).

The value of the chi-squared test statistic cannot be directly interpreted, like "Z." In some cases a value of chi-squared of 3.0 might be significant, whereas in other cases it might not. Interpreting chi-squared is more like interpreting "t." We need to take into account degrees of freedom in order to determine significance.

For the Pearson independence chi-squared test, the degrees of freedom are equal to the number of rows in the table less 1 times the number of columns in the table less 1; that is,

TABLE 10.3 Pearson (and Other) Chi-Squared Test Results: Marital Status by Race

	Chi-Squared Tests		
	Value	*df*	Asymp. Sig. (2-sided)
Pearson chi-squared	61.551	8	0.000
Likelihood ratio	51.356	8	0.000
Linear-by-linear association	25.150	1	0.000
N of valid cases	1,500		

One cell (6.7%) has an expected count less than 5.
The minimum expected count is 1.62.

$(r-1) * (c-1)$. Our example table has three columns (white, black, other). It has five rows (married, never married, etc.). So, for our example, the degrees of freedom is $[(5-1) * (3-1)] = 8$.

Table 10.3 presents the results of the chi-squared test for our example, as printed by SPSS.

We are not interested, here, in the likelihood ratio chi-squared test or the linear-by-linear association chi-squared test. But, do notice the footnote to the table warning that there is one cell (which is 6.7 percent of all the cells) that has a low frequency. Since this is less than 20 percent of the cells, this is not a big worry.

The Pearson chi-squared test statistic has the value of 61.551 in our example table. We saw that there were 8 degrees of freedom. The p-level for the test is (smaller than) 0.000. Since the probability that the null hypothesis is true is less than 0.05, we can conclude that it is unlikely that the null hypothesis of no group difference is true—so we can reject that idea in favor of the alternative of a group difference.

That's it. The Pearson independence chi-squared test can be used to assess confidence in asserting that there are group differences for any number of groups (columns in the table) for any number of possible categorical outcomes (rows in the table).

Once one has concluded that there are differences between groups that are statistically significant, it is wise look closely at the differences descriptively to decide whether they are substantively meaningful. We'll suggest some strategies for this in the next section. Before going on, though, take a few minutes to check your mastery of this section by taking the quiz, and reviewing if necessary.

CHECK QUIZ 10.1

1. A typical H_0 for a Pearson chi-squared test of independence is
   a. that the proportions of cases having each of various outcomes are different across the populations being compared.
   b. that the mean of one group on some variable is different from that of another group.

   c. that the proportions of cases having each of various outcomes are the same across the populations being compared.
   d. that the mean of one group on some variable is the same as that of another group.
2. When we say "expected frequency" in the context of a Pearson chi-squared test of independence, we mean
   a. the kind of numbers we expected given our theory.
   b. the distribution of scores if there were no association between the variables.
   c. the cell count based on the row and column proportions.
   d. b and c.
3. The chi-squared statistic gets larger if
   a. there is a small difference between the observed cell counts and the expected cell counts.
   b. there is a big difference between the observed cell counts and the expected cell counts.
   c. the variance in one variable is much larger than the variance in the other variable.
   d. the mean difference between the samples is large.
4. Among the assumptions for using the Pearson chi-squared test of independence is that the minimum expected frequency for cells is
   a. 1.
   b. 2.
   c. 5.
   d. 10.
5. Another assumption in the use of the Pearson chi-squared test of independence is that the groups are
   a. independent.
   b. dependent.
   c. normally distributed.
   d. representative samples.
6. Which assumption about level of measurement is made for the chi-squared test?
   a. All variables are at least ordinal.
   b. All variables are at least interval/ratio.
   c. All variables are nominal.
   d. At least one variable must be ordinal.
7. Which pattern of cell frequencies in a 2×2 table would indicate that the variables are independent?
   a. All cell frequencies are exactly the same.
   b. There is a different number of cases in each of the four cells.
   c. Only the cells in the top row of the table have cases in them.
   d. There are no cases in any cell.

Example

USING EXCEL TO SOLVE CHI-SQUARED PROBLEMS

For problems where we are comparing a small number of groups across a small number of possible outcomes (for example, a 2-by-2 table), it is very easy to calculate chi-squared by hand. A spreadsheet like Excel can also be used.

Study this example to see how the calculations are done for a very simple problem. Obviously, you can do by hand the same things that Excel is doing: taking sums, dividing, and so on.

In this problem we are interested in whether handedness (being right-handed, left-handed, or ambidextrous) is distributed in the same way for men and for women (the data are fictitious!). The independent variable is the groups being compared (men and women), so these categories are the columns of our data table. The dependent variable is whether persons are right-handed, left-handed, or both. So these three categories are the row variables in our data array.

Our actual data are the observed values. They have been placed in the first table in our Excel spreadsheet.

◇	A	B	C	D	E
1	Observed				
2			men	women	total:
3		right	58	35	=SUM(C3:D3)
4		left	11	25	=SUM(C4:D4)
5		ambidextrous	10	23	=SUM(C5:D5)
6		total:	=SUM(C3:C5)	=SUM(D3:D5)	=SUM(C6:D6)
7					
8					
9	Expected under null				
10			men	women	
11		right	=E3*C6/E6	=E3*D6/E6	
12		left	=E4*C6/E6	=E4*D6/E6	
13		ambidextrous	=E5*C6/E6	=E5*D6/E6	
14					
15			alpha	0.05	
16			P:	=CHITEST(C3:D5,C11:D13)	
17			Decision:	=IF(D16<=D15,"Reject H0","FTR")	
18					

In our spreadsheet, we've added formulas to calculate the row marginals (i.e., totals), column marginals (totals), and the grand total.

In the spreadsheet, you'll also notice that we have stated what our alpha level will be (0.05).

Before we calculate the test statistic, we should also determine our degrees of freedom. There are two columns ($c = 2$, so $c - 1 = 1$); there are three rows ($r = 3$, so $r - 1 = 2$). The degrees of freedom is $(c - 1) \times (r - 1)$, or $1 \times 2 = 2$. Using Excel, we don't have to calculate the degrees of freedom; it happens automatically when we tell Excel what rows and columns are included in the table.

Example

The tricky part about calculating chi-squared are the expected frequencies. We need to calculate an expected frequency for each of the $2 \times 3 = 6$ cells of the table. See how this has been done in the spreadsheet.

For right-handed men (cell 1, 1), we take the total number of right-handed persons (the row marginal, calculated and stored in cell E3), and multiply it by the proportion of all persons (regardless of handedness) who are males (this is the quantity C6/E6). This gives the expected number of males who should be right-handed if there are no differences between males and females.

We then repeat exactly the same logic for each of the other five cells. Pause a moment here and read the formulas in the spreadsheet for each of the other five expected cell frequencies. An alternative way to calculate expected frequencies for a given cell is to multiply the row marginal times the column marginal, and divide by the grand total.

The next spreadsheet shows the results of the calculations of row and column marginals, as well as expected cell frequencies (rather than the formulas).

◇	A	B	C	D	E
1	Observed				
2			men	women	total:
3		right	58	35	93
4		left	11	25	36
5		ambidextrous	10	23	33
6		total:	79	83	162
7					
8					
9	Expected under null				
10			men	women	
11		right	45.4	47.6	
12		left	17.6	18.4	
13		ambidextrous	16.1	16.9	
14					
15			alpha	0.05	
16			P:	0.000308910	
17			Decision:	Reject H0	
18					

We see that if there were no differences between men and women in the probability that persons are right-handed, we should have observed only 45.4 (on average) right-handed males, not the 58 right-handed men actually observed in our sample. So, there are more such people than we expected, assuming no group differences.

Similarly, we see that right-handed women are underrepresented, left-handed men are underrepresented, and ambidextrous men underrepresented.

But are these differences *in the sample* so big that they cause us to reject the idea that the proportions *in the population* are really the same? For this, we calculate the chi-squared test statistic and determine its p-level.

(*continued*)

Example

In Excel this is very easy to do. We use the function CHITEST(observed table, expected table). This was shown in the first panel of the example. Excel determines the degrees of freedom, calculates chi-squared, looks it up in the table of *p*-values, and reports that $p = 0.00030891$. Since this is less than the value we specified (alpha = 0.05), we can use the "IF" function to tell us whether to reject or accept the null hypothesis (see how to tell Excel to do this in the first panel of the example).

If we are doing the problem by hand, we need to do a bit more work. We know the observed values, and we've calculated the expected values. Now we need to apply the formula for chi-squared, Formula 10.1:

$$\chi^2_{(r-1)(c-1)} = \sum_{i=1}^{rc} \frac{(f_o - f_e)^2}{f_e} \tag{10.1}$$

The formula tells us (reading from the inside out) to first take the difference between an observed and an expected frequency in some cell); then square the difference; then divide that quantity by the expected frequency. Let's do this for the cell "right-handed men" (cell 1, 1).

The observed frequency is 58. The expected frequency is 45.5. So the difference is 58 − 45.4 or 12.6. We square this: $12.6 \times 12.6 = 158.8$ Then, we divide by the expected frequency: 158.8/45.4= 3.50.

We repeat this process for every one of the six cells in the table. We won't show all the work here, but for "ambidextrous women" the observed is 23 cases, the expected is 16.9 cases. The difference is $23 - 16.9 = 6.1$. This difference, squared, is $6.1 \times 6.1 = 37.21$. Dividing this by the expected frequency (16.9) gives us $37.21/16.9 = 2.20$.

After we have done this for all six cells, we have:

	Males	**Females**
Right-handed	3.50	3.34
Left-handed	2.45	2.37
Ambidextrous	2.31	2.20

The chi-squared test statistic is the sum of these six values, or 16.2.

To evaluate this, we need to know the degrees of freedom, and use our table of critical values.

We know the degrees of freedom are 2. Using a table of critical values of chi-squared, we see that a chi-squared test statistic at $p = 0.05$ with $df = 2$ must be at least 5.991. Since our test statistic is much larger than the critical value, we can reject the null hypothesis of no difference in handedness between men and women, in favor of the alternative of some difference.

Calculating the chi-squared test for more than a few groups or for outcomes with more than a few levels is very tedious and error-prone. Let's use statistical software to look at an example that is just a bit more complicated.

Example

USING SPSS FOR THE PEARSON INDEPENDENCE CHI-SQUARED TEST

The Pearson independence chi-squared test is widely used to test the null hypothesis that two categorical variables (nominal dichotomy, nominal polyotomy, grouped ordinal) are statistically independent. Where one of the variables is a grouping, or comparison, or independent variable, the test can also be interpreted as a test for differences in proportions between groups.

A major source of the continuing economic disparities among racial groups in the United States is differences in attaining formal educational credentials. Our researcher hypothesizes that there are statistically significant differences in the distributions of educational credentials earned among white, black, and other Americans. To test this hypothesis, data from the 1993 General Social Survey are used.

Stated in statistical terms, the null hypothesis is that there are no differences among the three racial groups in the population, in the proportions earning less than a high school degree, a high school degree only, a junior college degree, a bachelor's degree, or a graduate degree.

The first step is to examine the observed frequencies. (See Table 10.4.) Note that the independent variable, race, is the column variable; the dependent variable, respondent's highest degree, is the row variable.

TABLE 10.4 Educational Degree by Race, General Social Survey 1993, Observed Frequencies

R's Highest Degree * Race of Respondent Cross-Tabulation Count					
		Race of Respondent			
		White	**Black**	**Other**	**Total**
R's Highest Degree	Less than HS	214	48	17	279
	High school	658	92	30	780
	Junior college	74	13	3	90
	Bachelor's	209	7	18	234
	Graduate	99	7	7	113
Total		1,254	167	75	1,496

(continued)

Example

We see that the modal category for all three racial categories is "high school." But there do appear to be differences among the groups (we would see this more easily if we had used column percentages).

Next we calculate the expected frequencies under independence. That is, how many persons should appear in each cell if there truly were no differences between racial groups in educational outcomes? SPSS produces the expected frequencies in Table 10.5.

TABLE 10.5 Educational Degree by Race, General Social Survey 1993, Expected Frequencies

R's Highest Degree * Race of Respondent Cross-Tabulation Expected Count					
		Race of Respondent			
		White	Black	Other	Total
R's Highest Degree	Less than HS	233.9	31.1	14.0	279.0
	High school	653.8	87.1	39.1	780.0
	Junior college	75.4	10.0	4.5	90.0
	Bachelor's	196.1	26.1	11.7	234.0
	Graduate	94.7	12.6	5.7	113.0
Total		1,254.0	167.0	75.0	1,496.0

If there were no differences among racial groups in educational outcomes, then the observed and expected frequencies would be the same. They are not. To get a picture of what is going on, let's calculate the ***chi-squared residuals***. These are the observed frequencies minus the expected frequencies. These are shown in Table 10.6.

TABLE 10.6 Educational Degree by Race, General Social Survey 1993, Residuals

R's Highest Degree * Race of Respondent Cross-Tabulation Residual				
		Race of Respondent		
		White	Black	Other
R's Highest Degree	Less than HS	−19.9	16.9	3.0
	High school	4.2	4.9	−9.1
	Junior college	−1.4	3.0	−1.5
	Bachelor's	12.9	−19.1	6.3
	Graduate	4.3	−5.6	1.3

We can see that there are fewer whites with less than a high school degree than expected, and fewer blacks with graduate degrees than expected. The residuals are a useful way of examining where the differences are coming from, if chi-squared is significant.

After calculating the residuals, SPSS squares each residual, divides it by its expected frequency, and then adds them up to generate the chi-squared test statistic, shown in Table 10.7.

TABLE 10.7 Educational Degree by Race, General Social Survey 1993, Chi-Squared Test

Chi-Squared Tests			
	Value	***df***	**Asymp. Sig. (2-sided)**
Pearson chi-squared	36.482[a]	8	0.000
Likelihood ratio	41.135	8	0.000
Linear-by-linear association	3.656	1	0.056
N of valid cases	1,496		

We know that our table has three columns and five rows, so the degrees of freedom are $2 \times 4 = 8$. We are interested in the Pearson independence chi-squared (SPSS produces a number of related tests we won't discuss here).

Our chi-squared statistic is 36.482, with 8 degrees of freedom. SPSS calculates the *p*-value directly (rather than using a table of critical values), and finds that $p < 0.000$.

It is extremely unlikely (less than one chance in 1,000) that a chi-squared as large as 36.482 would be observed by chance in a sample drawn at random from populations where there truly were no group differences. We reject the null hypothesis. In 1993, there were clearly racial differences in educational outcomes in the United States (and there still are).

It is important to be confident that our sample results are reliable before we make too much of them, so we should always perform the chi-squared test before looking at the pattern. But once we are convinced that there is a pattern, we need to go further to describe it.

DESCRIBING GROUP DIFFERENCES

The Pearson independence chi-squared test is only the first step in understanding the ***differences in proportions*** across multiple groups. What chi-squared tells us is whether it is likely that there really are any differences of proportions in the whole populations from which our multiple samples were drawn.

If we cannot reject the null hypothesis of no group differences, we're done. The evidence does not support the research hypothesis, and it is time to go back to the drawing board.

But if we do reject the null hypothesis, all we know is that there probably are group differences. We don't yet know which groups are different in which ways from one another.

We would like to know two things about group differences, if we are confident that they do exist. The first is "strength." That is, how big are the differences? Does knowing what group a person is in reduce my uncertainty about predicting their outcome a lot, or just a little? The second is "form." Which groups differ in what ways from which others?

The Strength of Group Differences

A bit later in this book we will see how measures of the "strength of statistical association" can be applied to understanding whether the differences between groups are big enough to matter substantively.

For the moment, we'll examine some simple approaches to describing group differences in variables with proportional outcomes. In Table 10.8, again, are the data that we have been examining in our analysis of "race" group differences in marital status outcomes.

From our chi-squared test, we now are confident that there are probably differences in the proportional distributions of marital status among the "race" groups. But are these differences big enough to be important? "Big enough," of course, is a judgment call that depends on the research problem. However, there are some ways of summarizing the magnitude of the group effect.

The most obvious approach is to just compare the percentage (or proportion) distributions among the groups by looking at column percentages as we've done in the Table 10.8. It looks like "black" and "other" percentages are pretty much alike, and both differ from "white." Take a minute to look at the percentages—do you arrive at the same conclusion?

A somewhat more formal approach is to compare the proportions in the outcome categories for one group against another. If we subtract the proportions in the various categories for

TABLE 10.8 Differences in Proportions: Marital Status by Race

Marital Status by Race of Respondent (General Social Survey, 1978–1998)				
	White	**Black**	**Other**	**Total**
Married	727 (57.2%)	67 (38.3%)	22 (40.7%)	816 (54.4%)
Widowed	122 (9.6%)	22 (12.6%)	6 (11.1%)	150 (10.0%)
Divorced	173 (13.6%)	18 (10.3%)	8 (14.8%)	199 (13.3%)
Separated	24 (1.9%)	17 (9.7%)	4 (7.4%)	45 (3.0%)
Never married	225 (17.7%)	51 (29.1%)	14 (25.9%)	290 (19.3%)
Total	1,271 (100.0%)	175 (100.0%)	54 (100.0%)	1,500 (100.0%)

TABLE 10.9 Differences in Proportions between "White" and "Black"

	White	Black	Absolute Difference
Married	0.572	0.383	0.189
Widowed	0.096	0.126	0.030
Divorced	0.136	0.103	0.033
Separated	0.019	0.097	0.078
Never married	0.177	0.291	0.114
Sum of absolute differences			0.331
Sum divided by 2			0.166

one group from those for another, ignore the sign of the difference, sum the differences, and divide by 2 (we need to divide by 2 because a positive difference in one category necessarily matches a negative difference in another category, and we will be double counting if we don't divide by 2), we can create an index. Table 10.9 presents an example for the differences between "white" and "black."

The resulting number—0.166 in this case—summarizes the difference in the proportions on the outcome variable between the "white" group and the "black" group. This difference would be zero if the proportions were exactly the same for the two groups; the difference could be 1.000 if all the people in one group were in one category and all the people in the other group were in a different category. The difference in proportions between "white" and "other" in our example turns out to be 0.165. The difference in proportions between "black" and "other" is much lower—only 0.070. This agrees with our original observation that "black" and "other" were not very different, but both were rather different from "white."

The Form of Group Differences

Now that we know that the groups are different and how big the differences are, overall, among the groups, it is useful to describe the important differences in detail. For example, we now know that "whites" are different from "blacks" and "others," but that "blacks" and "others" are not very different from one another. But *how* are they different? In what way do the outcomes for one group differ from those for another?

The most obvious way to answer this question is to look again at the percentages. Where in the table are the big differences? When I look at the table, what I see is that "whites" are more likely than "blacks" or "others" to be married; they are less likely than "blacks" or "others" to be separated or never married.

Comparing percentages is a reasonable and correct way to describe the differences between groups. There is, however, an additional way that is sometimes helpful. This approach uses the residuals from the calculation of the chi-squared statistic (most computer programs for doing

TABLE 10.10 Analyzing Residuals to Describe Group Differences

Marital Status * Race of Respondent (General Social Survey, 1978–1998)				
		White	**Black**	**Other**
Married	Count	727	67	22
	Residual	35.6	−28.2	−7.4
Widowed	Count	122	22	6
	Residual	−5.1	4.5	0.6
Divorced	Count	173	18	8
	Residual	4.4	−5.2	0.8
Separated	Count	24	17	4
	Residual	−14.1	11.8	2.4
Never married	Count	225	51	14
	Residual	−20.7	17.2	3.6

chi-squared will print residuals if you ask for them). We have reproduced the results from SPSS in Table 10.10.

For each outcome, the table first reports the observed frequencies ("count"). For example, there were 727 respondents who were "white" and married.

The "residual" for each count is the difference between the actual number of cases (the observed frequency) and the number of cases that should have been in the category if there were no differences between the groups (i.e., the expected frequency). This residual, of course, is part of the formula for calculating chi-squared. But now let's look at the actual values and see what they mean.

The residual in the category "white-married" is +35.6; the residual in the category "black-married" is −28.2; the residual in the category "other-married" is −7.4. Notice that these residuals sum up to zero.

On the basis of the residuals, we can say, "White people are more likely to be married or divorced, and less likely to be widowed, separated, or never married than we would expect if the groups were all the same." We can draw similar portraits of the profiles for blacks (less likely to be married or divorced, more likely to be widowed, separated, or never married), and for others.

The pattern of residuals, then, lets us describe the profile of outcomes for each group, compared to what they would have been if the groups were the same. This approach is a bit more complicated than just looking at the percentages, but is based on deviations of the data from the idea of group equality, rather than group-to-group comparisons.

In this section, we've examined some approaches to how one can describe the differences in proportional outcomes among several groups once we have used the chi-squared test to be confident that the differences are real. Before reviewing the chapter as a whole, take a couple of minutes to review this section with the check quiz.

CHECK QUIZ 10.2

1. When we create an index based on the absolute difference of proportions (take the sum of the differences between proportions in the columns and divide by 2), the value of the index will be bounded by
   a. negative infinity to positive infinity.
   b. –1 to +1.
   c. 0 to 1.
   d. 1 to 10.
2. Such an index would have values close to zero if
   a. there were large differences between groups.
   b. there were small differences between groups.
   c. the variance in one group was small.
   d. the variance in one variable was large.

$$\chi^2_{(r-1)(c-1)} = \sum_{i=1}^{rc} \frac{(f_o - f_e)^2}{f_e} \tag{10.1}$$

3. Which part of Formula 10.1 for computing the Pearson chi-squared test of independence statistic tells us what the residuals are?
   a. the symbol to the left of the equal sign
   b. the denominator
   c. the numerator, including the squared term
   d. the numerator, not including the squared term
4. In order to identify large differences by looking at the chi-squared residuals, one should be on the lookout for
   a. large values.
   b. small values.
   c. nonzero values.
   d. empty cells.

SUMMARY

There are many times that social scientists are confronted with comparing more than two groups to see if (and how) they differ on outcome variables that are measured at the nominal or grouped ordinal level. In this chapter we have examined an overall test for multiple group differences in proportions—the Pearson chi-squared test of independence. We've also examined some approaches to describing the size and form of the group differences—if we are confident that they really do exist in the populations (not just the samples) being compared.

The Pearson independence chi-squared statistic is used to test the null hypothesis that the proportions of all outcomes are the same for all of the groups being compared. The alternative hypothesis is a very general one: the proportions of the various outcomes are not all the same.

The chi-squared test is based on comparing the observed frequencies in all the categories in a table against the numbers that should have occurred if the null hypothesis of no group difference was, in fact, true (the expected frequencies). It follows from this that the bigger the chi-squared statistic is, the bigger the difference between the real data and the null hypothesis, and the less likely it is that the null hypothesis is correct. So, big chi-squared statistics lead to the rejection of the null hypothesis of no difference between groups.

The chi-squared statistic's *p*-level needs to be interpreted in light of degrees of freedom (just like the t-tests for differences in means we studied earlier). The degrees of freedom for the Pearson independence chi-squared test are equal to the number of rows, less 1, times the number of columns, less 1.

Caution must be exercised with the Pearson chi-squared test when more than a small percentage of the cells (say 10 to 20 percent) in the table have small (less than 5) expected frequencies. Some caution is also needed when the number of cases is very large. Tables with very large expected cell frequencies may be statistically significant but substantively trivial. After we have rejected the null hypothesis of no group differences in proportions, it is important to examine and describe the differences.

The simplest and most obvious (and correct!) way to describe the differences between groups is simply to examine column percentages in the cross-tabulation. We can summarize whether the differences between groups are big or small by calculating overall indexes of differences in proportions or indexes of dissimilarity.

To describe the way in which the groups differ from one another, percentages can be used. We also showed how the residuals from the chi-squared test (i.e., the differences between the observed and expected frequencies) can be used to create a profile of how the groups differ from one another.

The Pearson independence chi-squared test is useful for comparing several groups when the outcome is categorical (nominal or grouped ordinal). When the outcome variable is measured on the interval/ratio level, we use the technique called "one-way analysis of variance" to test for differences among more than two groups. One-way ANOVA is the topic of the next chapter.

KEY TERMS

chi-squared residual

difference of proportions

expected cell count or frequency

observed cell count or frequency

Pearson independence chi-squared test

CHECK QUIZ ANSWERS

Quiz 10.1 Answers: 1. (c); 2. (d); 3. (b); 4. (c); 5. (a); 6. (c); 7. (a)
Quiz 10.2 Answers: 1. (c); 2. (b); 3. (c); 4. (a)

EXERCISES

1. Is there a gender gap in the use of computers? Data from the 1997 Statistical Abstract of the United States (Table 912) show that 41,260,000 of 130,782,000 men used computers; 39,753,000 of 137,001,000 women used computers. Create a cross-tabulation, and percentage it in the correct way. Calculate the Pearson independence chi-squared test, and interpret the result.
2. Is there a race gap in the use of computers? In 1997, according to the Statistical Abstract of the United States, 34.93 percent of white, non-Hispanic persons used computers (the total number of such persons was 194,746,000); 15.28 percent of 32,339,000 black, non-Hispanic persons used computers; and 13.98 percent of Hispanic persons used computers. Create a cross-tabulation, and percentage it in the correct way. Calculate the Pearson independence chi-squared test, and interpret the result.
3. Here are some sales figures collected by the Recording Industry Association of America describing the cash value of purchases (in millions of dollars) of several genres of music during the 1990s.

1990

Rock $2,722
Country $724
Rap/hip-hop $641
R & B $875
Pop $1,033
Religious $189
Classical $234
Jazz $362

1995

Rock $4,127
Country $2,057
Rap/hip-hop $825
R & B $1,392
Pop $1,244
Religious $392
Classical $357
Jazz $370

1999

Rock \$3,675
Country \$1,575
Rap/hip-hop \$1,576
R & B \$1,531
Pop \$1,502
Religious \$744
Classical \$510
Jazz \$438

One researcher hypothesizes that, during the 1990s, high-brow genres of music became less popular in the United States. Prepare a table that compares the proportions of all the sales in 1990 that were for high-brow genres (classical or jazz) versus all others, compared to 1999.

a. Lay out the table, and percentage it in the proper way to test the hypothesis that the proportion of all music sales that were sales of high-brow genres changed between 1990 and 1999.
b. State a null hypothesis and a research hypothesis.
c. Calculate the Pearson independence chi-squared statistic.
d. Should the null be accepted or rejected at $p < 0.05$?

4. Use the data on music sales reported in the preceding problem to do another analysis.

   This time, the researcher is interested in the more general question of whether there are any significant differences among the three years in the proportions of music of the various types that were purchased.

   a. Lay out the table, and percentage it in the proper way to test the hypothesis that the mix of music that the buying public likes was different among the three years.
   b. State a null hypothesis and a research hypothesis.
   c. Calculate the Pearson independence chi-squared statistic.
   d. Should the null be accepted or rejected at $p < 0.05$?

5. Do racial groups in American society differ in gun ownership? The General Social Survey gathered information on whether people had a gun in their home (or refused to answer the question), and their race ("white," "black," or "other"). Here are the results, as well as some chi-squared tests.

Have Gun in Home * Race of Respondent Cross-Tabulation

			Race of Respondent			
			White	**Black**	**Other**	**Total**
Have Gun in Home	**Yes**	Count	211	18	7	236
		Expected count	193.2	31.6	11.2	236.0
		Percent within race of respondent	42.1%	22.0%	24.1%	38.6%

			Race of Respondent			
			White	Black	Other	Total
	No	Count	288	63	21	372
		Expected count	304.5	49.8	17.6	372.0
		Percent within race of respondent	57.5%	76.8%	72.4%	60.8%
	Refused	Count	2	1	1	4
		Expected count	3.3	.5	.2	4.0
		Percent within race of respondent	0.4%	1.2%	3.4%	0.7%
Total		Count	501	82	29	612
		Expected count	501.0	82.0	29.0	612.0
		Percent within race of respondent	100.0%	100.0%	100.0%	100.0%

Chi-Squared Tests

	Value	*df*	Asymp. Sig. (2-sided)
Pearson chi-squared	18.451	4	0.001
Likelihood ratio	17.683	4	0.001
Linear-by-linear association	14.029	1	0.000
N of valid cases	612		

a. State the null hypothesis and the alternative hypothesis for the statistical test that has been performed.
b. Select the appropriate chi-squared statistic, and use it to accept or reject the null hypothesis, using a required confidence level of 99 percent.
c. Interpret your result.

6. A researcher asked, using the 1991 General Social Survey, whether there were "race" differences in the likelihood that respondents would report that they had been passed over for a promotion at work. The researcher expected that there would be significant differences. Here are the results of her test:

Cross-Tabulation

			Race of Respondent			
			White	Black	Other	Total
Being Passed Over for Promotion	**Yes**	Count	25	8	5	38
		Percent within race of respondent	3.1%	5.7%	15.6%	3.9%

(continued)

		Race of Respondent			
		White	Black	Other	Total
No	Count	773	133	27	933
	Percent within race of respondent	96.9%	94.3%	84.4%	96.1%
Total	Count	798	141	32	971
	Percent within race of respondent	100.0%	100.0%	100.0%	100.0%

Chi-Squared Tests

	Value	*df*	Asymp. Sig. (2-sided)
Pearson chi-squared	14.127	2	0.001
Likelihood ratio	9.235	2	0.010
Linear-by-linear association	11.716	1	0.001
N of valid cases	971		

a. What are the null and alternative hypotheses being tested?

b. Should the researcher accept or reject the null hypothesis at the 99 percent confidence level? (What is your evidence?).

c. Provide a one- or two-sentence interpretation of the meaning of the statistical results.

Chapter 11

MULTIPLE SAMPLE TESTS FOR MEANS: ONE-WAY ANOVA

LEARNING OBJECTIVES

When you have finished this chapter, you will be able to:

- Explain the purpose of one-way analysis of variance (ANOVA) and the null and alternative hypotheses.
- Understand the sum of squares total, sum of squares between groups, and sum of squares within groups.
- Calculate and interpret the eta-squared statistic.
- Determine the degrees of freedom of the F-test, and calculate mean squares.
- Calculate and interpret the F-statistic.
- Understand the idea of "experiment-wise error" and the purpose of post hoc tests.
- Interpret the differences between group means using the Scheffé protected t-test.

COMPARING SEVERAL GROUP MEANS WITH ANALYSIS OF VARIANCE

In the preceding chapter, we looked at a technique (the Pearson independence chi-squared test) that is useful for comparing proportions across multiple groups. This chi-squared test is very useful when the outcome that we are comparing across the groups is qualitative—measured as a categorical variable (nominal or grouped ordinal).

We can perform the same kind of comparisons in outcomes for multiple groups when the outcome is measured at the interval/ratio level. An approach that was developed for comparing multiple groups in experiments, called "***one-way***" (for one grouping variable) ***analysis of variance (ANOVA)*** is used for this purpose.

Analysis of variance is used to compare the means of multiple groups. Like chi-squared, we first test a global null hypothesis of no difference between groups. We will look at the hypotheses and process of doing a one-way ANOVA.

The name "analysis of variance" is well chosen. The "analysis" involves examining all of the variation across cases on the outcome (i.e., some people score high, others low) and dividing the total variation into two parts. One part is due to the differences between the groups we are comparing. This part of the variation in the outcomes can be attributed to or explained by the systematic differences among groups, which is what our theories are about. The other portion of the variation in outcomes cannot be attributed to systematic group differences, and must be left "unexplained" or "residual" or "due to individual differences." We will see how this division of the variance in the outcomes is done.

Once the variance has been analyzed, the component parts are used to construct a test (the F-test) to evaluate the null hypothesis of no differences among the outcome means for the multiple groups. We discuss the F-test and its interpretation.

If the F-test gives us sufficient confidence that there really are differences among the outcome means of groups, we then need to describe which groups are different from which others. This last step in ANOVA involves the use of protected t-tests to describe the differences between pairs of groups, and to test for the statistical significance of the difference. We discuss the use of post hoc protected t-tests to describe group differences.

Here's an example of a typical kind of research question that can be addressed with one-way ANOVA. The demographic behavior of people (e.g., fertility, mortality, age at marriage) tends to differ from one ethnic group to another in societies that display stratification and inequality along ethnic group lines. This is not to say that all members of one group behave differently than all members of another, but that the central tendencies of the groups are likely to differ.

Suppose we wanted to see if the desired completed family size (number of children) differs among people of different ethnicities in a sample of students at one university. Our general theory and past empirical work suggest the research hypothesis that the groups will probably differ.

If we collect information about desired family size from samples of persons of different ethnicities, we would expect the mean number of children to differ from one group to another if our theory is useful. Let's suppose that the sample means do differ. Is that the end of the story?

It's not. Since we are comparing means calculated from samples of university students (rather than a census of all the students), there is the possibility that the differences between means may be due to random sampling variability. So, before we do anything else, we must do an inference test. In ANOVA, we "analyze the variance" and use the results of this analysis to test hypotheses using the F-test.

ANALYZING VARIANCE AND THE F-TEST

To perform the F-test, we will need to analyze the variance, but let's first develop our hypotheses and assumptions.

Step 1: Null Hypothesis

One-way ANOVA tests the hypothesis that the means of multiple population groups are all equal:

$$H_0 : \mu_1 = \mu_2 = \mu_3 = \cdots = \mu_k$$

Notice that the null hypothesis is stated using the Greek letters μ (mu) to indicate population means. The null and alternative hypotheses are about the populations; we use information from the samples to make an inference about these (unobserved) population parameters.

The null hypothesis in one-way ANOVA is a very specific one. It asserts that the means of all groups are the same. The null hypothesis, then, can be rejected if any group or groups are different from any other group or groups.

Step 2: Alternative Hypotheses

If the null hypothesis is that the means of all population groups are the same, then the alternative hypothesis is that at least two groups differ.

This is a very general alternative hypothesis. But, before we try to examine and test particular group differences, we must be confident that they are probably true in the whole population.

Note that the alternative hypothesis is simply one of difference between any two means—it does not matter whether the difference is positive or negative. Unlike the t-test for the difference between two means, the research hypothesis in one-way ANOVA is not directional (i.e., it is one-tailed).

One-way ANOVA provides a test (the F-test) of the null hypothesis on no difference between any population means against the alternative hypothesis that at least one difference between means is not zero.

Step 3: Assumptions

The F-test, like the chi-squared test, is very widely used. Like the chi-squared test, its proper use involves making some assumptions.

First, we assume that the dependent or outcome variable we are studying is measured at the interval/ratio level, so that the use of means to describe central tendency is a reasonable approach.

Second, we assume independent random samples. That is, we need to assume that the selection of a person from one population has nothing to do with the probability that another person in that population or any other will be selected. Sometimes research designs select "matched" cases. For example, two identical twins might be split—one in the treatment group and one in the control group. Or for each Hispanic person we select at random, we may select a matched Anglo person who lives in the same neighborhood and has the same education and income. Simple one-way ANOVA does not apply to cases with matched samples.

Third, we assume that the dependent variable of interest is distributed (at least approximately) normally in the population groups we are comparing. Actually, as long as the shape and dispersion of the variable are the same across the population groups, ANOVA will be okay—even if the shape of the distribution is quite far from normal.

Fourth, we assume that the variance of the variable of interest is the same across the population groups we are comparing (the homoscedasticity or "equal group variance" assumption). The ANOVA test is an extension of the version of the t-test for differences between the means of two groups—where we assume the variances are equal. If there are really big differences in the variances across the sample groups, one should be suspicious of ANOVA results. Most statistical software will perform tests for equal group variances as a part of calculating ANOVA tests. It is wise to pay attention to the results of these tests in interpreting ANOVA results. Many statisticians feel, however, that the tests for homogeneity of variance are too conservative, particularly for large samples.

Step 4: Selecting an Error Level

There is nothing special about selecting a significance level, or alpha level, or *p*-level for the one-way analysis of variance. Usually, we want to be 95 percent sure that the null hypothesis is wrong before we reject it. Or, more properly, we want to be at least 95 percent confident that the samples we observed were not drawn from populations in which all the means were equal.

Okay, enough of the preliminaries. Let's talk now about analyzing the variance and constructing the F-test. Before we do, though, take just a minute to review your mastery of this section by taking the check quiz.

CHECK QUIZ 11.1

1. Note that, once again, although we're using a sample to test the hypothesis, the hypothesis is framed in terms of
   a. a theoretical "other."
   b. a population or populations.
   c. one or more parameters.
   d. b and c.
2. We will reject the null hypothesis if at least __________ group(s) differ(s) from the other groups in the ANOVA.
   a. zero
   b. one
   c. two
   d. three
3. The assumption of independent random samples means that, for one-way ANOVA,
   a. we shouldn't sample men and then place their girlfriends in another group.
   b. the potential sample should be stratified prior to sampling.
   c. cluster samples will be inadequate.
   d. it would be a bad idea to sample families with twins.
4. For one-way ANOVA, the variable of interest needs to have a level of measurement that is
   a. at least nominal.
   b. at least ordinal.
   c. at least interval/ratio.
   d. normally distributed.
5. The null hypothesis for ANOVA is
   a. that the variables are nominal.
   b. that the variables are associated.
   c. that the population means are equal.
   d. that the population means are different.
6. In ANOVA, we assume either that the variable of interest is distributed normally across population groups or
   a. that the shape and dispersion of the variable is the same across the population groups.
   b. that the means are the same across groups.
   c. that the variable has the same variance in at least two of the groups.
   d. that there is no "or": the variable of interest must be distributed normally across population groups.

ANALYZING VARIANCE

Testing for differences in population group means is only part of what ANOVA does. Maybe even more important, ANOVA partitions the variance of an outcome variable into two parts—variability that is due to or explained by the systematic differences among groups and variability that is unexplained or residual.

Dividing the variability into these components is useful because it tells us how important the differences are between the groups in terms of explaining differences among individual persons. We may be confident that population group means differ, but the differences may not be big enough to matter. Analyzing the variance provides a tool (eta-squared) for answering the question of how important the differences between groups are.

In this section, we need to use some formulas to explain the quantities into which ANOVA partitions variance. It's not necessary to memorize the formulas—we use computers to actually calculate the quantities—but you should try to understand the meaning of "sums of squares."

Sum of Squares Total

Let's begin with an important but very simple equation that summarizes the whole approach.

$$\text{SST} = \text{SSB} + \text{SSW} \tag{11.1}$$

Formula 11.1 says: "The ***sum of squares total*** is equal to the sum of squares between the groups plus the sum of squares within groups."

That doesn't mean much, yet.

The important idea here is: The total variation among cases on a variable (SST) can be divided into two parts. One part represents the variation that is due to differences between groups (SSB). The other part is due to differences between people within the groups (SSW). So, this equation asserts that the differences between people can be divided into (1) systematic differences between groups and (2) a residual variation due to individual rather than systematic factors.

Our theories and research hypotheses are always about how groups of people differ, on average, from one another. Our theories explain the differences between groups. Our theories, though, cannot explain the differences among the people within a group—which cannot be systematically due to the nature of the group.

This is a powerful and useful idea for testing theories. But we need to develop ways of measuring these sums of squares. We'll start with the sum of squares total (SST). Formula 11.2 is the most common formula for this quantity:

$$\text{SST} = \sum_{i=1}^{n} (Y_i - \overline{Y})^2 \tag{11.2}$$

Formulas are read inside out. We begin by subtracting individual *i*'s score from the average score. This measures how far individual *i* is from the average of all people in the sample. Next, we square this "mean deviation" so that the difference is a positive number. Last, we add up all the squared mean deviations for all individuals.

The sum of squares total is a measure of how far the cases in a sample are from the mean score of all the people in the sample. Since the distances from the mean are squared, we give it the name "sum of squares."

The sum of squares total measures the total amount of variability among the scores of people in the sample as deviations from the mean of the sample as a whole.

The numerical magnitude of the SST cannot really be directly interpreted. The size of the SST will depend on how many cases there are and the scale of measurement of the variable in question, as well as the total variation among the cases in the sample. However, the SST is a useful starting point, because it defines the total variability among the cases in the sample.

Sum of Squares between Groups

How much of the total variation among cases is due to systematic differences between the groups within which the cases are located? The ***sum of squares between groups*** is a measure of the amount of the total variation that is due to the differences between the groups. Formula 11.3 is one formula for the sum of squares between groups (SSB).

$$\text{SSB} = \sum_{k=1}^{K} N_k(\overline{Y}_k - \overline{Y})^2 \tag{11.3}$$

This formula is a bit more complicated. Let's walk through it one step at a time:

First, we take the mean of a particular group ($\overline{Y}_k$) and measure how far it is from the overall mean of all cases. This quantity tells us how different a particular group is from the sample as a whole. To make the difference positive, we square it. Next, we multiply the deviation of the group from the overall mean times the number of people in the group (N_k). This is saying: suppose that everyone in group k had the same score (the group mean); how much squared deviation from the overall mean would that add up to? Last, we repeat this calculation of deviations and weighting by group size for all groups ($k = 1$ to $k = K$) and add them up.

The SSB then is a measure, in terms of sums of squared deviations, of how much of the total variation is due to differences between the group means—or systematic differences between the groups. The "between groups" variation is the focus of our research hypothesis.

Of course, if we already knew the values of the other two sums of squares, we could easily find the value for SSB using Formula 11.4:

$$\text{SSB} = \text{SST} - \text{SSW} \tag{11.4}$$

That is, the variation between groups is equal to the total variation less the variation within groups.

Sum of Squares within Groups

Usually, the scores of the people within a group are not all the same. For example, there may be a difference between the means of men and women on some variable (a between-groups difference). But even after we take that into account there may still be differences between the people within each group. These residual individual differences are what are measured by the ***sum of squares within groups*** (SSW).

$$\text{SSW} = \sum_K \sum_I (Y_{ik} - \overline{Y}_K)^2 \qquad (11.5)$$

Formula 11.5 looks complicated, but it really isn't. Start from the inside, and work outward.

It says to take the score of person i within group k, and see how far it is from the mean of group k. Then square the distance. Do this for each person in group k, and add up the results. Then do the same thing within each of the other groups, and add up all the quantities.

The basic thing here is this: SSW measures how individuals deviate from the mean of the group they are in. So, SSW measures the part of the variation that cannot be due to group differences. Since our theory seeks to explain group differences, the variation between cases that is not due to group differences is "error" or "residual" or "unexplained."

Again, we can see this by rearranging the basic formula to produce Formula 11.6:

$$\text{SSW} = \text{SST} - \text{SSB} \qquad (11.6)$$

That is, the variability among people within groups is what is left when we take the total variability (SST) and remove the variability that is due to the differences between the groups (SSB).

Now that we have measures of total variability, the variability that is due to differences between the groups, and the variability that is residual within groups, we can do some interesting things.

Eta-Squared

The first useful thing that we can do with the sums of squares is to calculate a simple proportion called "eta-squared," as shown in Formula 11.7:

$$\eta^2 = \frac{\text{SSB}}{\text{SST}} \qquad (11.7)$$

Eta-squared takes the variability between the groups (SSB), and expresses it as a proportion of the total variability (SST).

CHECK QUIZ 11.2

1. Which of the following correctly states the relationship among the total sum of squares (SST), the sum of squares between groups (SSB), and the sum of squares within groups (SSW)?
   a. SST = SSB + SSW
   b. SST = SSB − SSW
   c. SSW = SSB + SST
   d. SSB = SST − SSW
2. The quantity SSW measures the amount of variation
   a. after subtracting the total variation (SST).
   b. within the categories.
   c. in the population.
   d. assuming the null hypothesis is true.
3. In the ANOVA test, if the null hypothesis is true, then
   a. SSB should be at least twice as much as SSW.
   b. SSW should be much greater than SSB.
   c. eta will be very large.
   d. the mean square between and the mean square within should be roughly equal in value.
4. SSW measures
   a. how much the mean of one group deviates from the mean of the other groups.
   b. how much variance there is in the largest group.
   c. how individuals deviate from the mean of the group they are in.
   d. the underlying concept.
5. Values for eta-squared range from
   a. negative infinity to positive infinity.
   b. −1 to +1.
   c. 0 to 1.
   d. 1 to 10.
6. The closer eta-squared is to 1,
   a. the greater the amount of variance explained by differences between groups.
   b. the greater the amount of variance explained by differences within groups.
   c. the more important degrees of freedom become.
   d. the less the amount of variance is explained by similarities among the groups.

Since SSB is the amount of the variability among the cases that is explained by differences between groups, and SST is the total variability, eta-squared tells us what proportion of the total variation among cases is due to differences between the groups—that is, how much of the variation is due to the systematic differences our theories predicted.

Eta-squared has a minimum value of zero. This would happen if all the group's means were the same, so that the sum of squares between groups was zero. This would mean, of course, that the groups don't differ at all—and that our theory that predicted group differences was probably wrong.

Eta-squared has a maximum value of 1. This would happen if the means of the groups were different, and every individual had the same score as every other individual in his or her group. In this case, the SSB would be the same as the SST. This would also mean that all of the differences that we could observe between individual cases were due to what group the cases were in.

Eta-squared is a useful statistic because it tells us, in a sense, how important the differences between groups are. If eta-squared is large, then group differences are an important part of understanding why individual cases are different. If eta-squared is small, then most of the differences among people are due to things other than what groups they are parts of.

The sums of squares are also used to test the hypothesis of differences in group means. Before we get to that, though, take a few minutes to review and take the check quiz.

Example

SUMS OF SQUARES AND ETA-SQUARED IN ONE-WAY ANALYSIS OF VARIANCE

The first stage of doing one-way analysis of variance is to compute the sums of squares (total, between groups, and within groups). These quantities can be used to describe the strength of the relationship between the group variable and the outcome by computing eta-squared.

Suppose that we were interested in exploring whether religious beliefs affect fertility behavior. We will analyze differences in the median number of children born to women in a number of world nations during the mid-1990s to explore this question.

We have divided the nations of the world into four groups, according to the predominant religion in each nation: Muslim, Protestant Christian, Catholic Christian, and Buddhist/Taoist (this excludes some nations that are none of these).

Since our interest is in comparing the groups of societies, rather than in representing the population of all world nations, we are going to use stratified sampling by drawing a sample of eight nations from each of the four religious groups, so that our final sample is 32 nations (eight Buddhist, eight Catholic, eight Muslim, and eight Protestant). Then, for each nation, we measure fertility.

First, we will calculate the sum of squares total.

Example

To calculate the SST we must first calculate the "grand mean" (mean of all group means). We then find the deviation of each score from the grand mean, and square the deviation. Here are the data, and the calculations for the sum of squares total:

Country	Religion	Fertility	Grand Mean	Deviation	Dev. square
Cambodia	Buddhist	5.81	3.57	2.24	5.04
Hong Kong	Buddhist	1.40	3.57	−2.17	4.69
Japan	Buddhist	1.55	3.57	−2.02	4.06
N. Korea	Buddhist	2.40	3.57	−1.17	1.36
Thailand	Buddhist	2.10	3.57	−1.47	2.15
Vietnam	Buddhist	3.33	3.57	−0.24	0.06
China	Taoist	1.84	3.57	−1.73	2.98
Singapore	Taoist	1.88	3.57	−1.69	2.84
Argentina	Catholic	2.80	3.57	−0.77	0.59
Burundi	Catholic	6.80	3.57	3.23	10.46
Croatia	Catholic	1.65	3.57	−1.92	3.67
El Salvador	Catholic	3.78	3.57	0.21	0.05
Honduras	Catholic	4.90	3.57	1.33	1.78
Lithuania	Catholic	2.00	3.57	−1.57	2.45
Paraguay	Catholic	4.30	3.57	0.73	0.54
Peru	Catholic	3.11	3.57	-0.46	0.21
Afghanistan	Muslim	6.90	3.57	3.33	11.12
Bangladesh	Muslim	4.70	3.57	1.13	1.29
Gambia	Muslim	6.29	3.57	2.72	7.42
Iraq	Muslim	6.71	3.57	3.14	9.89
Lebanon	Muslim	3.39	3.57	−0.18	0.03
Morocco	Muslim	3.83	3.57	0.26	0.07
Pakistan	Muslim	6.43	3.57	2.86	8.20
Somalia	Muslim	7.25	3.57	3.68	13.57
Australia	Protestant	1.90	3.57	−1.67	2.77
Cent. Afri. R.	Protestant	5.42	3.57	1.85	3.44
Estonia	Protestant	2.00	3.57	−1.57	2.45
Germany	Protestant	1.47	3.57	−2.10	4.39
Latvia	Protestant	2.00	3.57	−1.57	2.45
Norway	Protestant	2.00	3.57	−1.57	2.45
Sweden	Protestant	2.10	3.57	−1.47	2.15
United States	Protestant	2.06	3.57	−1.51	2.27
	Mean	3.57		SST	116.88

(*continued*)

Example

The mean number of children for the sample as a whole is 3.57. We next take the deviation of each of the 32 cases from the mean by subtracting the mean from the value for the case (e.g., Cambodia is 5.81 − 3.57 = +2.24). Then we square this deviation (e.g., 2.24 * 2.24 = 5.04). The sum of squares total is the sum of the squared deviations across all 32 cases. In our example, SST = 116.88. This amount represents the total variation among all the cases. It is this variance that the analysis of variance analyzes.

Next we calculate the sum of squares within groups (SSW).

We proceed by analyzing each group separately, and then summing the results.

For the first group of nations, the Buddhist/Taoist ones, we get:

Country	Religion	Fertility	Group Mean	Deviation	Dev. Square
Cambodia	Buddhist	5.81	2.54	3.27	10.69
Hong Kong	Buddhist	1.40	2.54	−1.14	1.30
Japan	Buddhist	1.55	2.54	−0.99	0.98
N. Korea	Buddhist	2.40	2.54	−0.14	0.02
Thailand	Buddhist	2.10	2.54	−0.44	0.19
Vietnam	Buddhist	3.33	2.54	0.79	0.62
China	Taoist	1.84	2.54	−0.70	0.49
Singapore	Taoist	1.88	2.54	−0.66	0.44
	Mean	2.54		SSW	14.74

The mean, here, is the mean within the group—not the grand mean. The deviations and squared deviations are deviations of each case from the mean of the group—not the grand mean. The sum of squared deviations within the Buddhist group is 14.74. We need to do this for each of the four groups.

Here are the numbers for each of the other three groups:

Catholic Christian					
Country	**Religion**	**Fertility**	**Group Mean**	**Deviation**	**Dev. Square**
Argentina	Catholic	2.80	3.67	−0.87	0.76
Burundi	Catholic	6.80	3.67	3.13	9.80
Croatia	Catholic	1.65	3.67	−2.02	4.08
El Salvador	Catholic	3.78	3.67	0.11	0.01
Honduras	Catholic	4.90	3.67	1.23	1.51
Lithuania	Catholic	2.00	3.67	−1.67	2.79
Paraguay	Catholic	4.30	3.67	0.63	0.40
Peru	Catholic	3.11	3.67	−0.56	0.31
	Mean	3.67		SSW	19.66

Example

Muslim					
Country	**Religion**	**Fertility**	**Group Mean**	**Deviation**	**Dev. Square**
Afghanistan	Muslim	6.90	5.69	1.21	1.46
Bangladesh	Muslim	4.70	5.69	−0.99	0.98
Gambia	Muslim	6.29	5.69	0.60	0.36
Iraq	Muslim	6.71	5.69	1.02	1.04
Lebanon	Muslim	3.39	5.69	−2.30	5.29
Morocco	Muslim	3.83	5.69	−1.86	3.46
Pakistan	Muslim	6.43	5.69	0.74	0.55
Somalia	Muslim	7.25	5.69	1.56	2.43
	Mean	5.69		SSW	15.58

Protestant Christian					
Country	**Religion**	**Fertility**	**Group Mean**	**Deviation**	**Dev. Square**
Australia	Protestant	1.90	2.37	−0.47	0.22
Cent. Afri. R.	Protestant	5.42	2.37	3.05	9.30
Estonia	Protestant	2.00	2.37	−0.37	0.14
Germany	Protestant	1.47	2.37	−0.90	0.81
Latvia	Protestant	2.00	2.37	−0.37	0.14
Norway	Protestant	2.00	2.37	−0.37	0.14
Sweden	Protestant	2.10	2.37	−0.27	0.07
United States	Protestant	2.06	2.37	−0.31	0.10
	Mean	2.37		SSW	10.91

The sum of squares within groups is the sum of the SSW across the four groups or:

$$\begin{aligned} \text{SSW} &= 14.74 + 19.66 + 15.58 + 10.91 \\ &= 60.89 \end{aligned}$$

Calculating the SSB is now very easy.

The sum of squares between groups can be calculated by taking the difference between each group's mean and the grand mean, squaring it, multiplying by the number of cases in the group, and then summing across the groups.

An easier way is to recognize that:

$$\text{SST} = \text{SSB} + \text{SSW}$$

or:

$$\text{SSB} = \text{SST} - \text{SSW}$$

(continued)

Example

Here:

$$\begin{aligned} SSB &= 116.88 - 60.89 \\ &= 55.99 \end{aligned}$$

To assess how much of the total variation can be explained by group differences, we calculate eta-squared.

Eta-squared is the ratio of the sum of squares between groups to the total sum of squares. It represents what portion of the total variation among cases (SST) is attributable to differences among the groups (SSB)—that is, what part of the total variation among cases is caused by or due to or explained by differences between groups.

In our example,

$$\begin{aligned} \text{Eta-squared} &= 55.99/116.88 \\ &= 0.479 \end{aligned}$$

That is, just less than half of the total variation in fertility rates among all the countries may be predicted by differences among nations grouped by predominant religion.

A word of caution is in order. This example offers an overly simplistic explanation of why fertility rates differ, on average, across societies, but nonetheless holds educational value. While religious beliefs and religious institutions do appear to have something to do with fertility differences, the complete story is much, much more complicated than this simple example suggests.

THE F-TEST

When we tested the difference between a single sample mean and some criterion value, we calculated a Z-distributed test statistic. To determine the *p*-level of the test statistic, we needed to take into account the size of the sample we were using and the fact that we had used the sample to calculate one mean.

When we tested the differences between two samples' means, we chose between a test statistic that was Z-distributed or one that was t-distributed. To determine the *p*-level of the test statistic, we needed to take into account the sizes of the two samples and the fact that we had calculated two means in order to do the test.

The F-test is another test statistic, like a Z-statistic or a t-statistic. It is a bit more complicated, though. In addition to taking into account the sample sizes, we need to take into account how many groups are being compared. The interpretation of the F-test is pretty simple. The calculation is a bit complicated.

Calculating the F-Statistic

There are various different (and equally valid) formulas for the F-test that you may find in different texts. We are going to start at the end and work our way backward. So, here's one formula to consider.

$$F_{dfb,\, dfw} = \frac{\text{MSB}}{\text{MSW}} \tag{11.8}$$

This says that the value of the F-test statistic, which needs to be interpreted paying attention to *dfb* and *dfw*, is equal to a ratio between MSB and MSW. So far, that means absolutely nothing to you.

The quantity in the top is the mean squares between groups (MSB). The MSB is a measure of the amount of variation that is due to differences between groups, corrected for the number of groups being compared.

The important thing is this: The numerator of the F-ratio is based on the sum of squares between groups, and gets bigger as the variation between groups gets bigger.

The quantity in the bottom is the mean squares within groups (MSW). The MSW is a measure of the amount of variation that is due to individual error, adjusted for the number of cases.

The important thing is this: The denominator of the F-ratio is based on the sum of squares within groups. So, as the error or residual variation becomes larger, the F-ratio becomes smaller.

Thus, the ***F-ratio*** is a ratio of the variance explained by group differences to the variance not explained by group differences. As the F-ratio becomes larger, the differences between groups are more important and the error or residual differences are less important. So, as the F-ratio gets bigger, we are more likely to believe that there really are group differences in the population.

Mean Squares

Even if there really were no group differences in the population, we might observe some in our samples just due to sampling variation. In order to assess this probability, we need to take into account how many groups we are comparing and how many cases there are.

The F-ratio is calculated by first calculating mean squares, as in Formula 11.9.

$$\text{MSB} = \frac{\text{SSB}}{dfb} \tag{11.9}$$

The ***mean squares*** between groups (the top of the F-ratio formula) is just the sum of squares between groups, divided by the degrees of freedom between groups (*dfb*). More on *dfb* in a minute. Note that because the MSB is based on the sum of squares between groups, as the variation between the groups gets larger (SSB), the mean squares between groups gets larger.

$$\text{MSW} = \frac{\text{SSW}}{dfw} \tag{11.10}$$

The mean squares within groups (MSW) (see Formula 11.10) is based on the sum of squares within groups, and gets larger as the error or residual gets larger. It too is corrected by degrees of freedom (i.e., degrees of freedom within groups or *dfw*).

Degrees of Freedom

The chance that we may observe a difference between groups simply as a result of sampling variability increases with the number of groups compared. If we examine 100 differences between groups, there is the possibility that at least some will be big in the sample (but not in the population). So, in calculating the F-ratio numerator, we need to take into account the number of groups. This is done by dividing the SSB by the number of groups, less 1 (Formula 11.11).

$$dfb = K - 1 \tag{11.11}$$

The amount of variation within groups (SSW) depends on how many cases there are. So, in calculating the F-ratio, we correct the SSW by dividing it by the number of cases, less the number of groups (Formula 11.12).

$$dfw = N - K \tag{11.12}$$

Making a Decision

Finally, we are ready to look at our F-test statistic and reach a decision about whether we should accept or reject the null hypothesis of no difference between population group means.

If you are using statistical software, this is easy. The software will print the *p*-level associated with the F-test.

CHECK QUIZ 11.3

1. ANOVA is a one-tailed test, and we are concerned only with those outcomes in which there is more variance
   a. within categories than between categories.
   b. between categories than within categories.
   c. within populations than within samples.
   d. within samples than within populations.
2. The sampling distribution for the ANOVA test is
   a. the Z distribution.
   b. the t-distribution.
   c. the F-distribution.
   d. none of the above.
3. In the ANOVA test, degrees of freedom within (*dfw*) are equal to ________, and degrees of freedom between are equal to $(k - 1)$.
   a. $(N - k)$
   b. $(k + 1)$
   c. $(N + k)$
   d. $(k - N)$
4. One limitation of the ANOVA test is that it is limited to
   a. only two categories.
   b. only two variables.
   c. only small samples.
   d. interval/ratio variables.

If you have done the calculation of the F-test value by hand, you will need to consult a table of critical values for the F-test. This critical value (the value which, if F is larger, leads to rejection of the null hypothesis) depends on the confidence level we selected in advance. It also depends on the *dfb* and *dfw*. Remember our original formula for F (Formula 11.8)?

$$F_{dfb,dfw} = \frac{\text{MSB}}{\text{MSW}} \tag{11.8}$$

This says that, when we seek to determine the critical value of F, we need to take into account the degrees of freedom between and the degrees of freedom within. Most statistical tables for critical values of F have columns that correspond to *dfb* and rows that correspond to *dfw*.

You've now reached the point where you have a *p*-value for your F-test. Now what?

Remember what the *p*-value means. The *p*-value is the chance that we are taking of being wrong if we reject the null hypothesis. Less correctly, but more usefully, you can think of the *p*-value as the probability the null hypothesis is really true in the population.

So, if p is less than our desired error tolerance, say 0.05, we conclude that we are sufficiently confident to reject the null hypothesis.

The null hypothesis is: All groups have the same mean in the population. We are rejecting this idea. The alternative is that the groups do not all have the same mean.

If we reach the conclusion that the groups may all have the same mean (that is, $p > 0.05$, usually), we're done. The theory that led us to the hypothesis that the groups would be different is not supported, and we need to think again.

If we reach the conclusion that there are group differences, the next step is to find out which ones, and to describe them. We'll show you how in the next section.

For now, pause for a few minutes to take the check quiz and make sure that you understand the F-test.

Example

THE F-TEST FOR ONE-WAY ANALYSIS OF VARIANCE

A researcher has selected samples from countries where the predominant religion is either Buddhist, Muslim, Catholic Christian, or Protestant Christian (each religion is represented by eight countries; i.e., total sample size is 32). For each nation, the median number of children ever born to women has been measured.

Our researcher believes, on the basis of past research and theory, that the predominant religion of a country influences fertility behavior. This leads to the H_a: The mean fertility of nations with different predominant religions differs. The null hypothesis is that there are no differences in the mean fertility rates of the populations of countries with the four different predominant religions.

An F-test is to be constructed to decide whether to accept or reject the null hypothesis at alpha = 0.05. The sums of squares have been computed elsewhere (see the previous example in this chapter).

We begin by setting up our analysis of variance summary table and entering the sums of squares:

Effect	Sum of Squares	Degrees of Freedom	Mean Squares
Between groups (religion)	55.99		
Within groups (error)	60.89		
Total	116.88		

Next, we need to add the degrees of freedom. For the between-groups effect (religion), the degrees of freedom is the number of groups being compared, less 1 (i.e., $k - 1$). Here, with four religious groups, the *df* is 3. The degrees of freedom for the within-groups sums of squares is the number of cases, less the number of groups ($N - k$). Here, the sample size is 32, and the number of groups is 4, so the degrees of freedom within groups is 28. The degrees of freedom for the total sums of squares is equal to the sample size, less 1 ($N - 1$). Here, that is $32 - 1 = 31$. We don't really need this quantity for calculating the F-test.

Effect	Sum of Squares	Degrees of Freedom	Mean Squares
Between groups (religion)	55.99	3	
Within groups (error)	60.89	28	
Total	116.88	31	

The F-test statistic is based on mean squares. Mean squares are calculated as the sum of squares for each effect, divided by its associated degrees of freedom (e.g., 55.99/3). The mean squares for the total sum of squares is not calculated, because it's not needed for the test statistic.

Effect	Sum of Squares	Degrees of Freedom	Mean Squares
Between groups (religion)	55.99	3	18.66
Within groups (error)	60.89	28	2.17
Total	116.88	31	

The F-test is defined as the mean squares between groups divided by the mean squares within groups:

$$F_{(dfb,dfw)} = MSB/MSW$$
$$F_{(3,28)} = 18.66/2.17$$
$$F_{(3,28)} = 8.6$$

Evaluating the F-test:

To determine the significance of the result, we must consult a table of critical values of the F-distribution (tables are in the appendix), based on the degrees of freedom for the between groups and within groups effects. Examining our table of critical values for $p = 0.05$, with 3 and 30 degrees of freedom (our particular table doesn't show exactly 28 *df*), we find the critical value of 2.92.

Since our test statistic exceeds the critical value ($8.6 > 2.92$), we may reject the null hypothesis of no group differences with 95 percent confidence. The alternative, which we accept, is that the mean fertility of at least one group of nations differs from at least one other.

COMPARING MEANS

If the results of our F-test have failed to convince us that there are differences between group means in the population, there is no need to proceed further. We need to go back and think about our theory.

If the results of the F-test suggest that there are differences between group means in the population, the next question is: which groups are different from which other ones?

This would seem to be an easy question to answer. Why not just calculate the mean of each group, and look at the list of groups and their means?

The problem with this is that each mean is a sample mean, and we need to be sure that the difference between any two groups that appears to exist in the sample is really true in the population, before we take seriously the difference between the sample means.

So, why not use a two-sample t-test to assess whether each pair of means is different? The problem is that the tests are not independent. Instead, we need to use a special procedure called the "protected" t-test to compare the multiple groups.

Let's work through an example of a complete analysis to put the discussion of comparing means in context.

Using data from subsamples of the General Social Surveys of 1978 through 1998, let's see whether "race" groups differ in their mean levels of education. Here is a plot of the sample means (prepared with SPSS "compare means" one-way ANOVA).

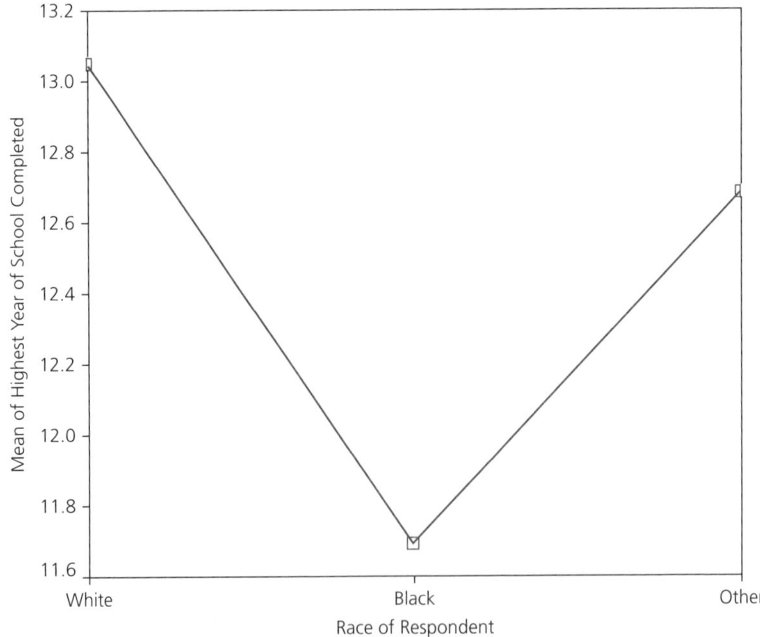

The means of the three groups in the samples appear to be somewhat different, with "white" at just over 13 years, "black" about 11.7 years, and "other" at about 12.7 years.

We need to be confident, though, that there are differences in population means, so let's perform an F-test. Before we do, let's look at the results of the ***Levene test for homogeneity of variances.***

Test of Homogeneity of Variances

Highest Year of School Completed			
Levene Statistic	df_1	df_2	**Sig.**
1.277	2	1,497	0.279

The Levene test has the null hypothesis that the groups *have* equal variances. So, we want to fail to reject this null hypothesis. Our *p*-level is 0.279, so we cannot reject the null hypothesis of equal population variances. Good. Now, let's do the F-test.

ANOVA

Highest Year of School Completed					
	Sum of Squares	*df*	**Mean Square**	**F**	**Sig.**
Between groups	283.443	2	141.722	7.659	0.000
Within groups	27,700.474	1,497	18.504		
Total	27,983.917	1,499			

The F-test has a value of 7.659 with 2 and 1,497 degrees of freedom. We are told that the *p*-level is (smaller than) 0.000. We conclude that there is little chance of error in rejecting the null hypothesis of no group mean differences in the population.

So, we believe that at least one pair of groups displays a significant difference. But, which one (or ones)?

Post Hoc Tests

To determine which populations are different from which other ones, we are going to compare all pairs of groups. In our example this is simple to do, because there are only three groups and three comparisons (white/black, white/other, black/other). In other cases there might be 10 groups and 45 comparisons $[K^* (K - 1)/2]$.

We are going to test whether the difference between each pair of means is zero (null hypothesis) or not (alternative hypothesis). But doing this uses the same groups over and over (actually each group is used $k - 1$ times). The ***post hoc tests***, then, are not independent tests, as is assumed by the standard formula for comparing two means.

There are a number of ways of dealing with this problem, and there are a large number of different (but similar) statistical post hoc tests. Most are based on the idea that we should increase the critical value to reject the null hypothesis to take account of the nonindependence of the tests. These tests are called "protected" t-tests, because they protect us against being too confident about the differences between pairs of groups when we are doing many nonindependent comparisons.

The details of all of the variations on protected t-tests are more than we want to discuss here. For most purposes, most tests will give the same basic answer. We will illustrate using one common (and one of the oldest and least sophisticated) tests, called the ***Scheffé test***, after its inventor.

Interpreting the Scheffé Test

Here are the results of the Scheffé test for the example of mean educational differences among "race" groups (as reported by SPSS).

Multiple Comparisons

Dependent Variable: Highest Year of School Completed
Scheffé

(I) Race of Respondent	(J) Race of Respondent	Mean Difference (I – J)	Std. Error	Sig.	95% Confidence Interval Lower Bound	95% Confidence Interval Upper Bound
White	Black	1.35	0.347	0.001	0.50	2.20
	Other	0.36	0.598	0.830	−1.10	1.83
Black	White	−1.35	0.347	0.001	−2.20	−0.50
	Other	−0.99	0.670	0.337	−2.63	0.65
Other	White	−0.36	0.598	0.830	−1.83	1.10
	Black	0.99	0.670	0.337	−0.65	2.63

The table reports the results of six protected t-tests for differences between two means. Three of these are redundant (i.e., there is a test of white – black, and also a test of black – white).

The first row compares "white" and "black." It says that the mean of whites is 1.35 years higher than the mean for blacks. The estimated standard error of this difference is 0.347 years. From the difference and the standard error, a t-statistic is constructed. The significance of this statistic ($p = 0.001$) is computed using corrected critical values. So, we can conclude that the mean for whites is probably higher than that for blacks in the population.

We cannot be confident, though, that the mean for whites and the mean for others are different. The p-level is 0.830. We would be taking an 83 percent chance of being wrong if we rejected the null hypothesis that the means are equal in the population.

CHECK QUIZ 11.4

1. We examine the Levene test for homogeneity of variance between groups prior to checking the F-test because
   a. it's the first thing in the output.
   b. there's very little entertainment in this town.
   c. the second assumption for ANOVA is that we have independent samples.
   d. the third assumption for ANOVA is that the shape and dispersion of the variable are the same across the population groups.
2. The null hypothesis for the Levene test of homogeneity is that
   a. the variance for the variable of interest is the same in the different groups.
   b. the variance for the variable of interest is different in the different groups.
   c. the standard deviation of at least one group will be larger than those of the other groups.
   d. the overall homogeneity will be larger than some arbitrary amount.
3. The text says that "we want to fail to reject this null hypothesis" for the Levene test. When we look at the output, we will fail to reject when
   a. the significance level is smaller than our alpha.
   b. the significance level is larger than our alpha.
   c. there are two or more degrees of freedom.
   d. H_a is supported.
4. If our theory leads us to believe that there is a mean difference between groups, we hope that the output shows that
   a. the significance level is larger than our alpha.
   b. there are two or more degrees of freedom in the sum of squares between groups.
   c. H_a is supported.
   d. the significance level is larger than our alpha.
   e. c and d.
5. We perform the Scheffé test because
   a. we're using interval/ratio data.
   b. we failed to reject the null hypothesis for the Levene test.
   c. it's the first option listed in SPSS.
   d. it adjusts for the fact that the tests of difference are not independent.
6. When we perform the Scheffé test, we'll know that significant differences exist between the groups if
   a. the value of the significance level for the group comparison is smaller than our alpha.
   b. there are two or more degrees of freedom in the equation.
   c. the value of the significance level is larger than our alpha.
   d. b and c.

The third possible comparison is between "black" and "other." We see from the results ($p = 0.337$) that we cannot be 95 percent sure that these groups are different.

So, we are left with a somewhat complicated conclusion: We're pretty sure that whites are higher than blacks, but we're not sure that whites are higher than others. And we're not sure that others are different from blacks. If you think about this, the conclusions do not seem entirely logically consistent—but they are right. Because we cannot be sure about the means due to sampling variability, only parts of the pattern of how these groups differ is certain.

Post hoc comparisons of all pairs of means, using protected two-group t-tests, are the most common tool for describing group differences—after the F-test has convinced us that there are at least some such differences.

Before proceeding to the chapter summary, take a couple of minutes to review by trying the check quiz.

SUMMARY

In this chapter we've looked at a test (the F-test) to assess whether there are differences among the mean scores on an outcome variable across multiple groups. The F-test is part of a bigger set of related procedures called the analysis of variance (ANOVA). We have only touched the surface of how ANOVA can be used. In fields where data are usually derived from experiments, you will want to know a lot more than we have discussed here. However, now you have the basic ideas.

There are many cases in experimental and quasi-experimental research where theory leads us to predict that the average scores of groups of subjects will differ. These might be control groups and treatment groups in experiments; they might be neighborhoods, organizations, or cities in quasi-experimental analysis; they might be naturally occurring categorical differences among groups—gender, ethnicity, and so on.

Theory usually leads us to the prediction that group means will differ (sometimes, theory may lead to stronger predictions about particular differences—contrasts can be used in ANOVA for more powerful analyses if the theory is stronger). The null hypothesis, then, is that the means of all the groups are the same in the populations from which we drew our samples.

We test the null hypothesis of no differences in group means using the F-test. The F-test is based on an analysis of the variance. The analysis of the variance in the outcome variable divides the total variation among cases (sum of squares total) into variation between the groups (sum of squares between groups—SSB) and variation within each group (sum of squares within groups—SSW).

It is the variation between groups that is explained by group differences; variation within groups is "residual." From this, the eta-squared statistic can be defined that describes the amount of variation that is due to group differences as a proportion of all of the variation.

Eta-squared tells us whether the differences between groups make a lot of difference in understanding the differences among all the individual cases.

The F-test statistic compares the variance explained (SSB) to the variance not explained (SSW). Each of these sums of squares is first converted into a "mean square" by dividing it by a different "degrees of freedom" value. The degrees of freedom are derived from the number of cases and the number of groups being compared.

The significance level (*p*) of the F-test is determined by the value of the F-statistic relative to critical values for the two degrees of freedom used in constructing the test statistic. Generally, the larger the F-test statistic, the more likely it is that we may reject the null hypothesis that the means are the same.

If we fail to reject the null hypothesis, we conclude that we cannot be confident that population means are really different. This is the end of the story, and we need to rethink our theory.

If we do reject the null hypothesis, we must then explore which means are different from which others. This is done by conducting "protected" two-group t-tests (like the Scheffé). Protected t-tests are used to guard against overconfidence that may arise when we are using the same samples to perform multiple and nonindependent tests.

This concludes our discussion of hypothesis testing. There is much more that you could study on this topic, but you now have a set of tools that will solve many of the problems you are likely to encounter.

In the last several chapters, on two-group and multiple-group tests, we have actually been doing bivariate (two-variable) statistics. We have been examining how an outcome variable differs (either its mean or its proportions) across two or more groups. You can have what group a person falls in as a variable, too. So, we are actually looking at how an independent variable (what group a person is in) affects a dependent variable (the outcome mean or proportion).

Tests for differences between two or more groups are actually one example of a bigger issue—the study of statistical association or independence of the scores on any two variables. For the remainder of the book, we are going to focus on this big idea of association.

KEY TERMS

analysis of variance (ANOVA)

degrees of freedom within and between

eta-squared

F-ratio

Levene test for homogeneity of variances

mean squares

one-way

post hoc test

Scheffé test

sum of squares between groups

sum of squares total

sum of squares within groups

CHECK QUIZ ANSWERS

Quiz 11.1 Answers: 1. (d); 2. (b); 3. (a); 4. (c); 5. (c); 6. (a)
Quiz 11.2 Answers: 1. (a); 2. (b); 3. (b); 4. (c); 5. (c); 6. (a)
Quiz 11.3 Answers: 1. (b); 2. (c); 3. (a); 4. (d)
Quiz 11.4 Answers: 1. (d); 2. (a); 3. (b); 4. (c); 5. (d); 6. (a)

EXERCISES

1. Are there regional differences in the United States in how satisfied people are with their lives? Here are data on 10 cases from each of four regions in the United States. Let's assign a score of 3 for people who report that they are "very happy" and a score of 2 for people who report that they are "pretty happy."

   Perform a one-way ANOVA to test whether there are significant differences among the regions in the average happiness of respondents.

   a. Present the null and alternative hypotheses.
   b. Calculate (by hand or with a calculator, spreadsheet, or statistical software) the sums of squares within groups, between groups, and total.
   c. Show the degrees of freedom for the within groups and between groups sums of squares.
   d. Show the mean squares between groups and within groups.
   e. Show the value of F. Determine whether this value is significant at $p = 0.05$ or less.
   f. Calculate eta-squared.
   g. Provide a brief interpretive conclusion.

Case Summaries

ID	General Happiness	Region of Interview
1	Very happy	South Atlantic
3	Pretty happy	South Atlantic
7	Pretty happy	South Atlantic
8	Very happy	South Atlantic
10	Very happy	South Atlantic
12	Very happy	South Atlantic
14	Very happy	South Atlantic
19	Very happy	South Atlantic
39	Pretty happy	South Atlantic
48	Pretty happy	South Atlantic
4	Pretty happy	Middle Atlantic
6	Very happy	Middle Atlantic

ID	General Happiness	Region of Interview
16	Very happy	Middle Atlantic
26	Very happy	Middle Atlantic
36	Pretty happy	Middle Atlantic
47	Pretty happy	Middle Atlantic
49	Very happy	Middle Atlantic
44	Pretty happy	Middle Atlantic
60	Pretty happy	Middle Atlantic
61	Very happy	Middle Atlantic
9	Pretty happy	Pacific
11	Pretty happy	Pacific
13	Very happy	Pacific
21	Pretty happy	Pacific
23	Very happy	Pacific
25	Very happy	Pacific
29	Pretty happy	Pacific
37	Pretty happy	Pacific
41	Pretty happy	Pacific
46	Very happy	Pacific
15	Very happy	E. North Central
5	Pretty happy	E. North Central
20	Pretty happy	E. North Central
22	Pretty happy	E. North Central
27	Very happy	E. North Central
33	Very happy	E. North Central
35	Pretty happy	E. North Central
45	Pretty happy	E. North Central
55	Pretty happy	E. North Central
57	Pretty happy	E. North Central

2. Do racial groups in the United States have differing political ideologies? A researcher using the General Social Survey asked respondents to rank themselves on an ordinal scale from 1 = extremely liberal to 7 = extremely conservative (we will treat this variable as if it were an interval-level variable). Respondents were also asked to identify themselves as "white," "black," or "other." Samples of 10 people of each racial group were randomly selected for analysis. Here are the data:

Scores of 30 Cases on the Political Conservativism Scale

White	Black	Other
4	4	6
4	4	4

(continued)

White	Black	Other
6	6	4
5	3	4
5	4	6
2	3	4
8	1	4
4	4	8
5	4	4
3	8	6

Perform a one-way ANOVA to test about whether there are significant differences among the race groups in their average political conservativism.

a. Present the null and alternative hypotheses.
b. Calculate (by hand or with a calculator, spreadsheet, or statistical software) the sums of squares within groups, between groups, and total.
c. Show the degrees of freedom for the within groups and between groups sums of squares.
d. Show the mean squares between groups and within groups.
e. Show the value of F. Determine whether this value is significant at $p = 0.05$ or less.
f. Calculate eta-squared.
g. Provide a brief interpretive conclusion.

3. Americans spend a lot of time watching TV. Do people with more education spend significantly more (or less) this way? Using General Social Survey data, we have compared self-reports of television watching between groups with different levels of educational credentials. Here are results from SPSS one-way ANOVA:

ANOVA

Hours per Day Watching TV					
	Sum of Squares	***df***	**Mean Square**	**F**	**Sig.**
Between groups	329.939	4	82.485	17.459	0.000
Within groups	6,278.796	1,329	4.724		
Total	6,608.735	1,333			

Multiple Comparisons

Dependent Variable: Hours per Day Watching TV Scheffé						
					95% Confidence Interval	
(I) R's Highest Degree	(J) R's Highest Degree	Mean Difference (I − J)	Std. Error	Sig.	Lower Bound	Upper Bound
LT high school	High school	0.50	0.150	0.025	0.04	0.96
	Junior college	0.89	0.301	0.069	−0.04	1.82
	Bachelor's	1.36	0.204	0.000	0.73	2.00
	Graduate	1.67	0.260	0.000	0.87	2.47
High school	LT high school	−0.50	0.150	0.025	−0.96	−0.04
	Junior college	0.39	0.286	0.765	−0.49	1.27
	Bachelor's	0.86	0.181	0.000	0.30	1.42
	Graduate	1.17	0.242	0.000	0.42	1.91
Junior college	LT high school	−0.89	0.301	0.069	−1.82	0.04
	High school	−0.39	0.286	0.765	−1.27	0.49
	Bachelor's	0.47	0.318	0.694	−0.51	1.46
	Graduate	0.78	0.356	0.313	−0.32	1.88
Bachelor's	LT high school	−1.36	0.204	0.000	−2.00	−0.73
	High school	−0.86	0.181	0.000	−1.42	−0.30
	Junior college	−0.47	0.318	0.694	−1.46	0.51
	Graduate	0.30	0.279	0.882	−0.56	1.16
Graduate	LT high school	−1.67	0.260	0.000	−2.47	−0.87
	High school	−1.17	0.242	0.000	−1.91	−0.42
	Junior college	−0.78	0.356	0.313	−1.88	0.32
	Bachelor's	−0.30	0.279	0.882	−1.16	0.56

The mean difference is significant at the 0.05 level. LT—less than.

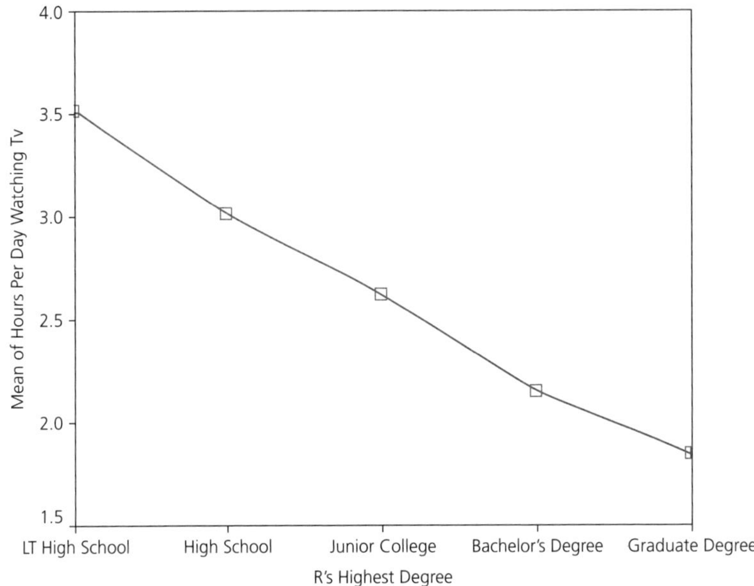

a. What is the null hypothesis being tested here?
b. What is the alternative hypothesis?
c. Should we accept or reject the null hypothesis? What is your evidence?
d. If we believe that some educational groups are significantly different from others, which groups differ from which other groups?
e. How would you summarize the results?

4. One measure of the level of gender inequality in a society is the ratio of the amount of formal education that women receive relative to that of men. A researcher has collected data on a sample of nations within each of four large world regions, and has used SPSS one-way ANOVA to examine differences in gender equality. Here are the researcher's results:

Descriptives

Female Years of School as a Percentage of Males

	N	Mean	Std. Deviation	Std. Error	95% Confidence Interval for Mean Lower Bound	95% Confidence Interval for Mean Upper Bound	Minimum	Maximum
Asia	42	57.5690	24.80143	3.82694	49.8404	65.2977	14.30	102.00
Africa	44	46.3364	26.76985	4.03571	38.1976	54.4751	20.00	148.10
Europe	34	91.9029	12.01119	2.05990	87.7120	96.0938	50.00	103.90

Female Years of School as a Percentage of Males								
					95% Confidence Interval for Mean			
	N	Mean	Std. Deviation	Std. Error	Lower Bound	Upper Bound	Minimum	Maximum
Americas	27	93.6963	11.57622	2.22784	89.1169	98.2757	60.00	110.80
Total	147	68.7837	29.45426	2.42935	63.9824	73.5849	14.30	148.10

ANOVA

Female Years of School as a Percentage of Males					
	Sum of Squares	*df*	Mean Square	F	Sig.
Between groups	62,383.310	3	20,794.437	46.261	0.000
Within groups	64,279.511	143	449.507		
Total	126,662.821	146			

Multiple Comparisons

Dependent Variable: Female Years of School as a Percentage of Males Scheffé						
					95% Confidence Interval	
(I) Recoded Region	(J) Recoded Region	Mean Difference (I − J)	Std. Error	Sig.	Lower Bound	Upper Bound
Asia	Africa	11.2327	4.57369	0.115	−1.7066	24.1720
	Europe	−34.3339	4.89115	0.000	−48.1713	−20.4965
	Americas	−36.1272	5.22981	0.000	−50.9228	−21.3317
Africa	Asia	−11.2327	4.57369	0.115	−24.1720	1.7066
	Europe	−45.5666	4.84116	0.000	−59.2626	−31.8706
	Americas	−47.3599	5.18310	0.000	−62.0233	−32.6966
Europe	Asia	34.3339	4.89115	0.000	20.4965	48.1713
	Africa	45.5666	4.84116	0.000	31.8706	59.2626
	Americas	−1.7934	5.46527	0.991	−17.2550	13.6683
Americas	Asia	36.1272	5.22981	0.000	21.3317	50.9228
	Africa	47.3599	5.18310	0.000	32.6966	62.0233
	Europe	1.7934	5.46527	0.991	−13.6683	17.2550

The mean difference is significant at the 0.05 level.

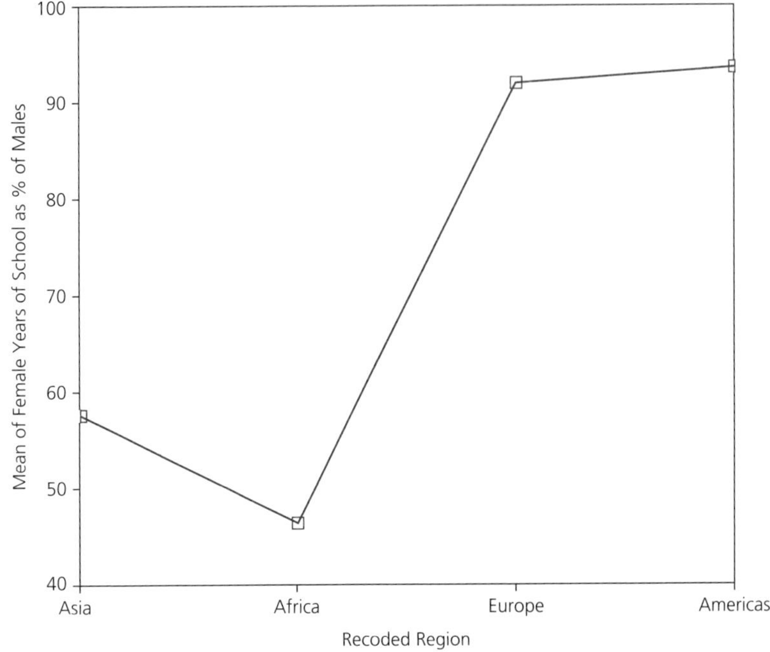

a. What is the null hypothesis being tested here?
b. What is the alternative hypothesis?
c. Should we accept or reject the null hypothesis? What is your evidence?
d. If we believe that some educational groups are significantly different from others, which groups differ from which other groups?
e. How would you summarize the results?

PART III

Association and Prediction

Chapter 12

Association with Categorical Variables

LEARNING OBJECTIVES

When you have finished this chapter, you will be able to:

- Understand the concepts of statistical association and independence.
- Master the process of analyzing statistical association: visualizing, significance testing, assessing strength, and form.
- Analyze association between two nominal variables using chi-squared type (phi, Cramér's V) and proportional reduction in error type (lambda, Goodman-Kruskal tau) measures of association.
- Analyze association between two grouped ordinal variables with gamma, Somers' d, tau-b, and tau-c.
- Analyze association between two full rank-order variables using Spearman's rho.

THE CONCEPT OF STATISTICAL ASSOCIATION

We've been examining how statistical procedures can be used to compare the central tendency of a variable between two or among several groups. These kinds of comparisons are very important for testing theories. Comparing groups is actually one application of the more general idea of statistical association (and the opposite, statistical independence).

The concept of statistical association is fundamental to all advanced statistics, so getting a firm intuitive grasp of this idea is important. We'll focus first on defining and illustrating statistical association, and on describing the questions that the analysis of association seeks to answer. Then, we'll apply these ideas to the association between two nominal variables, the association between two grouped ordinal variables, and two full rank-order variables.

Research on social stratification in the United States has found, over and over, that persons who have completed more formal schooling are likely to earn higher incomes than those with less schooling. Of course, not every person with many years of schooling earns more than every person with fewer years of schooling; but there is a tendency or a pattern in how scores on the two variables "co-occur" or "covary" or "co-relate."

This is an example of a statistical association between two variables: the levels of education and income. At the most basic level, statistical association means that there are patterns in the social world—that the social world is not random. The purpose of sociological theory, of course, is to provide explanations of why there are patterns, so the idea of association between variables is very closely related to theory. Theories imply associations, and we validate or reject theories by studying the associations they imply between variables.

So, a first intuitive notion of what it means to say that two variables are associated is to say that there is a pattern or nonrandomness in how the scores on one variable go with scores on the other variable.

A more formal definition of ***statistical association (correlation, covariance, relationship, going together)*** is: two variables are statistically associated if the distribution of Y, conditional on X, differs from the distribution of Y, not conditional on X.

Now let me translate that. The distribution of Y, not conditional on X, is just the relative frequencies on the variable Y. The distribution of Y, conditional on X, is the relative frequencies of Y calculated separately for each score on X. So, this is a fancy way of saying: if the scores on one variable (Y) differ depending on the scores on another variable (X), then the two variables are associated.

If two variables are associated, then, if I know what score a person has on one variable (call it X), then I will be able to make a more accurate prediction about that person's score on another variable (call it Y) than if I don't know their score on X. This is another definition of association. If knowing the score on one variable makes my predictions about the scores on the other variable more accurate than those guesses would be if I didn't know the score on the first variable, then the two variables are statistically associated.

So, there are three definitions of association: "certain scores on *X* tend to go with certain scores on *Y*," "the conditional distributions of *Y*, knowing *X*, are different from the overall distribution of *Y*," and "knowing *X* reduces error or uncertainty in predicting *Y*."

The opposite of association is ***statistical independence***: "there is no tendency for certain scores on *X* to go with particular scores on *Y*," "the conditional distributions of *Y*, knowing *X*, do not differ from the overall distribution of *X*," and "knowing *X* does not reduce error or uncertainty in predicting *Y*."

Take a look at the cross-tabulation shown as Table 12.1, with data from the General Social Survey (1993).

Are the variables "race of respondent" and "region of residence" statistically associated?

If we compare the conditional (percentage) distributions of region of residence across the categories of race, we see that there are large differences of the groups from one another, and from the total. White persons are relatively more likely to live in the Midwest, and black persons are likely to live in the South, for example. Where there are differences in the conditional distributions, there is evidence of statistical association.

If we were trying to predict where a person lives, would we be able to make more accurate predictions if we knew the person's race? Yes, we would make fewer errors in prediction, because, for example, we would want to predict more frequently that a person lives in the Midwest if we knew they were white than if we knew they were nonwhite.

TABLE 12.1 Cross-Tabulation of Region of Residence by Race

Region * Race of Respondent Cross-Tabulation

			Race of Respondent			
			White	**Black**	**Other**	**Total**
Region of Residence	**Northeast**	Count	105	20	11	136
		Percent within race of respondent	16.7%	25.3%	22.0%	18.0%
	Midwest	Count	206	10	5	221
		Percent within race of respondent	32.8%	12.7%	10.0%	29.2%
	South	Count	191	37	20	248
		Percent within race of respondent	30.4%	46.8%	40.0%	32.8%
	West	Count	126	12	14	152
		Percent within race of respondent	20.1%	15.2%	28.0%	20.1%
Total		Count	628	79	50	757
		Percent within race of respondent	100.0%	100.0%	100.0%	100.0%

We could not make a perfect prediction of a person's region of residence by knowing the person's race, though, so the association is not a perfect association. In real-world data, we rarely observe either complete absence of association or perfect association.

Okay, we're ready to get started on learning how to assess statistical association between variables. First, though, take a moment to check your knowledge.

CHECK QUIZ 12.1

	Nonvideo	Video	Total
Girls	34	102	136
Boys	68	204	272
Total	102	306	408

1. We interviewed 136 girls and 272 boys about whether they like to play video games; what can you say about the association of gender and game preference?
   a. A higher proportion of boys like to play video games.
   b. A smaller proportion of girls like to play video games.
   c. There seems to be a strong association between gender and game preference.
   d. There seems to be no association between gender and game preference.

	In Favor	Opposed	Total
Bikers	60	45	105
Skaters	40	70	110
Total	100	115	215

2. We interviewed 105 bikers and 110 skaters about a public safety measure; what can you say about the association of vehicle choice and support for the policy?
   a. There is a lot more variance in the skaters' responses.
   b. The table has 1 degree of freedom.
   c. There seems to be an association between the two variables.
   d. There doesn't seem to be any association between the two variables.
3. If one can predict the value of one variable with great precision based on the value of another variable, we say they have
   a. statistical independence.
   b. statistical precision.
   c. a strong association.
   d. a positive association.

ASSOCIATION WITH NOMINAL VARIABLES

In Chapter 10, we discussed the Pearson independence chi-squared statistic that can be used to test the hypothesis of no differences in proportions between or among two or more groups. Although we didn't say so at the time, when you learned to use this test, you were studying the association between two nominal variables. In the comparison of proportions across several groups, the variable that defines groups can also be thought of as an independent (X) variable; the proportions that are being compared across the groups are really a nominal "outcome" or Y or dependent variable.

In studying association, it is always a good idea to do four things: visualize the association; use a significance test to assess whether an association that we see in a sample is probably true for the whole population from which the sample was taken; measure the strength of association (is the association near "independent" or is it near "perfect"?); and describe the form (which scores on X tend to go with which scores on Y?).

Visualizing Nominal Association

It is a good idea to begin the study of nominal association by visualizing the relationship between X and Y. This is something you already know how to do. One approach is to create a proper cross-tabulation and compare the groups numerically. Another approach is to use a pie chart or bar chart to graphically display association.

A cross-tabulation (aka cross-tab, cross-break, table, etc.) displays the univariate and bivariate frequencies of two categorical variables. When we are using cross-tabulations to visualize the association between two nominal variables, one rule is particularly important. If one of the variables we are studying is considered to be the "grouping," test, X, or independent variable, that variable should define the columns of the table. The columns of the table are the x-axis, and this corresponds to treating X as the independent variable. When the table is properly laid out, the relative frequencies (as either percentages of proportions) should be calculated within each column—that is, summing up to 100 percent within each category of the independent variable.

If a table has been laid out properly, it is easy to see whether the two variables are associated. If the percentages (down the columns) are different across the columns, there is an association (in the sample, at least). Looking at Table 12.1, this is clearly the case—the relative frequencies of where respondents to the survey reside are quite different, depending on race. This means that, if we know race, we will be able to make more accurate predictions about residence than if we don't know race. We'll want to test whether the sample result is probably really true in the whole population.

We can also get a sense of the ***strength of the relationship*** by looking at the percentages. If the percentages are very different, then the independent variable makes a lot of difference and there is a strong relationship. Obviously, though, we need a more precise way of talking about "making a big difference." How big is "big"?

And we can describe the ***form of the relationship*** by simply looking at percentages, as well. Here (again looking at Table 12.1) we would say something like: "White folks are more likely to live in the Midwest than black folks are." Again, there is obviously a need to be a bit more precise about this, as well.

In studying association, social scientists almost always rely on numerical statistics and indexes of the existence, strength, and form of relationships. The indexes are precise, efficient, and easy to understand. But, for displaying or reporting associations, graphical displays can also be very helpful. With nominal variables, bar charts and pie charts are most often used to display frequencies (see Chapter 2 if you'd like to review this discussion). Look first at a comparative bar chart in Figure 12.1.

The bar chart is being used here to display the frequencies of the scores on the dependent variable (region of residence), separately for each score on the independent variable (race of

FIGURE 12.1 Comparative Bar Chart of the Association between Race and Region of Residence

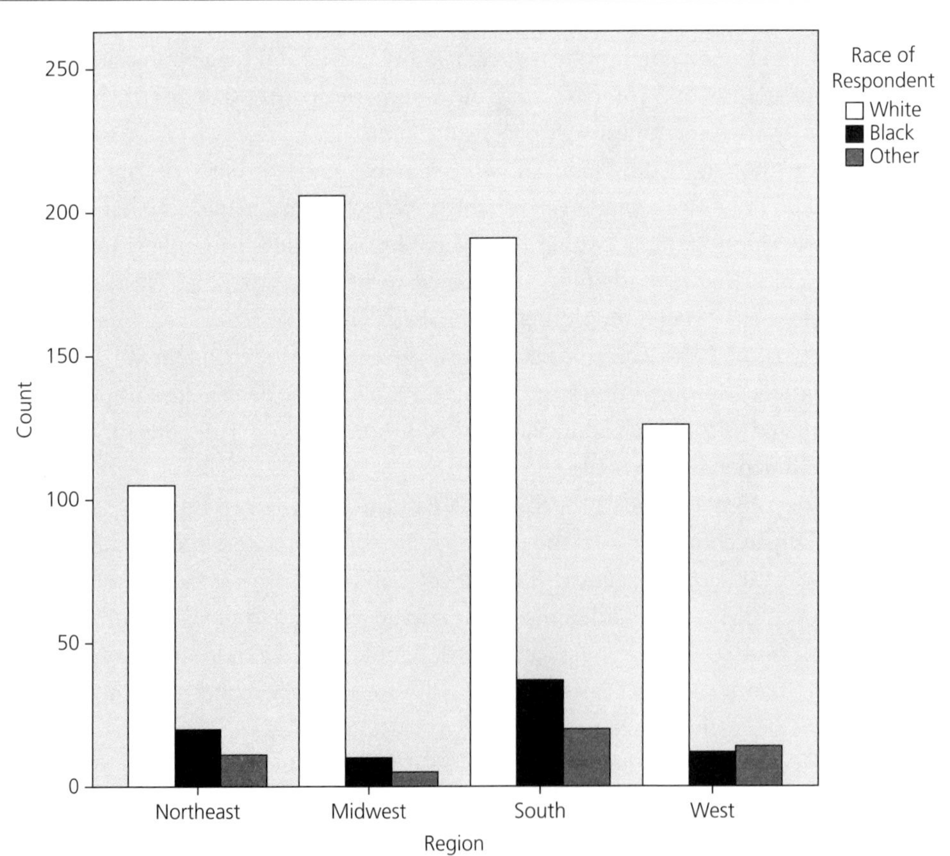

respondent). The most obvious thing in this graph is that there are many more "white" people in the sample than "black" or "other." But, if you focus on the relative heights of the bars within each group, you can see that the relative numbers of Southerners are greater among blacks than among whites. The fact that there are different-sized samples of whites, blacks, and others does not tell us about association. The fact that the relative sizes of the bars are different for the different groups does tell us that there is association in the sample.

The question of association really focuses on relative frequencies, not frequencies, so comparative pie charts are probably more useful graphical displays. Figure 12.2 shows three pie charts for the same data.

FIGURE 12.2 Comparative Pie Charts of the Association between Region of Residence and Race

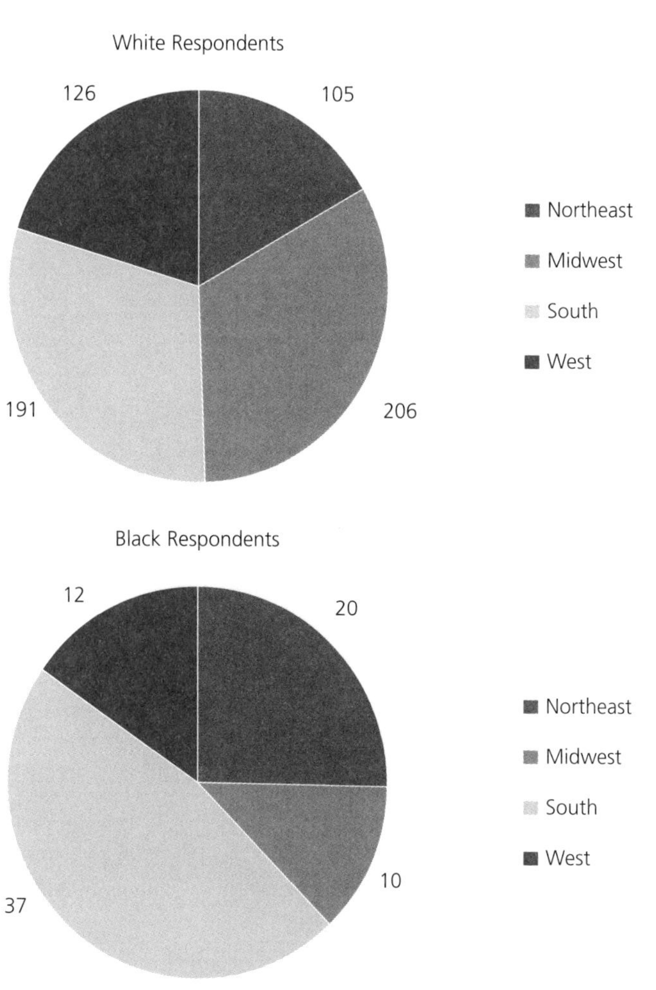

(continued)

FIGURE 12.2 Continued

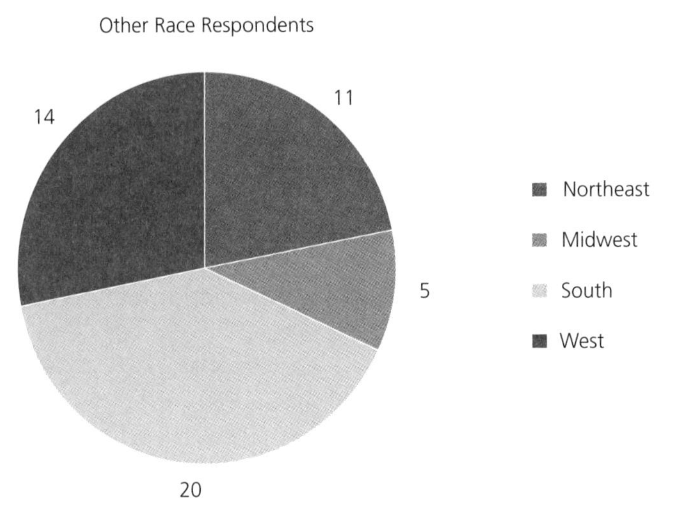

Even the quickest glance at the comparative pie charts should make it obvious that there are differences among whites, blacks, and others, that these difference are fairly large, and that Midwesterners are overrepresented among white respondents (among other differences). We can see whether there is an association (in the sample), we can see how strong the association is, and we can describe its form.

Before you go to the next section, take a minute with the short quiz to make sure you've mastered the main ideas. When you have, you're ready to learn some techniques that use more precise numerical statistics to analyze the existence, strength, and form of association.

Significance Testing for Nominal Association

It doesn't make much sense to worry about the strength of association or form of association between two nominal variables that we can visualize from sample data if we can't be pretty confident that there really is a relationship in the whole population. So, an important part of the analysis of association is to perform inference testing about association in the population.

Many statistics that are used to measure the strength of association between nominal variables have estimates of standard errors and significance tests associated with them (we'll see some examples later). An alternative procedure is to apply the Pearson independence chi-squared test to determine if we can be confident that there is an association between *X* and *Y* in the population.

The null hypothesis tested by the Pearson independence chi-squared and other significance tests for association is: "In the population, scores on *X* and *Y* are independent."

CHECK QUIZ 12.2

1. The traditional way of making a cross-tab is to put the grouping/independent variable in the
   a. rows.
   b. columns.
   c. jaws.
   d. title.
2. When showing percents in a cross-tab, they ought to add up to 100 percent
   a. in each column.
   b. in each row.
   c. in the spring.
   d. across all rows and columns.
3. Association is more about relative frequencies than absolute frequencies; for this reason, when displaying the association between nominal variables, researchers will often choose to use a
   a. bar chart.
   b. pie chart.
   c. histogram.
   d. candygram.
4. When looking at a cross-tab that has been laid out correctly, if the variables are associated, you ought to see
   a. similar percentages across the columns.
   b. different percentages across the columns.
   c. a footnote describing the association.
   d. a mix of similar and different percentages across the rows.

$$H_0: \chi^2_{(r-1)\times(c-1)} = 0$$

The alternative hypothesis is a simple one: "In the population, scores on X and Y are associated."

$$H_A: \chi^2_{(r-1)\times(c-1)} > 0$$

We assume both X and Y are nominal, and that the groups on X have been sampled randomly and independently. We evaluate the hypothesis test with a degrees of freedom value equal to the number of rows less 1 times the number of columns less 1. We select the 95 percent confidence level, or $p < 0.05$, for rejection of the null hypothesis.

Table 12.2 shows the cross-tabulation of the marital statuses of respondents to the General Social Survey (Y) by their race (X). Table 12.3 displays the output from SPSS for performing chi-squared tests.

There are several chi-squared tests. We will be concerned with only the Pearson (independence) chi-squared. The result shows a *p* of less than 0.000. That is, the probability that the null hypothesis of no association is true is considerably less than our criterion risk of 0.05. Thus, we would reach the conclusion that the null hypothesis (no association) should be rejected. This leaves the alternative: that the two variables are associated in the population.

In reporting results of significance tests in scientific literature, we usually use shorthand, because all of our readers have taken courses like the one you are taking. We would usually say something like: "Race and marital status are associated (chi-squared = 61.551 with 8 *df*, and $p < 0.05$)."

The Pearson independence chi-squared test is probably the most widely used tool to assess our confidence in the inference that X and Y are associated with each other in the whole

TABLE 12.2 Association between Marital Status and Race

Marital Status by Race of Respondent, 1998				
	White	**Black**	**Other**	**Total**
Married	727	67	22	816
	57.2%	38.3%	40.7%	54.4%
Widowed	122	22	6	150
	9.6%	12.6%	11.1%	10.0%
Divorced	173	18	8	199
	13.6%	10.3%	14.8%	13.3%
Separated	24	17	4	45
	1.9%	9.7%	7.4%	3.0%
Never married	225	51	14	290
	17.7%	29.1%	25.9%	19.3%
Total	1,271	175	54	1,500
	100.0%	100.0%	100.0%	100.0%

TABLE 12.3 Chi-Squared Tests for the Association of Marital Status and Race

Chi-Squared Tests			
	Value	***df***	**Asymp. Sig. (2-sided)**
Pearson chi-squared	61.551	8	0.000
Likelihood ratio	51.356	8	0.000
Linear-by-linear association	25.150	1	0.000
N of valid cases	1,500		

population that we drew our sample data from. You should recall, however, that when there are many cells with low expected frequencies, the chi-squared test needs to be used cautiously.

Take a moment now to see if you have mastered these ideas about inference testing for statistical association. When you're sure you've got it, you should go on to the next section, on the strength of association.

CHECK QUIZ 12.3

1. The null hypothesis for tests of association is that the variables are independent. This means
   a. that you want to disprove the alternative theory.
   b. that knowing one variable will help you predict the other.
   c. that the two variables are not associated.
   d. that the variables have different means, medians, and modes.
2. When we look at the results of the Pearson independence chi-squared test, if the significance of the test is less than our criterion of risk of type I error, then
   a. we reject the null hypothesis of independence.
   b. we reject the null hypothesis of association.
   c. we fail to reject the null hypothesis of independence.
   d. we fail to reject the null hypothesis of association.

The Strength of Nominal Association

There are many different statistics that have been designed to measure the strength of association between nominal variables. The measures are designed to capture somewhat different aspects of what it means to say that two variables are associated, and each of the various measures has certain strengths and weaknesses. We will discuss only a few of the measures that are most commonly used in applied social science work.

One way to think about all the various measures of the strength of association is to divide them into two groups: those based on chi-squared and those based on the "proportional reduction in error" (PRE) logic.

The older but still used approach to indexing the strength of association between two nominal variables starts with the Pearson independence chi-squared statistic.

In discussing the chi-squared statistic in Chapter 10, we noted that the value of the statistic increased as the differences in the relative frequencies of the groups being compared increased. That is, as association between two nominal variables gets stronger, the chi-squared statistic becomes a larger positive number. Because this is the case, we could use the value of chi-squared itself to measure the strength of association. But there are a couple serious problems with that idea.

The first problem with just using chi-squared itself to measure the strength of association is that it does not have an easy-to-interpret value. We would like a measure of association to take the value of zero when there is no association (and, actually, chi-squared does this). When two variables are perfectly associated, we would like our measure of strength to take a value of 1.0. Chi-squared does not do this.

The second, related problem is that the numerical value of chi-squared depends on the amount of association between two variables, the number of cases, and the number of cells in the table (or degrees of freedom). So, we cannot use the value of chi-squared to compare the strength of association between two samples that have different numbers of cases or different numbers of rows and columns (e.g., if we were comparing the strength of association between *X* and *Y* with the strength of association between *M* and *V*, and the variables had different numbers of categories).

Several measures have been developed that try to adjust the value of chi-squared so that it ranges between zero (no association) and 1.0 (maximum possible association) and so that its value is comparable across tables with different sample sizes.

For 2-by-2 tables, a commonly used measure is the ***phi*** coefficient, as shown in Formula 12.1.

$$\varphi = \sqrt{\chi^2/N} \tag{12.1}$$

That is, take chi-squared, divide it by the sample size, and take the square root of the result.

The phi coefficient ranges between zero (no association) and 1.0 (perfect association) for 2-by-2 tables. For larger tables, though, it should not be used, because its value can exceed 1.0. For larger tables, a different version, Cramér's V, is often calculated.

$$V = \sqrt{\frac{\chi^2}{[(N) \times (r-1, c-1)]}} \tag{12.2}$$

Cramér's V is the same as phi, except that we divide by the product of sample size times the smaller of the number of rows less 1, or columns less 1.

For the relationship between race and marital status that we examined in the previous section, SPSS produced the values for phi and V shown in Table 12.4.

Since the table is actually 3 by 5, we should not use phi (note that its value looks a bit inflated). Cramér's V has a value that is much closer to zero (no association) than to 1.0 (perfect association). Most analysts would probably characterize this as a weak association. However, there are no rules about what range of numerical values should be called "weak."

TABLE 12.4 Chi-Squared-Based Measures of Association for Marital Status by Race

Symmetric Measures			
		Value	**Approx. Sig.**
Nominal by nominal	Phi	0.203	0.000
	Cramér's V	0.143	0.000
N of valid cases		1,500	

Notice, also, that there are significance tests associated with phi and with Cramér's V. The null hypothesis is that the test statistic is zero (i.e., no association). The alternative hypothesis is that the test statistic is greater than zero.

It is important to remember that the values of chi-squared-based measures like phi and V can be interpreted only as "weak," "moderate," or "strong." It is *not* correct to say that an association of, say, 0.40 is twice as strong as an association of 0.20. This can make it difficult to explain the meaning of our results, and is a very good reason to use a different kind of measure based on the proportional reduction in error.

Most would agree that it is sensible for a statistic describing the strength of association to have a value of zero when there was no association. Most would also agree that it is sensible for perfect association to produce a statistic that has a value of 1.0. But, what about the values in between these two extremes?

One approach to measuring the strength of association, called "proportional reduction in error" (PRE), produces measures that describe the strength of relationships in terms of percentages of "reduction in prediction error" or "reduction in uncertainty" or "variance explained or accounted for." PRE approaches are particularly helpful because we can say that a relationship that is assessed at 0.40 is twice as strong as one that is assessed at 0.20. PRE approaches are also desirable because they make it somewhat easier to explain our results to people not trained in statistics. If a PRE measure has the value of 0.50, for example, we can say: "If we know the scores on the independent variable, we can reduce uncertainty in predicting scores on the dependent variable by half."

There are many different measures of the strength of association that use the PRE approach. They all have the same general logic that can be described in Formula 12.3.

$$\text{PRE} = \frac{(E_1\text{: Errors predicting } Y\text{, not knowing } X) - (E_2\text{: Errors predicting } Y\text{, knowing } X)}{(\text{E}_1\text{: Errors predicting } Y\text{, not knowing } X)} \times 100 \tag{12.3}$$

What the formula says is this: Suppose we tried to predict cases' scores on *Y*, not knowing their scores on *X*. We would make errors of prediction. Call this error E_1 or the unconditional error of prediction. Now, suppose that we were to try to predict cases' scores on *Y*, but this time we did know their scores on *X*. Call this error E_2, or the error in predicting *Y*, conditional on knowing *X*.

If *X* and *Y* are not associated, then knowing *X* won't help us; we will make the same number of errors predicting *Y* regardless of whether we know *X*. But, if *X* and *Y* are associated, then we will make fewer errors in predicting *Y* if we know *X*. Call the difference between the error not knowing (E_1) and the error knowing (E_2) the "reduction in error as a result of *X*."

Last, take the amount of reduction in error due to *X* ($E_1 - E_2$), and express it as a percentage of the original amount of error not knowing *X* (E_1). The result is the "percentage reduction in error in predicting *Y*, as a result of *X*." We can talk about his percentage reduction in error as the strength of the relationship, or as the "variation explained or accounted for by *X*."

Two commonly used PRE measures for studying nominal association are lambda and the Goodman and Kruskal tau (there are many others that we won't discuss here). The measures have the same general logic, but are calculated in different specific ways. While you should use statistical software to calculate the measures, it is useful to see where they are coming from. Table 12.5 shows SPSS output of these two statistics for the relationship between marital status and race.

Notice that there are three versions of lambda and two versions of tau. The "marital status dependent" version asks: What is the proportional reduction in error that we obtain in predicting marital status if we know race, compared to predicting not knowing race? The "race of respondent dependent" version asks: What is the proportional reduction in error that we obtain in predicting race when we know marital status, compared to predicting not knowing marital status? The "symmetric" version makes predictions in both directions (and the value of the statistic will fall between the values of the asymmetric versions). Here, we are

TABLE 12.5 PRE Measures of Association between Marital Status and Race

			Value	Asymp. Std. Error	Approx. T	Approx. Sig.
Nominal by nominal	Lambda	Symmetric	0.000	0.000		
		Marital status dependent	0.000	0.000		
		Race of respondent dependent	0.000	0.000		
	Goodman and Kruskal tau	Marital status dependent	0.011	0.004		0.000
		Race of respondent dependent	0.033	0.011		0.000

using race as the X variable and marital status as the Y variable, so we are interested only in the "marital status dependent" versions.

Let's look at lambda first. ***Lambda*** tells us that there is no association between the two variables—which contradicts our visualization! This is because lambda makes predictions based on the modal category of Y for each level of X. If the modal category of Y is the same for each level of X, lambda will be zero—even if the proportions differ. This isn't wrong, but it is often too conservative and crude.

An alternative PRE measure that is more sensitive than lambda is the ***Goodman and Kruskal tau***. For the GK tau, we do not guess the modal category on Y for all cases. Rather, we guess different scores on Y, in numbers proportional to the actual frequencies.

In the case of our example, the value of the Goodman and Kruskal tau turns out to be 0.011. This is a very weak association. Since the measure is PRE, we can describe the association by saying: "Knowing race reduces error in predicting marital status by 1.1 percent," or "Race explains 1.1 percent of the variation in marital status."

Notice that both PRE measures of association have values smaller than the chi-squared-based measures. This will usually be the case. PRE measures are preferred to chi-squared-based measures because they are more conservative and because they can be talked about in "percentage reduction" terms; chi-squared measures should never be described using the percentage reduction terminology.

Also note that measures of the strength of nominal association have their own significance tests that can be used instead of the global chi-squared test.

There are other measures of association for two nominal variables, but the few we have discussed will usually give you enough information to describe the strength of association. Take the short check quiz to review your knowledge.

The Form of Nominal Association

If we're confident that there really is an association between two variables in the population (which we've inferred from our sample), and if the association is strong enough to be of any interest (which we've determined by examining several measures of association), then we are ready to take the last step—describing the form of the association.

It's not enough to say that race and marital status are weakly associated and that we are 95 percent sure that the association of race and marital status in the whole population isn't zero. Our reader, and our theory, wants to know: "associated in what way?"

For nominal variables, to describe the form of the association is to say what categories of Y are overrepresented or underrepresented for which levels of X. Or, to be less technical: What groups on X are more likely to have which scores on Y?

There are a number of ways that one can validly describe the form of the relationship between two nominal variables. We have emphasized that examining column percentages in a properly prepared table or preparing comparative pie charts can be very effective ways of

CHECK QUIZ 12.4

1. True or False: The Pearson chi-squared test of independence is well suited for assessing the association of nominal variables, because chi-squared can range between 0 and 1.
2. The size of the chi-squared statistic depends on
   a. the amount of association between two variables.
   b. the number of cases.
   c. the number of cells in the table.
   d. all of these.
3. The text mentions two tests that adjust chi-squared so levels of association fall between 0 and 1; __________ is designed for 2×2 tables, while __________ is designed for larger tables.
   a. Cramér's thigh; phi
   b. phi; Fisher's exact
   c. Student's T; phi
   d. phi; Cramér's V
4. The problem with using phi to test the association of variables in tables that are larger than 2×2 is that
   a. the calculations are labor intensive.
   b. chi-squared is adequate in those cases.
   c. its maximum value may exceed 1.
   d. one is the loneliest number.
5. A key idea of PRE approaches to association is that
   a. they tell us how much better our prediction is, based on knowing the value of another variable.
   b. they are done before ("pre") other tests.
   c. they're like the F-test in ANOVA.
   d. they are unnecessary if chi-squared has already been computed.
6. Phi and Cramér's V are best used when the variables are both measured at the
   a. nominal level.
   b. ordinal level.
   c. interval/ratio level.
   d. continuous level.
7. In a 2×2 table, phi ranges in value from
   a. -1 to 1.
   b. 0 to 1.
   c. 0 to $+/-1$.
   d. 1 to 100.
8. Lambda compares the number of errors of prediction under two separate rules. In the first rule, the independent variable is
   a. ignored.
   b. squared.

c. taken into account.
d. percentaged.

9. According to the logic of proportional reduction in error (PRE), if two variables are associated, then information about the independent variable
   a. eliminates errors in the prediction of the dependent variable.
   b. reduces the number of errors in predicting the dependent variable.
   c. has no effect on the ability to predict the independent variable.
   d. decreases errors of prediction for negative relationships and increases errors for positive relationships.
10. While ignoring the independent variable, we make 92 errors when predicting the dependent variable. When taking the independent variable into account, we reduce the number of errors to 27. Therefore,
   a. the variables are not associated.
   b. the variables are associated.
   c. the independent variable is definitely a cause of the dependent variable.
   d. phi will be 0.

describing differences in Y between levels of X. In the chapter on chi-squared, we saw that calculating differences of proportions can also be useful. One additional method, "odds ratios" needs to be discussed, because it is widely used in fields such as demography and epidemiology.

An odds ratio is the ratio of the number of times that an event occurs (or a trait is present) to the *number of times that the event does not occur* (or the trait is absent). An odds ratio is similar to a proportion, but a proportion is the ratio of the number of times that event occurs to the *total number of cases*. If two people are married and one is single, we could calculate a proportion and say that two-thirds of all people (0.667) are married, or the probability that any one person is married is 0.667. Alternatively, we could say that the odds that a person was married were "2 to 1" (i.e., the number who are married in ratio to the number who aren't), or the odds of being married versus single are 2.0, or the odds of being married are twice as great as the odds of being single.

We can apply the same approach to the frequencies in a table that describes a nominal-by-nominal relationship.

Consider the data on marital status by race that we saw as Table 12.2.

In Table 12.2, among white people, 727 are married and 544 are not. So, the odds that a person is married if he or she is white are 727/544 or 1.34 to 1.0. White folks are slightly more likely to be married than not married.

In Table 12.2, among black people, 67 are married and 108 are not. So, the odds that a person is married if he or she is black are 67/108 or 0.62 to 1.0. Black folks are substantially less likely to be married than they are to be unmarried.

So, the odds that whites are married (1.34) are much larger than the odds that blacks are married (0.62). Indeed, the odds that whites are married are 2.16 times as large (1.34/0.62) as the odds for blacks. This number, 2.16, is the odds ratio.

The odds ratio is calculated by first calculating the odds of one outcome versus another (or versus all others) in each group that we are comparing (i.e., "white" and "black"). Then, the ratios of the odds of each of the groups to some particular group are calculated (i.e., the ratio of the odds of whites to the odds of blacks).

The resulting odds ratio can be interpreted as: the odds of a particular outcome are so many times as great if a case has one score on *X* versus having a different score on *X*. In our example, the odds that a person is married versus not married is 2.16 times as high for whites as for blacks. This suggests a meaningful difference in the outcomes.

Like differences in specific proportions, odds ratios are used to highlight a particular aspect of the relationship between *X* and *Y*. Many different odds ratios could be calculated for most tables. You need to focus on your research question in order to decide which odds are most meaningful to compare.

Take a moment to check your knowledge about describing the form of nominal association.

CHECK QUIZ 12.5

		Left-Handed	
		Yes	No
Friendly	**Yes**	30	80
	No	5	20

1. In the bogus data from the table, the odds that a lefty is friendly are:
   a. 30:80.
   b. 30:5.
   c. 30:20.
   d. 80:20.

		Left-Handed	
		Yes	No
Friendly	**Yes**	30	80
	No	5	20

2. In the table, the odds that a nonlefty is friendly are:
   a. 30:80.
   b. 30:5.
   c. 30:20.
   d. 80:20.

		Left-Handed	
		Yes	**No**
Friendly	**Yes**	30	80
	No	5	20

3. Just looking at the table, does it seem as though lefties or nonlefties are more likely to be friendly?
   a. It looks as though lefties are more likely to be friendly.
   b. It looks as though nonlefties are more likely to be friendly.
   c. It looks as though they're about equally likely to be friendly.
   d. It looks as though I should look for new friends.

		Left-Handed	
		Yes	**No**
Friendly	**Yes**	30	80
	No	5	20

4. The odds ratio of friendly lefties to friendly others is
   a. (30/5)/(80/20).
   b. (30 × 80)/(5 × 20).
   c. (30/20)/5/80).
   d. impossible to calculate.
5. If the odds ratio of friendly lefties to friendly others turned out to be 1.5, we could say
   a. that the odds of an "other" being friendly are one and a half times greater than those of a lefty being friendly.
   b. that the odds of a lefty being friendly are one and a half times greater than those of an "other" being friendly.
   c. that the odds of a lefty being friendly are three times greater than an "other" being friendly.
   d. that you should look among the ambidextrous if you want to find friendly people.

Example

MEASURES OF NOMINAL ASSOCIATION

In earlier examples, we examined the relationship between race and marital status using the U.S. General Social Survey. Many of the reasons why blacks and whites differ in their marital status distribution are thought to be associated with social class. Table 12.6 shows the association between survey respondents' self-identified social class and their marital status.

We will advance the research hypothesis that people of different social classes have different distributions of marital status, against the null hypothesis of no difference.

TABLE 12.6 Marital Statuses by Class Identification, General Social Survey 1996

	Class Identification				
Marital Status	**Lower**	**Working**	**Middle**	**Upper**	**Total**
Married	15	168	202	22	407
	27.8%	46.2%	50.6%	73.3%	48.1%
Widowed	15	40	44	2	92
	27.8%	11.0%	11.0%	6.7%	10.9%
Divorced	14	47	65	1	127
	25.9%	12.9%	16.3%	3.3%	15.0%
Separated	3	11	11	2	27
	5.6%	3%	2.8%	6.7%	3.2%
Never married	16	98	77	3	194
	29.6%	26.9%	19.3%	10%	22.9%
Total	54	364	399	30	847
	100.0%	100.0%	100%	100%	100%

We first want to just visualize the relationship by comparing the column percentages. It seems pretty clear that the social classes have quite different distributions of marital status. In the sample, it appears that the research hypothesis is supported.

Testing for statistical significance, we find chi-squared with 12 degrees of freedom has the value 28.894, with $p = 0.004$. We conclude that we may be more than 95 percent confident in rejecting the null hypothesis of no association.

The chi-squared-based measure phi should not be used with this table, because it is not a 2-by-2 table. Cramér's V has the value 0.107, with $p = 0.004$. We would conclude that there is a weak association. The PRE measure lambda with marital status dependent shows a value of 0.002, and $p = 0.857$. Using the definition of association that lambda indexes, we would conclude that there is no association. This contradicts

Example

our other evidence, particularly chi-squared. We recall that lambda can be a rather insensitive measure. The somewhat more sensitive Goodman-Kruskal tau measure shows an association of 0.014, but a $p < 0.000$. We would conclude that there is a significant association, but a very weak one. Knowing social class identification reduces errors in predicting marital status by only about 1.5 percent, compared to predicting marital status not knowing social class.

Despite the weak association, there are a number of quite interesting differences in the table that we might want to talk about. For this, odds ratios can be helpful. Let's suppose that we wanted to highlight how different the lower class is from the upper class in terms of never marrying versus being currently married. Note that we could form different odds ratios to highlight different features of the association.

We want to compare the lower class to the upper class, so we'll put lower-class people in the numerator of our odds ratio, and upper-class people in the denominator. Within lower-class people, we'll form the ratio of "never married" to "married." We'll do the same for upper-class people. This gives us:

$$(16/15)/(3/22) = 1.07/0.14 = 7.64$$

We can say that, compared to upper-class people, the odds that lower-class people are never married compared to married are more than 7 times as great. Lower-class people are 7 times more likely to never marry (compared to being married) as upper-class people are. Even though the overall statistical association between social class and marital status is not strong, there are some quite strong patterns in the form of the association!

ASSOCIATION WITH ORDINAL VARIABLES

The logic of analyzing the association between two ordinal variables is the same as the logic for studying two nominal variables. But, because ordinal variables tell us about rank and not just difference, we need to use a somewhat different approach to take advantage of the additional information.

Ordinal scales are of two types: full rank-order and grouped rank-order. Full rank-order scales assign each case a unique rank (i.e., there is one first-place case, one second-place case, etc.). Grouped rank-order data allow more than one case to share the same rank. Scales that divide people into "high," "medium," and "low," or Likert-type attitude items on surveys are grouped rank-order scales because any number of cases can share the same rank.

Visualizing Ordinal Association

Approaches to visualizing and indexing the association between two ordinal variables differ somewhat depending on whether the cases have been grouped into ranks.

A cross-tabulation between two full rank-order variables would make very little sense. The table would be extremely large, because each rank on *X* and each rank on *Y* would be a separate row and column. In each row (i.e., the scores on *Y*) there would be only one nonzero cell—because each score on *Y* corresponds with only one score on *X*. So, cross-tabulation is not a very useful approach to visualizing full rank-order association.

For grouped ordinal variables, cross-tabulation is a very good starting point to see whether the two variables are probably associated, as well as the strength and form of association. Take a look at the relationship between educational attainment (grouped ordinal *X*) and frequency of religious service attendance (grouped ordinal *Y*) shown in Table 12.7.

This is a fairly complex table because there are quite a few categories of each variable, but the idea for laying it out is quite simple. All the rules for a nominal table have been preserved. To represent the fact that the categories of grouped ordinal variables are ranked, we've made sure that the scores on the education variable (the independent variable here) increase as we move from left to right. Scores on the dependent variable, frequency of religious attendance, increase as we move from the bottom to the top of the table. Arranging the categories in rank order is necessary so that we can see the association in the cross-tabulation.

Scanning the cross-tabulation of a nominal-by-nominal table to see whether the two variables are associated is pretty simple—we just look to see if the column percentages differ from column to column. The idea of ordinal association is similar: if the two variables are associated, then the relative frequencies of *Y* will differ across levels of *X*. However, ordinal association goes beyond simple differences in outcomes. Ordinal association requires order!

Two variables have a positive ordinal association if cases that rank high on *X* are also likely to rank high on *Y*; two variables have a negative ordinal association if cases that rank

TABLE 12.7 Religious Service Attendance by Highest Educational Degree

Frequency of Religious Service Attendance by Highest Educational Degree (General Social Survey Sample, 1998)

Attends Services	Degree Less than High School	High School	Junior College	Bachelor	Graduate	Total
More than once a week	4 (8.2%)	16 (9.9%)	1 (5.0%)	2 (5.1%)	4 (18.2%)	27
Every week	7 (14.3%)	26 (16.0%)	4 (20.0%)	5 (12.8%)	5 (22.7%)	47
Nearly every week	1 (2.0%)	9 (5.6%)	2 (10.0%)	2 (5.1%)	1 (4.5%)	15
2–3 times per month	5 (10.2%)	14 (8.6%)	5 (25.0%)	9 (23.1%)	1 (4.5%)	34
Once a month	1 (2.0%)	12 (7.4%)	2 (10.0%)	2 (5.1%)	1 (4.5%)	18
Several times per year	4 (8.2%)	16 (9.9%)	3 (15.0%)	7 (17.9%)	1 (4.5%)	31
Once a year	4 (8.2%)	21 (13.0%)		3 (7.7%)	4 (18.2%)	32
LT once a year	4 (8.2%)	15 (9.3%)		4 (10.3%)	3 (13.6%)	26
Never	19 (38.8%)	33 (20.4%)	3 (15.0%)	5 (12.8%)	2 (9.1%)	62
Total	49 (100%)	162 (100%)	20 (100%)	39 (100%)	22 (100%)	292

high on X are likely to rank low on Y. In Table 12.7, we have shaded the cells in each column where most of the cases seem to lie. For people with less than a high school degree, almost 40 percent report that they never attend religious services; for those with graduate degrees, about 40 percent fall in the two highest categories of religious attendance. For educational levels in between, religious attendance also seems to be mostly in between.

There seems to be a pattern for people who have lower scores on X (i.e., lower levels of educational credentials) to also have low religious attendance. And as education increases (i.e., as we go from left to right across the table), the level of religious attendance tends to increase (that is, there are more cases at higher levels of attendance). Thus, what we are seeing in the table is a positive association of education and religious attendance: people who rank higher on education are likely to rank higher on religious attendance.

What would the table look like if there were a *negative* association? The column percentages would still vary across columns, but the pattern would be different. The relatively overrepresented cases would fall in a general pattern from the upper left to the lower right. That is, people with low ranks on education would tend to have high ranks on religious attendance; people with high education would tend to be low on attendance.

What if there were *no ordinal* association? If there were no differences in the percentages across columns, there would be no association (just like with nominal data). Suppose, though, that the percentages weren't the same from column to column—but that they didn't follow any consistent pattern of rising from lower left to upper right or consistently declining from lower left to upper right. The variables would display a nominal association if this were the case, but not an ordinal association. In visualizing ordinal association, then, we are looking for the existence of a pattern that tells us there is positive association or negative association—not just differences.

Take the quick quiz to see if you've mastered the basic ideas about seeing ordinal association. When you have, go on to learn some of the numerical statistics for measuring association with grouped ordinal variables.

Significance Testing for Ordinal Association

When we are working with ordinal variables, our research hypotheses are usually based on theoretical explanations of why a case that scores relatively high on one variable ought (on average) score high on another (for a hypothesis of positive association) or ought (on average) to score lower on another (for a hypothesis of negative association). That is, our research hypotheses are usually one-tailed.

$$H_a: \text{test statistic} > 0 \textit{ or } H_a: \text{test statistic} < 0$$

The null hypothesis in testing ordinal association is usually that knowing the rank of a case on one variable does nothing to improve our ability to predict its rank on another variable.

$$H_0: \text{test statistic} = 0$$

CHECK QUIZ 12.6

1. Ordinal data in which each case is assigned an individual rank are called
   a. grouped rank-order data.
   b. three-quarters rank-order data.
   c. half rank-order.
   d. full rank-order data.
2. Ordinal data in which many cases can share the same level of a variable are called
   a. grouped rank-order data.
   b. five-sixths rank-order data.
   c. half rank-order data.
   d. full rank-order data.
3. Why doesn't the cross-tabulation of two grouped rank-order variables make much sense?
   a. The table would be relatively large, and most cells would contain only zeros.
   b. You wouldn't be able to see any association between the variables in the table.
   c. You couldn't perform a chi-squared test on the table, because too many cells would have an expected value of zero.
   d. The table would be too wide for SPSS to print.
   e. It does make sense to do a cross-tabulation of these variables.
4. When making a table of grouped rank-order data, the columns
   a. should be in Times bold, 12 point.
   b. should be arranged from lowest value on the left to highest value on the right.
   c. should be arranged from highest value on the left to lowest value on the right.
   d. should always consist of nominal-level variables.
5. If the *Y* values in a cross-tabulation of grouped rank-order variables are arranged in the way recommended by the book, a negative association should show cells with higher counts
   a. on a diagonal from the lower left to the upper right.
   b. forming a straight line running down one of the columns.
   c. forming a straight line running across one of the rows.
   d. on a diagonal from the top left of the table to the bottom right of the table.
6. If there are only a few cases, you can probably spot association between two ordinal variables by
   a. arranging them in two columns, closing your eyes, and pointing to a random number in each column.
   b. arranging them in one column, sorting them, and finding the median.
   c. arranging them in two columns, sorting them by their order on the first column, and looking for positive or negative association.
   d. arranging them in two columns, finding the mean of each column, and comparing them.

For ordinal association, there are a number of alternative measures of the strength of association (we'll discuss the major ones in just a little bit). Each has a sampling distribution and standard error estimator. As a practical matter, statistics for ordinal association and their standard errors are almost always calculated using statistical software. You will find the value of the test statistic, (sometimes) the standard error, and (usually) a *p*-level for the rejection of the null hypothesis of no rank-order association. You need to pay attention to whether the test performed has been a one-tailed or a two-tailed test (one could have the alternative hypothesis that the association was not zero—although this is rare).

The Strength of Ordinal Association

There are several measures of the strength of ordinal association that are commonly used for grouped-ordinal variables (gamma, Somers' D, and tau-b/tau-c). For full rank-order ordinal data, the test statistic of choice is Spearman's rank-order correlation coefficient (Spearman's rho). While you will rarely calculate these by hand, it is important to understand how these measures index the strength of ordinal association.

Measures of association for grouped ordinal variables follow the proportional reduction in error (PRE) logic: can we reduce uncertainty in predicting *Y* if we know *X*, compared to predicting *Y* not knowing *X*. With nominal variables, we were interested in predicting which group a case fell in on *Y*, knowing or not knowing *X*. With ordinal variables, we are interested in predicting the rank order of a case on *Y*, knowing or not knowing its rank order on *X*.

Gamma, Somers' d, and tau-b/tau-c are all created by examining the ranks on *X* and *Y* of every pair of cases. Each pair of cases is classified as "concordant," "discordant," "tied on *X*," "tied on *Y*," or "tied on both *X* and *Y*."

Suppose there were three students—call them Fred, June, and Sandy. Suppose they performed as shown in Table 12.8. On the midterm Fred got an A, June got a B, and Sandy got a C. On the final exam, they performed in exactly the same way—Fred again got an A, June again got a B, and Sandy got a C.

Let's compare the ranks of Fred and June. Fred was higher than June on the midterm, and also higher on the final. Since they fell in the same rank order on the two tests (or variables), we will call their scores "concordant." Compare Fred and Sandy. They were in the same rank order on both tests (i.e., Fred was higher than Sandy on both), so this pair is also concordant. Last, compare June and Sandy. They are also concordant because June scored

TABLE 12.8 Perfect Positive Rank-Order Correlation: All Pairs Concordant

	Midterm Grade	Final Exam Grade
Fred	A	A
June	B	B
Sandy	C	C

higher than Sandy on both tests. So, of the three possible pairs, all are concordant. This is an example of a *perfect positive rank-order association*: all pairs of cases are in the same relative rank order on the two variables (in this case, on the two exams). The higher the rank on the midterm (X), the higher the rank on the final exam (Y).

Now, consider the result in Table 12.9, which is just the opposite.

If we compare Fred and June, we see that they in the opposite rank order on the midterm and final (Fred is higher than June on the midterm, but lower than June on the zfinal). Their rank order on the two exams are not in concordance. So, let's call this pair "discordant." If we compare Fred and Sandy, we find them discordant as well; and June and Sandy are also discordant. So, for all three pairs, the ranks on the two exams are discordant. This is an example of a *perfect negative rank-order association*: all pairs of cases are in the opposite rank order on the two variables. The higher the rank on the midterm (X), the lower the rank on the final exam (Y).

Associations are rarely perfect with real-world data, so we need to consider a few more possible outcomes of the two tests. Table 12.10 shows another possible result.

In this example, Fred and June are discordant (do you see why?). But Fred and Sandy are concordant (because they fall in the same rank order on both variables, with Fred ranking higher); June and Sandy are also concordant. So, two pairs are concordant and one pair is discordant. If we knew that any random person was higher than another on the midterm, our best guess about their rank order on the final would be that they fell in the same order. We would make fewer errors using this guessing rule than by guessing randomly. In fact, if we guessed "concordant" in all three possible pairs, we'd be right twice and wrong once. This is better than chance, so there is an association (a positive one)—but it is not a perfect association.

Rank-order associations do not have to be perfect positive or perfect negative associations. If more pairs are concordant than discordant (but there are some of each), we have a

TABLE 12.9 Perfect Negative Rank-Order Correlation: All Pairs Discordant

	Midterm Grade	Final Exam Grade
Fred	A	C
June	B	B
Sandy	C	A

TABLE 12.10 Less Than Perfect Positive Rank-Order Correlation

	Midterm Grade	Final Exam Grade
Fred	A	B
June	B	A
Sandy	C	C

tendency toward positive association or concordance; if more pairs are discordant than concordant, we have a tendency toward negative association or discordance. These tendencies can be stronger or weaker (if we had more than three cases).

There is one last complexity we need to deal with for thinking about association with grouped ordinal variables. Consider Table 12.11.

What is different here is that two students got the same grade on the final. With grouped ordinal data, of course, this happens all the time. Many students in a class will get the same letter grade; many respondents on a survey will answer "strongly disagree" to a particular question.

If we compare Fred and Sandy, there is no problem—they are clearly concordant. This is also true of the June and Sandy comparison—they are concordant. But, when we compare Fred and June, we can't say—because they share the same rank on the final exam (the Y variable in this example). So, the Fred/June comparison is neither concordant nor discordant. It is called "tied on Y." Of course, two or more cases could have the same score on X but different scores on Y. Again, we couldn't rank these pairs as concordant or discordant—they would be "tied on X." And maybe two cases have the same rank on both X and Y (e.g., what if Fred and June had both received A on both the midterm and the final?). In this case, the pair would be "tied on both X and Y."

All of the commonly used measures of the strength of association for grouped ordinal variables are based on the numbers of kinds of pairs. The measures differ from one another in how they deal with the ambiguous outcomes where pairs are tied on X, Y, or both.

Probably the most widely used measure of the strength of association for grouped ordinal data is ***gamma*** (see Formula 12.4).

$$G = \frac{N_c - N_d}{N_c + N_d} \tag{12.4}$$

where N_c is the number of concordant pairs and N_d is the number of discordant pairs. If there are equal numbers of concordant and discordant pairs, gamma will have the value of zero. If all pairs are concordant, gamma will take the value of $+1.0$. If all pairs are discordant, gamma will have the value of -1.0. Values in between indicate less than perfect association. Notice how gamma deals with the pairs of cases where ranking is ambiguous (tied on X, tied on Y, or tied on both). Gamma simply ignores these cases. Because gamma ignores ambiguous cases, it is the least conservative or cautious of the measures of association. Usually the value of gamma will be larger (i.e., closer to $+1.0$ or -1.0) than other measures.

TABLE 12.11 Rank-Order Correlation with Ties on Y

	Midterm Grade	Final Exam Grade
Fred	A	A
June	B	A
Sandy	C	C

Somers' d (see Formula 12.5) is a very close relative of gamma, but is a bit more conservative. The numerator for Somers' d is the same as for gamma: the number of concordant pairs minus the number of discordant pairs. The denominator, though, differs. It includes the number of pairs tied on *Y*.

$$d_{yx} = \frac{(N_c - N_d)}{(N_c + N_d + T_y)} \tag{12.5}$$

What this is saying is that cases that are tied on the dependent variable are pairs that might have been predicted if the association was a perfect one, but can't be in the real data. So, cases tied on *Y* ought to be regarded as failed predictions.

If we want to be more conservative still, we can use ***tau-b*** (for square tables; see Formula 12.6) or ***tau-c*** (for any table; see Formula 12.7). Tau-b and tau-c are symmetric measures of association. That is, we are hypothesizing covariation, not determination or the ability to predict one variable from the other.

$$\tau_b = \frac{(N_c - N_d)}{\sqrt{(N_c + N_d + T_y)(N_c + N_d + T_x)}} \tag{12.6}$$

$$\tau_c = (N_c - N_d)\left[\frac{2m}{\left(n^2(m-1)\right)}\right] \tag{12.7}$$

where m is the smaller of the number of rows or columns, and n is the sample size.

Both tau measures contain the same ratio of concordant and discordant pairs in the numerator. Tau-b counts the ties on both *X* and *Y* against the strength of association, whereas tau-c adjusts for possible inflation due to tied pairs by taking the number of cells into account. There is no one right measure. Use a computer and calculate them all!

So, take a moment now to check your knowledge with a little quiz. Then, we'll talk about how to study association when the two variables are measured as full rank-ordered, instead of grouped rank-ordered.

CHECK QUIZ 12.7

1. When talking about two rank-order variables, we say that two cases are "concordant" when
   a. they have the same relative order in both variables.
   b. we have nothing better to say about them.
   c. the variables they represent have the same mean.
   d. the difference between their rank orders is very small.

2. For variables measured at the ordinal level, gamma measures
    a. the statistical significance of the relationship.
    b. the proportional reduction in error gained by predicting one variable while taking the other into account.
    c. the relative importance of each variable to the association.
    d. all of the these.
3. One of the biggest differences between gamma and Somers' d is
    a. that Somers' d is not a PRE statistic.
    b. the way they handle tied cases.
    c. the way they tie handled cases.
    d. that Somers' d can be calculated by hand.
4. Gamma ranges from
    a. 0 to 1
    b. 1 to 100
    c. 0 to −1
    d. −1 to +1
5. In a negative relationship,
    a. if case A ranks below case B on one variable, it will rank below case B on the other variable.
    b. if case A ranks above case B on one variable, it will rank below case B on the other variable.
    c. if case A ranks above case B on one variable, it will rank above case B on the other variable.
    d. none of the these is true.
6. A gamma computed on the relationship between marital happiness and amount of TV viewing is 0.78. This means that
    a. if we know how pairs of couples compare on TV viewing, we would be 78 percent better at predicting their ranks on marital happiness.
    b. happily married couples don't watch TV.
    c. couples who watch a lot of TV tend to be unhappy.
    d. TV causes divorce.
7. Somers' d is more conservative than gamma because
    a. it includes scores tied on *Y* in the denominator, which results in lower Somers' d's overall.
    b. it wears pin-striped suits.
    c. it inflates the likely association.
    d. it is used more by Republicans.

Sometimes we collect data in the form of full rank-order scales, rather than grouped scores. That is, rather than knowing that five people scored "high," three scored "medium," and two scored "low," we could rank-order the people exactly from highest to lowest. Sometimes interval/ratio variables are treated as if they were ordinal variables. If interval/ratio variables have very skewed distributions or nonlinear associations, the correlation and regression methods discussed in upcoming chapters may not work well. So, sometimes we are willing to "lose information" about interval/ratio variables by treating them as ordinal variables.

We can extend the idea of concordance and discordance to the situation to take advantage of the greater amount of information that is available in full rank-order scales.

The most commonly used measure of the strength of association between two full rank-ordered variables, Spearman's rho (or rank-order correlation coefficient), is built on the idea that we can tell the amount of association by examining differences in ranks. Take a quick look at the formula for rho (Formula 12.8).

$$r_s = 1 - \frac{6\sum D^2}{N(N^2 - 1)} \tag{12.8}$$

The key part of the formula is the numerator ($\sum D^2$). This says, for each case, take the difference between the rank on X and the rank on Y (D) and square it, and then add up the differences. If the ranks on X and Y are identical (perfect positive association), this sum will be zero. If the ranks on X and Y are exactly the opposite of each other (perfect negative association), the sum of the squared differences in ranks will be the largest possible for any given number of cases. If the sum is an intermediate number, the association is weaker.

Take a minute now to check your knowledge of how to analyze the association of two full rank-ordered variables using Spearman's rho. When you've finished, you will probably want to review the chapter and read the summary.

CHECK QUIZ 12.8

1. Spearman's rho is appropriate for use with
   a. full rank-order ordinal variables.
   b. variables whose categories have been collapsed.
   c. tables larger than 2 × 2.
   d. negative relationships only.
2. Ordinal-level scales measuring religiosity and personal happiness range from 0 to 100. Which measure of association would be most appropriate?
   a. chi-squared
   b. phi
   c. gamma
   d. Spearman's rho
3. The square of Spearman's rho is the proportional reduction in error when predicting
   a. rank on one variable from rank on the other variable compared to predicting rank while ignoring the other variable.
   b. the rank of a case from its score.

c. rank on gamma versus rank on phi.
d. score on *X* while ignoring *Y*.

4. Many studies have explored the relationship between smoking and health problems. If one of those studies found a Spearman's rho of 0.78 between amount of smoking and seriousness of health problems, this would indicate
   a. that smoking causes health problems.
   b. a positive, causal relationship between these variables.
   c. a positive, strong relationship between these variables.
   d. a positive, statistically significant relationship.
5. Tests of significance based on gamma and Spearman's rho assume
   a. random sampling.
   b. ordinal level of measurement.
   c. normal sampling distribution.
   d. all of the these.
6. A reported significance level of 0.07 (two-tailed test) will be considered statistically significant only if
   a. our confidence interval is wider/larger than 0.07.
   b. we've set up the alternative hypothesis as a one-tailed test, and our confidence interval is wider/larger than 0.035.
   c. pigs are flying through the air at very high altitudes.
   d. both a and b.
7. Spearman's rho ranges from
   a. 0 to 1
   b. 1 to 100
   c. −1 to 1
   d. 25 or 6 to 4

ASSOCIATION FOR GROUPED ORDINAL VARIABLES

Example

Table 12.12 shows some data abstracted from the General Social Survey on the relationship between the independent variable "political conservativism" and the dependent variable, belief that "courts are too easy on criminals." Although we have only two categories of each variable, the interpretation we want is an ordinal one.

TABLE 12.12 Relationship between Conservativism and Sentencing Attitudes

	Liberal	Conservative	Total
Too easy	250	384	634
Too harsh	29	14	43
Total	279	398	677

(continued)

Example

To calculate the measures of association, we need to first calculate the numbers of pairs of cases of various types. These are shown in Table 12.13.

TABLE 12.13 Counts of Pairs for the Relationship between Conservativism and Sentencing Attitudes

Concordant pairs	11,136
Discordant pairs	3,500
Tied on X	12,626
Tied on Y	96,406
Tied on both X and Y	105,158
Total	228,826

We can plug these values into the formulas (or have software do it for us). What we find when we do is:

$$\text{Gamma} = 0.522$$
$$d_{yx} = 0.069$$
$$\text{T}_b = 0.139$$

The significance tests for all three statistics turn out to show $p < 0.05$. There appears to be a relationship in the whole population, based on the sample results.

How can we interpret these results? First, and most important, all three statistics have positive values. The higher the rank on conservatism, the higher the rank on perceiving sentencing as too easy. Or there is a positive rank-order association of conservatism with a preference for harsher sentences. This speaks to the form of the ordinal association.

But there is disagreement about the strength of the positive ordinal association. Looking at the numbers of pairs in Table 12.13, we can see why. A very large proportion of all cases are "tied on *Y*." Gamma simply ignores this fact. Somers' d penalizes the index of strength of association to the maximum possible extent. Tau-b also penalizes the index of association, but not as much. The most conservative interpretation (using d_{yx}) would conclude that knowing a person's rank on conservatism reduces error in predicting his or her sentencing attitudes by only 7 percent—quite a weak relationship. The most liberal interpretation (using gamma) would suggest that knowing a person's liberalism enables us to improve our predictions about the person's sentencing attitudes by over 50 percent!

There isn't any one right answer here. But watch out! If gamma is reported (and this is very common), it may somewhat overstate the strength and importance of the result. When you report results, it is a good idea to calculate all the statistics, and to report them all if they differ as much as the ones do here.

Example

ASSOCIATION FOR FULL RANK-ORDER VARIABLES

The number of children born to women in their lifetimes varies greatly across societies. One partial explanation for cross-national differences is that higher birthrates are the result of higher infant mortality. Where the chances are less that a child will survive to adulthood, families are more likely to make reproductive choices that increase the number of births.

If this reasoning is correct, then countries that rank high on the average rates of infant mortality (deaths of live-born children within the first year per 1,000 births) should also rank high on the average numbers of lifetime births per woman. That is, infant mortality rank and fertility rank should be positively associated. The null hypothesis is that there is no association.

We begin with raw data on infant mortality rates and fertility rates of 108 nations, as in Table 12.14.

TABLE 12.14 Partial Listing of Raw Infant Mortality and Fertility Data

Country	Infant Mortality	Fertility
Afghanistan	168.0	6.9
Argentina	25.6	2.8
Armenia	27.0	3.2
Australia	7.3	1.9
.	.	.
.	.	.
.	.	.
United States	8.1	2.1
Uzbekistan	53.0	3.7
Venezuela	28.0	3.1
Vietnam	46.0	3.3
Zambia	85.0	6.7

We are interested in the correlations of ranks, rather than quantities. The data here are actually measured at the interval level. We must first convert the data to ranks. First we sort the data in descending order on the independent variable (mortality). We then assign rank ordinal numbers (i.e., 1, 2, 3, . . .) to the cases, reflecting the highest rank on mortality, the second-highest rank, and so on. There are some countries that have exactly the same scores and are tied in rank. For cases having the same rank, we take the average (e.g., cases 8 and 9 each receive the rank 8.5). Next we resort the data and assign ranks to fertility (1 = highest fertility, 2 = second highest, etc.).

Next we calculate the difference in ranks (D in the Spearman's rho formula) by subtracting each country's rank on fertility from its rank on infant mortality. Since the

(continued)

Example

rho requires the squared difference, we've calculated it, too. Our data now look like those in Table 12.15, and we are ready to calculate the test statistic.

TABLE 12.15 Calculation of Differences in Ranks

Country	mortrank	fertrank	d	d_square
Afghanistan	1.0	3.5	−2.5	6.3
Argentina	58.5	58.0	0.5	0.3
Armenia	56.5	49.0	7.5	56.3
Australia	90.0	79.0	11.0	121.0
Botswana	46.0	27.0	19.0	361.0
Brazil	27.0	61.0	−34.0	1,156.0

Here is Formula 12.8, the formula for rho, again:

$$r_s = 1 - \frac{6\sum D^2}{N(N^2 - 1)} \tag{12.8}$$

Our N, or number of cases, is 107.

We calculate the sum of the differences in rank, squared, which turns out to be 30,878.

The denominator is $107 \times (11{,}449 - 1) = 1{,}224{,}936$.

So, the fraction becomes $185{,}268/1{,}224{,}936 = 0.1512$, and r_S is $1 - 0.1512 = +0.85$.

Since Spearman's rho is a PRE measure of association, we can say that knowing the rank of a country on infant mortality reduces uncertainty in predicting its rank on fertility by 85 percent—a very strong relationship. Nations that rank high on infant mortality display a strong tendency to also rank high on fertility.

The inferential significance of Spearman's rho can also be tested, using estimated standard errors and the t-distribution. Frankly, if you need to do this, we recommend using a statistics package with the algorithms built in.

SUMMARY

This whole chapter has been about one very important idea—the notion of "statistical association" (and its opposite, "statistical independence") of the scores on two variables. Our discussion in this chapter has been about the general idea of what association means, how to see association, and the steps involved in analyzing association. We have then applied these ideas to the relationship between two nominal variables, two grouped ordinal variables, and two full rank-order variables.

Often you will be interested in a relationship between variables of mixed types. Perhaps you want to know if gender (a nominal variable) helps us to predict political conservativism (an ordinal variable), for example. For many mixed pairs, the techniques of prediction that we discuss in Chapters 14 and 15 provide good approaches. But if all we want is a simple measure of association between two variables of mixed type, the rule is to use a measure of association that is appropriate for the variable measured at the lowest level. For example, if we are looking at an association between a nominal variable and an ordinal variable, we should select a measure for nominal association.

To say that two variables are associated, in the statistical sense, is to assert that certain scores on one variable tend to go with certain scores on the other—more than we would expect by chance. There are many everyday words that express the basic idea of association: we say that things "go together," that they "correlate," that they "covary," that they "co-occur." A more precise definition of association between two variables is that the conditional distributions of scores on one variable differ across levels of the other. If this is true, then knowing the scores on one variable enables us to make more accurate predictions about scores on the other variable. Association is often also defined as a reduction in uncertainty or an improvement in our ability to predict scores on one variable as a result of knowing the scores on the other.

Three questions guide all analyses of statistical association, regardless of the particular techniques of the kinds of variables we are studying. First, we must be sure that any association we observe in a sample of observations is real. That is, can we be confident that the association we observe in a sample is representative of an association in the whole population? If we cannot be confident that there is an association at the population level, there is usually no reason to go on to the second or third step. If we are confident that two variables are associated, the second question is about the strength of the relationship. It's useful to think about the strength of an association in terms of reduction in error in predicting scores on one variable as a result of knowing scores on the other. The third question in studying association is: What is the form of the effect or association? That is, in what way are scores on X related to scores on Y?

Next, we applied these ideas to studying the association between two nominal variables. Before calculating statistics and performing tests, it is always wise to visualize the relationship. The association between two nominal variables is best inspected by using a proper cross-tabulation with column percentages, or comparative pie charts. With nominal relationships, the Pearson independence chi-squared test is commonly used to test the hypothesis of "no association" or "independence." Sometimes, instead of chi-squared, inference tests associated with particular measures of the strength of association are used to do inference testing. It is wise to compare the results of these statistics with those of chi-squared.

Once we are confident that there is a relationship, its strength should be assessed. There are many measures of the strength of association between two nominal variables. Some measures are based on corrections to chi-squared (we discussed phi and Cramér's V).

An alternative approach is based on reduction in error in predicting which category each case falls in on *Y*, not knowing or knowing the scores on *X*. There are also a number of different PRE measures of association with somewhat different properties (we examined lambda and the Goodman-Kruskal tau). PRE measures can be interpreted as the percentage of uncertainty reduction or variance explained.

The form of a nominal-by-nominal association, overall, is most apparent from simple percentages in the table, or from comparative pie charts. To highlight certain aspects of the association that may be particularly important for a hypothesis test or policy evaluation, odds ratios may be useful supplemental descriptions of the form of association.

Next, we looked at association between two ordinal variables. Ordinal association is about ranking. For grouped ordinal variables, the idea of "concordant pairs" is used to index ranking; for full rank-ordered data, differences in rank are used.

We can visualize ordinal association for grouped variables in a cross-tabulation. The cross-tab should be arranged so that the categories of *X* increase in value as we move from left to right; values of *Y* should increase from the bottom to the top of the table. When arranged in this way, patterns of steadily increasing or steadily decreasing proportions in the top and bottom category indicate ordinal association as we scan the table from left to right.

With grouped ordinal variables, there are several commonly used measures of the strength of association. All of the measures are based on counts of the numbers of concordant, discordant, and tied pairs of cases. Gamma, Somers' d, and tau-b (and tau-c) are all PRE measures of association for grouped ordinal data. All three measures tell us both the direction and the strength of association. All three have inference tests associated with them that are routinely produced by statistical software. Gamma is the most liberal of the three measures (i.e., its values will usually be the largest for the same data table); Somers' d is a bit more conservative, and tau is the most conservative of the measures. It's a good idea to look at all three.

With full rank-ordered variables, the most commonly used measure of association is Spearman's rho. Rho is based on the difference of the ranks of cases on *X* and *Y*. The more similar the rankings on *X* and *Y*, the stronger the positive association; the less similar the rankings on *X* and *Y*, the stronger the negative association. Spearman's rank-order correlation coefficient (as rho is sometimes called) is also a PRE measure that has a value of zero for no association, -1.0 for perfect negative association, and $+1.0$ for perfect positive association.

When we work with interval/ratio variables, the questions also remain the same. But, again, the tools are different, as you will see in the next chapter.

KEY TERMS

Cramér's V

form of a relationship

gamma

Goodman and Kruskal tau

lambda

phi

Somers' d

statistical association (correlation, covariance, relationship, going together)

statistical independence

strength of a relationship

tau-b

tau-c

CHECK QUIZ ANSWERS

Quiz 12.1 Answers: 1. (d); 2. (c); 3. (c)
Quiz 12.2 Answers: 1. (b); 2. (a); 3. (b); 4. (b)
Quiz 12.3 Answers: 1. (c); 2. (a)
Quiz 12.4 Answers: 1. (F); 2. (d); 3. (d); 4. (c); 5. (a); 6. (a); 7. (b); 8. (a); 9. (b); 10. (b)
Quiz 12.5 Answers: 1. (b); 2. (d); 3. (a); 4. (a); 5. (b)
Quiz 12.6 Answers: 1. (d); 2. (a); 3. (e); 4. (b); 5. (d); 6.(c)
Quiz 12.7 Answers: 1. (a); 2. (b); 3. (b); 4. (d); 5. (b); 6. (a); 7. (a)
Quiz 12.8 Answers: 1. (a); 2. (d); 3. (a); 4. (c); 5. (d); 6. (d); 7. (c)

EXERCISES

1. Do people with different social class positions have different worldviews about the society they live in? Using the General Social Survey, a researcher asked respondents with different amounts of formal education what they thought about the motives of other people: Are other people likely to be helpful? Or are other people likely to be looking out for themselves? Or does it depend on the situation? A cross-tabulation was prepared to examine the association:

People Helpful or Looking Out for Selves * R's Highest Degree Cross-Tabulation

			R's Highest Degree						
			LT High School	**High School**	**Junior College**	**Bachelor**	**Graduate**	**NA**	**Total**
People Helpful or Looking Out for Selves	Helpful	Count	102	351	24	112	53		642
		% within R's Highest Degree	38.1%	56.8%	47.1%	66.3%	70.7%		54.3%
	Lookout for Self	Count	144	231	26	50	17	2	470
		% within R's Highest Degree	53.7%	37.4%	51.0%	29.6%	22.7%	100.0%	39.7%
	Depends	Count	22	36	1	7	5		71
		% within R's Highest Degree	8.2%	5.8%	2.0%	4.1%	6.7%		6.0%
Total		Count	268	618	51	169	75	2	1183
		% within R's Highest Degree	100.0%	100.0%	100.0%	100.0%	100.0%	100.0%	100.0%

a. Does there appear to be a relationship between educational attainment and trust of others? What is your evidence?
b. Describe the form of the relationship between the two variables. What is your evidence?
c. Does the relationship appear to be a strong one? What is your evidence?

2. In the General Social Survey, samples of males and females were asked their opinions about pornography. The researchers hypothesized that women would be less likely than men to agree that "pornography provides information about sex." And it was hypothesized that women would be more likely than men to agree that "pornography leads to rape."

   Here are the results:

   "Pornography provides information about sex"

   205 women said "no" and 326 said "yes."

   131 men said "no" and 287 said "yes."

   "Pornography leads to rape"

   346 women said "yes" and 173 said "no."

   198 men said "yes" and 205 said "no."

   a. Prepare proper cross-tabulations for each of the two relationships.
   b. Determine whether there is a statistically significant association (at $p = 0.05$) in each table.
   c. Calculate phi, Cramér's V, and lambda for each table, and comment on which association is stronger.
   d. For each table, describe the form of the association.

3. A researcher hypothesizes that people who believe in life after death are more likely to support the death penalty for serious criminal offenses. But the researcher thinks that this might not be equally true for male and female persons. Data are collected from a nationally representative random sample (note, however, that these results are fictitious), with the following results.

   Among male persons, 450 respondents believed in life after death. Of these, 400 favored the death penalty. Among 75 males who did not believe in life after death, 50 supported the death penalty.

   Among female persons, 450 respondents believed in life after death. Of these, 300 favored the death penalty. Among 125 women who reported that they did not believe in life after death, 100 supported the death penalty.

   a. Prepare two proper cross-tabs (one for men, one for women) to study the relationship between belief in life after death and support for the death penalty.
   b. Determine whether there is a statistically significant association (at $p = 0.05$) in each table.

c. Calculate phi, Cramér's V, and lambda for each table, and comment on which association is stronger.

d. For each table, describe the form of the association.

4. One theory suggests that people who obtain more education are more likely to be knowledgeable about the dangers of certain drugs, and are more likely to support legal regulation of their use. An alternative theory suggests that people who are more educated are more likely to question whether laws for (supposedly) victimless crimes should be eliminated.

   Here is an analysis of data from the General Social Survey, exploring the relationship between education and attitude toward the legalization of the use of marijuana.

Should Marijuana Be Made Legal? * R's Highest Degree Cross-Tabulation

			R's Highest Degree					
			LT High School	**High School**	**Junior College**	**Bachelor's**	**Graduate**	**Total**
Should Marijuana Be Made Legal?	Legal	Count	44	137	13	45	24	263
		% within R's Highest Degree	16.5%	22.0%	25.5%	26.6%	32.0%	22.2%
	Not Legal	Count	201	463	36	116	43	859
		% within R's Highest Degree	75.3%	74.3%	70.6%	68.6%	57.3%	72.5%
	Don't Know	Count	22	23	2	8	8	63
		% within R's Highest Degree	8.2%	3.7%	3.9%	4.7%	10.7%	5.3%
Total		Count	267	623	51	169	75	1,185
		% within R's Highest Degree	100.0%	100.0%	100.0%	100.0%	100.0%	100.0%

Chi-Squared Tests

	Value	*df*	Asymp. Sig. (2-sided)
Pearson chi-squared	23.975	8	0.002
Likelihood ratio	22.905	8	0.003
Linear-by-linear association	0.598	1	0.439
N of valid cases	1,185		

Directional Measures

			Value	Asymp. Std. Error	Approx. T	Approx. Sig.
Nominal by nominal	Lambda	Symmetric	0.000	0.000	.	.
		Should marijuana be made legal? dependent	0.000	0.000	.	.
		R's highest degree dependent	0.000	0.000	.	.
	Goodman and Kruskal tau	Should marijuana be made legal? dependent	0.010	0.005		0.003
		R's highest degree dependent	0.006	0.003		0.000
	Uncertainty coefficient	Symmetric	0.010	0.004	2.361	0.003
		Should marijuana be made legal? dependent	0.013	0.006	2.361	0.003
		R's highest degree dependent	0.008	0.003	2.361	0.003

Symmetric Measures

		Value	Approx. Sig.
Nominal by nominal	Phi	0.142	0.002
	Cramér's V	0.101	0.002
	Contingency coefficient	0.141	0.002
N of valid cases		1,185	

a. State a null hypothesis and alternative hypotheses.

b. Determine whether education and attitude toward legalization are associated at the 95 percent confidence level.

c. If associated, describe the strength of association using one or more appropriate measures of association.
d. If associated, describe the form of the association.
e. Reach a conclusion and comment on your findings.

5. Do racial groups in the United States differ in their access to firearms? Using data from the General Social Survey, we analyzed whether people who self-identified as "white," "black," or "other" race reported that they had a gun in their home. All possible measures of association were calculated (you may not want to use all of these). Here are the results:

Have Gun in Home * Race of Respondent Cross-Tabulation

			Race of Respondent			
			White	**Black**	**Other**	**Total**
Have Gun in Home	**Yes**	Count	211	18	7	236
		Percent within race of respondent	42.3%	22.2%	25.0%	38.8%
	No	Count	288	63	21	372
		Percent within race of respondent	57.7%	77.8%	75.0%	61.2%
Total		Count	499	81	28	608
		Percent within race of respondent	100.0%	100.0%	100.0%	100.0%

Chi-Squared Tests

	Value	***df***	**Asymp. Sig. (2-sided)**
Pearson chi-squared	14.170	2	0.001
Likelihood ratio	15.052	2	0.001
Linear-by-linear association	11.629	1	0.001
N of valid cases	608		

Directional Measures

			Value	**Asymp. Std. Error**	**Approx. T**	**Approx. Sig.**
Nominal by nominal	Lambda	Symmetric	0.000	0.000	.	.

(continued)

			Value	Asymp. Std. Error	Approx. T	Approx. Sig.
		Have gun in home dependent	0.000	0.000	.	.
		Race of respondent dependent	0.000	0.000	.	.
	Goodman and Kruskal tau	Have gun in home dependent	0.023	0.011		0.001
		Race of respondent dependent	0.018	0.009		0.000
		Uncertainty coefficient		Symmetric	0.020	0.010
2.020	0.001					
		Have gun in home dependent	0.019	0.009	2.020	0.001
		Race of respondent dependent	0.022	0.011	2.020	0.001

Symmetric Measures

		Value	Approx. Sig.
Nominal by nominal	Phi	0.153	0.001
	Cramér's V	0.153	0.001
	Contingency coefficient	0.151	0.001
N of valid cases		608	

a. State a null hypothesis and alternative hypotheses.
b. Determine whether the variables are associated at the 95 percent confidence level. (What is your evidence?)
c. If associated, describe the strength of association using one or more appropriate measures of association.
d. If associated, describe the form of the association. (What is your evidence?)
e. Reach a conclusion and comment on your findings.

6. Do our courts of law deal too leniently with criminals? A researcher hypothesizes that opinions on this specific subject differ according to people's general political conservatism. The researcher believes that people who are more politically conservative are more likely to believe that courts do not deal harshly enough with criminals. Using the General Social Survey, a table is prepared to examine the question.

Courts Too Easy on Criminals * Degree of Conservatism Cross-Tabulation

		Degree of Conservatism			Total
		Liberal	Middle of Road	Conservative	
Courts Too Easy on Criminals	Count	250	396	384	1030
	Percent within degree of conservatism	78.6%	86.3%	87.5%	84.7%
About Right	Count	39	42	41	122
	Percent within degree of conservatism	12.3%	9.2%	9.3%	10.0%
Courts Too Harsh on Criminals	Count	29	21	14	64
	Percent within degree of conservativism	9.1%	4.6%	3.2%	5.3%
Total	Count	318	459	439	1,216
	Percent within degree of conservativism	100.0%	100.0%	100.0%	100.0%

Directional Measures

			Value	Asymp. Std. Error	Approx. T	Approx. Sig.
Ordinal by Ordinal	Somers' d	Symmetric	0.079	0.025	3.165	0.002
		Courts too easy dependent	0.056	0.018	3.165	0.002
		Degree of conservatism dependent	0.137	0.042	3.165	0.002

Symmetric Measures

		Value	Asymp. Std. Error	Approx. T	Approx. Sig.
Ordinal by ordinal	Gamma	0.204	0.062	3.165	0.002
N of valid cases		1,216			

a. State a null hypothesis and a research hypothesis for this problem.
b. Which variable is independent, and which is dependent? Why?
c. Are the two variables associated at $p < 0.05$? What is your evidence?
d. Comment on the strength of association and its form. Are the data consistent with the researcher's hypothesis?

7. Do attitudes about capital punishment covary with formal education? Our researcher believes that, due to the liberal bias of educators, the more formal education one gets, the less likely one is to favor capital punishment for murder. Data from the 1998 General Social Survey are used to examine this question.

Oppose or Favor Death Penalty for Murder * R's Highest Degree Cross-Tabulation

Oppose or Favor Death Penalty for Murder			R's Highest Degree					Total
			LT High School	High School	Junior College	Bachelor	Graduate	
	Favor	Count	34	114	17	26	10	201
	Oppose	Count	9	40	3	9	12	73
Total		Count	43	154	20	35	22	274

Directional Measures

			Value	Asymp. Std. Error	Approx. T	Approx. Sig.
Ordinal by ordinal	Somers' d	Symmetric	0.092	0.056	1.628	0.104
		Oppose death penalty dependent	0.074	0.045	1.628	0.104
		Education dependent	0.120	0.073	1.628	0.104

Symmetric Measures

		Value	Asymp. Std. Error	Approx. T	Approx. Sig.
Ordinal by ordinal	Gamma	0.187	0.111	1.628	0.104
N of valid cases		274			

a. State a null and research hypothesis for this problem.
b. Which variable is independent, and which is dependent? Why?
c. Are the two variables significantly associated? What is your evidence?
d. Comment on the strength of association and its form. Are the data consistent with the researcher's hypothesis?

8. The "secularization" hypothesis in the sociology of religion suggests that more formal education tends to lead people to a secular and scientific worldview that lessens attachment to religion. As this occurs, people are less likely to engage in religious behavior, such as attending church services.

   Here is an analysis of data relevant to this hypothesis, from the General Social Survey.

How Often R Attends Religious Services * R's Highest Degree Cross-Tabulation

			RS Highest Degree					Total
			LT High School	High School	Junior College	Bachelor	Graduate	
How Often *R* Attends Religious Services	More Than Once a week	Count	27	54	5	15	11	112
		%	8.2%	6.9%	7.1%	7.4%	10.7%	7.5%
	Every Week	Count	59	162	17	42	19	299
		%	17.9%	20.6%	24.3%	20.7%	18.4%	20.1%
	Nearly Every Week	Count	20	47	4	16	5	92
		%	6.1%	6.0%	5.7%	7.9%	4.9%	6.2%
	2–3 Times a Month	Count	33	74	9	20	7	143
		%	10.0%	9.4%	12.9%	9.9%	6.8%	9.6%
	Once a Month	Count	12	56	7	21	9	105
		%	3.6%	7.1%	10.0%	10.3%	8.7%	7.0%
	Several Times a year	Count	40	89	10	24	15	178
		%	12.2%	11.3%	14.3%	11.8%	14.6%	11.9%
	Once a Year	Count	35	113	5	21	14	188
		%	10.6%	14.4%	7.1%	10.3%	13.6%	12.6%
	LT Once a Year	Count	30	76	5	14	4	129
		%	9.1%	9.7%	7.1%	6.9%	3.9%	8.7%
	Never	Count	73	115	8	30	19	245
		%	22.2%	14.6%	11.4%	14.8%	18.4%	16.4%
Total		Count	329	786	70	203	103	1,491
		%	100.0%	100.0%	100.0%	100.0%	100.0%	100.0%

Directional Measures

			Value	Asymp. Std. Error	Approx. T	Approx. Sig.
Ordinal by ordinal	Somers' d	Symmetric	0.045	0.021	2.106	0.035
		How often R attends religious services dependent	0.052	0.025	2.106	0.035
		R's highest degree dependent	0.039	0.019	2.106	0.035

Symmetric Measures

		Value	Asymp. Std. Error	Approx. T	Approx. Sig.
Ordinal by ordinal	Kendall's tau-b	0.045	0.021	2.106	0.035
	Kendall's tau-c	0.042	0.020	2.106	0.035
	Gamma	0.060	0.029	2.106	0.035
N of valid cases		1,491			

a. State the null and alternative hypotheses.
b. Characterize the strength, form, and statistical significance of the association.
c. Describe the form of the relationship.
d. Provide a brief conclusion: Is the secularization hypothesis supported?

9. One researcher argues that people with conservative political ideologies tend to place high value on individual freedom, and are likely to oppose all governmental regulation of individuals' behavior. Another researcher argues that conservative ideology is associated with the use of public policy to criminalize the behavior of those who are not members of the dominant groups in society.

   The question of legalization of marijuana would seem to be a good test case for seeing whether there is a relationship, and if so what kind of relationship, between ideological conservativism and the regulation of a social behavior that is less common among the elite classes. Here are some data from the 1998 General Social Survey, and an analysis with measures of association.

Should Marijuana Be Made Legal? * Think of Self as Conservative Cross-Tabulation

		Think of Self as Conservative							
Should Marijuana be Made Legal?		**Extremely Liberal**	**Liberal**	**Slightly Liberal**	**Moderate**	**Slightly Conservative**	**Conservative**	**Extremely Conservative**	**Total**
Legal	Count	4	5	9	11	6	3	1	39
	% within Think of Self as Conservative	80.0%	38.5%	45.0%	16.9%	23.1%	10.7%	25.0%	24.2%
Not Legal	Count	1	8	11	54	20	25	3	122
	% within Think of Self as Conservative	20.0%	61.5%	55.0%	83.1%	76.9%	89.3%	75.0%	75.8%
Total	Count	5	13	20	65	26	28	4	161
	% within Think of Self as Conservative	100.0%	100.0%	100.0%	100.0%	100.0%	100.0%	100.0%	100.0%

Chi-Squared Tests

	Value	*df*	Asymp. Sig. (2-sided)
Pearson chi-squared	19.304	6	0.004
Likelihood ratio	17.657	6	0.007
Linear-by-linear association	10.966	1	0.001
N of valid cases	161		

Directional Measures

			Value	Asymp. Std. Error	Approx. T	Approx. Sig.
Ordinal by ordinal	Somers' d	Symmetric	0.209	0.067	2.987	0.003
		Should marijuana be made legal? dependent	0.155	0.051	2.987	0.003
		Think of self as conservative dependent	0.320	0.103	2.987	0.003

Symmetric Measures

		Value	Asymp. Std. Error	Approx. T	Approx. Sig.
Ordinal by ordinal	Kendall's tau-b	0.223	0.072	2.987	0.003
	Kendall's tau-c	0.235	0.079	2.987	0.003
	Gamma	0.398	0.124	2.987	0.003
N of valid cases		161			

a. State the null and alternative hypotheses.
b. Characterize the strength, form, and statistical significance of the association.
c. Describe the form of the relationship.
d. Provide a brief conclusion: Which (if either) of our two researchers seems to be supported by the data?

10. Why do fertility rates differ from one society to another? One theory suggests that there is a connection between the survival rate of infants and the number of children that women bear: where infant death rates are high, women are likely to have more children.

    Here are data on the infant mortality rates and average fertility in 20 nations or regions during the mid-1990s. We want to know whether there is a relationship between the two variables. Since we are not sure about the relationship being linear, we have decided to use Spearman's rho (rank-order) correlation coefficient.

National Demographics ca. 1995

	Country or Region	Deaths, Age 0–1 per 1,000 Live Births	Average # of Children per Woman
1	Gaza Strip	33.00	7.50
2	Oman	27.00	7.00
3	Saudi Arabia	29.00	6.20
4	Maldives	30.00	6.60
5	Jordan	34.00	5.40
6	Solomon Islands	28.00	5.30
7	Libya	62.00	6.20
8	Syria	35.00	5.70
9	Comoros	77.00	6.90
10	Liberia	108.00	6.70
11	Iraq	127.00	5.60
12	Yemen	77.00	7.50
13	Paraguay	27.00	4.20
14	Tajikistan	32.00	4.80
15	Qatar	12.00	4.20
16	Togo	195.00	6.40
17	West Bank	27.00	4.40
18	United Arab Emirates	11.00	4.10
19	Ethiopia	128.00	6.90
20	Benin	94.00	7.00
Total	20		

a. Calculate rho.

b. Briefly interpret rho to inform us about the strength and form of the association between fertility and infant mortality.

11. A researcher studying modernization and development of nations in the world system believes that nations that rank high on urbanism (percent of people living in cities) are also likely to rank high on literacy (percent of the population who can read). Here are some data on 20 nations to examine this question.

Literacy and Urbanism 1995

	Country	People Who Read (%)	People Living in Cities (%)
1	Afghanistan	29	18
2	Argentina	95	86
3	Armenia	98	68
4	Australia	100	85

	Country	People Who Read (%)	People Living in Cities (%)
5	Austria	99	58
6	Azerbaijan	98	54
7	Bahrain	77	83
8	Bangladesh	35	16
9	Barbados	99	45
10	Belarus	99	65
11	Belgium	99	96
12	Bolivia	78	51
13	Bosnia	86	36
14	Botswana	72	25
15	Brazil	81	75
16	Bulgaria	93	68
17	Burkina Faso	18	15
18	Burundi	50	5
19	Cambodia	35	12
20	Cameroon	54	40
Total	20		

a. Calculate rho.

b. Briefly interpret rho to inform us about the strength and form of the association between literacy and urbanism.

Chapter 13

Association of Interval/Ratio Variables

LEARNING OBJECTIVES

When you have finished this chapter, you will be able to:

- Prepare a proper scatter plot.
- See positive and negative linear association and nonlinear association. You will be able to see strong and weak association in a scatter plot.
- Understand the Pearson zero-order product-moment correlation coefficient (r) and understand how it is used to test for linear association.
- Understand and interpret the coefficient of determination (R^2) as a measure of the strength of linear association.
- Interpret the linear regression equation to describe the association between two interval/ratio variables.

VISUALIZING INTERVAL/RATIO ASSOCIATION

With nominal variables, association means that certain kinds of X's tend to also be certain kinds of Y's. With ordinal variables, association means that if a case ranks higher than another on X, we can make a prediction that it will rank higher than the second on Y (positive association) or that the first case will rank lower on Y than the second (negative association).

If we have measured both X and Y on interval/ratio scales, we can go even further in describing association. If two interval/ratio variables are associated, we can say that each unit of X is associated with a specific amount of increase (or decrease) on Y. For example, a study might find that each additional year of education (X) is associated with an increase of $2,550 in annual income ($Y$).

Table 13.1 shows the relationship between two variables that describe the level of living in nations of the world: life expectancy at birth and infant mortality rates. One would reasonably hypothesize that high life expectancy and low infant mortality would tend to go together: the higher the score on one, the lower the score on the other; that is, there is expected to be a negative relationship between these two variables.

In Table 13.1, the two variables are treated as grouped ordinal variables. Life expectancy has been characterized as "very low," "low," "average," "high," or "very high." Infant mortality has been ranked as "low," "moderate," "high," or "very high."

There is clearly a negative ordinal association between these two variables, which we can see by noting the relatively large number of cases toward the upper left and lower right cells. If we used statistics to measure association, we would find that gamma $= -0.974$ and tau-b $= -0.775$ for this table (both significant at $p < 0.01$).

While an ordinal-by-ordinal table is a valid and useful way to examine this relationship, we can do better. The data were actually collected at the interval/ratio level—that is, the actual numbers of infant deaths per 100 live births was measured; the actual number of years of life expectancy were measured. While it's not wrong to collapse the data into categories like "very high" life expectancy, we are not taking full advantage of the information available.

TABLE 13.1 Ordinal Association of Infant Mortality and Life Expectancy

Infant Mortality by Life Expectancy, World Nations during Mid-1990s							
		Life Expectancy					
		Very Low	**Low**	**Average**	**High**	**Very High**	**Total**
Infant Mortality	Very high		4	1			5
	High	1	16	3	1		21
	Moderate	1	6	20	12		39
	Low				37	69	106
Total		2	26	24	50	69	171

FIGURE 13.1 Interval/Ratio Association of Infant Mortality and Life Expectancy

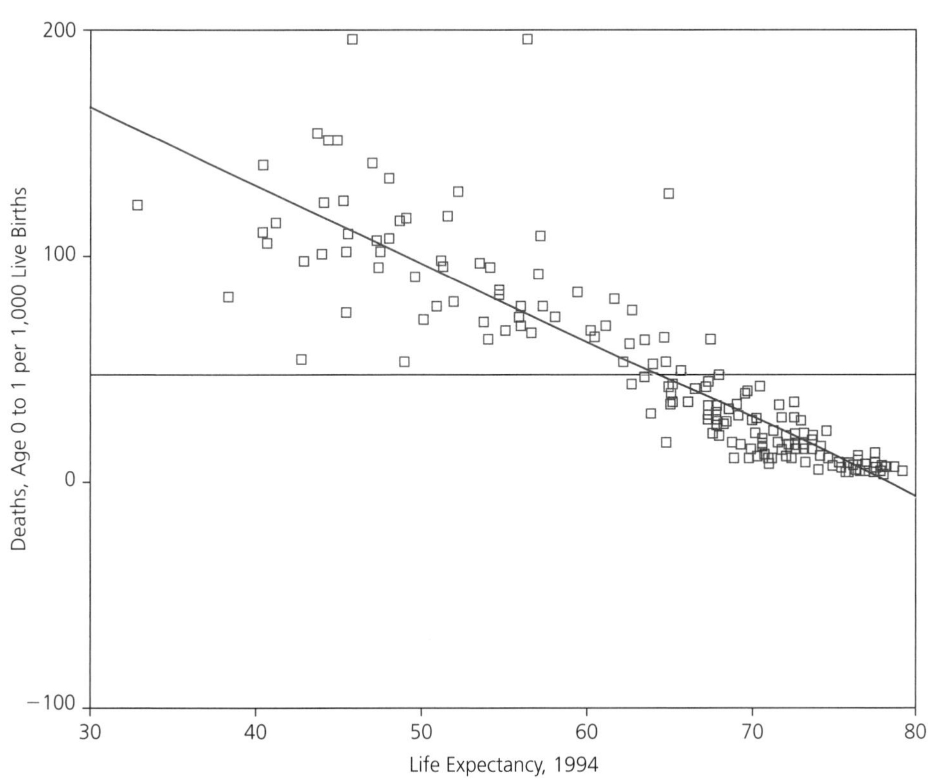

The 69 nations that have "very high" life expectancy do not all have the exact same life expectancy (actually, the values in the "very high" category are between 70 and 80 years).

Instead of grouping the values on X and Y, why not present the actual values? The graphic in Figure 13.1, called a scatter plot, does exactly that. Rather than grouping the cases into categories and counting them, a symbol is placed on the axes to reflect that actual exact scores of each case on X and Y (we'll talk about scatter plots in more detail in the next section).

If we took the scatter plot, drew grid lines on it for both X and Y, and then counted up the numbers of dots in each resulting square, we would have exactly the cross-tab that we presented in Table 13.1. The scatter plot is exactly the same as an ordinal cross-tab, but presents the exact ratio/interval values of X and Y.

In the next section we will discuss constructing and interpreting scatter plots that display the relationship between two interval/ratio variables. Following that, we will learn to answer our questions about association (are the variables associated? how strongly? what is the form of the relationship?) using statistical tools that take advantage of the additional information available when variables are measured at the interval/ratio level.

The tools that we will study in this chapter, linear correlation and regression, are particularly important to master. Most intermediate and advanced statistics use these tools extensively. So, while you may find the ideas in this chapter a bit challenging, it is worth the effort to master them.

Preparing a Scatter Plot

The best tool for visualizing the relationship between two interval/ratio variables is the ***scatter plot (aka scattergram)***. This very simple graphic is usually all that we need to see the strength and form of the relationship and whether the assumptions that we need to make to use correlation and regression analysis are satisfied.

A good scatter plot follows all the rules of a good cross-tabulation for nominal variables: it should have a title, axis labels, and explanatory notes that describe the source of the data and any changes that were made to the data. If we are interested in an asymmetric relationship (i.e., one variable is independent, the other dependent), then the independent variable is displayed along the horizontal (X) x-axis, and the dependent variable is displayed along the vertical (Y) y-axis.

A good scatter plot follows the additional rules for an ordinal cross-tabulation, as well. The values of X should be arrayed as increasing from left to right; the values of Y should be arrayed as increasing from the bottom to the top.

Because interval/ratio variables give us the exact score of each case on X and Y—rather than grouping these scores into categories—there are a few additional rules:

First, the scales along both the x-axis and the y-axis need to be graphed with equal intervals. That is, the space between, say, the values of 10 and 20 needs to be identical to the space between, say, 80 and 90. This may seem obvious, but using nonequal intervals for X and Y can distort and misrepresent the relationship.

Second, if possible, the scatter plot should include the "origin." The origin is the point where both the dependent and independent variables have the value of zero. If X and Y have negative, as well as positive values, it is helpful for the scatter plot to include reference lines that show $X = 0$ and $Y = 0$. Sometimes the values of X and/or Y that we are interested in are quite far away from zero. If this is the case, the graphic should make clear that the x-axis and y-axis of the scatter plot are not drawn at zero; this can be done by clear labeling of the values along the axes and, sometimes, by including a break in the axis line.

There are a couple of optional things that are sometimes done with scatter plots that can be very helpful in aiding interpretation.

Sometimes lines are added to the scatter plot to show the mean score on Y and/or X. In Figure 13.1, we've added a horizontal line at the mean score on the dependent variable.

This line can be a useful reference point to help identify the typical *X* scores of cases that are low (below the mean) or high (above the mean) on *Y*.

Sometimes we may have two or more kinds of cases. Using different symbols or colors for points in the scatter plot can be helpful in examining whether the same relationship between *X* and *Y* holds for different groups of cases. For example, we might want to identify all Asian nations in the graphic with blue squares instead of red used for the other nations. Statistical and spreadsheet software has built-in tools for creating scatter plots, and has many useful options.

Seeing Association in a Scatter Plot

Sometimes it is useful to add another line to the scatter plot—the "regression line" that we will discuss in some detail in a later section. We've added the regression line to the scatter plot in Figure 13.1—it is the downward-sloping line from the upper left to the lower right. The regression line is drawn in such a way that it comes as close as possible to all of the data points.

The regression line lets us quickly see if the relationship is positive or negative (does it slope upward or downward?). A negative or downward slope as we move from left to right tells us that, generally, as scores on *X* increase, scores on *Y* tend to decrease. A positive or upward slope indicates that the average scores on *Y* tend to get larger as *X* gets larger.

The regression line can also tell us how big the effect of *X* on *Y* is. In the plot, for example, when life expectancy goes up by 10 years, infant mortality goes down by about 35 deaths per thousand live births (compare the *Y* value of the regression line for any two points 10 years apart on life expectancy). If the regression line slopes sharply upward or downward, then small changes in *X* are associated with large changes or differences in *Y* (*X* has a large effect on *Y*). If the regression line is flat (i.e., parallel to the *X* axis), that means that *X* has no effect on *Y*, because changes in *X* are not associated with any difference or change in *Y*.

The scatter plot can also give us a feel for whether the relationship between *Y* and *X* is weak, moderate, or strong. What would the scatter plot look like if the relationship between *Y* and *X* was perfect? A perfect relationship means that, if I know *X*, I can predict *Y* without error. In correlation and regression analysis, this means that all of the points in the scatter plot fall right on a single straight line. That is, when all of the points in the scatter plot fall exactly on the regression line, the relationship is perfect.

What would the scatter plot look like if there were no relationship at all between *Y* and *X*? No association means that knowing *X* does not reduce uncertainty or error in predicting *Y*. If the points are, on average, far away from the regression line, predictions about any one case will be quite inaccurate—even though there may be an overall relationship. Very weak relationships between *Y* and *X*, then, can be seen as random "clouds" of points in the scatter plot.

Most relationships in real social science cases (like the earlier example of life expectancy and infant mortality) fall somewhere between "perfect relationship" and "statistical independence." The closer to independence, the more the scatter plot will resemble a circular cloud of points. The closer to a perfect relationship, the more the scatter plot will resemble a simple straight line.

What we can see in a scatter plot—whether there is a strong or weak relationship, whether the relationship is positive or negative, and the size of the effect—can all also be measured with numerical statistics. In the remaining sections of this chapter, we will take a look at these statistics. Before we do, though, there are just a couple more very important things to learn about visualizing interval/ratio-level relationships.

Linear and Nonlinear Association

Take a moment to study the new scatter plot that is shown as Figure 13.2. This one shows the relationship between the dependent variable of infant mortality (deaths in the first year of

FIGURE 13.2 Relationship of Infant Mortality to Education with Linear Regression Line

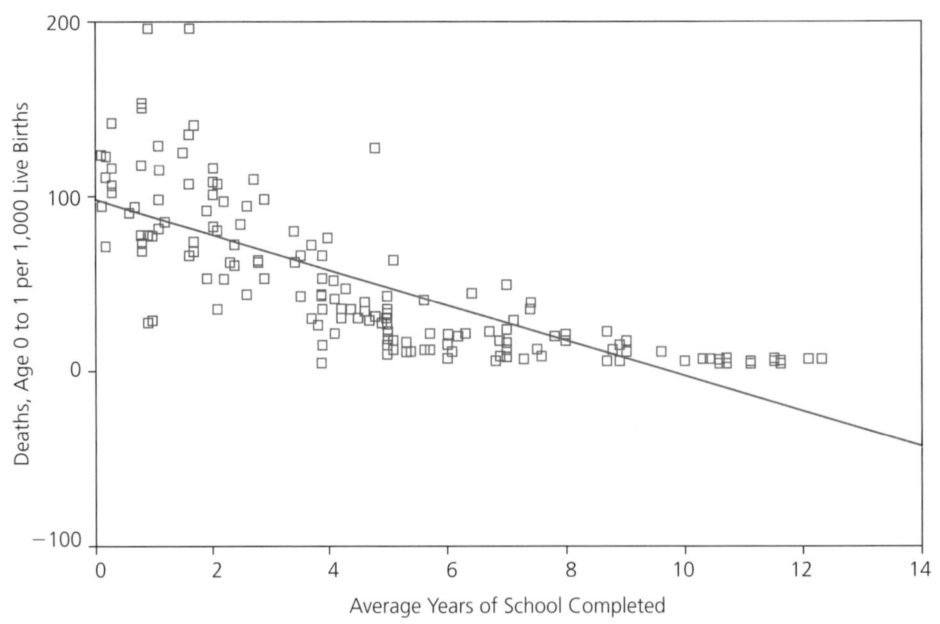

Note: Data from mid-1990s. Clearly, there is a relationship between these two variables—the plot displays a very clear pattern, not a random cloud of points. The relationship is a moderately strong one—the points are, on average, pretty close to the regression line. The relationship is negative: the higher the schooling, the lower the infant mortality.

life per 1,000 live births) and the independent variable of the average years of formal education completed. We've added the regression line to the scatter plot.

Notice, though, that the points are not randomly scattered around the regression line. Most points are above the regression line when education is zero to three years, and when education is eight or more years. When education is between three and eight years, most of the points are below the regression line. If we could draw a curved line rather than a straight one, our line would be a much better description of the scatter plot. We've done just that in Figure 13.3.

The numerical statistics that we will be discussing are called "linear" correlation and regression. That is, they are measures of the strength and form of linear relationships. When the relationship between X and Y is better described by some other kind of curve, linear correlation and regression statistics can be misleading.

In Figure 13.3, also notice that the points are more spread out around the trend line at low levels of education than they are at high education. This is a situation called "heteroscedasticity." Heteroscedasticity doesn't affect the form of the relationship estimated by regression statistics; but it does affect statistical tests of confidence in the existence of the relationship.

FIGURE 13.3 Relationship of Infant Mortality to Education with Nonlinear Regression Line

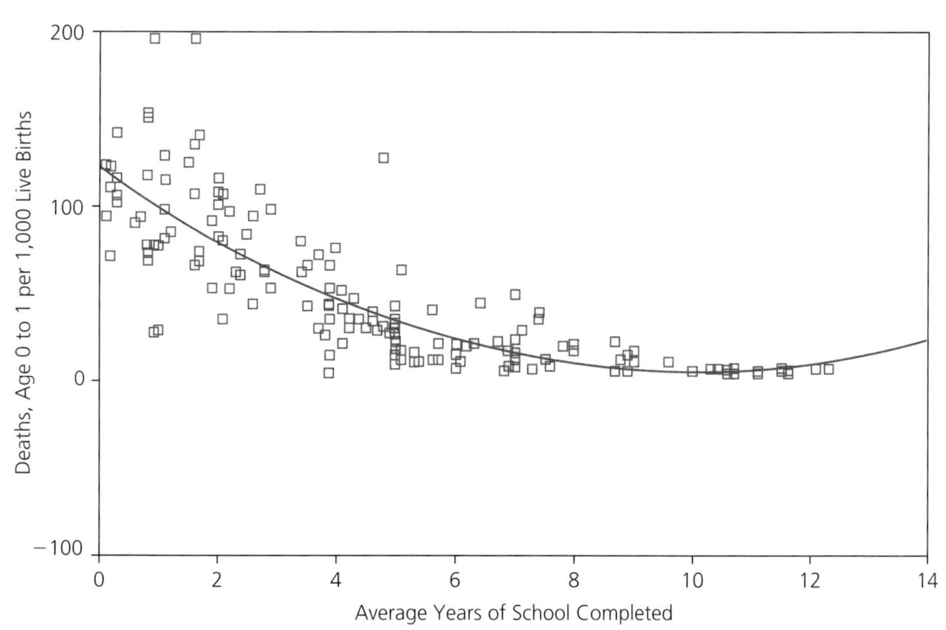

Note: Data from mid-1990s.

CHECK QUIZ 13.1

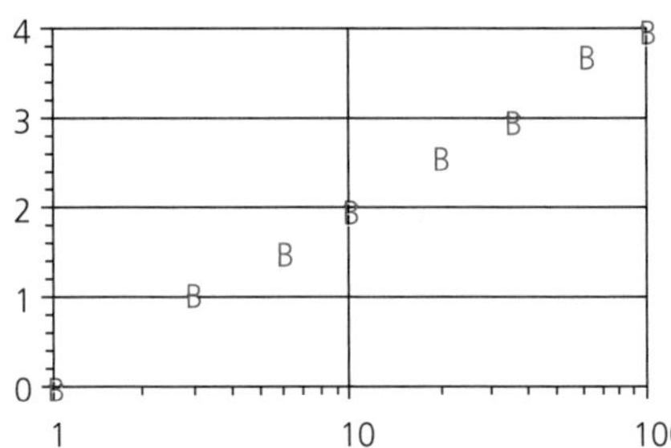

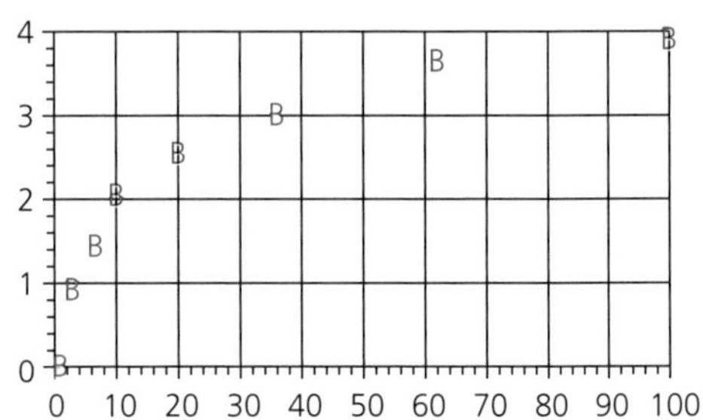

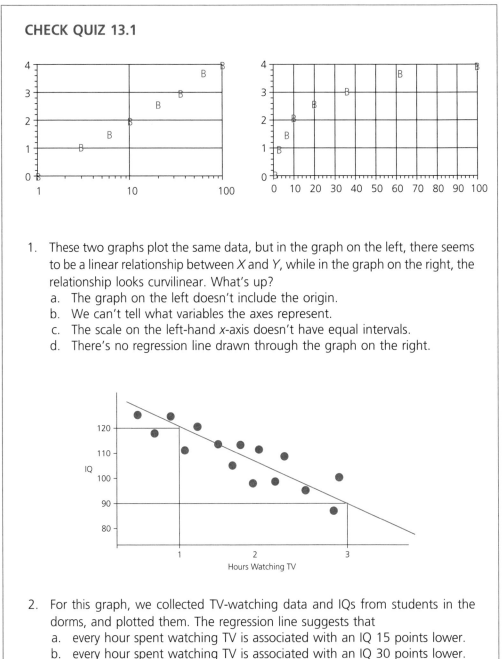

1. These two graphs plot the same data, but in the graph on the left, there seems to be a linear relationship between *X* and *Y*, while in the graph on the right, the relationship looks curvilinear. What's up?
   a. The graph on the left doesn't include the origin.
   b. We can't tell what variables the axes represent.
   c. The scale on the left-hand *x*-axis doesn't have equal intervals.
   d. There's no regression line drawn through the graph on the right.

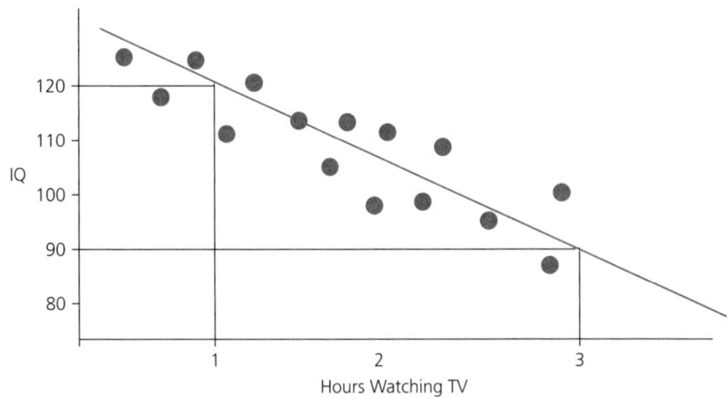

2. For this graph, we collected TV-watching data and IQs from students in the dorms, and plotted them. The regression line suggests that
   a. every hour spent watching TV is associated with an IQ 15 points lower.
   b. every hour spent watching TV is associated with an IQ 30 points lower.
   c. there's no association between TV watching and IQ.
   d. every hour spent watching *The Simpsons* increases IQ by 25 points.

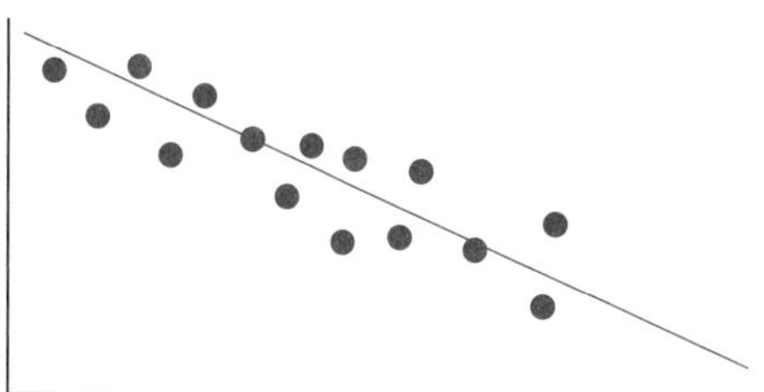

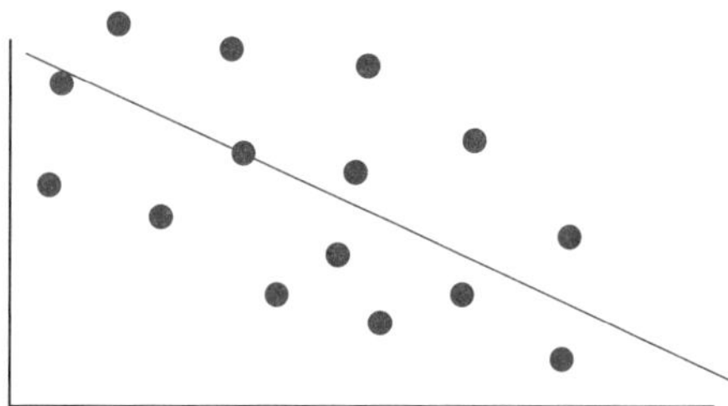

3. These two graphs have the same number of data points, and the regression lines have the same slope, but
   a. the mean value of *Y* is higher for the graph on the left.
   b. the relationship between the two variables is positive in the graph on the left.
   c. the graph on the right suggests a stronger relationship between the two variables than the graph on the left.
   d. there is a stronger relationship between the two variables in the graph on the left.
4. For interval/ratio level variables, the scatter plot is analogous to __________ for nominal- and ordinal-level variables.
   a. chi square
   b. percentages
   c. row marginals
   d. bivariate tables
5. When the values of *Y* are close to the regression line for some values of *X* and far from the regression line for other values of *X*, this is known as
   a. homoscedasticity.
   b. heteroscedasticity.
   c. correlation.
   d. curvilinear relations.
6. Cases far from the regression line are known as
   a. correlates.
   b. obfuscations.
   c. outliers.
   d. outlaws.

The regression line also helps us to see which cases are unusual. Cases that are very far from the regression line are called "outliers." They can be important for several reasons. Unusual cases may be wrong—one should always check out the scores and see if the data are correct. Unusual cases can affect our impression of where the regression line ought to be drawn. Also, outliers may have something in common that will help us to build a better theory. Suppose, for example, that all the positive outliers (points far above the regression line) were Muslim nations (they're not). This insight might lead us to think further about the relationship.

In this section we've seen that the scatter plot can be used to visualize all the important things about the strength and form of associations between two interval/ratio variables. You should always visualize the data before computing numerical statistics.

Take a minute to be sure that you've mastered the ideas here by taking the check quiz. When you're ready, we can move on to discuss the process of using numerical statistics to test statistical significance, define index strength, and describe the form of the relationship between interval/ratio variables.

SIGNIFICANCE TESTING FOR INTERVAL/RATIO ASSOCIATION

When we examine the scatter plot, we may see a pattern of linear association. Usually the data we are examining, though, are from a sample. Before we get too serious about describing the strength and form of the association, we need to be confident that the association exists in the population.

There is a commonly used approach to assess the confidence that we have in inferring a linear association between X and Y in a population on the basis of the information in a sample. After being clear about the null and research hypotheses, checking some very important assumptions, and setting a standard for acceptable confidence or error, the Pearson zero-order product-moment correlation coefficient is calculated. Then a test statistic is calculated and compared to the values of the t-distribution to decide whether to accept or reject the null hypothesis.

Null Hypothesis

The Pearson correlation coefficient is a multipurpose measure of linear association for interval/ratio data. We will examine it in detail as a measure of the strength and form of the relationship. Another one of its roles is to act as our criterion to assess our confidence that two variables are really associated in the population.

In studying the association between two interval/ratio variables, our research hypotheses almost always suggest reasons why we would expect X and Y to be associated. Of course, we never directly test the research hypothesis that two variables are associated; we try to reject the opposite notion, that they are independent. The null hypothesis that almost always interests us is:

$$H_0 : r_{xy} = 0$$

That is, in the whole population from which we drew our sample, the variables *X* and *Y* do not have any linear relationship. Or, if we had done a census and calculated Pearson's correlation coefficient (r_{xy}), it would have the value of zero. It is possible to test other null hypotheses (e.g., $r_{xy} = 0.25$), but this is so uncommon that almost all statistical software assumes that the null hypothesis value of r_{xy} is zero.

Alternative Hypotheses

The correlation coefficient is a measure of linear interval/ratio association, so it indexes both the direction and the amount of statistical association between *X* and *Y*. Usually our research and theory have led us to believe that the association between *X* and *Y* is either positive or negative (it can't be both!).

$$H_a : r_{xy} > 0 \text{ or } H_a : r_{xy} < 0$$

These are one-tailed alternative hypotheses. Of course, there is also an "alternative" alternative two-tailed hypothesis:

$$H_a : r_{xy} \neq 0$$

This states that we believe *X* and *Y* are associated, but we don't want to assert that the association is positive or that it is negative. Such a two-tailed alternative hypothesis is rare. But be careful, because statistical software usually prints the significance level for the two-tailed test; most often, you will want to divide it by 2 to find the *p*-level of the one-tailed test.

Assumptions

The assumptions of the significance test for correlation coefficients are quite important. The Pearson correlation coefficient turns out to be a very powerful tool, but—like other power tools—it can cause a lot of damage if not used properly!

We assume that both *X* and *Y* are measured at the interval/ratio level. If either *X* or *Y* is not interval/ratio, the Pearson correlation coefficient is simply not a valid measure of association, and our statistical test is meaningless.

Another important assumption is that the univariate distributions of both *X* and *Y* are (approximately) normal. This ***normality assumption*** is best tested by doing univariate statistics before looking at correlation and regression. Look to see that the distributions of *X* and *Y* are roughly bell-shaped (there are also statistical tests of normality that can sometimes be of use in large samples). Look also for outliers. In small samples, a few cases with extreme values can greatly influence the test statistic. Look also to be sure that both *X* and *Y* have a reasonable amount of variation (the coefficient of variation should be at least 20). And be sure that neither *X* nor *Y* has "floors" or "ceilings"—lower or upper limiting values that cause the scores to bunch up near the ends of the distribution.

Checking for normality in sample data is very important, because the correlation coefficient, regression line, and statistical significance tests can all be affected by violating the normality assumption. The good news, though, is that the violation of normality usually has to be pretty extreme (at least in large samples) before we are seriously misled.

The bad news is that many social science interval/ratio variables are just not normally distributed! Frequently it is necessary to transform either *X* or *Y* or both by taking a logarithm, calculating an inverse or square root, or applying some other function to make the distribution more normal. We won't discuss this matter further in this text. But, check this assumption—and if you have obvious departures from normality, consult an expert!

Probably the most important assumption is that the relationship between *X* and *Y* that we are studying is linear. That is, any unit change in *X*, regardless of the level on *X*, is associated with the same amount of change in *Y*. This ***linearity assumption*** is critical because Pearson's correlation coefficient and the regression line are measures of linear association only. If *X* and *Y* are associated in a nonlinear way (as in Figure 13.3), the correlation coefficient and regression line may be quite poor descriptions of the strength and form of association (and also of the significance).

The good news about the linearity assumption is that correlation and regression are quite robust (give pretty much correct answers most of the time) even when the relationship between *X* and *Y* is modestly nonlinear. There are ways of directly testing whether the relationship between *X* and *Y* is significantly nonlinear, which we won't discuss in this text. Generally, though, if you cannot see nonlinearity in a scatter plot, you are likely to be okay. Another item of good news is that it is often possible to fix nonlinearity (as well as nonnormality) by transforming *X* or *Y* or both with simple functions like logs, inverses, powers, and the like.

The last important assumption about the relationship between *X* and *Y* is the ***homoscedasticity assumption***. That is, the relative dispersion in scores on *Y* is about the same across all levels of *X*. In Figures 13.2 and 13.3, we see an example of the violation of this assumption. The scores on infant mortality (*Y*) are much more widely scattered around the regression line at low levels of education (*X*) than they are at high levels of education.

Violating the homoscedasticity assumption is mostly important with regard to prediction with the regression line, which we discuss in Chapter 14. The good news here is that looking at the scatter plot will usually diagnose this problem (again, there are additional statistical tests for this that we won't discuss here). And often transformations that solve other problems of nonnormal distributions or nonlinear relationships have the side benefit of also fixing heteroscedasticity.

That's a lot of assumptions! With correlation and regression, you need to spend some time with univariate analyses and scatter plots to test them. Once you have done this, it is relatively easy to test significance, and to describe the form and strength of association.

Selecting an Error Level

There is nothing new or different in thinking about selecting a type I error, alpha, or p-level for our significance test. The most common selection is 95 percent confidence or $p < 0.05$. There are circumstances, of course, when greater confidence is needed, or more error is acceptable.

Calculating the Test Statistic

To test the null hypothesis, the test statistic in Formula 13.1 is constructed.

$$t_r = r\sqrt{\frac{N-2}{1-r^2}} \tag{13.1}$$

The test statistic takes the value of Pearson's correlation coefficient (r) actually observed in the sample, and corrects it for the estimated sampling variability. We discuss the correlation coefficient in more detail later in this chapter. The estimated sampling variability of the correlation coefficient decreases with increasing sample size (note the N in the numerator of the standard error portion of the formula). The estimated sampling variability of the correlation coefficient also decreases as the strength of the correlation increases—that is, as the residual variation decreases.

The test statistic is distributed according to the t-distribution with $N - 2$ degrees of freedom. As you know by now, when sample sizes become reasonably large (say over 100 cases) the t-distribution and Z distribution are very similar.

You will probably never calculate this test by hand; it is built into all statistical software. Still, it is important to understand that the test statistic for hypotheses about the correlation coefficient has the same logic as all the others that we've examined. We are comparing the size of the deviation from the null hypothesis (i.e., the observed correlation coefficient less the null hypothesis that it is zero) to the estimated sampling variability in the statistic. The bigger the test statistic, as always, the more likely the null hypothesis is wrong, and the more confident we can be in rejecting the null hypothesis of no association.

Making a Decision

Testing statistical significance should be very familiar by now (probably too familiar!). The p or alpha level, type I error, or significance level guides us to reject the null hypothesis or to fail to reject it—as always.

If we fail to reject the null hypothesis, we're finished. We need to go back to the drawing board and consider why we have this outcome. Is our theory or research hypothesis really wrong? Did we get a biased sample? Did we fail to measure X or Y with reliable and valid instruments? In deciding to accept the null hypothesis, also give a moment's thought to the assumptions built into using the correlation coefficient as our measure of interval/ratio association. Are X and Y approximately normally distributed? Is the relationship between X and Y linear?

If there is a significant association, we can turn our attention to measuring its strength and form. These are the tasks we'll take up in the next sections.

Before we do, take the quick check quiz to see that you've mastered the ideas of the t-test as an inference test about the linear correlation between two interval/ratio variables.

CHECK QUIZ 13.2

1. Pearson's r tells us the strength and direction of association; the associated t-test tells us
   a. whether the variables are likely correlated with one another in the population.
   b. how often a correlation of that size might be expected to appear in the population.
   c. whether the variances have gotten too large.
   d. what the direction of association is (positive? negative?).
2. Which of these is not an important assumption for the statistical test of the significance of the Pearson correlation coefficient?
   a. linear relationship between X and Y
   b. normally distributed X and Y
   c. interval/ratio measurement of X and Y
   d. All of these are important assumptions.
3. When testing Pearson's r for significance, the null hypothesis is that
   a. there is no difference between the variables in the population from which the sample was drawn.
   b. there is no linear association between the variables in the population from which the sample was drawn.
   c. there is no difference between the sample and the population from which the sample was drawn.
   d. $r = 1.0$.
4. If the test of significance for a Pearson's r calculated from sample data fails to reject the null hypothesis, we assume that
   a. the association is not really there.
   b. no inference can be made about the relationship of the two variables in the population.
   c. the relationship exists but its direction and strength are unknown.
   d. the variables are related in the population.

Strength of Interval/Ratio Association

The ***Pearson zero-order product moment correlation coefficient*** has such a long name that nearly everyone calls it "*r*" or "***little r***." Little *r* is a measure of the direction and strength of linear association between two interval/ratio variables. It has the value of −1.0 for a perfect negative association, 0 for independence, and +1.0 for a perfect positive association. Even though it looks like a proportional reduction in error (PRE) measure, it is not (more on this shortly).

The Pearson correlation coefficient has a somewhat complicated formula (see Formula 13.2). There is no need to memorize the formula, but there are a couple of things about it that are worth noting.

$$r = \frac{\sum (x_i - \overline{X})(y_i - \overline{Y})}{\sqrt{\left[\sum (x_i - \overline{X})^2 \sum (y_i - \overline{Y})^2\right]}} \tag{13.2}$$

The numerator of the formula instructs us to first take the deviations of each case's *X* score from the mean of *X* and each case's *Y* score from the mean of *Y*. We are then instructed to multiply these "mean deviations" and sum the results. Suppose that Fred had a score on *X* that was above average and a score on *Y* that was below average. The *X*-deviation for Fred would be positive, the *Y*-deviation would be negative, and the product of the two would be negative. When Fred's scores are "discordant" (one is above the mean and the other is below the mean) the "cross product" of the deviations will be negative. When Fred's scores on "concordant" (scores on *X* and *Y* are either both above the mean or both below the mean), the cross product will be positive.

The numerator of the Pearson correlation coefficient is logically very similar to measures of ordinal association—except that the actual amount of positive or negative deviation (rather than just ranks) is counted. So, the greater the concordance of *X* and *Y* scores, on average across all the cases, the bigger the numerator in Formula 13.2 and the more positive the correlation coefficient. Since we have centered both *X* and *Y* on zero (by expressing them as deviations from their means), the numerator of the correlation will be zero when there is no association, an increasingly large negative number when there is a negative linear association, and an increasingly large positive number when there is a positive association between *X* and *Y*.

The denominator of the correlation formula is pretty complex. Basically, however, it measures the total amount of variation in both *X* and in *Y*. The correlation, then, is a measure of the "covariation" of *X* and *Y* (the numerator) to the total variation in *X* and *Y*. If all of the variation is "in common," the correlation will be +1.00 or −1.00. If none of the variability in X goes with the variability in Y, the covariation will be zero, and the correlation will be zero.

So, the Pearson correlation gives us a descriptive statistic measuring the strength and direction of linear association between X and Y in our sample. We can use the value of r to test the inference that there is also a correlation in the population from which the sample was drawn.

Little r is *not* a proportional reduction in error measure of the strength of association. A value of -1 does mean perfect negative association, a value of $+1$ does mean perfect positive association, and a value of zero does mean there is no association. However, the values of little r cannot be interpreted as the percentage of reduction in error or uncertainty in predicting Y knowing X versus not knowing X. This is a drawback.

Fortunately, there is a very easy solution. When the Pearson zero-order product-moment correlation coefficient (little r) is squared, it becomes a measure of association called the *coefficient of determination*, which does have a proportional reduction in error interpretation (see Formula 13.3).

$$R^2 = r \times r \tag{13.3}$$

The ***coefficient of determination*** is also known as "***big R-squared.***" It seems rather silly to have a special name of "big" R-squared when the coefficient is mathematically equal to little r, squared. The reason for this is that the coefficient of determination is also used in more complicated statistical procedures involving more than one X being used to predict Y. When there is only one X, as in the problems we are discussing, little r-squared has the same value as big R-squared.

The coefficient of determination does have a PRE interpretation. If $R^2 = 0.50$, we can say that knowing a person's score on X helps to reduce error in predicting his or her score on Y by 50 percent, compared to not knowing the person's score on X. This is a bit awkward, so most statisticians use the language "X accounts for 50 percent of the variance in Y" or even "X explains 50 percent of the variance in Y."

The coefficient of variation has a minimum possible value of zero, which happens when little r is zero. Big R-squared has a maximum value of $+1$ when little r is either -1 or $+1$. So the coefficient of determination tells us the strength of the association, but not whether the association is positive or negative.

So, we need to talk a bit more about describing the form of linear association between two interval/ratio variables. We'll do this in the next section. But first check your mastery of little r and big R-squared, and look at an example of how the Pearson correlation is calculated and interpreted.

CHECK QUIZ 13.3

1. The Pearson zero-order correlation coefficient is also known as
   a. big *P*.
   b. little *p*.
   c. big PZOCC.
   d. little *r*.
2. The formula for computing Pearson's zero-order correlation coefficient produces a number that gets larger in absolute value when
   a. the two variables are associated.
   b. there are fewer cases.
   c. the variances of the two variables are large.
   d. the standard deviations get larger.
3. Little *r* ranges from
   a. 0 to 1.
   b. 1 to 100.
   c. −1 to +1.
   d. 0 to infinity.
4. Big *R*-squared is also known as
   a. the coefficient of alienation.
   b. the coefficient of determination.
   c. the correlation coefficient.
   d. the residual correlation.
5. The coefficient of determination
   a. is a PRE measure of the strength of association.
   b. has the value of −1 or +1 when there is perfect association.
   c. tests whether *X* and *Y* are associated.
   d. tells us whether *X* and *Y* have a positive or negative association.
6. The coefficient of determination ranges from
   a. 0 to 1.
   b. 1 to 100.
   c. −1 to +1.
   d. 0 to infinity.

CALCULATING THE PEARSON CORRELATION COEFFICIENT

Example

Figure 13.4 shows a scatter plot of the relationship between the rate of property crimes in U.S. states in 1995 and rates of unemployment in 1996. Deprivation theory might

(*continued*)

Example

FIGURE 13.4 Property Crime Rates by Unemployment Rates in the United States

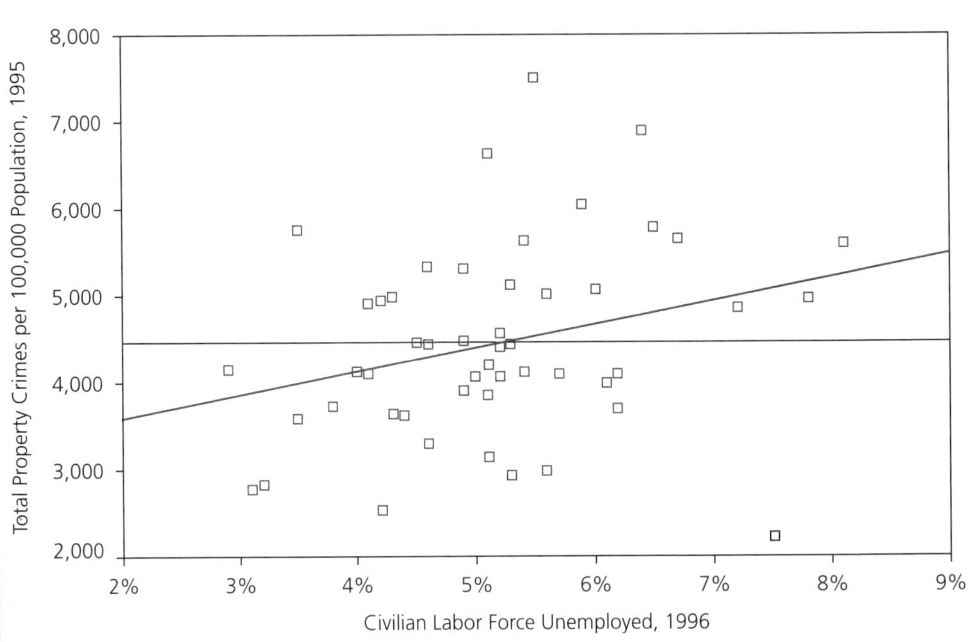

suggest the research hypothesis that higher property crime rates will be observed in states with higher unemployment rates.

The plot and the positive slope of the regression line suggest a modest positive relationship that would be consistent with our research hypothesis. But we want to test the reliability of this result by calculating a significance test.

The first step is to calculate the Pearson correlation coefficient. Recall Formula 13.2:

$$r = \frac{\sum (x_i - \overline{X})(y_i - \overline{Y})}{\sqrt{\left[\sum (x_i - \overline{X})^2 \sum (y_i - \overline{Y})^2\right]}} \tag{13.2}$$

Using a spreadsheet (see Table 13.2), we first record the score on X (unemployment) and Y (crimes per 100,000 population) for each case. Next, we calculate the sample mean score on X and the sample mean score on Y (last row of the table).

Example

TABLE 13.2 Spreadsheet Calculations for the Relationship of Property Crime and Unemployment Rates (Partial Listing)

State	Unemployment	Crime Rate	Xdev	Xdevsq	Ydev	Ydevsq	*XY*
Maine	5.1	3,153	0.0	0.00	−1,310	1,716,100	0.0
New Hampshire	4.2	2,541	−0.9	0.81	−1,922	3,694,084	1,729.8
Vermont	4.6	3,315	−0.5	0.25	−1,148	1,317,904	574.0
Massachusetts	4.3	3,654	−0.8	0.64	−809	654,481	647.2
.	.	.	.	.	.	.	.
.	.	.	.	.	.	.	.
.	.	.	.	.	.	.	.
California	7.2	4,856	2.1	4.41	393	154,449	825.3
Alaska	7.8	4,983	2.7	7.29	520	270,400	1,404.0
Hawaii	6.4	6,903	1.3	1.69	2,440	5,953,600	3,172.0
Mean/sum	5.1	4,463		65.99		60,385,981	17,798.5

We then subtract the mean unemployment rate from each case's rate (Xdev). Next, we square each case's deviation (Xdevsq). The deviation of each case from the mean of *Y* (Ydev) and the square of each case's deviation (Ydevsq) are then calculated. Sums for the squared deviations are shown in the last row. Finally, we multiply the *X* deviation times the *Y* deviation for each case (*XY*) and sum this column.

Having done all these calculations, we can plug the results into Formula 13.2.

The numerator of the correlation is the sum of the products of deviations (*XY*) or 17,798.5.

The denominator is:

$$\text{sqrt (sum of Xdevsq * sum of Ydevsq)}$$
$$\text{sqrt } (65.99 * 60{,}385{,}981) = 63{,}126$$

The correlation coefficient, then, is:

$$r = 17{,}799/63{,}126$$
$$r = 0.282$$

Pearson's *r* indicates a moderate positive linear association between the property crime rate and the unemployment rate across the 50 U.S. states during the mid-1990s.

(continued)

Example

To test whether this is a significant result, we now compute the t-test statistic using Formula 13.1.

$$t_r = r\sqrt{\frac{N-2}{1-r^2}} \tag{13.1}$$

With $N = 48$ (50 states minus two degrees of freedom), we do the arithmetic and come to the value 2.04.

Consulting the appendix table of t values, we see, for a one-tailed test with $df = 40$, a critical value at the $p = 0.05$ level of 1.68. The critical value for 60 *df* is 1.67 (our critical values table doesn't show the exact 48 degrees of freedom).

Our test statistic (2.04) exceeds the critical value (1.67). So, we reject the null hypothesis that $r = 0$, with 95 percent confidence.

We've determined that there is a statistically significant positive linear association: on average, the higher the unemployment rate, the higher the rate of property crime. The correlation is a modest value of 0.282. We can describe the strength of the relationship more effectively with the coefficient of determination.

$$R^2 = 0.282 * 0.282$$
$$R^2 = 0.0795 \text{ or } 7.95\%$$

By knowing unemployment rates, we are able to reduce error in predicting property crime rates by about 8 percent, compared to not knowing unemployment rates. Or, more commonly, unemployment "explains 8 percent of the variance" in property crime.

The Form of Linear Interval/Ratio Association

Correlation and regression statistics describe the *linear* association between two interval/ratio variables. The most efficient way to do this is to use a simple mathematical equation—the "regression prediction equation." In the scatter plots that we've examined in this chapter, we have graphed the regression equation, and said that the regression line is the line that comes as close as possible to all the data points. We need a much more precise understanding of this idea in order to use the regression equation for prediction—but we will put that off until the next chapter.

For the moment, a simple understanding of the regression equation will be sufficient. You might recall from basic mathematics that an equation that describes any straight line has the form of Formula 13.4. Sometimes the *a* and *b* are represented with different letters, and sometimes the terms are arranged a bit differently.

$$Y = a + bX \tag{13.4}$$

This very simple equation is able to describe exactly where the best-fitting ***regression line*** falls in a scatter plot, and tells us rather precisely about the form of the relationship between X and Y (intercept and slope).

According to Formula 13.4, what is the value of Y when X is zero? You should immediately see that the answer is a. This term (a) is the Y-intercept. It tells us where the regression line intersects with the y-axis. This anchors the regression line in the scatter plot.

The more interesting value in Formula 13.4 is b. This value is the slope of the line that describes how Y is related to X. Imagine that X changed from zero to 1. The slope (b) tells us how much Y would change. Suppose that X changed from 357 to 358. The slope still tells us that Y would change by b units.

The slope can be a big number or a small number. It can be positive or negative. It describes, on average, how much difference a change in X makes for a change in Y, and in what direction. This makes the slope our most complete measure of the size of the effect of X on Y.

In the next chapter, you will study the regression line and its interpretation in more detail. For now, it is enough to understand how the linear equation summarizes the direction (positive or negative) of association and answers the question: "How much difference in Y does a difference in X make?"

SUMMARY

In this chapter we've introduced some tools for examining the relationship between two interval/ratio variables.

It is always best to visualize the relationship before calculating numerical statistics. The scatter plot is a good technique for visualizing the relationship between X and Y, and for checking the key assumptions of linearity, normality, and homoscedasticity. A very important and useful enhancement of the scatter plot is to graph the regression prediction line along with the scatter of data points.

After visualizing the sample data, our next step is to assess our confidence that there really is a linear relationship between X and Y in the whole population from which the sample was drawn. To test the null hypothesis of no linear association between X and Y in the population, the Pearson zero-order product-moment correlation coefficient is used as an estimate of the magnitude of relationship in the sample. A t-test with $N - 2$ degrees of freedom is used to assess confidence in rejecting the null hypothesis in favor of the alternative that there is a linear relationship.

The Pearson correlation ("little *r*") is also a measure of the strength and direction of the relationship, but is not a proportional reduction in error (PRE) measure. For measuring the strength of association, the coefficient of determination ("big *R*-squared") is used. R^2 is a PRE measure of the strength of linear association.

The coefficient of determination tells us whether the relationship between *X* and *Y* is strong, moderate, or weak. It does not tell us the form or effect of *X* on *Y*. To describe the form of the relationship, the regression prediction equation is used.

We've not discussed the regression equation very much in this chapter, but you should be able to interpret the *Y*-intercept and the slope. These two numbers are our easiest and most efficient way of describing how much effect *X* has on *Y*, and whether this effect is positive or negative. There is much more to this topic, and we will discuss regression in more depth in the next chapter.

KEY TERMS

coefficient of determination (big R-squared)

homoscedasticity assumption

linearity assumption

normality assumption

Pearson zero-order product-moment correlation coefficient (little r)

regression line (intercept and slope)

scatter plot (aka scattergram)

CHECK QUIZ ANSWERS

Quiz 13.1 Answers: 1. (c); 2. (a); 3. (d); 4. (d); 5. (b); 6. (c)
Quiz 13.2 Answers: 1. (a); 2. (d); 3. (b); 4. (a)
Quiz 13.3 Answers: 1. (d); 2. (a); 3. (c); 4. (b); 5. (a); 6. (a)

EXERCISES

1. Here are some data on schooling, life expectancy, and urbanization for a sample of Middle Eastern and North African nations in the mid-1990s.

Country	Average Years of School Completed	Life Expectancy, 1994	Percent Urban
Saudi Arabia	3.70	67.32	78.00
Jordan	5.00	71.61	70.00

Country	Average Years of School Completed	Life Expectancy, 1994	Percent Urban
Libya	3.40	63.47	84.00
Syria	4.20	66.12	51.00
Iraq	4.80	64.96	73.00
Yemen	0.80	50.94	31.00
Qatar	5.60	72.25	90.00
United Arab Em.	5.10	72.00	82.00
Iran	3.90	65.26	57.00
Pakistan	1.90	57.11	33.00
Bahrain	3.90	73.12	89.00
Kuwait	5.40	74.62	95.00
Tunisia	2.10	72.54	56.00
Turkey	3.50	70.41	64.00
Algeria	2.60	67.35	53.00
Sudan	0.80	53.85	23.00
Morocco	2.80	67.50	47.00
Afghanistan	0.80	44.41	20.00
Lebanon	4.40	69.01	86.00

a. For each pair of variables, explain why you would take one to be the independent and the other to be the dependent for regression analysis.

b. Prepare a scatter plot of each of the three relationships (schooling * life expectancy; schooling * urban; life expectancy * urban). You may wish to draw these by hand, or you may use a spreadsheet or statistical package.

c. Sketch a regression line in each scatter plot (you may do this by eye or calculate the line using Excel or SPSS).

d. Comment on each relationship: Does there appear to be a relationship? Is it approximately linear? How strong is it? Is it a positive or negative relationship?

2. Here are some selected data on three variables for 20 U.S. states during the mid-1990s.

1995 Data on 20 Selected U.S. States

Name	Median Household Income, 1995 ($)	Percent of Population 25 Years and Older with College Degree, 1990	Percent Voting Democrat (Clinton), 1996
Maine	33,858	12.70	51.60
New Hampshire	39,171	16.40	49.30
Vermont	33,824	15.40	53.40
Massachusetts	38,574	16.60	61.50
Rhode Island	35,359	13.50	59.70

(continued)

Name	Median Household Income, 1995 ($)	Percent of Population 25 Years and Older with College Degree, 1990	Percent Voting Democrat (Clinton), 1996
Connecticut	40,243	16.20	52.80
New York	33,028	13.20	59.50
New Jersey	43,924	16.00	53.70
Pennsylvania	34,524	11.30	49.20
Ohio	34,941	11.10	47.40
Indiana	33,385	9.20	41.60
Illinois	38,071	13.60	54.30
Michigan	36,426	10.90	51.70
Wisconsin	40,955	12.10	48.80
Minnesota	37,933	15.60	51.10
Iowa	35,519	11.70	50.30
Missouri	34,825	11.70	47.50
North Dakota	29,089	13.50	40.10
South Dakota	29,578	12.30	43.00
Nebraska	32,929	13.10	35.00

a. For each pair of variables, explain why you would take one to be the independent variable and the other to be the dependent variable for regression analysis.

b. Prepare a scatter plot of each of the three relationships (income by education, income by Democrat, and education by Democrat). You may wish to draw these by hand, or you may use a spreadsheet or statistical package.

c. Sketch a regression line in each scatter plot (you may do this by eye or calculate the line using Excel or SPSS).

d. Comment on each relationship: Does there appear to be a relationship? Is it approximately linear? How strong is it? Is it a positive or negative relationship?

3. Here are descriptive statistics and Pearson correlation coefficients for the relationships among schooling, urbanization, and life expectancy in a larger sample (about 160 cases, compared to 19 nations in question 1) of nations in the mid-1990s.

Descriptive Statistics

	Mean	Std. Deviation	*N*
Average years of school completed	4.8000	3.27644	162
Percent urban	50.8293	24.13551	164
Life expectancy, 1994	64.3336	11.20671	172

Correlations

		Average Years of School Completed	Percent Urban	Life Expectancy, 1994
Average Years of School Completed	Pearson correlation	1	0.712*	0.817*
	Sig. (1-tailed)		0.000	0.000
	N	162	162	162
Percent Urban	Pearson correlation	0.712*	1	0.717*
	Sig. (1-tailed)	0.000		0.000
	N	162	164	164
Life Expectancy, 1994	Pearson correlation	0.817*	0.717*	1
	Sig. (1-tailed)	0.000	0.000	
	N	162	164	172

*Correlation is significant at the 0.01 level (1-tailed).

a. What is the null hypothesis for the one-tailed significance test shown? What is the alternative hypothesis?
b. Which correlations are statistically significant?
c. Briefly interpret the results.

4. Here are some descriptive statistics and bivariate correlations for the income, education, and political preference variables for all 50 U.S. states.

Descriptive Statistics

	Mean	Std. Deviation	*N*
Median household income, 1995	33,875.42	5,183.515	50
Percent of population 25 years and older with college degree, 1990	12.9	2.4	50
Percent voting Democrat (Clinton), 1996	47.2	6.8	50

Correlations

		Median Household Income, 1995	Percent of Population 25 Years and Older with College Degree, 1990	Percent Voting Democrat (Clinton), 1996
Median Household Income, 1995	Pearson correlation	1	0.655*	0.197*
	Sig. (2-tailed)		0.000	0.169
	N	50	50	50

(continued)

		Median Household Income, 1995	Percent of Population 25 Years and Older with College Degree, 1990	Percent Voting Democrat (Clinton), 1996
Percent of Population 25 Years and Older with College Degree, 1990	Pearson correlation	0.655*	1	0.099*
	Sig. (2-tailed)	0.000		0.492
	N	50	50	50
Percent Voting Democrat (Clinton), 1996	Pearson correlation	0.197*	0.099*	1
	Sig. (2-tailed)	0.169	0.492	
	N	50	50	50

*Correlation is significant at the 0.01 level (2-tailed).

a. What is the null hypothesis for the two-tailed significance test shown? What is the alternative hypothesis?
b. Which correlations are statistically significant?
c. Briefly interpret the results.

5. Our researcher has used SPSS to perform a linear regression of life expectancy (measured in years) on average schooling completed (also measured in years) for 162 nations during the mid-1990s. Here are some of the main results:

Model Summary

Model	*R*	*R*-Squared	Adjusted *R*-Squared	Std. Error of the Estimate
1	0.817	0.667	0.665	6.52143

ANOVA

Model		Sum of Squares	*df*	Mean Square	F	Sig.
1	Regression	13,626.599	1	13,626.599	320.407	0.000
	Residual	6,804.638	160	42.529		
	Total	20,431.236	161			

Coefficients

Model		Unstandardized Coefficients B	Std. Error	Standardized Coefficients Beta	t	Sig.
1	(Constant)	50.523	0.911		55.474	0.000
	Average years of school completed	2.808	0.157	0.817	17.900	0.000

a. Is there a significant linear relationship between the two variables? What is your evidence?

b. How strong is the relationship between the variables? Interpret the R^2.

c. What is the predicted life expectancy in a (hypothetical) nation with no formal education? What is the predicted life expectancy in a nation with an average of 10 years of education?

d. Interpret the meaning of the constant and the unstandardized slope.

6. Our researcher has used SPSS to perform a linear regression of median household income on the percentage of college graduates in all 50 U.S. states during 1995. Here are some of the main results:

Model Summary

Model	*R*	*R*-Squared	Adjusted *R*-Squared	Std. Error of the Estimate
1	0.655	0.429	0.417	3,957.30807

ANOVA

Model		Sum of Squares	*df*	Mean Square	F	Sig.
1	Regression	564,878,834.308	1	564,878,834.308	36.071	0.000
	Residual	751,693,781.872	48	15,660,287.122		
	Total	1,316,572,616.180	49			

Coefficients

Model		Unstandardized Coefficients B	Std. Error	Standardized Coefficients Beta	t	Sig.
1	(Constant)	15,475.524	3,114.336		4.969	0.000
	Percent of population 25 years and older with college degree, 1990	1,431.230	238.304	0.655	6.006	0.000

a. Is there a significant linear relationship between the two variables? What is your evidence?
b. How strong is the relationship between the variables? Interpret the R^2.
c. What is the predicted median income when the percentage of college graduates in a state is zero? When it is 10 percent?
d. Interpret the meaning of the constant and the unstandardized slope.

Chapter 14

REGRESSION ANALYSIS

LEARNING OBJECTIVES

When you have finished this chapter, you will be able to:

- Understand the notion of prediction for interval/ratio variables.
- Understand and interpret the linear regression equation to describe the association between two interval/ratio variables.
- Be able to understand and interpret simple regression from a computer output.
- Be able to understand and interpret multiple regression from a computer output.
- Understand and appreciate the meaning and role of the error term in regression.
- Be sensitive to how the regression equation is estimated, and some of the assumptions underlying its proper use.

PREDICTING OUTCOMES WITH REGRESSION

Linear regression is a technique that a researcher can use to analyze the relationship between a dependent variable and one or more independent variables. Regression builds on the idea of statistical association that we have been studying in the past several chapters. But regression changes our focus somewhat, by concentrating on predicting an outcome based on one or more independent variables.

Regression analysis is easily the most widely used technique in the social sciences. It is really a family of techniques that are used for almost all problems in advanced statistical analysis. In this chapter, we first provide an introduction to the key ideas by focusing on the case of an interval/ratio dependent variable and one interval/ratio independent variable. Then, we will explore a very important extension: adding more independent or predictor variables (multiple regression).

Regression analysis builds on the idea of statistical association: can we predict the scores on one variable better if we know the scores on another? But it focuses our attention on describing how a change or difference in the independent variable or variables affects or predicts outcomes. This is a very important change of focus, because almost all of social science work is concerned with predicting outcomes, and whether these outcomes differ in systematic ways with changes in causal conditions.

Almost all of the basic research questions of the social sciences can be thought of as problems of prediction. To name just a few:

- What are the determinants of property crimes in the United States?
- Does education affect racial prejudice?
- Do student SAT scores predict success in college?
- Does frequency of class attendance influence course grades?
- Does the number of people invited to a wedding predict marital duration?
- Does gestation influence birth weight?
- What individual characteristics predict personal income?

In every case, we are concerned with why some cases have different outcomes than others (why are crime rates high in some cities, but lower in others?). In every case, we have one or more theories of the causes that lead us to testable hypotheses (do people with more formal education display less racial prejudice than people with less formal education?). The simple regression model and its various extensions are the social scientists' tool of choice for testing whether theories provide valid explanations of our observations.

SIMPLE LINEAR REGRESSION

Simple linear regression is used to summarize the linear dependence of one variable (Y) on another (X). The researcher finds the best linear equation to describe how Y depends on X, usually provided in the form of a straight line. Then, the researcher assesses how adequate the prediction is (the ***goodness of fit***). The regression equation can then be used to describe the form of the relationship between X and Y in the sample. Once the linear relationship is estimated in the sample and described, the researcher can use regression to make inferences about the population from which the sample data utilized were obtained, and test hypotheses. Regression is a powerful tool, but it must be used carefully, so the third step in regression analysis is always to check assumptions and examine residuals. We'll discuss these issues in the next three sections.

The Regression Equation

The idea of describing the dependency of Y on X with a linear equation was introduced in Chapter 13, but it is worthwhile to review these ideas in a slightly different way here.

The simplest single-equation linear regression model is of the form:

$$Y = \beta_0 + \beta_1 X \tag{14.1}$$

Formula 14.1 states that Y, the dependent variable, is a linear function of X, the independent, explanatory, or predictor variable. In the equation, capital Greek letters are used because the coefficients obtained from a sample are estimates or best guesses of population values.

The linear equation has our two variables (Y and X), and also two parameters (β_0, β_1). β_0 is the average score on Y of the cases that have a score of zero on X. It is called, variously, the "***constant***" or "***Y-intercept.***" β_1 describes how a one-unit difference in scores on X impacts the scores on Y. It is called, variously, the "***slope***" or "***regression coefficient.***" Some texts use a for the intercept instead of β_0 and use b for the regression coefficient instead of β_1.

When we have estimated the values of β_0 and β_1 from the data in our sample, we can use the regression equation to describe the way that Y depends on X very simply. By inserting any value of X we might choose and doing a little math, we can see the predicted score of Y for that X. And, more generally, we can see (with β_1) how a unit change or difference on X is predicted to impact on Y: is the effect positive or negative, big or small?

The values of the Y-intercept and slope parameter are estimated from the data in our sample. For simple regression, this is done by the method of ***ordinary least squares (OLS).*** For more complicated regression models, the method of maximum likelihood is often used. We are not going to discuss the technical details of estimation very much in this book. Simply put, though, the method of ordinary least squares finds the sample estimates of the intercept and slope in a way that minimizes the sum of the squared residuals, or errors of prediction (more on residuals later). Another way of putting it is that ordinary least squares finds the values of the Y-intercept and slope that place the regression line as close as possible to all the data points.

In addition to describing how Y depends on X (the form of the relationship), simple regression analysis (when done by the least-squares method) also tells us about the strength of the relationship. The statistic used to describe the strength of the relationship is the *coefficient of determination* or "big R-squared" (R^2). We discussed the R^2 in Chapter 13, and need only say that it is a proportional reduction in error (PRE) measure that tells us what percentage of the variance in *Y* is accounted for by *X*, or (alternatively) how much of the error in predicting *Y* is reduced by knowing the effects of *X*.

Let's review the interpretation of the simple linear regression equation by looking at an example.

Example

SIMPLE LINEAR REGRESSION

Although we usually use computer software to calculate regression statistics, it is very helpful to study how it can be done by hand so you can see where the numbers are coming from.

Let's suppose (this is a hypothetical example!) that a researcher felt that the greater the number of factions (groups with varying views) in a social structure, the greater the difficulty that a leader will have in establishing legitimacy (popular acceptance of the "right to rule"). To test this idea, some data have been collected from 12 classes in the university. Each class has been scored on the amount of fractionalization (with the number of factions ranging from 2 to 16). In each class, the number of anti-instructor comments (taken from teaching evaluation forms) has been counted as our measure of lack of legitimacy. Table 14.1 shows the (hypothetical) data.

TABLE 14.1 Number of Class Factions and Anti-Instructor Comments (Hypothetical Data)

Class (Case)	Class Anti-Instructor Fractionalization	Comments
	X	Y
001	2	1
002	3	5
003	4	7
004	6	8
005	7	9
006	8	12
007	9	14
008	10	16
009	12	18
010	13	21
011	14	24
012	16	28

Regression statistics are based on sums of squared deviations from the mean of *X* (class fractionalization) and *Y* (anti-instructor comments), as well as the products of these deviations. The easiest way to calculate these is to use a spreadsheet.

Example

Step 1: Rearrange the data, and using a calculator or spreadsheet, proceed as shown.

X	Y	$\bar{X}-X$	$\bar{Y}-Y$	$(\bar{X}-X)(Y-Y)$	$(\bar{X}-X)^2$	$(\bar{Y}-Y)^2$
2	1	−6.667	−12.583	83.889	44.444	158.8
3	5	−5.667	−8.583	48.639	32.111	74.0
4	7	−4.667	−6.583	30.722	21.778	43.6
6	8	−2.667	−5.583	14.889	7.111	31.4
7	9	−1.667	−4.583	7.639	2.778	21.2
8	12	−0.667	−1.583	1.056	0.444	2.6
9	14	0.333	0.417	0.139	0.111	0.4
10	16	1.333	2.417	3.222	1.778	5.8
12	18	3.333	4.417	14.722	11.111	19.4
13	21	4.333	7.417	32.139	18.778	54.8
14	24	5.333	10.417	55.556	28.444	108.2
16	28	7.333	14.417	105.722	53.778	207.4
ΣX = 104	ΣY = 163			SP = 398.333	SSx = 222.667	SSy = 726.917

Note that the sums (bottom left), squared deviations from the means of X and Y (bottom right), and sum of cross products have been calculated and are shown in the last row of the table. They were calculated as shown in the next steps.

Step 2: Calculate the means of the two variables.
The mean of class fractionalization (X) is obtained as follows:

$$\Sigma\frac{X}{N}=\frac{104}{12}$$
$$=8.667$$

The mean of anti-instructor comments (Y) is obtained as follows:

$$\Sigma\frac{Y}{N}=\frac{163}{12}$$
$$=13.583$$

Step 3: Calculate the sum of the cross products of the deviations (SP), the sum of squares for $X(SS_x)$, and the sum of squares for $Y(SS_y)$.

$$\text{SP}=\sum(\bar{X}-X)(\bar{Y}-Y)$$
$$=398.333$$
$$\text{SS}_x=\sum(X-\bar{X})^2$$
$$=222.667$$
$$\text{SS}_y=\sum(Y-\bar{Y})^2$$
$$=726.917$$

(continued)

Example

Now we have all the parts that we need to calculate the key regression statistics: the coefficients that describe the *Y*-intercept and slope, and the measure of goodness of fit (the *R*-squared).

Step 4: Insert the computations into the formula for the regression coefficient (β_1), and the *Y*-intercept (β_0).

$$\begin{aligned}\beta_1 &= \frac{\text{SP}}{\text{SS}_x}\\ &= \frac{398.333}{222.667}\\ &= 1.789\\ \beta_0 &= \overline{Y} - \beta_1\overline{X}\\ &= 13.583 - (1.789)(8.667)\\ &= -1.921\end{aligned}$$

Step 5: Plot (draw) the regression line, and see how it can be used to predict the score on *Y* for any score we might choose on *X*.

In this case, the line is defined by $Y = -1.921 + 1.789(X)$. For example, if there are six factions in a class, we can predict or expect the number of comments against an instructor to be on average a little over 8. That is: Anti-instructor comments $= -1.921 + (1.789)(6) = 8.813$.

To draw the best-fitting or regression line, the data were input into computer software, SAS (SPSS or Excel could also be used).

In Figure 14.1, the line going from left to right is described as the best linear unbiased estimator (BLUE). It is the line that best minimizes errors or the distances between the values of the dependent variable predicted by our equation and the actual values observed or collected in the data. The crosses represent values of *Y* (anti-instructor comments). The line is the value predicted by the equation based on scores on class fractionalization (*X*). If an individual value (+) does not fall exactly on the line, then some error was made in predicting *Y* for that particular class or case. It is this distance between predicted values (the values that our equation says we should see) and the observed values in our data that is called the *residual.* The regression line is the best that we can come up with that minimizes the residuals squared and summed over all 12 observations in this data set. More will be said about residuals in the pages that follow.

Step 6: Calculate R^2, the coefficient of determination.

Given that a close relationship exists between r^2 and the *r* obtained in correlational analysis, one way to calculate an R^2 when there is only one independent variable in an equation is to first obtain the correlation coefficient between the two variables (independent and dependent) and then square the result. Alternatively, the following

Example

FIGURE 14.1 The Best-Fitting Equation and the Regression Line for Predicting Anti-Instructor Comments

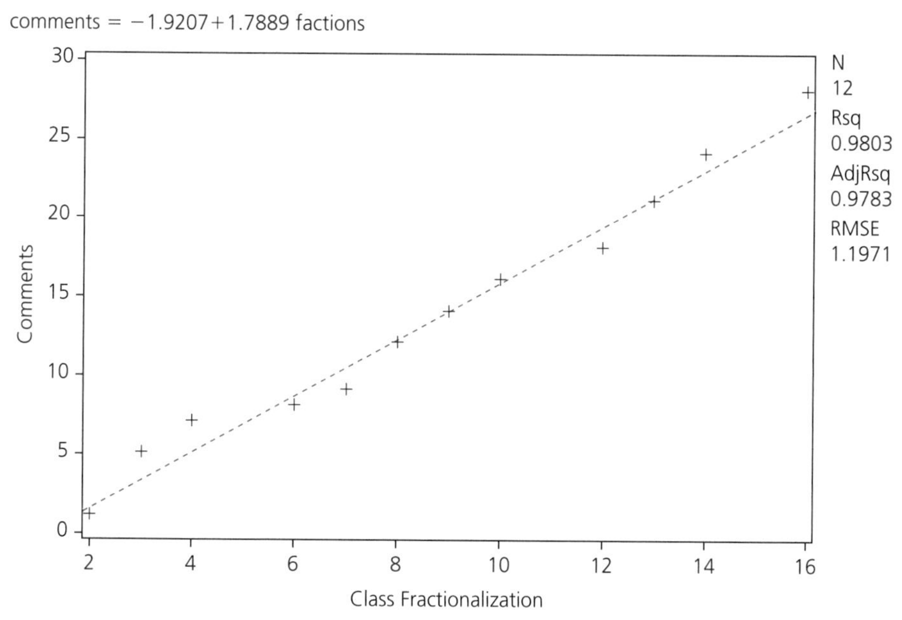

formula may be used:

$$r = \frac{\text{SP}}{\sqrt{(\text{SS}_x)(\text{SS}_y)}}$$

If we apply this to our data, we obtain:

$$\begin{aligned} r &= \frac{398.333}{\sqrt{(222.667)(726.917)}} \\ &= \frac{398.333}{\sqrt{161{,}860.428}} \\ &= \frac{398.333}{402.319} \\ &= 0.990 \end{aligned}$$

The correlation coefficient between class fractionalization and anti-instructor comments is 0.990, signifying a very high association. To obtain the R^2, simply take the square of this number.

$$R^2 = (0.990)^2 = 0.980$$

(continued)

Example

It is seen that 98 percent of variation in anti-instructor comments is accounted for by class fractionalization.

Step 7: R^2 gives proportion of variation due to the *X* variable. What about the proportion not due to the variable in the equation?

$$\begin{aligned} 1 - R^2 &= 1 - (0.990)^2 \\ &= 1 - 0.980 \\ &= 0.02 = 2\% \end{aligned}$$

Step 8: Calculate the total sum of squares, regression sum of squares, and error sum of squares (SS_{total}, SS_{reg}, and SS_{error}).

$$\begin{aligned} SS_{total} &= SS^Y = 726.917 \\ SS_{reg} &= R^2(SS_{total}) \\ &= (0.980)(726.917) \\ &= 712.379 \\ SS_{error} &= (1 - R^2)(SS_{total}) \\ &= (0.02)(726.917) = 14.538 \end{aligned}$$

Step 9: Calculate the mean square (MS) for regression and mean square for error.

$$\begin{aligned} df_{reg} &= 1 \text{ (We have only 1 independent variable)} \\ MS_{reg} &= \frac{SS_{reg}}{df_{reg}} \\ &= \frac{712.379}{1} = 712.379 \\ df_{error} &= N - 2 = 10 - 2 = 8 \\ MS_{error} &= \frac{SS_{error}}{df_{error}} \\ &= \frac{14.538}{8} = 1.817 \end{aligned}$$

Example

Step 10: Calculate the F-value and determine its statistical significance by comparing it with the critical value provided in the F-distribution table.

$$F = \frac{MS_{reg}}{MS_{error}}$$

$$= \frac{712.379}{1.817} = 392.063$$

$$df = 1 \text{ and } 8$$

$$\alpha = 0.05$$

$$\text{Critical } F = 5.32$$

Given that the calculated F is greater than the critical F, class fractionalization explains a significant amount of variance in anti-instructor comments (legitimacy).

Using Excel to Do the Calculations

First, open a new Excel file. Enter the values of X and Y variables in column A and column B, respectively. Next, calculate the average of X and Y variables. Find the icon "AutoSum" in the upper right corner, drop down the list, and select command "Average." Select all the values of X variable and the result is 8.667. Repeat for Y and the average of Y is 13.583.

In column C, calculate the difference between each X variable and average of X variable. Select cell C2, press the equal key (=), and write the equation "=A2−8.667." Then position your cursor at the lower right corner of cell C2. Your cursor will become +. Click on it and drag it down to fill in the rest of the cells with the same equation. Repeat again in column D to find out the difference between each Y variable and average of Y ("=B2 − 13.583").

In column E, try to calculate $(X - \overline{X})(Y - \overline{Y})$. Click on cell E2 and write the equation "=C2*D2." Similarly, write the equation "=C2*C2" in cell F2 to calculate $(X - \overline{X})(X - \overline{X})$ and "=D2*D2" in cell G2 to calculate $(Y - \overline{Y})(Y - \overline{Y})$.

To calculate SP, SS_x, and SS_y, respectively, sum up column E, column F, and column G using the icon "AutoSum."

Note: Due to rounding errors, results from Excel may not exactly match those obtained by hand calculations, but conclusions will be the same.

Before we go on, let's check and make sure that you have mastered the basic statistics calculated in linear regression analysis.

Hypothesis Tests in Regression

In regression analysis, there are two sets of hypotheses to be tested.

CHECK QUIZ 14.1

1. "Ordinary least squares" is
   a. the constant in a regression equation.
   b. the slope in a regression equation.
   c. a measure of the strength of the relationship.
   d. a method of estimating population parameters.
2. $Y = 20 + 6X$. What is the predicted score on Y when $X = 2$?
   a. 20
   b. 22
   c. 26
   d. 32
3. $Y = 20 + 6X$. If Fred is one unit higher than Sally on X, his predicted Y score is
   a. 20 points lower than Sally's.
   b. 20 points higher than Sally's.
   c. 6 points lower than Sally's.
   d. 6 points higher than Sally's.
4. R^2 is 0.50. This means that
   a. Y does not depend on X.
   b. X accounts for 50 percent of the variation in Y.
   c. Y accounts for 50 percent of the variation in X.
   d. X explains 0.25 of the variation in Y.

The first is a hypothesis about the equation or regression line as a whole, which is referred to as the ***global null hypothesis.*** It tests whether the model as whole fits the data in the population from which the sample was obtained. The second hypothesis to be tested is about the slope of the regression line.

In symbols, the global null hypothesis may be written as follows:

$$H_0 : R^2 = 0$$
$$H_a : R^2 > 0$$

To test the global null hypothesis, the researcher examines the top part of an output in most statistical packages like SAS, SPSS, or STATA and looks for values of multiple R or R^2. If the null hypothesis is correct, the multiple R or R^2 will invariably be zero or very close to it. The researcher next tries to determine whether the obtained R^2 is statistically significant. This is accomplished by examining the F-ratio or F-value and the associated probability that is printed by the software being used. In the absence of a printed probability, the researcher must look at the value of F relative to the specified degrees of freedom. Assuming that one is taking a 5 percent chance of being wrong ($\alpha = 0.05$), an F-value with a probability less than

0.05 will lead to the rejection of the null hypothesis. So, if the null hypothesis is correct, the F-ratio will be small and the *p*-level large.

In simple regression, we have only one X variable, so the global test is the same thing as saying that X does not affect Y. In multiple regression (discussed in the next section of this chapter) there are more X variables. In multiple regression, the global null hypothesis is that *none* of the X variables has any effect on Y in the population.

If we have concluded from the global test that X does affect Y, then we proceed to test the second hypothesis: whether the slope of the relationship is different from zero.

$$H_o : \beta_1 = 0$$
$$H_a : \beta_1 \neq 0$$
or
$$H_a : \beta_1 > 0$$
or
$$H_a : \beta_1 < -0.5$$

The null hypothesis states that the independent variable does not affect the dependent variable. That is, a change or difference in X has zero effect on Y—the slope is really zero in the population. There are alternative hypotheses. The most common one is that the slope is not zero in the population (a two-tailed test). But other hypotheses can be tested. For example, we might want to test if the slope was positive (a one-tailed test), or that it was less (or more) than some specific value.

Hypotheses about the value of regression coefficients are performed by estimating a standard error of the regression coefficient and calculating a t-statistic. In simple regression (with one X), we have a single set of hypotheses (about β_1). In the multiple regression model, there is a null hypothesis for every variable that one includes in the equation. If there are five independent variables, there will be five null hypotheses and five research hypotheses. This is true whether some variables are the focus of the investigation (focal or key variables) or merely control variables.

Regression Assumptions

Linear regression gives us an excellent tool to describe the effects of independent variables on outcomes and to test hypotheses. We need to be careful, though, because we have to make some assumptions.

Here are the most important assumptions in doing linear regression analysis:

- The dependent and independent variables are interval/ratio variables.
- The data were obtained by simple random sampling.
- The relationship between Y and X is approximately linear.
- The errors of prediction have an approximately normal distribution.

CHECK QUIZ 14.2

1. Which of the following is not an important assumption in regression analysis?
   a. simple random sampling
   b. linear relationships
   c. normally distributed dependent variable
   d. All of these are important assumptions.
2. If a relationship between Y and X is really nonlinear, and we use linear regression to estimate parameters, the result will be
   a. valid.
   b. a high value of R2.
   c. large residuals.
   d. homoscedasticity.
3. If the average prediction errors for cases that have high values on Y are larger than the average prediction errors for cases that have low values of Y, we are observing
   a. a violation of the assumptions.
   b. homoscedasticity.
   c. nonlinearity.
   d. heteroscedasticity.
   e. both a and d.

- Multiple independent variables are not highly correlated with one another.
- The independent variable(s) is/are not correlated with the residuals.
- The residuals are homoscedastic.

Most of these assumptions are familiar ones. By knowing about the sampling method and measurement instruments, we can check the first two assumptions. A close examination of the scatter plot (see Chapter 13) is useful for checking the ***linearity assumption.*** Our basic univariate statistics can be used to check on distributional normality. In multiple regression we have one additional assumption: no multicollinearity. The ***multicollinearity assumption*** states that the multiple independent variables are not strongly associated with one another.

The last two assumptions require that we look at the prediction errors or residuals from estimating the regression equation.

The Error Term: Examining Residuals

The simple linear regression equation shown as Formula 14.1 is an abstract model of the association between *Y* and *X*. To apply it, we use the measured scores for the cases on X_i and

Y_i to estimate the parameters β_0 and β_1. Formula 14.2 shows the form of the simple regression equation that is actually estimated from our data.

$$\hat{Y}_i = b_0 + b_1X_i + e_i \tag{14.2}$$

The equation says that we are predicting (Y hat) for each individual (sub i), based on the estimated regression parameters (b_0 and b_1) and the individual's score on X. However, the model or theory does not usually account for all of the variation in Y, the dependent variable. When dealing with social events, it is impossible to make predictions with 100 percent accuracy. We recognize this lack of precision by introducing into the model a symbol that represents variation in Y that cannot be explained by the included independent variables or X's. This is the error term or *residual* for an individual case (e_i).

There are many reasons why there are residuals in empirical regression analyses. It is impossible to avoid some sort of errors in measuring at least one of the variables in the equation. For example, some people do not give data collectors their real age when asked. The underlying theoretical equation might have a different shape than the one chosen by the researcher. If the relationship between X and Y is not actually linear, the linear regression equation will reflect this as prediction errors. And, very importantly, most social phenomena have complex causes. Unless our regression equation includes all of the variables that are actually relevant to explaining Y in the real world—and our equations usually do not—then this misspecification (called omitted variables) is reflected in prediction error.

It is important to examine the residuals when doing regression analysis. Most statistical packages provide built-in ways to look at the residuals to see if there is evidence of non-normality and nonlinearity. There is also an assumption called the ***homoscedasticity assumption***, which means that the variance (or standard deviations) of the error terms for observations should be constant across levels of Y. This implies that cases with larger values on the dependent variable should not provide larger error variances than cases with smaller values on the same variable. If we encounter more errors in prediction due to large predicted values, then we have a situation called heteroscedasticity. While minor violations of the aforementioned assumptions do not necessarily invalidate the results obtained, they often mean that our prediction is not as great or as accurate as it otherwise would have been.

APPLYING SIMPLE REGRESSION ANALYSIS

The first step in exploring any key relationship is the test of whether the two variables are associated with each other in a theoretically predicted way. A simple bivariate regression model helps in many circumstances. In the examples that follow, we use the statistical package for the social sciences, SPSS (version 17). You can follow along if you have the program available. Otherwise, just study the example.

Open the program by double-clicking on the SPSS icon on the desktop. Then, using the File menu, navigate to the "gss2008" data set (General Social Survey for 2008) and open it. The data set has already been saved as an SPSS machine-readable file.

Once in SPSS, choose the *Analyze* menu, then *Regression,* and then *Linear.* Select *realrinc,* that is, the survey respondent's annual income in constant dollars (the dependent variable) and *educ,* highest year of school completed, as the independent variable. Simply click OK, and you should get a bunch of results.

The first step in interpreting our regression is to examine the overall goodness of fit. The relevant result is shown in Table 14.2.

R-squared in the Model Summary box indicates the proportion of the total variance in the dependent variable explained by the independent variable, or the proportional reduction of error in predicting values of the dependent variable achieved by taking into consideration values on the independent variable. Our results indicate that 5.1 percent of the total variation in income is explained by individual differences in education. The R^2 is rather low, but this is not surprising given that there are many other factors that could affect income.

We also see the "Std. Error of the Estimate." This value (which we haven't talked about before) is the average size of a residual or the average size of a prediction error. In this case, when we predict income based on knowing education and the regression parameters, our average error is $76,489. We might compare this to the average income—but it is clear that our regression model is giving predictions that are very, very imprecise!

We can also test the global null hypothesis that no independent variable has an effect on *Y*, using the F-test. We don't show this here, because when there is only one independent variable, the global test (no effect of any independent variable) is the same thing as the specific test that education has no effect on income, which we see in the next part of the output (Table 14.3).

This panel of results shows us the estimated parameters for the constant and slope, as well as a few other things. The parameter estimates are found in the column labeled *B* under "Unstandardized Coefficients." They determine the straight line that best fits the observed scatter plot of income by education. This least-squares regression line is the straight line for which the sum of the squared prediction errors is minimized. The least-squares regression line has two components:

First, the coefficient labeled Constant is the *Y*-intercept of the regression and indicates the predicted value of the dependent variable for a case with a value of 0 on the independent

TABLE 14.2 Income and Education: Goodness of Fit Model Summary

Model	*R*	*R*-Squared	Adjusted *R*-Squared	Std. Error of the Estimate
1	0.227[a]	0.051	0.051	76,489.496

TABLE 14.3 Income and Education: Effects Analysis

Model		Unstandardized Coefficients		Standardized Coefficients		
		B	**Std. Error**	**Beta**	**t**	**Sig.**
1	(Constant)	−52,335.906	10,788.450		−4.851	0.000
	Highest year of school completed	6,178.689	762.609	0.227	8.102	0.000

variable. Someone with no education is predicted to have lost $52,335.91 in 2008. Note that the intercept can be negative or positive. Had the number here been positive, we would have been forced to conclude that someone with 0 on education is predicted to have gained $52,335.91 in 2008!

The slope or unstandardized regression coefficient next to the name of the independent variable indicates the substantive effect of the independent variable on the dependent variable. The slope for highest year of school completed indicates how much the predicted value of income changes for a one-unit change in education. The slope coefficient of $6,178.69 indicates that for each one-year increase in education, income is predicted to increase by about $6,178.69 on average.

As part of the effort to demonstrate the validity of our theoretical expectations, we need to determine whether the observed effect of education on income occurred as a result of random sampling error, or it denotes a real association that exists in the population from which the 2008 General Social Survey sample was drawn. In other words, we want to know whether the slope coefficient in the regression line is statistically significant. Answering this question involves setting up a test of the following hypotheses where β refers to the slope coefficient in the regression line for the population:

H_0: $\beta = 0$ (There is no association between the independent and dependent variables in the population; the sample association that appears in the sample data is a result of random sampling error or chance factors.)

H_a: $\beta \neq 0$ (The independent and dependent variables are associated in the population.)

We test this hypothesis by calculating the standard error for the slope coefficient and converting this slope coefficient to an appropriate test score (t-ratio). The ***standard error of the regression*** coefficient is (like all other standard errors we have studied) the average amount that we would expect the statistic (in this case, the slope) to vary from one sample to another. So, the test of the null hypothesis that the population slope is zero is just like any other hypothesis test that we have performed throughout this book. The t-value is obtained by dividing the slope or regression coefficient by its standard error. In other words, $t = \beta/se\ \beta$, where β is the slope coefficient and *se* is the standard error. We then compare the obtained test score to the theoretical sampling distribution of all such possible scores to figure out the probability of obtaining a test score of this magnitude if the sample was drawn from a population in which the coefficient was actually 0 (i.e., the probability that the null hypothesis is true).

The standard error (Std. Error) of the regression slope (coefficient) is the standard deviation of the sampling distribution of all regression slopes (coefficients) if we were to do the study over and over again. If you have difficulty understanding this, refer to earlier chapters where the sampling distribution was discussed. In general, standard errors close to zero are preferable. Large standard errors imply that if the study were repeated over and over on samples drawn from the same population, the slope coefficients would change for the variables involved. Thus, large standard errors essentially imply less confidence in the stability of our slope coefficients.

SPSS and other packages typically do all the necessary calculations, including the standard error, t-value, and even the *p*-value for the regression coefficients. Our only task is to interpret the results correctly. The standard error for the slope of our regression model is listed in the Std. Error column. The obtained t-value for each component is found in the column marked "t," and the probability (*p*-value) of obtaining such a t-value if the population value was actually 0 (if the null hypothesis was true) is found in the column marked Sig. (significance).

In order to answer the question about the statistical significance of our slope coefficient, we can refer to the Sig. column. If the *p*-value reported there is lower than the probability that we set at the beginning of the study, then we can say that the probability that the null hypothesis is true is so low that we do not believe that it is true. In the present example, the obtained t-value for the slope coefficient is 8.102, which has a *p*-value of 0.000. This indicates that there is no way that a coefficient of this magnitude ($6,178.69) could have occurred by chance as implied by the null hypothesis. We can confidently reject the null hypothesis in favor of the research hypothesis that the effect of education on income is not 0 in the U.S. population; the slope coefficient is statistically significant, supporting our theoretical expectations.

We are 95 percent confident, then, that education does predict income. However, we need to also be sure to report that the predictions are quite imprecise (the standard error of regression), and that education does not explain much of the variation among people's incomes (the R^2).

There is one last interesting piece of output in the column labeled "Standardized Coefficients." The standardized coefficient (called beta) expresses the impact of the independent variable in terms of standard deviation units. It tells us the number of standard deviations the dependent variable changes (increases or decreases) when the independent variable increases or decreases by one standard deviation. In the example at hand, the standardized coefficient of 0.227 indicates that income goes up by 0.227 standard deviations for each increase of one standard deviation in education.

The ***standardized regression (beta) coefficient*** is calculated by multiplying the unstandardized coefficient, β, by the ratio of the standard deviations for the independent and dependent variables. This information will be useful when we get to multiple regression. Given that they express all coefficients in terms of the same units (standard deviations), standardized coefficients may be useful in multivariable equations when we want to compare the size of the effects of different independent variables or rank-order variables in terms of their impact on the outcome variable.

Now that we have mastered the way in which linear regression talks about the relationships, as well as the statistical paraphernalia, we are ready to go a bit further. In the remaining sections of this chapter, we'll look at an important extension of the simple regression model. This extension—multiple regression—lets us study the effect of more than one *X* on *Y* at the same time. Another extension—logistic regression—lets us use the regression model to study relationships when *Y* is nominal, rather than interval/ratio, and will be treated in Chapter 15.

MULTIPLE REGRESSION

Multiple regression is a statistical technique for studying the relationship between a single dependent variable and two or more independent variables. Everything we said earlier about simple regression (assumptions, estimation, hypotheses, etc.) holds for multiple regression. The only differences between simple and multiple regression are the number of independent variables in the equation, and a variation in the interpretation of the slope or regression coefficients.

In simple regression, prediction of *Y* is based on one *X* (independent variable). In many cases, though, we may feel that an outcome is the outcome of more than one factor. Income, for example, may be affected by *both* years of schooling attained *and* years of job experience. To make matters more complicated, people who have more years of schooling probably, on average, have fewer years of job experience (because they were in school instead of working at full-time jobs). That is, the two independent variables (years of schooling, years of job experience) are not independent of each other!

Multiple regression enables us to answer two very important questions in cases where there is more than one independent variable.

First, we can measure the extent to which all the independent variables, jointly, help to predict the dependent variable. This is done using the coefficient of determination (R^2), which measures the association of all of the independent variables together with the dependent variable.

Second, we can describe the effect of each independent variable on the dependent variable net of the effects of other independent variables. This is done with the partial regression coefficient. The partial regression (or slope) coefficient in multiple regression will tell us, for example: What is the effect of each additional year of schooling on income among people who have the same job experience? And what is the effect of each additional year of job experience on income among people who have the same level of education? Standardized partial regression coefficients (beta coefficients) let us assess which independent variables have larger or smaller effects on the outcome, independent of (or "controlling for") the others.

The multiple regression equation takes the form of Formula 14.3:

$$Y = \beta_0 + \beta_1 X_1 + \beta_2 X_2 + \beta_3 X_3 + \varepsilon \tag{14.3}$$

In the equation, Y stands for the dependent variable; β_0 is the Y-intercept or the spot on the vertical axis (Y) where the regression line meets and crosses Y. In β_1, β is the slope or regression coefficient, which provides an estimate of the amount of force that a given variable exerts on the dependent variable. The subscript 1 simply means that this particular β is the first in the equation. X stands for a given independent variable, and the subscript 1 refers to the fact that the particular X in question is the first variable in the equation. The βs are multivariate regression coefficients, which now become more accurately viewed as partial regression or slope coefficients, and the Xs are variables whose effects are represented by the βs. Each observation in the data will have the same value on βs (the regression coefficients), but each person will have a different value on Y, X, and the error term.

The multiple regression coefficients serve to isolate the impact on Y of a change in one variable from the impact on Y of changes in the other variables. This is possible because multiple regression takes the changes in X_2 and X_3 into account when it estimates the coefficient of X_1, where X_2 and X_3 are predictors 2 and 3, respectively.

Estimating Multiple Regression with Ordinary Least Squares

The workhorse of regression analysis is an estimator called ordinary least squares (OLS). An estimator is a set of mathematical procedures for arriving at best guesses of population values (parameters) based on sample values (statistics). There are numerous estimators, and they arrive at estimates in different ways. Ordinary least squares calculates estimates by minimizing the squared differences (residuals) between values predicted by our equation (line) and actual values collected in the data for individual observations.

You will recall that regression is based on a straight-line relationship between the outcome variable and predictor variable(s). If there are no errors in prediction, the predicted values and the observed values of Y will fall on the regression line (at times called the line of best fit). In other words, predicted and observed values will be the same. Rarely, however, is this possible, because in real-world situations there is no perfection, especially in the social sciences. Thus, there will be differences between values predicted by our equation (the regression line) and actual sample values for the cases.

OLS works by selecting regression coefficients that make the squared errors in prediction (residuals) as small as possible. Why does OLS work with squared residuals? In making predictions of population values, some errors will be positive, whereas others will be negative. If, therefore, we just add up the errors, the positives will cancel out the negatives, and the sum will be zero. There will be no way to accurately assess the extent of prediction errors. However, if the errors (residuals) are squared, the problem of having positive and negative errors canceling each other out is eliminated. Despite squaring (and eventually summing) the squared residuals, the general rule is that we want the summed value to be as close to zero as possible, and if our model fits the data very well, the sum of squared residuals will indeed be close to zero.

Hypotheses in Multiple Regression

In multiple regression we begin with the same global null hypothesis about goodness of fit:

$$H_0 : R^2 = 0$$

That is, we first test the idea that there is no association between *any* of the independent variables and the dependent variable. This hypothesis is tested with an F-statistic. If we fail this test (fail to reject the null hypothesis), then we can go no further. If we pass the test, then we know that one, or more, or some combination of independent variables do predict on the outcome. We then search to find which ones, by testing the null hypotheses:

$$H_o : \beta_{YX1.2,3} = 0$$
$$H_o : \beta_{YX2.1,3} = 0$$
$$H_o : \beta_{YX3.1,2} = 0$$

That is: the partial slope of the effect on Y of X_1, while adjusting (or controlling) for X_2 and X_3, is zero. And the partial slope of the effect on Y of X_2, while adjusting for X_1 and X_3, is zero. And the partial slope of the effect on Y of X_3, while controlling for X_1 and X_2, is zero. These hypotheses are tested with t-tests.

The Estimated Regression Equation

When we estimate the parameters of our multiple regression equation using sample data, the process is very much the same as with simple regression. First we examine each variable by itself, and then each pair of variables—to see if the assumptions of normality and linearity are being met. Sometimes there are problems in satisfying these assumptions, and the scores on variables may need to be transformed or indexed.

The next step is to examine the global null hypothesis of no joint association of *Y* with all of the *X* variables. We do this using R^2 and the F-test. If no *X* or combination of *X*ss predicts *Y*, we're done—time to rethink our theory!

Assuming that one or more *X* variables do predict *Y*, we proceed to test the statistical significance of the partial slopes, and interpret the effects.

Finally, as in simple regression, we need to examine the residuals. Remember that the *residual* is defined as shown in Formula 14.4:

$$e_i = Y_i - \hat{Y}_i \tag{14.4}$$

The residual is not the same as the error term that we have met earlier. The error term is theoretical in nature. To understand the residual, one must think again of the fact that in regression analysis, there is an equation for each observation in the data. Furthermore, we are interested in predicting values of *Y* for each person on the basis of values of *X* for each individual. A question that has to be answered is the following: How accurate were our predictions for individuals in the population?

The residual is the difference between what we predicted for each person in the population and what the actual data values are for that person. The Y_i is the value for a given person in the data, and the $\hat{Y}_i$ is what we predicted that person's value to be. If we subtract the two numbers, the resulting difference is the residual or prediction error (what was left over). Residuals can be positive or negative. A positive value implies that we overestimated *Y* for the individual. A negative value, on the other hand, means that we underestimated *Y* for the person or observation. In general, residuals should be as close to zero as possible. If a given residual is zero, then our regression model was very accurate in making predictions for that observation.

A large residual for an individual in the sample indicates that the specified regression equation did not do a good job in predicting that person's value on the dependent variable (*Y*). If we have lots of cases characterized by large residuals, then even if the obtained R^2 and F-value are large, we ought to consider the possibility that there is something wrong with our theory or model. It may apply to some cases, but not to others. It is imperative that we identify the particular cases with large residuals and determine some unique properties about those cases or observations. Look at Table 14.4 to help you further understand residuals.

Extending Multiple Regression

The multiple regression equation is a powerful method for describing the joint and partial associations of two or more interval/ratio independent variables on an interval/ratio dependent variable. There are many very important research problems for which the multiple regression model is very helpful. With some minor modifications, multiple regression can be extended to many more research problems.

TABLE 14.4 Residuals for 10 Cases after Predicting Income with Education and Age: The 2008 General Social Survey

Case	R's Income ($)	Predicted Income ($)	Residual
01	14,728	38,884	−24,158
02	44,179	72,095	−27,916
03	24,098	29,638	−5,540
04	8,702	4,682	4,019
05	17,404	18,999	−1,596
06	480,144	42,532	437,612
07	64,260	62385	1,874
08	29,453	32,853	−3,401
09	44,179	58,705	−14,526
10	64,260	55,458	8,801

In simple linear and multiple regression, we have independent variables that are measured at the interval/ratio level. However, there are variables whose very nature is categorical, and not including them in the multiple regression equation could have deleterious consequences on our theoretical arguments. One could argue, for example, that education affects income differently for various racial/ethnic groups, or for different gender groups. If in fact race and gender influence income and their effects are not taken into account, our regression equation will not be adequate, and there could be lots of errors, resulting in large residuals. One way to include categorical variables in a regression model is to code each variable so that there is a suppressed or reference category. It is that reference category against which we compare the remaining categories with regard to their influence on the dependent variable. Categorical variables are often coded 1, 0, with 1 representing the group in the equation, and 0 representing the reference category or the suppressed group. Once coded in this manner, variables are called *dummy variables.* They are dummy not in terms of being stupid, but because they have been transformed and coded into 1 and 0. The slope or regression coefficients obtained are interpreted slightly differently from those derived from interval/ratio variables.

The multiple regression equation's partial slope coefficients tell us about the effect of each X on Y, holding constant or "partialling on" or controlling for all the others. But sometimes the effects of one X on Y depend on other X variables. For example, the effect of years of education on earnings may differ for men and for women. Multiple regression can be extended to examine this kind of *effect modification*, or *statistical interaction.*

To understand effect modification, think of a chemistry class that you had, maybe in high school. You probably recall that mixing sugar and sulfuric acid produced something that was neither sugar nor acid, but likely carbon. In other words, a synergistic effect was found. Likewise, in statistics, a variable like sex may have its own unique effect on income. Likewise, marital status (being married) may have its own unique effect. At the same time, a

CHECK QUIZ 14.3

1. In multiple regression, the constant or intercept is
   a. the predicted value of X1 when X2 is held constant.
   b. the predicted value of Y when all X values are zero.
   c. the predicted value of Y when all X values are dummy variables.
   d. the average score on Y.
2. The joint effect of all X variables on Y in multiple regression is measured by
   a. the coefficient of determination.
   b. the partial slope.
   c. the multicollinearity.
   d. the regression coefficient.
3. The effect of X1 on Y, controlling for X2 and X3, in multiple regression is described by
   a. the coefficient of determination.
   b. the t-test.
   c. the partial slope coefficient.
   d. the beta coefficient.
4. We can tell which independent variable has the largest partial effect on *Y* in multiple regression by examining the
   a. coefficient of determination.
   b. partial regression coefficient.
   c. standardized partial regression coefficient.
   d. F-test.

combination of the two may produce an effect that is also unique. The effect that is produced when two variables are cross multiplied is what is referred to as effect modification. Thus, gender may modify the effect of marital status on income. Think of it like this. It may well be that being married leads to higher income in general, but being married and at the same time being a woman may lead either to even higher income or to lower income. Effect modification is more popularly known in the social science literature as interaction. Two variables X_1 and X_2 may interact to produce a different effect that is not found when X_1 and X_2 are in the equation by themselves.

APPLYING MULTIPLE REGRESSION

Illustrating that that there is a meaningful bivariate association between education and income is only the first step in the process of building the case for the existence of a true relationship between the two variables in the population. The next steps involve eliminating alternative explanations for the association and considering multiple causes.

Let's study an example of how multiple regression is often applied in practice. Previously, we examined how income depends on education. But now we will extend this research by considering whether this effect might be spurious due to respondent's age. Then, we will see if the effect of education on income operates by way of the ***mediating variable*** of occupational prestige. Along the way, we will study the meaning and interpretation of multiple regression statistics.

Controlling for a Possible Spurious Effect

As you may have learned in your research methods classes, a relationship may exist between two variables X and Y not because that relationship is real, but because of some other variable that is causally prior to both X and Y. Once that extraneous variable's effect is removed, the original relationship between X and Y disappears. This situation is usually referred to as ***spuriousness.*** In the present case, one possible variable whose exclusion from the regression equation could cause X (education) and Y (income) to be related is respondent's age. It is plausible that older respondents have had more time to accumulate education and also have had more time to build a career. Since age is likely associated with both the independent and dependent variables and is causally prior to both, it represents a potential source of spuriousness that must be controlled if we are to build the case that education truly predicts income.

Let's examine the relationship between income and schooling, but control for respondent's age. In SPSS, we choose the *Analyze* menu, then *Regression*, and then *Linear.* We select *realrinc*, R's annual income in constant dollars, as the dependent variable. Now, however, our independent variables include both *educ* (highest year of school completed) and *age* (age of respondent).

First we examine the global null hypothesis of no joint effects and assess how well we do in predicting income in Table 14.5.

In an analysis that included only education as a predictor, we saw that the R^2 of income predicted by education was 0.051. After adding age as another predictor, we are now able to explain 5.8 percent of the total variance in income. This is not much of an improvement, but it is clear that age is adding something to our explanation. The F-test (not shown) convinces us that the two independent variables (education and age), taken together, do enable us to predict income (that is, R^2 is not equal to 0).

Having passed the global hypothesis test, we next look at the slope coefficients for the multiple regression (Table 14.6).

TABLE 14.5 Income, Education, and Age: Goodness of Fit

Model	R	R-Squared	Adjusted R-Squared	Std. Error of the Estimate
1	0.241[a]	0.058	0.056	75,349.393

TABLE 14.6 Income, Education, and Age: Partial Effects

Model	Unstandardized Coefficients	Standardized Coefficients	t	Sig.		
	B	Std. Error	Beta			
1	(Constant)	−70,153.503	12,395.253		−5.660	0.000
	Highest year of school completed	5,999.071	752.873	0.223	7.968	0.000
	Age of respondent	463.909	157.799	0.082	2.940	0.003

The *Y*-intercept (constant) is the predicted value of the dependent variable for a case with a value of 0 on *all* of the independent variables. So, a person age 0 with no education is predicted to have lost $37,590.50 in 2008. We should avoid placing too much emphasis on the substantive meaning on the value of this *y*-intercept since there are no members of the sample (or the population of interest) who have these characteristics.

Each slope coefficient in a multiple regression model reflects the effect of the given variable while controlling for all other variables included in the model. In our results, the coefficient for education indicates that, once the influence of age is removed, income increases by an average of $5,999.07 for each additional year of education. Each year of age appears to predict an income gain of $464. The t-tests tell us that both age and education have effects while controlling for one another.

But which (age or education) has the bigger effect, controlling for the other? The standardized coefficients provide the answer. Since they express all coefficients in terms of the same units (standard deviations), standardized coefficients are especially handy in multivariate models where we want to directly compare the size of the effects of different independent variables with regard to how they predict values on the dependent variable. In our example, the standardized coefficient for education is 0.223, indicating that an increase of one standard deviation in education is associated with an increase of 0.223 standard deviation in income. In comparison, an increase of one standard deviation in age is associated with an increase in income that is just 0.082 (beta = 0.082). Based on this information, we can say the predictive substantive role of education is greater than that of age. Gaining education may be more important than merely aging.

If education does really predict income, as our theoretical argument suggests, then we should observe a statistically significant effect of education even after we remove the effects of age (and any other influences on income). If the original association is wiped out (completely attenuated) when we statistically control for age, then the theoretical expectation of a causal relationship between education and income would be contradicted. Thus, comparing the partial coefficient for our key independent variable to the coefficient from the bivariate model provides an indication of how much of the original association was actually spurious, created by the influence of age on both education and income. In fact, after controlling for age, the effect of education changes very little. It goes from $6,178.68 in the bivariate model to $5,999.07 in the multivariable model and remains statistically significant with a *p*-value of 0.000. This adds a bit more support to the idea that there is a real predictive relationship between education and income.

Controlling for a Potential Intervening Variable

After you have eliminated all of the sources of redundancy and spuriousness that you can think of, it is time to move on to include more variables that make theoretical sense. In this example, we will test the theoretical argument that education predicts income through its influence on occupational prestige. That is, we expect that high levels of education increase the chances of ending up in a job that is prestigious and that this occupational location is associated with higher earnings. In this sense, occupational prestige can be thought of as an ***intervening variable*** linking education to income. We can classify the occupations of the workers in the sample using an occupational prestige score. The score ranges from 0 to 100, with higher scores indicating higher levels of occupational prestige. If our theoretical argument is correct, the coefficient for education should be attenuated (reduced) when we control for the influence of occupational prestige in the multivariate regression model, because the influence of a crucial link in the chain connecting education to income will be statistically removed.

We begin with the global null hypothesis of joint effect (Table 14.7).

According to the reported *R*-squared statistic, we account for 6.2 percent of the variation in income by taking into consideration a combination of education, age, and occupational prestige. While this is still a very weak joint relationship, we note that the R^2 does increase when we add the occupational prestige variable. Next, we examine the partial effects (Table 14.8).

Consistent with theoretical expectations, occupational prestige has positively predicted income. A one-unit increase in prestige leads to an increase in income of about $437.47. This may not seem like much in comparison to the large coefficient for education, but it is

TABLE 14.7 Income, Education, Age, and Occupational Status: Goodness of Fit

Model Summary				
Model	***R***	***R*-Squared**	**Adjusted *R*-Squared**	**Std. Error of the Estimate**
1	0.248[a]	0.062	0.059	73,845.126

TABLE 14.8 Income, Age, Education, and Occupational Status: Partial Effects

Coefficients						
		Unstandardized Coefficients		**Standardized Coefficients**		
Model		***B***	**Std. Error**	**Beta**	**t**	**Sig.**
1	(Constant)	−70,245.444	12,328.529		−5.698	0.000
	Highest year of school completed	4,875.003	868.544	0.184	5.613	0.000
	Age of respondent	366.402	157.074	0.066	2.333	0.020
	R's occupational prestige score (1980)	437.477	183.438	0.079	2.385	0.017

greater than that for age. A comparison of the standardized coefficients indicates that an increase of one standard deviation in occupational prestige produces a larger jump in income than does a one-standard-deviation increase in age. Using t-tests, we see that all three partial effects are statistically significant.

As before, attenuation of the education coefficient is of central interest to us given that our key relationship refers to the impact of education on income. As predicted in our theoretical arguments, the inclusion of occupational prestige in our model does result in a substantial reduction in the coefficient for education from $5,999.07 to $4,875.00. This attenuation of the coefficient is consistent with the theoretical argument that education predicts income, in part, by influencing the types of jobs that respondents end up in.

Multiple regression analysis allows us to extend simple regression analysis in some very powerful ways. The ideas of joint association (the ability of many independent variables, all together, predicting a dependent variable) and partial association (the effect of a variable adjusting for others) enable us to examine much more interesting and complex problems.

CHECK QUIZ 14.4

1. Linear regression analysis is used when the dependent variable is
   a. interval/ratio.
   b. a nominal dichotomy.
   c. a nominal polyotomy.
   d. ordinal.

2. Linear regression parameters are estimated from sample data using the method of
   a. guessing.
   b. ordinary least squares.
   c. maximum likelihood.
   d. extraordinary least squares.

SUMMARY

In this chapter we've introduced the simple linear regression model and seen one extension of it—multiple regression. The linear regression model is the basis for almost all advanced statistical analyses in the social sciences. The basic idea is to predict scores on an outcome variable as a linear and additive function of scores on one or more independent variables.

Two new concepts have been introduced. Joint association is the ability to reduce error in predicting a dependent variable by knowing the scores on multiple independent variables. The global null hypothesis in all regression analysis is that the joint association is zero. The other new concept is partial association. Partial association describes the effect of one independent variable on a dependent variable while holding constant (or "partialling on" or controlling for) other independent variables. The local hypothesis tests of regression analysis are that the partial effects (or partial slopes, or partial regression coefficients) are zero—indicating no effect of an independent variable, net of the effects of others.

We first examined simple regression (one interval/ratio dependent variable and one interval/ratio independent variable). The global null hypothesis is tested with an F-test of the R^2, which is estimated by ordinary least squares. The linear effect of X is tested with a t-test of the slope coefficient. We saw how the linear regression equation describes the effect of X on Y. The idea of prediction errors or residuals was introduced. The assumptions of linear regression analysis were also examined.

Next, we extended the simple regression model to multiple regression. In multiple regression, an interval/ratio dependent variable is a linear additive function of more than one independent variable. The multiple regression model lets us examine the ideas that the relationship between a given Y and X may be spurious due to the effects of antecedent other causes (i.e., additional X variables). The multiple regression model also lets us study whether the effect of one X on Y is mediated by another, intervening X variable.

KEY TERMS

global null hypothesis
goodness of fit
homoscedasticity assumption
intercept or constant
intervening variable
linearity assumption
mediating variable
multicollinearity assumption
multiple regression
normality of distribution assumption
ordinary least squares (OLS)
residual
simple regression
slope or regression coefficient
spuriousness
standard error of regression
standardized regression (beta) coefficient

CHECK QUIZ ANSWERS

Quiz 14.1 Answers: 1. (d); 2. (d); 3. (c) 4. (b)
Quiz 14.2 Answers: 1. (d); 2. (c); 3. (e)
Quiz 14.3 Answers: 1. (b); 2. (a); 3. (c); 4. (c)
Quiz 14.4 Answers: 1. (a); 2. (b)

EXERCISES

1. A researcher is interested in evaluating two alternative theories. One theory views television watching as part of American mass culture and a low-brow form of entertainment. This theory suggests that television viewing should be negatively related to socioeconomic status. The other theory suggests that television viewing is a way of gaining access to information and culture. This view suggests that television viewing should be positively related to socioeconomic status.

   Data are collected from the General Social Survey, and a regression analysis is performed with hours per week of television viewing being predicted by socioeconomic status. Here are a number of results of the analysis.

Model Summary				
Model	***R***	***R*-Squared**	**Adjusted *R*-Squared**	**Std. Error of the Estimate**
1	0.238	0.057	0.056	2.512

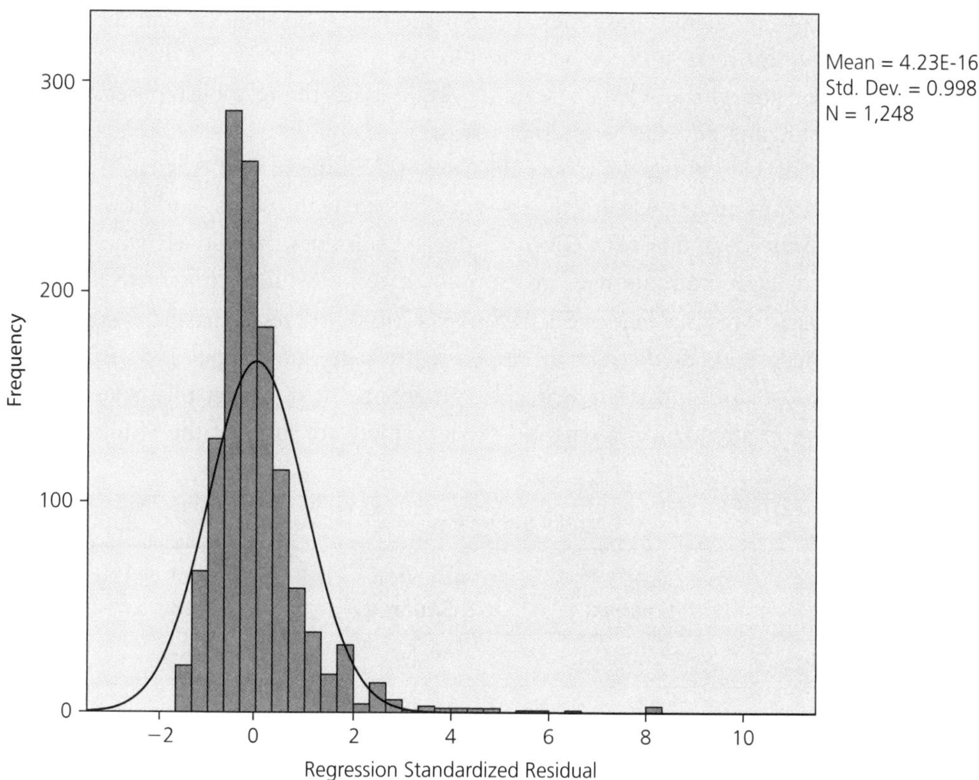

Histogram of Residuals Dependent Variable: Hours per Day Watching TV

Coefficients						
		Unstandardized Coefficients		**Standardized Coefficients**		
Model		***B***	**Std. Error**	**Beta**	**t**	**Sig.**
1	(Constant)	4.493	0.191		23.515	0.000
	Socioeconomic index	−0.032	0.004	−0.238	−8.689	0.000

a. Is there a significant linear relationship between the two variables? What is your evidence?
b. How strong is the relationship between the variables? Interpret the R^2.
c. What is the predicted television watching level of a person with a socioeconomic index score of 50? With a score of 75? With a score of 25?

d. Interpret the meaning of the constant and the unstandardized slope.
e. Comment on whether the residuals from the regression indicate that the assumptions of linear regression are being met.
f. What conclusion should the researcher reach about the relationship between television watching and socioeconomic status?

2. A sociologist of religion has the theory that one of the functions of religion in society is to regulate norms about sexual activity—who has sex with whom, and how often. In Western, advanced capitalist societies, the researcher argues, individuals who are more attached to religious communities are more likely to be sexually conservative.

   Using data from the General Social Survey (2008), the researcher performs a linear regression analysis to predict survey responses to a question about the respondent's frequency of sex during the last year. The variable used to predict this is an index of the frequency of attendance at religious services. Here are some of the results:

Model Summary

Model	***R***	***R*-Squared**	**Adjusted *R*-Squared**	**Std. Error of the Estimate**
1	0.054	0.003	0.002	2.016

ANOVA

Model	**Sum of Squares**	***df***	**Mean Square**	**F**	**Sig.**	
1	Regression	20.342	1	20.342	5.006	0.025
	Residual	6,834.330	1,682	4.063		
	Total	6,854.672	1,683			

Coefficients

		Unstandardized Coefficients		**Standardized Coefficients**		
Model		***B***	**Std. Error**	**Beta**	**t**	**Sig.**
1	(Constant)	2.849	0.080		35.567	0.000
	How often R attends religious services	−0.040	0.018	−0.054	−2.237	0.025

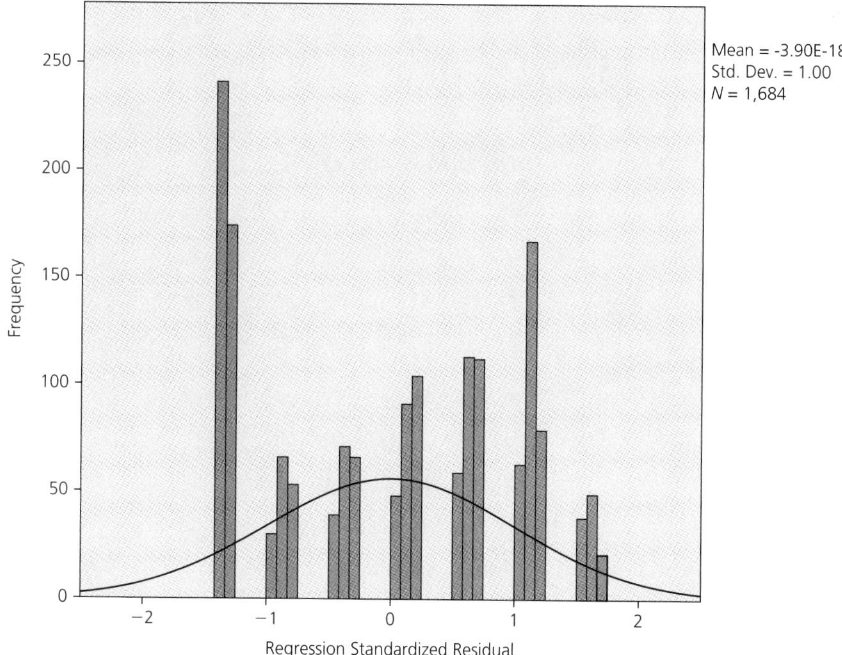

a. Is there a significant linear relationship between the two variables? What is your evidence?
b. How strong is the relationship between the variables? Interpret the R^2. Is the relationship statistically significant, according to the F-test?
c. What is the predicted sexual frequency index score of persons with a religious attendance index score of 5? Of 3? Of 1?
d. Interpret the meaning of the constant and the unstandardized slope.
e. Comment on whether the residuals from the regression indicate that the assumptions of linear regression are being met.
f. What conclusion should the researcher reach about the relationship between the frequency of sexual intercourse and religious service attendance?

3. Our researcher who is studying television watching has decided to add some independent variables to the statistical model predicting average daily hours of watching. To the previous bivariate regression equation with socioeconomic index, the researcher has added: respondent's age (older people are more likely to watch TV, especially if they have retired); number of persons in respondent's household (HOMPOP; a higher number of persons in a household will likely generate greater conflict over choice of programs to be watched; such households may also have lower income, and thus fewer TV sets, with the possible consequence of lower TV watching per individual); and last, female. We suspect that although female labor force participation has increased tremendously in the United States (and across the world), women might still outnumber men in terms of those staying at home (e.g., to take care of children). Women are also greater targets of TV executives in terms of

advertising products. Women will therefore be expected to watch more TV per week. The female effect might be negligible, however, given social change in the United States.

Here are the descriptive statistics for all of the variables:

Descriptive Statistics

	Mean	Std. Deviation	*N*
Hours per day watching TV	2.95	2.591	1,248
Age of respondent	47.41	16.843	1,248
Respondent socioeconomic index	48.333	19.3421	1,248
Number of persons in household	2.58	1.435	1,248
Female	0.5240	0.49962	1,248

Next, we see information about goodness of fit.

Model Summary

Model	*R*	*R*-Squared	Adjusted *R*-Squared	Std. Error of the Estimate
1	0.301[a]	0.091	0.088	2.474

ANOVA[a] Model		Sum of Squares	*df*	Mean Square	F	Sig.
1	Regression	760.586	4	190.147	31.065	0.000
	Residual	7,608.334	1,243	6.121		
	Total	8,368.920	1,247			

Next, we have the results describing the estimated multiple regression equation.

Coefficients

		Unstandardized Coefficients		Standardized Coefficients		
Model		*B*	Std. Error	Beta	t	Sig.
1	(Constant)	3.717	0.344		10.800	0.000
	Age of respondent	0.022	0.004	0.142	4.896	0.000
	Respondent socioeconomic index	−0.034	0.004	−0.251	−9.265	0.000

Coefficients						
	Unstandardized Coefficients		Standardized Coefficients			
Model	*B*	Std. Error	Beta	t	Sig.
Number of persons in household	−0.120	0.053	−0.066	−2.277	0.023
Female	0.244	0.140	0.047	1.735	0.083

Finally, the researcher examines a histogram of the prediction errors.

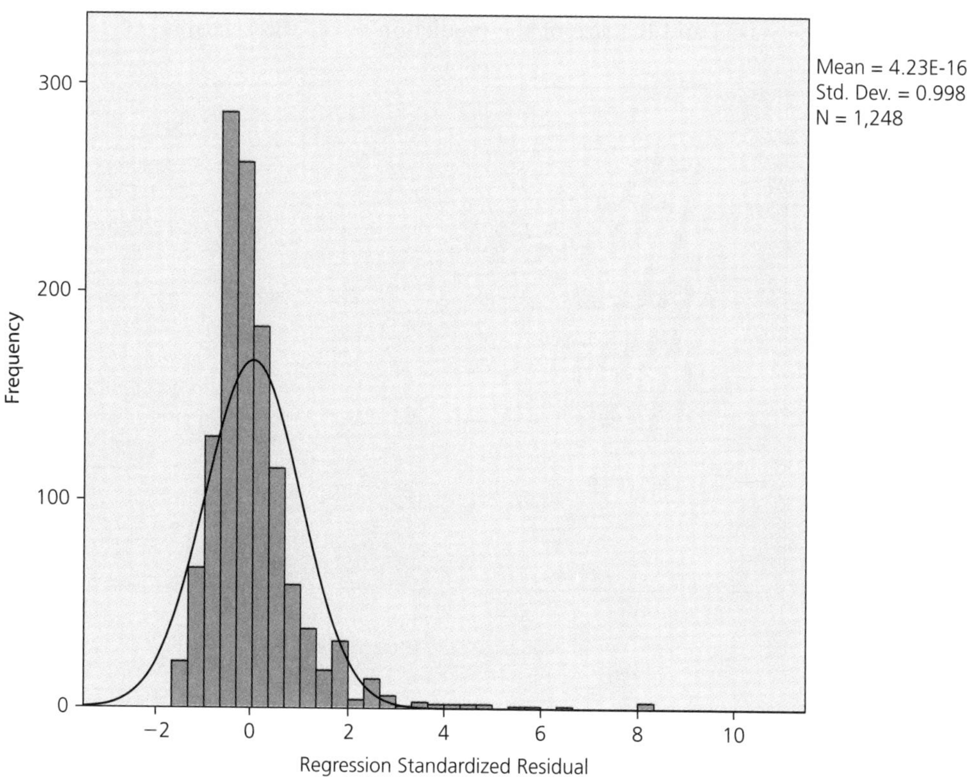

a. Is there a statistically significant joint relationship between the independent variables and TV watching? What is your evidence?
b. How strong is the joint relationship? What is your evidence? Are we able to predict TV watching better using more variables than just social class?
c. Which independent variables have statistically significant partial effects on the dependent variable? What is your evidence?

d. Describe the partial effects by interpreting the unstandardized regression coefficients.
e. Which independent variable has the largest effect on TV watching, controlling for the others? What is your evidence?
f. Comment on the residuals plot. Does it appear that the assumptions of linear regression have been satisfied?
g. What should the researcher conclude about the hypotheses?

4. In the problems on predicting TV watching, the dependent variable was measured as the number of hours per day that respondents reported watching television. After doing the regression analyses, the researcher prepared a plot having to do with the residuals from the regression.

In the plot, we see the relationship between the predicted score on television watching (the y-axis) and the size of the prediction error (the x-axis).

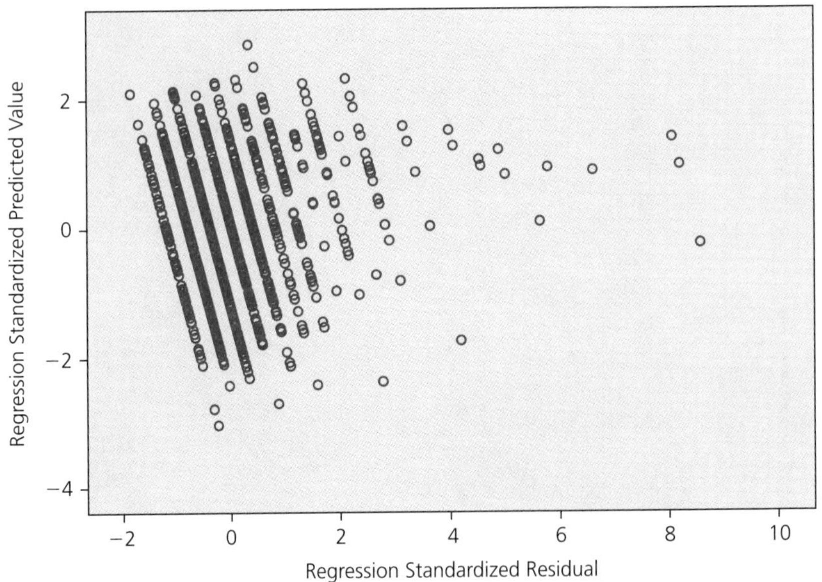

a. Describe the pattern of distribution of the residuals. Are there outliers? Does the plot display homoscedasticity?
b. Why do there appear to be stripes in the plot?

5. Our researcher is continuing the exploration of predictors of the frequency of sexual intercourse. In an earlier analysis, it was found that as the frequency of attendance at religious services increased, reported sexual activity declined. Our researcher's original results have been criticized, and a number of additional independent variables have been suggested.

In addition to the index of the frequency of church attendance, the respondent's age has been added to the model. Among persons over 18 in the General Social Survey sample, it is hypothesized that sexual frequency declines with age. Whether persons are married or not (1 = married, 0 = not) has been added. It is hypothesized that married persons have higher rates of sexual intercourse. The variable "male" has been added (1 = male, 0 = not). Previous studies have shown that males are more likely to report (and overreport) sexual frequency than females are. Education has been added as well (highest year of schooling completed). The researcher doesn't have a hypothesis about education, but feels that it may make a difference. Last, the researcher adds a measure of health (1 = excellent health, 2 = good health, 3 = fair health, and 4 = poor health). The researcher hypothesizes that ill health inhibits sexual activity.

First we see the basic descriptive statistics for the variables in the new analysis.

Descriptive Statistics

	Mean	**Std. Deviation**	***N***
Frequency of sex during past year	2.72	1.995	1,127
How often R attends religious services	3.63	2.783	1,127
Age of respondent	46.70	17.445	1,127
Married	0.4765	0.49967	1,127
Condition of health	2.03	0.803	1,127
Male	0.4561	0.49829	1,127
Highest year of school completed	13.57	3.016	1,127

Next, we have information on the goodness of fit of the new model.

Model Summary

Model	***R***	***R*-Squared**	**Adjusted *R*-Squared**	**Std. Error of the Estimate**
1	0.584	0.341	0.337	1.624

and

ANOVA

Model	**Sum of Squares**	***df***	**Mean Square**	**F**	**Sig.**	
1	Regression	1,528.030	6	254.672	96.564	0.000
Residual	2,953.805	1,120	2.637			
Total	4,481.835	1,126				

Finally, we receive the results with the estimated parameters of the regression equation.

Coefficients

Model		Unstandardized Coefficients: B	Unstandardized Coefficients: Std. Error	Standardized Coefficients: Beta	t	Sig.
1	(Constant)	5.767	0.312		18.504	0.000
	How often R attends religious services	0.013	0.018	0.018	0.697	0.486
	Age of respondent	−0.059	0.003	−0.519	−20.453	0.000
	Married	1.267	0.101	0.317	12.566	0.000
	Condition of health	−0.172	0.063	−0.069	−2.716	0.007
	Male	0.323	0.099	0.081	3.271	0.001
	Highest year of school completed	−0.053	0.017	−0.080	−3.193	0.001

a. Is there a statistically significant joint relationship between the independent variables and the frequency of sexual intercourse? What is your evidence?
b. How strong is the joint relationship? What is your evidence? Are we able to predict sexual frequency better using more variables than just religious service attendance?
c. Which independent variables have statistically significant partial effects on the dependent variable? What is your evidence?
d. Describe the partial effects by interpreting the unstandardized regression coefficients.
e. Which independent variable has the largest effect on sexual frequency, controlling for the others? What is your evidence?
f. What should the researcher conclude about the hypotheses?

Chapter 15

Logistic Regression Analysis

LEARNING OBJECTIVES

When you have finished this chapter, you will be able to:

- Distinguish between linear and nonlinear relationships.
- Understand what to do when an outcome variable is nonlinear.
- Understand what to do when the outcome variable has only two values.
- Understand logistic regression theory.
- Estimate and interpret logistic regression.

PREDICTING WITH NONLINEAR RELATIONSHIPS

A predictive association between two variables need not always follow a linear (straight-line) pattern. Indeed, there are many nonlinear relationships encountered in research. For example, it is known from sociological and epidemiologic studies that the risk of human mortality is high at birth. Thereafter, for each extra minute that an infant survives, its risk of death declines until middle age. It should be noted of course that as long as a person is alive, his or her mortality risk is never zero. Mortality risk declines rapidly after birth, stays somewhat flat in youth and early adult ages, but begins to rise again beyond age 50. After age 65, mortality risk rises sharply, and accelerates even faster beyond age 70. Investigating whether a person is alive or dead given that he or she was born would not assume a linear relationship between mortality and any covariates utilized as risk factors.

In sociology, it is known that a relationship exists between age and the probability of owning a home, but this relationship does not follow a linear (straight-line) manner. In the teenage years (say up to age 15), the home ownership probability for ordinary individuals is likely 0. This may continue through the college years while individuals are acquiring human capital and other needed skills to enter the labor market. With completion of college education and subsequent acquisition of employment along with marriage for some, home ownership probabilities begin to rise rather rapidly above 0, until they plateau at age 65. If we were to draw a curve describing the relationship between home ownership and age, we would most likely end up with a curve that resembles an *S*. Figure 15.1 is a sketch of what we would expect this relationship to look like.

A social scientist may be interested in estimating whether there are sex differences in preference for gun ownership in a home. Preference for gun ownership may be measured as 1 = yes and 0 = no. Similarly, another researcher may divide the nations of the world into those that have experienced civil wars in the post-Soviet era (1 = yes) and those that have not (0 = no). An epidemiologist may be interested in studying whether frequency of cell phone use leads to the development of brain tumors. From a population of cell phone users and nonusers after some years of follow-up, the researcher might divide the sample into those who developed tumors and those who did not. The estimating strategy would be to determine if the odds of developing tumors are elevated by cell phone use.

As may be seen in Figure 15.1, a logistic curve (as opposed to a straight line) shows an *S* shape. It begins flat, goes on for a while, and then begins to rise and quickly accelerate. At some point, it begins to curve again smoothly until the top becomes almost as flat as how it started. Applying this to home ownership rates, the curve is flat (hovering at 0) when people are young. It is rare (though not impossible) for individuals below 20 to own their own homes; typically, they are in school learning. At age 30, however, a substantial number have completed their education, possibly gotten married, and begun to raise families. Accordingly, home ownership rates rise rather sharply. This rise is even sharper at age 40 when a substantial proportion of the population now owns their homes. Ownership here means they hold

FIGURE 15.1 Logistic Curve Showing the Relationship between Age and Percent of Homeowners

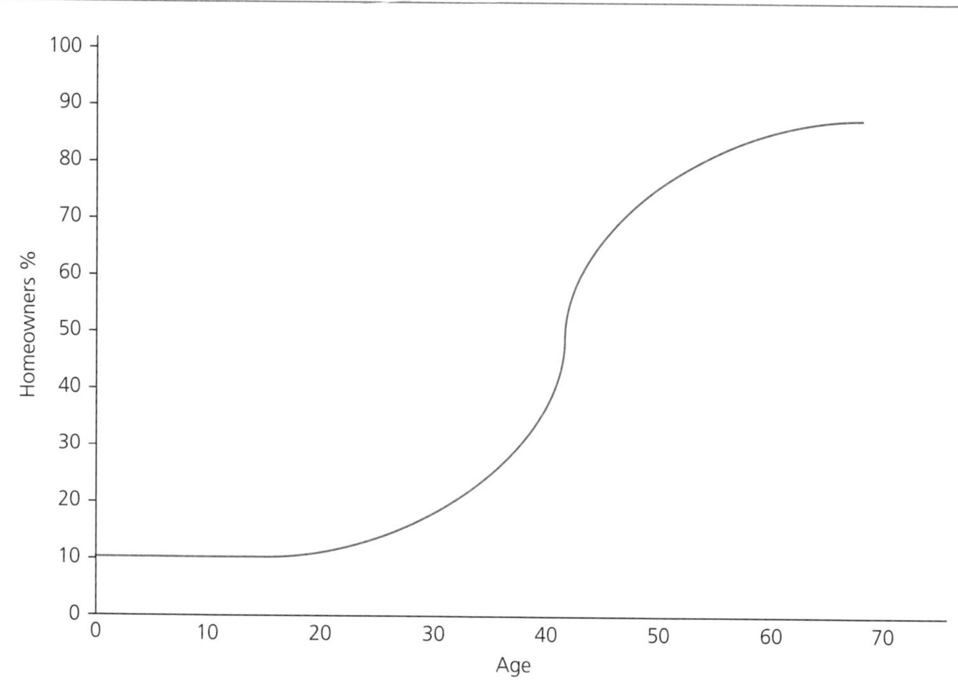

mortgages and do not, strictly speaking, own their homes (the banks do). The curve flattens beyond age 55. Clearly, those who wanted to own homes and had the means have already purchased homes; they are not after new ones. Beyond 65, people enter retirement age and again do not begin owning new homes.

One relationship that is definitely not linear is that which may exist between a dependent variable that has only two values and an independent variable with any number of values. The former is often described as a binary response variable, given that a given unit of analysis can take one of only two possible outcomes. There are many relationships of interest in the social sciences where the outcome, or dependent, variable has only two values: true/false, yes/no, alive/dead, event happened/did not happen.

Where the outcome has two values, a researcher who attempts to fit a linear model through ordinary least squares (OLS) regression will have many errors in the process, and any resulting estimates will not be precise or accurate. The rule, then, in statistics is that the researcher should understand the underlying relationship between variables before deciding whether to fit a straight line (using linear regression) or a curved (*S*-shaped) line using logistic regression. ***Logistic regression*** is almost always the preferred technique because the dependent variable has two values.

LOGISTIC REGRESSION

Up to this point, we have assumed that the dependent variable was measured at the interval/ratio level. It was further assumed that a straight-line relationship existed between the dependent variable and the independent variable(s). Suppose, however, we are confronted with doing research that involves predicting a dependent variable that is not interval/ratio, but instead is discrete, say with only two values, 1 and 2 or 1 and 0. Let us suppose further that the underlying theoretical relationship between a key independent variable and the outcome variable is not linear.

Dependent variables with only two outcomes (e.g., 1 or 0) are also called binary dependent variables. In the social sciences, examples include divorced/not divorced; favor marijuana decriminalization/do not favor marijuana decriminalization; employed/unemployed; in the labor force/not in the labor force; voted for Barack Obama in the 2008 election/did not vote for Obama. In public health and epidemiology, interest might be in death from suicide/death from other causes; dead/alive; smoked during pregnancy/did not smoke during pregnancy; suffers from depression/does not suffer from depression. As you can see, the applications are limited only by the imagination of the researcher.

When an outcome is dichotomous, it is often unrealistic to assume that the effect of X on it is linear. Suppose that X has a positive effect on a dichotomous Y. As X increases, Y increases; as X decreases, Y decreases. But suppose that X keeps increasing. If Y has already reached 1, it has no place left to go! When dependent variables are dichotomous, the OLS regression model can often predict scores on Y that are higher than 1, or lower than 0—which are logically impossible!

As we have seen, the OLS model assumes a straight line between the dependent variable and the independent variable(s); however, suppose the true model is not linear, but a threshold model. In some cases, this alternative (true) model makes more substantive and mathematical sense. If we force a straight line on a model that is clearly nonlinear, the result will be systematic correlation between X values and disturbances (ε). This is a violation of the regression assumption of no correlation between the independent variables and the error term. The consequences of this violation are grave: First, regression coefficients are no longer consistent, but inconsistent. Second, regression coefficients are no longer unbiased. Third, even a large sample will not save us here; tests of statistical significance are meaningless, as standard errors and t-values cannot be trusted.

Where the outcome is dichotomous and/or the effects of X are not linear, logistic regression can be used instead of OLS regression. This requires both a different model and a different approach to estimating the parameters from sample data.

THE LOGISTIC REGRESSION MODEL

The logistic regression model is used to predict a categorical variable by an independent variable or set of independent variables. The dependent variable may be binary, ordinal, or multicategorical—but we will consider only the case of a binary dependent variable. The independent variables may be interval/ratio, dichotomous, discrete, or a mixture of all. In addition, one may have interaction variables in a logistic regression equation. The model is shown as Formula 15.1:

$$P(Y_i = 1) = \frac{1}{1 + e^{-(\beta_0 + \beta_1 X_{1i} + \beta_2 X_{2i} + \ldots + \beta_k X_{ki})}} \tag{15.1}$$

where P is the probability of observing a case i on the outcome variable Y with a value of 1; P is equal to 1 over: 1 plus e to minus the quantity β_0 plus the sum of regression coefficients multiplied by values of individual cases on the various independent variables. The symbol e is Euler's constant, approximately equal to 2.71828.

The logistic regression model shown in Formula 15.1 states that the probability that a case will score 1 (instead of 0) is a multiplicative function of the effects of various X values (because, in the denominator, the effects are powers of e). This model makes mathematical sense, but is rather difficult to talk about in everyday language. So the logistic regression model, as we actually use it, is estimated in terms of effects of X on the ***log of the odds*** that $Y = 1$.

INTERPRETING EFFECTS IN LOGISTIC REGRESSION

The ***odds*** that an event will occur is the ratio of the expected number of times that an event will occur to the expected number of times it will not occur. For example, an odds of 6 means that we expect 6 times as many occurrences as nonoccurrences. An odds of 1/5 means that we expect only one-fifth as many occurrences as nonoccurrences. The general mathematical form is shown in Formulas 15.2 and 15.3).

$$O = \frac{P}{1 - P} = \frac{\text{Probability event occurs}}{\text{Probability event does not occur}} \tag{15.2}$$

$$P = \frac{O}{1 + O} \quad \text{where } O = \text{Odds and } P = \text{Probability} \tag{15.3}$$

There is a direct relationship between the odds that $Y = 1$ and the probability that $Y = 1$, as shown in Table 15.1.

This relationship between the odds and probabilities, plus a little algebra, allows us to restate Formula 15.2 in such a way that the log of the odds of $Y = 1$ is a linear and additive function of the effects of X, as shown in Formula 15.4.

$$\log[\text{odds}(Y_i = 1)] = \beta_0 + \beta_1 X_{1i} + \beta_2 X_{2i} + \ldots + \beta_k X_{ki} \tag{15.4}$$

For estimation and predictive purposes, however, probabilities have serious limitations. The first is that they are constrained to range from 0.0 to 1.0. This implies that if a given variable's real effect on an outcome variable exceeds 1, interpretation could be problematic. The second limitation is that a probability value cannot be negative. Again, suppose a given

TABLE 15.1 How Odds and Probabilities Are Related

Probability	Odds
0.1	0.11
0.2	0.25
0.3	0.43
0.4	0.67
0.5	1.00
0.6	1.50
0.7	2.33
0.8	4.00
0.9	9.00

independent variable's effect on a categorical variable is negative; interpretation of that effect (in the form of a logistic regression coefficient) would be meaningless. A researcher who does not resolve these limitations makes a grave mistake because an analyst should never place constraints on values of coefficients. They should be allowed to achieve their true value as they exist in the population and on the basis of the theory being tested.

How do we solve these two problems? Let us refer to the first as the "upper boundedness" problem, and to the second as the "positive only" problem for regression coefficients.

Solution takes a two-step approach through which we perform two transformations. First, we convert probabilities in odds as shown in Formula 15.2. Given that odds can take on infinite values, moving away from probabilities to odds now means that regression coefficients can take on any value that is zero or above. Next, we rely on left-hand side of Formula 15.4 to solve the second problem by taking the (natural) log of the odds and getting what is called the logit.

This two-step approach can be illustrated by an example. Let us calculate the logit for a case chosen at random in the population for the value on an independent variable or covariate. Suppose that our dependent variable has values 1 (voted for Barack Obama in the 2008 election) and 0 (voted for John McCain in the 2008 election). Let us further assume that the probability of that individual voting for Obama $P(Y=1)$ was 0.218. Based on Formula 15.2, we must divide this probability (occurrence) of voting by that of not voting (nonoccurrence).

If $P(Y=1)=0.218$, it follows that $1-P(Y=1)=0.782$. We take the ratio of these two numbers (voting for Obama versus not voting for Obama) to convert to odds. That is:

$$\text{Odds} = \frac{P(Y=1)}{1-P(Y=1)}$$

$$= \frac{0.218}{0.782}$$

$$= 0.279$$

Since we have only managed to obtain odds (removed upper boundedness), we must now strive to ensure that the associated logistic coefficient is in the correct direction. Hence, we take the log of the odds as in Formula 15.4.

Accordingly, the natural log of the odds in our example (ln 0.279) is equal to −1.276. Thus, the logit of the probability of voting for Obama is −1.276. The conversion to the logit teaches us an important two-part lesson: First, if we had stopped only at predicting probabilities without conversations, we would have come to the wrong conclusion (a positive number). Second, the true effect of the covariate involved would have been underestimated.

A major advantage of taking the log of the odds is that obtained coefficients have no bounds and they can take on negative as well as positive values, ranging from negative infinity to positive infinity.

Stated this way, logistic regression looks exactly like multiple regression on the right-hand side of the equation. The left-hand side of the equation is not the score on Y, though. Rather, it is the log of the odds that $Y = 1$. This means that each unit of X has the effect of β on the log of the odds of Y. The log of the odds of Y is not an easy idea, so we will show you some other ways to talk about effects in logistic regression in the following pages.

ESTIMATING LOGISTIC REGRESSION MODELS WITH MAXIMUM LIKELIHOOD

Because logistic regression operates on a categorical dependent variable, the method of ordinary least squares cannot be used (it assumes a normally distributed dependent variable). Instead, a more general method of estimation is used to find the best-fitting values of the parameters. This method is called maximum likelihood.

Maximum likelihood (ML) is an iterative estimation technique that chooses coefficient estimates that maximize the likelihood of the sample data set being observed. In logistic regression, the ML program chooses coefficient estimates that maximize the log of the probability (or likelihood) of observing the particular set of values of the dependent variable in the sample for a given set of X values.

The underlying question addressed by ML is the following: What values of population parameters have in fact given rise to the sample that we have observed? In other words, it selects estimates of parameter values that, if true, would maximize the probability of observing what we have in fact observed (the data). It accomplishes its task using a two-step sequence.

The first step is *constructing the likelihood function*. Here, the program relies on the researcher, who specifies a model by selecting a probability distribution for the dependent variable and choosing a functional form that relates the parameters of this distribution to the values of the independent variables. In the case of logistic regression, the binary dependent variable is presumed to have a binomial distribution. As in regular regression, we assume independent random sampling.

CHECK QUIZ 15.1

1. Logistic regression analysis is used when the dependent variable is
   a. interval/ratio.
   b. a nominal dichotomy.
   c. a nominal polyotomy.
   d. ordinal.
2. Logistic regression parameters are estimated from sample data using the method of
   a. guessing.
   b. ordinary least squares.
   c. maximum likelihood.
   d. extraordinary least squares.
3. The regression coefficients in logistic regression analysis show the effects of a one-unit change in X on
   a. the score on Y.
   b. the odds that $Y = 1$.
   c. the log of the odds that $Y = 1$.
   d. the probability that $Y = 1$.
4. True or False: The right-hand side of the logistic regression equation has the same form as it does in simple and multiple regression.

The second step is *maximization*. ML begins work by coming up with what are called starting values (initial estimates) of the parameters. The program then makes passes through the data to determine if improvements could be made to the initial estimates through maximizing the ***log likelihood***. It makes passes, called iterations, until no further improvements to the parameter estimates are possible.

Because logistic regression uses maximum likelihood, our old friend the coefficient of determination (R^2) cannot be directly estimated. So, we have two puzzles for interpreting logistic regression: First, how do we assess ***goodness of fit*** (the ***global null hypothesis***)? Second, how do we assess the partial effects of each X? It is easiest to understand the answers by working through an example. But first, a quick check quiz.

APPLYING LOGISTIC REGRESSION

Using data from the 2008 General Social Survey, let's apply logistic regression to predict the log of the odds of favoring marijuana decriminalization ($Y = 1$) versus not favoring decriminalization ($Y = 0$). Our key predictor is education. Our research hypothesis is that higher education increases the odds of favoring decriminalization. Age, sex (male $= 1$), and frequency of attendance at religious services are included as control variables.

Goodness of Fit in Logistic Regression

The first step in interpreting regression is to evaluate the global null hypothesis that none of the independent variables have any relationship to *Y*. In OLS regression, we do this by testing whether R^2 might be zero in the population, given what we observe in our sample, using an F-test. Since logistic regression uses maximum likelihood, not OLS, we need to do this test a different way.

We first estimate a model that assumes the null hypothesis is correct:

$$H_o: \beta_1 = \beta_2 = \beta_3 = 0$$

We measure the size of the residuals from this model with a log likelihood statistic.

Then we estimate the model again, assuming that the null hypothesis is wrong; that is, we find the maximum likelihood values of the β coefficients, given what see in the sample. Again, we measure the size of the residuals from this model with a log likelihood statistic.

Finally, we compare the two statistics by calculating a test statistic (Formula 15.5).

$$-2(\ln L_{\text{Null}} - \ln L_{\text{Model}}) \tag{15.5}$$

This statistic tells us how much the residual, or prediction error, has been reduced by using the *X* variables. The null hypothesis would suggest that this reduction is zero; if the statistic is large enough (in a chi-squared test with $df =$ number of independent variables), we reject the null hypothesis. Here, we conclude that at least one independent variable has an effect on the log odds of favoring decriminalization of marijuana. Table 15.2 shows the SPSS output.

SPSS also produces some pseudo-R^2 statistics that help to assess the strength of the joint association. The *R*-squared calculated in logistic regression may not be interpreted as a proportional reduction in error measure the same way as it would in OLS. Recall that the dependent variable is categorical with values of 1 and 0. Our aim is to come up with independent variables that can accurately classify the observations into 1 or 0 accurately on the basis of the independent variables. Through maximum likelihood, logistic regression attempts to classify cases correctly into category 1 or category 0. The higher the percentage of cases correctly classified into 1 or 0, the higher the predictive power of the model and, presumably, the higher the *R*-squared value.

TABLE 15.2 Goodness of Fit in Predicting Support for Decriminalization

Model Summary			
Step	**−2 Log Likelihood**	**Cox & Snell *R*-Squared**	**Nagelkerke *R*-Squared**
1	1,517.446	0.036	0.049

In the current case, we are very confident that there is a joint association in the population, but we are led to believe that the three independent variables do not reduce uncertainty very much in predicting who does, and who does not, favor decriminalization of marijuana.

ASSESSING PARTIAL EFFECTS

Having determined that we reject the global null hypothesis, we can turn to assessing the partial effects of the predictor variables. Table 15.3 shows the results of our analysis from SPSS; other software packages will produce the same results, but they will be formatted differently.

As in multiple linear regression, in logistic regression there is an implied null hypothesis for each independent variable included in the equation. In Table 15.3 we see parameter estimates, their associated standard errors, and test statistics for the null hypothesis that each logistic regression coefficient is equal to 0, or it has no effect on the log odds of favoring marijuana decriminalization.

The parameter estimates are logistic regression coefficients (*B*). Each has an estimated standard error—how much, on average, we would expect *B* to vary from one sample to another, just by chance. A test statistic (not t, but the Wald chi-squared) is calculated, and tested with one degree of freedom. In our example, we see that we cannot be confident (at $p < 0.05$) that men and women differ in their attitudes toward decriminalization ($p = 0.216$). Also, we cannot be confident that younger and older people differ (something of a surprise!). We can be confident, however, that people with more education and less differ in their attitudes. In addition, we can be confident that those who attend religious services more regularly have different attitudes about decriminalization than those who attend religious services less regularly.

So, we must now describe the form of the significant effects.

Remember that the *B* coefficient expresses the effect of a unit change in *X* on the log odds that a person favors decriminalization. For education, this effect is positive, whereas for religious attendance the effect is negative. So, as education increases, the log odds favoring decriminalization increase; and, as religious attendance increases, the log odds of favoring decriminalization decrease.

TABLE 15.3 Partial Effects on the Odds of Favoring Decriminalization of Marijuana

Variables in the Equation							
		B	Std. Error	Wald	*df*	Sig.	Exp(*B*)
Step 1	gender1(1)	−0.153	0.124	1.533	1	0.216	0.858
	educ	0.053	0.021	6.273	1	0.012	1.054
	attend	−0.126	0.023	29.894	1	0.000	0.882
	age	−0.004	0.004	0.981	1	0.322	0.996
	Constant	−0.334	0.344	0.944	1	0.331	0.716

Talking about effects on the log odds is awkward. So, what we usually do is to take the antilog (i.e., we exponentiate) the *B* coefficient so we can talk about how a change in *X* affects the odds of *Y*, as shown in the last column of Table 15.3.

In taking the antilog, we move from an additive to a multiplicative way of talking about effects. The exp(*B*) for the effect of education is 1.054. This means that (controlling for the effects of the other *X* variables) when education increases by one unit (i.e., a year), the odds that a person favors decriminalization are multiplied by 1.05 (or are increased by about 5 percent). The exp(*B*) for religious attendance is 0.882. This means that (controlling for the effects of other *X* variables) when religious attendance increases by one unit, the odds of favoring decriminalization are multiplied by 0.88 (or are reduced to 88 percent of what they were at the lower level of religious attendance).

EXTENDING LOGISTIC REGRESSION

Since the right-hand side of the logistic regression model is exactly the same as any other regression model, we can include categorical and continuous independent variables in logistic regressions. We can also include interaction effects, as we do in regular regression. So it is possible to test exactly the same kinds of hypotheses about binary outcome variables that we can test with interval/ratio variables.

It is also possible to extend the logistic regression model in two additional ways that are often helpful, but which we will only mention here.

Ordinal logistic regression uses the regression model to analyze the cumulative log odds of scoring at the next highest rank of a grouped ordinal variable. For example, many attitude surveys ask respondents to choose among "strongly disagree," "disagree," "neutral," "agree," and "strongly agree." We can use the ordinal logistic regression model to examine whether each unit of *X* increases the log odds of choosing "disagree" instead of "strongly disagree," or choosing "agree" instead of "neutral."

Multinomial logistic regression uses the regression model to analyze multiple-choice kinds of outcomes. For example, we might want to predict whether a person is married, divorced, separated, or never married. If these are mutually exclusive and jointly exhaustive, we can analyze the log odds of each outcome compared to one baseline. For example, we can analyze the log odds of being married versus never married, divorced versus never married, and separated versus never married. We can test hypotheses about the effects of predictor variables on each of these odds. The multinomial logistic regression model then lets us examine nominal polyotomies.

There are many further extensions of the regression model to deal with other kinds of outcomes (e.g., counts of events, times until an event happens, variables that cannot have scores below or above some value, etc.). These are advanced topics that we can't cover here. But, now that you understand the basic linear regression model, the multiple regression model, and the logistic regression model, you are ready to deal with these advanced topics.

In this chapter we've introduced the binary logistic regression model and seen two extensions of it: cumulative logistic regression and multinomial regression. The linear regression model encountered in Chapter 14 is the basis for almost all advanced statistical analyses in the social sciences. The basic idea was to predict scores on an outcome variable as a linear and additive function of scores on one or more independent variables.

In this chapter, we extended the linear regression model to the case in which the outcome is binary, rather than interval/ratio. Many important social science hypotheses deal with "yes/no" or "true/false" or "present/absent" kinds of outcomes, and logistic regression is a good tool. Logistic regression predicts the log of the odds of the outcome as a linear function of X variables. We saw how to interpret partial slope coefficients in logistic regression. We also looked at how logistic regression models are estimated with maximum likelihood (instead of least squares), and how this affects the test of the global null hypothesis with -2 log likelihood (instead of R^2).

Finally, we briefly introduced two extensions of the binary logistic regression model. Ordinal logistic regression allows us to apply the regression model to grouped ordinal dependent variables. Multinomial logistic regression extends the model to study nominal polyotomies.

SUMMARY

Many outcome variables of interest are not measured at the interval/ratio level. But the regression model, with some modifications, can be used to predict these outcomes as a linear and additive function of one or more independent variables.

Where the outcome is a nominal dichotomy or binary variable, logistic regression analysis by the method of maximum likelihood is often used instead of linear regression by the method of ordinary least squares.

Logistic regression predicts the log of the odds that a case will have a score of 1 on the outcome of interest, instead of the score of 0. Using the method of maximum likelihood, logistic regression finds the best-fitting linear function of independent variables to account for why some cases score 1 and others score 0 on the outcome.

As in regular regression, we first examine the global null hypothesis that none of the Xs predict Y. In logistic regression, this is done using a likelihood ratio test and the pseudo-R-squared statistic. We then test which independent variables, if any, have significant effects on the outcome (while controlling the other independent variables) using the Wald chi-squared test.

Last, we interpret the partial (logistic) regression coefficients for any variables that have significant effects. The regression coefficients in logistic regression describe the effect of a one-unit change or difference in X on the log of the odds that the case scores 1 on Y.

Sometimes, to make interpretation easier, we take the log of the regression coefficient. When we have done this, we interpret the log(β) to tell how a one-unit change in X multiplies the odds of scoring 1 on the outcome.

There are many other variations of the multiple regression model that are used when outcomes are not interval/ratio. For nominal polyotomies, the multinomial logistic regression model is often used. For grouped ordinal outcome variables, the ordered logistic regression model is often used.

KEY TERMS

global null hypothesis

goodness of fit

log likelihood

log odds

logistic regression

maximum likelihood

multinomial logistic regression

odds

ordinal logistic regression

CHECK QUIZ ANSWERS

Quiz 15.1 Answers: 1. (b); 2. (c); 3. (c); 4. (T)

EXERCISES

1. Are persons who favor the death penalty for murder more likely to have guns at home? A researcher believes that persons who have more punitive attitudes toward criminals (favor the death penalty) are also more likely to own guns.

   Using data from the 2008 General Social Survey, the researcher codes persons who own guns as 1, and those who don't as 0. Respondents to the survey were also asked whether they favored the imposition of the death penalty. Those who favored the death penalty ($N = 830$) were coded 1, and those who opposed the death penalty ($N = 421$) were coded 0.

   Since the outcome is a dichotomous variable, logistic regression analysis was performed using SPSS. Here are portions of the output.

   Model with only a constant −2 log likelihood: 1,618.857

   Model with constant and covariates −2 log likelihood: 1,554.970

Omnibus Tests of Model Coefficients

		Chi-Squared	df	Sig.
Step 1				
	Model	63.887	1	0.000

Model Summary

Step	−2 Log Likelihood	Cox & Snell *R*-Squared	Nagelkerke *R*-Squared
1	1,554.970[a]	0.050	0.069

Variables in the Equation

								95% CI for Exp(*B*)	
		B	Std. Error	Wald	*df*	Sig.	Exp(*B*)	Lower	Upper
Step 1	cappun(1)	1.068	0.140	58.029	1	0.000	2.911	2.211	3.832
	Constant	−1.374	0.121	128.156	1	0.000	0.253		

Prepare a short research report including:

a. Is there a significant relationship between the two variables? What is your evidence?
b. How strong is the relationship between the variables? Interpret the −2 log likelihood statistics and the chi-squared omnibus null hypothesis test and pseudo-R^2. Is the relationship statistically significant, according to the chi-squared test?
c. What are the predicted log odds that a person who opposes the death penalty will own a gun? What are the predicted log odds that a person who favors the death penalty will own a gun?
d. Interpret the meaning of the slope (*B*) and exp(*B*).
e. What conclusion should the researcher reach about the relationship between the attitudes toward the death penalty and toward gun ownership?

2. Were there social class differences in voting for George Bush in 2004? A political sociologist theorizes that persons who hold more privileged positions in a society are more likely to be more politically conservative, because they seek to protect their statuses. Applying this theory to modern American presidential elections, the researcher hypothesizes that people who see themselves as upper-class and middle-class were more likely to support George Bush in the 2004 election than people who see themselves as working-class or lower-class.

Using data from the 2008 General Social Survey, the researcher studies whether respondents voted for Bush (coded 1), or for anyone else (coded 0). A series of dummy independent variables is created to measure whether a respondent identifies as middle-class ($N = 579$), working-class ($N = 478$), or lower-class ($N = 59$). The category "upper-class" ($N = 54$) is treated as the reference group.

A logistic regression is run using SPSS to predict the log odds of voting for Bush versus anyone else, using the social class dummy variables as predictors. Here is a portion of the results.

Omnibus Tests of Model Coefficients

		Chi-Squared	*df*	Sig.
Step 1	Step	10.967	3	0.012
	Block	10.967	3	0.012
	Model	10.967	3	0.012

Model Summary

Step	−2 Log Likelihood	Cox & Snell *R*-Squared	Nagelkerke *R*-Squared
1	1,610.656[a]	0.009	0.012

Variables in the Equation

								95% CI for Exp(*B*)	
		B	Std. Error	Wald	*df*	Sig.	Exp(*B*)	Lower	Upper
Step 1[a]	class			10.238	3	0.017			
	class(1)	−0.967	0.396	5.961	1	0.015	0.380	0.175	0.826
	class(2)	−0.957	0.312	9.424	1	0.002	0.384	0.208	0.707
	class(3)	−0.786	0.309	6.445	1	0.011	0.456	0.249	0.836
	Constant	0.865	0.298	8.424	1	0.004	2.375		

Prepare a short research report including:

a. Is there a significant joint relationship between the voting for Bush and the social class categories? What is your evidence?

b. How strong is the relationship between the variables? Interpret the −2 log likelihood statistics and the chi-squared omnibus null hypothesis test and pseudo-R^2. Is the relationship statistically significant, according to the chi-squared test?

c. Which independent variables have significant partial effects on the dependent variable? What is your evidence?
d. Interpret the meaning of the slope (*B*) and exp(*B*) coefficients.
e. Calculate the predicted log odds that a working-class person voted for Bush, that a lower-class person voted for Bush, that a middle-class person voted for Bush, and that an upper-class person voted for Bush.
f. What conclusion should the researcher reach about the research hypothesis that people in the upper and middle classes were more likely to vote for Bush than persons in the working and lower classes?

APPENDIX

CHI-SQUARED DISTRIBUTION: CRITICAL VALUES FOR COMMONLY USED ALPHA = 0.05 AND ALPHA = 0.01

USING THE TABLE OF CRITICAL VALUES OF THE CHI-SQUARED TEST

The table that follows shows critical values for the chi-squared independence test at alpha = 0.05 and alpha = 0.01. Critical values for up to 30 degrees of freedom (*df*) are shown. Sometimes, other alpha levels may be desired. Sometimes, your table may have more than 30 degrees of freedom. But the values here will meet your needs most of the time.

To use the table:

- Determine the degrees of freedom for the cross-tabulation you are examining. The Pearson independence chi-squared test has degrees of freedom equal to $(R - 1) * (C - 1)$—that is, the number of rows in the table less one, times the number of columns in the table less one. For example, a 3-by-2 table has 2 * 1 or two degrees of freedom.
- Determine whether you want to test the hypothesis at the 95 or 99 percent confidence level (alpha = 0.05 or alpha = 0.01).
- Find the critical value for your test by locating the cell at the intersection of the degrees of freedom and alpha level that you chose.

If the value of your chi-squared test statistic is larger than the critical value, you may reject the hypothesis of no association (or no differences between groups); if your test statistic is less than the critical value, you should not reject the null hypothesis. Be a little cautious, though. Tables that are sparse (i.e., have a substantial proportion of cells with low expected frequencies) may give false positive results with the Pearson chi-squared test.

	Alpha Level	
df	0.05	0.01
1	3.841	6.635
2	5.991	9.210
3	7.815	11.345
4	9.488	13.277
5	11.070	15.086
6	12.592	16.812
7	14.067	18.475
8	15.507	20.090
9	16.919	21.666
10	18.307	23.209
11	19.675	24.725
12	21.026	26.217
13	22.362	27.688
14	23.685	29.141
15	24.996	30.578
16	26.296	32.000
17	27.567	33.409
18	28.869	34.805
19	30.144	36.191
20	31.410	37.566
21	32.671	38.932
22	33.924	40.289
23	35.172	41.638
24	36.415	42.980
25	37.652	44.314
26	38.885	45.642
27	40.113	46.963
28	41.337	48.278
29	42.557	49.588
30	43.773	50.892

F-DISTRIBUTION: CRITICAL VALUES FOR COMMONLY USED ALPHA = 0.05 AND ALPHA = 0.01

USING THE TABLES OF CRITICAL VALUES OF THE F-TEST

In order to use the tables that follow to determine whether your F-statistic is significant (allowing you to reject the null hypothesis), you need to know three things:

1. What is the desired alpha (or *p*, or significance, or error) level of your test? Only two tables are given here, corresponding to the most commonly chosen alpha levels. The first shows values for the 0.05 level; the second shows values for the 0.01 level.
2. Degrees of freedom (*df*) for the numerator of the F-ratio. For one-way ANOVA, this is equal to the number of levels of the independent variable less one. Other uses of the F-test may have different degrees of freedom.
3. Degrees of freedom for the denominator of the F-ratio. For one-way ANOVA, this is equal to the number of cases less one, less the number of levels of the independent variable.

To use the tables:

1. Choose either the first table or the second table, depending on your desired *p*-level.
2. Locate the column with the degrees of freedom for the numerator of your F-ratio.

3. Locate the row with the degrees of freedom for the denominator of your F-ratio.
4. The intersection of the row and column gives the critical value. For example, at alpha = 0.05, with six and four degrees of freedom, the critical value is 6.16.

If your test statistic exceeds the critical value, you may reject the null hypothesis at the alpha level chosen; if your test statistic does not exceed the critical value, you must accept the null hypothesis.

Critical Values of the F-Distribution for $p = 0.05$

	df_1									
df_2	1	2	3	4	5	6	8	12	24	More
1	161.40	199.50	215.70	224.60	230.20	234.00	238.90	243.90	249.00	254.30
2	18.51	19.00	19.16	19.25	19.30	19.33	19.37	19.41	19.45	19.50
3	10.13	9.55	9.28	9.12	9.01	8.94	8.84	8.74	8.64	8.53
4	7.71	6.94	6.59	6.39	6.26	6.16	6.04	5.91	5.77	5.63
5	6.61	5.79	5.41	5.19	5.05	4.95	4.82	4.68	4.53	4.36
6	5.99	5.14	4.76	4.53	4.39	4.28	4.15	4.00	3.84	3.67
7	5.59	4.74	4.35	4.12	3.97	3.87	3.73	3.57	3.41	3.23
8	5.32	4.46	4.07	3.84	3.69	3.58	3.44	3.28	3.12	2.93
9	5.12	4.26	3.86	3.63	3.48	3.37	3.23	3.07	2.90	2.71
10	4.96	4.10	3.71	3.48	3.33	3.22	3.07	2.91	2.74	2.54
15	4.54	3.68	3.29	3.06	2.90	2.79	2.64	2.48	2.29	2.07
20	4.35	3.49	3.10	2.87	2.71	2.60	2.45	2.28	2.08	1.84
25	4.24	3.38	2.99	2.76	2.60	2.49	2.35	2.16	1.96	1.71
30	4.17	3.32	2.92	2.69	2.53	2.42	2.27	2.09	1.89	1.62
40	4.08	3.23	2.84	2.61	2.45	2.34	2.18	2.00	1.79	1.51
60	4.00	3.15	2.76	2.52	2.37	2.25	2.10	1.92	1.70	1.39
120	3.92	3.07	2.68	2.45	2.29	2.17	2.02	1.83	1.61	1.25
More	3.84	2.99	2.60	2.37	2.21	2.09	1.94	1.75	1.52	1.00

Critical Values of the F-Distribution for $p = 0.01$

	df_1									
*df*2	1	2	3	4	5	6	8	12	24	More
1	4,052.00	4,999.00	5,403.00	5,625.00	5,764.00	5,859.00	5,981.00	6,106.00	6,234.00	6,366.00
2	98.49	99.01	99.17	99.25	99.30	99.33	99.36	99.42	99.46	99.50
3	34.12	30.81	29.46	28.71	28.24	27.91	27.49	27.05	26.60	26.12
4	21.20	18.00	16.69	15.98	15.52	15.21	14.80	14.37	13.93	13.46
5	16.26	13.27	12.06	11.39	10.97	10.67	10.27	9.89	9.47	9.02
6	13.74	10.92	9.78	9.15	8.75	8.47	8.10	7.72	7.31	6.88
7	12.25	9.55	8.45	7.85	7.46	7.19	6.84	6.47	6.07	5.65
8	11.26	8.65	7.59	7.01	6.63	6.37	6.03	5.67	5.28	4.86
9	10.56	8.02	6.99	6.42	6.06	5.80	5.47	5.11	4.73	4.31
10	10.04	7.56	6.55	5.99	5.64	5.39	5.06	4.71	4.33	3.91
15	8.68	6.36	5.42	4.89	4.56	4.32	4.00	3.67	3.29	2.87
20	8.10	5.85	4.94	4.43	4.10	3.87	3.56	3.23	2.86	2.42
25	7.77	5.57	4.68	4.18	3.86	3.63	3.32	2.99	2.62	2.17
30	7.56	5.39	4.51	4.02	3.70	3.47	3.17	2.84	2.47	2.01
40	7.31	5.18	4.31	3.83	3.51	3.29	2.99	2.66	2.29	1.80
60	7.08	4.98	4.13	3.65	3.34	3.12	2.82	2.50	2.12	1.60
120	6.85	4.79	3.95	3.48	3.17	2.96	2.66	2.34	1.95	1.38
More	6.64	4.60	3.78	3.32	3.02	2.80	2.51	2.18	1.79	1.00

Standard Normal Scores (Z-Scores), and Cumulative Probabilities (Proportion of Cases Having Scores below Z)

USING THE Z-SCORE TABLE

The table gives Z-scores from −3.00 through +3.00, which will provide the information you need for almost all hypothesis testing.

The probability associated with each Z-score is the proportion of the area of the standard normal distribution that falls at or below the score. With a little cleverness, you can use this to find the proportions below, above, or between any Z-scores you might want. Here are some hints for the most common situations:

We want to know the proportion of cases that fall below that of a given case. After finding the Z-score of the given case, simply look up the Z-score in the table. The proportion you want is shown.

We want to know the proportion of cases that fall above that of a given case. After finding the Z-score of the given case, look up the proportion in the table. Since this is the proportion of cases below Z and you want the proportion above Z, subtract the proportion you find in the table from 1.0 (since the area below plus the area above any given Z-score must sum to 1.0).

We want to know the proportion of cases that fall between two scores. Find the Z-score for each of the scores. Find the proportion of cases that have scores lower than the lower of the two scores you're interested in, by using the table. Then find the proportion of all cases that have scores lower than the higher of the two scores you're interested in, by using the table. The difference between the two probabilities is the area between the two scores. Do not subtract the Z-scores! Find the probabilities first, and then subtract them.

Z-Score	Probability	Z-Score	Probability	Z-Score	Probability
−3.00	0.0013	−2.63	0.0043	−2.26	0.0119
−2.99	0.0014	−2.62	0.0044	−2.25	0.0122
−2.98	0.0014	−2.61	0.0045	−2.24	0.0125
−2.97	0.0015	−2.60	0.0047	−2.23	0.0129
−2.96	0.0015	−2.59	0.0048	−2.22	0.0132
−2.95	0.0016	−2.58	0.0049	−2.21	0.0136
−2.94	0.0016	−2.57	0.0051	−2.20	0.0139
−2.93	0.0017	−2.56	0.0052	−2.19	0.0143
−2.92	0.0018	−2.55	0.0054	−2.18	0.0146
−2.91	0.0018	−2.54	0.0055	−2.17	0.0150
−2.90	0.0019	−2.53	0.0057	−2.16	0.0154
−2.89	0.0019	−2.52	0.0059	−2.15	0.0158
−2.88	0.0020	−2.51	0.0060	−2.14	0.0162
−2.87	0.0021	−2.50	0.0062	−2.13	0.0166
−2.86	0.0021	−2.49	0.0064	−2.12	0.0170
−2.85	0.0022	−2.48	0.0066	−2.11	0.0174
−2.84	0.0023	−2.47	0.0068	−2.10	0.0179
−2.83	0.0023	−2.46	0.0069	−2.09	0.0183
−2.82	0.0024	−2.45	0.0071	−2.08	0.0188
−2.81	0.0025	−2.44	0.0073	−2.07	0.0192
−2.80	0.0026	−2.43	0.0075	−2.06	0.0197
−2.79	0.0026	−2.42	0.0078	−2.05	0.0202
−2.78	0.0027	−2.41	0.0080	−2.04	0.0207
−2.77	0.0028	−2.40	0.0082	−2.03	0.0212
−2.76	0.0029	−2.39	0.0084	−2.02	0.0217
−2.75	0.0030	−2.38	0.0087	−2.01	0.0222
−2.74	0.0031	−2.37	0.0089	−2.00	0.0228
−2.73	0.0032	−2.36	0.0091	−1.99	0.0233
−2.72	0.0033	−2.35	0.0094	−1.98	0.0239
−2.71	0.0034	−2.34	0.0096	−1.97	0.0244
−2.70	0.0035	−2.33	0.0099	−1.96	0.0250
−2.69	0.0036	−2.32	0.0102	−1.95	0.0256
−2.68	0.0037	−2.31	0.0104	−1.94	0.0262
−2.67	0.0038	−2.30	0.0107	−1.93	0.0268
−2.66	0.0039	−2.29	0.0110	−1.92	0.0274
−2.65	0.0040	−2.28	0.0113	−1.91	0.0281
−2.64	0.0041	−2.27	0.0116	−1.90	0.0287

Z-Score	Probability	Z-Score	Probability	Z-Score	Probability
−1.89	0.0294	−1.46	0.0721	−1.03	0.1515
−1.88	0.0301	−1.45	0.0735	−1.02	0.1539
−1.87	0.0307	−1.44	0.0749	−1.01	0.1562
−1.86	0.0314	−1.43	0.0764	−1.00	0.1587
−1.85	0.0322	−1.42	0.0778	−0.99	0.1611
−1.84	0.0329	−1.41	0.0793	−0.98	0.1635
−1.83	0.0336	−1.40	0.0808	−0.97	0.1660
−1.82	0.0344	−1.39	0.0823	−0.96	0.1685
−1.81	0.0351	−1.38	0.0838	−0.95	0.1711
−1.80	0.0359	−1.37	0.0853	−0.94	0.1736
−1.79	0.0367	−1.36	0.0869	−0.93	0.1762
−1.78	0.0375	−1.35	0.0885	−0.92	0.1788
−1.77	0.0384	−1.34	0.0901	−0.91	0.1814
−1.76	0.0392	−1.33	0.0918	−0.90	0.1841
−1.75	0.0401	−1.32	0.0934	−0.89	0.1867
−1.74	0.0409	−1.31	0.0951	−0.88	0.1894
−1.73	0.0418	−1.30	0.0968	−0.87	0.1922
−1.72	0.0427	−1.29	0.0985	−0.86	0.1949
−1.71	0.0436	−1.28	0.1003	−0.85	0.1977
−1.70	0.0446	−1.27	0.1020	−0.84	0.2005
−1.69	0.0455	−1.26	0.1038	−0.83	0.2033
−1.68	0.0465	−1.25	0.1056	−0.82	0.2061
−1.67	0.0475	−1.24	0.1075	−0.81	0.2090
−1.66	0.0485	−1.23	0.1093	−0.80	0.2119
−1.65	0.0495	−1.22	0.1112	−0.79	0.2148
−1.64	0.0505	−1.21	0.1131	−0.78	0.2177
−1.63	0.0516	−1.20	0.1151	−0.77	0.2206
−1.62	0.0526	−1.19	0.1170	−0.76	0.2236
−1.61	0.0537	−1.18	0.1190	−0.75	0.2266
−1.60	0.0548	−1.17	0.1210	−0.74	0.2296
−1.59	0.0559	−1.16	0.1230	−0.73	0.2327
−1.58	0.0571	−1.15	0.1251	−0.72	0.2358
−1.57	0.0582	−1.14	0.1271	−0.71	0.2389
−1.56	0.0594	−1.13	0.1292	−0.70	0.2420
−1.55	0.0606	−1.12	0.1314	−0.69	0.2451
−1.54	0.0618	−1.11	0.1335	−0.68	0.2483
−1.53	0.0630	−1.10	0.1357	−0.67	0.2514
−1.52	0.0643	−1.09	0.1379	−0.66	0.2546
−1.51	0.0655	−1.08	0.1401	−0.65	0.2578
−1.50	0.0668	−1.07	0.1423	−0.64	0.2611
−1.49	0.0681	−1.06	0.1446	−0.63	0.2643
−1.48	0.0694	−1.05	0.1469	−0.62	0.2676
−1.47	0.0708	−1.04	0.1492	−0.61	0.2709

Z-Score	Probability	Z-Score	Probability	Z-Score	Probability
−0.60	0.2743	−0.17	0.4325	0.26	0.6026
−0.59	0.2776	−0.16	0.4364	0.27	0.6064
−0.58	0.2810	−0.15	0.4404	0.28	0.6103
−0.57	0.2843	−0.14	0.4443	0.29	0.6141
−0.56	0.2877	−0.13	0.4483	0.30	0.6179
−0.55	0.2912	−0.12	0.4522	0.31	0.6217
−0.54	0.2946	−0.11	0.4562	0.32	0.6255
−0.53	0.2981	−0.10	0.4602	0.33	0.6293
−0.52	0.3015	−0.09	0.4641	0.34	0.6331
−0.51	0.3050	−0.08	0.4681	0.35	0.6368
−0.50	0.3085	−0.07	0.4721	0.36	0.6406
−0.49	0.3121	−0.06	0.4761	0.37	0.6443
−0.48	0.3156	−0.05	0.4801	0.38	0.6480
−0.47	0.3192	−0.04	0.4840	0.39	0.6517
−0.46	0.3228	−0.03	0.4880	0.40	0.6554
−0.45	0.3264	−0.02	0.4920	0.41	0.6591
−0.44	0.3300	−0.01	0.4960	0.42	0.6628
−0.43	0.3336	0.00	0.5000	0.43	0.6664
−0.42	0.3372	0.01	0.5040	0.44	0.6700
−0.41	0.3409	0.02	0.5080	0.45	0.6736
−0.40	0.3446	0.03	0.5120	0.46	0.6772
−0.39	0.3483	0.04	0.5160	0.47	0.6808
−0.38	0.3520	0.05	0.5199	0.48	0.6844
−0.37	0.3557	0.06	0.5239	0.49	0.6879
−0.36	0.3594	0.07	0.5279	0.50	0.6915
−0.35	0.3632	0.08	0.5319	0.51	0.6950
−0.34	0.3669	0.09	0.5359	0.52	0.6985
−0.33	0.3707	0.10	0.5398	0.53	0.7019
−0.32	0.3745	0.11	0.5438	0.54	0.7054
−0.31	0.3783	0.12	0.5478	0.55	0.7088
−0.30	0.3821	0.13	0.5517	0.56	0.7123
−0.29	0.3859	0.14	0.5557	0.57	0.7157
−0.28	0.3897	0.15	0.5596	0.58	0.7190
−0.27	0.3936	0.16	0.5636	0.59	0.7224
−0.26	0.3974	0.17	0.5675	0.60	0.7257
−0.25	0.4013	0.18	0.5714	0.61	0.7291
−0.24	0.4052	0.19	0.5753	0.62	0.7324
−0.23	0.4090	0.20	0.5793	0.63	0.7357
−0.22	0.4129	0.21	0.5832	0.64	0.7389
−0.21	0.4168	0.22	0.5871	0.65	0.7422
−0.20	0.4207	0.23	0.5910	0.66	0.7454
−0.19	0.4247	0.24	0.5948	0.67	0.7486
−0.18	0.4286	0.25	0.5987	0.68	0.7517

Z-Score	Probability	Z-Score	Probability	Z-Score	Probability
0.69	0.7549	1.12	0.8686	1.55	0.9394
0.70	0.7580	1.13	0.8708	1.56	0.9406
0.71	0.7611	1.14	0.8729	1.57	0.9418
0.72	0.7642	1.15	0.8749	1.58	0.9429
0.73	0.7673	1.16	0.8770	1.59	0.9441
0.74	0.7704	1.17	0.8790	1.60	0.9452
0.75	0.7734	1.18	0.8810	1.61	0.9463
0.76	0.7764	1.19	0.8830	1.62	0.9474
0.77	0.7794	1.20	0.8849	1.63	0.9484
0.78	0.7823	1.21	0.8869	1.64	0.9495
0.79	0.7852	1.22	0.8888	1.65	0.9505
0.80	0.7881	1.23	0.8907	1.66	0.9515
0.81	0.7910	1.24	0.8925	1.67	0.9525
0.82	0.7939	1.25	0.8944	1.68	0.9535
0.83	0.7967	1.26	0.8962	1.69	0.9545
0.84	0.7995	1.27	0.8980	1.70	0.9554
0.85	0.8023	1.28	0.8997	1.71	0.9564
0.86	0.8051	1.29	0.9015	1.72	0.9573
0.87	0.8078	1.30	0.9032	1.73	0.9582
0.88	0.8106	1.31	0.9049	1.74	0.9591
0.89	0.8133	1.32	0.9066	1.75	0.9599
0.90	0.8159	1.33	0.9082	1.76	0.9608
0.91	0.8186	1.34	0.9099	1.77	0.9616
0.92	0.8212	1.35	0.9115	1.78	0.9625
0.93	0.8238	1.36	0.9131	1.79	0.9633
0.94	0.8264	1.37	0.9147	1.80	0.9641
0.95	0.8289	1.38	0.9162	1.81	0.9649
0.96	0.8315	1.39	0.9177	1.82	0.9656
0.97	0.8340	1.40	0.9192	1.83	0.9664
0.98	0.8365	1.41	0.9207	1.84	0.9671
0.99	0.8389	1.42	0.9222	1.85	0.9678
1.00	0.8413	1.43	0.9236	1.86	0.9686
1.01	0.8438	1.44	0.9251	1.87	0.9693
1.02	0.8461	1.45	0.9265	1.88	0.9699
1.03	0.8485	1.46	0.9279	1.89	0.9706
1.04	0.8508	1.47	0.9292	1.90	0.9713
1.05	0.8531	1.48	0.9306	1.91	0.9719
1.06	0.8554	1.49	0.9319	1.92	0.9726
1.07	0.8577	1.50	0.9332	1.93	0.9732
1.08	0.8599	1.51	0.9345	1.94	0.9738
1.09	0.8621	1.52	0.9357	1.95	0.9744
1.10	0.8643	1.53	0.9370	1.96	0.9750
1.11	0.8665	1.54	0.9382	1.97	0.9756

Z-Score	Probability	Z-Score	Probability	Z-Score	Probability
1.98	0.9761	2.33	0.9901	2.68	0.9963
1.99	0.9767	2.34	0.9904	2.69	0.9964
2.00	0.9772	2.35	0.9906	2.70	0.9965
2.01	0.9778	2.36	0.9909	2.71	0.9966
2.02	0.9783	2.37	0.9911	2.72	0.9967
2.03	0.9788	2.38	0.9913	2.73	0.9968
2.04	0.9793	2.39	0.9916	2.74	0.9969
2.05	0.9798	2.40	0.9918	2.75	0.9970
2.06	0.9803	2.41	0.9920	2.76	0.9971
2.07	0.9808	2.42	0.9922	2.77	0.9972
2.08	0.9812	2.43	0.9925	2.78	0.9973
2.09	0.9817	2.44	0.9927	2.79	0.9974
2.10	0.9821	2.45	0.9929	2.80	0.9974
2.11	0.9826	2.46	0.9931	2.81	0.9975
2.12	0.9830	2.47	0.9932	2.82	0.9976
2.13	0.9834	2.48	0.9934	2.83	0.9977
2.14	0.9838	2.49	0.9936	2.84	0.9977
2.15	0.9842	2.50	0.9938	2.85	0.9978
2.16	0.9846	2.51	0.9940	2.86	0.9979
2.17	0.9850	2.52	0.9941	2.87	0.9979
2.18	0.9854	2.53	0.9943	2.88	0.9980
2.19	0.9857	2.54	0.9945	2.89	0.9981
2.20	0.9861	2.55	0.9946	2.90	0.9981
2.21	0.9864	2.56	0.9948	2.91	0.9982
2.22	0.9868	2.57	0.9949	2.92	0.9982
2.23	0.9871	2.58	0.9951	2.93	0.9983
2.24	0.9875	2.59	0.9952	2.94	0.9984
2.25	0.9878	2.60	0.9953	2.95	0.9984
2.26	0.9881	2.61	0.9955	2.96	0.9985
2.27	0.9884	2.62	0.9956	2.97	0.9985
2.28	0.9887	2.63	0.9957	2.98	0.9986
2.29	0.9890	2.64	0.9959	2.99	0.9986
2.30	0.9893	2.65	0.9960	3.00	0.9987
2.31	0.9896	2.66	0.9961		
2.32	0.9898	2.67	0.9962		

STUDENT'S T-DISTRIBUTION: CRITICAL VALUES FOR COMMONLY USED ALPHA LEVELS

USING THE TABLE OF CRITICAL T-SCORES

Before using this table to figure out the probability of your t-test statistic, you will need to know three things:

1. Degrees of freedom for the test you are doing (be careful, as there are several common statistical tests that use the t-distribution). Be sure to use the right degrees of freedom for your test (e.g., for a one-sample test of a mean, $df = N - 1$; for a two-sample test of the difference between independent sample means, $df = N_1 + N_2 - 2$).
2. Whether your alternative hypothesis is one-tailed or two-tailed.
3. The alpha (or p, or significance, or error) level that you have decided on for your test (most commonly, 0.05).

Begin by locating the row that corresponds to the degrees of freedom for your test. Next, look at the header of the table to find the column for the type of test (one-tailed or two-tailed) and significance (alpha) level. Locate the critical value that is at the intersection of the row and column. For example, for a two-tailed test at the 0.02 level with three degrees of freedom, the critical value is 4.541.

If your test statistic is bigger than the critical value, you may reject the null hypothesis. If your test statistic is not larger than the critical value, you may not reject the null hypothesis.

This table does not give the exact *p*-levels for your test, but does allow you to make the decision to accept or reject the null hypothesis.

	Alpha Level for One-Tailed Test					
	0.10	**0.05**	**0.025**	**0.010**	**0.005**	**0.0005**
	Alpha Level for Two-Tailed Test					
df	**0.20**	**0.10**	**0.050**	**0.020**	**0.010**	**0.0010**
1	3.078	6.314	12.706	31.821	63.657	636.619
2	1.886	2.920	4.303	6.965	9.925	31.598
3	1.638	2.353	3.182	4.541	5.841	12.941
4	1.533	2.132	2.776	3.747	4.604	8.610
5	1.476	2.015	2.571	3.365	4.032	6.859
6	1.440	1.943	2.447	3.143	3.707	5.959
7	1.415	1.895	2.365	2.998	3.499	5.405
8	1.397	1.860	2.306	2.896	3.355	5.041
9	1.383	1.833	2.262	2.821	3.250	4.781
10	1.372	1.812	2.228	2.764	3.169	4.587
15	1.341	1.753	2.131	2.602	2.947	4.073
20	1.325	1.725	2.086	2.528	2.845	3.850
25	1.316	1.708	2.060	2.485	2.787	3.725
30	1.310	1.697	2.042	2.457	2.750	3.646
40	1.303	1.684	2.021	2.423	2.704	3.551
60	1.296	1.671	2.000	2.390	2.660	3.460
120	1.289	1.658	1.980	2.358	2.617	3.373
More	1.282	1.645	1.960	2.326	2.576	3.29

INDEX

A

Absolute zero, 17, 18, 20

Age, and home ownership rates, 490–491

Age of vehicle, and cars in use in U.S., 107

Alpha (type 1) error, defined, 230, 249, 255

Alpha level: most commonly used, 230; selecting an, 229–230, 255; and table of critical t-scores, 517–518

Alternative hypotheses (H_a): explanation of, 249, 251–254; for tests about one mean, 259; for tests about one proportion, 267–268

Analysis of variance (ANOVA), one-way: analyzing variance, 339, 342–346; comparing means, 356–358, 360; defined, 98, 314, 338; exercises, 362–368; F-test, 350–354; F-test example, 354–355; hypotheses and assumptions, 339–341; key terms, 361; quiz answers, 362; quizzes, 341, 345, 353, 359; summary on, 360–361

Analysis ToolPak, Excel's: installing, 50–51; for summary tables, 51–55

Anti-instructor comments, and number of class factions, 456–461

Arithmetic mean: defined, 82, 95–96, 102; formula for, 96, 97; from grouped data, 101; and interval/ratio data, 96–98; of list of values, 100–101; two mathematical properties of, 97; working with the, 98–99

Association of interval/ratio variables: exercises, 446–452; form of linear interval/ratio association, 444–445; key terms, 446; quiz answers, 446; quizzes, 432–433, 438, 441; and regression line (intercept and slope), 429, 444–445; significance testing for, 434–445; strength of, 439–441; summary on, 445–446; visualizing, 426–434

Association with categorical variables: concept of statistical association, 372–374; exercises, 407–423; key terms, 406–407; nominal association, 375–391; ordinal association, 391–404; quiz answers, 407; quizzes, 374, 379, 381, 386–387, 388–389, 394, 398–399, 400–401; summary on, 404–406

Assumptions: in general hypothesis testing process, 254–255; and one-way ANOVA, 339–341; regression, 463–464; in testing about one mean, 259–260; in testing about one proportion, 268

Average, defined, 82, 96, 98, 102. *See also* Mean

B

Bar charts: defined, 30–31; examples of, 30, 83, 84; exercise in making, 71–72; histograms versus, 36; modified, 31–32; and nominal association, 376–377; stacked, 37, 56, 86, 89

Bell curve: defined, 188, 189; properties of, 189–202. *See also* Normal distribution

Beta error (type II error), defined, 249–250

Bias and efficiency, 220–221

Bimodal, defined, 151, 160

Binary variable, 18

Bins (categories), defined, 39–40

Box-and-whiskers plot: description of, 152, 153–154, 177; drawing, 155–158; exercise using, 181; quiz on, 159–160

C

Cartesian coordinate way of representing and reading quantitative information, 36
Case, defined, 14, 15, 21
Cases or observations, describing scores of a sample of, 26
Categorical data, dispersion of: example of, 115–117; index of qualitative variation (IQV), 118–119, 144–145; and proportion in nonmodal categories, 117–118; segregation index, 119–121, 145–146
Categories, and interval/ratio data, 39–40
Census bureau, data collected by, 12
Central tendency: basic idea of, 82–83; Excel for finding measures of, 108–109; exercises, 103–107; key terms, 102; mean, 82, 95–101; median, 82, 88–95; mode, 82, 83–88; quiz answers, 103; quizzes, 87, 92, 100; SPSS for finding measures of, 109–112; summary on, 102
Central tendency estimates: bias and efficiency, 220–221; introduction to, 219; point estimates, 220, 229–240; standard error of a mean, 221–225, 229; standard error of a proportion, 225–227, 229
Charts. *See* Bar charts; Histograms; Pie charts
Chi-squared: calculating, 318–319; comparing proportions across several groups, 314–315; defined, 177, 314; Excel for solving chi-squared problems, 322–324; exercises, 333–336; key terms, 332; quiz answers, 333; quizzes, 320–321, 331; SPSS for, 325–327; summary on, 331–332; table of critical values of the chi-squared test, 505–506; testing for multiple group differences, 315–320
Class factions, and anti-instructor comments, 456–461
Cluster samples, defined, 215–216
Coefficient of determination (big *R*-squared): defined, 440, 455–456; example using, 458–460
Coefficient of kurtosis, formula for, 173
Coefficient of skewness, 167–168
Coefficient of variation (CV): description of, 134–135, 139; example of calculating, 136–137; Excel for working with, 147–148
Comparing two groups, 280
Comparing two groups' means, 280–289
Comparing two groups' proportions, 289–294
Concordant pairs, 395–396
Confidence intervals: boundaries of, 230–231; defined, 212; importance of, 213; for means, 231–235; for proportions, 236–241; setting, 229
Confirmatory application of statistics, 7
Confirmatory phase of research, 10
Conservatism and sentencing attitudes, relationship between, 401–402
Constant: in regression equation, 455; variable versus, 15
Continuous variables: defined, 16; exercises illustrating, 22–23
Cramér's V: description of, 382, 383, 405; example of, 390; formula for, 382
Critical value, defined, 254, 257
Cross-tabulations, and nominal association, 375
Cumulative percentages: description of, 34, 35, 89–91; rounding, 91
Cumulative relative frequencies, defined, 35

D

Data, defined, 14, 21
Death penalty: formal education and attitude toward, 416; and gender and beliefs about life after death, 409
Decision-making, in hypothesis testing process, 256–257
Degrees of freedom, and Pearson chi-squared test of independence, 318, 319–320
Degrees of freedom between groups (*dfb*), 352, 353

Degrees of freedom within groups (*dfw*), 352, 353
Dependent variables: defined, 15–16; exercises for identifying, 23–24
Deprivation theory, 441–442
Descriptive statistics, 5
Discordant pairs, 395, 396
Discrete variables: defined, 16; exercises illustrating, 22–23
Discussion section, of research report, 13–14
Dispersion: basic idea of, 114–115, 139; of categorical data, 115–121; Excel for working with, 144–148; exercises related to, 140–144; of interval/ratio data, 121–139; key terms, 140; quiz answers, 140; quizzes on, 122, 138; summary on, 139
Dispersion of categorical data: example of, 115–117; index of qualitative variation (IQV), 118–119, 144–145; and proportion in nonmodal categories, 117–118; segregation index, 119–121, 145–146
Dispersion of interval/ratio data: coefficient of variation (CV), 134–137, 139, 147–148; interquartile range, 123–126; mean absolute deviation (MAD), 127–129, 147; quiz on, 138; the range, 122–123; standard deviation, 130–134; two approaches to, 121–122; variance, 130, 132, 134
Displaying one distribution: exercises related to, 57–60; frequency distributions for interval/ratio variables, 38–43; frequency distributions for nominal variables, 26–32; frequency distributions for ordinal variables, 32, 34–37; key terms, 56; quiz answers, 57; quizzes, 33, 38, 43; and SPSS (statistical software), 61–79; summarizing data with Excel, 43–56; summarizing variation in one variable, 26; summary on, 55
Distinctiveness, 17, 18, 20
Distributional shape: basic ideas of, 150–152; box-and-whiskers plot, 152, 153–160; common distributional shapes, 175–177; exercises on describing, 178–182; kurtosis, 152, 169–175; of nominal and ordinal variables, 152–158; normal distribution, 151–152; quiz answers on, 178; quizzes on, 159–160, 161, 172; skewness, 152, 163–168; SPSS for comparing numerical indexes and graphics of, 183–185; summary on, 177–178; unimodality, 151, 158, 160–163
Dummy variables: creating, 269–270; defined, 18, 270; and regression model, 473; two-sample test for proportions using, 290, 291–292, 307

E

Ecological fallacy, 14
Educational degree by race, from General Social Survey, 327. *See also* Formal education
Effect modification, 473–474
Effect sizes, 305
Efficient estimates, 221
Empirical generalizations, 10
Equal intervals, 17, 18, 20
Equal probabilities, 176
Eta-squared: defined, 344–346; example, 346–350
Euler's constant (*e*), 493
Excel: Analysis ToolPak, 50–55; for chi-squared problems, 322–324; and confidence interval for a mean, 234–235; and confidence interval for a proportion, 238–240; functions for summarizing data, 43–50; and kurtosis, 175; for linear regression analysis, 461; and measures of central tendency, 108–109; and measures of variation, 144–148; and the normal distribution, 199, 206–207; and skewness, 175; and SPSS, 65, 68–70; for standard error of a mean, 224–225; for two-sample tests, 301–302
Excel's Analysis ToolPak: installing, 50–51; for summary tables, 51–55
Expected cell counts or frequencies, 318, 319
Expected value of the statistic, 218, 240
Exploratory application of statistics, 7

Exploratory phase of research, 10
Exponential distributions, 176

F

50th percentile of a distribution, 89
Firearms, racial groups and their access to, 413–414. *See also* Gun ownership
Fisher's exact test, 317
Form of group differences, 329–330
Form of the relationship, 376
Formal education: among adults in the U.S., 89, 90; and attitude toward death penalty, 416; and church attendance, 417, 418, 419
Formula Builder, in Excel, 45, 46, 54
Formula for: coefficient of kurtosis, 173; coefficient of skewness, 168; confidence interval of a mean, 231–234; confidence interval of a proportion, 236, 237; Cramér's V, 382; gamma, 397; index of qualitative variation (IQV), 118; kurtosis (coefficient of kurtosis), 170; large-sample hypothesis test about a single sample proportion, 268–269; logistic regression model, 493; mean, 96–97; mean absolute deviation (MAD), 127; multiple regression, 470; Pearson zero-order product-moment correlation coefficient, 437, 442; phi coefficient, 382; proportional reduction in error (PRE), 383; relative frequencies (percentages and proportions), 28–29; segregation index, 119; skewness, 164; Somers' d, 398; Spearman's rho, 400; standard deviation, 130, 131; standard error of the mean, 221–222; standard error of a proportion, 225; tau-b, 398; tau-c, 398; test statistic, 256, 283, 284, 288, 289; testing a hypothesis about a single population mean, 260; variance, 130, 132; Z-score, 193
F-ratio, defined, 351. *See also* F-test
Frequency chart, defined, 26
Frequency chart rules: and interval/ratio variables, 40–41; and nominal variables, 27–28; and ordinal variables, 34–35
Frequency distributions: and Excel tools, 43–55; exercises using, 57–60; for interval/ratio variables, 38–43, 56; for nominal variables, 26–32, 56; for ordinal variables, 32, 34–38, 56
Frequency polygon, 41, 43, 56
Frequency tables (exercise 1 using SPSS), 65–70
F-test: and analyzing variance, 339, 342–346; calculating the F-statistic, 351; degrees of freedom, 352; description of, 177, 338–339, 350–351; making a decision, 352–354; mean squares, 351–352; for one-way analysis of variance, 354–355; tables of critical values of, 507–509
Full rank-order ordinal variables, 20, 34, 85

G

Gamma: defined, 395, 406; in example, 402; formula for, 397
Gender and game preference, 374
Gender gap in computer use, 333
General Social Surveys (GSS), examples of data taken from, 59, 60, 61, 72, 103–105, 294, 315, 325–327, 334–335, 363, 364, 373, 379, 409, 410, 413, 414, 416, 417, 419, 480, 482, 501, 503
Global null hypothesis, 462, 496
Goodman and Kruskal tau, 384, 385, 391, 406
Goodness of fit: defined, 7, 455; in examples, 458, 484; in logistic regression, 496, 497–498
Graphical displays: and interval/ratio variables, 41–43, 56; and nominal variables, 29–32, 56; and ordinal variables, 36–38, 56. *See also* Bar charts; Histograms; Pie charts
Gross national product (GNP) per capita, frequency charts of, 40, 41
Group differences, describing, 327–330
Grouped ordinal data, finding the median in, 92–93
Grouped ordinal variable type, defined, 18, 34, 85
Gun ownership: and attitude toward death penalty, 501–502; General Social Survey data on, 334–335

H

Height, finding the median, 88, 89
Heteroscedasticity, defined, 431
Histograms: bar charts versus, 36–37; defined, 36, 56; examples of, 36, 52, 150, 151, 180, 244, 481; in Excel, 51, 52; of normal distribution, 188, 189, 190–191; for ordinal data, 36; for visualizations of interval/ratio variables, 41, 95, 96
Home ownership rates, and age, 490–491
Homogeneity of variances, Levene test for, 282, 285, 292, 307, 309, 310, 311, 312, 357
Homoscedasticity assumption, 436, 465
Hypothesis: defined, 10; and research problem, 12
Hypothesis testing: alternative hypotheses, 251–254; assumptions, 254–255; calculating test statistics, 255–256; defined, 7, 248; exercises, 275–278; key terms, 275; making a decision, 256–257; null hypothesis, 249, 250–251; quiz answers, 275; quizzes, 258, 263, 271; selecting an error level, 255; summary on, 273–275; and theory, 248–249; and type 1 error, 249; and type II error, 249–250
Hypothesis testing about one mean: alternative hypotheses, 259; assumptions, 259–260; brief explanation of, 258; example of, 264–265; Excel for, 266; making a decision, 262; null hypothesis, 259; selecting an error level, 260; the t-test, 260–262; usefulness of, 263
Hypothesis testing about one proportion: alternative hypotheses, 267–268; assumptions, 268; example of, 272–273; making a decision, 270; null hypothesis, 267; selecting an error level, 268; the test statistic, 268–270; two approaches for, 267
Hypothesis testing for two samples: comparing two groups, 280; comparing two groups' means, 280–289; comparing two groups' proportions, 289–294; Excel for, 301–302; exercises on, 308–312; interpreting group differences, 302–305; key terms, 308; Levene's test for equality of variances, 282, 285, 292, 307; nonindependent samples, 296–300; quiz answers, 308; quizzes, 286, 293, 298, 306; significance versus importance, 304, 307; summary on, 307–308; testing the difference between two groups' proportions, 294–296
Hypothesis testing in regression, 461–463

I

i (subscript *i*), 97
Income distribution for nonblack and black American families, histograms showing, 150–151
Independent variables, 15–16
Index of dissimilarity: defined, 119–121; Excel for computing, 145–146
Index of qualitative variation (IQV): defined, 118–119; Excel for computing, 144–145
Infant mortality and fertility data, example using, 403–404
Infant mortality and life expectancy: interval/ratio association of, 427; ordinal association of, 426
Infant mortality to education with linear regression line, relationship of, 430
Infant mortality to education with nonlinear regression line, relationship of, 431
Inference, defined, 212
Inferential statistics: assessing confidence in point estimates, 229–240; basic problem of, 6, 212–213; central tendency estimates, 219–229; exercises, 242–246; key terms, 241; quiz answers, 241; quizzes, 218, 228–229, 239; sampling concepts, 214–219; summary on, 240–241; uses of, 213–214
Integrated Public Use Microdata Series (IPUMS) project, 12
Intercept (*Y*-intercept), 445, 455
Interquartile range, calculating the, 123, 124–126

Inter-University Consortium for Political and Social Research (ICPSR), 12
Interval variables, defined, 20
Interval/ratio association: exercises, 446–452; form of linear, 444–445; key terms, 446; quiz answers, 446; quizzes, 432–433, 438, 441; and regression line (intercept and slope), 429, 444–445; significance testing for, 434–445; strength of, 439–441; summary on, 445–446; visualizing, 426–434
Interval/ratio data: and the mean, 96–98, 102, 108–109; and the median, 88, 91, 108; and the mode, 87–88, 108
Interval/ratio data, dispersion of: coefficient of variation (CV), 134–137, 139, 147–148; interquartile range, 123–126; mean absolute deviation (MAD), 127–129, 147; quiz on, 138; the range, 122–123; standard deviation, 130–134; two approaches to, 121–122; variance, 130, 132, 134
Interval/ratio scales, description of, 38–39
Interval/ratio variables: frequency distributions for, 38–43, 56; and SPSS software, 72–79
Intervening variable, controlling for, 477–478

J

Jointly exhaustive categories, 39

K

Kurtosis: coefficient of, 170–174; defined, 152, 169, 178; Excel for calculating, 175; negative, 169, 170, 175; positive, 169, 170; quiz on, 172; skewness and kurtosis together, 174–175; statistical measures of, 169–171

L

Lambda, 384, 385, 390
Legalization of marijuana, relationship between education and attitude toward, 410–413
Leptokurtic distribution, 169, 170
Levels of measurement, 16–18, 20
Levels or values of a variable, 15
Levene's test for equality of variances, 282, 285, 292, 307, 309, 310, 311, 312, 357
Linearity assumption, 436, 464
Literacy and urbanism, link between, 422–423
Little *r*: and coefficient of determination, 440; defined, 434, 439–440; example using, 441–444; formula for, 439; quiz on, 441
Log likelihood, 496, 501, 502
Log of the odds, 493, 495, 498–499, 500, 503
Logistic regression analysis: applying, 496–498; exercises, 501–504; extending, 499–500; goodness of fit in, 496, 497–498; interpreting effects in, 493–495; key terms, 501; logistic curve, 490–491; logistic regression model, 492–493; and maximum likelihood (ML), 495–496; and partial effects, 498–499; quiz answers, 501; quizzes, 496; summary, 500–501; when to use, 492
Logit, 494, 495
Lower bound, 230

M

Margin of error, 212
Marginal totals, 28
Marijuana, relationship between education and attitude toward legalization of, 410–413
Marital status and race, association between, 315, 328, 380, 384
Marriage, testing theories about prevalence of, 294–296
Maximum likelihood (ML), 495–496
Mean: defined, 82, 95–96, 102; Excel for finding mean of interval/ratio variable, 108–109; formula for, 96, 97; from grouped data, 101; and interval/ratio data, 96–98, 108–109; of list of values, 100–101; SPSS for finding mean of a distribution, 112; two mathematical properties of, 97; working with the, 98–99
Mean absolute deviation (MAD): calculating the, 127–129; Excel for working with, 147; formula for, 127
Median: defined, 82, 88, 102; Excel for finding, 108; in grouped ordinal data, 92–93; height,

88, 89; and interval/ratio data, 91; in list of values, 94–95; and ordinal data, 89–91, 102; quiz on, 92; SPSS for finding median of a distribution, 111–112
Mediating variable, 475
Methods section, of research report, 12–13
Mode: defined, 82, 83, 102; Excel for finding mode of nominal data, 108; and interval/ratio data, 87–88; and nominal data, 83–85, 102; and ordinal data, 85–86; quiz on, 87; SPSS for finding mode of variables, 109–111
Multicollinearity assumption, 464
Multimodal, defined, 160, 161
Multinomial logistic regression, 499, 500
Multiple regression: applying, 474–478; defined, 469–470; estimated regression equation, 471–472; extending, 472–474; formula for, 470; hypotheses in, 471; ordinary least squares (OLS) for estimating, 470–471; quiz, 474
Mutually exclusive categories, 39

N

N, sample size, 29, 96, 97
$n - 1$, 131
National Center for Health Statistics (NCHS), 12
National Health Interview Survey, 12
National Opinion Research Center (NORC), 60, 61
Negative kurtosis, 169, 170, 175
Negative skew, 163, 166, 168
Nominal and ordinal distributions, shape of, 152–153
Nominal association: form of, 385, 387–389; measures of, 390–391; significance testing for, 378–381; strength of, 381–385; visualizing, 375–378
Nominal data, mode of: Excel for finding, 108; explanation of, 83–85, 102
Nominal dichotomy variable type, 18
Nominal polyotomy variable type, 18
Nominal variables: defined, 18; frequency distributions for, 26–32, 56
Nonindependent samples: description of, 296–297; quiz, 298; test for difference in mean differences, 297–299; testing two nonindependent means (example), 299–300
Nonprobability samples, 214
Normal distribution: defined, 151–152, 178, 188; Excel for working with, 206–207; exercises, 203–206; finding areas "under the curve", 197–201; properties of, 189–191; quiz answers, 203; quizzes, 192, 194, 197; shape of curve of histogram of, 190–191; standard normal or Z distribution, 188, 192–194; summary on, 201–202; working with Z-scores, 194–197
Normal distribution function in Excel (NORMDIST), 199
Normality assumption, 435–436
Null hypothesis: defined, 249, 250–251; global, 462; for a test about one mean, 259; for a test about one proportion, 267

O

Observation, units of, 14, 21
Observed cell counts or frequencies, 318, 319
Observing a datum, 10
Odds ratio, 387
Odds that an event will occur, 493
One mean, tests about: alternative hypotheses, 259; assumptions, 259–260; description of, 258; example, 264–265; Excel for, 266–267; making a decision, 262; null hypothesis, 259; quiz, 263; selecting an error level, 260; six steps to, 259–262; t-test, 260–262
One sample, hypothesis testing for: alternative hypotheses, 251–254; assumptions, 254–255; calculating test statistics, 255–256; defined, 7, 248; exercises, 275–278; key terms, 275; making a decision, 256–257; null hypothesis, 249, 250–251; process of, 250–258; quiz answers, 275; quizzes, 258, 263, 271; selecting an error level, 255; summary on, 273–275; tests about

one mean, 258–267; tests about one proportion, 267–273
One-tailed alternative hypothesis: and chi-squared test, 317; defined, 252; examples of, 257, 259; and significant findings, 304; and table of critical t-scores, 517, 518; for tests comparing two-group means, 281–282
One-way ANOVA: analyzing variance, 339, 342–346; comparing means, 356–358, 360; defined, 338; exercises, 362–368; F-test, 350–354; F-test example, 354–355; hypotheses and assumptions, 339–341; key terms, 361; quiz answers, 362; quizzes, 341, 345, 353, 359; summary on, 360–361
Ordering in magnitude, 17, 18, 20
Ordinal association: significance testing for, 393, 395; strength of, 395–401; visualizing, 391–393
Ordinal data: histograms for, 36; and the median, 89–9, 92–93, 102, 108; and the mode, 85–86, 108
Ordinal logistic regression, 499, 500
Ordinal variables: defined, 18; frequency distributions for, 32, 34–38, 56; two kinds of, 34, 85
Ordinary least squares (OLS), 455, 470–471
Overrepresented in survey research, 267

P

Parameter, defined, 6, 7
Partial effects, assessing, 498–499
Pearson chi-squared test of independence: and association between two nominal variables, 375; calculating, 318–319; comparing proportions across several groups, 314–315; defined, 314; Excel for solving chi-squared problems, 322–324; exercises, 333–336; key terms, 332; quiz answers, 333; quizzes, 320–321, 331; SPSS for, 325–327; summary on, 331–332; testing for multiple group differences, 315–320
Pearson zero-order product-moment correlation coefficient: and coefficient of determination, 440; defined, 434, 439–440; example using, 441–444; formula for, 439; quiz on, 441
Perfect negative rank-order association, 396
Perfect positive rank-order association, 395, 396
Phi coefficient, 382, 405
Pie charts: description of, 32; Excel for creating, 71; and nominal association, 376, 377–378; quiz question on, 33
Platykurtic distribution, 169, 170, 171, 175
p-level: defined, 230, 255; selecting the, 255, 260, 262; and table of critical t-scores, 517–518
Point estimates: assessing confidence in, 229–241; defined, 212, 220
Policy implications of findings, 13
Political conservatism and sentencing attitudes, relationship between, 401–402
Pooled estimator, defined, 283
Population, inferring to the, 5–7
Population parameter, 212
Population proportion (P_u), 236
Pornography, gender and opinions about, 409
Positive kurtosis, 169, 170
Positive skew, 163, 165, 166
Post hoc tests, 357–358, 360
Predicting outcomes with regression analysis: basic description of, 454; exercises, 480–488; key terms, 480; multiple regression, 469–479; quiz answers, 480; quizzes, 462, 464, 474, 478–479; simple linear regression, 454–469; summary on, 479
Predicting with nonlinear relationships, 490–491. *See also* Logistic regression analysis
Predictions, use of statistics for, 7–8
Probability sampling: kinds of, 214–215; methods, 6–7
Promotion, data on being passed over for, 335–336
Proportion: confidence interval for a, 238–240; standard error of a, 225–227; tests about one, 267–273
Proportional reduction in error (PRE) logic, 381, 383

Q

Qualitative variables, 17–18
Qualitative variation, index of (IQV): defined, 118–119; Excel for computing, 144–145
Quantitative variables, 18
Quiz answers for chapter quizzes on: association of interval/ratio variables, 446; association with categorical variables, 407; central tendency, 103; chi-squared, 333; dispersion, 140; displaying one distribution, 57; distributional shape, 178; general introduction to statistics, 21–22; hypothesis testing for one sample, 275; hypothesis testing for two samples, 308; inferential statistics, 241; logistic regression analysis, 501; normal distribution, 203; one-way ANOVA, 362; regression analysis, 480
Quizzes on: association of interval/ratio variables, 432–433, 438, 441; association with categorical variables, 374, 379, 381, 386–387, 388–389, 394, 398–399, 400–401; central tendency, 87, 92, 100; chi-squared, 320–321, 331; dispersion, 122, 138; displaying one distribution, 33, 38, 43; distributional shape, 159–160, 161, 172; general introduction to statistics, 6, 8, 11, 15, 17, 19; hypothesis testing for one sample, 258, 263, 271; hypothesis testing for two samples, 286, 293, 298, 306; inferential statistics, 218, 228–229; logistic regression analysis, 496; normal distribution, 191, 194, 197; one-way ANOVA, 341, 345, 353, 359; regression analysis, 462, 464, 474, 478–479

R

Random samples, 214–215
Range: calculating the, 122–123; as feature of the normal distribution, 190; interquartile, 123, 124–126
Rank-order associations, 395–397
Rank-order correlation coefficient (Spearman's rho): defined, 395, 406; example using, 403–404; exercises using, 421–423; formula for, 400; quiz on, 400–401
Ratio variables, 20
Real class boundaries, 39
Recode into fewer categories (using SPSS), 72–79
Regression analysis: exercises, 480–488; key terms, 480; multiple regression, 469–479; predicting outcomes with, 454; quiz answers, 480; quizzes, 462, 464, 474, 478–479; simple linear regression, 454–469; summary on, 479
Regression line (intercept and slope): description of, 429, 444–445; example of, 458, 459
Regression prediction equation, 444
Rejection region, defined, 254
Religious services, formal education and attendance at, 417, 418, 419
Research, basic elements of: dependent and independent variables, 15–16; discrete and continuous variables, 16; exercises, 22–24; key terms, 21; levels of measurement, 16–18, 20; quiz answers, 21–22; quizzes on, 15, 17, 19; summary on, 20–21; units of analysis, 14; variables, 15
Research hypothesis, defined, 10, 248–249. *See also* Hypothesis testing
Research report: common format for, 11; discussion, 13; methods, 12–13; peer review and publication of, 13–14; research problem, 12; results, 13
Research studies, identifying variables in, 23–24
Residuals: analyzing, 329–330; and multiple regression, 464–465; and simple regression, 458

S

Sales figures collected by the Recording Industry Association of America, 333–334
Sample, defined, 5, 14
Sample survey, 212
Sample variance (s^2), 130
Samples: cluster, 215–216; stratified, 215
Sampling distributions, defined, 217, 240
Sampling error, 216–217
Sampling variability, 217
Scatter plot: example of, 427; preparing a, 428–429; seeing association in a, 429–430

Scheffé test, interpreting the, 358, 360
Scientific theories, defined, 9
Secularization hypothesis in sociology of religion, 417–419
Segregation index: defined, 119–121; Excel for computing, 145–146
Sexual activity and religious service attendance, relationship between, 482–483
Shape of a distribution: basic ideas of, 150–152; box-and-whiskers plot, 152, 153–160; common distributional shapes, 175–177; exercises on describing, 178–182; kurtosis, 152, 169–175; of nominal and ordinal variables, 152–158; normal distribution, 151–152; quiz answers on, 178; quizzes on, 159–160, 161, 172; skewness, 152, 163–168; SPSS for comparing numerical indexes and graphics of, 183–185; summary on, 177–178; unimodality, 151, 158, 160–163
Sigma, 97, 221
"Sigma hat," 221
Significance, importance versus, 304, 307
Significance testing. *See* Hypothesis testing
Simple linear regression: applying, 465–469; defined, 454–455; example of, 456–461; hypothesis test in regression, 461–463; regression assumptions, 463–464; regression equation, 455–456
Skewed distribution, description of, 99
Skewness: basic idea of, 163–164; coefficient of, 167–168; defined, 152, 163; Excel for calculating, 175; formula for, 164; and kurtosis together, 174–175; negative skew, 163, 166, 168; and nominal variables, 152; positive skew, 163, 165, 166; quiz on, 166; statistical measures of, 164–166
Slope (*b*), 445, 455
Social class differences, in voting for George Bush, 502–504
Social research and theories, 9–11
Software, statistical. *See* Excel; SPSS
Somers' d: defined, 395, 406; in example, 402; formula for, 398
Spearman's rho (rank-order correlation coefficient): defined, 395, 406, example using, 403–404; exercises using, 421–423; formula for, 400; quiz on, 400–401
SPSS (software): Data View, 62; and distributional shape, 183–185; exercises using, 65–79; introduction to, 61–64; launching, 61; and measures of central tendency, 109–112; for Pearson independence chi-squared test, 325–327; Variable View, 63–64
Spuriousness, controlling for, 475–477
Squared deviations from the mean, 98
Stacked bar charts, 37, 56, 86, 89
Standard deviation: defined, 130–131; example of calculating variance and, 132–134; formula for, 130, 131
Standard error of a mean: calculating, 222–224; and confidence intervals, 229; Excel for calculating, 224–225; formula for, 221–222
Standard error of a proportion, 225–227
Standard error of the regression coefficient, 467
Standard errors, 217–219
Standard normal distribution: description of, 188, 192–194; working with Z-scores, 194–197
Standardized regression (beta) coefficient, 469
Statistic, defined, 6
Statistical association: concept of, 372–374; exercises, 407–423; key terms, 406–407; nominal association, 375–391; ordinal association, 391–404; quiz answers, 407; quizzes, 374, 379, 381, 386–387, 388–389, 394, 398–399, 400–401; summary on, 404–406
Statistical independence, defined, 373
Statistical inference: basic problem of, 212–213; central tendency estimates, 219–229; confidence in point estimates, 229–240; exercises, 242–246; key terms, 241; quiz answers, 241; quizzes, 218, 228–229, 239; sampling concepts, 214–219; summary on, 240–241; uses of, 213–214

Statistics: descriptive, 5; exercises after introduction to, 22–24; four tasks for, 4–8; for hypothesis testing, 7; inferential, 5–7; key terms, 21; for prediction, 7–8; quiz answers, 21–22; quizzes on, 6, 11, 15, 17, 19; reasons for studying, 4; in research process, 9–14; summary on role of, 20–21
Stem-and-leaf plot, 185
Stratified samples, defined, 215
Strength of group differences, 328–329
Strength of the relationship, 375
Student's t-distribution: defined, 177, 260; for hypothesis testing about one mean, 255, 260; table of critical t-scores, 517–518
Subscripts, in statistics, 29, 97
Sum of deviations from the mean, 97
Sum of squares between groups (SSB): description of, 343–344; example, 349–350
Sum of squares total (SST): description of, 342–343; example, 346–347
Sum of squares within groups (SSW): defined, 344; example, 348–349
Symmetry, of the normal distribution, 190

T

Tables: critical values of the chi-squared test, 505–506; critical values of the F-test, 507–509; table of critical t-scores, 517–518; Z-score table, 511–516
Tau-b: defined, 395, 406; in example, 402; formula for, 398
Tau-c: defined, 395, 406; formula for, 398
Television watching: predicting average daily hours of, 483–486; two theories on, 480–482
Test statistic: calculating, 255–256, 265; for small samples, 284
Testing, hypothesis: alternative hypotheses, 251–254; assumptions, 254–255; calculating test statistics, 255–256; making a decision, 256–257; null hypothesis, 250–251; quiz, 258; selecting an error level, 255; summary on, 273–275; and theory, 248–249; and type 1 error, 249; and type II error, 249–250
Testing about one mean: alternative hypotheses, 259; assumptions, 259–260; description of, 258; example, 264–265; Excel for, 266–267; making a decision, 262; null hypothesis, 259; quiz, 263; selecting an error level, 260; six steps to, 259–262; t-test, 260–262; usefulness of, 263
Testing about one proportion: alternative hypotheses, 267–268; assumptions, 268; example of, 272–273; making a decision, 270; null hypothesis, 267; selecting an error level, 268; the test statistic, 268–270; two approaches for, 267
Theories and social research, 9–11
Theory, observation, and hypothesis testing, 250–251. *See also* Hypothesis testing
t-tests: Excel for two-sample t-tests, 301–302; formula for, 260; paired sample, 302; SPSS one-sample t-test results, 261–262; table of critical t-scores, 517–518; unpaired or independent, 301
Tukey, J., 155, 185
Two-sample tests: comparing two groups, 280; comparing two groups' means, 280–289; comparing two groups' proportions, 289–294; Excel for, 301–302; exercises on, 308–312; interpreting group differences, 302–305; key terms, 308; nonindependent samples, 296–300; quiz answers, 308; quizzes, 286, 293, 298, 306; summary on, 307–308; testing the difference between two groups' proportions, 294–296
Two-tailed alternative hypothesis: defined, 252; examples of, 257, 259; and table of critical t-scores, 517, 518; for tests comparing two-group means, 281–282
Type I (or alpha) error, defined, 230, 249, 255
Type I error level: most commonly used, 230; selecting a, 229–230, 255; and table of critical t-scores, 517–518
Type II (or beta) error, defined, 249–250

U

Unbiased point estimate, 220
Unemployment and property crimes, relationship between, 441–444
Unimodality: description of, 151, 158, 160; of a normal distribution, 190; in real-world applications, 160–163
United States Bureau of the Census, data collected by, 12
Units of analysis, 14, 21
Univariate descriptive statistics, 55
Upper bound, 230
Urbanism and literacy, examining link between, 422–423

V

Valid frequencies (Valid Percent), 35
Variables: defined, 15, 21; dependent and independent, 15–16; discrete and continuous, 16, 22–23; dummy variable, 269–270, 473; exercises for identifying, 22–24; levels of measurement of, 16–18, 20
Variance: analyzing, 339, 342–346; defined, 130; example of calculating the, 132–134; formula for, 130, 132
Voting for Bush, and social class differences, 502–504

W

Wald chi-squared test, 498, 500

X

X bar, 96, 97
x-axis of bar chart, 31

Y

y-axis of bar chart, 31
Y-intercept, 445, 455

Z

Z distribution: defined, 177, 188; properties of, 192–193; and Z-scores, 193–194
Z-scores: and confidence intervals for means, 231–234; and confidence intervals for proportions, 236, 237; defined, 192–194, 232; Excel for working with, 206–207; quiz on, 197; using the Z-score table, 511–516; working with, 194–197, 202